COMPLETE PROSE WORKS

OF

John Milton

This publication is made possible
through grants from
the Lucius N. Littauer Foundation
the Andrew W. Mellon Foundation
the National Endowment for the Humanities

Complete Prose Works

OF

John Milton

VOLUME VIII
1666–1682

New Haven and London: Yale University Press

MCMLXXXII

Designed by John O. C. McCrillis
and set in Old Style No. 7 type.
Printed in the United States of America by
The Vail-Ballou Press, Binghamton, N.Y.

Library of Congress Cataloging in Publication Data

Milton, John, 1608–1674.
  Complete prose works.

  Includes bibliographies.
  CONTENTS: v. 1. 1624–1642.—v. 2. 1643–1648.—[etc.]
—v. 8. 1666–1682.
PR3569.W6   828'.408   52-5371
                                     AACR1

  ISBN 0-300-01288-8 (set)
      0-300-02561-0 (vol. 8)

10 9 8 7 6 5 4 3 2 1

EDITOR OF VOLUME VIII

MAURICE KELLEY

DON M. WOLFE
1902–1976

Don Wolfe's dedication to the militant Milton was first embodied in *Milton in the Puritan Revolution* (1941). To his account of Milton's ideas and activities he appended selections from some leftist pamphleteers, a line of interest he followed up in *Leveller Manifestoes of the Puritan Revolution* (1944). The broad base of his allegiance is recalled by Christopher Hill, formerly Master of Balliol College and author of many books on the period, whose *Milton and the English Revolution* (1978) "is dedicated in gratitude to the memory of Don M. Wolfe, who devoted a lifetime to the study of Milton, but never forgot Richard Overton and Gerrard Winstanley." And Wolfe's sympathy with Milton and other reformers was quickened by his earnest concern for the common man in his own country. His name is chiefly identified with the *Complete Prose Works of John Milton* in eight massive volumes (1953–82), an edition he conceived, managed, and carried almost to its completion. Such a project required the talents of a devoted scholar, organizer, financier, and diplomat who had to surmount the innumerable problems of heavy costs and collaborative labor over many years. Parts of that labor were shared by an editorial board, general editors of the individual volumes (Wolfe himself took the first), and special editors of various writings. The result has been a set of carefully edited texts, with new translations of the Latin prose (including the big *De Doctrina Christiana*), and elaborate commentaries on the works and their background. "Si monumentum requiris, circumspice."

ABBREVIATIONS

LIBRARIES

BM	British Museum
BN	Bibliothèque nationale
CAM	University Library, Cambridge
FSL	Folger Shakespeare Library
HCL	Harvard College Library
HHL	Huntington Library
NLM	National Library of Medicine
PML	Pius XII Memorial Library, Saint Louis University
PUL	Princeton University Library
RUL	Rutgers University Library
UBB	Universitätsbibliothek, Basel
UIL	University of Illinois Library
UTSL	Union Theological Seminary Library
YUL	Yale University Library

WORKS

Columbia	*The Works of John Milton,* New York: Columbia University Press, 1931–38.
Complete Prose	*Complete Prose Works of John Milton,* New Haven: Yale University Press, 1953–82.
CSPD	*Calendar of State Papers Domestic.*
DNB	*Dictionary of National Biography.*
French, *Life Records*	J. Milton French, *The Life Records of John Milton,* New Brunswick: Rutgers University Press, 1949–58.
Masson, *Life*	David Masson, *The Life of John Milton,* Cambridge: Cambridge University Press, 1875–94.
NED, OED	*New English Dictionary.*
Parker, *Milton*	William R. Parker, *Milton: A*

Biography, Oxford: Clarendon Press, 1968. (Because the two volumes are continuously paginated, page numbers alone are given.)

STC   A. W. Pollard and G. R. Redgrave, *A Short-Title Catalogue of Books Printed in England . . . 1475–1640,* London, 1946; Donald Godard Wing, *Short-Title Catalogue of Books Printed in England . . . 1641–1700,* New York, 1945–51.

PERIODICALS

BHR	*Bibliothèque d'Humanisme et Renaissance*
DAI	*Dissertation Abstracts International*
ELH	*ELH: A Journal of English Literary History*
ES	*English Studies*
HLQ	*Huntington Library Quarterly*
HTR	*Harvard Theological Review*
JEGP	*Journal of English and Germanic Philology*
JHI	*Journal of the History of Ideas*
MLR	*Modern Language Review*
MP	*Modern Philology*
N&Q	*Notes and Queries*
NDJFL	*Notre Dame Journal of Formal Logic*
PMLA	*Publications of the Modern Language Association*
PQ	*Philological Quarterly*
RenQ	*Renaissance Quarterly*
Ren&R	*Renaissance and Reformation*
RES	*Review of English Studies*
SB	*Studies in Bibliography: Papers of the Bibliographical Society of the University of Virginia*
SCN	*Seventeenth-Century News*
SEL	*Studies in English Literature, 1500–1900*

SP	*Studies in Philology*
SRen	*Studies in the Renaissance*
TCBS	*Transactions of the Cambridge Bibliographical Society*
TLS	*London Times Literary Supplement*
UMCMP	University of Michigan Contributions in Modern Philology
UTQ	*University of Toronto Quarterly*

PREFACE

With the Restoration in 1660, Milton's public political life and new writings on contemporary issues come virtually to a close. His published works in prose from 1666 to 1682 consist of one familiar letter, commentary on *Paradise Lost* and *Samson Agonistes,* and earlier undertakings— a Latin grammar, a treatise on logic, and an account of the geography of Russia—on which he probably made editorial revisions and additions in readying his manuscripts for the printer. Not until 1673–74 did he break his political silence with a fourteen-page plea for toleration for all Protestant sects and a twelve-page translation of a Latin proclamation of the election of a Polish king—a document whose pertinence to English politics is not clear.

So, unlike volumes I–IV and VII, volume VIII of *Complete Prose* contains no long, general introduction relating Milton and his prose writings to the history and politics of his time. Rather, like the introductions to volumes V–VI, which treat of Milton as a historian and a theologian, the introductory materials of volume VIII consist of several special introductions discussing Milton's place in the field of endeavor to which each individual work belongs (literary criticism, grammar, logic, toleration, and geography), with each introduction immediately preceding the work that it discusses.

Appearing also in volume VIII, as Appendix A, is Milton's *Outlines for Tragedies,* the collection of notes on possible subjects for an epic poem found in the Trinity College, Cambridge, Manuscript. The date of these notes (1639?–1642?) dictates that they should have been printed in volume I, immediately following Milton's *Commonplace Book;* but only after publication of that volume did the Editorial Board of *Complete Prose* recognize that the *Outlines* could quite properly, like the *Commonplace Book,* be considered a "work"—a continuing endeavor constituting a unit in Milton's literary activities. The manuscript notes are consequently edited and printed belatedly here in volume VIII.

Not appearing in volume VIII, though announced on the book jackets of earlier volumes of *Complete Prose,* is the *Marginalia.* When the Editorial Board decided to include this section on Milton's annotated Greek texts, the copy of Pindar at Harvard (Sumner 123) was commonly believed to have been annotated by Milton, and the many annotations citing works outside the Pindar volume promised to enable exploration of Milton's classical studies in the manner that Hanford had used the *Commonplace Book* to map Milton's private studies in history, etc. (*PMLA,* XXXVI

[1921], 251–314). Subsequent to this decision, however, Maurice Kelley's and Samuel D. Atkins's "Milton and the Harvard Pindar" (*SB*, XVII [1964], 77–82) indicated that the Pindar volume had no clear place in the Milton canon and its manuscript annotations could not safely be used to chart Milton's private classical studies. Since Milton's remaining six Greek texts contain autograph references to fewer than a dozen works outside his annotated volumes, and since these references are only incidental to the primary purpose of his annotations, the materials left after elimination of the Harvard Pindar are not sufficient to constitute a "work" in any significant sense of the term; so the contemplated *Marginalia* was dropped from the *Complete Prose Works*.

For preparation of this final volume, I have had excellent helpers. For assembling manuscripts and even marking some of them for the press, I am particularly indebted to Rose Mintz, who served as secretary to Don Wolfe in his late days. Elaine Miller and Dennis Moore have labored diligently in the vineyard of manuscript checking. Samuel D. Atkins has generously given time to a critical reading of the introduction to Milton's *Accedence Commenc't Grammar*. The contributing editors to volume VIII have been uniformly cooperative and agreeable in the preparation of their manuscripts for the printer. And finally I am indeed grateful to three ladies of the Yale University Press: Maureen MacGrogan for her constructive copyediting of the manuscripts and Anne Mackinnon and Mary Alice Galligan for their patient and diplomatic handling of matters in the proof.

Maurice Kelley

CONTENTS

COMPLETE PROSE WORKS

OF

John Milton

MILTON'S PRIVATE CORRESPONDENCE

1666

PREFACES, TRANSLATIONS, AND NOTES BY ROBERT W. AYERS

LETTER XXXIII, PETER HEIMBACH TO MILTON, MAY 27 / JUNE 6, 1666

This is the last known letter to Milton by any correspondent and renews a correspondence carried on in 1656–57.[1] Heimbach had sought Milton's recommendation for appointment as secretary to George Downing, minister to The Hague, in 1657. During the nine years between letters, Heimbach had returned to his native duchy of Cleves, where his father, Weinand von Heimbach, was chancellor and where he himself since 1664 had become state councillor to the Elector of Brandenburg for the affairs of Cleves.[2]

The winter of 1665–66 was a time of plague in London, and Heimbach, having earlier heard that Milton had been taken by the epidemic, writes to express his pleasure that the report was untrue and to wish the distinguished poet—whose greatest poems were yet to be published—a serene and quiet retirement. The tone is fulsome and fawning. The Latin is awkward, sometimes incorrect, and erratically punctuated; Masson (*Life*, VI, 501) describes it as "dreadful, with false case-constructions and a syntax defying analysis."

[1] Letters 30, 36, *Complete Prose*, VII, 494–95, 507.

[2] For our meager information about Heimbach, see Alfred Stern, *Milton und seine Zeit* (Leipzig, 1879), III, 184. John Shawcross ("The Familiar Letters," in *The Prose of John Milton*, ed. J. Max Patrick [Garden City, N.Y.: Doubleday, 1967], p. 626, n. 2) suggests that Heimbach "may have in part owed his governmental appointment to Milton's recommendation through Henry Lawrence, minister to Holland." This conjecture is unnecessary if not far-fetched, particularly since Heimbach's father was chancellor. Also questionable is the so-called Heimbach presentation copy of Milton's 1645 *Poems* (Columbia, XVIII, 270, 549; French, *Life Records*, IV, 109, and V, 449; Parker, *Milton*, pp. 918, 929; and Shawcross, "Familiar Letters," p. 626). The inscription, hailing Heimbach as an elegant poet, flowery orator, and keen philosopher, is not in the hand of a recognizable Milton amanuensis; in 1656–57 Heimbach was a young man (in Letter 30, Milton addressed him as "adolescenti"); and Heimbach's Latin, even now in 1666, hardly evidences the accomplishments the inscription accords him. Indeed, considering also his taste for fulsome compliment, one might uncharitably suggest that Heimbach was himself responsible for the inscription.

Original letter in British Museum, Add. MS 5016*, ff. 6–7v; first published in
The Works of John Milton, ed. John Mitford, 8 vols. (London, 1851), I, cxcvi–ii;
Latin text and translation in Columbia, XII, 316–19, and French, *Life Records,*
IV, 421–24 (see V, 465, for correction of date); translation in Masson, *Life,* VI,
501.

TO JOHN MILTON, A MAN ABOVE PRAISE, PETER HEIMBACH SENDS HIS GREETINGS.

HAD we earlier learned that you, John Milton (an exceptional man in every way), were still in the land of the living, I should also earlier have returned to London and attested to our most affectionate regard.[1] But it was reported that you had been restored to your heavenly *patria,* and that, freed from our earthly follies, from on high you now looked down upon them. And, since no correspondence is allowed into that kingdom, I have hitherto had to restrain and repress my pen so eager to write to men such as you.[2] I, who used to admire in you not so much the individual virtues themselves as the marriage of various virtues, do now respect [3] in you (along with many other things) that union (which a countenance most worthy of a man displays) of gravity with the fairest humanity, of charity with prudence, of piety with policy, of policy with immeasurable erudition, and—may I add— of a magnanimous and not the least bit timorous spirit with a solicitous love of peace, even where younger souls become dis- heartened [4]—a union altogether remarkable, and beyond the de- serts of the age. So now I pray to God that all things may conclude according to your prayer and your heart's desire—but with one exception: for filled with years [5] and full of honors (even those you have refused), you long for nothing more than the prize of quiet and the crown of justice, and what seems the same choice as that of Simeon of old, "Lord, now lettest thou thy servant depart in peace." [6] But my prayer is far different from this—namely, that

---

[1] There is in this first sentence an awkward shift from accusative subject to the vocative form of address; also, Heimbach's pluperfect subjunctive *testatus fuissem* (should have attested) should be *testatus essem.*

[2] Heimbach's *ad tui similes* should be either *cum aliis multis* or *inter alia multa.*

[3] Heimbach's *suspicio,* in classical Latin "to look up to," thus "to respect," and so used by Heimbach, but by Milton's time, "to suspect." See Milton's punning play.

[4] Heimbach's *animos laborentur* should be either *animi laborentur* or *animos laborent.*

[5] Heimbach's *saturus annis,* but an adjective formed from *satis* should be *satur.*

[6] Luke 2:29. Simeon, mentioned this once in the Bible, was an aged Pharasaic quietist who had long waited for "the consolation of Israel" and whose "just and devout" life and expectation of the Messiah had been rewarded by a divine

the blessed Almighty God Himself may for a very long time permit you to participate and be pre-eminent in our literary affairs. So, may you and yours be well and happy, most learned Milton, with our best wishes to all of yours. I wrote this on June 6, 1666, of the common Christian era, where we live at Cleves, the electoral seat of the councils. Again, farewell, and continue to love us as earnestly as you now do, and as soon as possible make us happy with the most delightful of all replies.

[Endorsed:]   To a most noble and celebrated man,
          John Milton, Englishman. By a friend.
          at London.

LETTER 41, TO PETER HEIMBACH, AUGUST 15, 1666

This, the last known letter from Milton to any correspondent,[1] is in reply to Heimbach's letter of May/June. It is interesting and entertaining, both for its ironic indulgence of Heimbach's fulsome phrases and patronizing tone, and for its playfulness, as Milton deftly criticizes Heimbach's rhetoric, his diction, and his punctuation.

Letter 31 in Milton, *Epistolarum Familiarum Liber Unus* (1674), pp. 65–66; Latin text and translations in Columbia, XII, 112–15, and French, *Life Records*, IV, 424–26; translation in Masson, VI, 501–2; Phyllis B. Tillyard, *Milton: Private Correspondence and Academic Exercises* (Cambridge, 1932), pp. 51–52; Shawcross, "Familiar Letters," Patrick, pp. 625–26.

TO THE MOST ILLUSTRIOUS PETER HEIMBACH, COUNCILLOR TO THE ELECTOR OF BRANDENBURG.

IF, among so many deaths of my countrymen, and in a year so poisonous and plague-ridden, especially because of some rumor you believed that I too (as you write) had been borne away, it is no wonder; and if (as it seems) that rumor sprang up among your people because they were concerned about my welfare, it is not displeasing to me, for I take that as evidence of their good will towards me. But by the blessing of God, who had prepared a safe place for me in the country,[1] I am both alive and well. Let me not

---

intimation that he should not die until he had seen the Christ. As the infant Jesus was presented in the temple following the Circumcision, Simeon took him up in his arms and uttered the quoted words, in expression of the idea that since his life was without further purpose or end, he was now ready for death. But in the "Coming" of the Son in 1660, Milton had not beheld the consolation of the English Israel, and with his major poems yet to be published in 1667 and 1671, his life was not without further purpose. The allusion is grossly inept.

[1] For lost letters and fragments, see Columbia, XII, 412–15, and XVIII, 520–24.

[1] At Chalfont St. Giles, Buckinghamshire, somewhat more than twenty miles from London. By the time this letter was written, the plague had much abated, and Milton had returned to his house in Artillery Walk.

be useless, whatever remains for me in this life.[2] But that thoughts of me should come to your mind after so long a time [3] is pleasant indeed, even though as you embellish the fact with words—*admiring* (as you write) the marriage of so many various virtues, you seem to support some *suspicion* [4] that you have forgotten me instead. I should most certainly dread the multifarious offspring of so many marriages, were it not well-known that virtues grow and flourish most in straitened and difficult circumstances.[5] One of those Virtues has not so pleasantly repaid to me the charity of hospitality, however, for the one you call *Policy* (and which I would prefer you call *Patriotism*), after having allured me by her lovely name, has almost *expatriated* me, as it were. The singing of the others sounds well together, however. One's *Patria* is wherever it is well with him. Let me conclude (if I may first beg this of you), that if you should find here anything badly written or not punctuated, blame it on the boy who wrote this down while utterly ignorant of Latin,[6] for I was forced while dictating—and not without some difficulty—to completely spell out every single letter. In the meanwhile, I am pleased that your merits as a man (whom I knew as a youth of exceptional promise) have brought you to a place of such honor in the favor of your prince; and I wish and hope for you all good fortune.[7] Farewell.

London, August 15, 1666.

[2] This terse sentence is Milton's wry response to Heimbach's blundering Simeon allusion, which to Milton suggests uselessness.

[3] The last known earlier letter from Heimbach to Milton was dated December 18, 1657 (*Complete Prose,* VII, 507).

[4] Heimbach's *suspicio,* in classical Latin "to look up to," thus "to respect," and so used by Heimbach, but by Milton's time, "to suspect." Through the pun Milton calls attention to Heimbach's faulty Latin diction.

[5] A description of Milton's own situation following the Restoration.

[6] By his parentheses and word play Milton has deftly criticized the faults and follies of Heimbach's letter, but, he says, "If you should find any defects in *my* letter, blame it on the *boy!*" For the suggestion that this boy may be Amanuensis B of the *De Doctrina* manuscript, see *Complete Prose,* VI, 30, n. 13.

[7] The English were at war with the Dutch, and Masson (*Life,* VI, 502 n.) suggests the "fancy" that "Milton may not merely have been ironically rebuking Heimbach for his adulation and silly phraseology, but may also have been suspicious of the possibility of some trap laid for him politically. Certainly, if this letter of Milton's to a Councillor of the Elector of Brandenburg had been intercepted by the English Government, it is so cleverly worded that nothing could have been made of it.—But Heimbach may have been as honest as he looks. Even then, however, Milton, knowing little or nothing of Heimbach for the last nine years, had reason to be cautious."

PROSE ACCOMPANYING
PARADISE LOST
1668 & 1674
PREFACE AND NOTES BY ROBERT J. WICKENHEISER

Six succeeding title pages (two in 1667, two in 1668, and two in 1669) [1] witness the continuing sale of the first edition of *Paradise Lost;* and at some time before the poem appeared with the 1668[2] title page, Milton, or possibly his printer, Samuel Simmons, decided to include prose synopses of the ten books of the epic and a description (as well as a defense) of the verse of the poem.

To effect these additions without jettisoning the remaining unsold sheets of the 1667 printing, Simmons inserted at the beginning of the 1668[2] issue two preliminary four-leaf gatherings [A, a] laid out as follows: [A], title page; [Av], blank; [A2]–[a3], eleven pages of synopses of the ten books of *Paradise Lost,* headed "The Argument"; [a3v]–[a4], a two-page essay entitled "The Verse"; [a4v], a thirteen-item *errata,* also published for the first time.

The top of the first page of the synopses [A2] is headed by a line *The Printer to the Reader,* which is followed by a three-line statement:

> COurteous Reader, There was no Argument at first intended to the Book, but for the satisfaction of many that have desired it, is procured.   S. Simmons.

---

[1] Designated here as 1667[1], 1667[2], 1668[1], 1668[2], 1669[1], 1669[2]. For discussions of the publication of *Paradise Lost,* see Helen Darbishire, "The Printing of the First Edition of *Paradise Lost," RES,* XVII (1941), 415–27, and *The Manuscript of Milton's Paradise Lost, Book I* (Oxford, 1931); James H. Pershing, "The Different States of the First Edition of *Paradise Lost," The Library,* XXII (1942), 34–66; Harris F. Fletcher, ed., *John Milton's Complete Poetical Works Reproduced in Photographic Facsimile,* 4 vols. (Urbana: University of Illinois Press, 1943–48), II, 100–212, III, 7–59, and W. W. Greg's review in *MLR,* XLII (1947), 133–37.

In a succeeding form of the first printing, still carrying the 1668[2] title page, these three lines were expanded to a more grammatical five-line statement:

> COurteous Reader, There was no Argument at first intended to the Book, but for the satisfaction of many that have desired it, I have procur'd it, and withall a reason of that which stumbled many others, why the Poem Rimes not.   *S. Simmons.*

Except for the additional two lines after "desired it," in the printer's prefatory statement, the text of each Argument, the essay, and the *errata* is identical with that headed by the three-line *The Printer to the Reader,* and so it remained in the 1669[1] issue of the epic.

For the 1669[2] issue, however, the entire set of preliminary leaves was reset and reprinted, but with less care than that exercised in the earlier issues of the first and in the second edition. The format, however, remained the same, although *The Printer to the Reader* was now eliminated: the eleven pages of Argument [beginning on A2], the essay on *The Verse* [a3v], and the *errata* [occupying a4v].

The second edition of *Paradise Lost* (1674) presented the Argument for each book separately, with the ten books of the first edition now turned into twelve and the Arguments distributed accordingly. That of Book VII was divided to serve for VII and VIII, and X for XI and XII, as indicated in textual notes, below, pp. 23, 24, 26, 28, 29. With this division, the essay on the verse appeared for the first time in the place that we know it: after Marvell's poem and before Book I begins with its Argument.

As we have few facts about the publication of the 1674 edition of *Paradise Lost,*[2] as indeed about the publication of 1668[2], in which the prose Arguments first appeared, it is not surprising that we know even less about why Milton thought it fitting to add an Argument for each book of his epic poem and a brief defense of the verse or why he supplied such additional material to Simmons, who states in *The Printer to the Reader* that "There was no Argument at first intended to the Book, but for the satisfaction of many that have desired it, I have procur'd it." If we accept that Milton carefully watched over the first publication of *Paradise Lost,* that he supplied a list of *errata* to be printed on the blank page resulting from the inclusion of the Arguments and essay on the verse, that he "revised the text once more for a second edi-

---

[2] Fletcher has observed that "the full and exact history of the printing and publication of this edition is shrouded in uncertainty, if not mystery," III, 7.

tion," [3] that he carried out his own division of the books and emended certain lines to suit his new twelve-book format, then we should also allow that the poet himself initially supplied the Arguments and the essay on the verse and that he divided the Arguments for his revised second edition or at least oversaw their proper division, especially since the title page of the second edition reads: "Revised and Augmented by the same Author."

Milton was certainly aware that the most popular epics in the Renaissance, including those he admired, made use of Arguments; that Arguments in verse or prose had, in fact, become part of the epic format. Chapman, for example, supplied a brief Argument for each book in his 1598–1615 translations of Homer's *Iliad* and *Odyssey;* Tasso had done the same for his *Gerusalemme Liberata* some twenty years earlier (translated into English by Edward Fairfax in 1600). [4] Three additional writers, whose long poems became immensely popular in their day, also provided an Argument for each major division in their work: Du Bartas in *Divine Weeks* (translated into English by Joshua Sylvester, 1592–99), Francis Quarles in *A Feast For Worms* (1620), and Abraham Cowley in *Davideis* (1656). Dryden, later in the century, maintained the tradition by supplying an Argument for each book in his translation of Virgil's *Aeneid* (1697).

Milton's Arguments are too appropriately detailed to be considered simply the compilation of a printer, although they may well have been requested of the poet by Simmons. In the Argument for Book XII (1674 edition), for instance, Milton not only changed the 1668[2] version to suit the new distribution of the Arguments but also added two important details not found in the earlier version: "in the mention of *Abraham*" and "which was promised *Adam* and *Eve* in the Fall." [5] Such details demand a more substantial knowledge of the narrative than one might expect of the printer.

More significantly, while the Arguments read essentially as prose synopses of the narrative action that follows, occasionally they

---

[3] Helen Darbishire (*The Manuscript of Milton's Paradise Lost, Book I,* p. xlvi) tells us that "Milton took unusual pains to prepare an accurate text for his printer, employing a careful scribe, and careful correctors; he supervised proof-correction of the first edition in 1667, overhauled the book for a page of errata in 1668, and revised the text once more for a second edition in 1674. The urge to perfection was there."

[4] Ariosto, in *Orlando Furioso* (translated by John Harington in 1591), and Spenser, in *The Faerie Queene* (1590–96), likewise supplied brief verse synopses for each canto.

[5] See nn. 1, 3, and 4 to Argument XII.

contain observations that are more than mere narrative summary.[6]
Two such instances, for example, are in the first Argument, where,
in the midst of a synopsis of the narrative, the author observes,
"for Heaven and Earth may be suppos'd as yet not made," and
again, "for that Angels were long before this visible Creation, was
the opinion of many ancient Fathers." Both interjections refer to
complex theological considerations concerning creation (see notes
5 and 10 to Argument I), and it is unlikely that admissions of this
kind, along with others that also reflect the poet's stance on controversial theological issues and that detail matters appropriate to
his own theodicy, originated in someone other than Milton.

   Milton's reasons for defending his nonrhyming verse are perhaps
clearer to us than his reasons for adding the Arguments, although
even the Arguments themselves can be seen to reflect something
of the poet's own rhetorical training and persuasions as well as
something of his endeavor to provide his epic with a more "traditional" format. Yet the sentiments expressed in the essay concerning whether or not a "Heroic Poem" should rhyme are more
openly "Miltonic" and appear to be more immediately and more
evidently the poet's own.

   But while the sentiments are clearly "Miltonic," the occasion or
reason for Milton's including a defense of his epic blank verse in
the 1668[2] issue of *Paradise Lost* is perhaps less clear to us. The
revised *Printer to the Reader,* quoted above, simply states: "There
was no Argument at first intended to the Book, but for the satisfaction of many that have desired it, I have procur'd it, *and withall
a reason of that which stumbled many others, why the Poem Rimes
not*" (italics mine). The early twentieth-century critic, George
Saintsbury, for example, believed that the publisher pressed Milton
for this statement in the hope that an explanation of the lack of
rhyme would satisfy dubious readers. "The insertion of the paragraph," Saintsbury adds, "was an afterthought; and that Milton
was not in the best of tempers at having to write it, is pretty
evident." [7] More recently, however, Morris Freedman has pointed

   [6] As *OED* points out, "Argument" may refer either to the "theme or the subject-
matter of discussion or discourse in speech or writing," or, more obviously, to
"the summary or abstract of the subject-matter of a book." Milton uses his Arguments in the most obvious sense, as synopses or summaries of narrative action.
But he also has in mind a more rhetorically oriented usage as well, whereby the
Argument is used to provide an introduction to what follows, detailing or setting
forth by way of exposition the subject matter as well as the theme of the book.
See also n. 1 to Argument I.
   [7] George Saintsbury, *A History of English Prosody* (London, 1908), II, 236.

out that Milton's paragraph on the verse of *Paradise Lost,* despite its brevity, embodies all of the major issues in the Dryden-Howard exchange: "Milton stepped into the brawl impatiently; there is no fuss about his manner and not much grace or patience either; the issues are simple enough to state and dispose of quickly. His attention in the paragraph is directed toward the immediate problem raised by Dryden and Howard with particular reference to *Paradise Lost:* What is the proper form for epic poetry in our time? Milton deals with the questions summarily, often in the phraseology and the formulations used by Dryden and his brother-in-law. There is not a waste word or idea in Milton's paragraph, and almost every phrase is the distillation of lengthy matter in Dryden and Howard." [8] E. M. W. Tillyard, on the other hand, states that "the acrid tone of Milton's note on *Paradise Lost*" sprang from his dislike of the rhymed couplets of Cowley's *Davideis,* "the first original poem in English to affect the growingly fashionable neo-classic form in all its strictness and using the couplet in a new and vital way." [9] And indeed the success of the *Davideis* (published in 1656), as well as the Dryden-Howard controversy and perhaps even the urgings of Milton's own publisher, may well have spurred the poet to write his defense of using blank verse in heroic poetry, although Milton's reasons for believing in the superiority of blank verse were by now bone-deep.

About Milton's opinion that the "Heroic Poem" should be free "from the troublesom and modern bondage of Rimeing," much has been written. One view focuses upon Milton's sharing the general Renaissance disgust for rhyming as being "a vulgar and easie kind of poetry." [10] Another emphasizes not only the skill with which Milton himself handles rhyme but the extent to which it continues to figure in his own verse to the very end. [11] G. Stanley Koehler perhaps puts the matter best when he writes, "In spite of recurring

[8] Morris Freedman, "Milton and Dryden on Rhyme," *HLQ,* XXIV (1960–61), 343. See also note 3 to The Verse.

[9] E. M. W. Tillyard, *The Miltonic Setting* (Cambridge, 1938), p. 204.

[10] Arthur M. Clark, "The Difficulty of Rhyming," *Studies in Literary Modes* (Edinburgh and London, 1946), p. 167, here quoting Thomas Campion, *Observations in the Art of English Poesie,* 1602, in *Elizabethan Critical Essays,* ed. G. Gregory Smith (Oxford, 1904), II, 378. See, too, Clark's chapter on "Milton and the Renaissance Revolt against Rhyme." Also see n. 6 to The Verse.

[11] See, for example, Ants Oras, "Milton's Early Rhyme Schemes and the Structure of *Lycidas,*" *MP,* LII (1954), 12–14, and John S. Diekhoff, "Rhymes in *Paradise Lost,*" *PMLA,* XLIX (1934), 539–43, who suggests that Milton obviously did not take his own rejection of rhyme too literally since almost two hundred instances of rhyme occur in the blank verse of *Paradise Lost.*

expressions of surprise, there is really nothing peculiar in Milton's attitude toward rime, nor anything remarkable in his rejection of it in the Preface to *Paradise Lost*. Milton appears never to have thought too well of couplet rime, using it for the most part for exercises, paraphrases, and occasional verse. And I suspect that his complaint is directed against rime only in this more specialized form." [12]

About the more troublesome phrases, "apt numbers" and "fit quantity of syllables," Koehler has also argued that the former "refers probably to the rhythm of the foot—or, at very most, of the line—as a basis for regularity in the rhythm" and that Milton's emphasis upon "quantity" involves an emphasis upon "the kind of reading which brings out the sense rather than the meter of the lines." [13] Koehler argues further that "such a 'fit quantity of syllables' itself can involve either pattern or variety, according to whether this quantity coincides with and emphasizes the iambic rhythm or counters and obscures it." [14] Unlike Clark, who has suggested that Milton's objection to rhyme involved "a dislike which drew its main strength from his respect for classical modes and his scorn for the monkish and medieval," [15] Koehler concludes that "in such a balancing of opposites [i.e., regularity of rhythm as opposed to the liberating effect of enjambment], even a free rime may tip the scales heavily toward monotony; and it is hardly surprising that Milton should have condemned rime, particularly in its couplet form, as an especially troublesome bondage, fatal to variety, inhibiting the poet just at the moment when he is most aware of his need for freedom." [16]

Regardless of why Milton finally saw fit to incorporate the prose Arguments and essay on the verse into *Paradise Lost*, once he did so they became a standard part of the poem's format. Fletcher's claim, for example, that "the second edition of *Paradise Lost* presents the text of the poem to us about as Milton wanted it presented," [17] can be seen to apply to the poem in its entirety, including the poet's prose Argument for each book and his defense of blank verse. The text here, consequently, is that of the second edition (1674), which represents the poet's final version of his epic poem.

[12] G. Stanley Koehler, "Milton on 'Numbers,' 'Quantity,' And 'Rime,' " *SP*, LV (1958), 214.

[13] Ibid., pp. 216, 209.

[14] Ibid., p. 216.

[15] Clark, "Difficulty of Rhyming," pp. 166–67.

[16] "Milton on 'Numbers,' " p. 217.

[17] *Milton's Poetical Works*, III, 51.

Although certain variations exist among the 1668, 1669, and 1674 texts for the Arguments and for the essay on the verse, most notably between the 1669 and 1674 texts, the text of the second edition exhibits little revision of outstanding importance by Milton or by someone representing him. I have, therefore, noted only significant textual variations, [18] in addition to supplying appropriate annotations.

[18] Changes in spelling, punctuation, and type are meticulously recorded in Fletcher's photofacsimile edition of the 1674 edition of *Paradise Lost* (vol. III), where reproductions of the text may be inspected.

THE VERSE.

THE *Measure is* English *Heroic Verse without Rime,*[1] *as that of* Homer *in* Greek, *and of* Virgil *in* Latin; *Rime being no necessary Adjunct or true Ornament of Poem or good Verse, in longer Works especially, but the Invention of a barbarous Age,*[2] *to set off wretched matter and lame Meeter; grac't indeed since by*

[1] Numerous studies on Milton's style and versification in *Paradise Lost* have appeared since 1900, and some, more than others, have concerned themselves with the claims Milton makes here about rhyme being "the Invention of a barbarous Age," "a fault avoyded by the learned Ancients both in Poetry and all good Oratory," and the cause of the loss "of ancient liberty," which must be "recover'd to [the] Heroic Poem from the troublesom and modern bondage of Rimeing." See especially Walter Thomas, "Milton's Heroic Line Viewed from a Historical Standpoint," *MLR*, II (1907), 302–3; George Saintsbury, *A History of English Prosody* (London, 1908); Robert Bridges, *Milton's Prosody*, rev. ed. (Oxford, 1921; rpt. 1967); Enid Hamer, *The Metres of English Poetry* (London, 1930), pp. 85–105; Arthur M. Clark, "The Difficulty of Rhyming," and "Milton and the Renaissance Revolt against Rhyme," in *Studies in Literary Modes* (Edinburgh and London, 1946); Herbert H. Petit, "Milton, Aristotle, and the Modern Critics," *Classical Bulletin*, XXV (1948), 8–10; George A. Kellogg, "Bridges' Milton's Prosody and Renaissance Metrical Theory," *PMLA*, LXVIII (1953), 268–85; Ernest S. Sprott, *Milton's Art of Prosody* (Oxford, 1953), particularly pp. 39 ff.; F. T. Prince, *The Italian Elements in Milton's Verse* (Oxford, 1954), pp. 108–45; G. Stanley Koehler, "Milton on 'Numbers,' 'Quantity,' and 'Rime,' " *SP*, LV (1958), 201–17; Morris Freedman, "Milton and Dryden on Rhyme," *HLQ*, XXIV (1960–61), 337–44; Vernon Hall, Jr., "Milton," in *A Short History of Literary Criticism* (New York: New York University Press, 1963), pp. 52–55; Christopher Ricks, *Milton's Grand Style* (Oxford: Clarendon Press, 1963); John Steadman, "Verse without Rime: Sixteenth-Century Italian Defences of Versi Sciolti," *Italica*, XLI (1964), 384–402, and "Demetrius, Tasso, and Stylistic Variation in *Paradise Lost,*" *ES*, XLVII (1966), 329–41; Hilda M. Hulme, "On the Language of *Paradise Lost*: Its Elizabethan and Early Seventeenth Century Background," *Language and Style in Milton: A Symposium in Honor of the Tercentenary of Paradise Lost,* ed. Ronald D. Emma and John T. Shawcross (New York: Frederick Ungar, 1967).

[2] See also William Webbe (*Discourse of English Poetry,* 1586), who dismisses rhyming as a "barbarous custome" (*Elizabethan Critical Essays,* ed. G. Gregory Smith [Oxford, 1904], I, 278), and note 6 below.

the use of some famous modern Poets,[3] *carried away by Custom,*
but much to thir own vexation, hindrance, and constraint to express
many things otherwise, and for the most part worse then else they
would have exprest them.[4] *Not without cause therefore some both*
Italian *and* Spanish *Poets* [5] *of prime note have rejected Rime both*
in longer and shorter Works, as have also long since our best English

---

[3] As Arthur Clark observes (*Studies in Literary Modes*, p. 106), "we can assume
with reason that he [Milton] was fully aware of the deliberate choice of rhyme
for the two most notable of recent epics, Davenant's *Gondibert* (1650) and Dryden's
Annus Mirabilis (1667) and of what they and Hobbes had to say in recommendation of the heroic quatrain as an epic vehicle, and we can be as sure that he
knew Dryden to be the leading practitioner of rhyme in the drama and the
champion of its dramatic use in several critical essays. For one thing, there is on
record the Miltonic dictum (undated, it is true, but recorded by his widow and
presumably uttered in the late sixteen-sixties or early sixteen-seventies) to the
effect that Dryden was 'a rhymist but no poet' " (quoted from Masson, *Life*, VI,
682).

[4] Thomas Campion, for example, was disgusted by the facility of rhyme, which
he considered a "vulgar and easie kind of poetry" (*Observations in the Art of
English Poesie*, 1602, in *Elizabethan Critical Essays*, ed. Smith, II, 239). See also
note 6 below. Even more contemptuous than Milton's judgment here are the lines
by Marvell which Milton admitted to the 1674 edition of *Paradise Lost:*

>   Well mightst thou scorn thy Readers to allure
>   With tinkling Rhime, of thy own sense secure;
>   While the *Town-Bayes* writes all the while and spells,
>   And like a Pack-horse tires without his Bells:
>   Their Fancies like our Bushy-points appear,
>   The Poets tag them, we for fashion wear.

[5] Among the Italian poets might be included Trissino, who abandoned the use
of rhyme in his heroic poem, *L'Italia Liberata dai Goti* (1547), and Rucellai, who
did likewise in his didactic poem, *Le Api* (1525). Luigi Alamanni's imitation of
Sophocles' *Antigone* (1532) and his poem *La Coltivazione* (1546) are also in blank
verse. The sixteenth-century Italian translator of the classics, poet, and critic,
Felice Figliucci, also urged the rejection of rhyme in Italian poetry. F. T. Prince,
Italian Elements in Milton's Verse, pp. 108–45, argues that Milton was following
basically the unrhymed hendecasyllables as used by Torquato Tasso in his religious epic *Il Mondo Creato*. Among the Spanish poets in the latter half of the
sixteenth century Francisco de Aldana translated the *Epistles* of Ovid into Spanish
blank verse and Gonsalvo Perez the *Odyssey* of Homer. Carl W. Cobb discusses
"Milton and Blank Verse in Spain," *PQ*, XLII (1963), 264–67, concluding that
while "no Spanish poets at all actually 'rejected' rhyme," two Spanish poems,
both translations, "perhaps formed the basis for Milton's statement"—Perez's
translation of the *Odyssey* and Juan de Jáuregui's blank verse translation of
Tasso's long pastoral poem *Aminta* (1607). Like Milton, Cobb observes, Jáuregui
also felt it necessary to defend blank verse.

Tragedies, as a thing of it self, to all judicious ears, triveal and of no true musical delight; which consists onely in apt Numbers, fit quantity of Syllables, and the sense variously drawn out from one Verse into another, not in the jingling sound of like endings, a fault avoyded by [A4] *the learned Ancients both in Poetry and all good Oratory. This neglect then of Rime so little is to be taken for a defect, though it may seem so perhaps to vulgar Readers, that it rather is to be esteem'd an example set,*[6] *the first in* English, *of ancient liberty recover'd to Heroic Poem from the troublesom and modern bondage of Rimeing.* . . . [A4v]

[6] See also Roger Ascham's *The Schoolmaster* (1570), where, in reference to the "good iudgement" of Lord Surrey who "auoyded the fault of Ryming," Ascham concludes: "And, therfore, euen as *Virgill* and *Horace* deserue most worthie prayse, that they spying the vnperfitness of *Ennius* and *Plautus,* by trew Imitation of *Homer* and *Euripides,* brought Poetrie to the same perfitnes in *Latin,* as it was in *Greke,* euen so those, that by the same way would benefite their tong and contrey, deserue rather thankes than disprayse in that behalfe" (*English Works of Roger Ascham,* ed. W. A. Wright [Cambridge, 1904], p. 292). Throughout his defense of blank verse Milton echoes many other of Ascham's sentiments expressed in *The Schoolmaster* and even some of his phrases: that "rude beggerly ryming" is the invention of "barbarous nations," received "into England by men of excellent wit in deede, but of small learning, and lesse iudgement in that behalfe"; that "Ryming . . . hath bene long misliked of many, and that of men of greatest learnyng, and deepest iudgement"; that poets should, as "that worthie Senese Felice Figliucci . . . earnestlie [exhorted] all the *Italian* nation . . . leaue of[f] their rude barbariousnesse in ryming, and folow diligently the excellent *Greke* and *Latin* examples, in trew versifying," for "the worthie Poetes in *Athens* and *Rome,* were more carefull to satisfie the iudgement of one learned, than rashe in pleasing the humor of a rude multitude"; and that poets, therefore, should use "diligence, in searchying out, not onlie iust measure in euerie meter . . . but also trew quantitie in euery foote and sillable" so that the fashion for "rude ryming of verses" might be curtailed (*English Works,* pp. 289–92).

PARADISE LOST.

BOOK I.
THE ARGUMENT.[1]

This first Book proposes, first in brief, the whole Subject, *Mans disobedience, and the loss thereupon of Paradise wherein he was plac't:* Then touches *the prime cause of his fall, the Serpent, or rather* Satan *in the Serpent;* [2] *who revolting from God, and drawing to his side many Legions of Angels, was by the command of God driven out of Heaven with all his Crew into the great Deep.* Which action past over,[3] the Poem hasts into the midst of things, presenting *Satan with his Angels now fallen into Hell,* describ'd here, *not in the Center* [4] (for Heaven and Earth may be suppos'd as yet

---

[1] See prefatory remarks above, and in particular n. 6 to the preface. The Arguments provide a prose synopsis for each book consistent with the poet's grand rhetorical design, to "assert Eternal Providence, / And justifie the wayes of God to men" (I, 25–26). At times (see nn. 5 and 10, below) parenthetical observations are included that do more than simply contribute to a brief summation of what is to follow; they actually point up the poet's position on a controversial theological issue. The Arguments, then, not only provide an introduction to the subject matter and theme of each book but also help establish the framework for Milton's own theodicy.

[2] In *Christian Doctrine*, I, xi, Milton observes: "This sin [of 'our first parents'] was instigated first by the devil" (*Complete Prose,* VI, 382–83).

[3] Because the narrative of Milton's epic begins *in medias res* and because that "action" (i.e., the revolt and battle in heaven) will be narrated later.

[4] Hell is described here not at the center of the earth but somewhere else, "in a place . . . fitliest call'd Chaos." In *Christian Doctrine*, I, xxxiii (*Complete Prose,* VI, 629–30), Milton argues that hell must be "situated outside this world" because "The devil's fall preceded that of man" and therefore "it is highly improbable that hell should have been prepared within this world . . . when the earth had not yet been cursed." "Besides," he adds, "if the whole world must eventually be destroyed by fire [which Milton himself believed] . . . [hell would then] have to be destroyed as well, along with the earth . . . [and this] would be very nice for the damned, no doubt!" Earlier, in *Doctrine and Discipline* (1643), Milton leaves the exact location of hell undecided; see *Complete Prose,* II, 294.

not made,[5] certainly not yet accurst) [6] *but in a place of utter* [7] *darkness, fitliest call'd* Chaos: [8] *Here* Satan *with his Angels lying on the burning Lake, thunder-struck and astonisht, after a certain space recovers, as from confusion, calls up him who next in Order and Dignity lay by him; they confer of thir miserable fall.* Satan *awakens all his Legions, who* [1] *lay till then in the same manner confounded; They rise, thir Numbers, array of Battel, thir chief Leaders nam'd, according to the Idols known afterwards in Ca-naan* [9] *and the Countries adjoyning. To these* Satan *directs his Speech, comforts them with hope yet of regaining Heaven, but tells them lastly of a new World and new kind of Creature to be created, according to an ancient Prophesie or report in Heaven;* for that Angels were long before this visible Creation, was the opinion of many ancient Fathers.[10] *To find out the truth of this Prophesie, and what to determin thereon he refers to a full Councel. What his Associates thence attempt.* Pandemonium *the Palace of* Satan *rises, suddenly built out of the Deep:* [11] *The infernal Peers there sit in Councel. . . .* [2] [12]

[5] The parenthetical observation refers to the created universe, i.e., heaven and earth, which was not yet made when Satan and his angels fell. Of the creation of hell, Milton states in *Christian Doctrine*, I, xxxiii (*Complete Prose*, VI, 629): "The hell of the damned is the same as the place which was prepared for the devil and his angels, Matt. xxv."

[6] See nn. 4, above, and 8, below.

[7] Either "outer" or "utter" (i.e., extreme, complete).

[8] Chaos existed before the creation of man and of his universe. "It is clear, then," Milton states in *Christian Doctrine*, I, vii (*Complete Prose*, VI, 307), "that the world was made out of some sort of matter." He defines (p. 308) "this original matter" as "not an evil thing, nor to be thought of as worthless: it was good, and it contained the seeds of all subsequent good. It was a substance, and could only have been derived from the source of all substance. It was in a confused and disordered state at first, but afterwards God made it ordered and beautiful."

[9] I.e., Palestine. The "Idols" are those false gods enumerated in the Old Testament.

[10] Milton acknowledges in *Christian Doctrine*, I, vii (*Complete Prose*, VI, 312–13) that "Most people argue that the angels should be understood as included in and created along with 'the heavens' at the creation of the world." But he holds that "Certainly many of the Greek Fathers, and some of the Latin, were of the opinion that angels, inasmuch as they were spirits, existed long before this material world. Indeed it seems likely that that apostacy, as a result of which so many myriads of them fled, beaten, to the lowest part of heaven, took place before even the first beginnings of this world."

[11] Lines 700 ff., however, describe Pandemonium as being built out of materials taken from the floor of hell.

[12] Here and later, three spaced periods followed by a bracketed page number indicate that the Argument does not occupy all of the indicated page.

BOOK II.[1]

The Consultation begun, Satan *debates whether another Battel be to be hazarded for the recovery of Heaven: some advise it, others dissuade: A third proposal is prefer'd, mention'd before by* Satan, *to search the truth of that Prophesie or Tradition in Heaven concerning another world, and another kind of creature equal or not much inferiour to themselves, about this time to be created:*[2] *Thir doubt who shall*[3] *be sent on this difficult search:* Satan *thir chief undertakes alone the voyage, is honourd and applauded. The Councel thus ended, the rest betake them several wayes and to several imployments, as thir inclinations lead them, to entertain the time till* Satan *return. He passes on his Journey to Hell Gates, finds them shut, and who sat there to guard them, by whom at length they are op'nd, and discover to him the great Gulf between Hell and Heaven; with what difficulty he passes through, directed by* Chaos, *the Power of that place,*[4] *to the sight of this new World which he sought.* [27]

BOOK III.

God sitting on his Throne sees Satan *flying towards this world, then newly created;*[1] *shews him to the Son who sat at his right hand; foretells the success of* Satan *in perverting mankind; clears his own Justice and Wisdom from all imputation, having created*

---

[1] 1674 repeats the three-line heading reprinted at the heading of our Book I, changing only the number of the book. In the interest of economy, we omit the first and third lines, retaining only the second, which gives the number of the book.

[2] This phrase is repeated verbatim in Book II, 348–49. Milton accords with Origen's doctrine (condemned by Aquinas in *Summa Theologica,* I, 961, a.33) that God created the world and man after the revolt of the angels.

[3] For *shall* 1669[2] reads *should.*

[4] Milton's conception of Chaos stems from Hesiod's mythological account as well as from Ovid's rationalized treatment of the primeval chaotic mass of "warring seeds of things" before the world began (*Metamorphoses,* I, 5–20). As Merritt Y. Hughes observes (*John Milton: Complete Poems and Major Prose* [New York, Odyssey Press, 1957], p. 180), "In Boccaccio's *Genealogy of the Gods* Chaos is represented as a crowned figure sitting on a throne with his consort Night, as Hesiod described those first parents of all things in the *Theogony.* In Milton's 'anarch' enthroned on the 'wasteful Deep' in *Paradise Lost,* II, 960, his readers would recognize Boccaccio's Chaos. Thus, in some mysterious way, Milton's 'anarch' was identifiable with a Chaos bounded by Heaven above and more or less by Hell below it and also by our universe, which had recently been excavated out of it somewhere not far below the floor of Heaven."

[1] See n. 2 to Argument II.

Man free and able [2] *enough to have withstood his Tempter;* [3] *yet declares his purpose of grace towards him, in regard he fell not of his own malice, as did* Satan, *but by him seduc't.* [4] *The Son of God renders praises to his Father for the manifestation of his gracious purpose towards Man; but God again declares, that Grace cannot be extended towards Man without the satisfaction of divine Justice; Man hath offended the majesty of God by aspiring to God-head,* [5] *and therefore with all his Progeny* [6] *devoted to death must dye, unless some one can be found sufficient to answer for his offence, and undergo his Punishment. The Son of God freely offers himself a Ransome for Man:* [7] *the* [60] *Father accepts him, ordains his incarnation,* [8] *pronounces his exaltation above all Names in Heaven and Earth;* [9] *commands all the Angels to adore him; they obey, and hymning to thir Harps in full Quire, celebrate the Father and the*

[2] In *Christian Doctrine*, I, iii (*Complete Prose*, VI, 160–67), Milton argues God's freedom from responsibility despite his foreknowledge. "By virtue of his wisdom God decreed the creation of angels and men as beings gifted with reason and thus with free will" (p. 164), so that their fall would therefore depend upon their own volition. "From the concept of freedom, then," Milton states, "all idea of necessity must be removed" (p. 161). And with regard to man in particular: "Whatever was a matter of free will for the first created man, could not then have been immutably or absolutely decreed from all eternity" (p. 162).

[3] The temptation of Adam and Eve is to be seen as one of those "Good temptations," which, Milton says in *Christian Doctrine*, I, viii (*Complete Prose*, VI, 338), "God uses to tempt even righteous men, in order to prove them. He does this not for his own sake—as if he did not know what sort of men they would turn out to be—but either to exercise or demonstrate their faith or patience, as in the case of Abraham and Job, or to lessen their self-confidence and prove them guilty of weakness, so that they may become wiser, and others may be instructed."

[4] *Christian Doctrine*, I, xi (*Complete Prose*, VI, 382–83): "This sin was instigated first by the devil, as is clear from the course of events. . . . Secondly it was instigated by man's own inconstant nature."

[5] In *Christian Doctrine*, I, xi (*Complete Prose*, VI, 384), Milton says bluntly of Adam's and Eve's fall that "each was . . . cunningly aspiring to divinity."

[6] In *Christian Doctrine*, I, xi (*Complete Prose*, VI, 384), Milton observes: "For Adam, the parent and head of all men, either stood or fell as a representative of the whole human race."

[7] Cf. Matt. 20:28: "Even as the Son of man came not to be ministered unto, but to minister, and to give his life a ransom for many." (Unless otherwise noted, all biblical quotations are from the King James Bible.) In *Christian Doctrine*, I, xiv (*Complete Prose*, VI, 415–16), Milton states: "Redemption is that act by which Christ, sent in the fulness of time, redeemed all believers at the price of his own blood, which he paid voluntarily, in accordance with the eternal plan and grace of God the Father."

[8] I.e., God "ordains" according to his divine plan.

[9] Cf. Phil. 2:10: "That at the name of Jesus every knee should bow, of things in heaven, and things in earth, and things under the earth."

Son.[10] *Mean while* Satan *alights upon the bare Convex of this Worlds outermost Orb;* [11] *where wandring he first finds a place since call'd The Lymbo of Vanity;* [12] *what persons and things fly up thither; thence comes to the Gate of Heaven, describ'd ascending by staires,*[13] *and the waters above the Firmament that flow about it: His passage thence to the Orb of the Sun; he finds there* Uriel *the Regient of that Orb,*[14] *but first changes himself into the shape of a meaner Angel; and pretending a zealous desire to behold the new Creation and Man whom God had plac't here,*[15] *inquires of him the place of his habitation, and is directed; alights first on Mount* Niphates.[16] . . . [61]

BOOK IV.

Satan *now in prospect of* Eden, *and nigh the place where he must now attempt the bold enterprize which he undertook alone against God and Man, falls into many doubts with himself, and many passions, fear, envy, and despare; but at length confirms*

[10] Milton discusses the relationship of the Father and the Son, that God begot his only Son in accordance with his decree, in *Christian Doctrine,* I, v (*Complete Prose,* VI, 209).

[11] Not the earth but the convex outer shell of the universe.

[12] Milton's "Paradise of Fools" (III, 496), as opposed to the Limbo, according to Catholic doctrine, where the souls of good people who died before the Christian era, as well as those of unbaptized infants, reside in joyful, though limited, bliss.

[13] I.e., the ladder whose top Jacob dreamed "reached to heaven, and behold the angels of God ascending and descending on it" (Gen. 28:12).

[14] Uriel is not mentioned in the Bible. Milton's depiction of him as regent of the sun (lines 622–29) is like the angel whom John saw "standing in the sun" (Rev. 19:17). Likewise, according to Jewish tradition Uriel was one of the four great archangels (along with Michael, Gabriel, and Raphael) who ruled the four quarters of the world, Uriel's being the South. In Hebrew the name Uriel means "the fire or light of God."

[15] For *here,* the text of 1669² reads *there.*

[16] "A mountain range of western Asia, part of the Taurus range, thus described by Strabo: 'To the south across the Euphrates . . . the mountains which separate Sophena and the rest of Armenia from Mesopotamia are called Taurus. Among these mountains is Masium . . . ; then the range rises higher and is called Niphates. Here are the springs of the Tigris' (11. 12. 4)" (Allan H. Gilbert, *A Geographical Dictionary of Milton* [New Haven, 1919], p. 210). "There is no evidence for the interesting speculation that Niphates may be the same mountain from which Adam later contemplates the world, or on which Christ is tempted (xi. 376–84)." (John Carey and Alastair Fowler, eds., *The Poems of John Milton* [London: Longmans, 1968], p. 607).

*himself in evil, journeys on to Paradise,[1] whose outward prospect
and scituation [2] is discribed, overleaps the bounds, sits in the shape
of a Cormorant [3] on the Tree of life, as highest in the Garden to
look about him. The Garden describ'd; Satans first sight of Adam
and Eve; his wonder at thir excellent form and happy state, but
with resolution to work thir fall; overhears thir discourse, thence
gathers that the Tree of knowledge was forbidden them to eat of,[4]
under penalty of death; and thereon intends to found his Temptation, by seducing them to transgress: then leaves them a while,
to know further of thir state by some other means. Mean while
Uriel descending on a Sun-beam warns Gabriel, who had in
charge [5] the Gate of Para-[84] dise, that some evil spirit had escap'd
the Deep, and past at Noon by his Sphere in the shape of a good
Angel down to Paradise, discovered after by his furious gestures
in the Mount. Gabriel promises to find him [6] ere morning. Night
coming on, Adam and Eve, discourse of going to thir rest: thir
Bower describ'd; thir Evening worship. Gabriel drawing forth his
Bands of Night-watch to walk the round of Paradise, appoints two
strong Angels to Adams Bower, least the evill spirit should be there
doing some harm to Adam or Eve sleeping; there they find him at
the ear of Eve, tempting her in a dream, and bring him, though
unwilling, to Gabriel; by whom question'd, he scornfully answers,
prepares resistance, but hinder'd by a Sign from Heaven, flies out
of Paradise. . . . [85]*

---

[1] I.e., Eden (a Hebrew word meaning "delight" or "place of pleasure"), the
region in which Paradise was located. *Paradise:* from *paradeisos,* the Greek form
of a word of Persian origin (cf. Sanscrit *paradesa;* Arabic *firdaus;* Hebrew *pardes*)
meaning "park" or "pleasure ground."

[2] I.e., outward appearance and character, as described in IV, 132–42.

[3] "like a Cormorant" (IV, 196). The cormorant is a voracious sea bird (of the
family *Phalacrocorcacidae*), having a long neck and a distensible pouch under
the bill for holding captured fish.

[4] See n. 5 to Argument IX.

[5] In making the angel Gabriel guardian of Paradise Milton accepts a long-
standing tradition that had made Gabriel (along with Michael and Raphael) one
of the three protecting angels to whom "the Catholic church sanctioned prayer
by name" (Robert West, *Milton and the Angels* [Athens, Ga., 1955], p. 62). None
of the scriptural references to Gabriel, however (Dan. 8:16; 9:21; and Luke 1:19),
implies his guardianship of Paradise. See also n. 14 to Argument III.

[6] For *find him,* the text of both 1668[2] and 1669[2] reads *find him out.*

BOOK V.

Morning approach't, Eve *relates to* Adam *her troublesome dream; he likes it not, yet comforts her: They come forth to thir day labours:* [1] *Thir Morning Hymn at the Door of thir Bower. God to render Man inexcusable sends* Raphael [2] *to admonish him of his obedience, of his free estate,*[3] *of his enemy near at hand; who he is, and why his enemy, and whatever else may avail* [4] Adam *to know.* Raphael *comes down to Paradise, his appearance describ'd, his coming discern'd by* Adam *afar off sitting at the door of his Bower; he goes out to meet him, brings him to his lodge, entertains him with the choycest fruits of Paradise got together by* Eve; *thir discourse at Table:* Raphael *performs his message,*[5] *minds* [6] Adam *of his state and of his enemy; relates at* Adams *request who that enemy is, and how he came to be so, beginning from his first revolt in Heaven,*[7] *and the occasion thereof; how he drew his Legions*

---

[1] I.e., natural duties consistent with living in a prelapsarian world, for Milton says in *Christian Doctrine,* I, x (*Complete Prose,* VI, 351–52), "Adam was not required to perform any works; he was merely forbidden to do one thing," and, "he was in fact drawn to these [good works] by his own natural impulses, without being commanded."

[2] The name means "medicine of God," and this corresponds with the angel's role in the Book of Tobit as it is reflected in *Paradise Lost,* IV, 166–71. In Jewish tradition Raphael is one of the four angels who stand in the presence of God; the other three are Michael, Gabriel, and Uriel. See also n. 14 to Argument III.

[3] In *Christian Doctrine,* I, x (*Complete Prose,* VI, 351–52) Milton states, "It was necessary that one thing at least should be either forbidden or commanded, and above all something which was in itself neither good nor evil, so that man's obedience might in this way be made evident. For man was by nature good and holy, and was naturally disposed to do right, so it was certainly not necessary to bind him by the requirements of any covenant to something which he would do of his own accord. And he would not have shown obedience at all by performing good works, since he was in fact drawn to these by his own natural impulses, without being commanded." See also n. 5 to Argument IX. With regard to *free estate,* see n. 2 to Argument III.

[4] I.e., profit, for it is important that Adam be told "whatever else" he needs to know about evil, since his innocence was often regarded as one of the formal causes of original sin.

[5] I.e., as God's messenger Raphael carries out his assignment. *Angel* comes from the Greek *angelos* (a translation of the Hebrew *mal'ākh*), meaning "messenger."

[6] I.e., reminds. Earlier in this Argument we are told that Raphael is sent to "admonish" Adam, i.e. [from the Latin *admonere*], *to remind* him of his primary duty to obey God.

[7] See n. 4 to Argument VI.

after him to the parts of the [116] *North, and there incited them to rebel with him, perswading all but only* Abdiel [8] *a Seraph, who in Argument diswades and opposes him, then forsakes him.* .... [117]

BOOK VI.

Raphael [1] *continues to relate how* Michael [2] *and* Gabriel [3] *were sent forth to battel* [4] *against* Satan *and his Angels. The first Fight describ'd:* Satan *and his Powers retire under Night: He calls a Councel, invents devilish Engines, which in the second dayes Fight put* Michael *and his Angels to some disorder; but they at length pulling up Mountains overwhelm'd both the force and Machins of* Satan: *Yet the Tumult not so ending, God on the third day sends*

[8] The name means "servant of God" and occurs only as a human name in the Bible (1 Chron. 5:15). Milton invented his character, whom he has God address directly in VI, 29, with the title "Servant of God," as an embodiment of that "eager desire to sanctify the divine name, together with a feeling of indignation against things which tend to the violation or contempt of religion," which he says "is called zeal" (*Christian Doctrine*, II, vi [*Complete Prose*, VI, 697]). *Seraph*, i.e., Seraphim, one of the ranks of angels.

[1] See n. 2 to Argument V.

[2] Michael is identified in Book VI as "of Celestial Armies Prince" (44). Milton notes in *Christian Doctrine*, I, ix (*Complete Prose*, VI, 347) that in Jewish tradition Michael (which in Hebrew means the "God-like" or "strength of God") "is the first of the chief princes" and "the greatest prince" (Dan. 10:13; 12:1), and that he is also the "leader of the angels" and "antagonist of the prince of devils." In making the name Michael signify the first of the Angels, not Christ, Milton accepts Catholic rather than Protestant opinion (see West, *Milton and the Angels*, p. 125). In Rev. 12:7, Michael "and his angels fought against the dragon." See also n. 14 to Argument III.

[3] See n. 5 to Argument IV.

[4] As Merritt Y. Hughes observes, "Probably Milton regarded the war in Heaven as both allegorical and historical. For centuries various commentators had regarded the drawing off of a 'third part of the angels' by Lucifer, in Revelation xii, 4–11, and his battle there with Michael, as a record of angelic war before the creation of Adam. . . . But Milton was too much a humanist and at the same time too much interested in the historical truth to be found in the Bible to be content to treat the battle in heaven as sheer allegory. The biblical warrant for it as history might be small, but in the traditions of battles between the Olympian gods and the Titans which Hesiod tells, and which left their marks widely in classical literature and sculpture, Milton—like most of his contemporaries—saw a survival of sacred history in the legends of the pagans. . . . [and] for Milton the legends about the Titans' war with the gods of light on Olympus were proof of a core of some kind of historical truth in the revolt of the angels" (*John Milton*, p. 178).

Messiah *his Son,*[5] *for whom he had reserv'd the glory* [6] *of that Victory: Hee in the Power of his Father* [7] *coming to the place, and causing all his Legions to stand still on either side, with his Chariot and Thunder driving into the midst of his Enemies, pursues them unable to resist towards the wall of Heaven; which opening, they leap down with horrour and confusion into the place of punishment prepar'd for them in the Deep:* Messiah *returns with triumph to his Father.* [145]

BOOK VII.[1]

Raphael *at the request of* Adam *relates how and wherefore this world was first created;* [2] *that God, after the expelling of Satan and his Angels out of Heaven, declar'd his pleasure to create another World and other Creatures to dwell therein; sends his Son* [3] *with Glory and attendance of Angels to perform the work of Creation* [4] *in six dayes:* [5] *the Angels celebrate with Hymns the performance thereof, and his reascention into Heaven. . . .* [173]

[5] The anointed of the Father and man's appointed Savior.

[6] Milton argues in *Christian Doctrine* I, v (*Complete Prose,* VI, 274), that "the glory which the Father gives the Son is not lost to him, since the Son everywhere glorifies the Father."

[7] The chapter on "The Son of God" in *Christian Doctrine* (I, v) begins with a reference to Col. 1:15: "Who is the image of the invisible God, the firstborn of all created things." In the discussion that follows, Milton focuses upon how "when these things [i.e., actions] are ascribed to the Son, it is done in such a way as to make it easily intelligible that they should all be attributed primarily and properly to the Father alone" (*Complete Prose,* VI, 211, 233).

[1] The Argument of 1674 for Book VII is the first half only of the Argument of the 1668/69 Book VII, since this book was divided into two books (VII and VIII) for the second edition. See prefatory remarks.

[2] For Milton, God created man and his universe "after the expelling of Satan and his Angels out of Heaven," as he states here.

[3] Throughout his chapter on "The Son of God" (*Christian Doctrine* I, v [*Complete Prose,* VI, 203–80, esp. 267]), Milton insists that the Son was voluntarily begotten by the Father and that creation was accomplished through him by the Father.

[4] Milton regarded the act of creation as the imposition or "addition of forms" upon unformed matter, i.e., upon chaos, which Milton considered to be "confused and disordered" or formless (*Christian Doctrine,* I, vii [*Complete Prose,* VI, 308]). See also n. 8 to Argument I and n. 4 to Argument II.

[5] As Maurice Kelley states (*Complete Prose,* VI, 88): "the work of the six days does not mark, in Milton's chronology, the beginning of time. The first of all created things was the Son, whom the Father begot by a decree. Since the decree must precede the execution of the decree, time began with the generation of the Son; and not until much later, probably after the defection of the evil angels, did the Father begin the work described in the first chapter of Genesis." See *Christian Doctrine,* I, iii (VI, 166), v (VI, 209), and vii (VI, 313).

BOOK VIII.[1]

Adam *inquires concerning celestial Motions, is doubtfully answer'd, and exhorted to search* [2] *rather things more worthy of knowledg:* Adam *assents, and still desirous to detain* Raphael, *relates to him what he remember'd since his own Creation, his placing in Paradise, his talk with God concerning solitude and fit society, his first meeting and Nuptials with* Eve, *his discourse with the Angel thereupon; who after admonitions repeated departs.* . . . [193]

BOOK IX.[1]

Satan *having compast the Earth, with meditated guile returns as a mist by Night into Paradise, enters into the Serpent sleeping.* Adam *and* Eve *in the Morning go forth to thir labours,* [2] *which* Eve *proposes to divide in several places, each labouring apart:* Adam *consents not, alledging the danger, lest that Enemy, of whom they were forewarn'd, should attempt* [3] *her found alone:* Eve *loath to be thought not circumspect or firm enough, urges her going apart,* [4] *the rather desirous to make tryal of her strength;* Adam *at last yields: The Serpent finds her alone; his subtle approach, first gazing, then speaking, with much flattery extolling* Eve *above all other Creatures.* Eve *wondring to hear the Serpent speak, asks how he attain'd to human speech and such understanding not till now; the Serpent answers, that by tasting of a certain Tree in the Garden*

---

[1] The Argument of 1674 Book VIII is the last half of the Argument of 1668/69 Book VII, beginning here with "Adam inquires" rather than "Adam then inquires." See prefatory remarks.

[2] For *search,* the text of 1669[2] reads *seek.*

[1] The Argument of 1674 Book IX is the same as that of 1668/69 Book VIII.

[2] See n. 1 to Argument V. As Milton states, *Christian Doctrine,* I, x (*Complete Prose,* VI, 351), "The providence which relates to his [man's] prelapsarian state is that by which God placed man in the garden of Eden and supplied him with every good thing necessary for a happy life."

[3] I.e., should "attempt" to seduce Eve, while alone, to disobey God; but also, should "try" Eve, i.e., tempt her.

[4] Different views prevail. (1) According to pre-Christian commentaries on Genesis, Eve was originally assigned the care of part of the garden; (2) Eve's effective pleading to work alone on the day of temptation is Milton's representation of "obstinate presumption" (see Sister M. I. Corcoran, *Milton's Paradise* [Chicago, 1945], pp. 54, 126); (3) the manner of Eve's arguing foreshadows the sophistries of modern efficiency experts (see J. C. Ransom, *God without Thunder* [New York, 1931], pp. 133–34); (4) Eve's proposal and the manner in which she makes it are a "final stroke of art in the characterization of the mother of all women" (see Hughes, ed., *John Milton,* p. 383n).

he attain'd both to Speech and Reason, till then void of both: Eve
requires him [213] *to bring her to that Tree, and finds it to be the*
Tree of Knowledge forbidden: [5] *The Serpent now grown bolder,*
with many wiles and arguments induces her at length to eat; she
pleas'd with the taste [6] *deliberates a while whether to impart thereof*
to Adam *or not, at last brings him of the Fruit, relates what per-*
swaded her to eat thereof: Adam *at first amaz'd,*[7] *but perceiving*
her lost, resolves through vehemence [8] *of love to perish with her;* [9]
and extenuating the trespass [10] *eats also of the Fruit: The Effects*
thereof in them both; they seek to cover thir nakedness; [11] *then fall*
to variance and accusation of one another. . . . [214]

[5] In *Christian Doctrine,* I, x (*Complete Prose,* VI, 351–52), Milton states: "so
that there might be some way for man to show his obedience, God ordered him
to abstain only from the tree of the knowledge of good and evil, and threatened
him with death if he disobeyed." "It was necessary," Milton goes on to say, "that
one thing at least should be either forbidden or commanded, and above all something which was in itself neither good nor evil, so that man's obedience might in
this way be made evident." About the "tree of the knowledge of good and evil"
itself, Milton observes, it "was not a sacrament . . . but a kind of pledge or
memorial of obedience" (See n. 3 to Argument V). "It was called the tree of
knowledge of good and evil because of what happened afterwards: for since it
was *tasted* [italics mine, see note 6 following], not only do we know evil, but also
we do not even know good except through evil."

[6] In Milton's time this important word meant to learn by "proof," "test," or
"experience," as well as "to try, examine, or explore by touch," "to handle," and
"to have carnal knowledge of"; it also meant "to perceive or recognize as by the
sense of taste or smell" (*OED*).

[7] *OED* defines *amazed* as "stunned or stupified," "out of one's wits," "struck
with sudden terror," "alarmed," and "lost in wonder or astonishment."

[8] I.e., "impetuosity," "great force or violence," "excessive ardor, eagerness, or
fervor of personal feeling or action; passionate force, violence, or excitement"
(*OED*).

[9] Concerning the nature of Adam's and Eve's sin, Milton emphatically states
in *Christian Doctrine,* I, xi (*Complete Prose,* VI, 383–84): "For what fault is there
which man did not commit in committing this sin? He was to be condemned both
for trusting Satan and for not trusting God; he was faithless, ungrateful, disobedient, greedy, uxorious; she, negligent of her husband's welfare; both of them
committed theft, robbery with violence, murder against their children (i.e., the
whole human race); each was sacrilegious and deceitful, cunningly aspiring to
divinity although thoroughly unworthy of it, proud and arrogant."

[10] I.e., underrating or minimizing Eve's sin; allowing for mitigating circumstances.

[11] In *Christian Doctrine,* I, xii (*Complete Prose,* VI, 394), Milton interprets
"they knew that they were naked" (Gen. 3:7) as signifying a "degradation of the
mind . . . [for] the whole man is defiled." The result, he adds, is "shame," citing
Gen. 3:7, "they sewed leaves together and made themselves aprons."

BOOK X.[1]

Mans transgression known, the Guardian Angels forsake Paradise, and return up to Heaven to approve thir vigilance, and are approv'd, God declaring that The entrance of Satan could not be by them prevented.[2] *He sends his Son*[3] *to judge*[4] *the Transgressors, who descends and gives Sentence accordingly;*[5] *then in pity cloaths them both,*[6] *and reascends.* Sin and Death *sitting till then at the Gates of Hell, by wondrous sympathie*[7] *feeling the success of* Satan *in this new World, and the sin by Man there committed, resolve to sit no longer confin'd in Hell, but to follow* Satan *thir Sire up to the place of Man: To make the way easier from Hell to this World to and fro, they pave a broad Highway or Bridge over* Chaos,[8] *according to the Track*[9] *that* Satan *first made; then preparing for Earth, they meet*[10] *him proud of his success returning to Hell; thir mutual gratulation.* Satan *arrives at* Pandemonium, *in full of assembly*[11] *relates with boasting his* [250] *success against Man; instead of applause is entertained with a general hiss by all his audience, transform'd with himself also suddenly into Serpents,*

---

[1] The Argument of 1674 Book X is the same as that of 1668/69 Book IX. Some of the most curious and interesting textual variations found among the 1668, 1669, and 1674 texts occur in this Argument. See, e.g., nn. 3, 9, 10, 11, 13 below.

[2] Cf. III, 682–85: "For neither Man nor Angel can discern / Hypocrisie, the only evil that walks / Invisible, except to God alone, / By his permissive will, through Heav'n and Earth." In X, 37, God simply says: "your sincerest care could not prevent."

[3] For *Son,* the text of 1669[2] reads *Angels.*

[4] John 5:22: "For the Father judgeth no man, but hath committed all judgment unto the Son." The Son, says Milton in *Christian Doctrine,* I, v (*Complete Prose,* VI, 238), "was a God on both counts, as messenger and as judge"; and of the Son's "coming to judge the world" in the fullness of time (p. 270) Milton had no doubt. See also n. 6 to Argument XII.

[5] I.e., according to the Father's decree *and* in relation to the heinousness of man's having sinned against his God.

[6] Gen. 3:21 says simply that "the Lord God" made "coats of skins and clothed them," but Milton's judge also has "pity" for Adam and Eve, indicative of mercy to come.

[7] Here and in X, 246–49, Milton uses *sympathie* to mean a "wondrous" (i.e., astonishing, remarkable) attraction at great distance: "Powerful at greatest distance to unite / With secret amity things of like kinde / By secretest conveyance."

[8] Cf. heaven's ascending stairs in Argument III.

[9] For *Track,* the text of 1669[2] reads *Tract.*

[10] Some 1674 copies read *met,* others *meet* (as is also found in both states of the first edition). Possibly *met* was an early printing error in the second edition, later discovered and corrected to read *meet.*

[11] For *in full of assembly,* the text of both 1668[2] and 1669[2] reads *in full assembly,* a more grammatically satisfying phrase.

according to his doom giv'n in Paradise; [12] *then deluded with a shew of the forbidden Tree springing up before them, they greedily reaching to take* [13] *of the Fruit, chew dust and bitter ashes.* [14] *The proceedings of* Sin *and* Death; *God foretels the final Victory of his Son over them, and the renewing of all things;* [15] *but for the present commands his Angels to make several alterations in the Heavens and Elements.* Adam *more and more perceiving his fall'n condition heavily bewailes, rejects the condolement of* Eve; *she persists and at length appeases him: then to evade the Curse likely to fall on thir Ofspring,* [16] *proposes to* Adam *violent wayes which he approves not, but conceiving better hope, puts her in mind of the late Promise made them, that her Seed should be reveng'd on the Serpent,* [17] *and exhorts her with him to seek Peace of the offended Deity, by repentance and supplication.* [18] . . . [251]

[12] I.e., the *promise* to man. See note 17 below.

[13] For *take,* the text of both 1668² and 1669² reads *taste.*

[14] As Hughes notes (*John Milton,* pp. 419–20), "Throughout the popular encyclopaedias—Swan's *Speculum Mundi* and Caxton's *Mirrour of the World* especially—[Kester] Svendsen (*M[ilton] & S[cience,* Cambridge, 1956], pp. 28–29) traces repetitions of Josephus' story of *that bituminous Lake* (the Dead Sea) and the city of *Sodom,* which, 'for the impiety of its inhabitants, was burnt by lightning; . . . and the traces are still to be seen, as well as the ashes growing in their fruits, which fruits have a color as if they were fit to be eaten; but if you pluck them with your hands, they dissolve into smoke and ashes' (*Wars* IV, viii, 4) . . . [and as a background for Milton's narrative there is also the] popular belief that snakes eat nothing but dust which Topsell in his *Historie of Serpents,* p. 16, challenged, though he thought it possible that snakes of the kind that figures in Eve's temptation might have no food but dust."

[15] *Christian Doctrine,* I, xxxiii (*Complete Prose,* VI, 632): "Our glorification will be accompanied by the renovation of, and our possession of, heaven and earth and all those creatures in both which may be useful or delightful to us."

[16] In his response to Eve (X, 820 f.) Adam conjectures that through his fall all men have fallen. His reasoning is similar to that of Milton's in *Christian Doctrine,* I, xi (*Complete Prose,* VI, 384), where Milton argues that Adam's and Eve's posterity are "judged and condemned in them . . . so they must obviously have sinned in them as well." See also n. 6 to Argument III.

[17] The mystery of this "Promise" is explained in *Christian Doctrine,* I, xiv (*Complete Prose,* VI, 416), where Milton says that "in pronouncing punishment upon the serpent, at a time when man had only grudgingly confessed his guilt, God promised that he would raise up from the seed of the woman a man who would bruise the serpent's head, Gen. 3:15. This was before he got as far as passing sentence on the man. Thus he prefaced man's condemnation with a free redemption."

[18] Adam's and Eve's "repentance" and "supplication" partake of the four steps involved in regeneration discussed by Milton in *Christian Doctrine,* I, xix (*Complete Prose,* VI, 466): "Repentance . . . is the gift of God by virtue of which the

BOOK XI.[1]

The Son of God presents to his Father the Prayers of our first Parents [2] *now repenting, and intercedes for them:* [3] *God accepts them, but* [4] *declares that they must no longer abide in Paradise;* [5] *sends* Michael *with a Band of Cherubim* [6] *to dispossess them; but first to reveal to* Adam *future things:* [7] Michaels *coming down.* Adam *shews to* Eve *certain ominous signs;* [8] *he discerns* Michaels *approach, goes out to meet him: the Angel denounces* [9] *thir departure.* Eve's *Lamentation.* Adam *pleads, but submits: The Angel leads him up to a high Hill,* [10] *sets before him in vision what shall happ'n till the Flood. . . .* [285]

---

regenerate man, seeing with sorrow that he has offended God by his sins, detests and avoids them and, through a sense of the divine mercy, turns to God with all humility, and is eager in his heart to follow what is right."

[1] The Argument of 1674 Book XI consists of approximately the first half of the Argument of 1668/69 Book X. See prefatory remarks.

[2] The Son of God makes intercession for man, Milton says in *Christian Doctrine*, I, xv (*Complete Prose*, VI, 434–35), "first, *by appearing on our behalf in God's presence*, Heb. ix, 24 . . . secondly, *by making our prayers pleasing to God.*"

[3] Milton states in *Christian Doctrine*, I, xv (*Complete Prose*, VI, 430), that the Son's "mediatorial office, for which he was chosen by God the Father, is the office by virtue of which he willingly performed, and still performs all those things through which peace with God and eternal salvation for the human race are attained."

[4] For *but,* the text of 1669[2] reads *and.*

[5] One of the immediate consequences of the fall. See Gen. 3:22–23.

[6] For *Cherubim,* the text of 1669[2] reads *Cherubims.*

[7] I.e., pertaining to the history of man's salvation.

[8] For *signs;* there is *signs,* in the text of 1669[2]. After the fall nature was believed to have reflected man's changed condition. In *Christian Doctrine*, I, xiii (*Complete Prose*, VI, 399), Milton interprets Gen. 3:17, as meaning that after the fall nature became subject to mortality and a curse on account of man: "The curse of death extends to the whole of nature, because of man." For a discussion of the "pathetic fallacy" involved in Milton's presenting nature as degenerating after man's fall, see A. Z. Butler, *Essays in Honor of Walter Clyde Curry* (Nashville, 1954), pp. 274–76.

[9] *de* + *nuntiare:* to make known or to report; also, to give formal, authoritative, or official information; to proclaim, announce, declare (*OED*).

[10] See n. 16 to Argument III.

BOOK XII.[1]

The Angel Michael *continues from the Flood to relate what shall succeed;* [2] *then, in the mention of* Abraham,[3] *comes by degrees to explain, who that Seed of the Woman shall be, which was promised* Adam *and* Eve *in the Fall;* [4] *his Incarnation, Death, Resurrection, and Ascention; the state of the Church* [5] *till his second Coming.*[6] Adam *greatly satisfied and recomforted by these Relations* [7] *and Promises descends the Hill with* Michael; *wakens* Eve, *who all this while had slept, but with gentle dreams compos'd to quietness of mind and submission.*[8] Michael *in either hand leads them out of*

[1] The Argument of 1674 Book XII consists of approximately the last half of the Argument of 1668/69 Book X. Most of the first five lines (from "The Angel" to "in the Fall") of the 1674 Argument were supplied for this edition and are not found in the Argument of 1668/69 Book X, which reads: "thence from the Flood relates, and by degrees explains, who that Seed of the Woman shall be; his Incarnation." See prefatory remarks.

[2] I.e., pertaining to the promised salvation of man, identified specifically in this Argument as Christ's "Incarnation, Death, Resurrection, and Ascention" and "the state of the Church till his second Coming." The doctrinal elements involved here, and expressed by Adam in XII, 401–58, are affirmed by Milton in his detailed discussion of "The Administration of Redemption" in *Christian Doctrine,* xvi. Milton emphasizes that Christ "submitted himself voluntarily, both in life and in death, to the divine justice, in order to suffer all the things which were necessary for our redemption" and that his resurrection and ascension leads "to immortality and to the highest glory" and was carried out "on behalf of all men" (*Complete Prose,* VI, 438, 440, and 444).

[3] I.e., the promise made to Abraham "that in his Seed / All Nations shall be blest (XII, 125–26). This phrase was added in the second edition (1674).

[4] See n. 17 to Argument X. The phrase, "which was promised Adam and Eve in the Fall," was added in the second edition (1674); "in the Fall" means "in the judgment given *after* man's Fall."

[5] In *Christian Doctrine,* I, xxix (*Complete Prose,* VI, 568), Milton describes the "universal visible church" as "the whole multitude of those who are called from any part of the whole world, and who openly worship God the Father in Christ either individually or in conjunction with others."

[6] In *Christian Doctrine,* I, xxxiii (*Complete Prose,* VI, 621), Milton interprets Christ's second coming as the time when he "with the Saints, arrayed in the glory and the power of the Father, will judge the fallen angels and the whole human race."

[7] I.e., revelations.

[8] Though Eve's failure to submit to her husband and Adam's failure in turn to exert his rightful authority lead to their fall, Milton sees Eve's submission to

Paradise, the fiery Sword waving behind them, and the Cherubim
taking thir Stations to guard the Place,[9] [313]

Adam as being even more necessary and complete after the fall. In *Christian Doctrine*, I, x (*Complete Prose*, VI, 355), he interprets Gen. 3:16 ("your obedience will be toward your husband") as meaning that "The husband's authority became still greater after the fall." See also Books X, 195–96 ("and to thy Husbands will / Thine shall submit, hee over thee shall rule"), and XI, 290–91 ("with thee goes / Thy Husband, him to follow thou art bound").

[9] The text of both 1668[2] and 1669[2] ends with a period instead of a comma.

ACCEDENCE COMMENC'T
GRAMMAR

1669

INTRODUCTION BY DAVID P. FRENCH

PREFATORY NOTE

The present edition of the *Accedence Commenc't Grammar* was originally undertaken by the late J. Milton French. By the time of his death, he had published an article about the illustrative quotations that the work contains, but he had neither prepared a text for publication nor begun the commentary about its place in literary history. Thus my father is in no way responsible for deficiencies in the present edition, which he unfortunately neither prepared nor saw.

For various kinds of help I am grateful to a number of people: to Professors Don M. Wolfe and Maurice Kelley of the editorial board; to Miss Isabel Fry and the staff of the Henry E. Huntington Library; to the Alumni Development Fund of the University of Oklahoma for a travel grant to that library; to the Faculty Research Committee of the University of Oklahoma for financial aid in collation and in the preparation of the manuscript; to Professor Bruce Granger and the late John Paul Pritchard of the Department of English at the University of Oklahoma; to Dean James Sims of the University of Southern Mississippi; and to my wife, who has generously devoted countless hours to collation of the texts, rectification of errors, and many other kindnesses.

I. PUBLICATION, RECEPTION, AND COMPOSITION

According to Anthony à Wood, John Milton's *Accedence Commenc't Grammar* first appeared in October 1661, a claim he continued to maintain in the revision of *Fasti Oxonienses* as well as in the original.[1] Since no such edition seems to be extant, however, it must at present be considered a ghost, despite the odd definiteness about the month of supposed publication. The first known actual appearance, therefore, was that announced in the June 28, 1669, issue of *Mercurius Librarius* (number 4), which prices the work at 8d bound; presumably it appeared almost immediately thereafter.[2] This version now exists with two different title pages, the one listing the author as "J.M." and the other openly calling him "John Milton," an indecisiveness the same publisher, Samuel Simmons, also demonstrates in the various title pages of *Paradise Lost*. Masson's suggestion that Simmons feared losing sales by explicit identification of the notorious author seems at least plausible.[3]

---

[1] Cited in French, *Life Records,* IV, 359.
[2] Ibid., p. 449.
[3] Masson, *Life,* VI, 622–23.

Because of the "conjugacy of title page with author's name in full," Harris Fletcher has suggested that the latter of the two forms may be the earlier printing.[4] The only important variants are in the title pages themselves, in any case, and the same printed sheets occur in both versions (see below, pp. 80–81). The book has never been separately printed since its presumed first appearance in 1669, though it has appeared in all major editions of Milton's collected prose.

Insofar as I can tell, the *Accedence* had no effect whatever upon either the schoolmasters of the day or the reading public at large. Though Solomon Lowe's *Grammar of the English Tongue* once lists Milton in 1726 as the author of such a book,[5] it was apparently never used in schools or even discussed by other grammarians. In the year after its publication, for instance, William Walker's *Royal Grammar . . . Explained*—which was variously reprinted until at least 1695—refers by name to over two dozen writers on Latin grammar, but Milton's name never appears.[6] General critical response was equally sparse. Printing history suggests that the work sold slowly, since the printer was still advertising it at the same price as late as 1680.[7] In a life of James Harrington in 1699, John Toland goes out of his way to state that had he been consulted about the choice of Milton's prose for the edition of 1698 he would have omitted the *Accedence* as negligible.[8] In his scrupulous investigation of Milton's early reputation, W. R. Parker finds only two references to the book,[9] and both of these are merely attempts to discredit the Latinity of Andrew Marvell's *Rehearsal Transpros'd* (1673) through mocking reference to schoolmaster Milton. Neither makes any useful estimate of the actual grammar. Even the interesting fact that certain editions of Milton include the *Accedence* but omit some other works is probably the result of a blanket decision to leave out all Latin writings, not an implied judgment of comparative worth. Nor has the book fared better in later ages.

---

[4] Harris Fletcher, *An Exhibition of Some Latin Grammars Used or Printed in England, 1471–1697* (Urbana: University of Illinois Press, 1955), p. 39.

[5] Foster Watson, *The English Grammar Schools to 1660* (Cambridge, 1908), p. 288; hereafter cited as Watson.

[6] For variant titles and editions of Walker's book, see *STC*.

[7] John Starkey listed Milton's text in his catalogue in Paul Rycaut's *History of the Turkish Empire*, 1680. See French, *Life Records*, V, 33.

[8] French, *Life Records*, V, 300.

[9] W. R. Parker, *Milton's Contemporary Reputation* (Columbus, Ohio, 1940), pp. 115–16.

With only two recent exceptions,[10] no modern critic or biographer
has ever discussed the book carefully: most pass it by silently, while
the rest either dutifully chronicle its existence without comment or
dub it mere hackwork, with judgments ranging from "innocuous"
to "shabby." [11] Without much doubt, it is Milton's least popular
production.

Though details of publication and reception thus seem reasonably clear, those of composition are not. Most modern scholars
seem to think that Milton wrote the *Accedence* while he was teaching school in the mid-1640s; early biographers suggest a period
either shortly before or even after the Restoration of 1660.[12] Though
it is impossible to be sure which view is correct, the three possibilities at least warrant exploration.

According to Masson, Milton began teaching his nephews as
early as 1639–40, added more pupils in the period 1640–45, and
reached the peak of his endeavors in 1647; thereafter, despite ru-
mors that he intended to found an academy like that described in
Of Education, he suddenly abandoned teaching entirely, perhaps
because he had received a sufficient bequest at his father's death
to allow him to live independently.[13] Phillips also agrees that Milton
had planned an academy but changed his mind in 1647—possibly
in connection with a shadowy scheme to make the poet an "Ad-
jutant-General in Sir *William Waller's* army." [14] Such a theory
might also explain various puzzling notes by Samuel Hartlib, who
at about the same time wrote and then canceled several references
to "Mr. Milton's Academy" among his own papers.[15] By such
reckoning, then, we should date the *Accedence* at some time prior
to 1647, and we should explain the delayed publication by Milton's
need for money after 1660. Several points support such a theory.
One would normally expect a man to write a school text while he

[10] J. Milton French, "Some Notes on Milton's *Accedence Commenc't Grammar*,"
in *Milton Studies in Honor of Harris Fletcher* (Urbana: University of Illinois
Press, 1961), pp. 33–42; also in *JEGP*, LX (1961), 641–50; hereafter cited as
French "Notes"; Gordon Campbell, "Milton's *Accedence Commenc't Grammar*,"
Milton Quarterly, X (1976), 39–48.

[11] Parker, *Milton's Reputation*, p. 49, and Masson, *Life*, VI, 640.

[12] See, for example, Masson, *Life*, VI, 640, and French, *Life Records*, IV,
449–50.

[13] Masson, *Life*, III, 656–67.

[14] French, *Life Records*, II, 122.

[15] Ibid., pp. 168–69. It is perhaps worth noting that Hartlib's notes are not
dated and thus may refer to another year entirely; yet 1647 would of course fit
perfectly with the suggested abandonment of a planned academy because of a
bequest.

was active in the profession, not over two decades later, and it seems natural to assume that the same impulse that produced *Of Education* could bring forth a Latin grammar. Again, with one exception the grammarians from whom Milton draws techniques and illustrative examples were published before 1647 (see below), and J. Milton French suggests that the one exception, James Shirley's *Via ad Linguam Latinam Complanata,* may have been available in some other form before its nominal publication date.[16] Finally, an ordinary man would be most likely to undertake a work involving much minute research in many texts only when he was capable of reading, not when he was stone blind.

Yet much can be said for the Commonwealth era as well. In the first place, Milton was apparently working upon his Latin dictionary in 1655, by which time he had been blind for some three years.[17] The two tasks of defining terms and finding grammatical illustrations, obviously, might well be done at the same time, and the use of an amanuensis for the one would allow for the other as well. In the second place, two of the early biographers agree with this hypothesis: the "earliest" biography claims that the grammar was "finish'd after the Restoration," which implies that it was begun earlier, and Aubrey states flatly that Milton wrote it "After he was blind." [18] Third, after 1655 he was granted a substitute for most of his governmental duties, and apparently he had time to work on his *History of Britain,* his Latin dictionary, and his Greek thesaurus.[19] It would not be surprising to learn that the grammar also occupied part of his thoughts as well.

The other major possibility, obviously, is the period following his compulsory retirement from politics after the return of the king. Political upheavals had made it impossible for him to write of state affairs; at the same time, financial losses that reduced his income by at least one-half and perhaps two-thirds by 1670 would make every possible honorable source of income seem attractive. Masson suggests that at one stroke he had lost £2,000 in the Excises in 1660, that he had heavy expenses because of his short imprisonment, and that the Great Fire, in burning the Bread Street house, reduced his income even further, perhaps from £200 in 1662 to about £100 in 1670.[20] Again, Charles Gildon asserts that after 1660 Milton once more turned schoolteacher, a rumor that is perhaps

---

[16] French, "Notes," pp. 34–35, n. 5; 37.
[17] French, *Life Records,* IV, 3–6.
[18] Ibid., p. 450.
[19] Ibid., pp. 3–6.
[20] Masson, *Life,* VI, 718.

strengthened by taunts against the poet for just that reason in 1673.[21] While such claims are very possibly distortions, built up on the fact that men like Ellwood welcomed the chance to read aloud to Milton in return for the pleasure of his conversation, they are perhaps not impossible—and if true would again turn his thoughts to the problems of textbooks. Finally, as we shall see later, a movement was afoot in the 1660s to replace the hitherto prescribed royal grammar with another more modern and usable one. Milton may well have hoped to gain considerable profit if his work could qualify as the official replacement. In other words, salient reasons make each of the three time spans a reasonable conjectural date of composition for the *Accedence*. At present, however, there seems no decisive way to choose among the possibilities.

II. MILTON'S *ACCEDENCE* AND LILY'S *GRAMMAR*

Unlike many of Milton's other works, the *Accedence* makes few demands upon the reader's historical, philosophical, and theological background; it is merely a textbook, designed for young school-boys or for adults with no previous training in Latin. In order to evaluate it properly, therefore, one needs to know what other books of the same sort were currently popular in 1669, which older ones were still in use, and what improvements Milton himself may have provided. The basic influence, quite clearly, was the authorized royal grammar written in large part by William Lily. This section will discuss the origin and nature of Lily's work and then compare it with Milton's recension. The following section will treat the possible influence of other grammars and grammarians. The results of both discussions should help to define the nature and extent of Milton's own contribution.

A. Grammars before Lily

All instruction in the Latin language since the Middle Ages must go back eventually to the works of Donatus, the great fourth-century grammarian upon whose *Ars Minor* nearly all later texts, including Milton's *Accedence,* are ultimately based. It is undoubtedly one of the most popular and widely circulated books ever written, having served as the standard school text for over a thousand years; it was reprinted in England as late as the sixteenth century and has been used in Italy even in the twentieth. Its very

---

[21] French, *Life Records,* V, 49.

form determined the mold of later works, and its terminology established the vocabulary of grammar in use ever since. Parts of speech (noun, pronoun, verb, adjective), case (nominative, genitive, ablative), and many other concepts appear fully developed in Donatus. Even the illustrations chosen—*musa* for a first-declension noun, *amo* for a first-conjugation verb—have continued as frequent choices until the present. The importance of the *Ars Minor* is almost impossible to overstate; despite increasing competition, most notably perhaps from Priscian in the sixth century, it held the field until the Renaissance.[1]

The first important challenge was that of scholastic philosophy, whose adherents from the middle of the twelfth century on became dissatisfied with mere handbooks of usage and wanted semantic and philosophical insights into the patterns underlying usage; these men sought not mere codifications of actual practice but a revelation of the fixed laws underlying that practice. The difference between the two approaches was clear even in so basic a matter as definition of terms. In Donatus, for instance, a pronoun is a word used in place of a noun to convey the same meaning and refers to someone or something already mentioned.[2] By 1499, however, the following was thought more illuminating: "The term *pronoun* signifies a substance or entity under the inward mode of a lasting concept of quality and state of rest under a precisely formal state of comprehension."[3] Another example would be the use of an absolute construction. Earlier grammarians merely recorded the classical usage of such a form with an ablative; the later sought to know the special "ablativity" of the "absolute" concept, the *modus significandi* of the device.[4] From a rationalistic point of view, such an approach brought under the realm of law the mere helter-skelter records of thoughtless practice; for busy schoolmasters, however, it contaminated grammatical training with irrelevant and chimerical speculation.

[1] My discussion is based primarily upon the excellent edition of Wayland Johnson Chase, *The "Ars Minor" of Donatus* (Madison, 1926).

[2] Ibid., p. 32; "pars orationis, quæ pro nomine posita tantundem pæne significat personamque interdum recepit."

[3] Cited in William Harrison Woodward, *Desiderius Erasmus Concerning the Aim and Method of Education* (Cambridge, 1904), pp. 102–3, from a 1499 printed grammar for beginners: "Pronomen . . . significat substantiam seu entitatem sub modo conceptus intrinseco permanentis seu habitus et quietis sub determinate apprehensionis formalitate." My discussion follows Woodward, who wisely evades any attempt at translation—a precedent that perhaps I should have perpetuated here.

[4] Ibid., pp. 102–3.

It is on this latter ground that Erasmus bitterly attacks the works of Johannes de Garlandia, which had attained sufficient popularity to be printed in England by both de Worde and Pynson.[5] Similarly, Lorenzo Valla (1415–65) flatly asserted that whatever good authors of antiquity had written was to him sufficient warrant of good Latinity: "I accept as law whatever great authors have practiced." [6] Latinity for Valla depends therefore upon authoritative practice, not upon logical consistency. His comment seems almost a direct rebuttal of Helias, who had condemned Priscian on rationalistic grounds:

> In as much as Priscian failed to display grammar through every possible mode of knowledge, to that degree his exposition lessened in worth. Because of this limitation, he stated many rules whose causes he did not explain, asserting them solely on the authority of classical practice. For this reason he does not really teach, since true teachers are those who assign reasons to explain their rules.[7]

Valla's *De Linguæ Latinæ Elegantia,* interestingly enough, was reprinted in England as late as 1688. And humanistic writers followed his lead, the first systematic grammar of the group perhaps being that of Petrottus, a pupil of Vittorino da Feltre, which was published in 1473.[8]

In England, publication of grammatical works began early and rapidly increased in quantity. *STC,* for instance, lists some twenty-one different authors and nearly three hundred editions of works on grammar by the year 1542. Some of these were continental—there are ten editions of Donatus and nineteen of Garland, for example—but most are English, the palm going to Whittington with 138 different entries and Stanbridge with 62. Since the first known fragment of any grammatical work printed in England dates only from c. 1481,[9] the rate of increase was clearly large. Yet most of these works, perhaps because of the Reformation, stopped being printed by about 1535; none of the voluminous productions of Stanbridge, Linacre, or Whittington—the three most impor-

---

[5] Ibid., p. 103, n. e; *STC.*

[6] Woodward, *Desiderius Erasmus,* p. 104: "Ego pro lege accipio quidquid magnis auctoribus placuit."

[7] Ibid., p. 102, n. 2: "Cum Priscianus non docuerit grammaticam per omnem modum sciendi possibilem, in eo sua doctrina est valde diminuta. Unde constructiones multas dicit, quarum tamen causas non assignat, sed *solum eas declaret per auctoritates antiquorum grammaticorum.* Propter quod non docet, quia illi tantum docent qui causas suorum dictorum assignant."

[8] Ibid., p. 104.

[9] See Harris Francis Fletcher, *The Intellectual Development of John Milton* (Urbana: University of Illinois Press, 1956–61), I, 118.

tant—was reissued after that date, and Cardinal Wolsey's *Æditio*, perhaps itself originally designed as the royal grammar, disappeared with Wolsey's own fall from grace.

Yet these books influenced later writers and deserve notice in their own right. Lily refers with high praise to "our Linacre," for example,[10] and Milton objects to him only on the ground that he is too learned for school use, which is hardly a damning comment.[11] Robert Whittington's *Vulgaria* (1525) remained sufficiently accessible for John Clarke to reprint much of it in his own *Dux Grammaticus Tyronem Scholasticum* in 1633. Furthermore, these works are by no means rote lists in Latin for the quivering seven-year-old to memorize without comprehension. The *Lac Puerorum* of John Holt (1510), for instance, explains in plain, simple English the rudiments of Latin: "There ben viii partes of speche. Noun, pronoune. . . ." Of these, he goes on, four are "declyned and moveable," and four are not. Thereafter he summarizes such matters as declensions and conjugations in compact, easy forms, using the simple examples of *musa* and *amo* which had started with Donatus. In fact, he even makes a point of using illustrations that might render the lessons both memorable and pleasant: he shows a man's hand with the appropriate forms of *hic-hœc-hoc* on each finger, he has another such for the second declension, and he uses a six-starred candelabrum to make case endings clear. Also, following a trick of medieval grammarians that we shall later see in Lily, he puts many of his rules into verses that the children might learn more easily than dry lists.[12] All of these methods, clearly, are intended to make schooling as pleasant as possible; they do not depend upon brutal floggings to enforce student effort.

Furthermore, the good grammarians of the day make it clear that conjugations and syntax are not ends in themselves but merely the entrance to the treasury of Latin literature: in fact, they frequently protest against overemphasis upon the rules. In his at times charming *Rudimenta Grammatices* (1529?), Cardinal Wolsey first insists that his only purpose has been to make rules clearer to "young wits" than they had been before and then firmly states that

[10] Vincent J. Flynn, ed., *A Shorte Introduction of Grammar by William Lily* (New York: Scholars' Facsimiles & Reprints, 1945), sig. E2 of the *Brevissima Institutio*, which comprises the second half of the volume. I shall use this edition for all citations from Lily with the short titles *Shorte Introduction* and *Brevissima Institutio*. Lack of pagination unfortunately calls for location through signatures.

[11] John Milton, *Accedence Commenc't Grammar*, see below, p. 86; hereafter cited as *Accedence*.

[12] John Holt, *Lac Puerorum* (1510; BM), sigs. A3–A3v, A4, A5v, A7v.

children should begin actual readings as soon as they have learned
the basic declensions and conjugations; rules follow usage, he observes, and not the contrary—and thus one should go as directly
as possible to the texts themselves.[13] Two years later, Sir Thomas
Elyot makes exactly the same plea in *The Boke Named the Governour* (1531): "Grammar being but an introduction to the understanding of authors, if it be made too long or too exquisite [minutely
detailed] to the learner, it . . . mortifieth his courage."[14]

For Wolsey and Elyot, as well as for Erasmus, grammar was
a humanistic art designed to advance men in general wisdom, not
to exercise them in the intricacies of syntactical hairsplitting. Thus
the grammars of these early years obviously discard the scholastic
emphasis upon the philosophical basis for rules and align themselves firmly with the empirical traditions of Donatus and Valla.

B. Lily's *Grammar* and Its Opponents

In 1540 occurred the most decisive single event in the history of
Latin grammars in England: Henry VIII decreed that all schoolmasters and all schools in the kingdom should thereafter use one
and only one text, the authorized grammar commonly called Lily's.
This official monopoly was later confirmed by edicts of Edward
VI, Elizabeth I, and various sessions of both Houses of Convocation. That of 1571, for instance, spoke as follows: "Schoolmasters
shall teach no grammar book but that which the king's majesty
has ordained for use in all schools throughout the realm." That of
1604 confirmed the same order: "they shall teach the grammar set
forth by Henry the Eighth, and continued in the times of King
Edward the Sixth, and Queen Elizabeth of noble memory, and
none other. And if any schoolmaster, being licensed . . . shall
[disobey, he shall] . . . be suspended from teaching school any
longer."[1] As Foster Watson wryly notes, even today Lily's grammar is apparently the only lawful text in English schools.[2] Thus
all later texts, including Milton's, were at least nominally illegal

---

[13] *Rudimenta Grammatices* (1529; BM), sig. G4.

[14] Sir Thomas Elyot, *The Boke Named the Governour*, ed. Foster Watson
(London, 1907), p. 35.

[1] Cited in Edward Cardwell, *Synodalia: A Collection of Articles of Religion,
Canons, and Proceedings of Convocations in the Province of Canterbury*
[1547–1717], 2 vols. (Oxford, 1842), II, 128: "Ludi magistri nullam docebunt
grammaticam, nisi eam, quam solam regia majestas per omne regnum in omnibus
scholis legi mandavit." The second passage (ibid., II, 292) is in English.

[2] Watson, p. 258.

for any schoolmaster to assign to his pupils—though not, perhaps, to publish, buy, or use himself.

The book itself is a curious combination of quite different sections, composed by various men and basted into a single cover. In part, it was written by John Colet, the Dean of Saint Paul's Cathedral; in part, it comes from William Lily, the headmaster of Saint Paul's School; additions and revisions were provided by Erasmus himself; and various others including a royal committee combined to provide the final form of the 1542 edition.[3] Certain of its details need not detain us here: the royal proclamation for its use, a short section on orthography, a discussion of Latin prosody, and an index translating the major words used in the rules. There are also a few rather innocuous prayers, suggesting perhaps the hope of the compilers to avoid doctrinal disputes without becoming entirely secular. Beyond these peripheral matters, the book falls essentially into two parts: a *Shorte Introduction of Grammar,* covering about one-third of the volume, and a far more elaborate *Brevissima Institutio seu Ratio Grammatices Cognoscende* comprising the rest. The *Shorte Introduction* is entirely in English; the *Brevissima Institutio* is entirely in Latin. A preface to the reader explains the scope and rationale of the whole work.

In general, the longer *Brevissima Institutio*—whose title J. Milton French aptly calls ironic [4]—is a detailed elaboration and very frequently a repetition of matters treated in the *Shorte Introduction.* Each of the two sections is a nearly complete Latin grammar in itself, the only major difference being fullness of coverage. Also, in form both follow the same pattern. First of all, the parts of speech are listed in two groups: those that are declined, such as the noun and verb, and those that are not, such as the conjunction. Then the writer methodically treats each in turn, explaining its nature, forms, and uses. After discussing the parts of speech by themselves—their etymology or accidence, in contemporary terminology—he treats syntax, the ways in which one word links to others in the sentence. First come the three concords or agreements: of subject with verb, of noun with adjective, of relatives with their antecedents. Then he treats each part of speech in relation to others: how nouns are fitted to other nouns in apposition, which adjectives take the genitive, which verbs use an ablative, and other such matters. By the end, he has both shown the variant forms of

---

[3] For the quite complicated history of the early editions, see among others the works of Fletcher, Flynn, and Watson listed above.

[4] French, "Notes," p. 35.

individual words and explained how they combine in Latin sentences.

Apart from the language in which each is written, the main differences between the two parts are matters of degree, not of kind. Leaving aside such minor points as prosody, which occurs only in the Latin *Brevissima Institutio,* Lily's *Grammar* is thus a double work, not a single one. While the English tends to state main rules without exceptions, the Latin adds a wealth of special cases and subrules. The most famous parts of the latter are its three hexameter poems: the *Propria quæ maribus,* dealing with the genders of regular nouns; the *Quæ genus,* treating irregular nouns; and the *As in præsenti,* treating the principal parts of verbs. These are long, detailed, and complex, often providing a versified listing of dozens of special cases:

> As in præsenti, perfectum format in avi,
> Ut no nas navi, vocito vocitas vocitavi.
> Deme lavo lavi, iuvo iuvi, nexoque nexui,
> Et seco quod secui, neco quod necui, mico verbum
> Quod micui, plico quod plicui, frico quod fricui dat.[5]

In five lines here, a general rule with two regular examples is followed by eight exceptions—and more follow in the poem itself. The *Shorte Introduction,* on the other hand, merely conjugates a single sample verb for each class, omitting both the principle behind the relation of parts and the possible exceptions thereto.

The intended use of the work is made clear in the preface "To the Reader." [6] Because a grammar is necessary for beginners, one is provided; since a single universal text is preferable to a multitude of competing and conflicting ones, this one is prescribed, though schoolmasters are urged to submit possible improvements. In actual class use, the master should first teach thoroughly the various conjugations and declensions, the necessary foundation to all later work; a student should be able to complete this preliminary task in only three months. Next he should learn the three concords. Thereafter, however, instead of continuing methodically with the grammar, he should go directly to writing simple Latin from English models. Thus the second or Latin part was designed not as a text but as a reference book, through which the pupil might solve whatever perplexities he found in his own efforts at composition.

On the whole, then, the preface advocates a sensible and humane approach to the teaching of Latin. Yet, both then and since, its

---

[5] Lily, *Brevissima Institutio,* sig. C6.
[6] Lily, *Shorte Introduction,* sigs. A2–A3v.

intent has been often misunderstood. It is frequently asserted or implied, for instance, that pupils were forced to memorize, in Latin, the whole grammar of a language they did not yet understand in the least. By implication, of course, Renaissance schoolmasters become insensitive tyrants whose only goal was to make their pupils miserable. These charges have been exaggerated and distorted, even by unusually sensitive scholars. Donald L. Clark, for instance, makes the following comment about Saint Paul's School, which was both Milton's and Lily's and thus is an especially appropriate example: "And I say 'learn' advisedly, for the tradition of the grammar school required the boy to memorize his Latin grammar. . . . In some of the more popular textbooks the rules were put into verse to make memorizing easier." [7] Elsewhere he notes that the *Carmen de Moribus,* an eighty-six-line Latin poem by Lily about proper manners for schoolchildren, was first parsed and then memorized in the first or second form.[8] Yet Clark also carefully points out [9] that good teachers never made children learn anything they did not already thoroughly understand. Sensible contemporary writers frequently insist upon the same point. In his influential *Ludus Literarius* (1612), for example, John Brinsley introduces a dialogue between Spondeus, a discouraged and ineffective teacher, and Philoponus, an enlightened representative of Brinsley himself who insists that memorization without understanding is futile.[10] Thus one-half of the usual charge seems unjustified: uncomprehending memorization was not the goal. The other half is a misleading partial truth. Parts of the Latin grammar were memorized in the upper forms, to wit, the *Quæ genus,* the *As in præsenti,* and the *Propria quæ maribus.* Their very verse form, which is perhaps a relic of medieval days when books were too expensive for mere pupils to own and when only memorization could lead to learning, is obviously designed for that purpose. Yet this fact is quite different from Clark's phrase, "memorize his Latin grammar," and comes much nearer to the standard modern requirement that a boy learn the principal parts of irregular verbs, and the like, along the way. At Ipswich, for instance, Cardinal Wolsey assigned the three poems to three different forms for three different years.[11] In length the poems take up, respectively, five, ten, and five pages of Lily.

[7] Donald Lemen Clark, *John Milton at St. Paul's School* (New York: Columbia University Press, 1948), p. 128.

[8] Ibid., p. 54.

[9] Ibid., p. 168.

[10] John Brinsley, *Ludus Literarius* (1627, CAM; originally 1612), pp. 53–54.

[11] Cited in Clark, *Milton at St. Paul's,* p. 117.

Thus the student was asked, in the course of three years, to memorize a total of twenty pages of versified rules, or something under seven a year. Furthermore, since the whole *Brevissima Institutio* is 138 pages long, the sections marked for memorization take up less than 15 percent of the space, a fact that significantly reduces the supposed cruelty of teaching at the time. Unless one completely rejects all memorization whatever—a precept that would make any language teaching apparently impossible—both the education of the day and Lily's grammar itself seem more sinned against than sinning.

Despite its very real virtues, however, the work does have obvious limitations. The Latin poems are difficult to use for reference purposes because they are not alphabetically arranged; the repetition of material in two separate grammars is needlessly cumbersome; the advantages of treating grammar in the language being learned are at best debatable; and the prescription of a single required text would inevitably antagonize every grammarian who thought that he could write a better one. Thus it is not surprising that Lily's monopoly was frequently challenged. Some of the protests were purely economic, like Michael Sparke's *Scintilla* (1641), which is essentially a plea that all publishers and not merely the patent holder be allowed to reprint Lily. In addition, however, a good many books either attacked Lily's imperfections openly or, by offering to supplement his work, implied his inadequacy. Some of these seem to have disappeared; there are references to an attack upon the book in about 1620 by one Ralph Gittins, for instance, which I have been unable to track down. Yet others can still be found, such as the following:

1616   Thomas Granger, *Syntagma Grammaticum, or an Easie Explanation of Lillies Grammar*
1625   Thomas Wise, *Animadversions upon Lillies Grammar*
1642   William Hayne, *Lillies Rules Construed*
1651   Charles Hoole, *Lilly's Latin Grammar Fitted for the Use of Schools*
1659   Bassett Jones, *Hermæologium . . . A Supplement to Lilly's Grammar*
1665   Edward Leedes, *Vossius in Supplementum Vulgaris Grammatices*
1670   William Walker, *The Royal Grammar . . . Explained*
1684   G., R., *A Censure upon Lilly's Grammar*

One neither supplements, censures, animadverts upon, nor fits out that which is already satisfactory. And these titles are merely samples, chosen at approximately decade intervals from a list that could be lengthened.

Another evidence of dissatisfaction can be found in full-fledged attempts to supplant the royal grammar. As early as 1551, for example, less than a decade after the royal mandate, John Fox submitted to the Privy Council certain "tables of grammar" designed to reduce the prolixity of Lily. Furthermore, he had the written support of eight lords of the Council to back him up.[12] Again, Thomas Farnaby's popular *Systema Grammaticum* of 1641 is said to have been written at the express command of King Charles I, another indication of a desire for change.[13] During the Commonwealth period, several attempts were made to replace Lily with the textbooks of Comenius and his followers. And after the Restoration, at least two frontal attacks were mounted. The first is to be found in at least three records, those of the Convocation of the Church of England and of Parliament itself. On May 4, 1661, the future Bishop John Pearson, famous for his explanation of the Creed, submitted an alternative grammar that was seriously considered: "There was introduced a book of grammar written by John Pierson, S.T.P., a member of the Lower House; and the said reverend father, with the approbation of his fellows, committed its care, review, and examination to the reverend father . . . and other bishops."[14] Two years later, on March 28, 1663, another proposal was made for a text that would teach both Latin and Greek grammar simultaneously; the matter was then adjourned until the following May, and nothing came of it.[15] The third main attack occurred in the House of Lords in 1675, where "Lilly's Etc. Grammar Bill" was introduced "to enjoin the Teaching of Lillie's and Cambden's Grammar in Free Schools."[16] This move to bolster traditional standards (Camden's Greek grammar was widely used) apparently failed to gain sufficient support to get beyond a first reading, an indication of strong opposition.

The most striking proof of discontent, however, lies in the enormous number of other grammar books that did not pose as supplements to Lily but were written, published, and presumably even used after the promulgation of the royal decree. A reading of both *Short-Title Catalogues* nets well over 150 different titles between 1540 and 1700, and this number omits all reprintings—an important fact in that several of these went through seven or eight dif-

---

[12] Watson, p. 241.

[13] Ibid., p. 274.

[14] Cardwell, *Synodalia,* II, 782: "Liber grammaticalis per Johannem Pierson S.T.P. unus de gremio domus inferioris fuit introduct': et dictus reverendissimus pater, de et cum concensu confratrum suorum, curam, revisionem, et examinationem ejusdem commisit reverendissimo patri . . . [et aliis] episcopis."

[15] Ibid., II, 674.

[16] *House of Lords Journals,* XI, 703b [27 Car. II (1674)].

ferent editions. To put it differently, despite Lily's monopoly, one new book on the topic appeared almost every year. Milton's *Accedence Commenc't Grammar* should consequently be viewed not as an isolated and exceptional occurrence but as one of many varied attempts to improve the work prescribed for the use of schools and schoolmasters. Somewhat later in this essay, I shall look in more detail at the nature and contents of these competitive offerings.

In practice, though, none of these attacks completely accomplished its goal; Lily continued throughout the eighteenth century, underwent a major revision by Christopher Wordsworth (the poet's brother) in the early nineteenth, and carried on until its final displacement by Dr. Hornby of Eton in 1868.[17] The book was, then, enormously successful for over three hundred years. Cumulatively, however, the various forays traced above indicate that there was dissatisfaction with it almost from the beginning and that many thoughtful men felt that it was inadequate to its purpose. One of these was John Milton.

C. Milton's Departures from Lily

Several seventeenth-century grammarians such as Farnaby and Danes are good enough to list in their prefaces what they consider their major innovations. Milton unfortunately is less specific, but in his short "To the Reader" he does mention at least three sorts of changes he has made from Lily: consolidation into a single and unified English volume, judicious compressions and omissions, and certain structural alterations. All in all, these represent a distinct improvement over his source.

1. Consolidation into One English Grammar

Milton's first prefatory complaint involves the "making two labours of one, by learning first the Accedence, then the Grammar in Latin, ere the Language of those Rules be understood." [1] This statement is rather ambiguous, however, and even seems to contradict the very title of his book: *Accedence Commenc't Grammar:* the one objects to beginning grammar with accidence while the other promises just that. *Accedence,* which Milton never defines, is usually equated with *etymology* or what he calls *right-wording,* the separate examination of each part of speech by itself; he and others distinguish the term from *syntax* or *right-joyning,* which treats the methods of connecting separate words in a proper man-

---

[17] Flynn's introduction to Lily, p. ix.
[1] *Accedence,* p. 86 below.

ner. *Grammar* Milton defines as "right understanding, speaking, or writing Latine," [2] a highly inclusive statement that of course comprehends both accidence and syntax. Thus his prefatory statement implies a bewildering opposition between the whole and one of its parts. Furthermore, since no major grammarian ever suggested beginning language training with syntax, the very title of the book seems to belabor the obvious or to say nothing at all.

No solution to these issues seems entirely convincing, but perhaps two possibilities are worth mention. First, Milton may be trying to suggest that he is writing a grammar that begins with the accidence and not, as Lily had, with orthography; in fact, he specifically mentions omitting among other things "*That of Grammar, touching Letters and Syllables.*" [3] Secondly and perhaps more probably, he may be trying in his title to emphasize the singleness of his own book. Many grammarians talked as if Lily's *Shorte Introduction* were nothing but a description of the eight parts of speech, an accidence and not a syntax, even though in fact it treats concords and questions of construction for a full eighteen pages. Thus, perhaps Milton is accepting the common though fallacious view as a way of saying that he has joined into one both the *Shorte Introduction* and the *Brevissima Institutio*. Perhaps the kindest answer, however, would be to assume that the publisher, Simmons, chose the title after reading Milton's ambiguous prefatory note and that the poet himself was not responsible for what seems at best clumsy and unclear.

In any case, his solution to the prefatory problem is clear: "to joyn both Books into one, and in the English Tongue." [4] This statement actually fuses two quite different matters, the ordering of materials and the language they are written in. As to the former, Lily's double plan inevitably brought about repetition in some spots and confusing omission in others. The English section, for example, says that a noun is the "name of a thinge, that may be seene, felte, hearde, or understande: As the name of my hande in Latine is Manus: the name of an House is Domus: the name of goodnes is Bonitas"; in the Latin, it is "a part of speech which signifies a thing, without any distinction of time or person." [5] The first defines by example, the second by genus and differentiae; the whole involves both repetition and possible confusion. Milton's single text

---

[2] Ibid., p. 87 below.

[3] Ibid., p. 86 below.

[4] Ibid., p. 86 below.

[5] Lily, *Shorte Introduction,* sig. A5; *Brevissima Institutio,* sig. A5: "Nomen, est pars orationis, quæ rem significat, sine ulla temporis aut personæ differentia."

avoids the whole issue: "A Noune is the Name of a Thing, as *Manus* a Hand, *Domus* a House, *Bonus* good, *Pulcher* fair." [6] Again, Lily defines the cases of nouns for twenty-one lines of the *Shorte Introduction* and then repeats exactly the same materials, with no significant differences, for sixteen lines of the *Brevissima Institutio*.[7] On the other hand, a long section in the latter about the kinds of nouns—in all twenty-three, from primitive and derivative through adverbial and participial—occurs nowhere in the former; [8] likewise, the extremely important discussion of principal parts of verbs that makes up the *As in præsenti* can be found only in the more complete handbook.[9] Yet the sample conjugations of verbs and declensions of nouns that are, after all, the very heart of the Latin language are never repeated in the *Brevissima Institutio*. The student trying to solve a problem, therefore, was obliged to thumb through the equivalent of two volumes to find an answer he dimly remembered having seen somewhere. Milton's organization here is distinctly better.

At least for most twentieth-century readers, the substitution of a purely English commentary will bring few regrets. Even if we assume, as Lily's preface advises, that the *Brevissima Institutio* is a reference work rather than a textbook, and even if we assume yet more hopefully that the student seeking tips on the supine had thoroughly learned the *Shorte Introduction* some time earlier, it still does not follow that he could read with no trouble a Latin discussion of grammatical difficulties. Despite praxis, phrase book, and colloquy, he would still need to seek subject and verb methodically to answer in an hour a problem that five minutes might otherwise dispose of. At one stroke, in other words, Milton dispensed with at least half the difficulty the tyro must have felt in using Lily.

2. Omission and Compression

A second virtue that Milton specifies in his preface is his greater "brevity." [10] His claim is quite justified in regard to Lily: the *Accedence* is only sixty-five pages long, which is little more than the *Shorte Introduction* alone with its sixty-three pages in Lily—and the addition of the *Brevissima Institutio* brings the total to 203. This saving comes partly through omission and partly through

[6] *Accedence*, p. 89 below.

[7] Lily, *Shorte Introduction*, sig. A5v; *Brevissima Institutio*, sig. A6.

[8] Lily, *Brevissima Institutio*, sig. A5–A6r.

[9] Ibid., sig. C65 ff.

[10] *Accedence*, p. 86 below.

compression. Milton's decision to use a single volume in place of Lily's yoked twins of course explains much of the latter; the gain here is clearly great. But the same principle can be seen in individual sections as well. When he comes to define *etymology,* for instance, Lily includes eight lines that discuss alternate historical word sources, make a donnish pun about a single life and its heavenly nature, furnish us with alternative terms from Cicero (*notatio* or *veriloquium*), and derive the word itself from its Greek roots.[11] Milton shortens all this to a single sentence: *"Etymologie,* or Right-wording, teacheth what belongs to every single word or part of Speech." [12] Without losing any crucial part of the original, he has pared away much that was superfluous.

Milton frequently leaves out needless ramifications of the rules. Lily, for instance, lists six different modes of verbs (indicative, imperative, infinitive, optative, potential, and subjunctive) and follows each drearily through all four sample conjugations, one after another.[13] Milton, on the other hand, reduces these to four: indicative, imperative, infinitive, and "the Potential or Subjunctive." [14] The principle here seems to be quite different. Milton arranges words by their case endings so that the student may easily recognize and use each; Lily, on the other hand, is differentiating terms through their signification. The optative, the subjunctive, and the potential are identical in form: *laudarem* is the first person singular imperfect of each of the three, as *audivissent* is the third plural pluperfect. Thus Milton here is clearly the more empirical of the two, with emphasis on the actual endings in use, while Lily still shows traces of the scholastic desire to categorize by essences. The same distinction is also at work elsewhere. Lily names seven genders: masculine, feminine, neuter, common of two, common of three, doubtful, and epicoene; [15] Milton has only the first three, and while he notes that some words are of two genders or even of three, he omits the epicoene entirely.[16] Since the case endings are the same in the latter three, he clearly views them as a needless elaboration of classes. The most striking example, perhaps, is the adverb, which Lily elaborately breaks into some thirty forms: place, time, number, calling, affirming, excluding, choosing, re-

---

[11] Lily, *Brevissima Institutio,* sig. A4v.
[12] *Accedence,* p. 87 below.
[13] Lily, *Shorte Introduction,* sigs. B3v ff.
[14] *Accedence,* p. 98 below.
[15] Lily, *Shorte Introduction,* sigs. A5v f.
[16] *Accedence,* pp. 87–88 below.

mitting, and so on almost forever.[17] Milton's statement is refreshingly simple: "Of Adverbs, some be of *Time,* as *hodiè* to day, *Cras* to morrow &c. Some be of *Place,* as *Ubi* where, *ibi* there, &c. And of many other sorts needless to be set down here." [18] The firmness of phrase here shows clearly Milton's emphasis upon the learning of usable Latin, not of a philosophical framework within which to view it.

Milton saves even more space through complete omission of several whole sections in Lily: various prayers and graces to be read at meal times, a *Carmen de moribus* with its hints about schoolboy etiquette, a short treatment of orthography and Latin pronunciation, a summary of prosody, and an index of Latin nouns and verbs in the versified rules. While the last might have been a helpful addition, few of the rest would be missed. John Milton, whose *Of Education* is after all designed in part to counteract the effects of original sin and whose educational curriculum worked outward from simple biblical stories to the heights of theology, would certainly not object to religious instruction, but he might well find Lily's offerings somewhat perfunctory and easily expendable. The section on orthography is, as he observes, left out "as learnt before, and little different from the English spelling." [19] In *Of Education,* Milton proposes that children should begin grammar school not at six but at twelve, by which time they would have learned English literacy at a petty school; [20] for such a pupil, definitions of the vowels or lists of English letters in upper and lowercase forms would be needless, and they would be even less helpful to "the Elder Sort" who might use the book. As to pronunciation, Milton's well-known complaint to Ellwood that few Englishmen would ever try to speak Latin with the "correct" Italian sounds may well have discouraged him from any attempt: [21] "few will be perswaded to pronounce Latin otherwise than thir own English." [22]

At least two reasons may help to explain his omission of a prosody, even though obviously Milton thought poetry important. First, his somewhat utilitarian educational program included few Latin poets in the early years; Edward Phillips' list of his school reading includes in all only two, Manilius and Lucretius, both of

[17] Lily, *Shorte Introduction,* sigs. C2v f.

[18] *Accedence,* p. 111 below.

[19] Ibid., p. 86 below.

[20] *Complete Prose,* II, 379 and n. 59.

[21] See, for instance, James Holly Hanford, *A Milton Handbook,* 3rd ed. (New York, 1941), p. 62.

[22] *Accedence,* p. 86 below.

whom he presumably came to rather late in his career.[23] Second, Milton himself notes that by the time a student has learned this grammar well, prosody "will not need to be Englisht for him who has a mind to read it."[24] Thus apparently Milton views versification as a late stage of education, in opposition to many schoolmasters of the day who asked for Latin poems from a quite early age. And by the time a student was reading Horace and Catullus, he would be far beyond the elementary materials in Lily with their definitions of feet, catalogues of meters, and simple discussions of quantity. Like the previous sections, then, that on metrics disappears from Milton's text, and since all of these together fill almost one-quarter of Lily's volume, their omission distinctly sharpens the outlines of the *Accedence*.

A third method of shortening the work stems from his admirable resolve to omit exceptional cases entirely: "What will not come under Rule, by reason of too much variety in Declension, Gender, or Construction, is also here omitted, least the course and clearness of method be clog'd with Catalogues instead of Rules, or too much interruption between Rule and Rule."[25] He then instances Linacre's final decision to list alphabetically all idioms involving verbs, in a book that "though very learned, [was] not thought fit to be read in Schools." Milton's own solution is simple: instead of such catalogues, a "Dictionary stor'd with good Authorities will be found the readiest guide."[26] The major victims here are the three rhymed poems in Lily: the *Quæ genus* with its discussion of irregular nouns, the *As in præsenti* containing the principal parts of verbs, and the *Propria quæ maribus* with the genders of regular nouns. In the main, Milton's version is a distinct improvement over Lily's, though unfortunately he does not always remember his own excellent rule and thus at times also falls into pedantry.

His greatest success, as one might expect, comes with the *Quæ genus,* which by definition deals with exceptions that "reading will best teach." Five pages of Lily's verse are thus compressed into two paragraphs stating briefly that some nouns lack either singular or plural forms, that some switch their gender in changing from singular to plural, and that still others take various genders in the plural. We consequently escape in Milton from a profusion of aptotes, monoptotes, diptotes, triptotes, and redundants within which Lily piles up several hundred defective or irregular nouns, many

[23] Helen Darbishire, ed., *The Early Lives of Milton* (London, 1932), p. 60.
[24] *Accedence,* p. 86 below.
[25] Ibid.
[26] Ibid.

of which are both unusual and quite useless to a schoolboy working up his theme.[27] In the *As in præsenti,* on the other hand, Milton faced more difficult problems, some of which will be treated later (pp. 59–60) and others of which compression could not shorten. Many examples in Lily's *Quæ genus* have no pedagogical value and are present merely to satisfy a lust for completeness—like the statement that Juvenal once uses *balneum,* a watering-place, in the plural—but no one can use Latin at all without a thorough grounding in the principal parts of common verbs, many of which are highly irregular. Thus Milton was forced to provide an extensive list, and he did so.

The *Propria quæ maribus* is much improved in the *Accedence,* but here Milton himself descends to mechanical lists of exceptions, especially in his treatment of third-declension nouns. After a brave start that summarizes the main rules of the Latin poem in concise English prose, he falters by including two particular exceptions (the proper names *Agragas* and *Sulmo*) and cannot resist showing that *oleaster,* usually masculine, is once feminine in Cicero.[28] He does classify third-declension nouns by a general rule involving unaccented or accented forms of the genitive singular, but he is so aware of numerous exceptions that he tries to deal with these too. Having begun with a perhaps defensible series of subrules—e.g., nouns ending in *-do, -go, -as,* and *-ix* are feminine[29]—he then adds catalogues of examples and exceptions that are not defensible. Dealing with neuters, for instance, he includes this imposing aggregation: "mel, fel, lac, far, ver, cor, æs, vas vasis, os ossis, os oris, rus, thus, jus, crus, pus."[30] To crown all, the list is copied exactly, with no change whatever, from the *Propria.*[31] Nor is this the only case: he borrows a similar list of over twenty nouns to illustrate one general rule and then immediately adds ten more exceptions—also mostly from Lily, though apparently he stuck one of his own on at the end.[32] Finally, he interlards his discussion of the other declensions with similar anomalies, as if he had at this point forgotten his previously declared goal. Though his section on nouns is considerably shorter than that in his source, then, the difference is less than strict adherence to his own rule of avoiding catalogues would provide; in fact, as the text now stands, the

[27] Lily, *Brevissima Institutio,* sigs. B6 ff.
[28] *Accedence,* pp. 87–88 below.
[29] Ibid., p. 92 below.
[30] Ibid.
[31] Lily, *Brevissima Institutio,* sig. B1.
[32] *Accedence,* p. 91 below.

reader must search for some time in order to disentangle the three supposedly basic accentual rules for the third declension.

The fourth and final method of achieving brevity is Milton's frequent compression of individual details into fewer words than Lily's equivalent achieves. As J. Milton French has pointed out, one device was to condense his illustrative examples, leaving out all parts of the original that do not clarify the immediate grammatical issue.[33] Thus, for instance, Lily illustrates the use of an understood noun by using the sentence "Ubi ad Dianæ veneris, ito ad dexteram," or "When you reach [the temple] of Diana, turn right."[34] In appropriating the same example, Milton omits entirely the main clause; he prints only "Ubi ad Dianæ veneris."[35] When Lily's sentences are needlessly long, such surgery is excellent: it prevents distraction and confusion of the present grammatical problem with possible other issues elsewhere in the sentence. At times, however, the result can be so cryptic as to make the remaining words almost impossible for a beginner to understand— and thus destroys the whole value of the illustration. A second and even more doubtful economy was Milton's decision not to translate his examples. On the whole, Lily gives English versions of each in the *Shorte Introduction* but consistently omits them in the *Brevissima Institutio,* presumably on the assumption that a student capable of using the second section could do his own translating. Milton follows a similar pattern, occasionally translating short examples in the passages about the parts of speech but more often not—and never giving translations in the syntax. In view of the fact that in 1657 Charles Hoole methodically spent one whole section of his *Common Rudiments of Latine Grammar* in translating each of Lily's examples throughout the whole book,[36] it seems obvious that here Milton badly overestimated student proficiency. Still a third attempt at compression comes in changed phrasing of the rules themselves. At times, the result is cryptic to the point of obscurity, as in the following: "And if the Nominative cases be of several persons, or the Substantives and Antecedents of several Genders, the Verb shall agree with the second person before the third, and with the first before either; And so shall the Adjective or Relative in thir Gender."[37] As other authors make plain, he is

[33] French, "Notes," p. 36, n. 8.

[34] Lily, *Brevissima Institutio,* sig. E4.

[35] *Accedence,* p. 115 below.

[36] Charles Hoole, *The Common Rudiments of Latine Grammar* (London, 1657; HCL), pt. III.

[37] *Accedence,* p. 114 below.

here saying that just as one prefers the first to the second person and the second to the third, so one should prefer the masculine to the feminine gender and the feminine to the neuter when a choice of agreement appears. Thus, in the statement "Frater & Soror quos vidisti," or "the brother and sister whom you saw," *quos* (whom) is in the masculine because that is what other writers call the more worthy gender. In his desire to save words here, Milton produces a rule that no student could possibly hope to understand.

By all these means, then, Milton succeeds in drastically reducing Lily's book to about one-quarter of its original size. Some of them, it is true, seem ill advised, such as the omission of the glossary, the failure to translate examples, and the occasional obscure phrasing of rules. At other times, Milton fails to sustain his own promise to omit exceptions and piles up the pedantic lists that he condemns in others. In general, however, the reducing diet succeeds; by using it, Milton slims both parts of Lily into a single volume about the size of the *Shorte Introduction* alone. This feat by itself would deserve credit.

3. Alterations

In his note "To the Reader," Milton briefly mentions "*addition or alteration from other Grammars*" as part of his purpose, but he does not specify any details, saying merely that his own book will "declare sufficiently to them who can discern." [38] And certainly there are dozens of changes throughout the work. Some are mere matters of detail, ranging from redefinition of terms to the correction of apparent errors in Lily. Some involve the revision and often the expansion of the illustrative examples that Lily joins to his rules. And finally, there are a number of more sweeping structural changes that reorder whole sections to make them simpler, clearer, or more effective. Some examples of each of the three might be helpful.

a. Details. In describing the formation of superlative adjectives, Lily says that one adds "s + simus" to the "firste case of his positive that endeth in i," as in *durus, duri, durissimus* (hard . . . hardest). [39] Milton has a slightly different phrasing; the superlative "is formd of the first case of his Positive that endeth in *is,* by putting thereto *simus,* as of [*durus*] *duris durissimus.*" [40] The results are obviously the same in both cases, but Milton has shortened the process by

[38] *Accedence,* p. 86 below.
[39] Lily, *Shorte Introduction,* sig. A8.
[40] *Accedence,* p. 95 below.

one step and thus simplified one problem for the learner of Latin. He is equally helpful at times in his definitions of terms. The main structural distinction in all grammars of the day came between the accidence and the syntax. In the *Shorte Introduction,* where help is most needed, Lily makes no real attempt to explain the difference but instead goes directly into his subject matter: "For the due joyninge of wordes in construction, it is to be understanded, that in Latine speache there be three Concordes. The first betweene [&c.]." [41] Milton, on the other hand, clarifies his terms:

> Hitherto the Eight Parts of speech Declin'd and Undeclin'd have been spoken of single, and each one by it self: Now followeth *Syntaxis* or *Construction,* which is the right joyning of these parts together in a Sentence.
> Construction consisteth either in the agreement of words together in Number, Gender, Case, and Person, which is call'd Concord; or the governing of one the other in such Case or Mood as is to follow. [42]

In other words, the reader now realizes where he has been and where he is going, a most helpful bit of information. Lily defines *grammar* itself as "recte scribendi atque loquendi ars," [43] the art of writing and speaking well; Milton, more humanistically, expands the term to be "the Art of right understanding, speaking, or writing Latine, observd from them who have spoken or written it best." [44] Lily would undoubtedly accept both of the added propositions, namely that grammar appeals to the mind as well as to the memory and that it is empirical and not scholastic in origin, but he here failed to say so, whereas Milton explicitly added the points.

Not all of the changes seem equally helpful, however. Lily calls an adverb "a part of speache joyned to the Verbes, to declare theyr signification." [45] Presumably noting that such a definition omits adverbs modifying adjectives—as in "the book was *almost* ruined"—Milton tried to enlarge his scope to cover such cases: "An Adverb is a part of Speech joynd with some other to explain its signification." [46] The greater inclusiveness here produces a corresponding error, as it would presumably include all adjectives, which also are joined to words to explain their signification: "the *brown* book." Again, Milton's definitions of the cases are far less

[41] Lily, *Shorte Introduction,* sig. C4.
[42] *Accedence,* p. 113 below.
[43] Lily, *Brevissima Institutio,* sig. A2.
[44] *Accedence,* p. 87 below.
[45] Lily, *Shorte Introduction,* sig. C2v.
[46] *Accedence,* p. 111 below.

adequate than those in the royal grammar. The nominative, says Lily, "commeth before the verbe, and aunswereth to this question, Who or What"; [47] for Milton it is merely "the first Case, and properly nameth the thing." [48] Had he said "the case usually given in rules and dictionaries," he might have defined the awkward word *first,* but he still would not have told us how to use the form.

On a number of occasions, Milton also makes corrections in Lily's assertions. Lily, for example, includes the Greek derivative name *Androgeos* with the second declension and puts *Sappho* with the third.[49] For Milton, "Proper names in *os* and *o* long pertaining to the Fourth Declension Greek, may belong best to the fourth in Latin, as *Androgeos* . . . [and] *Sappho.*" [50] Again, Lily says [51] that when a vowel precedes a -*us* adjective, it should be compared with *magis* and *maxime* and not changed of itself, as in English one says "more nearly" and not "nearlier." His example is *assiduus,* whose superlative he gives as *maxime assiduus.* Milton, after citing the same generalization, says "Yet some of these follow the general Rule, as *Assiduus, assiduissimus.*" [52] Though other examples might be given—he calls Lily's future infinitive a participle, for instance, and denies the existence of a perfect passive tense[53]— these may suffice to show the kind of careful weighing and checking that Milton used in his own work. Though both authors, at first glance, often seem to be saying the same thing, Milton's boast that differences "will declare sufficiently" to a careful reader is by no means unfounded.

b. Examples. In his article about the *Accedence,* J. Milton French deals specifically with the nature and origin of Milton's illustrative materials. The text as a whole, he observes, contains about 530 different examples, of which 330 or nearly 60 percent come directly from Lily.[54] It seems fair to conclude then that here as elsewhere Lily's text is the clear original for Milton's work and that the *Accedence* is an attempt to improve, not to reject completely, the product of his predecessor. Yet the converse of the statistic above is also important: Milton added some two hundred examples of his own, or 40 percent of the total number, and thus obviously did far

---

[47] Lily, *Shorte Introduction,* sig. A5v.
[48] *Accedence,* p. 88 below.
[49] Lily, *Brevissima Institutio,* sigs. B3v, B5v.
[50] *Accedence,* p. 93 below.
[51] Lily, *Shorte Introduction,* sig. A8v.
[52] *Accedence,* p. 95 below.
[53] Ibid., p. 113 below.
[54] French, "Notes," p. 37.

more than merely repeat Lily by rote. In fact, this increase is so large that Milton's failure to specify it among his own improvements seems rather curious. Quite clearly, he was aware that generalizations and rules are meaningful to young students only when they are attached to particular cases. The sheer bulk and variety of these sentences are impressive proof of Milton's meticulous effort.

The sources he used for these examples are not certain. J. Milton French could find only a couple of dozen in other grammars of the day, which seems to suggest that such was not their origin. There is always the possibility of a phrase book *Florilegium* or other shortcut, but he could find none. Thus he concludes that they originate in Milton's "own reading in the original writers." [55] To this proposition I can add only one interesting but unverifiable footnote, the suggestion that Milton may well have combined research for the grammar with that for his proposed dictionary of Latin phrases based on the work of Stephanus.[56] The tasks are sufficiently alike to allow useful quarrying back and forth. Though the dictionary has since disappeared, it apparently was extant after Milton's death and formed the partial basis for the fifth edition (but not the first) of Adam Littleton's *Latin Dictionary* of 1723. That work speaks of using

> A Manuscript Collection, in three *Large Folios* digested into an *Alphabetical Order*, which the learned Mr. *John Milton* had made out of *Tully, Livy, Caesar, Sallust, Quintus Curtius, Justin, Plautus, Terence, Lucretius, Vergil, Horace, Ovid, Manilius, Celsus, Columella, Varo, Cato, Palladius;* in short, out of the best and purest *Roman* Authors.[57]

Even more tantalizing is the statement that Milton seldom omits "naming not only the Author, but the place in him, whence they fetch their Authorities. This is known to be *Stephen's* method, and the same may be seen in Mr. Milton's Manuscript, by the curious or doubtful." [58] It thus seems more than possible that those quotations that J. Milton French did not find might well be available in this now lost manuscript. It is perhaps worth noting that all but three authors in this list—Palladius, Manilius, and Quintus Curtius—are those to whom Milton did go for the *Accedence;* although they obviously do represent the "best and purest Roman Authors"

---

[55] Ibid., p. 42.
[56] See p. 35 above.
[57] Adam Littleton, *Linguæ Latinæ Liber Dictionarius Quadripartitus,* 5th ed. (London, 1723; RUL), sigs. A2–A2v. The imprimatur is dated January 1, 1677.
[58] Ibid., sig. A2v.

and thus the natural sources, the fact might be mildly suggestive of simultaneous compilation.

c. Structural changes. Milton's third alteration involves reorganization of certain sections of the text. Matters of illustrative details and examples are at best improvements upon an already completed work; structural alterations attempt to rethink the raw data in original terms. They are thus of some importance to any estimate of Milton's contribution to the history of Latin grammars. And Milton makes such changes in both major and minor matters.

For example, some five pages of the *Shorte Introduction* and four more of the *Brevissima Institutio* deal with the three concords or kinds of agreement: subject with verb, adjective with noun, and relative pronoun with its antecedent.[59] Lily takes up each separately in turn; as such matters are basic to all translation, the result is quite helpful to any beginner. Milton, however, organizes the same material around the concepts of gender, case, and the like.[60] The result is a totally different approach, much like the change in a pile of notes shifted from alphabetical to chronological order; though the materials may be the same, the emphasis is radically different. Which is the better way is perhaps problematical, but each is surely a logical approach to a fundamental problem, and Milton has made a major change from Lily.

A similar condition obtains in the handling of pronouns. Lily states that there are four declensions of these, differentiated by the ending of the genitive singular case: *-i,* as in *mei* or *tui; -ius,* as in *ipsius* and *huius; -i-œ-i,* as in *nostri-nostrœ-nostri;* and *-atis,* as in *nostratis.*[61] Milton, on the other hand, insists that the personal pronouns like *meus* and *tuus* are really adjectives, are declined like them, and should not be considered under pronouns at all. In addition, he believes that certain words in Lily's lists in fact have the genitive form *-jus* instead of *-ius.* Consequently, Milton asserts that there are really only three declensions of pronouns, which he classifies as Lily's first (presumably in *-i,* though he fails to say so), a second ending in *-ius (ille, iste,* and *ipse),* and a new third declension of the *-jus* words, which are *hic, is, qui,* and *quis.*[62] In at least two ways, then, Milton rejects Lily's ordering and consequently evolves a quite different alternative of his own.

---

[59] Lily, *Shorte Introduction,* sigs. C4–C5v; *Brevissima Institutio,* sigs. E2–E3v.
[60] *Accedence,* pp. 113–14 below.
[61] Lily, *Shorte Introduction,* sigs. B1–B2.
[62] *Accedence,* pp. 96–97 below.

A third major distinction occurs in the syntax, where both consider the construction of verbs with other words. Lily has the advantage of clarity and a logical order: he treats verbs in relation to each case in turn. Thus, with the nominative he discusses predicate adjectives with the verb *to be* and other substantive verbs, as in "Malus cultura fit bonus," a bad man is made good through training and discipline; with the dative, such cases as "Huic habeo, non tibi"—I have it for him, not for you—with the *huic* in the dative.[63] The result is easy to remember schematically. On the other hand, it is scarcely arranged in order of importance. The direct object in the accusative is surely the most frequent and most used instance of such governance, but it occurs over halfway through Lily's discussion. Perhaps with this fact in mind, Milton rearranges the whole discussion by topics and, at least partly, in order of importance. Furthermore, he makes it clear that most of the other cases occur in addition to a direct object, not apart from one. His scheme, therefore, is to treat first the various uses of the verb *to be,* then to discuss direct objects with an accusative and exceptions to that rule, and finally to analyze the secondary problems: an accusative with a genitive, an accusative with a dative, a double accusative (as in "Rogo te pecuniam," I ask you [for] money), and an accusative with an ablative (as in "Ferit eum gladio," he strikes him with a sword).[64] Schematically viewed, Milton's method is less immediately clear, but it might be judged superior in the last analysis—and it is very definitely a major change from the original.

Fourth and perhaps most important is his handling of the *As in præsenti.* In addition to blending it into the text itself (above, pp. 105–10), he also makes an improvement in its arrangement. Lily, aware that pupils need to know not merely the present but also the perfect tense of verbs, methodically goes through the present tenses of both regular and some irregular examples, showing how each forms its perfect tense. Thus, in the first conjugation, verbs forming -*as* in the second person singular present change to -*avi* in the perfect. *Lavo,* I wash, has *lavas,* you wash, as the second person; thus it becomes *lavi,* I have washed, in the perfect. After going through the appropriate forms for all four conjugations, Lily then faces the other main problem of the supines, or what are sometimes called the perfect passive participles. His next step consequently is to list rules for translating the perfect tenses into su-

---

[63] Lily, *Shorte Introduction,* sigs. C8–D2.
[64] *Accedence,* pp. 120–21 below.

pines, and he tells us that *-vi* perfects change into *-tum* supines. Thus *potavi,* I have drunk, becomes *potatum.*[65] Lily is logical and clear. He would be extremely annoying to use, however, because he makes us use two rules instead of one: if we know the present and want the supine, we must first find the perfect from the present and then look up the supine from the perfect. The process is roughly like translating Italian into English by way of German. To avoid this confusion, Milton usefully combines both sets of rules in one, giving all principal parts of the verb at once. Thus he says that "Verbs of the first Conjugation form thir Preterperfect Tense in *avi,* Supine in *atum,* as *Laudo laudavi laudatum.*" [66] His lists are in general similar to those of Lily and at times identical, but the reordering of materials provides a distinctly more usable and less exasperating solution to the problem of principal parts. Though his carpet contains exactly the same threads, he has woven them into a far more effective design.

These four matters, then, are major changes from Lily, representing quite different approaches to material and using Lily's data merely for reference. Even in less serious matters, moreover, he frequently reorders Lily more effectively. Lily, like Milton, separates questions of accidence from questions of syntax—but he does not follow his own distinction consistently. The outstanding instance, perhaps, comes when he discusses prepositions in the section on accidence. Logically, he ought merely to define the part of speech and show how it operates in practice. Instead, he gives elaborate lists of over fifty prepositions in terms of the cases they govern: *ad* with an accusative, *cum* with an ablative, and the like.[67] These issues, of course, are part of syntax, or the "right joyning" of words, not of accidence. Milton therefore sharply abbreviates the one and one-half pages of the *Shorte Introduction* to a bare half-dozen lines and leaves the problem of governing cases for the syntax proper, where it belongs.[68]

Another similar change is mentioned in the preface, where Milton says that *"Of figurate Construction what is usefull is digested into several Rules of* Syntaxis." [69] The methodical Lily devotes six and one-half pages of the *Brevissima Institutio* to a treatment of fourteen figures of speech, which he divides into two groups: *figuræ dictionis* and *figuræ constructionis.* The first six deal essentially

[65] Lily, *Brevissima Institutio,* sigs. C6–D3v.
[66] *Accidence,* p. 105 below.
[67] Lily, *Shorte Introduction,* sigs. C3–C3v.
[68] *Accidence,* pp. 112, 127–28 below.
[69] Ibid., p. 86 below.

with the addition or subtraction of a syllable or a letter in a given word, as in the English words *loved* and *beloved* or *evening* and *eve*.[70] These Milton does briefly list in a separate section at the end of the accidence before he begins the syntax.[71] The other eight, which take up most of Lily's discussion, are entirely absent except when appropriate grammatical rules call for them. Thus Lily discusses synecdoche, which occurs when "that which pertains to a part is attributed to the whole" and which may take either an accusative or an ablative case, as in "*Saucius frontem* vel *fronte*," hurt in the forehead.[72] Under his treatment of construction of substantives with an accusative, Milton states that "All words expressing part or Parts of a thing, may be put in the Accusative, or sometimes in the Ablative; as *Saucius frontem* or *fronte*."[73] Lily lists no such rules in either the English or the Latin syntax. Here, in other words, Milton has chosen rather to blend the principle into the text than to tabulate it methodically in an appendix. Much of the gist of Lily's treatment of syllepsis—the inclusion of the less under the more worthy person or gender—appears (albeit clumsily) in Milton's discussion of the concords, where he discusses the preference for first person above the other two and like matters.[74] And in discussing the construction of substantives, Milton brings in apposition: "But if both the substantives be spoken of one thing, which is call'd apposition, they shall be both of the same case; as *Pater meus vir, amat me puerum*."[75] Lily gives the same example under construction of nouns substantive in the *Shorte Introduction* without naming the figure of speech, repeats the rule in Latin with the term itself in the *Brevissima Institutio*, and lists it under figures of speech, thus in effect stating the point in three separate places.[76] Milton's reordering is thus considerably more terse and, for a student who is learning grammar and not rhetoric, equally effective.

Some changes are less drastic but nevertheless improve clarity. Lily begins the *Shorte Introduction* with a heading "Of the Noune," which begins with short sections about numbers, cases, articles, and genders.[77] Milton gives a better overall perspective by follow-

---

[70] Lily, *Brevissima Institutio*, sigs. G1–G4.

[71] *Accedence*, p. 112 below.

[72] Lily, *Brevissima Institutio*, sig. G4: "Synecdoche, est cum id quod partis est, attribuitur toti."

[73] *Accedence*, p. 116 below.

[74] Ibid., p. 114 below.

[75] Ibid., p. 115 below.

[76] Lily, *Shorte Introduction*, sig. C6v; *Brevissima Institutio*, sigs. E3v, G1v.

[77] Lily, *Shorte Introduction*, sig. A5.

ing his list of declined and undeclined parts of speech with this statement: "Nounes, Pronounes, and Participles, are declin'd with Gender, Number, and Case; Verbs, as hereafter in the Verb." [78] Thereafter, he treats the concepts of gender, number, and case separately before beginning his treatment of any one part of speech. He has thus made generally applicable to several parts of speech those elements that Lily overrestricts to nouns only, and he has indicated the relation between these particular accidentals and those of the verb, which he shows to be coming up later; when he introduces mood, tense, and person, number has already been made clear. Also, since he will treat *hic-hæc-hoc* under pronouns, he omits entirely Lily's short section on articles, which do not properly exist in Latin. As another example, Lily conjugates the active forms of verbs and then stops to teach the verb *to be* before going on to the passive, which of course depends upon it. His phrasing is lame: "Here, before we decline any Verbes in *Or,* for suplying of many tenses, lacking in all suche verbes, we muste learne to decline this Verb *Sum,* in this wise." [79] Milton, on the other hand, wisely conjugates *sum* completely in his preliminaries before beginning the four conjugations [80] and thus avoids needless interruptions of structure. Other similar instances could also be shown: Milton omits the treatment of datives with the passive at the point where Lily takes the matter up; Milton includes gerunds under case forms in his syntax where Lily separates the two topics; Milton has a separate discussion of gerunds and supines where Lily combines them with other matters; and Milton helpfully devotes a separate section to defining the voices of verbs by themselves while Lily blends these without comment into his introductory remarks on the topic.[81] All of these changes, in other words, are departures from Lily designed to describe as clearly as possible the crucial aspects of Latin grammar, a topic with which the beginner surely needs as much help as he can find.

In all of these various ways, then—consolidation, omission, compression, and a host of alterations—Milton undoubtedly changes and usually though not always improves upon the royal grammar. It would be quite inaccurate, therefore, to view the *Accedence* as a mere restatement of Lily; despite limitations, it constantly shows Milton's desire to improve upon the established school text.

[78] *Accedence,* p. 87 below.
[79] Lily, *Shorte Introduction,* sig. B5.
[80] *Accedence,* pp. 98–99 below.
[81] Ibid., pp. 105, 100 below; Lily, *Shorte Introduction,* sigs. D2, D2v, C8.

III. MILTON'S *ACCEDENCE* AND OTHER GRAMMARS

It seems clear, then, that Milton set out to revise the royal grammar into a more usable text for young schoolboys and that the number of his improvements was considerable. As has already been shown, however, Milton was only one of many men who attempted such a task. The very year of the *Accedence* itself, for instance, saw three other entries into the race: an anonymous *Examen of the Way of Teaching the Latin Tongue;* Arthur Brett's *A Demonstration How the Latin Tongue May Be Learned;* and William Walker's *Some Improvements to the Art of Teaching,* which reached at least a ninth edition by the end of the century. It seems important then to ask whether Milton was entirely original in his improvements upon Lily or whether at times he was merely using methods that had already been incorporated in the works of his competitors. Though perhaps incapable of complete resolution, these questions require at least some discussion.

It is surprising that Milton discusses so few major grammarians of the sixteenth and seventeenth centuries. Lily himself turns up once in *Of Education;* the *Accedence* makes a single casual reference to Thomas Linacre, whose fine scholarship in some ways set standards for English Latinists for the next two centuries; and Samuel Hartlib, whose multifarious interests included the reform of Latin teaching along with practically everything else, is of course the man to whom Milton dedicated *Of Education,* which also contains a few slighting words about the Comenian tradition.[1] Otherwise, as a glance at the index to Columbia will show, Milton makes no reference whatever to the grammatical works of his illustrious predecessors or contemporaries. Roger Ascham is mentioned for *Toxophilus* but not for pedagogy; Melanchthon and Erasmus are praised for learning but not for teaching; Ramus and Wolsey and Priscian (except for a mild joke in Prolusion VI) might never have dealt with the topic for all that Milton says; and names like Robert Whittington, John Brinsley, Charles Hoole, and Joshua Poole—all well enough known to appear today in the *Dictionary of National Biography*—never occur at all. From explicit references alone, then, one would be forced to conclude that Milton believed himself the only improver upon Lily. Such a conclusion is, however, almost certainly wrong. As writers like Hoole and Brinsley make clear, good schools of the day—and Milton's Saint Paul's was among the very best—used many of these other works as

---

[1] *Complete Prose,* II, 362 ff.

subsidiary texts; [2] thus, even as a schoolboy Milton would have come to know many of them. It has been usually asserted that a copy of Thomas Farnaby's *Systema Grammaticum* now at Harvard once belonged to Milton; if so, since Farnaby there discusses two other major writers, Vossius and Danes, Milton was thus presumably aware of them as well.[3] It would seem difficult to believe that he could miss the *Logonomia* of Alexander Gill, Sr., whom Milton praised as a Latin poet and who was a strong admirer of Farnaby.[4] In addition, in the *Accedence* itself Milton mentions "other grammars," which he does not name; though annoyingly vague to the literary historian, the remark does show awareness of competition.[5] Finally, J. Milton French has suggested,[6] on the basis of probable borrowings of certain illustrative examples, that Milton "seems to have known" at least the works of Peter Ramus, John Brinsley, John Bird, Charles Butler, Thomas Farnaby, and James Shirley. And so the circle grows; by inference if not by demonstration, then, it is reasonably clear that Milton knew at least a good number of the Latin grammatical texts of the day.

How far any particular one of these directly influenced him is hard to tell. Many of the improvements in the *Accedence* do appear in these and similar volumes, but it seems impossible to say whether Milton found the idea there, whether both follow a quite different common source, or whether Milton arrived at the idea in question independently. The safest procedure, therefore, seems to be double: first to discuss the variety of these other attempts as a way of anchoring Milton within certain traditions; and then to show possible resemblances between them and the *Accedence* in cases where both deviate from Lily. Though any single parallel might be coincidental, the sum total suggests that Milton was using a number of ideas already current in his own day.

A. Lily's Competitors

After the publication of Lily, the earlier flow of Latin grammars in England itself dried to a mere trickle, perhaps because the royal

---

[2] See, for example, John Brinsley, *A Consolation for Our Grammar Schooles*, ed. Thomas Clark Pollock (New York: Scholars' Facsimiles & Reprints, 1943), pp. 59 ff., and Charles Hoole, *A New Discovery of the Old Art of Teaching School*, ed. E. T. Campagnac (Liverpool and London, 1913), p. xvii.

[3] Thomas Farnaby, *Systema Grammaticum* (London, 1641; HCL). The dedication to Vossius discusses Danes. See French, *Life Records*, II, 29.

[4] Masson, *Life*, I, 78 ff.

[5] *Accedence*, p. 86 below.

[6] French, "Notes," pp. 34–35, n. 5.

monopoly was then most strongly enforced. Where twenty-four major authors dominated the sixty years of 1481–1542, I have found only half that number for the seventy years 1542–1612. Even among the works of these, four were reprints of continental writers like Despauterius, three were by Scots to whom the royal edict apparently did not apply, and two were merely anonymous pamphlets.[7] In fact, the only solid contributions of the period were four books by John Stockwood, a celebrated teacher and Heidelberg graduate who was under the protection of Sir Robert Sidney. Two of Stockwood's works were sufficiently distinguished to warrant republication over half a century later;[8] no other author of the period seems even to have been mentioned. From about 1612 to 1669, however—an even shorter period—the publication rates swell rapidly. In fact, well over 150 editions of Latin grammars are still known, or on the average about three a year. Part of the increase may possibly be due to a desire for education among rising social classes; part may stem from the victory of Puritanism with its ardent interest in schooling; conceivably under the Commonwealth enforcement of the royal monopoly withered away, becoming a purely token affair. In any case, a series of detailed and carefully wrought treatments of ways of learning Latin became rapidly available. Of these, three varieties warrant notice: the januists, the innovators, and the traditionalists.

1. The Januists

The most radical of the three was undoubtedly the *janua* approach, first developed by William Bathe, an Irish Jesuit stationed in Spain. In the preface to the 1615 edition of his *Janua Linguarum*, the gate of languages, he summarizes the rationale behind the movement.[9] There are two ways of learning a foreign language, he notes: the regular, through study of the grammatical rules, and the irregular, through concentration on vocabulary alone without any study of accidence and syntax. The former offers stylistic perfection, but the latter hastens facility, as men show who quickly pick up the vernacular of a foreign country. In order to save learning time, therefore, Bathe tries to attach language study not to

[7] *STC*.

[8] Stockwood's *Disputatiuncularum Grammaticalium Libellus* of 1598 reached a sixth edition of 1650 and was recommended by Charles Hoole (*A New Discovery*, p. xvii) in 1660. Stockwood's *Treatise of the Figures* of rhetoric of 1609 appeared as late as 1748 (HHL). See also *DNB*.

[9] [William Bathe], *Janua Linguarum, sive Modus Maxime Accommodatus, quo Patefit Aditus ad Omnes Linguas Intelligendas* (London, 1615; HHL), preface.

grammatical rules but to groups of related words, offered in short sentences designed to implant each in the memory. To ensure brevity, he also attempts to use each word only once. By memorizing these groups of sentences, one might also absorb through osmosis the grammatical structure of the tongue as well—just as a child does. He thus solves very simply the problems of declensions and concords: he teaches no grammar at all.

Bathe's work was extremely popular throughout Europe; in England alone, *STC* records nine editions by 1640 and implies the existence of at least two others, while many more appeared on the Continent. From the 1630s onward, however, he faced increasingly strong competition from similar publications by the Moravian bishop J. A. Comenius, the friend of Samuel Hartlib and other Commonwealth projectors.[10] The *Short-Title Catalogues* show well over a dozen works on education by Comenius and list almost forty editions of these between 1631 and 1700. One apparently went through fourteen different editions in only thirty years, a remarkable popularity. Comenius had apparently received his inspiration from several sources, including Bathe, whose originality and importance he frequently underrates. According to T. Corcoran, Comenius happened to see the 1617 Leipzig edition of Bathe's *Methodus Institutionis Nova Quadruplex,* which was printed without Bathe's preface; if so, then Comenius underestimated Bathe, and the Bathe tradition has been unduly neglected in educational history.[11]

Certainly their aims were similar, since Comenius too would teach Latin through memorized vocabulary arranged in sentences of increasing difficulty. Yet there are differences. Though both arrange their sentences topically, they proceed by different organizational principles. Bathe's structure was moral: his first "century" or group of sentences dealt with vice and virtue, the second with wisdom and folly, and so on, with a catchall at the end for indifferent things. Comenius, on the other hand, divides words by the processes of everyday life and has sections about parts of the body, cookery and hunting, the building trades, aspects of the weather, and the like. In both cases, the end is clearly Latin for conversational use, not for its humanistic and literary values; it is a utilitarian tool, not a prelude to the reading of classical authors.

[10] For Comenius, see especially M. W. Keatinge, *The Great Didactic of John Amos Comenius,* 2 vols., 2nd ed. (London, 1921), and G. H. Turnbull, *Hartlib, Dury, and Comenius* (London: University Press of Liverpool, 1947).

[11] T[imothy] Corcoran, *Studies in the History of Classical Teaching: Irish and Continental, 1500–1700* (Dublin and Belfast, 1911), pp. 44–49.

In some ways, the method was actually quite ancient: colloquies and phrase books had long been used to supplement formal grammar. The *Colloquies* of Erasmus immediately come to mind, but many other examples exist. In England, for instance, John Brinsley's *Pueriles Confabulatiunculæ* (1617) and—a whole century earlier—William Horman's *Vulgaria* (1519) were both well known. The latter is divided into groups of sentences about domestic life, cooking, marriage, and many other topics that appear in Comenius as well. It is highly concrete and topical; we learn from one sentence, for example, that there were fifty-two parish churches in London, and another useful one, "Dentium dolore graviter infestor," is translated as "I am sore troubled with the tooth ache." [12] In his *New Discovery of an Old Art* (1660), Charles Hoole recommends two of John Brinsley's collections and the *Janua Linguarum* as well for use in the lower forms. [13] Thus the two groups were potentially complementary. Yet the aims were really quite different: the *Vulgaria* was designed to supplement and the *Janua* to displace grammatical training. And there was a distinct feeling that the two modes were basically incompatible. As early as 1614, Eilhard Lubin attacked the very notion of grammatical rules as inappropriate to children:

> For boyes are bid to apprehend those things, whereof that age is not yet capable; and are commanded to learn those things without book [i.e., by heart]. . . . And far madder than which hitherto were those, who propounded to boyes the Precepts of Grammar, obscure in themselves; and besides that, inclosed in Verses, in Verses J say, so obscure, as may seem even to us who are farther grown in years, to stand in need of some Oedipus to understand them. [14]

Nor will tinkering with the rules help, he thinks: strict brevity omits too much, while inclusiveness is merely bewildering, and "Scholar-like become choler-like employments." [15] To the devout januist, traditional grammar was a demon to be exorcised.

Yet the januist unhappily found several motes in his own eye as well. By his effort to use each word only once, Bathe rings so many ingenious changes on his centuries that Keatinge finds some of the later ones practically meaningless. [16] Also, restriction to a

---

[12] William Horman, *Vulgaria* (London, 1519; HHL), p. 27 and passim.

[13] See n. 8, above.

[14] Samuel Hartlib, *The True and Ready Way to Learn the Latin Tongue* (London, 1654), p. 12. The work reprints books by Lubin, Richard Carew, and Montaigne.

[15] Ibid., p. 13.

[16] Keatinge, *Great Didactic,* I, 20.

single occurrence loses entirely the advantage of that other major teaching device, repetition, and the student who forgot a single sentence might irretrievably lose a crucial term. For this reason, some *januas* were indexed, yet even this precaution was presumably inadequate, since in 1634 Wye(?) Saltonstall published a *Clavis ad Portam,* a key to the gate or *janua,* offering an alphabetical reminder of terms. Finally, in the long run even the januists admitted that while osmosis may serve for modern languages (and several of the works were tri- or quadrilingual), Latin, Greek, and Hebrew regrettably do seem to need rules as well.[17] And Comenius actually went so far as to write two Latin grammars himself, though one of these is no longer extant.[18] The "universal panacea" produced problems of its own.

During the Commonwealth period, Samuel Hartlib almost persuaded Parliament to adopt Comenianism as the national method of language instruction.[19] After the Restoration, however, the general conservative reaction in all other fields showed up in matters of schooling as well. In fact, there was for some men sinister identification between the januist movement and the late reign of the saints. One bishop, hearing a nontraditional answer from a schoolboy during an examination, was heard to reply "What . . . Puritanism in Schools too?"[20] And in 1678 Christopher Wase specifically links the dire effects of political change with the evils of januism: "But to demolish foundations out of privat opinion daily changeable is a presumption of ill consequence to the publick. Our modern *Januists* of the Latine and Greek tongue seem in great measure to leave grammar and to build upon Dictionary; as do others who practice without Rule, or by a Rule not Catholick."[21] The result was in no way a prohibition of Comenius's works, since at least fourteen editions were published between 1660 and 1700. Yet just as Protestant pressures may have contributed to the disappearance of Bathe's Jesuit *Janua* (whose last English edition, perhaps significantly, is listed as 1640), so the petering out of Comenianism may be due in good part to a political change of atmosphere. I know of no such book first published after the Restoration.

[17] See Comenius's own grammar in *Opera Didactica Omnia,* 3 vols. (Prague: Academiæ Scientiarum Bohemoslovencæ, 1957), I, pars II, 304 ff.

[18] Keatinge, *Great Didactic,* I, 25, 67.

[19] See, for instance, William Boyd, *The History of Western Education* (London: Black, 1954), pp. 273–74.

[20] N. [Nedham?] M., *A Discourse Concerning Schools and School-Masters, Offered to Publick Consideration* (London, 1663; HHL), pp. 5–6.

[21] [Christopher Wase], *Considerations Concerning Free-Schools as Settled in England* (Oxford, 1678; HHL), pp. 87–88.

For all of these reasons, it does not seem strange that Milton in 1669 avoided the reforming zeal of januism. Its connotations would have made any hope of popular adoption seem vain. Furthermore, he had long before shown that he had little faith in such shortcuts, when he spoke contemptuously in the 1640s of "what many modern *Janua's* and *Didactics* more than ever I shall read, have projected." [22] As Ernest Sirluck has shown, [23] Milton and the Comenians did agree in some matters—dislike of the slowness of the traditional program, for instance, and the belief that languages are means, not ends—but they were far apart in others: Milton was humane where they were vocational; he would teach literature where they would eliminate it; they sought a key to universal knowledge where he was less sanguine about the human nature of fallen man. The *Accedence,* therefore, implicitly rejects Comenian pidgin Latin for the precision of stylistic correctness.

2. The Innovators

A second group is made up of authors who suggest that language training can be speeded up or made more thorough through the use of some particular approach or device that had hitherto been neglected. These men were obviously far less radical than the januists, as most of them wished to improve grammatical teaching, not abolish it. Their faith in some one single technique, however, sets them apart from the traditional full coverage of Lily.

One interesting example is Joseph Webbe, whose two works suggest that since rigid application of regular rules produces a mechanical and wooden Latin which no man ever used, the student should concentrate instead upon the larger unit of the clause. [24] Though this suggestion scarcely seems surprising today, it is interesting to note that neither Lily nor Milton discusses clauses as central elements of language; perhaps Webbe was thus among the first to use a concept now so traditional in language instruction. In 1654, John Webster praised Webbe but implied that the "Clausary method," despite its advantages, had been methodically disregarded by hidebound traditionalists who were unwilling to consider any new methods. [25] He may well be right; though Webbe was on occasion praised, his suggestions had little effect on later seventeenth-century writers.

[22] *Complete Prose,* II, 364.

[23] Ibid., p. 184 ff.

[24] Joseph Webbe, *An Appeal to Truth* (London, 1622; HHL), and *A Petition to the High Court of Parliament* (London, 1623; HHL).

[25] John Webster, *Academiarum Examen* (London, 1654; HHL), pp. 22–23.

A somewhat related issue is that of idioms. Impressed by the fact that much actual speech is idiomatic and thus irregular, several writers suggested that a student would do better to memorize usual expressions than to learn often inapplicable rules. Webbe shares this view, pointing out that, since in fact any language changes its dialect every twenty miles or so and almost every generation as well, the search for immutable rules leads only to a regularized language that never existed.[26] This surprisingly modern belief in linguistic relativity leads him to insist that in language teaching custom is a far safer guide than formal syntax. Nor was he alone in this belief, as the abundance of phrase books and lists of idioms makes clear. And the *Hermes Anglo-Latinus: or Directions for Young Latinists, to Speake Latine Purely* (London, 1639; HHL) by Philip Munck (?) strongly protests that student writers make errors because they "work onely verbatim (which is nowhere necessary but in parsing . . .)" and fail "to reserve to each idiom its own propriety." [27] Munck thus specializes in meticulous discussion of shades of meaning.

The influence of Ramian logic can be found in grammatical texts as well, both in the grammar of Ramus himself (HHL photostat; London, published in English in 1585) and in John Bird's *Grounds of Grammar Penned and Published* (Oxford, 1639; CAM). For Bird—whose work Milton may have known—grammar falls into rudiment and regiment, the former being in turn either elementary or accidentary, terms that seem to correspond to orthography and accidence. His method in general is a subdivision of concepts into two parts, followed by other subdivisions of each half. Thus regiment splits into plain and figurative, whereas plain in turn may be that of conveniency ("when there is a Rection joyned with Concordancy") and confrequency ("a rection joyned with a discrepancy of the words").[28] The result is undoubtedly logical, but its complexity might well discourage many readers. Basically, the text is excellent; were it not for needless complexity of method, it might well rival or even surpass Lily in clarity and orderliness.

A fourth device was the attempt to put grammatical rules into verse for easy memorizing by schoolboys. This will-of-the-wisp may well have been necessary in the Middle Ages, when the average pupil could not own a book and was forced to depend upon his memory for all he knew, and it died hard in later practice.

[26] Webbe, *Appeal to Truth,* sig. C4.
[27] My tentative ascription of authorship stems from a handwritten note in the Huntington copy: "Phillipo Munckero, authore." See sigs. A3v–A4v.
[28] Bird, *Grounds of Grammar,* pp. 107 ff.

James Shirley the playwright, for instance, issued in 1649 a *Via ad Latinam Linguam Complanata,* which not merely retains the rhymed Latin poems but matches them with rhymed English translations of his own. Against a shortened version of the *Propria quæ maribus,* for example, he put this:

> The proper names of Angels, every winde,
> Of Moneths and Rivers, are like Males declin'd.[29]

Nor was Shirley the last. As late as 1689, Richard Busby was again resurrecting a method that had been tried for many centuries.[30]

Other solutions could be added, such as the valiant attempt of Edward Leedes, who discovered that his workbook was being hawked from class to class and who therefore issued *More English Examples to Be Turned into Latin* to prevent student plagiarism.[31] Forms A and B are not unknown today in the textbook industry. Or there is the other fond hope of teaching both Greek and Latin concurrently, on the assumption that the same grammatical rules frequently apply to both languages—a goal that we have already noted in 1663 (see above, p. 45) and that Richard Busby revived in his *Rudimentum Grammaticæ Græco-Latinæ Metricum* in 1689.[32] Yet enough have been mentioned to suggest the scope and variety of such attempts at innovation. They reinforce, of course, the fact that grammatical texts were common in the seventeenth century and that Milton was one of many in choosing to write another. In addition, however, they also emphasize one other point: Milton was not an innovator in any of these senses; he did not seek salvation through clauses, idioms, Ramian dialectic (despite his version of Ramus's logic), versified rules, workbooks, or the simultaneous teaching of several languages. By contrast, the *Accedence* seems much more balanced than many of these works, despite their very real virtues.

3. The Traditionalists

In addition to these various attempts at novelty, there were also a good number of rivals to Lily within his own terms, the methodical discussion of all basic aspects of Latin grammar. A useful

---

[29] James Shirley, *Via ad Latinam Linguam Complanata* (London, 1649; HHL), p. 50.

[30] [Richard Busby], *Rudimentum Grammaticæ Græco-Latinæ Metricum* (London, 1689; HHL). The authorship is debatable; see G. F. Russell Barker, *Memoir of Richard Busby D.D.* (London, 1895), p. 43.

[31] [Edward Leedes? preface signed E.L.], *More English Examples to Be Turned into Latin* 3rd ed. (London, 1692; HHL).

[32] See n. 30, above.

focus is perhaps Charles Hoole's *A New Discovery of the Old Art of Teaching School* (1660), in which the author lists those grammars that seem to him most useful as supplements to Lily.[33] Because the book appeared within a decade of the *Accedence,* it offers a representative view of those books most in favor at the time. For the first three forms, he lists little beyond construes and a few readers, and in the fifth and sixth he switches to either encyclopedic grammarians like Linacre or eminent continental ones like Vossius. For the fourth form, however, he suggests seven authors whom he finds valuable for student reference: Danes, Bird, Farnaby, Shirley, Burles, Hawkins, and Gregory, in addition to his own multifarious textbooks, which he neatly puffs along the way. None of these openly tries to displace Lily; Danes, for instance, says "my care and endeavour hath bin to alter nothing therein, further than Method, Perspicuitie, and Truth it self shall give countenance thereto," [34] and Hoole himself elsewhere warily speaks of his work as a *"Subsidiary School-book"* [35] and not as an autonomous production. In actual fact, however, all are clearly designed to offer direct competition—as Hoole himself implicitly admits by claiming that one of his books contains everything a child would need for the first year's study of Latin.[36]

Of these seven, that by Gregory I have not seen. That by Hawkins, *A Brief Introduction to Syntax* (1631), is essentially a reprinting of the Spanish grammarian Nebrissa with merely a slight added commentary by Hawkins. Despite prefatory poems of congratulation by James Shirley, the work seems clumsier than most of the rest. Bird's *Grounds of Grammar Penned and Published* (1639) has already been mentioned for its reliance upon the Ramian method of subdivision by two's; otherwise, it is a thorough and quite traditional approach to grammar in the manner of Lily. And we have also discussed Shirley's *Via ad Latinam Linguam Complanata* (1649) as an example of the fad for versified grammatical rules. Except for the clumsy rhymes, it too is a clear, methodical text that might well give basic instruction to any schoolchild.

The other three are worth more comment, for they are typical of the best texts of the age. One, John Danes's *A Light to Lily* (1637), demonstrates the author's judgment just as a companion

---

[33] Hoole, *New Discovery,* p. xvii.

[34] John Danes, *Light to Lilie* (London, 1637; FSL), sig. A6.

[35] Charles Hoole, *The Common Rudiments of English Grammar* (London, 1657; HHL), dedication.

[36] Charles Hoole, *Aditus Facilis ad Linguam Latinam* (London, 1649; UIL), sig. A8.

book, *Paralipomena* (1638), does his learning. The latter is an attempt to provide advanced discussion of grammatical niceties for those already well grounded in the fundamentals. It apparently came into being from Danes's observation that no one since Linacre had even tried to provide such a discussion: "I was both grieved and vexed to discover that, since the time of our most learned Linacre, whose *Emendata Structura* was inadequate to drive out barbarity, no Englishman has again appeared to take upon himself the tasks of grammar." [37] He thereupon published a book of above four hundred pages to remedy that defect. Entirely in Latin, it provides a *scholion* upon the perplexities of Lily, whom he follows generally in organization. The *Light to Lily,* on the other hand, methodically tries to simplify the subject for the young beginner: he avoids dividing pronouns into primitive and derivative, relative and demonstrative, for example, because he thinks the topic too difficult for children; he omits Lily's special rules for telling gender by accent in nouns increasing long or short and instead describes gender by declension endings wherever possible. Though Danes does not entirely escape the Lilyan shadow—he retains the set-off Latin poems, for instance—he does produce a much simpler and more usable book,[38] clearly written for the tender student.

The most respected volume in Hoole's list is undoubtedly Thomas Farnaby's *Systema Grammaticum* (1641), which Milton very probably knew. In general, Farnaby was looked upon as the standard for other writers; in his complaint about the absence of thorough grammarians since Linacre, for example, Danes was careful to make a partial exception of Farnaby,[39] and other writers also mention him with evident respect. In some ways, the book is harder to use than those of Danes and Bird, since it perpetuates the double-grammar tradition in English and Latin of Lily, but it does offer a good number of significant improvements. Irregular verbs like *volo, eo,* and *possum,* which are separately treated in Lily, here appear with their appropriate conjugations; Farnaby avoids duplication of rules from one section of his text to the next; he so shortens the rules of syntax that these are "few and short, not 150. lines to be learned *memoriter*"; he obligingly distinguishes main from subordinate ideas through differences in type size; and he is proud of the fact that his own section on etymology is "not half so

[37] John Danes, *Paralipomena Orthographiæ, Etymologiæ, Prosodiæ* . . . (London, 1638; HHL), dedicatory epistle.

[38] Danes, *Light to Lilie,* preface; the poems occur in a separate section between the accidence and the syntax.

[39] Danes, *Paralipomena,* dedication.

much as the now taught *Accidents.*" [40] The work is, therefore, a careful and successful improvement upon Lily.

Edward Burles's *Grammatica Burlesa; or, A New English Grammar* is in some ways the most impressive of the lot. In a prefatory note, he humbly suggests that he had originally intended to call the book "Pedissequa Farnabiana," a footman to Farnaby, but that some "objected mightily" to Farnaby's name[41]—perhaps because of presumed involvement with a royalist uprising some years before, though Burles professes to know no cause.[42] The most refreshing aspect of the book is its simple English prose throughout, a decision he not merely practices but sturdily defends: "if any *Aristarchus* carp at my Translation of Rules . . . Let such a one know that I doe not *aucupate praise,* but have studied *plainness.* . . . What would it profit the Scholar [i.e., pupil] to read Latin words, and yet being asked for the English should be altogether to seek for an answer?" [43] Nor does he merely give a skeletal outline of essentials; the work fills six books and nearly four hundred pages of text. His only concession to Lily is his practice at times of listing the usual Latin rules in a second column—and even then he clips away the irregular examples. In the first four lines of the *Propria quæ maribus,* for instance, he sharpens structure by separating two main rules and by omitting twelve specific examples which blur the sequence of generalization; these anomalies appear later in a quite separate part of the book called *Observations and Annotations.*[44] The result is much clearer than Lily, is immensely better in organization, and puts the whole matter in simple English. There was, in short, no dearth of intelligent and thoughtful traditional grammars in the middle years of the seventeenth century.

B. Milton's Use of Other Grammars

Milton himself is somewhat ambiguous about claiming originality for the *Accedence,* which he calls "*A work suppos'd not to have been done formerly; or if done, not without such difference here in brevity and alteration, as may be found of moment.*" [1] To begin with, in the preface it is not clear whether he sees his major contribution in the single-volume format or in the complete use of English. In either case, he is more derivative than his words might

---

[40] Farnaby, *Systema Grammaticum,* "To the Reader."
[41] Edward Burles, *Grammatica Burlesa* (London, 1652; HHL), sig. A7.
[42] See *DNB.*
[43] Burles, *Grammatica Burlesa,* sig. A7v.
[44] Ibid., pp. 141–42.
[1] *Accedence,* p. 86 below.

imply, for even if we assume a very early date of composition in the 1640s he is literally wrong. Also, he clearly hedges his bets, first suggesting that he is quite original and then retreating to the claim that he has merely done better what others had already performed. Yet even the lesser assertion is not entirely valid, as many of his own improvements had appeared in the works of other grammarians. The text is in general rather selective and eclectic than novel.

Throughout the century, authorities disagreed about the advisability of using a completely English text. To his *Short Introduction to Grammar* (1632), for instance, David Wedderburn adds a defensive postscript justifying his partial use of English by analogy to Greek, which he believes no one would think of teaching without the crutch of a Latin commentary.[2] Yet he himself gradually shifts from English to Latin as the work progresses until the last half or so is entirely in the older tongue. Another example of these two interacting forces is Lily's own work, which Foster Watson claims could be found entirely in English by the year 1657.[3] As a matter of fact, it was never really translated; instead, a number of men—Stockwood, Hampton, Haines, Reeve—prepared construes for the use of beleaguered schoolboys who needed help in parsing the original. The result is scarcely a translation, however, as a specimen passage easily shows:

> Quæ *nouns which* variant *vary* genus *their gender* et *and* flexum *declining* quæcunque *whatever* novato ritu *after a new manner* deficiunt *fall short* vel *or* superant *exceed* sunto *let them be* heteroclita *heteroclites.*[4]

Such a passage is perfectly unreadable, of course, but its very existence shows both the pull toward preservation of the Latin and the companion desire to put the material in a more usable form.

As early as 1585, however, *The Latin Grammar of P. Ramus, Englished and Newly Corrected,* had appeared entirely in the vernacular, and John Bird's *Grounds of Grammar Penned and Published* (1639) had appeared in similar garb by the time Milton first began to teach school. Even if we assume that the *Accedence* dates from the early 1640s—and then we should need to explain why the author failed to revise his assertion some three decades later in

---

[2] David Wedderburn, *A Short Introduction to Grammar, Compyled for the Instruction of Youth, by Publique Authoritie* (Aberdeen, 1632; HHL), sig. E1. Presumably the royal mandate to use Lily did not apply in Scotland.

[3] Watson, p. 266.

[4] This and other construes are included in the 1732(?) *Short Introduction of Grammar* printed "for W. Lilly and John Ward" (London, n.d.; PUL), p. 151.

1669—his major claim seems to be wrong. And by the time of the Restoration a number of other texts had followed the same lead, such as Edward Burles's *Grammatica Burlesa* (1652) with its revealing subtitle *A New English Grammar,* or the better-known *Aditus Facilis ad Linguam Latinam* (1649) of Charles Hoole. Because all four of these books also treat grammar in a single, sequential volume, they effectively destroy Milton's first assertion. One might conclude that Milton's work came at just about the time when grammarians in general were giving up their previous tendency to "aucupate praise" by writing in the tongue being taught. While Milton's decision was thus up to date, it was not revolutionary.

His competitors could also match his second claim to "brevity." Like Milton, for example, John Brinsley reduces Lily's seven genders to three, saying that the rest are "compounded or made of these three." [5] In 1625, in fact, Thomas Wise stoutly asserts that the very concept of the epicoene "belongs not to a Grammarian, but to a Philosopher" and comes to the same conclusion.[6] Again, Milton is not original in reducing the number of modes of verbs, since John Danes's *Light to Lillie* (1637) points out that the "Optative and Potential are the same with the Subjunctive, differing only in manner of signifying" and firmly asserts that if one categorizes by signification there will be no end to modes.[7] Where Milton omits categories of adverbs, Danes had already claimed credit for the same innovation "because I have found them by experience a distraction to children." [8] In all three of these improvements, then, Milton is merely following informed public opinion.

Nor is his decision to omit some parts of Lily a new method of shortening his book. Both Shirley and Farnaby omit the section on orthography; Shirley and Brinsley leave out the prosody; none of the other major grammarians includes the prayers and verses on etiquette that grace Lily. The latter's religious emphasis was apparently out of date by the middle of the seventeenth century, and authorities were at least divided about the need for versification and orthography. Though Milton is more extreme in his excisions than some others—Brinsley's *Posing* has the vowels and conso-

---

[5] John Brinsley, *Posing of the Parts* (London, 1615; CAM). An odd system of pagination gives a single number for both recto and verso of the same sheet; see p. 4v.

[6] Thomas Wise, *Animadversions upon Lillies Grammar* (London, 1625; FSL), pp. 35–36.

[7] Danes, *Light to Lilie,* sig. A7v.

[8] Ibid., sigs. A7v–A8.

nants, Burles includes metrics—he is by no means unique; all of his omissions can be matched in other popular texts. His ways of obtaining brevity, in other words, were already well known.

The third claim of improvement through alteration also depends heavily upon changes already developed by others. When Milton adds to Lily the idea that prepositions may be used not merely before nouns but also in "composition" as prefixes to other words—and he gives six examples[9]—he is merely echoing the same list in Bird.[10] In the same source he could have found his own defective definition of an adverb (see above, p. 111), which there appears as a part of speech "added to words to declare their signification: Principally and frequently to a Verb." [11] The reduction of Lily's five tenses to three and so small a detail as building the superlative form of an adjective upon an *er* base instead of an *r* also appear in the same work.[12] And other of his alterations appear in other authors of the day. The plan of joining the perfect with the supine form of a verb, which represents so distinct an improvement over Lily's cumbersome two sections, turns up in Shirley; [13] Milton's decision to omit from the accidence the cases governed by prepositions occurs in Danes, who relegates them "to the Syntaxis, where they must necessarily be treated to shew their construction"; [14] Farnaby in 1641 had omitted the supposed adjectives *hic, hæc,* and *hoc* as camouflaged pronouns and had also melded the relevant sections of etymological figures into the proper parts of the text itself.[15] Milton's admission that he had made "addition or alteration from other Grammars," then, seems perfectly accurate.

In general, therefore, it seems safe to say that Milton's book attempts to choose wisely among the various improvements his competitors had produced. Yet in a few places he does seem to have added something of his own. His decision to discuss all three concords together in terms of their accidents of case and number,[16] for example, I did not notice in other contemporary texts. Again, where there are various treatments of pronouns—Danes, for instance, drops entirely the concept of their declension and instead

---

[9] *Accedence,* p. 112 below.

[10] John Bird, *Grounds of Grammar Penned and Published* (Oxford, 1639; CAM), p. 104.

[11] Ibid., p. 96.

[12] Ibid., pp. 62, 42.

[13] Shirley, *Via ad Latinam Linguam Complanata,* p. 75.

[14] Danes, *Light to Lilie,* sig. D2v.

[15] Farnaby, *Systema Grammaticum,* "To the Reader."

[16] *Accedence,* p. 113 below.

insists that they should be treated like the adjectives *bonus, solus,* and *felix,*[17] an approach Milton incorporates into his own scheme— I have seen no other use of three declensions including *jus* genitives.[18] And Milton's attempt to discuss construction of verbs in terms of the frequency of occurrence of the rule, though it has some relationship to the methods of Danes and Farnaby, is also possibly unique. In at least some cases, then, Milton may have introduced innovations of his own; in general, however, he was codifying the best current usage.

IV. THE SIGNIFICANCE OF MILTON'S *ACCEDENCE*

Throughout the seventeenth and much of the eighteenth century as well, a solid knowledge of Latin was a necessary prerequisite to almost any kind of professional life. As the pugnacious Thomas Morrice, M.A., points out in his passionate *Apology for Schoole-Masters* (1619), most important serious books required Latinity; with it one might travel throughout "all Christian Kingdomes"; and it could even ward off criminal execution by virtue of benefit of clergy.[1] The fact that eight different authors were impelled in the next century to turn Gray's *Elegy in a Country Churchyard* into the enduring tongue [2] is merely one of thousands of signs that Latin continued as the "parole of the learned." It is thus scarcely surprising that many writers sought ways to simplify the long and complicated processes of language instruction.

Some methods were radical, such as the Comenian and Bathean elimination of grammar in favor of vocabulary and memorized phrases; others sought panaceas in particular methods like emphasis upon idiom, the use of versified rules, and heavy dependence upon the clause as the unit of learning. Milton uses no such novelties: in the long tradition of Wolsey, Lily, Farnaby, and others, he seeks merely to clarify and simplify the traditional divisions of accidence and syntax. Linguistically, then, he is conservative. Other writers again claimed only to supplement the royal grammar through question-and-answer forms or construes of Lily. Milton is also apart from this group, for he is clearly determined to supersede, not to bolster, that currently in use, whose cumbersome

[17] Danes, *Light to Lilie,* sig. A6v. He points out that only Priscian among the ancients makes any such division.

[18] *Accedence,* pp. 96–97 below.

[1] Thomas Morrice, *An Apology for Schoole-Masters* (London, 1619; HHL), sigs. D6–D6v.

[2] Clark Sutherland Northrup, *A Bibliography of Thomas Gray* (New Haven, London, and Oxford, 1917), pp. 74 ff.

prolixity wastes the *"tenth part of mans life, ordinarily extended."* [3]

On the other hand, he also avoids the company of those who seek completeness in a grammar school text, who would answer every conceivable question of syntax in a single volume—scholars like Linacre, Farnaby, and Burles. Though highly complimentary to learned men, he was too humanistic, too much the product of Saint Paul's, to fall into the role of dedicated grammarian; as *Of Education* makes clear, he would dispatch the necessary preliminaries as quickly as possible so that the student might begin to savor the sweetness of classical learning itself. [4] The man who condemned the "despicable quibbles" [5] and the "capricious *Pœdantie* of hotliver'd Grammarians" [6] would be unlikely to confuse the instruments of learning with learning itself. He thus sought to distill the minimal knowledge a student would need to read Cato and Palladius, Varro and Livy. In short, Milton tried to do better what had often been done before.

The result is, in many ways, a distinct improvement upon the authorized text. Milton has pared away much that was needless, compressed much that was prolix, and sharpened the order and structure of traditional materials. In addition, he has combined the best insights of many other writers into his own work: he can take from Bird the prepositions used in composition without losing his way in Bird's thirty kinds of adverbs; he can omit orthography with Shirley without following the *ignis fatuus* of versified rules; he can follow Ramus's totally English format without the constant multiplication of Ramian alternate possibilities. Similarly, though he clearly intends to displace Lily, he does not hesitate to found his whole work on the received grammar, whose order of presentation he follows and whose very lists and catalogues he appropriates when they seem fit to his purposes. Though much of the *Accedence* appears also in Lily, in general Milton improves whatever he alters.

Yet the book is not entirely successful. Where Lily's versified rules at least are capable of being memorized, Milton's corresponding lists of special cases would at times lead a neophyte to despair—as in his elaborate discussion of third-declension nouns, where he instances over 170 exceptions and subclassifications. [7] Similarly, seven whole pages pile up lists of the principal parts of verbs, but

[3] *Accedence,* p. 86 below.
[4] *Complete Prose,* II, 372 ff.
[5] Ibid., I. 300.
[6] Ibid., p. 666.
[7] *Accedence,* pp. 90–92 below.

they are not even in alphabetical order.[8] Though they do have a method to them, they are neither fit for memorization nor usefully arranged for reference. When to these problems one adds occasional obscurity and awkwardness of definition, the result is a less than perfect handbook. It most certainly testifies, as J. Milton French suggests,[9] to Milton's constant desire to improve the world he lived in, but it is a distinctly minor achievement. Perhaps the fairest judgment would be an analogy with the present-day scholar who at one point in his career writes a new handbook for English composition classes. If the man is worthy, the result will do its job competently, it will include the insights of other writers, and it will make certain improvements upon its competitors. Milton himself, I think, would claim no more for the *Accedence Commenc't Grammar*.

V. THE TEXT

The present text ("A" text) follows the Huntington Library copy (shelf number 105,677). Collation: 12mo: A–B^{12}, C^{11} [$5 (-A1, title page) signed]; pp. [4] 1–65 [1]. Contents: [A1], title page (verso blank); A2–A2v, "To the Reader"; A3–C11, the work (errata also on C11). This copy has been collated with microfilms of the following:

B.   Yale University Library (Z77.147) [used in Columbia Milton]
C.   Trinity College, Cambridge (II.12.1796)
D.   University Library, Cambridge (Christ's College) (Cc.6.13^3)
E.   Harvard College Library (14496.15.25*)
F.   University of Illinois Library (Uncat., RBR)
G.   British Museum (C 123 a 15)
H.   Columbia University Library (470/1669/M64)
 I.   Bodleian Library, Oxford (Ashm A4)
J.   Bodleian Library, Oxford (8° C89 Art)
K.   Bodleian Library, Oxford (Douce MM 297).

The existence of two quite different title pages (see below, pp. 84–85) would at first suggest two editions. In fact, there seems to have been only one, to which all of the above copies belong. The printing is in general careless and sloppy, and obvious mistakes are repeated in all copies that would surely have been caught had the type been reset. On p. 29, next-to-last and last lines, all copies print the word "thir" twice in a row. On p. 33, five lines up, as the editor of the Columbia Edition notes, "vincio" appears as

[8] Ibid., pp. 105–11 below.
[9] French, "Notes," p. 42.

"vinclo" and "vinctum" as "vinctumo." On p. 38, lines 8 and 10, the italicized word "*Laudandum*" begins with a roman, not an italic, "L," while two lines later an italicized upper-case "*P*" begins the roman word "*Passive*." On p. 52, the last line begins with "hese" instead of "these"—and begins flush with the margin, leaving no space for a letter "t," which did not print. On the first line of the same page, the typesetter left far too much space between words and letters even though the first word on the next line, "only," could easily have been added. Thus there was but one edition.

There are, however, several variants among the copies. Many of these seem to be the result of type slippage, like that on p. 45, line 4, where most copies have as a last word "n" instead of the appropriate "in." There is room in all for the missing "i," however, and in the Yale copy there is at least a trace of it. Though frequent, these variants seem to me meaningless. There are, however, three more significant differences:

1. There are several peculiarities in pagination: in copy "D," p. 9 is wrongly numbered "I." In copies "B" and "I," p. 56 has no page number. These variants are not present in the other copies.
2. On p. 5, fifth line from the bottom, the "A" text reads "Voc. *Parens*." The Bodleian copy "J," however, reads "Voc. *hic Parens*." None of the other copies has the variant.
3. Toward the bottom of p. 25 in the "A" text, the word "*Plur*." is placed at right angles to the other printing and runs upward from bottom to top, as does the other phrase "*Pres. Sing*." across the page. In copies "G," "H," and "K," however, the word "*Plur*." is reversed and runs downward from top to bottom. All other copies follow the "A" text.

There seems to be no obvious connection between these variants and the two title pages. The "A" text and copies "C," "D," "J," and "K" have the title page reading "John Milton." The others have that reading "J.M." I thus conclude that the three significant variations listed above probably result from casual proofreading and correction during the actual press run of the edition.

In general, my aim has been to reproduce *literatim* the text of the Huntington Library copy. Thus my text reads *vinclo,* not *vincio;* and *vinctumo,* not *vinctum*—even though both forms are clearly wrong (see text below, p. 108). I have, however, made two exceptions to this customary rule. Although I print the original errata sheet at the end of the book, I have also silently corrected in the text the five errors it lists. And very occasionally, where a letter has dropped from a word in the Huntington copy but is present in the others, I have replaced it. Thus, on p. 33 (below,

p. 108), where the "A" text reads *salio alui saltum,* I have printed
salio salui saltum. This exception occurs only in the absence of a
letter, not in its emendation. Yet it must be admitted that other
errors will be present, not merely because of my own fallibility but
also because the printing is sometimes so unclear that transcription
becomes a guess, not a certainty. On p. 33 (below, p. 108), where
George Philip Krapp in the Columbia Milton read *sarcio sarsi*
sartum, sarcio sarsi sartum, I read *sarcio sarsi sartum, farcio farsi*
fartum. Where he read *libes* in the Yale copy, I read *lebes* in both
Huntington and Yale copies (below, p. 91). Thus, in the latter case
his corrected and my uncorrected text agree, yet I am certainly not
positive that his reading is demonstrably wrong. Apart from these
very few particular instances, however, my textual principle has
been the reproduction, not the improvement, of the 1669 edition.

I am deeply grateful to the Huntington Library, San Marino,
for allowing me to use its copy as my basic text and to reproduce
the title page of that edition. I am also most grateful to the Yale
University Library for its kindness in allowing me to reproduce
here the alternative title page from its copy.

In one way, the *Accedence* is quite different from Milton's other
works: it is a reworking of commonly known materials, not a fully
original contribution to knowledge. As a result, it asks for special
editorial treatment. In most of the writings, a reader has frequent
questions about details that are now obscure: the source of an odd
name, the history of an idea, the significance of an event, the point
of an allusion. Here, however, the text requires no such background
knowledge, and the footnotes appropriate to Milton's other works
would be pointless. To define the accusative case or to say that
other grammarians agree that the nominative plural of *rosa* is *rosæ*
seems futile. The only other obvious use for annotation would be
to identify the sources of examples with which the author illustrates
Latin rules. After some deliberation, I have decided to omit these,
especially since J. Milton French's article (listed above) says all
that I could say on the topic. Their bulk would be enormous, as
there are some 530 of them; well over 60 percent were merely
transferred from Lily and other grammars; few scholars probably
care whether a phrase like *procul muros* comes from Livy or Sallust;
the source of at least 20 percent is still unknown; and even when
an apparent source in a classical writer exists, it is impossible to
be sure whether Milton went directly to the original, found the
phrase in another writer, picked it up from another grammar, or
discovered it in someone's florilegium. Instead of such footnotes,

therefore, I have instead utilized the available space for a longer introduction dealing with what seem to me the most important questions: How does Milton's grammar differ from Lily's and the works of his competitors? How is it like them? What influence and effects did it have? These matters, I hope, may be of more interest to the reader.

ACCEDENCE
Commenc't
GRAMMAR,

Supply'd with sufficient
RULES,

For the use of such as,
Younger or Elder, are desirous, without more trouble
then needs, to attain the *Latin*
Tongue; the elder sort especially, with little teaching, and
thir own industry.

J. M.

LONDON,

Printed by *S. Simmons*, next door to
the *Golden Lion* in *Aldersgate-street*, 1669.

ACCEDENCE
Commenc't
GRAMMAR,

Supply'd with sufficient

RULES,

For the use of such (Younger
or Elder) as are desirous, without more trouble than
needs to attain the

LATIN TONGUE;

The Elder sort especially, with
little Teaching, and their
own Industry.

By JOHN MILTON.

LONDON, Printed for *S. S.* and are
to be sold by *John Starkey* at the Miter in *Fleet-
street*, next *Temple-bar.* 1 6 6 9.

TO THE
READER

IT hath been long a general complaint, not without cause, in the bringing up of Youth, and still is, that the tenth part of mans life, ordinarily extended, is taken up in learning, and that very scarcely, the Latin Tongue. *Which tardy proficience may be attributed to several causes: In particular, the making two labours of one, by learning first the* Accedence, *then the* Grammar *in Latin, ere the Language of those Rules be understood. The only remedy of this, was to joyn both Books into one, and in the* English Tongue; *whereby the long way is much abbreviated, and the labour of understanding much more easie: A work suppos'd not to have been done formerly; or if done, not without such difference here in brevity and alteration, as may be found of moment. That of* Grammar, *touching Letters and Syllables, is omitted, as learnt before, and little different from the* English [A2] *Spelling-book; especially, since few will be perswaded to pronounce* Latin *otherwise then thir own* English. *What will not come under Rule, by reason of too much variety in Declension, Gender, or Construction, is also here omitted, least the course and clearness of method be clog'd with Catalogues instead of Rules, or too much interruption between Rule and Rule: Which* Linaker *setting down the various Idiomes of many verbs, was forc't to do by Alphabet; and therefore, though very learned, not thought fit to be read in Schools. But in such words, a* Dictionary *stor'd with good* Authorities *will be found the readiest guide. Of figurate Construction what is usefull is digested into several Rules of* Syntaxis: *and* Prosodie, *after this* Grammar *well learnt, will not need to be Englisht for him who hath a mind to read it. Account might be now givn what addition or alteration from other Grammars hath been here made, and for what reason. But he who would be short in teaching, must not be long in Prefacing: The Book it self follows, and will declare sufficiently to them who can discern.*

J.M. [A2v]

ACCEDENCE
Commenc't
GRAMMAR

LATIN Grammar is the Art of right understanding, speaking, or writing Latine, observed from them who have spoken or written it best.

Grammar hath two Parts: Right-wording, usually call'd *Etymologie;* and right-joyning of words, or *Syntaxis.*

Etymologie, or Right-wording, teacheth what belongs to every single word or part of Speech. [1]

Of Latin *SPEECH*
are Eight General Parts:

Noun			Adverb		
Pronoun	De-		Conjunction		Unde-
Verb	clin'd.		Preposition		clin'd.
Participle			Interjection		

*DE*clin'd are those Words which have divers endings; as *Homo* a man, *hominis* of a man; *Amo* I love, *amas* thou lovest. *Undeclin'd* are those words which have but one ending, as *bene* well, *cum* when, *tum* then.

Nounes, Pronounes, and Participles, are declin'd with Gender, Number, and Case; Verbs, as hereafter in the Verb.

Of Genders.

GEnders are three, the Masculin, Feminin, and Neuter. The Masculin may be declin'd with this Article *Hic,* as *hic Vir* a Man; The Feminin with this Article *Hæc,* as *hæc Mulier* a Woman; The Neuter with this Article *Hoc,* as *hoc Saxum* a Stone.

Of the Masculin are generally all Nounes belonging to the Male kind, as also the Names of Rivers, Months, and Winds.

Of the Feminin, all Nounes belonging to the Female kind, as also the names of Countries, Cities, Trees, some few of the two latter excepted: Of Cities, as *Agragas* and *Sulmo,* Masculin; *Argos,*

Tibur, Præneste, and such as end in *um,* [2] Neuter; *Anxur* both. Of Trees, *Oleaster* and *Spinus,* Masculin; but *Oleaster* is read also Feminin, *Cic.* verr. 4. *Acer, siler, suber, thus, robur,* Neuter.

And of the Neuter are all Nouns, not being proper Names, ending in *um,* and many others.

Some Nouns are of two Genders, as *hic* or *hæc dies* a Day; and all such as may be spoken both of Male and Female, as *hic* or *hæc Parens* a Father or Mother; some be of three, as *hic haec* and *hoc Felix* Happy.

Of Numbers.

WOrds Declin'd have two Numbers, the Singular, and the Plural. The Singular speaketh but of one, as *Lapis* a Stone. The Plural of more then one, as *Lapides* Stones; yet sometimes but of one, as *Athenae* the City *Athens, Literæ* an Epistle, *ædes ædium* a House.

Note that some Nounes have no Singular, and some no Plural, as the nature of thir signification requires. Some are of one Gender in the Singular; of another, or of two Genders in the Plural, as reading will best teach.

Of Cases.

NOunes, Pronounes, and Participles are declin'd with six Endings, which are called Cases, both in the Singular and Plural Number. The Nominative, Genitive, Dative, Accusative, Vocative, and Ablative.

The *Nominative* is the first Case, and properly nameth the thing, as *Liber* a Book.

The *Genitive* is Englisht with this Sign *of,* as *Libri* of a Book.

The *Dative* with this Sign *to,* or *for,* as *Libro* to or for a Book. [3]

The *Accusative* hath no sign.

The *Vocative* calleth or speaketh to, as *O Liber* O Book, and is commonly like the Nominative.

But in the Neuter Gender the Nominative, Accusative, and Vocative, are like in both Numbers, and in the *Plural* end alwayes in *a.*

The *Ablative* is Englisht with these Signs, *in, with, of, for, from, by,* and such like, as *de Libro* of or from the Book, *pro Libro* for the Book And the Ablative Plural is alwayes like the Dative.

Note, that some Nouns have but one ending throughout all Cases, as *Frugi, nequam, nihil;* and all words of number from three to a hundred, as *quatuor* four, *quinque* five, *&c.*

Some have but one, some two, some three Cases only, in the Singular or Plural, as use will best teach.

Of a Noune.

A Noune is the Name of a thing, as *Manus* a Hand, *Domus* a House, *Bonus* Good, *Pulcher* Fair.

Nounes be Substantives or Adjectives.

A Noun Substantive is understood by it self, as *homo* a man, *domus* a house.

An Adjective, to be well understood, requireth a Substantive to be joyn'd with it, as *bonus* good, *parvus* little, which cannot be well understood unless somthing good or little be either nam'd, as *bonus vir* a good man, *parvus puer* a little boy; or by use understood, as *honestum* an honest thing, *boni* good men. [4]

The Declining of Substantives.

NOunes Substantive have five Declensions or forms of ending thir Cases, chiefly distinguisht by the different ending of thir Genitive Singular.

The first Declension.

THe first is when the Genitive and Dative singular end in *æ*, &c. as in the Example following.

Singular.	Plural.
Nom. Voc. Abl. *musa*	Nom. Voc. *musæ*
Gen. Dat. *musæ*	Gen. *musarum*
Acc. *musam*	Dat. Abl. *musis.*
	Acc. *Musas*

This one word *familia* joyn'd with *pater, mater, filius,* or *filia,* endeth the Genitive in *as,* as *pater familias,* but somtimes *familiæ: Dea, mula, equa, liberta,* make the Dative and Ablative plural in *abus; filia* and *nata* in *is* or *abus.*

The first Declension endeth alwayes in *a,* unless in some words deriv'd of the Greek: and is always of the Feminin Gender, except in names attributed to men, according to the general Rule, or to Stars, as *Cometa, Planeta.*

Nounes, and especially proper Names derived of the Greek, have here three endings, *as, es, e,* and are declin'd in some of thir Cases after the Greek form. *Æneas,* acc *Ænean,* voc *Ænea. Anchises,* acc. *Anchisen,* voc *Anchise* or *Anchisa,* abl. *Anchise. Penelope, Penelopes, Penelope, Penelopen,* voc. abl. *Penelope.* Somtimes following the Latin, as *Marsya, Philocteta,* for *as* and *es; Philoctetam, Eriphylam,* for *an* and *en.* Cic. [5]

The second Declension.

THe second is when the Genitive Singular endeth in *i,* the Dative in *o, &c.*

Sing.		Plur.
Nom. Voc. *Liber*		Nom. Voc. *Libri*
Gen. *libri*		Gen. *librorum*
Dat. Abl. *libro*		Dat. Abl. *libris*
Acc. *librum*		Acc. *libros.*

Note that when the Nominative endeth in *us*, the Vocative shall end in *e*, as *Dominus ô Domine*, except *Deus ô Deus*. And these following, *Agnus, lucus, vulgus, populus, chorus, fluvius, e* or *us*.

When the Nominative endeth in *ius*, if it be the proper name of a man, the Vocative shall end in *i*, as *Georgius ô Georgi;* hereto add *filius ô fili*, and *genius ô geni*.

All Nounes of the Second Declension are of the Masculin or Neuter Gender; of the Masculin, such as end in *ir, or,* or *us*, except some few, *humus, domus, alvus*, and others deriv'd of the Greek, as *methodus, antidotus*, and the like, which are of the Feminin, and some of them somtimes also Masculin, as *atomus, phaselus;* to which add *ficus* the name of a disease, *grossus, pampinus*, and *rubus*.

Those of the Neuter, except *virus, pelagus*, and *vulgus* (which last is sometimes Masculin) end all in *um*, and are declin'd as followeth:

Sing.		Plur.
Nom. Ac. Voc. *Studium*		Nom. Ac. Voc. *Studia*
Gen. *studii*		Gen. *studiorum*
Dat. Abl. *studio*		Dat. Abl. *studiis.*

Some Nouns in this Declension are of the first Example Singular, of the second Plural, as [6] *Pergamus* the City *Troy*, Plur. *Hæc Pergama;* and some names of hills, as *Mænalus, Ismarus, hæc Ismara;* So also *Tartarus*, and the Lake *Avernus;* others are of both, as *sibilus, jocus, locus, hi loci*, or *hæc loca*. Some are of the Second Example Singular, of the first Plural, as *Argos, Cælum*, Plur. *hi Cæli;* others of both, as *Rastrum, Capistrum, Filum, Frænum;* Plur. *fræni* or *fræna*. *Nundinum*, & *Epulum*, are of the first Declension Plural, *Nundinæ, Epulæ; Balneum* of both, *balneæ* or *balnea*.

Greek proper names have here three endings, *os, on*, and *us* long from a Greek Diphthong. *Hæc Delos, hanc Delon. Hoc Ilion.* the rest regular, *Hic panthus, ô panthu*, Virg.

The third Declension.

THe third is when the Genitive singular endeth in *is*, the Dative in *i*, the Accusative in *em* and somtimes in *im*, the Ablative in *e*,

and somtimes in *i*, the Nom. Acc. Voc. Plural in *es*, the Genitive
in *um* and somtimes in *ium*, &c.

Sing.			Plur.
Nom. Gen. Voc. *Panis*			Nom. Ac. Vo. *panes*
Dat. *pani*			Gen *panum*
Acc. *panem*			Dat. Abl. *panibus*.
Abl. *pane*			

Sing			Plur.
Nom. Voc. *parens*			No. Ac. Voc. *parentes*
Gen. *parentis*			Gen. *parentum*
Dat. *parenti*			Dat. Abl. *parentibus*.
Acc. *parentem*			
Abl. *parente*			[7]

This third Declension, with many endings, hath all Genders,
best known by dividing all Nounes hereto belonging into such as
either increase one syllable long or short in the Genitive, or increase
not at all.

Such as increase not in the Genitive are generally Feminin, as
Nubes nubis, Caro carnis.

Except such as end in *er*, as *hic venter ventris*, and these in *is*
following, *natalis, aqualis, lienis, orbis, callis, caulis, collis, follis,
mensis, ensis, fustis, funis, panis, penis, crinis, ignis, cassis, fascis,
torris, piscis, unguis, vermis, vectis, postis, axis*, and the Compounds of *assis*, as *centussis*.

But *Canalis, finis, clunis, restis, sentis, amnis, corbis, linter,
torquis, anguis, hic* or *hæc;* To these add *vepres.*

Such as end in *e* are Neuters, as *mare, rete*, and two Greek in
es, as *hippomanes, cacoëthes.*

Nounes encreasing Long.

Nounes encreasing one syllable long in the Genitive are generally
Feminin, as *hæc pietas pietatis, virtus virtutis.*

Except such as end in *ans* Masculin, as *dodrans, quadrans,
sextans;* in *ens*, as *oriens, torrens, bidens* a pick-axe.

In *or*, most commonly deriv'd of Verbs, as *pallor, clamor;* In *o*,
not thence deriv'd, as *ternio, senio, sermo, temo*, and the like.

And these of one syllable, *sal, sol, ren, splen, as, bes, pes, mos,
flos, ros, dens, mons, pons, fons, grex.*

And words deriv'd from the Greek in *en*, as *lichen;* in *er*, as
crater; in *as*, as *adamas;* in *es*, as *lebes;* to these, *hydrops, thorax,
phœnix.*

But *scrobs, rudens, stirps* the body or root of a tree, and *calx*
a heel, *hic* or *hæc*. [8]

Neuter, these of one syllable, *mel, fel, lac, far, ver, cor, æs, vas
vasis, os ossis, os oris, rus, rhus, jus, crus, pus.* And of more
syllables in *al* and *ar,* as *capital, laquear,* but *halec hoc* or *hæc.*

Nounes encreasing Short.

Nounes encreasing short in the Genitive are generally Masculin,
as *hic sanguis sanguinis, lapis lapidis.*

Except, Feminin all words of many syllables ending in *do* or *go,*
as *dulcedo, compago, arbor, hyems, cuspis, pecus, pecudis:* These
in *ex, forfex, carex, tomex, supellex:* In *ix, appendix, histrix, cox-
endix, filix.* Greek Nounes in *as* and *is,* as *lampas, iaspis:* To these
add *chlamys, bacchar, syndon, icon.*

But *margo, cinis, pulvis, adeps, forceps, pumex, ramex, imbrex,
obex, silex, cortex, onix,* and *sardonix, hic* or *hæc.*

Neuters are all ending in *a* as *problema,* in *en,* except *hic pecten,*
in *ar* as *jubar,* in *er* these, *verber, iter, uber, cadaver, zinziber,
laser, cicer, siser, piper, papaver;* somtimes in *ur,* except *hic furfur,*
in *us* as *onus,* in *ut* as *caput;* to these, *marmor, æquor, ador.*

Greek proper names here end in *as, an, is* and *eus,* and may be
declin'd some wholly after the Greek form, as *Pallas pallados pal-
ladi pallada;* others in some Cases, as *Atlas,* acc. *Atlanta,* voc.
Atla. Garamas, plur. *garamantes,* acc. *garamantas. Pan panos
pana. Phyllis phyllidos,* voc *phylli,* plur. *Phyllides,* acc. *phyllidas.
Tethys, tethyos,* acc. *tethyn,* voc. *tethy. Neapolis, neapolios,* acc.
neapolin. Paris, paridos or *parios,* acc. *parida* or *parin. Orpheus
orpheos orphei orphea orpheu.* But Names in *eus* borrow somtimes
thir Genitive of the Se- [9] cond Declension, as *Erechtheus, er-
echthei.* Cic. *Achilles* or *Achilleus, Achillei;* and somtimes their
Accusative in *on* or *um,* as *Orpheus Orpheon, Theseus Theseum,
Perseus Perseum,* which somtimes is formd after Greek words of
the First Declension Latin, *Perseus* or *Perses, Persæ Persæ Persen
Persæ Persa.*

The fourth Declension.

THe fourth is when the Genitive Singular endeth in *us,* the
Dative Singular in *ui,* and somtimes in *u,* Plural in *ibus* and sometimes in *ubus.*

Sing.		Plur.
Nom. Gen. Vo. *Sensus*		Nom. Ac Voc. *Sensus*
Dat. *sensui*		Gen. *sensuum*
Acc. *sensum*		Dat. Abl *sensibus.*
Abl. *sensu*		

The fourth Declension hath two endings, *us* and *u; us* generally
Masculin, except some few, as *hæc manus, ficus* the fruit of a tree,

acus, porticus, tribus: but *penus* and *specus hic* or *hæc. U* of the
Neuter, as *gelu, genu, veru;* but in the Singular most part defective.

Proper Names in *os* and *o* long pertaining to the Fourth Declension Greek, may belong best to the fourth in Latin, as *Andro-*
geos, Gen. *Androgeo,* Acc. *Androgeon.* Hic *Athos,* hunc *Atho,* Virg.
Hæc *Sappho,* Gen. *Sapphus,* Acc. *Sappho.* Better Authors follow
the Latin form as *Dido didonis didonem.* But *Iesus Iesu Iesu*
Iesum Iesu Iesu.

The fifth Declension.

THe fifth is when the Genitive and Dative Singular end in *ei,*
&c. [10]

Sing.			Plur.
Nom. Voc. *Res*			Nom. Acc. Voc. *res*
Gen. Dat. *rei*			Gen. *rerum*
Acc. *rem*			Dat. Abl. *rebus.*
Abl. *re*			

All Nounes of the fifth Declension are of the Feminin Gender,
except *dies hic* or *hæc,* and his Compound *meridies hic* only.

Some Nounes are of more Declensions then one, as *vas vasis* of
the third in the Singular, of the second in the Plural *vasa vasorum.*
Colus, laurus, and some others, of the second and fourth. *Satur-*
nalia saturnalium or *saturnaliorum saturnalibus,* and such other
names of feasts, *Poëmata poëmatum, Poëmatis* or *poëmatibus,* of
the second and third Plural. *Plebs* of the third and fifth, *plebis* or
plebei.

The declining of Adjectives.

A Noun Adjective is declin'd with three Terminations, or with
three Articles.

An Adjective of three terminations is declin'd like the first and
second Declension of Substantives joyn'd together after this
manner.

Sing.			Plur.
Nom. *bonus bona bonum*			Nom. Vo. *boni bonæ bona*
Gen. *boni bonæ boni*			Gen. *bonorum bonarum bonorum*
Dat. *bono bonæ bono*			Dat. Abl. *bonis*
Ac. *bonum bonam bonum*			Ac. *bonos bonas bona.*
Voc. *bone bona bonum*			
Abl. *bono bona bono*			

In like manner those in *er* and *ur,* as *sacer sacra sacrum, satur*
satura saturum: but *unus, totus, solus, alius, alter, ullus, uter,*
with their compounds [11] *Neuter, uterque,* and the like, make thir
Genitive Singular in *ius,* the Dative in *i,* as *Unus una unum,* Gen.

unius, Dat. *uni,* in all the rest like *bonus,* save that *alius* maketh in the Neuter Gender *aliud,* and in the Dative *alii,* and somtimes in the Genitive.

Ambo and *duo* be thus declin'd in the plural only.

Nom. Voc. *Ambo ambœ ambo.*

Gen. *amborum ambarum amborum.*

Dat. Abl. *Ambobus ambabus ambobus.*

Acc. *ambos* or *ambo, ambas ambo.*

Adjectives of three Articles have in the Nominative either one ending, as *hic, hœc, & hoc felix;* or two, as *hic & hœc tristis, & hoc triste;* and are declin'd like the Third Declension of Substantives, as followeth.

Sing.	Plur.
Nom. *hic hœc & hoc Felix*	Nom. *hi & hœ felices, & hœc felicia*
Gen. *felicis*	Gen. *felicium*
Dat. *felici*	Dat. Abl. *felicibus*
Acc. *hunc & hanc felicem, & hoc felix*	Acc. *hos & has felices, & hœc felicia*
Voc. *ô felix*	Voc. *ô felices, & ô felicia.*
Abl. *felice* or *felici*	

Sing.	Plur.
No. *hic & hœc tristis, & hoc triste*	Nom. *hi & hœ tristes; & hœc tristia*
Gen. *tristis*	Gen. *tristium*
Dat. Abl. *tristi*	Dat. Abl. *tristibus*
Acc. *hunc & hanc tristem, & hoc triste*	Acc. *hos & has tristes, & hœc tristia*
Voc. *ô tristis, & ô triste*	Voc. *ô tristes, & ô tristia.* [12]

There be also another sort which have in the Nominative Case three Terminations and three Articles, as *hic acer, hic & hœc acris, hoc acre.* In like manner be declined *equester, volucer,* and some few others, being in all other cases like the Examples beforegoing.

Comparisons of Nounes.

ADjectives, whose signification may increase or be diminish't, may form Comparison, whereof there be two degrees above the positive word it self, The Comparative, and Superlative.

The Positive signifieth the thing it self without comparing, as *durus* hard.

The Comparative exceedeth his Positive in signification, compar'd with some other, as *durior* harder; and is formd of the first Case of his Positive that endeth in *i,* by putting thereto *or* and *us,* as of *duri, hic & hæc durior, & hoc durius;* of *dulci, dulcior dulcius.*

The Superlative exceedeth his Positive in the highest degree, as *durissimus* hardest; and it is formd of the first case of his Positive that endeth in *is,* by putting thereto *simus,* as of *duris durissimus, dulcis dulcissimus.*

If the Positive end in *er,* the Superlative is formd of the Nominative case by putting to *rimus,* as *pulcher pulcherrimus.* Like to these are *vetus veterrimus, maturus maturimus;* but *dexter dextimus,* and *sinister sinisterior sinistimus.*

All those Nouns ending in *lis* make the Superlative by changing *is* into *limus,* as *humilis, similis, facilis, gracilis, agilis, docilis docillimus.*

All other Nounes ending in *lis* do follow [13] the general Rule, as *utilis utilissimus.*

Of these Positives following are formd a different sort of Superlatives; of *superus, supremus* and *summus; inferus, infimus* and *imus; exterus, extimus* and *extremus; posterus postremus.*

Some of these want the Positive, and are form'd from Adverbs; of *intra, interior intimus, ultra ulterior ultimus, citra citerior citimus, pridem prior primus, prope propior proximus.*

Others from Positives without Case, as *nequam nequior nequissimus.*

Some also from no Positive, as *ocior ocissimus.* Some want the Comparative, as *novus novissimus, sacer sacerrimus.*

Some the Superlative, as *senex senior, juvenis junior, adolescens adolescentior.*

Some ending in *us,* frame thir Comparative as if they ended in *ens, benevolus, maledicus, magnificus magnificentior magnificentissimus.*

These following are without Rule, *Bonus melior optimus, Malus pejor pessimus, Magnus major maximus, Parvus minor minimus; Multus plurimus, multa plurima, multum plus plurimum.*

If a Vowel come before *us,* it is compared with *magis* and *maximè,* as *pius, magis pius, maximè pius; idoneus, magis* and *maximè idoneus.* Yet some of these follow the general Rule, as *Assiduus assiduissimus, strenuus strenuior, exiguus exiguissimus, tenuis tenuior tennuissimus.*

Of a Pronoun.

A Pronoun is a part of Speech that standeth for a Noun Substantive, either at present or before spoken of, as *ille* he or that, *hic* this, *qui* who. [14]

There be Ten Pronounes, *Ėgo, tu, sui, ille, ipse, iste, hic, is, qui* and *quis,* besides their Compounds, *egomet, tute, hicce, idem, quisnam, aliquis,* and such others. The rest so call'd, as *meus, tuus, suus, noster, vester, nostras, vestras, cujus* and *cujas,* are not Pronouns, but Adjectives thence deriv'd.

Of Pronounes such as shew the thing present are called *Demonstratives,* as *ego, tu, hic;* and such as refer to a thing antecedent or spoken of before are called Relatives, as *qui* who or which.

Quis, and often *qui,* because they ask a question, are called Interrogatives, with their Compounds *ecquis, namquis.*

Declensions of Pronouns are three.

Ego, tu, sui, be of the First Declension, and be thus declin'd.

Sing.	Plur.
Nom. *Ego*	Nom. Acc. *Nos*
Gen. *mei*	Gen. *nostrum* or *nostri*
Dat. *mihi*	Dat Abl. *nobis*
Acc. Abl. *me*	Voc. *Caret.*
Voc. *Caret*	

Sing.	Plur.
Nom. Voc. *Tu*	Nom. Acc. Voc *vos*
Gen. *tui*	Gen. *vestrum* or *vestri*
Dat. *tibi*	Dat. Abl. *vobis.*
Acc. Abl. *te*	

Sing.	Nom. Voc. *Caret*		Dat. *sibi*
Plur.	Gen. *sui*		Acc. Abl. *se.*

From these three be deriv'd *meus, tuus, suus, noster, vester, nostras, vestras,* (which are called [15] Possessives) whereof the former five be declin'd like Adjectives of three Terminations, except that *meus* in the Vocative Case maketh *mi, mea, meum; Nostras, Vestras,* with three Articles, as *hic & hœc nostras & hoc nostras* or *nostrate, vestrate.* In other Cases according to Rule.

These three, *ille, iste, ipse,* be of the Second Declension, making thir Genitive singular in *ius,* their Dative in *i;* and the former two be declin'd like the Adjective *alius,* and the Third like *unus* before spoken of.

	Nom. *ille illa illud,*	Gen. *illius,*	Dat. *illi.*
Sing.	Nom. *iste ista istud,*	Gen. *istius,*	Dat. *isti.*
	Nom. *ipse ipsa ipsum,*	Gen. *ipsius,*	Dat. *ipsi.*

These four, *hic, is, qui* and *quis,* be of the third Declension, making thir Genitive singular in *jus,* with j consonant, and be declin'd after this manner.

Sing.	Plur.
Nom. *hic hæc hoc*	Nom. *hi hæ hæc*
Gen. *hujus*	Gen. *horum harum horum*
Dat. *huic*	Dat. Abl. *his*
Acc. *hunc hanc hoc*	Acc. *hos has hæc*
Voc. *Caret*	Voc. *Caret*
Abl. *hoc hac hoc*	

Of *iste* and *hic* is compounded *istic istæc, istoc* or *istuc.* Acc. *istunc istanc, istoc* or *istuc.* Abl. *istoc istac istoc.* Plur. *istæc* only.

Sing.	Plur.
Nom. *is ea id*	Nom. *ii eæ ea*
Gen. *ejus*	Gen. *eorum earū eorum*
Dat. *ei*	Dat. Abl. *iis* or *eis*
Acc. *eum eam id*	Acc. *eos eas ea*
Voc. *Caret*	Voc. *Caret*
Abl. *eo ea eo*	[16]

Sing.	Plur.
Nom. *qui quæ quod*	Nom. *qui quæ quæ*
Gen. *cujus*	Gen. *quorum quarum quorum*
Dat. *cui*	Dat. Abl. *quibus* or *queis*
Acc. *quem quam quod*	Acc. *quos quas quæ*
Voc. *Caret*	Voc. *Caret*
Abl. *quo qua, quo* or *qui*	

In like manner *quivis, quilibet,* and *quicunque* the Compounds. Sing. Nom. *Quis, qua* or *quæ, quid.* Gen: &c. like *qui.* So *quis-quam, quisnam,* Compounds.

Of *Quis* are made these Pronoun Adjectives, *Cujus cuja cujum,* whose; and *hic* & *hæc cujas* and *hoc cujate,* of what Nation.

Quisquis is defective, and thus declin'd,

No. { *Quisquis* / *Quicquid* }   Ac. { *Quicquid* }   Ab. { *Quoquo* / *Quoqua* / *Quoquo* }

Of a Verb.

A Verb is a part of Speech, that betokeneth *being,* as *Sum* I am, or *doing,* as *Laudo* I praise; and is declin'd with Mood, Tense, Number and Person.

Moods.

THere be four Moods, which express the *manner of doing;* the Indicative, the Imperative, the Potential or Subjunctive, and the Infinitive.

The Indicative Mood *sheweth* or *declareth,* as *Laudo* I praise.

The Imperative *biddeth* or *exhorteth,* as *Lauda* praise thou.

The Potential or Subjunctive is Englisht with [17] these Signs, *may, can, might, would, could, should;* Or without them as the Indicative, if a Conjunction go before or follow. As *Laudem,* I may or can praise. *Cum Laudarem* when I praised. *Cavissem, si præ-vidissem,* I had bewar'd if I had foreseen.

The Infinitive is englisht with this sign *To,* as *Laudare* to praise.

Tenses.

THere be three Tenses which express the *time of doing:* The Present, the Preterit or past, and the Future.

The Present Tense speaketh of the time that *now is,* as *Laudo* I praise.

The Preterit speaketh of the time *past,* and is distinguisht by three degrees: the Preterimperfect, the Preterperfect, and the Preterpluperfect.

The Preterimperfect speaketh of the time *not perfectly past,* as *Laudabam* I praised or did praise.

The Preterperfect speaketh of the time *perfectly past,* as *Laudavi* I have praised.

The Preterpluperfect speaketh of the time *more then perfectly past,* as *Laudaveram* I had praised.

The Future Tense speaketh of the time *to come,* as *Laudabo* I shall or will praise.

Persons.

THrough all Moods, except the Infinitive, there be three Persons in both Numbers, as, Sing. *Laudo* I praise, *laudas* thou praisest, *laudat* he praiseth; Plur. *Laudamus* we praise, *laudatis* ye praise, *laudant* they praise. Except some Verbs which are declin'd or form'd in the Third Person only, and have before them this sign, *It;* as *Tædet* it irketh, *oportet* it behoveth, and are called Impersonals. [18]

The Verb which betokeneth *being,* is properly this Verb *Sum* only, which is therefore call'd a Verb Substantive, and formd after this manner.

Indicative.

Pres. *sing.*	{ *I am.* Sum, es, est, *Plur.* sumus, estis, sunt.
Pret. *imp.*	{ *I was.* Eram, eras, erat, *Pl.* eramus, eratis, erant.
Pret. *perfect*	{ *I have been.* Fui, fuisti, fuit, *Plur.* fuimus, fuistis, fuerunt *or* fuere.
Pret. *plup.*	{ *I had been.* Fueram, fueras, fuerat, *Pl.* fueramus, fueratis, fuerant.
Fu- *ture.*	{ *I shall or will be.* Ero, eris, erit, *Pl.* erimus, eritis, erunt.

Imperative.

Be thou.

Sing.			*Plur.*		
{ Sis, es, esto.		Sit, esto.	{ Si- mus,	Sitis, este, estote.	Sint, sunto

Potential.

Pres. *sing.*	{ *I may or can be.* Sim, sis, sit, *Pl.* simus, sitis, sint.
Preter *imperf*	{ *I might or could be.* Essem *or* forem, es, et, *Pl.* essemus, esse- tis, essent *or* forent.
Preter- *perfect*	{ *I might or could have been.* Fuerim, ris, rit, *Pl.* rimus, ritis, rint. [19]
Preterplup. *with a con-* *junction.* Si	{ *If I had been.* Fuissem, es, et, *Pl.* emus, etis, ent.
Future Si	{ *If I shall be or shall have been.* Fuero, ris, rit, *Pl.* rimus, ritis, rint.

Infinitive.

Pres. and *Preter-* *imperf*	{ Esse, *to be.* }	{ *Preter-* *perfect,* *& pret.* *pluper.* }	Fuisse, *to have or had been.*
Future	{ Fore, *to be hereafter.*		

In like manner are form'd the Compounds; *Absum, adsum, desum, obsum, prœsum, prosum, possum;* but *possum* somthing varies after this manner.

Indicat. Pres. Sing. *Possum, potes, potest,* Plur. *possumus, pot-estis, possunt.* The other are regular, *poteram, potui, potueram, potero.*

Imperative *it wants.*

Potent. Pres. *Possim,* &c. Preterimperfect, *Possem*

Infin. *Pres. Posse.* Preterit. *Potuisse.*

Voices.

IN Verbs that betoken *doing* are two Voices, the *Active* and the *Passive.*

The Active signifieth *to do,* and always endeth in *o,* as *Doceo,* I teach.

The Passive signifieth *what is done to one by another,* and always endeth in *or,* as *Doceor* I am taught.

From these are to be excepted two sorts of [20] Verbs. The first are called *Neuters,* and cannot take *or* in the Passive, as *Curro* I run, *Sedeo* I sit; yet signifie somtimes passively, as *Vapulo* I am beaten.

The second are call'd *Deponents,* and signifie actively, as *Loquor* I speak; or Neuters, as *Glorior* I boast: but are form'd like Passives.

Conjugations.

VErbs both Active and Passive have four Conjugations, or forms of declining, known and distinguisht by thir Infinitive Mood Active, which alwayes endeth in *re.*

In the first Conjugation, after *a* long, as *Laudare* to praise.

In the second, after *e* long, as *habere* to have.

In the third, after *e* short, as *legere* to read.

In the fourth, after *i* long, as *audire* to hear.

In these four Conjugations, Verbs are declin'd or formd by Mood, Tense, Number, and Person, after these Examples.

Indicative Mood,
Present Tense

Singular.	Plural.

I *Thou* *He*	*We* *Ye* *They*
praise. praisest. praiseth	*praise. praise. praise.*
Laudo, laudas, laudat,	laudamus, laudatis, laudant.
Habeo, habes, habet,	habemus, habetis, habent.
Lego, legis, legit,	legimus, legitis, legunt.
Audio, audis, audit,	audimus, auditis, audiunt. [21]

Preter-imperfect tens. sing.	Laudabam, Habebam, Legebam, Audiebam,	*I praisd* or *did praise.* bas, bat, *Plur.* bamus, batis, bant.
Preter-perfect tens. sing.	Laudavi Habui Legi Audivi	*I have praisd.* isti, it, *Plur.* imus, istis, erunt *or* ere.
Preter-pluperfect tense sing.	Laudaveram Habueram Legeram Audiveram	*I had praisd.* ras, rat, *Plur.* ramus, ratis, rant.
Future tense sing.	Laudabo Habebo	*I shall* or *will praise.* bis, bit, *Plur.* bimus, bitis, bunt.
	Legam Audiam	es, et, *Plu.* emus, etis, ent.

Imperative Mood.

	Praise thou.	*Let him praise.*	*Let us praise.*	*Praise ye.*	*Let them praise.*
Pres. Sing.	Lauda, laudato.	Laudet laudato.	*Pl.* laudemus.	Laudate, laudatote.	Laudent, laudanto.
	Habe, habeto.	Habeat habeto.	*Pl.* habeamus,	Habete, habetote.	Habeant, habento.
	Lege, legito.	Legat legito.	*Pl.* legamus.	Legite, legitote.	Legant, legunto.
	Audi, audito.	Audiat audito,	*Pl.* audiamus.	Audite, auditote.	Audiant, audiunto. [22]

Potential Mood.

I may or *can praise.*

Present tense sing.	Laudem, laudes, laudet, *Pl.* laudemus, laudetis, laudent. Habeam, Legam, Audiam,	as, at, *Pl.* amus, atis, ant.
Preterim-perfect tense sing.	Laudarem, Haberem, Legerem, Audirem,	*I might* or *could praise.* res, ret, *Plur.* remus, retis, rent.

I might or *should have praisd.*

| *Preter-perfect tense sing.* | Laudaverim, Habuerim, Legerim, Audiverim, | ris, rit, *Pl.* rimus, ritis, rint. |

If I had praisd.

| *Preterplu. sing. with a Conjun- ction.* Si | Laudavissem, Habuissem, Legissem, Audivissem, | ses, set, *Pl.* semus, setis, sent. |

If I shall praise or *shall have praisd.*

| *Future tense sing.* Si | Laudavero, Habuero, Legero, Audivero, | ris, rit, *Plur.* rimus, ritis, rint. |

Infinitive Mood.

| *Present and Pre-terimper-fect tense* | Laudare, Habere Legere, Audire, | *To* | *Praise.* *Have.* *Read.* *Hear.* [23] |
| *Preterper-fect & Pre-terpluper-fect tense.* | Laudavisse, Habuisse, Legisse, Audivisse, | *To have or had* | *Praised.* *Read.* *Heard.* |

Verbs of the third Conjugation irregular
in some Tenses of the Active Voice.

Indicative Mood

Present Tense singular.

| Volo, vis, vult, Nolo, —— *The rest is want* Malo, mavis, ma-vult | | *Plur.* | Volumus, vultis, volunt. Nolumus, —— nolunt. *ing in this Tense.* Malumus, mavultis, ma-lunt. |

| *Preterit.* | Volui. Nolui. Malui. |

Volo and *Malo* want the Imperative Mood.

Imperative.

| *Sing.* | Noli, Nolito. | *Plur.* | Nolite, Nolitote. |

Potential.

Present *tens. sing.*	{ Velim, Nolim, Malim, }	is, it, *Plur.* imus, itis, int.
Preterim- perfect tens. sing.	{ Vellem, Nollem, Mallem, }[24]	es, et, *Pl.* emus, etis, ent.

Infinitive.

Present.   { Velle, Nolle, Malle.

Indicat. Pres. *Edo, edis* or *es, edit* or *est;* Plur. *Editis* or *estis.*

Imper. *Ede* or *es, edito* or *esto. Edat, edito* or *esto.* Plur. *Edite este editote estote.*

Poten. Preterimperfect Tense, *Ederem* or *essem.*

Infinit. *Edere* or *esse.*

Verbs of the fourth Conjugation irregular in some Tenses Active.

EO and *queo,* with his Compound *Nequeo,* make *eunt* and *queunt* in the Plural Indicative present, and in thir Preterimperfect *ibam* and *quibam,* thir Future *ibo* and *quibo.*

Imperat. *I, ito. Eat, ito.* Plur. *Eamus. Ite, itote. Eant, eunto.*

Potent. *Eam. Irem.* &c.

The forming of the Passive Voice.
Indicative.

Pres. Sing

I am praised.

Laudor, aris *or* are, atur,	*Plur.*	amur, amini, antur.
Habeor, eris *or* ere, etur,		emur, emini, entur.
Legor, eris *or* ere, itur,		imur, imini, untur.
Audior, iris *or* ire, itur,		imur, imini, iuntur. [25]

I was praisd.

Preterim- perfect tens. sing.	{ Laudabar, Habebar, Legebar, Audiebar, }	baris *or* bare, batur, *Plur.* bamur, bamini, bantur.

Note that the *Passive Voice* hath no Preterperfect, nor the Tenses deriv'd from thence in any Mood.

I shall or *will be praisd.*

Future	Laudabor,	beris *or* bere, bitur, *Plur.*
Tense sing.	Habebor,	bimur, bimini, buntur.
	Legar,	eris *or* ere, etur, *Plu.* emur,
	Audiar,	emini, entur.

Imperative.

Be thou praisd.	*Let him be praisd.*	*Let us be praisd.*	*Be ye praisd.*	*Let them be praisd.*
Laudare, laudator.	laudetur, laudator.	*Pl.* lau-demur.	laudamini, laudaminor.	laudentur, laudantor
Habere, habetor.	habeatur, habetor.	*P.* habe-amur.	habemini, habeminor.	habeantur, habentor.
Legere, legitor.	legatur, legitor.	*Pl.* lega-mur.	legimini, legiminor.	legantur, leguntor.
Audire, auditor.	audiatur, auditor.	*P.* audi-amur.	audimini, audiminor.	audiantur, audiuntor. [26]

Present Singular.

Potential.

I may or *can be praisd.*

Present sing.	Lauder, eris *or* ere, etur, *Plur.* emur,	emini, entur.
	Habear,	
	Legar,	aris *or* are, atur, *Plu.* amur,
	Audiar,	amini, antur.

I might or *should be praisd.*

Preterim-perfect sing.	Laudarer,	
	Haberer,	reris *or* rere, retur, *Pl.*
	Legerer,	remur, remini, rentur.
	Audirer,	

Infinitive.

Present & Preterim-perfect	Laudari	*To be*	*Praisd.*
	Haberi		*Had.*
	Legi		*Read.*
	Audiri		*Heard.*

Verbs irregular in some Tenses
Passive.

EDor, editur or *estur:* The rest is Regular.

The Verb *Fio,* is partly of the Third, and partly of the Fourth Conjugation, and hath only the Infinitive of the Passive Form.
Indicat. Pres. Sing. *Fio, fis, fit,* Plur. *fimus, fitis, fiunt.* Preter-imperfect, *Fiebam.* Preterperfect *it wants.* Future *Fiam,* &c. [27]
Imperat. *Fi, fito.* Plur. *fite, fitote. Fiant, fiunto.*

Potent. Pres. *Fiam,* &c. Preterimperfect. *Fierem.*
Infinit. *Fieri.*

Also this Verb *Fero,* is contracted or short'n'd in some Tenses, both Active and Passive, as *Fers, fert,* for *feris, ferit,* &c.
Indicat. Pres. Sing. *Fero, fers, fert,* Plur.———— *fertis,*————
Preterperfect, *Tuli*
Imperat. *Fer ferto,* &c. Plur. *Ferte fertote.*
Potent. Preterimperfect, *Ferrem,* &c.
Infinit. *Ferre.*

Passive.

Indicat. Pres. Sing. *Feror, ferris* or *ferre, fertur,* &c.
Imperat. Sing. *Ferre, fertor,* &c.
Potent. Preterimperfect, *Ferrer.*
Infinit. *Ferri.*

Of Gerunds and Supines.

THere be also belonging to the Infinitive Mood of all Verbs certain Voices called Gerunds and Supines, both of the Active and Passive signification

The first Gerund endeth in *di,* as *Laudandi* of praising or of being praisd. The second in *do,* as *Laudando* in praising or in being praisd. The third in *dum,* as *Laudandum* to praise or to be praisd.

Note that in the two latter Conjugations, the Gerunds end somtimes in *undi, do, dum,* as *dicendi* or *dicundi:* But from *Eo* alwayes *eundi,* except in the Compound *ambiendi.*

Supines are two. The first signifieth Actively, [28] as *laudatum* to praise; the latter Passively, as *laudatu* to be praised. Note that most Neuters of the second Conjugation, and *volo, nolo, malo,* with many other Verbs, have no Supine.

Verbs of the four Conjugations irregular in the Preterperfect Tense or Supines.

VErbs of the first Conjugation form thir Preterperfect Tense in *avi,* Supine in *atum,* as *Laudo laudavi laudatum.*
Except,

Poto potavi potatum or *potum; neco necavi necatum* or *nectum.*

Domo, tono, sono, crepo, veto, cubo, form *ui, itum,* as *cubui cubitum;* but *secui sectum, fricui frictum, mico micui:* yet some of these are found Regular in the Preterperfect Tense or Supine, especially compounded, as *increpavit, discrepavit, dimicavit, sonatum, dimicatum, intonatum, infricatum,* and the like.

Plico and his Compounds form *ui* or *avi*, as *explicui explicavi explicitum* or *explicatum;* except *supplico,* and such as are compounded with a Noun, as *Duplico Multiplico* in *avi* only.

But *Lavo lavi lautum lotum* or *lavatum, juvo juvi, adjuvo adjuvi adjutum.*

Do dedi datum, Sto steti statum, in the Compounds, *stiti, stitum* and somtimes *statum,* as *Presto prestiti prestitum* and *prestatum.*

VErbs of the second Conjugation form thir thir Preterperfect Tense in *ui,* thir Supine [29] in *itum,* as *habeo habui habitum.*

Some are Regular in thir Preterperfect Tense; but not in thir Supines, as *doceo docui doctum, misceo miscui mistum, teneo tenui tentum, torreo torrui tostum, censeo censui censum, pateo patui passum, careo carui cassum* and *caritum.*

Others are Irregular both in Preterperfect Tense and Supines, as *Jubeo jussi jussum, sorbeo sorbui sorpsi sorptum, mulceo mulsi mulsum, luceo luxi.*

Deo in *di,* as *sedeo sedi sessum, video vidi visum, prandeo prandi pransum.* And some in *si,* as *suadeo suasi suasum, rideo risi risum, ardeo arsi arsum.* Four double thir first Letters, as *Pendeo pependi pensum, mordeo momordi morsum, spondeo spopondi sponsum, tondeo totondi tonsum,* but not in thir Compounds, as *dependi depensum.*

Geo in *si,* and some in *xi,* as *urgeo ursi, mulgeo mulsi mulxi mulctum, augeo auxi auctum, indulgeo indulsi indultum, frigeo frixi, lugeo luxi.*

ieo leo and *neo nevi, vieo vievi vietum,* But *Cieo cievi citum, deleo delevi deletum, fleo flevi fletum, compleo complevi completum;* as also the Compounds of *Olec,* except *redoleo* and *suboleo;* but *adolevi adultum, neo nevi netum,* but *maneo mansi, torqueo torsi tortum, hæreo hæsi.*

Veo in *vi,* as *serveo servi,* but *deferveo deferbui, conniveo connivi* and *connixi, movi motum, vovi votum, cavi cautum, favi fautum.*

THe third Conjugation formeth the Preterperfect Tense, by changing *O* of the Present Tense into *I;* the Supine without certain Rule, as *lego legi lectum, bibo bibi bibitum, lambo lambi, scabo scabi, ico ici ictum, mando mandi mansum, pando pandi passum, edo edi esum* or *estum,* in like manner *comedo,* [30] the other compounds *esum* only; *rudo rudi, sallo salli salsum, psallo psalli, emo emi emptum, viso visi visum, verto verti versum, solvo solvi solutum, volvo volvi volutum, exuo exui exutum,* but *ruo rui ruitum,* in compound *rutum,* as *derui derutum; ingruo, metuo metui.*

Others are irregular both in Preterperfect Tense and Supine.

In *bo*, *scribo scripsi scriptum, nubo nupsi nuptum, cumbo cubui cubitum*.

In *co, vinco vici victum, dico dixi dictum*, in like manner *duco, parco peperci* and *parsi parsum* and *parcitum*.

In *do*, these three loos *n, findo fidi fissum, scindo scidi scissum, fundo fudi fusum*. These following, *vado, rado, lædo, ludo, divido, trudo, claudo, plaudo, rodo, si* and *sum*, as *rosi rosum*, but *cedo cessi cessum*. The rest double thir first Letter in the Preterperfect Tense, but not compounded, as *tundo tutudi tunsum, contundo contudi contusum*, and so in the other Compounds. *Pendo pependi pensum, dependo dependi, tendo tetendi tensum* and *tentum, contendo contendi, pedo pepedi peditum, cado cecidi casum, occido, recido recidi recasum*. The other Compounds have no Supine. *Cædo cecidi cæsum, occido occidi occisum*. To these add all the compounds of *do* in this Conjugation, *addo, credo, edo, dedo, reddo, perdo, abdo, obdo, condo, indo, trado, prodo, vendo vendidi venditum*, except the double Compound, *abscondo abscondi*.

In *go, ago egi actum, dego degi, satago sategi, frango fregi fractum, pango* to joyn *pegi pactum, pango* to sing *panxi, ango anxi, jungo junxi junctum;* but these five, *fingo, mingo, pingo, stringo, ringo*, loos *n* in their Supines, as *finxi fictum, ningo ninxi, figo fixi fixum*, [31] *rego rexi rectum; diligo, negligo, intelligo, lexi lectum, spargo sparsi sparsum*. These double thir first Letter, *tango tetigi tactum*, but not in his Compounds, as *contingo contigi, pango* to bargain *pepigi pactum, pungo* and *repungo pupugi* and *punxi punctum* the other Compounds *punxi* only.

Ho in *xi, traho traxi tractum, veho vexi vectum*.

In *lo, vello velli* and *vulsi vulsum, colo colui cultum; excello, precello, cellui celsum; alo alui alitum altum*. The rest, not compounded, double thir first Letter, *Fallo fefelli falsum, refello refelli, pello pepuli pulsum, compello compuli, cello ceculi, percello perculi perculsi perculsum*.

In *mo, vomo vomui vomitum, tremo tremui, promo pressi pressum, como, premo, demo, sumo*, after the same manner, as *sumpsi, sumptum*.

In *No, sino sivi situm, sterno stravi stratum, sperno sprevi spretum, lino levi lini* and *livi litum, cerno crevi cretum, temno tempsi, contemno contempsi contemptum, gigno genui genitum, pono posui positum, cano cecini cantum, concino concinui concentum*.

In *Po, rumpo rupi ruptum, scalpo scalpsi scalptum*, the rest in *ui*, as *strepo strepui strepitum*.

In *quo, linquo liqui, relinquo reliqui relictum, coquo coxi coctum.*

In *Ro, verro verri* and *versi versum, sero* to sow *sevi satum,* in compound *situm,* as *insero insitum; sero* of another signification most us'd in his compounds, *Assero, consero, desero, exero, serui sertum, uro ussi ustum, gero gessi gestum, quæro quæsivi quæsitum, tero trivi tritum, curro, excurro, præcurro, cucurri cursum,* the other compounds double not, as *concurro concurri.*

In *So, accerso, arcesso, incesso, lacesso, ivi itum, capesso* both *i* and *ivi, pinso pinsui pistum* and *pinsitum.* [32]

In *sco, pasco pavi pastum; compesco, dispesco,* ui; *posco poposci, disco didici, quinisco quexi, nosco novi notum,* but *agnosco agnitum, cognosco cognitum.*

In *to, sisto stiti statum, flecto flexi flexum, pecto pexui pexi pexum* and *pectitum, necto nexui nexi nexum, plecto plexi plexum, sterto stertui, meto messui messum, mitto misi missum, peto petivi petitum.*

In *vo, vivo vixi victum.*

In *xo, texo texui textum, nexo nexui nexum.*

In *cio, facio feci factum, jacio jeci jactum, lacio lexi lectum, specio spexi spectum,* with thir Compounds, but *elicio elicui elicitum.*

In *dio, fodio fodi fossum.*

In *gio, fugio fugi fugitum.*

In *pio, capio cepi captum, rapio rapui raptum, cupio cupivi cupitum, sapio sapui sapivi sapitum.*

In *rio, pario peperi partum.*

In *tio, quatio quassi quassum, concutio concussi concussum.*

In *uo, pluo plui pluvi plutum, struo struxi structum, fluo fluxi fluxum.*

THe fourth Conjugation formeth the Preterperfect Tense in *ivi,* the Supine in *itum.*

Except, *Venio veni ventum, comperio, reperio, reperi repertum, cambio campsi campsum, sepio sepsi septum, sarcio sarsi sartum, farcio farsi fartum, fulceo fulsi fultum, sentio sensi sensum, haurio hausi haustum, sancio sanxi sanctum sancitum, vinclo vinxi vinctumo salio salui saltum,* in Compound *sultum,* as *desilio desilui desultum, amicio amicui amictum, aperio, operio perui pertum, veneo venivi venum, singultivi singultum, sepelivi sepultum.* [33]

Of Verbs Compounded.

THese Verbs Compounded change *a* into *e* throughout, *Damno, lacto, sacro, fallo, arceo, tracto, partio, farcio, carpo, patro, scando, spargo,* as *conspergo conspersi conspersum.*

These following change thir first vowel into *i,* and some of them thir Supines into *e, habeo, lateo, salio, statuo, cado, lædo, cano, quæro, cædo, tango, egeo, teneo, taceo, sapio, rapio, placeo, displiceo, displicui displicitum;* Except *complaceo, perplaceo, posthabeo.*

Scalpo, calco, salto, change *a* into *u,* as *exculpo.*

Claudo, quatio, lavo loos *a,* as *excludo, excutio, eluo.*

These following change thir first Vowel into *i,* but not in the Preterperfect Tense, and somtimes *a* into *e* in the Supine, *emo, sedeo, rego, frango, capio, jacio, lacio, specio, premo,* as *comprimo compressi compressum, conjicio conjeci conjectum, pango* in two only, *compingo, impingo: Ago,* in all but *perago, satago, circumago, dego* and *cogo coegi: Facio* with a Preposition only, not in other Compounds, as *inficio, olfacio: Lego* in these only, *diligo, eligo, intelligo, negligo, seligo,* in the rest not, as *prælego,* add to these *supersedeo.*

Of Verbs Defective.

VErbs called Inceptives ending in *sco,* borrow thir preterperfect Tense from the Verb whereof they are deriv'd, as *tepesco tepui* from *tepeo, ingemisco ingemui* from *ingemo;* as also these Verbs, *cerno* to see, *vidi* from *video, sido sedi* from *sedeo, fero tuli* from *tulo* out of use, in the Supine [34] *latum, tollo sustuli sublatum* from *suffero.*

These want the Preterperfect Tense.

Verbs ending in *asco,* as *puerasco;* in *isco,* as *fatisco;* in *urio,* except *parturio, esurio:* these also, *vergo, ambigo, ferio, furo, polleo, nideo,* have no Preterperfect Tense.

Contrary, these four, *Odi, cæpi, novi, memini,* are found in the Preterperfect Tense only, and the Tenses thence deriv'd, as *odi, oderam, oderim, odissem, odero, odisse,* except *memini,* which hath *memento mementote* in the Imperative.

Others are defective both in Tense and Person, as *Aio, ais, ait,* Plur. *aiunt.* The Preterimperfect *aiebam* is intire. Imperative, *ai.* Potential, *aias, aiat,* Plur. *aiamus, aiant.*

Ausim for *ausus sim, ausis, ausit,* Plur. *ausint.*

Salveo, salvebis, salve salveto, salvete salvetote, salvere.

Ave aveto, avete avetote.

Faxo, faxis, faxit, faxint.

Quæso, Plur. *quæsumus.*

Infit, infiunt

Inquio or *inquam, inquis inquit,* Plur. *inquiunt. Inquibat,* Cic. Topic. *inquisti, inquit.* Future, *inquies, inquiet* Imperat. *Inque inquito.* Potent *Inquiat.*

Dor the first person Passive of *do,* and *for* before *faris* or *fare* in the Indicative, are not read, nor *der* or *fer* in the Potential.

Of a Participle.

A Participle is a part of Speech, partaking with the Verb from whence it is deriv'd in Voice, Tense, and signification, and with a Noun Adjective in manner of Declining. [35]

Participles are either of the Active or Passive Voice.

Of the *Active* Two. One of the Present Tense ending in *ans,* or *ens,* as *laudans* praising, *habens, legens, audiens,* and is declin'd like *fœlix,* as *hic hœc* and *hoc habens,* Gen. *habentis,* Dat. *habenti,* &c. *Docens docentis,* &c. But from *eo, euns,* and in the compounds *iens euntis,* except *ambiens ambientis.* Note that some Verbs otherwise defective, have this Participle, as *aiens, inquiens.*

The other of the Future Tense is most commonly formd of the first Supine, by changing *m* into *rus,* as of *laudatum laudaturus* to praise or about to praise, *habiturus, lecturus, auditurus;* but some are not regularly formd, as of *sectum secaturus,* of *jutum juvaturus, sonitum sonaturus, partum pariturus, argutum argui-turus,* and such like; of *sum, futurus:* This, as also the other two Participles following are declin'd like *bonus.*

This Participle, with the Verb *Sum,* affordeth a second Future in the Active Voice, as *laudaturus sum, es, est,* &c. as also the Future of the Infinitive, as *laudaturum esse* to praise hereafter, *futurum esse,* &c.

Participles of the Passive Voice are also two, one of the Preterperfect tense, another of the Future.

A Participle of the Preterperfect Tense, is formd of the latter Supine, by putting thereto *s,* as of *laudatu laudatus* praisd, of *habitu habitus, lectu lectus, auditu auditus.*

This Participle joyn'd with the Verb *Sum,* supplyeth the want of a Preterperfect and Preterpluperfect Tense in the Indicative Mood passive, and both them and the Future of the Potential; as also [36] the Preterperfect and Preterpluperfect of the Infinitive, and with *ire* or *fore* the Future; as *laudatus sum* or *fui* I have been praisd, *Plur. lauditi sumus* or *fuimus* we have been praisd, *laudatus eram* or *fueram,* &c. Potential, *laudatus sim* or *fuerim, laudatus essem* or *fuissem, laudatus ero* or *fuero,* Infinit. *laudatum esse* or *fuisse* to have or had been praisd; *laudatum ire* or *fore* to be praisd hereafter.

Nor only Passives, but some Actives also or Neuters, besides thir own Preterperfect Tense, borrow another from this Participle; *Cœno Cœnavi* and *Cœnatus sum, Juravi* and *juratus, Potavi* and *potus sum, Titubavi* and *titubatus, Careo carui cassus sum, Prandeo prandi* and *pransus, Pateo patui* and *passus sum, Placeo placui placitus, Suesco suevi suetus sum, Libet libuit* and *libitum est, Licet licuit licitum, Pudet puduit puditum, Piget piguit pigitum, Tœdet teduit pertœsum est,* and this Deponent *Mereor merui* and *meritus sum*

These Neuters following, like Passives, have no other Preterperfect Tense, but by this Participle, *Gaudeo gavisus sum, fido fisus, audeo ausus, fio factus, soleo solitus sum.*

These Deponents also form this Participle from Supines irregular; *Labor lapsus, patior passus, perpetior perpessus, fateor fassus, confiteor, diffiteor diffessus, gradior gressus, ingredior ingressus, fatiscor fessus, metior mensus, utor usus, ordior* to spin *orditus,* to begin *orsus, nitor nisus* and *nixus, ulciscor ultus, irascor iratus, reor ratus, obliviscor oblitus, fruor fructus* or *fruitus, miserior misertus, tuor* and *tueor tuitus, loquor locutus, sequor secutus, experior expertus, paciscor pactus, nanciscor nactus, apiscor aptus, adipiscor adeptus, queror questus, proficiscor profectus, expergiscor experrectus, comminiscor commentus, nascor natus, morior mortuus, orior ortus sum.* [37]

A Participle of the Future Passive is formd of the Gerund in *dum,* by changing *m* into *s,* as of *laudandum laudandus* to be praisd, of *habendum habendus,* &c. And likewise of this Participle with the Verb *Sum,* may be formd the same Tenses in the Passive, which were form'd with the Participle of the Preterperfect Tense, as *laudandus sum* or *fui,* &c.

Infinit. *Laudandum esse,* or *fore.*

Of Verbs Deponent come Participles, both of the Active and Passive form, as *loquor loquens locutus locuturus loquendus;* whereof the Participle of the Preter Tense signifieth somtimes both Actively and Passively, as *dignatus, testatus, meditatus,* and the like.

Of an Adverb.

AN Adverb is a part of Speech joynd with some other to explain its signification, as *valdè probus* very honest, *benè est* it is well, *valdè doctus* very learned, *benè mane* early in the morning.

Of Adverbs, some be of *Time,* as *hodiè* to day, *Cras* to morrow, &c.

Some be of *Place,* as *Ubi* where, *ibi* there, &c. And of many other sorts needless to be here set down.

Certain Adverbs also are compar'd, as *Doctè* learnedly, *doctiùs doctissimè, fortiter fortiùs fortissimè, sœpe sœpius sœpissime,* and the like. [38]

Of a Conjunction.

A Conjunction is a part of Speech, that joyneth Words and Sentences together.

Of conjunctions some be Copulative, as *et* and, *quoque* also, *nec* neither.

Some be Disjunctive, as *aut* or.

Some be Causal, as *nam* for, *quia* because, and many such like.

Adverbs when they Govern Mood and Tense, and joyn Sentences together, as *cum, ubi, postquam,* and the like, are rather to be call'd Conjunctions.

Of a Preposition.

A Preposition is a part of Speech most commonly, either set before Nouns in Apposition, as *ad patrem,* or joyn'd with any other words in Composition, as *indoctus.*

These six, *di, dis, re, se, am, con,* are not read but in Composition.

As Adverbs having Cases after them, may be call'd Prepositions, so Prepositions having none, may be counted Adverbs.

Of an Interjection.

AN Interjection is a part of Speech, expressing some passion of the mind.

Some be of sorrow, as *heu, hei.*

Some be of marvelling, as *papœ.*

Some of disdaining, as *vah.*

Some of praising, as *euge.*

Some of exclaiming, as *ô, proh,* and such like. [39]

Figures of Speech.

WOrds are somtimes encreast or diminisht by a Letter or Syllable in the beginning, middle or ending, which are call'd *Figures of Speech:*

Encreast

In the beginning, as *Gnatus* for *Natus, Tetuli* for *tuli Prothesis.*

In the middle, as *Rettulit* for *Retulit, Cinctutus* for *Cinctus. Epenthesis.*

In the end, as *Dicier* for *dici. Paragoge.*

Diminisht

In the beginning, As *Ruit* for *Eruit. Apherisis.*

In the middle, as *Audiit* for *Audivit, Dixti* for *dixisti, Lamna* for *lamina Syncope.*

In the end, as *Consili* for *consilii; scin* for *scisne. Apocope.* [40]

The second part of Grammar,
commonly called *Syntaxis,*
or *Construction.*

Hitherto the Eight Parts of speech Declin'd and Undeclin'd
have been spoken of single, and each one by it self: Now
followeth *Syntaxis* or *Construction,* which is the right
joyning of these parts together in a Sentence.

Construction consisteth either in the agreement of words together
in Number, Gender, Case, and Person, which is call'd Concord;
or the governing of one the other in such Case or Mood as is to
follow.

Of the Concords.

THere be *Three* Concords or Agreements.

The *First* is of the Adjective with his Substantive.

The *Second* is of the Verb with his Nominative Case.

The *Third* is of the Relative with his Antecedent.

An Adjective (under which is comprehended both Pronoun and
Participle) with his Substantive or Substantives, a Verb with his
Nominative Case or Cases, and a Relative with his Antecedent or
Antecedents, agree all in number, [41] and the two latter in person
also: as *Amicus certus. Viri docti. Præceptor prælegit, vos vero
negligitis.* Xenophon & Plato *fuere æquales. Vir sapit, qui pauca
loquitur. Pater & Præceptor veniunt.* Yea though the Conjunction
be disjunctive, as *Quos neque desidia neque luxuria vitiarant.*
Celsus. *Pater & Præceptor, quos quæritis.* But if a Verb singular
follow many Nominatives, it must be applyed to each of them
apart, as *Nisi foro & curiæ officium ac verecundia sua constiterit.*
Val. max.

An Adjective with his Substantive, and a Relative with his Antecedent agree in Gender and Case; but the Relative not in case
alwayes, being oft-times govern'd by other constructions: as *Amicus
certus in re incerta cernitur. Liber quem dedisti mihi.*

And if it be a Participle serving the Infinitive Mood future, it
oft-times agrees not with the Substantive neither in Gender nor in
Number, as *Hanc sibi rem præsidio sperat futurum.* Cic. *Audierat
non datum ire filio Uxorem.* Terent. *Omnia potius actum iri puto
quam de provinciis.* Cic.

But when a Verb cometh between two Nominative cases not of
the same number, or a Relative between two Substantives not of

the same Gender, the Verb in Number, and the Relative in Gender may agree with either of them; as *Amantium iræ amoris integratio est. Quid enim nisi vota supersunt. Tuentur illum globum qui terra dicitur. Animal plenum rationis, quem vocamus hominem. Lutetia est quam nos Parisios dicimus.*

And if the Nominative cases be of several persons, or the Substantives and Antecedents of several Genders, the Verb shall agree with the second person before the third, and with the first [42] before either; And so shall the Adjective or Relative in thir Gender; as *Ego & tu sumus in tuto. Tu & Pater periclitamini. Pater & Mater mortui sunt. Frater & Soror quos vidisti.*

But in things that have not life, an Adjective or Relative of the Neuter Gender, may agree with Substantives or Antecedents, Masculin or Feminin, or both together; as *Arcus & calami sunt bona. Arcus & calami quæ fregisti. Pulcritudinem, constantiam, ordinem in Consiliis factisque conservanda putat.* Cic. Off. I. *Ira & ægritudo permista sunt.* Sal.

Note that the Infinitive Mood, or any part of a Sentence may be instead of a Nominative Case to the Verb, or of a Substantive to the Adjective, or of an Antecedent to the Relative, and then the Adjective or Relative shall be of the Neuter Gender; And if there be more parts of a Sentence then one, the Verb shall be in the plural number; *Diluculo surgere saluberrimum est. Virtutem sequi, vita est honestissima. Audito proconsulem in Ciliciam tendere. In tempore veni, quod omnium rerum est primum. Tu multum dormis & sæpe potas, quæ duo sunt corpori inimica.*

Somtimes also an Adverb is put for the Nominative Case to a Verb, and for a Substantive to an Adjective; as *Partim signorum sunt combusta. Propè centies & vicies erogatum est.* Cic. verr. 4.

Somtimes also agreement, whether it be in Gender or Number, is grounded on the sense, not on the words; as *Illum senium* for *illum senem. Iste scelus* for *iste scelestus.* Ter. *Transtulit in Eunuchum suam,* meaning *Comœdiam.* Ter. *Pars magna obligati,* meaning *Homines.* Liv. *Impliciti laqueis nudus uterq;* for *Ambo.* Ov. *Alter in alterius jactantes lumina vultus,* Ovid. that is, *Alter & alter. Insperanti ipsa refers* [43] *te nobis,* for *mihi.* Catul. *Disce omnes.* Virg. Æn. 2. for *tu quisquis es. Duo importuna prodigia, quos egestas tribuno plebis constrictos addixerat.* Cic. pro Sest. *Pars mersi tenuere ratem. Rhemus cum fratre Quirino jura dabant.* Virg. that is, *Rhemus & frater Quirinus. Divillimur inde Iphitus & Pelias mecum.* Virg.

Construction of Substantives.

HItherto of Concord or agreement; the other part followeth, which is *Governing,* whereby one part of Speech is govern'd by another, that is to say, is put in such Case or Mood as the word that governeth or goeth before in construction requireth.

When two Substantives come together, betokening divers things, whereof the former may be an Adjective in the Neuter Gender taken for a Substantive; the latter (which also may be a Pronoun) shall be in the Genitive Case; as *Facundia Ciceronis. Amator studiorum. Ferimur per opaca locorum. Corruptus vanis rerum.* Hor. *Desiderium tui. Pater ejus.*

Somtimes the former Substantive, as this word *Officium* or *Mos,* is understood; as *Oratoris est,* It is the part of an Oratour. *Extremæ est dementiæ,* It is the manner of extream madness. *Ignavi est,* It is the quality of a sloathful man. *Ubi ad Dianæ veneris; Templum* is understood. *Justitiæne prius mirer belline laborum.* Virg. Understand *Causâ. Neque illi sepositi Ciceris, neque longæ invidit avenæ.* Hor. Supply *partem.*

But if both the Substantives be spoken of one thing, which is call'd apposition, they shall be [44] both of the same case; as *Pater meus vir, amat me puerum.*

Words that signifie Quality, following the Substantive whereof they are spoken, may be put n the Genitive or Ablative Case; as *Puer bonæ indolis,* or *bona indole.* Some have a Genitive only; as *Ingentis Rex nominis.* Liv. *Decem annorum puer. Hujusmodi pax. Hujus generis animal.* But *genus* is sometimes in the Accusative: as *Si hoc genus rebus non proficitur.* Varr. *de re rust.* And the cause or manner of a thing in the Ablative only; as *Sum tibi natura parens, preceptor consiliis.*

Opus and *Usus* when they signifie Need, require an Ablative; as *Opus est mihi tuo judicio. Viginti minis usus est filio.* But *Opus* is somtimes taken for an Adjective undeclin'd, and signifieth Needful; as *Dux nobis & Author opus est. Alia quæ opus sunt para.*

Construction of Adjectives, Govern-
ing a Genitive.

ADjectives that signifie Desire, Knowledge, Ignorance, Remembrance, Forgetfulness, and such like; as also certain others deriv'd from Verbs, and ending in *ax,* require a Genitive; as *Cupidus auri. Peritus belli. Ignarus omnium. Memor præteriti. Reus furti. Tenax propositi. Tempus edax rerum.*

Adjectives call'd Nouns Partitive, because they signifie part of some whole quantity or number, govern the word that signifieth the thing parted or divided, in the Genitive; as *Aliquis nostrum. Primus omnium. Aurium mollior est sinistra. Orato-* [45] *rum eloquentissimus.* And oft in the Neuter Gender; as *Multum lucri. Id negotii. Hoc noctis.* Sometimes, though seldom, a word signifying the whole is read in the same Case with the Partitive, as *Habet duos gladios quibus altero te occisurum minatur, altero villicum,* Plaut. For *Quorum altero. Magnum opus habeo in manibus; quod jampridem ad hunc ipsum (me autem dicebat) quædam institui.* Cic. Acad. I. *Quod quædam* for *cujus quædam.*

A Dative.

ADjectives that betoken Profit or Disprofit, Likeness or Unlikeness, Fitness, Pleasure, Submitting, or Belonging to any thing, require a Dative; as *Labor est utilis corpori. Æqualis Hectori. Idoneus bello. Jucundus omnibus. Parenti supplex. Mihi proprium.*

But such as betoken Profit or Disprofit have somtimes an Accusative with a Preposition; as *Homo ad nullam partem utilis.* Cic. *Inter se æquales.*

And some Adjectives signifying Likeness, Unlikeness, or Relation, may have a Genitive. *Par hujus. Ejus culpæ affines. Domini similis es. Commune animantium est conjunctionis appetitus. Alienum dignitatis ejus.* Cic. Fin. I. *Fuit hoc quondam proprium populi Romani longè a domo bellare.* But *propior* and *proximus* admit somtimes an Accusative; as *proximus Pompeium sedebam.* Cic.

An Accusative.

NOuns of Measure are put after Adjectives of like signification in the Accusative, and somtimes in the Ablative; as *Turris alta centum* [46] *pedes. Arbor lata tres digitos. Liber crassus tres pollices,* or *tribus pollicibus.* Sometimes in the Genitive; as *Areas latas pedum denûm facito.*

All words expressing part or Parts of a thing, may be put in the Accusative, or somtimes in the Ablative; as *Saucius frontem* or *fronte. Excepto quòd non simul esses cætera lætus.* Hor. *Nuda pedem.* Ov. *Os humerosque deo similis.* Virg. Somtimes in the Genitive, as *Dubius mentis.*

An Ablative.

ADjectives of the Comparative degree, englisht with this sign *then* or *by,* as also *Dignus, Indignus, Præditus, Contentus,* and these words of Price, *Carus, vilis,* require an Ablative; as *Frigidior glacie. Multo doctior. Uno pede altior. Dignus honore. Virtute præditus. Sorte sua contentus. Asse charum.*

But of Comparatives, *plus, amplius,* and *minus,* may govern a Genitive, also a Nominative, or an Accusative; as *Plus quinquaginta hominum. Amplius duorum millium. Ne plus tertia pars eximatur mellis.* Varro. *Paulo plus quingentos passus. Ut ex sua cujusque parte ne minus dimidium ad fratrem perveniret.* Cic. Verr. 4. And *Dignus, Indignus,* have somtimes a Genitive after them; as *Militia est operis altera digna tui. Indignus avorum.* Virg.

Adjectives betokening Plenty or Want, will have an Ablative, and somtimes a Genitive; as *Vacuus ira,* or *iræ. Nulla Epistola inanis re aliqua. Ditissimus agri. Stultorum plena sunt omnia. Integer vitæ, scelerisque purus. Expers omnium. Vobis immunibus hujus esse mali dabitur.* [47]

Words also betokening the cause, or form, or manner of a thing, are put after Adjectives in the Ablative Case; as *Pallidus ira. Trepidus morte futura. Nomine Grammaticus, re Barbarus.*

Of Pronouns.

PRonouns differ not in Construction from Nouns, except that Possessives, *Meus, tuus, suus, noster, vester,* by a certain manner of speech, are sometimes joyn'd to a Substantive, which governs thir Primitive understood with a Noun or Participle in a Genitive Case; as *Dico mea unius opera rempublicam esse liberatam.* Cic. For *Mei unius opera.* In like manner *Nostra, duorum, trium, paucorum, omnium virtute,* for *nostrum duorum, &c. Meum solius peccatum,* Cic *Ex tuo ipsius animo,* For *Tui ipsius. Ex sua cujusque parte,* Id. Verr. 2. *Ne tua quidem recentia proximi Prætoris vestigia persequi poterat.* Cic. verr. 4. *Si meas presentis preces non putas profuisse,* id. *Pro* Planc. *Nostros vidisti flentis ocellos.* Ovid.

Also a Relative, as *qui* or *is,* sometimes answers to an Antecedent Noun or Pronoun Primitive understood in the Possessive; as *Omnes laudare fortunas meas qui filium haberem tali ingenio præditum.* Terent.

Construction of Verbs.

VErbs for the most part govern either one case after them, or more then one in a different manner of Construction.

Of the Verb Substantive Sum, and such like, with a Nominative, and other oblique Cases.

VErbs that signifie Being, as *Sum, existo, fio;* and certain Passives, as *dicor, vocor, salutor,* [48] *appellor, habeor, existimor, videor;* also Verbs of motion or rest, as *incedo, discedo, sedeo,* with such like, will have a Nominative Case after them as they have before them, because both Cases belong to the same person or thing, and the latter is rather in apposition with the former, then govern'd by the Verb; as *Temperantia est virtus. Horatius salutatur Poeta. Ast ego quæ divum incedo regina.*

And if *est* be an impersonal, it may sometimes govern a Genitive, as *Usus Poetæ, ut moris est, licentia,* Phædrus 1. 4. *Negavit moris esse Græcorum, ut &c* Cic. verr. 2.

But if the following Noun be of another person, or not directly spoken of the former, both after *Sum* and all his Compounds, except *possum,* it shall be put in the Dative; as *Est mihi domi pater. Multa petentibus desunt multa.*

And if a thing be spoken of, relating to the person, it may be also in the Dative; as *Sum tibi præsidio. Hæc res est mihi voluptati. Quorum alteri Capitoni cognomen fuit.* Cic. *Pastori nomen Faustulo fuisse ferunt.* Liv.

Of Verbs Transitives with an Accusative, and the Exceptions thereto belonging.

VErbs Active or Deponent, call'd Transitive, because thir action passeth forth on some person or thing, will have an Accusative after them of the person or thing to whom the action is done; as *Amo te. Vitium fuge. Deum venerare. Usus promptos facit. Juvat me. Oportet te.*

Also Verbs call'd Neuters, may have an Accusative of thir own signification; as *Du-* [49] *ram servit servitutem. Longam ire viam. Endimionis somnum dormis. Pastillos Rufillus olet. Nec vox hominem sonat. Cum Glaucum saltasset.* Paterc. *Agit lætum convivam.* Horat. *Hoc me latet.*

But these Verbs, though Transitive, *Misereor* and *Miseresco,* pass into a Genitive; as *Miserere mei.* Somtimes into a Dative. *Huic misereor.* Sen. *Dilige bonos, miseresce malis.* Boet.

Reminiscor, Obliviscor, Recordor, and *Memini,* somtimes also require a Genitive; as *Datæ fidei reminiscitur. Memini tui. Obliviscor carminis.* Somtime retain the Accusative; as *Recordor pueritiam. Omnia quæ curant senes meminerunt.* Plaut.

These Impersonals also, *interest* and *refert,* signifying to concern, require a Genitive, except in these Ablatives Feminine, *Mea, tua, sua, nostra, vestra, cuja.* And the measure of concernment is often added in these Genitives, *magni, parvi, tanti, quanti,* with thir Compounds; as *Interest omnium rectè agere. Tua refert teipsum nosse. Vestra parvi interest.*

But Verbs of Profiting or Disprofiting, Believing, Pleasing, Obeying, Opposing, or being angry with, pass into a Dative; as *non potes mihi commodare nec incommodare. Placeo omnibus. Crede mihi. Nimium ne crede colori. Pareo Parentibus. Tibi re-pugno. Adolescenti nihil est quod succenseat.* But of the first and third sort, *Juvo, adjuvo, lædo, offendo,* retain an Accusative.

Lastly, these Transitives, *fungor, fruor, utor, potior,* and Verbs betokening want, pass direct into an Ablative. *Fungitur officio. Aliena frui insania. Utere sorte tua.* But *fungor, fruor, utor,* had antiently an Accusative. Verbs of want, and *potior,* may have also a Genitive. *Pecuniæ indiget. Quasi* [50] *tu hujus indigeas patris. Potior Urbe,* or *Urbis.*

Somtimes a phrase of the same signification with a single Verb, may have the Case of the Verb after it; as *Id operam do,* that is to say, *id ago. Idne estis authores mihi?* for *id suadetis. Quid me vobis tactio est?* for *tangitis.* Plaut. *Quid tibi hanc curatio est rem?* Id.

The Accusative with a Genitive.

HItherto of Transitives governing thir Accusative, or other Case, in single and direct Construction: Now of such as may have after them more Cases then one in Construction direct and oblique, that is to say, with an Accusative, a Genitive, Dative, other Accusative, or Ablative.

Verbs of Esteeming, Buying or Selling, besides thir Accusative, will have a Genitive betokening the value of price, *flocci, nihili, pili, hujus,* and the like after Verbs of Esteeming: *Tanti, quanti, pluris, minoris,* and such like, put without a Substantive, after Verbs of Buying or Selling; as *Non hujus te æstimo. Ego illum flocci pendo. Æqui boni hoc facio* or *consulo. Quanti mercatus es hunc equum? Pluris quam vellem.*

But the word of Value is somtimes in the Ablative; as *Parvi* or *parvo æstimas probitatem.* And the word of Price most usually; As *Teruncio eum non emerim.* And particularly in these Adjectives, *Vili, paulo, minimo, magno, nimio, plurimo, dimidio, duplo,* put without a Substantive, as *Vili vendo triticum. Redimete captum quàm queas minimo.* And somtimes *minore* for *minoris. Nam a Cælio propinqui minore centessimis nummum movere non possunt.* Cic. [51] Att. 1. 1. But Verbs Neuter or Passive have only the oblique Cases after them; as *Tanti eris aliis, quanti tibi fueris. Pudor parvi penditur.* Which is also to be observ'd in the following Rules.

And this Neuter *Valeo* governeth the word of value in the Accusative; as *Denarii dicti quod denos æris valebant.* Varr.

Verbs of admonishing, accusing, condemning, acquitting, will have, besides thir Accusative, a Genitive of the Crime, or Penaltie, or Thing; as *Admonuit me errati. Accusas me furti? Vatem sceleris damnat. Furem dupli condemnavit.* And somtimes an Ablative with a preposition, or without; as *Condemnabo eodem ego te crimine. Accusas furti, an stupri, an utroque? De repetundis accusavit,* or *damnavit.* Cic.

Also these impersonals, *pœnitet, tœdet, miseret, miserescit, pudet, piget,* to thir Accusative will have a Genitive, either of the person, or of the thing; as *Nostri nosmet pœnitet. Urbis me tœdet. Miseret me tui. Pudet me negligentiœ.*

An Accusative with a Dative.

VErbs of Giving or Restoring, Promising or Paying, Commanding or Shewing, Trusting or Threatning, add to thir Accusative a Dative of the person; as *Fortuna multis nimium dedit. Hœc tibi promitto. Æs alienum mihi numeravit. Frumentum imperat civitatibus. Quid & cui dicas, videto. Hoc tibi suadeo. Tibi* or *ad te scribo. Pecuniam omnem tibi credo. Utrique mortem minatus est.*

To these add Verbs Active compounded with hese prepositions, *prœ, ad, ab, con, de, ex, ante, sub,* [52] *post, 'ob, in* and *inter;* as *Prœcipio hoc tibi. Admovit urbi exercitum. Collegœ suo imperium abrogavit. Sic parvis componere magna solebam.*

Neuters have a dative only; as *Meis majoribus virtute prœluxi.* But some compounded with *prœ* and *ante* may have an accusative; as *Prœstat ingenio alius alium. Multos anteit sapientia.* Others with a Preposition; as *Quœ ad ventris victum conducunt. In hœc studia incumbite.* Cic.

Also all Verbs Active, betokening acquisition, likening, or relation, commonly englisht with *to* or *for,* have to thir accusative a dative of the person; as *Magnam laudem sibi peperit. Huic habeo non tibi. Se illis œquarunt. Expedi mihi hoc negotium:* but *mihi, tibi, sibi,* sometimes are added for Elegance, the sense not requiring; as *Suo hunc sibi jugulat gladio.* Terent. Neuters a dative only; as *Non omnibus dormio. Libet mihi. Tibi licet.*

Somtimes a Verb Transitive will have to his accusative a double dative, one of the person, another of the thing; as *Do tibi vestem pignori. Verto hoc tibi vitio. Hoc tu tibi laudi ducis.*

A double Accusative.

VErbs of asking, teaching, arraying, and concealing, will have two accusatives, one of the person, another of the thing; as *Rogo te pecuniam. Doceo te literas. Quod te jamdudum hortor. Induit se calceos. Hoc me celabas.*

And being Passives, they retain one accusative of the thing, as *Sumptumque recingitur anguem*, Ovid. Met. 4. *Induitur togam.* Mart. [53]

But Verbs of arraying somtimes change the one accusative into an ablative or dative; as *Induo te tunica* or *tibi tunicam. Instravit equum penula*, or *equo penulam.*

An Accusative with an Ablative.

VErbs Transitive may have to thir accusative an ablative of the instrument or cause, matter, or manner of doing; and Neuters the ablative only; As *Ferit eum gladio. Taceo metu. Malis gaudet alienis. Summa eloquentia causam egit. Capitolium saxo quadrato substructum est. Tuo consilio nitor. Vescor pane. Affluis opibus. Amore abundas.* Somtimes with a Preposition of the manner; as *Summa cum humanitate me tractavit.*

Verbs of endowing, imparting, depriving, discharging, filling, emptying, and the like, will have an ablative, and somtimes a genitive; as *Dono te hoc annulo. Plurima salute te impertit. Aliquem familiarem suo sermone participavit. Paternum servum sui participavit consilii. Interdico tibi aqua & igni. Libero te hoc metu. Implentur veteris Bacchi.*

Also Verbs of comparing, or exceeding, will have an ablative of the excess; as *Præfero hunc multis gradibus. Magno intervallo eum superat.*

After all manner of Verbs, the word signifying any part of a thing, may be put in the genitive, accusative, or ablative; as *Absurdè facis qui angas te animi. Pendet animi. Discrucior animi. Desipit mentis. Candet dentes. Rubet capillos. Ægrotat animo, magis quàm corpore.* [54]

Nouns of Time and Place after Verbs.

NOuns betokening part of time, be put after Verbs in the ablative, and somtimes in the accusative; as *Nocte vigilas, luce dormis. Nullam partem noctis requiescit.* Cic. *Abhinc triennium ex Andro comigravit.* Ter. *Respondit triduo illum, ad summum quatriduo periturum*, Cic. Or if continuance of time, in the accusative, somtimes in the Ablative; as *Sexaginta annos natus. Hyemem totam stertis. Imperium deponere maluerunt, quam id tenere punctum temporis contra Religionem.* Cic. *Imperavit triennio, & decem mensibus.* Suet. Somtimes with a Preposition; as *Ferè in diebus paucis, quibus hæc acta sunt.* Ter. Rarely with a genitive; as *Temporis angusti mansit concordia discors.* Lucan.

Also Nouns betokening Space between places are put in the accusative, and somtimes in the ablative; as *Pedem hinc ne dis-*

cesseris. Abest ab Urbe quingentis milibus passuum. Terra marique gentibus imperavit.

Nouns that signifie Place, and also proper Names of greater places, as Countries, be put after Verbs of moving or remaining, with a Preposition, signifying *to, from, in,* or *by,* in such case as the Preposition requireth; as *Proficiscor ab Urbe. Vivit in Anglia. Veni per Galliam in Italiam.*

But if it be the Proper Name of a Lesser Place, as of a City, Town, or Lesser Island, or any of these four, *Humus, Domus, Militia, Bellum,* with these signs, *on, in,* or *at* before them, being of the first or second Declension, and singular number, they shall be put in the genitive; if of the third Declension, or Plural Number, or this word *rus,* in [55] the dative or ablative; as *Vixit Romæ, Londini. Ea habitabat Rhodi. Conon plurimum Cypri vixit.* Cor. Nep. *Procumbit humi bos. Domi bellique simul viximus. Militavit Carthagini* or *Carthagine. Studuit Athenis. Ruri* or *rure educatus est.*

If the Verb of moving be to a Place, it shall be put in the accusative; as *Eo Romam, Domum, Rus.* If from a Place, in the ablative; as *Discessit Londino. Abiit Domo. Rure est reversus.*

Somtimes with a Preposition; as *A Brundisio profectus est.* Cic. Manil. *Ut ab Athenis in Bœotiam irem.* Sulpit. apud. Cic. Fam. 1. 4. *Cum te profectum ab domo scirem.* Liv. 1. 8.

Construction of Passives.

A Verb Passive will have after it an ablative of the doer, with the Preposition *a* or *ab* before it, somtimes without, and more often a dative: as *Virgilius legitur a me. Fortes creantur fortibus.* Hor. *Tibi fama petatur.* And Neutropassives, as *Vapulo, veneo, liceo, exulo, fio,* may have the same Construction; as *Ab hoste venire.*

Somtimes an accusative of the thing is found after a Passive; as *Coronari Olympia.* Hor. Epist. I. *Cyclopa movetur.* Hor. for *saltat* or *agit. Purgor bilem.* Id.

Construction of Gerunds and Supines.

GErunds and Supines will have such cases as the Verb from whence they come; as *Otium scribendi literas. Eo auditum Poetas. Ad consulendum tibi.* [56]

A Gerund in *di* is commonly govern'd both of Substantives and Adjectives in manner of a genitive; as *Causa videndi. Amor habendi. Cupidus visendi. Certus eundi.* And sometimes governeth a genitive Plural; as *Illorum videndi gratia.* Ter.

Gerunds in *do* are us'd after Verbs in manner of an ablative, according to former Rules, with or without a preposition; as *Defessus sum ambulando. A discendo facile deterretur. Cæsar dando, sublevando, ignoscendo, gloriam adeptus est. In apparando consumunt diem.*

A Gerund in *dum* is us'd in manner of an accusative after prepositions governing that case; as *Ad capiendum hostes. Ante domandum ingentes tollent animos.* Virg. *Ob redimendum captivos. Inter cœnandum.*

Gerunds in signification are oft-times us'd as Participles in *dus; Tuorum consiliorum reprimendorum causa.* Cic. *Orationem Latinam legendis nostris efficies pleniorem.* Cic. *Ad accusandos homines præmio ducitur.*

A Gerund in *dum* joyn'd with the Impersonal *est,* and implying some necessity or duty to do a thing, may have both the Active and Passive construction of the Verb from whence it is deriv'd; as *Utendum est ætate.* Ov. *Pacem Trojano a rege petendum.* Virg. *Iterandum eadem ista mihi.* Cic *Serviendum est mihi amicis. Plura dixi quam dicendum fuit.* Cic. pro Sest.

Construction of Verb with Verb.

WHen two Verbs come together without a nominative case between them, the latter shall be in the Infinitive Mood; as *Cupio discere.* [57] Or in the first Supine after Verbs of moving; as *Eo cubitum, spectatum.* Or in the latter with an adjective; as *Turpe est dictu. Facile factu opus scitu.*

But if a Case come between, not govern'd of the former Verb, it shall alwayes be an accusative before the Infinitive Mood; as *Te rediisse incolumem gaudeo. Malo me divitem esse, quam haberi.*

And this Infinitive *esse,* will have alwayes after it an accusative, or the same case which the former Verb governs; as *Expedit bonos esse vobis. Quo mihi commisso, non licet esse piam.* But this accusative agreeth with another understood before the Infinitive; as *Expedit vobis vos esse bonos. Natura beatis omnibus esse dedit. Nobis non licet esse tam disertis.* The same Construction may be us'd after other Infinitives Neuter or Passive like to *esse* in signification; as *Maximo tibi postea & civi, & duci evadere contigit.* Val. Max. L.6.

Somtimes a Noun Adjective or Substantive governs an Infinitive; as *Audax omnia perpeti. Dignus amari. Consilium ceperunt ex oppido profugere.* Cæs. *Minari divisoribus ratio non erat.* Cic. verr. I.

Somtimes the Infinitive is put absolute for the preterimperfect or preterperfect Tense; as *Ego illud sedulo negare factum.* Ter. *Galba autem multas similitudines afferre.* Cic. *Ille contra hæc omnia ruere, agere vitam.* Ter.

Construction of Participles.

PArticiples govern such cases as the Verb from whence they come, according to their Active or Passive signification; as *Fruiturus amicis. Nun-* [58] *quam audita mihi. Diligendus ab omnibus. Sate sanguine divûm. Telamone creatus. Corpore mortali cretus.* Lucret. *Nate deâ. Edite regibus. Lævo suspensi loculos tabulasque lacerto.* Hor. *Census equestrem summam.* Id. *Abeundum est mihi. Venus orta mari. Exosus Bella.* Virg. *Exosus diis.* Gell. *Arma Perosus.* Ovid. But *Pertæsus* hath an accusative otherwise then the Verb; as *Pertæsus Ignaviam. Semet ipse pertæsus.* Suet. To these add participial adjectives ending in *bilis* of the Passive signification, and requiring like case after them; as *Nulli penetrabilis astro lucus erat.*

Participles chang'd into Adjectives have thir Construction by the Rules of Adjectives; as *Appetens vini. Fugitans litium. Fidens animi.*

An Ablative put absolute.

TWo Nouns together, or a Noun and Pronoun with a Participle exprest or understood, put absolutely, that is to say, neither governing nor govern'd of a Verb, shall be put in the ablative; as *Authore Senatu bellum geritur. Me duce vinces. Cæsare veniente hostes fugerunt. Sublato clamore prælium committitur.*

Construction of Adverbs.

EN and *ecce* will have a Nominative, or an accusative, and somtimes with a dative; as *En Priamus. Ecce tibi status noster. En habitum. Ecce autem alterum.*

Adverbs of quantity, time, and place require a genitive; as *Satis loquentiæ, sapientiæ parum. Satis* also compounded with a Verb; as *Is rerum sua-* [59] *rum satagit. Tunc temporis. Ubique gentium. Eò impudentiæ processit. Quoad ejus fieri poterit.*

To these add *Ergo* signifying the cause; as *Illius ergo.* Virg. *Virtutis ergo. Fugæ atque formidinis ergo non abiturus.* Liv.

Others will have such case as the Nouns from whence they come; as *Minime gentium. Optime omnium. Venit obviam illi. Canit similiter huic. Albanum, sive Falernum te magis appositis delectat.* Hor.

Adverbs are joyn'd in a Sentence to several Moods of Verbs.

Of Time, *Ubi, postquam, cum* or *quum,* to an Indicative or

Subjunctive; as *Hæc ubi dicta dedit. Ubi nos laverimus. Postquam excessit ex Ephebis. Cum faciam vitula.* Virg. *Cum canerem reges.* Id.

Donec while, to an Indicative. *Donec eris felix. Donec* untill, to an Indicative or Subjunctive; *Cogere donec oves jussit.* Virg. *Donec ea aqua decocta sit.* Colum.

Dum while, to an Indicative. *Dum apparatur Virgo. Dum* untill, to an Indicative or Subjunctive; as *Dum redeo. Tertia dum Latio regnantem viderit æstas. Dum* for *dummodo* so as, or, so that, to a Subjunctive. *Dum prosim tibi.*

Quoad while, to an Indicative. *Quoad expectas contubernalem. Quoad* untill, to a Subjunctive. *Omnia integra servabo, quoad exercitus huc mittatur.*

Simulac, simulatque to an Indicative or Subjunctive; as *Simulac belli patiens erat simulatque adoleverit ætas.*

Ut as, to the same Moods. *Ut salutabis, ita resalutaberis. Ut sementem feceris, ita & metes.* Hor. *Ut* so soon as, to an Indicative only: as *Ut ventum est in Urbem.* [60]

Quasi, tanquam, perinde, ac si, to a Subjunctive only; as *quasi non norimus nos inter nos. Tanquam feceris ipse aliquid.*

Ne of forbidding, to an Imperative or Subjunctive; as *Ne sævi. Ne metuas.*

Certain Adverbs of quantity, quality, or cause; as *Quam, quoties, cur, quare,* &c. Thence also *qui, quis, quantus, qualis,* and the like, coming in a sentence after the principal Verb, govern the Verb following in a Subjunctive; as *videte quàm valdè malitiæ suæ confidat.* Cic. *Quid est cur tu in isto loco sedeas?* Cic pro Cluent. *Subsideo mihi diligentiam comparavi quæ quanta sit intelligi non potest, nisi* &c. Cic. pro Quint. *Nam quid hoc iniquius dici potest, Quam me qui caput alterius fortunasq; defendam, Priore loco dicere.* Ibid. *Nullum est Officium tam sanctum atq; solenne, quod non avaritia violare soleat.* Ibid. *Non me fallit, si consulamini quid sitis responsuri.* Ibid. *Dici vix potest quam multa sint quæ respondeatis ante fieri oportere.* Ibid. *Docui quo die hunc sibi promisisse dicat, eo die ne Romæ quidem eum fuisse.* Ibid. *Conturbatus discedit neq; mirum, cui hæc optio tam misera daretur.* Ibid. *Narrat quo in loco viderit Quintium.* Ibid. *Recte majores eum qui socium fefellisset in virorum bonorum numero non putarunt haberi oportere.* Cic. pro Rosc. Am. *Quæ concursatio percontantium quid Prætor edixisset, ubi caenaret, quid enuntiasset.* Cic. Agrar. I.

Of Conjunctions.

COnjunctions Copulative and Disjunctive, and these four, *Quam, nisi, præterquam, an,* couple like cases; as *Socrates docuit*

Xenophontem & Platonem. Aut dies est, aut nox. Nescio albus an
[61] *ater sit. Est minor natu quàm tu. Nemini placet prœterquam*
sibi.

Except when some particular construction requireth otherwise;
as *Studui Romœ & Athenis. Emi fundum centum nummis &*
pluris. Accusas furti, an stupri, an utroque?

They also couple for the most part like Moods and Tenses; as
Recto stat corpore, despicitque terras. But not alwayes like Tenses;
as *Nisi me lactasses, & vana spe produceres. Et habetur, & refe-*
retur tibi a me gratia.

Of other Conjunctions, some govern an Indicative, some a Subjunctive, according to thir several significations.

Etsi, tametsi, etiamsi, quanquam an Indicative; *quamvis* and
licet most commonly a Subjunctive; as *Etsi nihil novi afferrebatur.*
Quanquam animus meminisse horret. Quamvis Elysios miretur
Grœcia campos. Ipse licet venias.

Ni, nisi, si, siquidem, quod, quia, postquam, posteaquam, an-
tequam, priusquam an Indicative or Subjunctive; as *Nisi vi mavis*
eripi. Ni faciat. Castigo te, non quòd odeo habeam, sed quòd amem.
Antequam dicam. Si for *quamvis* a Subjunctive onely. *Redeam?*
Non si me obsecret.

Si also conditional may somtimes govern both Verbs of the sentence in a Subjunctive; as *Respiraro, si te videro.* Cic. ad Attic.

Quando, quandoquidem, quoniam, an Indicative; as *Dicite*
quandoquidem in molli consedimus herba. Quoniam convenimus
ambo.

Cum seeing that, a Subjunctive; as *Cum sis officiis Gradive*
virilibus aptus.

Ne, an, num, of doubting, a Subjunctive; as *Nihil refert, fece-*
risne, an persuaseris. Vise num redierit. [62]

Interrogatives also of disdain or reproach understood govern a
Subjunctive; as *tantum dem, quantum ille poposcerit?* Cic. verr.
4. *Sylvam tu Scantiam vendas?* Cic. Agrar. *Hunc tu non ames?*
Cic. ad Attic. *Furem aliquem aut rapacem accusaris? Vitanda*
semper erit omnis avaritiœ suspicio. Cic. verr. 4. Sometimes an
Infinitive; as *Méne incœpto desistere victam?* Virg.

Ut that, lest not, or although, a Subjunctive; as *Te oro, ut redeat*
jam in viam. Metuo ut substet hospes. Ut omnia contingant quœ
volo.

Of Prepositions.

OF Prepositions, some will have an accusative after them, some
an ablative, some both, according to thir different signification.

An accusative these following, *Ad, apud, ante, adversus adversum, cis citra, circum circa, circiter, contra, erga, extra, inter, intra, infra, juxta, ob, ponè, per, propè, propter, post, penes, præter, sucundùm, supra, secùs, trans, ultra, usque, versus;* But *versus* is most commonly set after the case it governs, as *Londinum versus.*

And for an accusative after *ad,* a dative somtimes is us'd in Poets; as *It clamor cœlo.* Virg. *Cœlo si gloria tollit Æneadum.* Sil. for *ad cœlum.*

An ablative these, *A, ab, abs, absque, cum, coram, de, e, ex, pro, præ, palàm, sine, tenus,* which last is also put after his case, being most usually a genitive, if it be Plural; as *Capulo tenus. Aurium tenus.*

These, both cases, *In, sub, super, subter, clam, procul.* [63]

In, signifying *to, towards, into,* or *against,* requires an accusative; as *Pisces emptos obolo in cœnam seni. Animus in Teucros benignus. Versa est in cineres Troja. In te committere tantum quid Troes potuere?* lastly, when it signifies *future time* or *for;* as *Bellum in trigesimum diem indixerunt. Designati consules in annum sequentem. Alii pretia faciunt in singula capita canum.* Var. Otherwise *in* will have an ablative; as *In Urbe. In Terris.*

Sub, when it signifies *to,* or *in time, about,* or *a little before,* requires an accusative; as *sub umbram properemus. Sub id tempus. Sub noctem.* Otherwise an Ablative. *Sub pedibus. Sub umbra.*

Super signifying *beyond,* or *present time,* an accusative; as *Super Garamantas & Indos. Super cœnam.* Suet. at supper time. *Of* or *concerning,* an ablative; as *Multa super Priamo rogitans. Super hac re.*

Super, over or *upon,* may have either case; as *Super ripas Tiberis effusus, Sæva sidens super arma. Fronde super viridi.*

So also may *subter;* as *pugnatum est super subterque terras. Subter densa testudine.* Virg. *Clam patrem* or *patre. Procul muros.* Liv. *Patria procul.*

Prepositions in composition govern the same cases as before in apposition. *Adibo hominem. Detrudunt naves scopulo.* And the Preposition is somtimes repeated; as *Detrahere de tua fama nunquam cogitavi.* And somtimes understood, governeth his usuall case; as *Habeo te loco parentis. Apparuit humana specie. Cumis erant oriundi.* Liv. *Liberis parentibus oriundus.* Colum. *Mutat quadrata rotundis.* Hor. *Pridie Compitalia. Pridie nonas* or *calendas. Postridie Idus. Postridie ludos.* Before which accusatives *ante* or *post* is to be understood, *Filii id ætatis.* Cic. *Hoc noctis.*

Liv. Understand *Secundum*. Or refer to [64] part of time. *Omnia Mercurio similis*. Virg. Understand *per*.

Of Interjections.

CErtain Interjections have several cases after them. *O,* a Nominative, Accusative or Vocative; as *O festus dies hominis. O ego lævus.* Hor. *O fortunatos. O formose puer.*

Others a Nominative, or an Accusative; as *Heu prisca fides! Heu stirpem invisam! Proh sancte Jupiter! Proh deum atque hominum fidem! Hem tibi davum!*

Yea, though the Interjection be understood; as *Me miserum! Me cæcum, qui hæc ante non viderim!*

Others will have a Dative; as *Hei mihi. Væ misero mihi.* Terent.

FINIS.

ERRATA.

PAge 16. Line 5. for *hoc nostrate* Read *hoc nostras* or *'nostrate.*
p. 31. L. 11. f. *visi* r. *vici.*
P. 35. 1. 21: f. *Quæsimus* r. *Quæsumus.*
P. 54. 1. 8. f. *Transitives* r. *Transitive.*
P. 55. 1. 8. f. *Tit.* r. *Ter.* [65]

PROSE PRELIMINARY TO
SAMSON AGONISTES

1671

PREFACE AND NOTES BY ROBERT J. WICKENHEISER

Unlike the Argument and essay on the verse of *Paradise Lost,* which Milton added to his epic poem one year after it was published, the essay on tragedy and the Argument of *Samson Agonistes* were included with the drama when it first appeared in print, together with *Paradise Regained,* in 1671. And again unlike *Paradise Lost,* only one text of Milton's tragedy and preliminary prose was printed during the poet's life, that of the first edition. The prose of *Samson* consequently poses no significant publishing or textual problems.

But although there is just one text of *Samson Agonistes,* printed most probably by John Macocke, one of the largest printers of London, considerable and conflicting speculation has focused in modern times on the date of composition: Is *Samson*—and in our case, the preliminary prose—early or late work of Milton?

As early as c. 1640, as the Trinity College Manuscript indicates (below, p. 130), Milton was considering Samson as a possible subject for poetic treatment; and in 1642 he was openly speculating on the *kind* of great work he should devote his life to and was considering among other forms "those Dramatic constitutions, wherein *Sophocles* and *Euripides* raigne." [1] These dates would seem to offer a reasonable *terminus a quo* for Milton's tragedy and the accompanying prose.

The earliest printed notice of *Samson Agonistes* occurs in a 1670 catalogue of books offered for sale by the bookseller John Starkey, for whom Macocke printed Milton's brief epic and drama. Although the catalogue is dated "29th. *May,* 1670," it includes titles of books that were offered for sale with title pages dated as late as 1672 and was presumably intended to advertise both books in

---

[1] *The Reason of Church Government, Complete Prose,* I, 814.

print and books about to be printed.[2] Except for furnishing a *terminus ad quem,* neither this notice nor others shortly after help in determining the actual date of composition.

The earliest date proposed is that offered by Allan H. Gilbert— a date perhaps not later than Milton's draft of plans for Samson plays appearing in the Trinity College Manuscript, that is, c. 1640. "The manuscript perhaps lay with him until he had *Paradise Regained* ready for printing." When the publisher asked for more material to fill out the *Paradise Regained* volume, Milton "thought of his old tragedy, had it found, and turned it over to the bookseller. I am inclined to think that he did no further work on it." And "it is easy to suppose that when Milton prepared his argument, he lifted it from notes—now lost—such as the [Trinity College] MS gives for other subjects." [3] W. R. Parker, however, has advanced reasons for believing that Milton began writing his drama in 1646–47 and then took it up again in 1652–53, by and large completing it about this time; [4] whereas A. S. P. Woodhouse has argued that *Samson* was written sometime during the "year before the Restoration (May, 1660) and spring of 1661." [5] Finally, the view inherited from Masson and furthered by Grierson and Hanford, that Milton wrote *Samson* late in life (1667–70) and that in his hero he embodied much of himself and his own life,[6] still holds primary credence; and in support of this dating, Morris Freedman has

[2] All notices of the publication of *Paradise Regain'd . . . To which is added Samson Agonistes* are dated 1670; see Harris F. Fletcher, ed., *John Milton's Complete Poetical Works . . . in Photofacsimile,* 4 vols. (Urbana: University of Illinois Press, 1943–48), IV, 15–16, and Parker, *Milton,* pp. 1136–39. The volume was licensed July 2, 1670, and entered in the *Stationers' Registers* September 10, 1670. All known title pages have the date 1671. Both Fletcher and Parker suggest that the delay in publishing may have been due to the time taken by the blind Milton in supervising proofreading.

[3] Allan H. Gilbert, "Is *Samson Agonistes* Unfinished?," *PQ,* XXVIII (1949), 98–106, quoting pp. 106, 98.

[4] W. R. Parker, "The Date of *Samson Agonistes,*" *PQ,* XXVIII (1949), 145–66; and "The Date of *Samson Agonistes:* A Postscript," *N&Q,* n.s. V (1958), 201–2.

[5] A. S. P. Woodhouse, "*Samson Agonistes* and Milton's Experience," *Transactions of the Royal Society of Canada,* 3rd ser. XLIII (1949), 145–56; and *The Heavenly Muse* (Toronto: University of Toronto Press, 1972), pp. 292–319.

[6] James Holly Hanford, *Samson Agonistes and Milton in Old Age* (New York: Haskell House, 1964); first published in *Studies in Shakespeare, Milton, and Donne* (New York: Macmillan, 1925); and *John Milton, Englishman* (New York: Crown Publishers, 1949), pp. 200–29. Ernest Sirluck ("Some Recent Suggested Changes in the Chronology of Milton's Poems," *JEGP,* LX [1961], 749–85) questions both Gilbert's and Parker's arguments for an early date of composition of *Samson* and reaffirms the traditional view. Ants Oras (*Blank Verse and Chronology in Milton,* University of Florida Monographs, Humanities, no. 20 [Gaines-

sought to relate the preface to *Samson* to Dryden's *Essay of Dramatic Poesie,* printed in 1668. [7]

Anyone who investigates this problem of date will discover that no real documentary evidence has so far been uncovered that will solve it or the temporal relationship of the preliminary prose to the drama: Was the preface composed at the same time as the tragedy, or was it written specially for publication in the 1671 volume? With Edward Phillips one is forced to acknowledge that the date of composition of Milton's drama "cannot certainly be concluded." [8] Yet, regardless of when Milton may have begun and completed *Samson* and its preface, the preliminary prose was published together with the drama from the very outset, and the opinions expressed in it reflect the poet's mature views concerning drama in general and the kind of dramatic tragedy in particular that he was trying to write.

Although Milton's preface may not lay to rest all issues that have troubled readers of *Samson Agonistes* and in fact has given rise to many probing questions regarding the play's structure, spirit, and tragic stature, it does contain the emphases the poet himself thought most fitting for those who "will," as he says, "best judge" his work. Perhaps Woodhouse is closest to the mark when he concludes: "To say that *Samson Agonistes* is a classical tragedy with a Christian theme and outlook does not completely define the effect or the means used to obtain it; but it puts us, I think, on the right track. It gives us a point of view from which to read and judge the poem." [9] And that point of view is itself something that Milton had seen fit to provide already in his own prefatory observations on "that sort of Dramatic Poem which is call'd Tragedy."

The texts of the preface and Argument here are those of the first edition, which, as Fletcher concludes, "On the whole . . . represent

---

ville: University of Florida Press, 1966]) provides statistical analyses supporting the traditional chronology. For a recent survey of the controversy, see Christopher Hill, *Milton and the Puritan Revolution* (London: Faber and Faber, 1978), pp. 481–86, who concludes: "On the evidence so far produced, I see no reason to date *Samson Agonistes* before 1660, and many reasons for dating it after the Restoration."

[7] Morris Freedman, "Milton and Dryden" (Ph.D. diss., Columbia University, 1953); abstract, *DAI,* XIV (1954), 109, an account of which appears in *SCN,* July 1955; also Freedman's *"All for Love* and *Samson Agonistes," N&Q,* n.s. III (1956), 514–17, and "Milton and Dryden on Rhyme," *HLQ,* XXIV (1960–61), 337–44.

[8] Helen Darbishire, *The Early Lives of Milton* (London, 1932), p. 75.

[9] A. S. P. Woodhouse, "Tragic Effect in *Samson Agonistes," UTQ,* XXVIII (1959), 222.

perhaps as well as can be expected the texts . . . as Milton wanted them to be."[10] Because there is no manuscript of this prose and no later editions during Milton's life, no textual notes are necessary,[11] but annotations have been supplied here where they seemed appropriate.[12] Within these annotations, quotations from Greek and Latin authors are from the Loeb Classical Library.

[10] Fletcher, *Milton's Poetical Works*, IV, 37. The text of *Paradise Regained* ends on p. 111 (H8[r]) with the verso blank and unnumbered. The title page of *Samson* (I[r]) faces this blank page, and the verso is blank. The prose essay, "Of that sort of Dramatic Poem which is call'd Tragedy," begins on the following page (I2[r]), numbered 3; it ends on I3[r], p. 5. "The Argument" occupies [I3v], p. 6.

[11] As Fletcher points out (ibid., IV, 40), the second edition of 1680, also printed for John Starkey, seems to contain no alterations of the 1671 texts that originated with Milton.

[12] Although I have used various studies and editions of *Samson*, I am particularly indebted in my annotations to James Holly Hanford, *The Poems of John Milton*, 2nd ed. (New York: Ronald Press, 1953); Merritt Y. Hughes, *John Milton: Complete Poems and Major Prose* (New York: Odyssey Press, 1957), and John Carey and Alastair Fowler, *The Poems of John Milton* (London: Longmans, 1968).

SAMSON AGONISTES[1]

Of that sort of Dramatic Poem which is call'd Tragedy.

Tragedy, as it was antiently compos'd, hath been ever held the gravest, moralest, and most profitable of all other Poems: therefore said by *Aristotle* [2] to be of power by raising pity and fear, or terror, to purge the mind [3] of those and such like passions, that is to temper and reduce them to just measure with a kind of delight, stirr'd up by reading or seeing those passions well imitated. Nor is Nature wanting in her own effects to make good his assertion: for so in Physic things of melancholic hue and quality are us'd against melancholy, sowr against sowr, salt to remove salt humours. Hence Philosophers and other gravest

[1] In Greek the word means both a "contestant in athletic games" and a "champion." Carey and Fowler (*Poems of Milton*, p. 331) note that "[Edward] Phillips's *New World of Words* (1658 and 1663) defines 'agonize' as 'play the champion' "; Paul R. Sellin ("Milton's Epithet Agonistes," *SEL*, IV [1964], 137–62) discusses still other seventeenth-century connotations; and for F. Michael Krouse (*Milton's Samson and the Christian Tradition* [Princeton: Princeton University Press, 1949], pp. 108–16), the term means first of all simply an athlete struggling for a prize in the Olympic games; metaphorically, the champion of truth in terms of exertion of the mind and spirit called for in the Platonic ethic; and finally, the Christian athlete, Saint Paul's champion armed with "the whole armor of God," about whom Augustine wrote in his *De Agone Christiano*.

[2] Milton paraphrases the Aristotelian definition of tragedy in *Poetics,* chap. VI, from which he quotes in the Greek and in Latin translation on the title page.

[3] Here Milton gives the classic statement in English of Aristotle's psychological effect of tragedy. Milton has long been considered to be drawing upon the Italian critics Minturno (*Arte Poetica*, 1563) and Guarini (*Il Compendio della Poesia Tragicomica*, 1601), who applied the popular Renaissance principle that "like cures like" to Aristotle's theory of tragic catharsis. As Hughes points out (*Milton,* p. 549), Minturno states: "Medicine has no greater power, by means of poison, to expel poison from an afflicted body than tragedy has to purge the soul of its impetuous passions by the skilful expression of strong emotion in poetry." Hughes adds that "Minturno developed the idea no further than Milton did, but he came close to Milton's 'agonistic' conception by adding that tragedy is properly a kind of spiritual athletic discipline like the hard physical training of the Spartans, and that it trains men to endure reversals of fortune." Paul R. Sellin, however ("Sources of Milton's Catharsis: A Reconsideration," *JEGP* LX [1961], 712–30), notes that both Minturno's and Guarini's conceptions of Aristotelian catharsis differ from Milton's. Minturno conceived of catharsis as the expelling of unde-

Writers, as *Cicero, Plutarch* and others, frequently cite out of Tragic Poets, both to adorn and illustrate thir discourse. The Apostle *Paul* himself thought it not unworthy to insert a verse of *Euripides* [4] into the Text of Holy Scripture, I *Cor.* 15.33. and *Parœus* [5] commenting on the *Revelation*, divides the whole Book as a Tragedy, into Acts distinguisht each by a Chorus of Heavenly Harpings and Song between. Hereto-[3]fore Men in highest dignity have labour'd not a little to be thought able to compose a Tragedy. Of that honour *Dionysius* [6] the elder was no less ambitious, then before of his attaining to the Tyranny. *Augustus Cæsar* also had

---

sirable passions rather than, as Milton emphasizes, the reduction of all passions to a norm. Guarini considered Aristotle's τοιούτων παθημάτων to refer only to the emotions of pity and fear, not, as Milton has it, to "those and such like passions." Sellin suggests that Daniel Heinsius (*De Tragœdiæ Constitutione,* 1611) proposes a theory closer to Milton's, although even Heinsius stresses that pity and fear are the only emotions involved in tragic catharsis. Hanford notes (*Poems of Milton,* p. 553) that the homeopathic analogy, as outlined by Milton here, "almost certainly points the way to what Aristotle meant, or ought to have meant. The difficulty of incorporating such a principle in the general theory of tragedy, as expressed in this Preface, is obvious. How is the delight of seeing the passions well imitated related to the emotional identification demanded by the theory of like curing like? Milton raises basic æsthetic questions but by no means solves them. As he proceeds he seems to be content to accept 'gravest, moralest and most profitable' in the conventional sense of Satan's characterization of the tragedians in *Paradise Regained* [IV, 262–63] as 'teachers best / Of moral prudence, with delight receiv'd.' "

[4] Milton attributed this verse, "Evil communications corrupt good manners," to Euripides both here and in *Areopagitica* (*Complete Prose,* II, 508). J. J. Lynch (*N&Q,* III [1956], 477) notes that this maxim is from Menander's *Thais,* not Euripides; but the fragment in which it has survived is found in editions of both Menander and Euripides.

[5] Milton also makes this point in *The Reason of Church Government, Complete Prose,* I, 815. David Pareus was a German Reform theologian (1548–86). His discussion of Revelation as a drama may be found in his *In Divinam Apocalypsin . . . Commentarius,* "Procemiun ad Auditores," cap. VIII, and in "Phænomena et Personæ, quibus hoc propheticum Drama, septem visionibus revelatum peragitur," *Operum Theologicorum Exegeticorum* (Francofurti, 1647), II, 627, 630–31 (misnumbered 549–50).

[6] A tyrant of Syracuse (431–367 B.C.). Diodorus Siculus (XIV, 109; XV, 6–7, 73–74) relates that Dionysius was "madly addicted to poetry," and though audiences at two Olympic games laughed at his verses, he "did not give up his devotion to writing." His tragedy, *The Ransom of Hector,* won a prize at the Wine Press Festival at Athens, and in the celebration of his victory, he died from overdrinking.

begun his *Ajax*,[7] but unable to please his own judgment with what he had begun, left it unfinisht. *Seneca* the Philosopher is by some thought the Author of those Tragedies [8] (at lest [9] the best of them) that go under that name. *Gregory Nazianzen* a Father of the Church, thought it not unbeseeming the sanctity of his person to write a Tragedy, which he entitl'd, *Christ Suffering.*[10] This is mention'd to vindicate Tragedy from the small esteem, or rather infamy, which in the account of many it undergoes at this day with other common Interludes; hap'ning through the Poets error of intermixing Comic stuff with Tragic sadness [11] and gravity; or introducing trivial and vulgar persons, which by all judicious hath bin counted absurd; and brought in without discretion, corruptly to gratifie the people. And though antient Tragedy use no Prologue,[12] yet using sometimes, in case of self defence, or explanation, that which *Martial* calls an Epistle; in behalf of this Tragedy coming forth after the antient manner,[13] much different from what among us passes for best, thus much before-hand may be Epistl'd;

[7] The story is told by Suetonius (*Lives of the Caesars,* II, lxxxv): "Though he began a tragedy with much enthusiasm, he destroyed it because his style did not satisfy him."

[8] Ten tragedies bear the name of the Stoic philosopher Lucius Annaeus Seneca (3 B.C.–A.D. 65). "The doubt as to his authorship of the tragedies," as Carey and Fowler note (*Poems of Milton,* p. 344), "is due to a mistake of Sidonius Apollinaris, *Carmen,* ix, 230–38, who clearly distinguishes between Seneca the philosopher and Seneca the tragedian."

[9] I.e., least.

[10] The play has also been ascribed to Apollinarius the elder, but Milton, like his contemporaries, believed the tragedy written by Gregory of Nazianzen (325?–390?), Bishop of Constantinople. Hughes (*Milton,* p. 550) observes that Milton "admired its Euripidean echoes and must have been interested in a long-standing controversy as to whether the 'Playe of Christ' by Nazianzenus, as Stephen Gosson called it in his *Schoole of Abuse,* was intended for acting or was composed 'dialogue-wise, as Plato and Tullie did their philosophye, to be reade, not to be played.' "

[11] I.e., seriousness.

[12] Milton employs "Prologue" here in the sense of a preliminary address to the audience intended to serve as a defense of the play, much like Ben Jonson's "To the Reader," in which he defends his having executed the high "offices of a tragic writer" in *Sejanus*.

[13] Hanford notes (*Poems of Milton,* p. 553) that "Milton touches on the essential points of superiority claimed by Renaissance criticism of classical as opposed to modern drama: (1) purity of genre, violated by the mixture of comic and tragic; (2) decorum in the dramatis personae, violated by the portrayal of common men; (3) concentration of action and unity of time; (4) the use of chorus." For a discussion of some length of Milton's theories of drama and epic and their relation to the precepts of classical and Renaissance critics, see Ida Langdon, *Milton's Theory of Poetry and Fine Art* (New Haven, 1924), pp. 83–153.

that *Chorus* is here introduc'd after the Greek manner,[14] not antient only but modern, and still in use among the *Italians*.[15] In the modelling therefore of this Poem, with good reason, the Antients and *Italians* [16] are rather follow'd, as of much [4] more authority and fame. The measure of Verse us'd in the Chorus is of all sorts, call'd by the Greeks *Monostrophic*,[17] or rather *Apolelymenon*,[18] without regard had to *Strophe, Antistrophe* or *Epod*, which were a kind of Stanza's fram'd only for the Music, then us'd with the Chorus that sung; not essential to the Poem, and therefore not material; or being divided into Stanza's or Pauses, they may be call'd *Allæostropha*.[19] Division into Act and Scene referring chiefly to the Stage (to which this work never was intended) is here omitted.

It suffices if the whole Drama be found not produc't beyond the fift Act, of the style and uniformitie, and that commonly call'd the Plot,[20] whether intricate or explicit, which is nothing indeed but such œconomy, or disposition of the fable as may stand best with verisimilitude and decorum; they only will best judge who are not

[14] To comment on the action and to enrich its background by appropriate references to the past.

[15] For instance, in Tasso's *Aminta* (1581) and Guarini's *Il Pastor Fido* (1590).

[16] In *Of Education* (*Complete Prose*, II, 404–5) Milton emphasizes that the Italians are the best representatives, after the ancients, of "that sublime art which in *Aristotles poetics*, in *Horace*, and the *Italian* commentaries of *Castelvetro, Tasso, Mazzoni*, and others, teaches what the laws are of a true *Epic* poem, what of a *Dramatic*, what of a *Lyric*, what decorum is, which is the grand master peece to observe."

[17] I.e., one stanza only.

[18] Meaning "freed" or "loosened"—here in the sense that the choruses are free, because "not essential to the Poem," from the restraints of the strict identical pattern that divides stanzas into the *strophe* (sung by the chorus while moving from right to left), *antistrophe* (sung while moving in the opposite direction and corresponding exactly to the strophe in structure), and concluding *epode* (sung while standing still).

[19] Meaning "of irregular strophes." Milton intends the term to be used in reference to choruses that may seem at times to divide into stanzas, even though the stanzas or strophes themselves vary in length (i.e., since "The measure of Verse us'd in the chorus is of all sorts").

[20] In *Poetics*, VI, Aristotle places first among his six elements of tragedy the plot, "which," for Milton, "is nothing indeed but such economy," i.e., management of the events, or, as Aristotle calls it, the "arranging of the incidents or episodes" in the drama. Aristotle divides plots into two classes, simple (ἁπλοῖ) and complex (πεπλεγμένοι), which Milton refers to here as "explicit" and "intricate."

unacquainted with *Æschulus*,[21] *Sophocles,* and *Euripides,* the three Tragic Poets unequall'd yet by any, and the best rule to all who endeavour to write Tragedy. The circumscription of time [22] wherein the whole Drama begins and ends, is according to antient rule, and best example,[23] within the space of 24 hours. [5]

The ARGUMENT.[1]

S Amson *made Captive,*[2] *Blind, and now in the Prison at* Gaza,[3] *there to labour as in a common work-house, on a Festival day,*[4] *in the general cessation from labour, comes forth into the open Air, to a place nigh, somewhat retir'd there to sit a while and bemoan his condition. Where he happens at length to be visited by certain friends and equals* [5] *of his tribe, which make the Chorus,*[6] *who seek to comfort him what they can; then by his old Father* Manoa, *who endeavours the like, and withal tells him his purpose*

---

[21] According to J. C. Maxwell ("Milton's Knowledge of Aeschylus: The Argument from Parallel Passages," *RES,* n.s. III [1952], 366–71), Aeschylus was not popular in the seventeenth century, even among scholars, and it is therefore unusual for Milton to rank him here with Sophocles and Euripides.

[22] I.e., "unity of time," a principle read into Aristotle's *Poetics* by Renaissance criticism, which requires that a drama ideally not exceed twelve, or at most twenty-four, hours in the duration of its action. Milton adheres strictly to this principle.

[23] As Carey and Fowler note (*Poems of Milton,* p. 345), "there are five exceptions among surviving Greek tragedies: Aeschylus' *Persians, Agamemnon* and *Eumenides,* Sophocles' *Trachiniæ,* and Euripides' *Suppliants.*"

[1] For a discussion of the term "Argument" and Milton's use of it, see above, p. 15, n. 1. Milton's Argument indicates the crucial stages in the action of his drama: Manoa's visit to Samson, Samson's first refusing the officer who summons him but later yielding, Manoa's return full of hope, and finally a Hebrew's relating what Samson had done. It is curious, however, that neither Dalila nor Harapha— characters who have attracted the attention of modern readers—receives more than passing reference in the brief statement: "who in the mean while is visited by other persons."

[2] Samson begins *in medias res,* a feature that allows Milton the flexibility he needs to adapt the story as found in Judg. 13–16 and to treat it as he intends.

[3] Chief of the five federated cities of the Philistines, located some fifty miles south and west of Jerusalem.

[4] Milton identifies the occasion later in the Argument as "a day of Thanksgiving for thir deliverance from the hands of Samson." Cf. Judg. 16:23: "Then the lords of the Philistines gathered them together for to offer a great sacrifice unto Dagon their god, and to rejoice: for they said, Our God hath delivered Samson our enemy into our hand."

[5] A Latinism signifying "contemporaries" and meaning "persons of about the same age."

[6] I.e., make up the Chorus.

to procure his liberty by ransom; lastly, that this Feast was pro-
claim'd by the Philistins [7] *as a day of Thanksgiving for thir deliv-*
erance from the hands of Samson, *which yet more troubles him.*
Manoa *then departs to prosecute his endeavour with the* Philistian
Lords for Samson's *redemption; who in the mean while is visited*
by other persons; and lastly by a publick Officer to require his
coming to the Feast before the Lords and People, to play or shew
his strength in thir presence; he at first refuses, dismissing the
publick Officer with absolute denyal to come; at length perswaded
inwardly that this was from God, he yields to go along with him,
who came now the second time with great threatnings to fetch him;
the Chorus yet remaining on the place, Manoa *returns full of joyful*
hope, to procure e're long his Sons deliverance: in the midst of
which discourse an Ebrew comes in haste confusedly at first; and
afterward more distinctly relating the Catastrophe, what Samson
had done to the Philistins, *and by accident to himself; wherewith*
the Tragedy ends. [6]

---

[7] An aggressive people of as yet undetermined origin, occupying southwestern
Palestine, who figure most prominently in Judg. 13–16 and 1 Sam. They oppressed
the Israelites, captured the ark of God and took it into the house of Dagon, but
returned it after the Lord twice struck down the idol. Subsequently they were
successively defeated by Samuel, by Saul, and by David.

A FULLER COURSE IN THE ART OF LOGIC CONFORMED TO THE METHOD OF PETER RAMUS

1672

EDITED AND TRANSLATED BY
WALTER J. ONG, S.J.
AND
CHARLES J. ERMATINGER

CONTENTS

Introduction by Walter J. Ong, S.J.

A Fuller Course in the Art of Logic Conformed to the
Method of Peter Ramus (1672)
Translated and Edited by Walter J. Ong, S.J., and
Charles J. Ermatinger.

Book the First

[The Invention of Arguments]

Book the Second

[The Disposition of Arguments]

INTRODUCTION

By Walter J. Ong, S.J.

I. THE WORK AND ITS DATE

Milton's *Artis Logicæ Plenior Institutio ad Petri Rami Methodum Concinnata* is a textbook on logic, composed in Latin as schoolbooks in all subjects normally had been in Western Europe from antiquity. It consists of the text of the *Dialectic* or *Logic* by the French philosopher and educational reformer Pierre de la Ramée or Petrus Ramus (1515–72), taken from Ramus's final revision of 1572, virtually intact, amalgamated into a longer explanation of the same material worked up by Milton from George Downame (or Downham) and other commentators on Ramus and from some ideas of his own, the whole supplemented with an exercise in logical analysis adapted from Downame and an abridgment of the *Petri Rami vita* by Johann Thomas Freige (Freigius). The logic text proper is presented so that the work of Ramus, Milton, Downame, and the other commentators form one continuous text. We can render the complete title of the work into English as *A Fuller Course in the Art of Logic Conformed to the Method of Peter Ramus* and can use as the short title simply Milton's *Logic* or the *Logic*.

The *Logic* was first published in 1672, when Milton was sixty-four years old and had only two more years to live. When it was written we do not know for sure, but we can be virtually certain that it was a much earlier composition. Ramist logic, as will be seen, was well known at Saint Paul's School when Milton was a pupil there and was a live concern at Christ's College when Milton was at Christ's in 1625–32. By 1672 it was losing its grip everywhere it had flourished. Various times have been proposed for the composition of the *Logic,* all of them reviewed and expertly reevaluated by the late Professor William Riley Parker and more recently by Dr. Francine Lusignan [1]: (1) Milton's postbaccalaureate

---

[1] Parker, *Milton,* pp. 259, 325, 468, 612, 621–22, 862, 905, 938, 1139, etc. Francine Lusignan, "L'*Artis Logicæ Plenior Institutio* de John Milton: État de la Question et Position" (Ph.D. diss., University of Montreal 1974), pp. 37–136. Mme. Lusignan's work is thoroughgoing and definitive.

years at Cambridge University, 1629–32; (2) the years 1640–47, when he was teaching first his nephews, Edward and John Phillips, and later a few other boys; (3) more precisely, the spring and summer of 1648, when it is hard to point with certainty to anything else he was doing; (4) the period after the Restoration (at least for "finishing" the work).[2]

Professor Parker favored early in 1648, though "with no great confidence," remarking that the years 1640–44 were a particularly "busy period of teaching." [3] Parker himself, however, notes that Milton's greatest motivation for producing a logic textbook would have been when he was organizing the subject in his own mind in order to teach it—many, and perhaps most, logic and other elementary textbooks were and still are produced under such motivation. This would suggest that the work was got up earlier than 1648, for around August 1647 Milton had given up his large house in Barbican [4] for a much smaller one in High Holborn and had apparently discontinued his teaching. Had he been teaching in 1648, if the Phillips boys began their schooling in 1640, one could argue in favor of the date on the grounds that Milton's own curriculum plans, as seen in his treatise *Of Education* (1644) and elsewhere, call for logic in the seventh or eighth year of schooling. Milton's actual practice, as Parker notes, did often substantiate his expressed ideas on the curriculum, but we cannot at all be sure that it did so in every detail. To Parker's considerations Mme. Lusignan has added others, largely based on her computer-assisted studies of the frequency in Milton's prose works of the terms "logic" and "dialectic" and their cognates. Her results favor the years 1641–47 and, within this period, most probably 1645–47 as dates for Milton's composition of his *Logic*. The 1645–47 dating, it might be added, would accord fairly well with Milton's curriculum plans for his pupils.

In any event, the *Logic* fits in with Milton's procedures and with some other textbooks he was using in teaching the Phillips boys and his other pupils. Parker notes Milton's programmatic use of "method" in curriculum design. Although Parker does not specify further, this method was unmistakably Ramist. For example, the order meteorology, mineralogy, botany, biology, anatomy, which Parker identifies as that of the Great Chain of Being,[5] is even more

---

[2] Parker, *Milton,* p. 1139.
[3] Ibid., pp. 325, 938, n. 67; cf. 852, n. 64.
[4] Ibid., p. 312.
[5] Ibid., p. 209.

immediately that of Ramist method, proceeding from the more general (wider forces of nature) to the more specific (animal life). In individual subjects Milton was employing several textbooks "methodized" along Ramist lines: for example, the *Elementa Arithmeticæ Logicis Legibus Deducta* (Basel, 1579) by Christianus Urstitius and the *Quæstiones Geometricæ* (Frankfurt, 1600, 1612, etc.) by Petrus Ryff, whom Professor Parker mentions but without noting that these authors were from the Ramist milieu.[6] Milton certainly knew Ramist logic from his days at Cambridge, but this specific advocacy of Ramist method and methodized textbooks in the 1640–48 period favors the view that at this time he may well have been working hard with Ramist logic, where method is given its classic treatment. Leo Miller calls attention to a high incidence of Ramist terminology in Milton's *Tetrachordon*, which appeared in 1645. Rolf Dahlø argues that because Milton's treatment of *definitio* in *Tetrachordon* varies from his treatment of *definitio* in the *Logic*, the *Logic* belongs to an earlier period. The variation, however, appears to be basically an *ad hoc* adaptation to a particular subject that does not rule out what the *Logic* has to say.[7]

My own balancing of the evidence in the light of pedagogical practice in the sixteenth and seventeenth centuries inclines me to the view that Milton most likely got up his *Logic* whenever—or just before—he was first teaching it to John and/or Edward Phillips (John stayed with him longer than Edward, it appears)[8] and/or other pupils. It is most unlikely that a routine work of this sort would have been composed except in fairly close association with the teaching of the subject matter. Moreover, Milton's discontinuation of teaching in 1647 could well have cooled for the time being any thought he may have had of publishing what was essentially a schoolbook.

The 1641–47 date would of course not preclude Milton's touching up the manuscript much later, before he gave it to Spencer Hickman for publication in 1672, particularly in the two or three places where asides in the *Logic* may reflect more fully matured theological preoccupations. But references to theology would not have been unmanageable in a course in logic for his pupils even in 1640–48—

---

[6] Ibid., p. 852, nn. 65, 68. See also Walter J. Ong, *Ramus and Talon Inventory* (Cambridge: Harvard University Press, 1958), pp. 528, 532. The fuller title of Ryff's book is *Quæstiones Geometricæ in Euclidis et P. Rami στοιχείωσιν*.

[7] Leo Miller, "Milton Edits Freigius' 'Life of Ramus,' " *Ren&R*, VIII (1972), 112. Rolf Dahlø, "The Date of Milton's *Artis Logicæ* and the Development of the Idea of Definition in Milton's Works," *HLQ*, XLIII (1979), 25–36.

[8] Parker, *Milton*, pp. 304, 391.

however much they may have been contrary to his own pronouncements regarding the proper content of logic[9]—because the pupils would already have studied theology and church history in their sixth year. Milton proposed to cap rather than begin his entire educational program with logic, rhetoric, and poetics in that order.[10]

Major revisions, however, would appear ruled out, as Mme. Lusignan, too, believes, because the technicalities, massive quotations, and cross-references would seem to make visual access to the text imperative for extensive modifications. The question of possible minor revisions remains. It might perhaps be soluble if, as one unsupported and unidentified opinion had it, the manuscript of the *Logic* were somehow still extant.[11] One or two minor features in Milton's abridgment of Freige's "Life of Peter Ramus" suggest that he may have made some slight later revisions but do not at all prove that he did.[12]

II. MILTON'S *LOGIC* IN INTELLECTUAL HISTORY

(A) The Western Heritage.

Milton's *Logic* does not deviate in any significant way from the logic of Ramus on which it explicitly structures itself. To Ramus's treatment, Milton's text adds a few theological asides, but its relevance to the history of logic is the same as that of Ramus's own work. Ramus's logic was hardly a major event in the internal development of logic as a science, for Ramus was not a speculative or a structural innovator. His position in Renaissance logic has been detailed by Risse and, in the overall history of logic, briefly and pointedly by Bocheński and more cursorily by William and Martha Kneale [13] and need not be reviewed here. Ramus belonged

---

[9] Milton, *Logic*, Preface, pp. 210–11 herein.

[10] Parker, *Milton*, pp. 256–57.

[11] "One university professor writes to me that he believes the MS. [of Milton's *Artis Logicæ Plenior Institutio*] is in existence, but gives no reasons to support his belief, for which I can find no particle of evidence." John Walker McCain, Jr., "Milton's *Artis Logicæ*," *N&Q*, CLXIV (1933), 149–50. And that is that.

[12] Miller, "Milton Edits Freigius' 'Ramus,' " p. 113.

[13] Wilhelm Risse, *Die Logik der Neuzeit*, vol. I, *1500–1600* (Stuttgart-Bad Canstatt: Friedrich Frommann Verlag, 1964), pp. 122–200 and passim (see the index); I. M. Bocheński, *A History of Formal Logic*, trans. and ed. Ivo Thomas (Notre Dame, Ind.: University of Notre Dame Press, 1961), pp. 4–5, 232, 254–56, 466, 497–500; William and Martha Kneale, *The Development of Logic* (Oxford: Clarendon Press, 1962), pp. 301–6.

to an age when the massive and original developments of medieval logic had been programmatically set aside and ridiculed by humanists, who were commonly more preoccupied with the human life world than with the formal structures of science. Like most humanist logics, Ramus's is a residual logic,[14] not really a "reform" in any other sense than a random and superficial simplification.

But despite its intrinsic inconsequentiality, Ramist logic is exceedingly important in the psychological and cultural development of mankind because of the way it emerged in the logical tradition of Western culture.[15] Without some familiarity with this logical tradition and with Ramist logic in particular, it is impossible to understand the intellectual and literary milieu of John Milton or his contemporaries or to grasp many of the conscious aims and procedures in Milton's writing, whether prose or poetry, or, for that matter, to know adequately Milton's experience of himself or his feel for the human life world and the physical universe.

Milton lived toward the end of what we may call the age of logic,[16] in a culture that had assumed, quite explicitly for over four hundred years and before that less intently for some fifteen hundred years, that the study of logic was somehow central to liberal education, to each individual man's full realization of his potential as man. The age of logic continued through and beyond the Renaissance until the romantic movement realigned cultural and psychic structures. Logic has an abiding effect on us still—and indeed an intensified effect, for it makes possible our computer culture—but since the romantic and technological revolutions its position in the curriculum and in consciousness has shifted: Logic is taken to be specialized equipment, the possession of some highly theoretical boondogglers and also of some direct users, often im-

---

[14] See Joseph T. Clark, *Conventional Logic and Modern Logic* (Washington, D.C.: American Catholic Philosophical Association, 1952); Bocheński, *History of Formal Logic*, pp. 254–64, 14; E. J. Ashworth, in her study, "Some Notes on Syllogistic in the Sixteenth and Seventeenth Centuries," *NDJFL*, XI (1970), 17–33, applies to Ramus's "reform" the neatly summary term "random simplification."

[15] See Walter J. Ong, *Ramus, Method, and the Decay of Dialogue* (Cambridge: Harvard University Press, 1958); Wilbur Samuel Howell, *Logic and Rhetoric in England, 1500–1700* (Princeton: Princeton University Press, 1956); Walter J. Ong, *Rhetoric, Romance, and Technology* (Ithaca, N.Y.: Cornell University Press, 1971), pp. 1–103.

[16] This paragraph and a few others here have been used almost verbatim in my study, "Logic and the Epic Muse," in John T. Shawcross and Michael Lieb, eds., *Achievements of the Left Hand* (Amherst: University of Massachusetts Press, 1974), pp. 240–41.

portant and powerful users, particularly if they work at decision making with the support of computers. But these groups are relatively few in numbers. Logic is their special concern; it is not part of the knowledge of every well-educated man. For the well-educated man in Milton's day, logic was essential—more so than, for example, arithmetic or English grammar or geography.

To understand in any but the most superficial sense what logic meant to Milton and his contemporaries, we must ask ourselves why there was an age of logic at all. Few histories of culture even raise this question. Logic has often been thought of as though it had no history outside itself or even no interior history, as though it could have arisen at almost any time, so that its appearance at one time rather than another is simply fortuitous and not worth inquiring about. Philosophers by the score, including Immanuel Kant and others of his stature, have been spectacularly ignorant of the fact that logic has indeed a long and involved history: like many others, Kant actually believed and stated that the development of logic ended with Aristotle.[17] To assess the significance of Milton's logic, we have really not attended to logic as a development in human psychological and cultural history: we rake through Milton's prose and poetry for structures identified in his logic, we assure ourselves that even in poetry he liked quite formal logical control, we assume that this was either more or less a good thing or possibly a bad thing, and we drop the subject there. Questions regarding the larger reasons for the conspicuous preoccupation with logic so manifest in the culture of the time are hardly raised. But such questions are essential for a twentieth-century understanding of Milton.

In the West what we have called the age of logic grew out of the vastly longer preceding age, which we can style the age of rhetoric. The sequence rhetoric-to-logic constitutes a major event or series of events in the evolution of consciousness. In the perspectives traced by Erich Neumann,[18] who does not, however, treat of this

---

[17] See Bocheński, *History of Formal Logic,* p. 6, where Kant's statement is quoted, and pp. 6–9. Bocheński, whose work is invaluable in its aims and achievement, is single-minded in the pursuit of his objective, the history of *formal* logic, and treats the interior history of logic with total disregard of the cultural and psychological history in which logic comes into being. There is every justification for this procedure, but it of course calls for supplementation.

[18] Erich Neumann, *The Origins and History of Consciousness,* with a foreword by C. G. Jung, trans. R. F. C. Hull (New York: Pantheon Books, 1954). Neumann cites abundantly other historians of culture. See also Ong, *Rhetoric, Romance, and Technology,* chap. 1, "Rhetoric and the Origins of Consciousness."

rhetoric-to-logic sequence as such, the development of logic and particularly the maximizing of the subject in the European Middle Ages can be made out to be one of the major manifestations of the continuous process through which "the conscious system has absorbed more and more unconscious contents and progressively extended its frontiers." [19]

Formal logic had been developed by the ancient Greeks out of reflection on discussion or dispute.[20] Discussion and dispute and the persuasive oratory that is their forensic manifestation have roots too far back in prehistory ever to be fully charted. In one form or another they are seemingly as old as man himself. By the time of the Sophists in Greece, however, the kind of intellectual and verbal operations that went into these activities, particularly oratory, were codified to some degree in an "art" of rhetoric. As an art, or sequential set of reflective principles describing and prescribing for rhetorical performance, rhetoric was the product of writing, for purely oral modes of thought cannot produce lengthy, linear, or analytic schemata,[21] such as even the simplest textbook. Gilbert Durand has pointed out in his brilliant psychocultural study, *Les Structures Anthropologiques de l'Imaginaire,* how rhetoric is intermediary between the unreflective use of symbols and the formalism of logic.[22] It grows out of the preconceptual by antithesis. Ancient Greek culture knew a high development of rhetoric by the time of the Sophists, who were at their first apogee just before Plato. This rhetoric encouraged reflective discussion of the relationship of competing propositions in oratory and other argumentation. How far does what I say refute what you say? And why? Out of such discussion formal logic grew.

Formal logic blossomed suddenly. Historians of logic can state quite simply that Aristotle "was the first formal logician," who was not bragging but simply reporting fact when he said of his *Topics* and *De Sophisticis Elenchis* that although other works of his had antecedents, "this inquiry" did not, for in its field before it "nothing existed at all." [23]

[19] Neumann, *Origins and History of Consciousness,* p. xviii.

[20] Bocheński, *History of Formal Logic,* pp. 10–18, 26–39 (esp. 31–39), 417.

[21] See Walter J. Ong, *The Presence of the Word* (New Haven and London: Yale University Press, 1967), pp. 28–31.

[22] Gilbert Durand, *Les Structures Anthropologiques de l'Imaginaire* (Paris: Presses universitaires de France, 1960), pp. 541–59.

[23] Bochenski, *History of Formal Logic,* pp. 40, 29, where the relevant texts from Aristotle are also given.

It has been pointed out that formal logic shows no evenly continuous evolution but that its history develops in a broken line: A
century of rapid development is followed by a decline, and when
new beginnings are made after some centuries, often the search
begins anew, the older achievements having been lost except for
a few fragments.[24] Nevertheless, if we look at the history of logic
in the very long perspectives of the total history of mankind, we
can readily discern an overall pattern of growth and increment.

After it was developed for the first time in the history of mankind
among the ancient Greeks, beginning, as we have seen, with
Aristotle (384?–322 B.C.), formal logic languished, particularly after Boethius (A.D. 480?–524?). The scholastic philosophers revived
it in the twelfth century and starting in the latter half of the same
century constructed a new logic unknown to antiquity, formulated
metalogically with an extremely sophisticated semiotics (Latin
based, of course).[25] Many of the developments of this medieval
scholastic logic, unexamined by anyone since the early 1500s, still
remain to be explored by modern scholars. Historically this logic
is of incalculable psychological and cultural importance. Scholastic
logic, with the scholastic philosophy accompanying it, is inseparable from the development of the medieval universities and thus
ultimately not only of Milton's Cambridge but also of all the universities of today which, without exception throughout the world,
trace essentially if not in detail to the universities of medieval
Europe. This itself shows something about the way consciousness
"rises" and, once risen, spreads itself.

The drives toward quantification of all sorts that formal logic
fosters grow stronger and stronger through the Middle Ages and
with the advent of print result in some of the characteristic "simplifications" of logic promoted by Peter Ramus, turning largely on
the use of diagrams or of thought patterns readily assimilable to
diagrams.[26] The Renaissance marks a temporary regression in the
interior development of logic but by no means the total disappearance of interest in the subject, for the medieval curricular
emphasis that had made logic central to the entire educational
enterprise continues through the Renaissance, to a great extent
unimpaired. Despite humanist antipathy to logical formalism, logic
in a residual and scientifically uneventful form remains with very

[24] Ibid., p. 12.
[25] Ibid., pp. 12–13 ff.
[26] See Ong, *Ramus, Method, and Decay of Dialogue,* pp. 306–18 and passim;
Frances Yates, *The Art of Memory* (Chicago: University of Chicago Press, 1966),
pp. 231–42 and passim.

few exceptions absolutely integral to the curriculum. The Renaissance expresses its continuing adherence to logic by producing the
first histories of formal logic, the earliest of them by Peter Ramus
and the second by a "systematic" certainly known to Milton,
Bartholomæus Keckermann (Keckermannus), 1571–1608.[27] They
were not very good histories, but they showed that even at the
center of humanism logic could not be ruled out of the intellectual
tradition. Indeed, humanist rhetoric, which was calculated to dis-
lodge logic, in some ways preserved it: compared to rhetoric as
this subject is taught today, humanist rhetoric is quite close to
formal logic in its vaunting of formal structures in thought and
communication.[28]

Modern logic, or "mathematical logic" (also called "symbolic
logic" and "logistic"), which has its indecisive beginnings more or
less with Leibnitz (1646–1716) but takes its effective rise from the
work of George Boole starting in 1847, branched out first from the
object-language of ancient logic supplemented with its own rich
use of variables but only after 1930 picked up again the medieval
interest in semantics that the humanists generally had discarded.[29]

This account covers in distressingly brief summary the development of logic in the West. The Indian variety of logic, the only
other formal logic besides the Western variety ever to appear,
shows the same initial relationship to rhetoric as does logic in the
West in that the Indian logic, too, grew out of examination of the
methodology of discussion. In India formal logic as such comes
into being some five centuries later than in Greece, in the first
century after Christ. Although it would be hard to show that it
rose in complete independence of Greek influence, this Indian formal logic may have been an independent development.[30] It has its
own modest but perhaps novel achievements, but it needs no more
than to be noted here, as it has no influence on the tradition af-
fecting Milton.

Seen in the long view, Western culture is characterized by a
gradual and somewhat intermittent but ultimately irresistible intensification of the logical component of the intellectual heritage.
Despite the fact that we no longer live in what has here been styled
the age of logic, the intensification of logic has reached its peak in
our time with continued development of formal logic and, for the

[27] Bocheński, *History of Formal Logic,* p. 4.
[28] See Ong, *Rhetoric, Romance, and Technology,* chap. 3, "Tudor Writings on
Rhetoric, Poetic, and Literary Theory," esp. pp. 48–58.
[29] Bocheński, *History of Formal Logic,* pp. 267–70 ff.
[30] Ibid., pp. 416–17, 430–40.

first time, the beginnings of a comprehensive understanding of the entire formal logic heritage. These perspectives have been sketched in some detail here because they are absolutely needed for a decent understanding of Milton's *Logic* and because this *Logic* has never been set before in anything like full historical perspective.

(B) Logic and Rhetoric before Ramus.

Throughout its development formal logic often distracted from the art of rhetoric, which had codified the less formalized operations of discussion and oratory, and at times logic even apparently threatened to overwhelm rhetoric. But in fact formal logic never drove rhetoric out of existence or even seriously impaired it. From antiquity through Milton's age and beyond, rhetoric, understood as the art of persuasion, continued to be studied alongside logic, understood as the study of the formal structures of thought. Indeed, on the whole rhetoric remained the more pervasive of the two long-interrelated disciplines in its effect on the curriculum, on intellectual development, and on culture generally. In antiquity the philosophy of Socrates, Plato, and Aristotle, and of the Stoics and other schools, despite its intrinsic merit and long-range effect, played a relatively minor role in a culture that remained fundamentally rhetorical, committed on the whole much more to oratory than to abstract philosophic investigation.[31] In the Middle Ages, when logic was far more widely studied than it was in classical antiquity, rhetoric still played a major intellectual role,[32] and, as we have just seen, in the Renaissance humanists saw the strengthening of rhetoric as a crucial objective in their program and indeed their world view.[33]

A formal logic concerns itself with logical theorems, that is, with utterances in which if something is posited something else follows. It thus has to do with what we may call the structure of thought and is of itself completely dispassionate or, in this sense, "objective." However, such an art or science does not come into existence fully conscious of its aims and possibilities but is worked up ar-

[31] Henri-Irénée Marrou, *A History of Education in Antiquity,* trans. George Lamb (New York: Sheed and Ward, 1956), pp. 194–205.

[32] See Richard McKeon, "Rhetoric in the Middle Ages," *Speculum,* XVII (1942), 1–32.

[33] See Jerrold E. Seigel, *Rhetoric and Philosophy in Renaissance Humanism* (Princeton: Princeton University Press, 1968), esp. pp. 137–39 (on Lorenzo Valla, a most outspoken proponent of rhetoric as a subject touching human decision making and action and a most downright scorner of philosophy, including logic, as unrelated to real existence).

duously out of vague and ill-understood antecedents over many generations and centuries and millennia.

We have noted earlier that formal logic grew out of reflection on the methodology of discussion and dispute. In effect, this means that it grew out of an economy of knowledge that can be characterized as dominantly rhetorical, where all thought and communication is much involved with the human life world, with persons and personalities, and with commitment on issues, many of them practical and emotional rather than theoretical. It has been the business of formal logic, as it has been of all sciences, to disengage issues that can be articulated in dispassionate terms from what we may call enthymematic issues, issues that are not dispassionate. Aristotle had defined an enthymeme as the rhetorical equivalent of the logical syllogism,[34] meaning by an enthymeme not what the term has commonly meant since Boethius (a syllogism, one premise of which is not expressed but understood: All men are mortal, therefore Peter is mortal) but a reasoning process that proceeds from probable premises to a probable conclusion. Rhetoric is deliberative, says Aristotle, and "about certainties no one deliberates." [35] (We should probably send soldiers against anyone invading our land. Our former allies are seemingly invading our land. Therefore we should probably send soldiers against our former allies.) In an enthymeme the reasons for the conclusion and the action that follows are not all articulated or even necessarily articulable but are grounded elsewhere, "in the feelings or heart" (*en*, in; *thymos*, feelings, heart—today, we might say in the subconscious). Rhetoric aims not merely at establishing a truth or at showing how one articulated truth follows from another but at persuasion, at eliciting action, although it of course wants this action aligned with articulated truth as far as possible. But most often we have to act with less than total articulate command of every issue involved: we cannot program every decision in life on a computer and indeed probably cannot program even one of them totally. It was from this economy of "reasoning" on half-articulated, half-inarticulated grounds that formal logic had to be disengaged.

Individual logicians have been relatively successful in detaching logic from its original rhetorical bedding, but if we look at the overall history of logic and the milieux in which it flourished, we see that the detachment has never been complete. For one thing, in the mainstream of the pedagogical tradition, formal logic was

[34] *Rhetoric* i.2 (1356b–1357a); cf. i.1 (1355a).
[35] *Rhetoric* i.2 (1357a).

from antiquity until romanticism or beyond commonly taught in more or less close association with the art of rhetoric as one of the *artes sermocinales* or arts of expression that constituted the trivium, grammar, rhetoric, and logic (sometimes the order of the last two was reversed). Secondly, despite its formal base, logic tended to be defined before the age of print in terms of communication between persons, as Ramus defined it, following Cicero: it was *ars disserendi,* the art of discourse. The definition of logic as the art of thinking, with the implication that thinking was independent of discourse, became a favorite only after print had had its effect.[36]

The posttypographic desocialization of logic suggests some perspectives for Milton's own work. Milton's shift from the original Ramist definition, "art of discourse" (*ars bene disserendi*), to the later favorite, "art of reasoning well" (*ars bene ratiocinandi*),[37] situates him farther out than Ramus had been along the trajectory moving logic from an art of communication to an art of presumably solipsistic thought. Thirdly, in the mainstream of pedagogical tradition again, logic had often been more or less equated with dialectic, as it is in both Ramus and Milton, although with many careful thinkers dialectic was taken to be a study concerned not with the totally "necessary" connections treated in formal logic but with what is the more probable, as in a debate: Dialectic lay between the somewhat weaker probabilities of rhetoric and the inevitabilities of formal logic.[38]

In the main current of teaching as this flowed into the Renaissance on the continent and later in the British Isles, rhetoric and logic appeared to overlap one another also in the way they were theoretically organized and taught. The pattern inherited from Cicero and widely adopted by Renaissance humanists presented rhetoric as made up of five "parts," which Cicero had suggested might well be called separate arts [39] and which were in fact present in the pedagogical heritage because they more or less corresponded to stages in liberal education (that is, education for public speaking, education of the orator) among the ancient Greeks and Romans.[40] Because these arts were commonly taught in Latin and there were

---

[36] Ong, *Ramus, Method, and Decay of Dialogue,* pp. 178–80; Ong, *Presence of the Word,* pp. 59–63, 293, etc.

[37] Milton, *Logic,* pp. 217–18 below.

[38] Ong, *Ramus, Method, and Decay of Dialogue,* pp. 215–17; Ong, "The Province of Rhetoric and Poetic," in Joseph Schwartz and John A. Rycenga, eds., *The Province of Rhetoric* (New York: Ronald Press, 1965), pp. 48–56.

[39] Cicero, *Brutus* vi.25; see Howell, *Logic and Rhetoric,* pp. 66 ff.

[40] Marrou, *Education in Antiquity,* pp. 197–200.

no established English terms for the concepts they used, the Latin terms are indicated here to make their English equivalents specific. The five parts were: (1) invention (*inventio*), or the discovery of "arguments" to prove what one wished to prove (in the disputatious climate of the ancient oral cultures, communication was commonly taken to consist paradigmatically not in simple assertion but in assertion-against-opposition—more will be said shortly about the reasons for this disputatiousness); (2) disposition or arrangement (*dispositio*), sometimes called also "judgment" (*iudicium*), of the material one had discovered; (3) style (*elocutio*), or the investing of "naked reasons" with variously effective trappings such as metaphor, synecdoche, or other devices; (4) memory (*memoria*), or mnemonic control of the entire speech for oral presentation (which normally did not at all mean verbatim memorization but mnemonic control of the parts of the oration and of one's themes and formulas); and finally (5) delivery itself (*pronuntiatio*) on the orator's platform.

These last two parts of rhetoric make it clear that the art of rhetoric in principle concerned oral, not written, communication. Although rhetoric as a scientifically organized "art" could come into existence only with script, its roots and its concerns are those of the older preliterate culture. Indeed, even in Milton's day the old oral culture remained so assertive that in teaching verbal expression the oration was still commonly taken as the paradigm of all utterance, even epistolary correspondence. Few had yet explicitly recognized the problem of adjusting this originally oral art to composition in writing.

In the pedagogical tradition where rhetoric was commonly assigned its five parts, dialectic or logic was commonly thought of as consisting of two "parts," which in a general way matched the first two parts of rhetoric: (1) invention (*inventio*) or discovery and (2) judgment (*judicium*). The coincidence of these two parts with the first two parts of rhetoric was due to some degree to the fact that logic had grown out of rhetoric and to some degree to the fact that, once separated, however ineffectively from a theoretical point of view, each of the two arts tended to develop its own interior structure and theory independently of the other. Few teachers of rhetoric or logic could adequately explain and none could totally explain how the two parts of dialectic or logic and the first two parts of rhetoric contrasted or overlapped or coincided.

(C) Logic and Rhetoric in Ramist Theory.

By 1543 Ramus decided to remove all this confusion. The essence of the Ramist reform was to separate logic (or, synonymously, dialectic) from rhetoric absolutely as an art (that is, in theoretical presentation—Ramus insisted that logic and rhetoric were joined in practice or "use," in the sense that in composing a given bit of discourse one relied simultaneously on logic and rhetoric, as well as on grammar). Excised from the art of rhetoric, invention and judgment were to belong to logic alone. Style and delivery belonged to rhetoric alone. Memory was dropped as a separate part: Ramus assigns it to dialectic or logic,[41] but since he allowed this art, as every other art, only two parts,[42] memory is assimilated to the second of these parts, judgment or disposition. The alleged reason for thus doing away with memory as a separate part was that if one observed the "order of nature" (in actuality, this meant the order in which a subject was presented in accord with Ramist "method") things followed one another in the mind readily and correctly without demanding any effort specifically for memorization—memory was automatic.[43]

The real but unacknowledged (and probably unnoticed) reasons for dropping memory were somewhat different: (1) the entire Ramist arrangement of an art was itself an elaborate structure designed to implement recall; [44] and (2) there remained in Ramus's day little pedagogical need for exhaustively cultivated memory because of the developments in means for storing and retrieving knowledge extramentally. First, the buildup in the use of written materials that had marked the Middle Ages, as against a less chirographic, more highly oral classical antiquity, continued through the Renaissance, so that educators were, mostly unwittingly, training far less for oratory and far more for writing than their counterparts had done in classical antiquity. Secondly, print had made spatial organization and retrieval of knowledge far more effective than was possible even in the preceding manuscript culture. With several thousands of copies of a text presenting everything in exactly the same place on the same page, indexing became a major feature of printed books, particularly in academic and

---

[41] Petrus Ramus, *Scholæ Rhetoricæ*, Lib. III, in *Scholæ in Liberales Artes*, ed. Walter J. Ong (1569; facs. rpt., Hildesheim and New York: Georg Olms Verlag, 1970), col. 254 ff.

[42] Ibid., Lib. II, cap. viii, in *Scholæ in Liberales Artes*, cols. 53–66.

[43] Petrus Ramus, *Dialecticæ Institutiones* (Paris: Iacobus Bogardus, 1543; PML), fols. 54–56: here Ramus works out a "dialectical analysis" of Penelope's complaint in Ovid, explaining that this is the best possible method to enable the schoolboy to memorize Ovid's lines. See Ong, *Ramus, Method, and Decay of Dialogue*, p. 194 (cf. pp. 195, 208, etc.), and Yates, *Art of Memory*, pp. 231–42.

[44] Ong, *Ramus, Method, and Decay of Dialogue*, p. 280; Yates, *Art of Memory*, pp. 231–42.

technical fields. Indexing had been impracticable on any large scale in a manuscript culture because two manuscripts of the same work seldom if ever match page for page, so that each would require a separate index. Ramus's organization of knowledge is geometrical, in terms of dichotomized charts: Milton's *Logic* can be plotted in such charts with no effort at all. Modern encylopedias, which begin with Ramism, build on the new print economy of extramentally localized knowledge storage and retrieval.

Ramus was here riding the wave of the future, although, because print had not been fully interiorized in the consciousness, neither he nor his contemporaries were entirely aware of the forces that the foregoing paragraph has tried to indicate and to which the sixteenth century was responding. The next big step in extramentally localized knowledge retrieval would be the computer, but the computer was three centuries away.

It has at times been suggested that at some point between their beginnings in antiquity and Ramus's reform, rhetoric and logic had become "confused" with one another.[45] In fact, as we now know, they had never been unconfused; they had come into existence rooted in the same ground and had never had their roots effectively disentangled. Ramus managed to disentangle them only at the cost of construing rhetoric as an art of pure ornamentation calculated to add beauties to the naked reasons of logic and thus always liable to charges of meretriciousness. Treating rhetoric as an art of ornamentation was not at all new; Alcuin, for example, had so treated it in his *Book on Schemes and Tropes (Liber de Schematibus et Tropis)*, and so had many others. But doing so with an eye to keeping logic and rhetoric totally distinct as arts shows a particular Ramist emphasis.

In definitively separating logic and rhetoric, if Ramus incapacitated or discredited rhetoric, in theory he exalted formal logic to a height virtually unknown before. For he insisted that there was only one logic, that is, the "art" of logic or formal logic as he taught it, which supplanted all the probable logics projected by earlier philosophers. This logic was founded on and formulated out of the "natural logic" that governed all acceptable mental processes. The one and only logic ruled in imperious supremacy, solitary and uncontested, over all thinking, from formal science to poetry, and

---

[45] See Norman E. Nelson, *Peter Ramus and the Confusion of Logic, Rhetoric, and Poetry,* UMCMP, no. 2 (Ann Arbor: University of Michigan Press, 1947). Quite rightly, Professor Nelson warns against ascribing too much inner consistency to Ramus's thought on this subject.

over the most practical decision making. Other implications of the Ramist view of logic will be discussed below.

Ramus's distinction between the two arts, however admirable its aim, was insecure not only because it laid rhetoric open to the charge of meretriciousness but, more profoundly, because it was based on ukase prompted by impatience and pedagogical convenience rather than on any profound insight into the nature of thought and expression. Separating logic and rhetoric in pure theory might not work; no matter, they must be separated for better teaching. No one in Ramus's age could as yet explain historically the "confusion" he undertook to right, but many before him and in his own day, including his adversaries Antonio de Gouveia, Jean Riolan, and Jacques Charpentier, had more penetrating insights than his into the complex and indeed mysterious relationship of rhetoric and logic.[46] Ramus largely neglects such insights and, to account for the mixed-up state of affairs he met with before his reform, in his *Aristotelicæ Animadversiones,* his *Scholæ Rhetoricæ,* his *Scholæ Dialecticæ,* and elsewhere, postulates either a widespread and enduring delinquency or a deliberate malice on the parts of students and teachers of these and other arts (all of which should be governed by logic, he maintains). Aristotle, or at least "the Aristotelians," were intellectual reprobates, and that was why thinking had become so complicated and learning so arduous.

(D) Logic, Rhetoric, and the Polemic Style of Life.

Ramus's suggestion that true understanding even of formal logic had been blocked or derailed because of some kind of moral turpitude was of course not original and has its own historical roots. Formal logic, as we have seen, grew out of reflection on the methodology of discussion and dispute, which is to say, out of a more or less polemic setting. Whatever the success of logic in achieving neutral formalization, its practitioners have always kept alive a strong sense of this polemic setting, in which, in the nature of things, the conviction that the adversary is mistaken in his opinions can shift to a persuasion that he is perversely evil, or at least guilty of malfeasance.

Moreover, the polemic operations out of which logic had grown remained central to virtually all activity in Ramus's and Milton's academic world. Indeed, they constituted the academic world. From as far back as we can go in classical antiquity until, roughly, the age of romanticism, all formal academic training was de-

[46] See Ong, *Ramus, Method, and Decay of Dialogue,* pp. 214–24.

signedly polemic. The one exception might be the study of language itself (which meant, in effect, Latin and in the better Renaissance schools some study of Greek). But even here the polemic spirit was high, and grammarians were in fact, if not in professed intent, often the most quarrelsome of scholars.[47] Elsewhere polemic was not merely present but also consciously and conspicuously planned. From the faculty of arts (mostly logic and physics or natural philosophy, with some metaphysics and ethics) through law, theology, and medicine in its speculative and to some degree in its practical aspects,[48] one was trained not in "objectivity"—though individuals might well achieve this—but always in either taking a stand and defending it or in attacking the stand another took. Disputation ruled all. There were no objective tests and indeed nothing even so objective as written examinations or papers. One proved one's mastery of a subject by opting for certain positions (theses) and defending them orally in the disputations that were structured all through academic life and that linger today, in their last, moribund stage, in the "defense" of doctoral dissertations.

The institutionalized polemic climate of academic life from as far back as we can go in antiquity to romanticism must be understood if the impact of logic on Milton's world is to be grasped. The adversary procedures suggested by Milton's announced purpose in his greatest epic, "to justifie the ways of God to men," reflect the polemic educational heritage, as does much else in *Paradise Lost,* as for example the heading "The Argument" that labels the prose summary prefixed by Milton to each book. "Argument" had been partly neutralized and had come to mean something like what we mean by "summary" today, but not quite, for it was never entirely divested of its original polemic overtones. In his poem Milton intended to prove something and to show that others were wrong. All speech, poetry included, was assumed to be probatory or disprobatory unless there were positive indications to the contrary—as there almost never were. Indeed, following Ramus (and many others), Milton can discern "proof" and "refutation" in passages that to the twentieth-century mind appear patently nonpolemic

[47] See Richard Foster Jones, *The Triumph of the English Language* (Stanford, Calif.: Stanford University Press, 1953), passim, for the countless quarrels generated around the study of language in the sixteenth and seventeenth centuries.

[48] See Hastings Rashdall, *The Universities of Europe in the Middle Ages,* new ed. by F. M. Powicke and A. B. Emden (Oxford: Clarendon Press, 1936), I, 436–37; for a particular example of the polemic thesis method in medical education, see Dean Putnam Lockwood, *Ugo Benzi: Medieval Philospher and Physician, 1376–1439* (Chicago: University of Chicago Press, 1951), passim.

utterances of fact or fancy. Thus, for example, in Book I, chapter xx, of the *Logic,* p. 279 below, Milton cites a line from Ovid's *Tristia* iii, "You are more fierce than the harsh Busiris," as providing an "argument" offering "proof": "Here the lesser ferocity of Busiris argues the greater ferocity of the person against whom the poet inveighs." Hundreds of such examples are to be found in the *Logic*.

Like all Ramist logic and that part of Aristotelian logic that connects with dialectic or debate, Milton's logic is basically geared to invention, teaching ways of locating arguments proving or disproving something, that is, it is ordered to achieving preconceived aims rather than to descriptively dispassionate theory, and in this sense is a rhetorical logic. The theory is there in webby abundance but encrusted with polemic. In Book II, chapter x, p. 358 below, for example, Milton's *Logic* presents the structure of the syllogism in terms of how to move to a desired conclusion: One starts with the conclusion (or "question"), and "logic" thereupon consists in searching for an argument to warrant linking the subject and predicate terms, or to warrant dissociating them if what one needs is a negative answer. Ramist logic of course moves beyond the part strictly called invention to its second part, disposition or judgment, but its practically programmatic nature shows in this second part also, for one "disposes" or arranges arguments with deliberate goals in mind. One goes to this logic not merely to discern and describe noetic structures but to get somewhere.

The polemic climate of this academic world might be labeled "existentialist" or "activist" in the sense that it constituted ultimately a context for action rather than a framework for pure speculation. In an age when the written examination had apparently not yet even been thought of as a possibility, the practice of testing mastery of a subject by oral dispute, pro and con, thrust the most abstruse speculation into active confrontation with living and present adversaries. This is the climate in which Milton's logic, like the logics before it and like Marxist dialectic since, came into existence. Logical theory had never risen completely clear of its origins in real discussion and dispute. You knew you were right largely because no one could prove you were wrong.

Thus, even though logic is formally conceived as moving toward objectivity and, in our age, into the utterly dispassionate structures of the computer, in fact the art stood in Milton's day not simply for structure but also for struggle. The state of affairs reveals the kind of paradox that always governs human operations at their depths, where the "objective" or impersonally formal demands of logic by their very nature generate contentiousness. For human knowledge necessarily has always its dark as well as its light side, and the demands made by formal logic to translate everything into the explicit, the "light" side of knowing, to the total suppression of the "dark" or unconscious side, push the I-and-the-world antithesis to its extreme limits (the object world in effect smothers the ego), imposing on the psyche strains that result in feelings of extreme hostility and hence in quarrelsomeness.[49] The humanists' quarrel with scholastic logicians for being so quarrelsome as well as our persistent folkloric images of sharp-tongued or tyrannical logicians remind us, if the endless Ramist disputes did not, of the threat of hostile passion that has haunted the objectivities of logic from its beginnings in ancient Greeks' reflections on disputation through Abelard's *Sic et Non,* the scurrilities of Renaissance devotees of logic, and on down to the present.

To see Milton's logic in its full setting within what we have styled the age of logic, we should also note the psychological realities of this polemic world and their connections with the still larger movements in culture marking the gradual growth of human consciousness. The polemic world of academia, populated from the beginning exclusively by males (with totally negligible exceptions), operated in fact as the intellectualized phase of the larger world of male ritual combat, which is not restricted to the human species but rules the animal kingdom and, as Charles Darwin already knew, so largely sets the patterns in animal evolution.[50] Ritual or ceremonial combat between males of the same species throughout the animal kingdom has been the object of many biological and anthropological studies today, particularly in connection with the territoriality of individuals and breeding groups. Such fighting is normally never lethal, being immediately terminable by specific signals on the part of the vanquished. But it is serious and normally preserves and improves the species. The academic contests powered by logic (and its correlatives dialectic—insofar as this was kept distinct from formal logic—and rhetoric) followed the same pattern: They showed who was the more competent man and developed both individual intellectual prowess and knowledge itself.

Academic polemic, as long as it lasted in full form, was always between males: To all intents and purposes education by thesis and disputation is coextensive with all-male schools and vanishes

[49] Durand, *Les Structures Anthropologiques de l'Imaginaire,* pp. 191–99, 453 ff.

[50] See Walter J. Ong, *Fighting for Life: Contest, Sexuality, and Consciousness* (Ithaca and London: Cornell University Press, 1981).

with coeducation.[51] In the West, from antiquity until its demise with romanticism, academic jousting was conducted always in Latin, which from about A.D. 500 or 600 was constituted an all-male tribal language, learned outside the family in all-male institutions from all-male teachers normally with regular physical punishment in such a way that Latin language study can be recognized as a puberty rite, a *rite de passage,* featuring physical and mental hardships and marking off those who had undergone it from all other members of society.[52] With coeducation, both institutionalized physical punishment and the use of Latin as a medium of instruction quite promptly disappear. Simultaneously there disappears the orality that characterized all academic education from antiquity to the romantic age and that had been connected with the ascendency of rhetoric and dialectic (in the sense of formalized debate) together with logic as combatic oral arts. By the romantic age, testing had been effectively oriented toward writing. These seemingly disconnected changes—disappearance of institutionalized ceremonial contest (involving substitution of writing for combative oral debate as a test of learning), the phasing out of Latin as a medium of thought and instruction, the suppression of physical punishment, and the development of coeducation—appear historically to be so closely associated as to be de facto correlatives, and they mark the limits, on our side, of the life world that gave rise to Milton's *Logic.*

The decisively male cast of this intellectual world where the age of logic took form helps situate the age in terms of the shifts in male-female polarities that help pattern cultural and psychic evolution. The ascent of logic is part of the ascent of masculinity characteristic of the point in Western cultural development when the "ego consciousness has achieved independence" and the "total personality has detached itself from the natural context of the surrounding world and the unconscious."[53] With logic, in other words, a decisive stage in "objectivity" is reached. Logic treats human thought not in its full human framework but as a structure, a "thing." The world, the "way *things* are," is set off decisively from the human life world and its interpersonal, subjective reactions: Although these latter may not be denied, they are sharply distinguished from something other than themselves, something

[51] See Ong, *Presence of the Word,* pp. 192–255, *Rhetoric, Romance, and Technology,* pp. 113–41, 268–69, 280, and "Communications Media and the State of Theology," *Cross Currents,* XIX (1969), 462–80.

[52] Ong, *Rhetoric, Romance, and Technology,* pp. 113–41.

[53] Neumann, *Origins and History of Consciousness,* p. 131.

irrefragable, obdurate, fixed, unsusceptible to persuasion or to any other typically rhetorical action.

The relationship of logic to the ascent of masculinity is also indispensible for a fuller understanding of the *Artis Logicæ Plenior Institutio* in the consciousness of the man who wrote *Paradise Lost*. For the same ascent of masculinity that is marked by the age of logic is marked, although not quite synchronously, by the cult of the hero. Like the cult of logic, the cult of the hero has remote beginnings in antiquity, and after its climacteric perdures for centuries in more and more attenuated forms: The warring heroes of ancient and medieval romances are incontestably viable and credible, but by the time of Milton's *Paradise Lost* heroes are in trouble, as later disputes regarding the identification of Milton's hero clearly show. By the eighteenth century, epic heroes will have been reduced to mock heroes in mock epics. At the onset of the new wave of femininity that marks the romantic movement, the once glorious military hero shows morbid symptoms, which Byron both satirizes and aggravates. Eventually, in *Fear and Trembling,* Kierkegaard will find himself sufficiently distanced from the heroic myths to achieve the insight that the Christian message is incompatible with the typical heroic mold, which it transcends—thus, by implication, suggesting the deepest reasons for Milton's problem with his great epic. And in our day the old-style hero remains for the most part only as refracted in the antiheroes of works typified by those of Samuel Beckett.

The cult of logic and the cult of the hero work partly with and partly against one another. In its drive toward masculine "objectivity," logic tends to program the sensibility away from the world of narrative and myth that is the hero's natural, and virtually only, habitat. But as a masculine symbol the hero appeals to the deep drives powering the age of logic. Indeed, heroes arise, before and during Milton's time, in the academic world itself, as an academic mythology squares off giants against one another, each with his group of adherents—the typical product of male bonding patterns, the fighting team, the *comitatus,* the "gang": These are the Thomists and Scotists and Ockhamists and Ramists and Aristotelians and Philippo-Ramists and Systematics. Milton's *Logic* and his *Paradise Lost* and his polemic tracts all grow out of similar agonistic soil.

(E) Ramus's Logic in Fuller Cultural Perspectives.

If what we have styled the age of logic marks a specific stage in the development of consciousness, Ramist logic marks a special moment in the age of logic itself. Ramism was one of several humanist reactions to late medieval logic, and it can be interpreted in terms of our growing knowledge of medieval logic. Far from being "decadent"—whatever that could mean for a formal discipline such as logic or mathematics—late medieval logic was a highly developed and rigorous discipline, which had gone far beyond ancient logic, notably in the development of metalogic (formulas are not exhibited but abstractly described) and of semiotics (the relationship of logic to a particular language structure).[54] Its semiotics had encouraged development of highly philosophical grammars, among other things, such as the *Doctrinale* of Alexander of Villa-dei, composed about 1199 and commented on for over three centuries. The logics and grammars had become so highly developed and academically powerful that they were crowding into the lower ranges of the curriculum, where, instead of being trained for expressing themselves in the Latin in which academic work and thought went on (there was no way adequately to talk about grammar or logic or medicine or law in the vernaculars, which did not have current words for the concepts in play), little boys in their early teens or younger were being made to attempt the most abstruse scientific or philosophical linguistic and logical analysis. A rough parallel would be to imagine an elementary school today where in the fifth through eighth grades all other subjects were laid aside and the pupils were simply trained in mathematics up through calculus and into a bit of topology. This was the situation the humanists decried,[55] and it signaled not a "decadent" logic but quite the opposite: an almighty logic threatening to eat up everything else.

Still, one had to have logic. Following earlier humanists, notably Rudolph Agricola (1444–85), Peter Ramus set out to produce a logic that would meet the ineradicable feeling of the age of logic that logic was an important and all-permeating subject but at the same time would avoid intricacies. Logic without pain. The recipe Ramus hit upon was, inevitably, an agglomerate. Ramus's logic is an amalgam of various ingredients from the logical tradition of the West: Platonic doctrine on ideas, considerably attenuated, Aristotle's logic in snippets, some Ciceronian dialectic and rhetoric, scraps of medieval syllogistic, the medieval drive toward greater and greater quantification of models for thought—all this put to-

[54] Bocheński, *History of Formal Logic,* pp. 152, 148–251.
[55] See Terrence Heath, "Logical Grammar, Grammatical Logic, and Humanism in Three German Universities," *SRen,* XVIII (1971), 9–64.

gether with humanist impatience over elaborated scientific formalism and a real concern for the realities of the human life world, a concern shading in Ramus and others into a concern for the useful and practical.

The drive to simplification was powered not by philosophical insight [56] but by pedagogical practicality, and it was implemented by print, which could foster tight diagrammatic organization of verbalized materials in the dichotomized charts (arduous to duplicate in manuscript but in print as easy to reproduce as straight text) that often appear in Ramist works. For what he sacrificed in scientific logical formality Ramus substituted a forthright neatness, adapted to and supported by the "objectivity" of the printed page. [57] His logic can be made "clear and distinct" to the eye and easy to remember.

(F) Milton's Own Training in Logic.

Ramist logic had begun to attract attention in England by the 1550s and reached its first peak in the 1570s and 1580s, with the major center of interest at Cambridge. [58] In the 1640s when, as has been seen, Milton pretty surely got up his *Logic,* Ramism was still much in evidence at Cambridge and in northwest Europe generally, though it was declining by the time Milton published his *Logic* in 1672. Interest in Ramism was always highest in more or less Calvinist circles, and hence chiefly in northern Europe, not so much because of Ramus's own doctrinal commitments, which tended to be rather Zwinglian, as because of the congeniality Calvinists found in the Ramist bookkeeping approach to philosophy and all learning [59] and in Ramism as a memory system that abolished Ciceronian and medieval mnemonic arrangements of symbolic figures in favor of charts of printed words for storing and retrieving knowledge—the Calvinist preference for an exterior world free of statuary found the Ramist imagination comfortably clean as the result of what has been deftly named "inner iconoclasm." [60]

Ramist logic was thus readily available in the British academic world when Milton entered Saint Paul's School around 1620. And

---

[56] "It seems quite clear that there was no formal basis for his [Ramus's] so-called reforms. His only apparent principle was one of random simplification." Ashworth, "Syllogistic in the Sixteenth and Seventeenth Centuries," pp. 17–33.

[57] Ong, *Ramus, Method, and Decay of Dialogue,* pp. 306–18. Cf. Risse, *Logik der Neuzeit,* vol. 1, *1500–1640,* pp. 122 ff.

[58] Howell, *Logic and Rhetoric,* pp. 173–246.

[59] Ong, *Rhetoric, Romance, and Technology,* pp. 165–89.

[60] Yates, *Art of Memory,* pp. 234–35.

indeed, because of its simplification, it adapted admirably as "petty logic," the elementary version of the subject, which young boys needed early in their schooling, often even before rhetoric, and which they could flesh out later at the university in more advanced logical studies. Ramism, in fact, throughout its history tended to drift into the secondary schools and away from the universities, where it was often scorned.[61] Donald L. Clark and Harris F. Fletcher thus have warrant for conjecturing that Milton was taught something of Ramus's *Dialectica* at Saint Paul's, where Clark suggests also that he may have memorized Talon's Ramist *Rhetorica* or Charles Butler's abridgment of this work.[62] Clark also suggests that Milton's preference for the term *logica* over *dialectica* (see Book I, chapter i, pp. 217–18 below) may reflect some influence of Alexander Gill (or Gil), Sr., high master at Saint Paul's School in Milton's time there and author of *Logonomia Anglica* (which included logic as its second part). Clark points out that Ramus's *Scholæ in Liberales Artes* (which included Ramus's lectures on dialectic, though not the *Dialectica* or *Logic* proper) was in the Saint Paul's School library.[63] But no one has been able to show for certain that Milton was actually indoctrinated in Ramus's logic at Saint Paul's.

Milton's own Christ's College was the strongest of all Ramist strongholds, both before and during Milton's years there, 1625–32. As reader in logic in the public schools of the university, Laurence Chaderton (or Chatterton), a fellow of Christ's, had lectured on Ramus's logic between 1568 and 1577. Following him, William Perkins (1558–1602), who took his bachelor's degree from Christ's in 1581, and George Downame (or Downham, d. 1634), who took his there in 1585, both became enthusiastic Ramists and fellows of Christ's College. Downame also became university professor of logic and author of the *Commentary* used by Milton. At Christ's Milton had been a fellow student of the younger George Downame, nephew of the elder George.[64] Milton's familiarity with Ramism traces clearly to Christ's.

[61] Ong, *Ramus, Method, and Decay of Dialogue*, p. 303.

[62] Donald L. Clark, *John Milton at St. Paul's School* (New York: Columbia University Press, 1948), pp. 13, 147–51; Harris F. Fletcher, *The Intellectual Development of John Milton* (Urbana: University of Illinois Press, 1956), I, 219–28.

[63] Clark, *Milton at St. Paul's*, p. 13.

[64] Parker, *Milton*, p. 261; cf. *DNB* articles on the brothers George and John Downham (Downame).

(G) Milton's Adaptation of Ramus.

The simplicity of Ramist logic paradoxically generated commentaries to explain what Ramus meant—commentaries that were in turn suppressed for being too distracting or discouraging and alternately revived and revised and amalgamated again. The first of the commentaries, by Ramus's literary lieutenant Omer Talon (in Latin Audomarus Talæus, ca. 1510–62), was revised after Talon's death by Ramus himself.[65] Milton's *Logic* is one of the late enlargements, in which, as noted above, Ramus's work and Milton's commentary, itself in great part from the *Commentary* by George Downame or Downham (Dounamus),[66] are amalgamated into one continuous text. Since, as earlier noted, in no significant way does Milton's adaptation deviate from or alter Ramus's pattern of organization, the description of Ramus's logic or dialectic here is also a description of the basic organization of Milton's *Logic*. Milton's infrequent deviations from Ramus will be given specific mention as the present description proceeds and in notes to Milton's text itself.

Logic or dialectic was an international possession, and Milton's work was much more part of an international heritage than it was anything distinctively British. This is shown preeminently by its Latin. It was still awkward in Milton's age, though becoming less so than formerly, to explain technical matters in English or the other vernaculars, which did not have an established vocabulary for academic or scientific subjects, and thus through the mid-seventeenth century most textbooks, like Milton's *Logic,* were done the easier way, in Latin. No matter where they were published, such books in Latin had an immediate international market. Downame's *Commentary* is a case in point. It appeared in at least six editions,[67] published at the site of the great semiannual international book fair, Frankfurt-am-Main, before its one British edition put in its appearance in London in 1669, too late to have been used by Milton. Milton thus knew this work of his fellow Englishman

[65] See below, p. 187.

[66] *Commentarii in P. Rami Dialecticam, quibus ex classicis quibusque auctoribus præciptorum Rameorum perfectio demonstratur, sensus explicator, usus exponitur* (Francofurti: Impensis Nicolæ Bassæi typis Ioannis Saurii, 1601; CAM).

[67] Ong, *Ramus and Talon Inventory,* nos. 372 (1601—copies in Cambridge University Library and Biblioteca nacional, Lisbon), 379 (1605), 381 (1610), 389 (1610), 406 (1616), and 424 (1631). All available before the 1640s, any of these could have been used by Milton. The 1631 edition has been used for collations here (copy in PML). The 1605 edition is given as the first edition by Howell, *Logic and Rhetoric,* p. 208; the 1610, in *DNB*.

and fellow member of Christ's College through Continental presses. The fact that Milton's *Logic* identifies Milton himself on its title page as "the Englishman" of course also advertises the international context of his work itself. Learned Latin books commonly identified their authors by country or locale.

(H) Influence of Milton's *Logic*.

Milton's *Logic* was read by some students at Harvard in the late seventeenth and early eighteenth century and was used in England at Rathmell Academy, founded in 1669.[68] I know of no other indications of its academic use, and the fact that after its first edition of 1672 (1673) it was never reprinted except as part of a collection of Milton's works makes it unlikely that it had any widespread effective currency. One copy at Christ's College, Cambridge, as noted later here, is signed on the title page "W. Wordsworth," but mere possession of a book hardly "argues" its intensive use. Although Ramist logic was of major import, Milton's own edition of Ramus would appear to have had very little impact on intellectual or educational history except perhaps in forming the sensibilities of Milton's two nephews and his other pupils. Edward Phillips, one of the nephews, became an editor of miscellanea, as Ramists sometimes tended to become.

III. THE STRUCTURE AND CONTENT OF RAMIST LOGIC, INCLUDING MILTON'S

Ramist logic or dialect had two "parts," as has been seen. This meant that it dealt with two operations, set down successively in the Book I and Book II into which Ramist logic textbooks are always divided: discovery or invention (*inventio*), which implemented finding the needed elements for thought and discourse, and judgment (*iudicium*) or arrangement (*dispositio*), which taught how to put the elements of discourse together once they had been found. The model resorted to here is engagingly simple: The carrying on of thought and discourse consists of locating singularized elements and joining them.

(A) Invention.

Invention (*inventio*) or discovery, the first "part" of Ramist logic, treated always in Book I of Ramist texts, is an operation whereby a person faced with a question, Is *A B?* can locate a middle term or "argument" that will either join or separate the two terms, *A*

[68] Lusignan, "L'*Artis Logicæ*," p. 9.

and *B,* in the question and thereby provide and prove the answer: *A* is *B* or *A* is not *B.* Is John mortal? Well, John is a man. All men are mortal. Therefore John *is* mortal. "Man" is the middle term or "argument": it "argues" mortality here.

   Discovery of such a term was achieved by running through certain "headings," as one might style them today, which might suggest one or another "argument," Ramus's word for a "term." But "heading" did not fit into the way Ramus's or Milton's age thought about these matters. From antiquity the sources for arguments had been thought of not as headings but as "places"—*topoi* in Greek or *loci* in Latin—imagined noetic locales where the elements of thought are somehow stored. The term is favored by familiarity with writing, which situates otherwise "winged" words in static space, though we do not know what the prechirographic history of the term may have been. In these places are to be found the various arguments by which proof or disproof can be achieved. Quintilian, following Cicero, says that the *loci* are "seats of arguments." [69] Ramus, however—and Milton following him—does not explicitly resort to the idea of places as such, although he derives directly from the topical or place tradition, where his immediate predecessor, Rudolph Agricola, had exploited the term *locus* or "place" quite vigorously.[70] Ramus used the term "argument" instead of "place." Where others would, for example, refer to the locus or place called "contraries," out of which arguments based on contraries were to be drawn, Ramus simply refers to "contraries" (*contraria*), that is, "contrary arguments" in the plural, and lets it go at that. But even so, the tendency to think of the arguments as somehow localized is quite evident in the dichotomized outline tables found in so many editions of Ramus's *Logic:* In these diagrams the loci or places where arguments lodge have been transferred from some vague mental arena to specific places or slots in a chart on the visible printed page.

   It should be noted that, although Ramus and Milton use *argumentum* to refer to a middle term in the sense explained above, they also use it in a larger sense to mean any term at all, as is noted below. Warrant for this might be found in the fact that under suitable circumstances any term could function as a middle term.

   The arguments or places in Milton's Ramist listing include efficient cause, material cause (or matter, that out of which a thing is made), formal cause (or form, which constitutes a thing as what

---

[69] *Institutiones Oratoriæ* V.x.20.
[70] See Ong, *Ramus, Method, and Decay of Dialogue,* pp. 104–12.

it is), final cause (or purpose, end), effect, subject, related things, contraries, and so on. Thus, faced with the question, Is Peter a human being? and running through these arguments (or these places), one notes that among efficient causes are "procreant causes," such as father and mother. (Each argument, in Ramus's sense of place or heading, is broken down into subheadings, regularly dichotomized, two by two, as will be explained.) Knowing that Peter had a human father (and/or mother), that is, a human procreant cause, one can argue that he is a human being, for when a being acts as a procreant cause it produces an effect of the same nature as itself. Or, noting that Peter's father (and/or mother) was a rabbit, one can argue that Peter is not human but a rabbit, as his procreant cause was a rabbit.

To situate this first "part" of Ramus's and Milton's logic, namely invention, within the logical tradition, it is important to note that these places and the arguments in them are not in the technical sense "categories." Categories (*katēgoriai, prædicamenta*) in Aristotle, and in the logical tradition generally, were not exact equivalents of the English term "categories," which today can refer to virtually any kind of classification. Aristotle's *katēgoriai* are not middle terms but are specifically classifications of predicates found in propositions, that is, of "accusations" (for the Greek term *katēgoria* means that, an accusation) that could be "brought against" a subject, that is, could be said of a subject. The categories link Aristotle's study of being with his study of predication, and formal logic with metaphysics. Thus, the dog is an animal (here the category or predicate, "animal," is a substance), the dog is large (here the category or predicate, "large," is a quantity), the dog is white (here the category or predicate, "white," is a quality), the dog is seated (here the category or predicate, "seated," is a bodily position), and so on. Aristotle lists categories in varying numbers, but his maximum number is ten. Lists of the *topoi* or loci or places vary over the ages and from author to author in the same age but commonly run much longer than this list of categories: Aristotle's list has been calculated at 338 to 360 (classifiable under four headings), Cicero's at 17, Themistius's at 22; Rudolph Agricola gives 24, and Ramus 20 in his final tally but fewer in his earlier lists.[71] Occasionally a place might bear the same name as a category or a related name, but basically place and category refer to quite different things. Lists of places tend to be looser, rule-of-thumb agglomerates of headings to stimulate thought. The Ramist ar-

[71] Ibid., pp. 122–23.

guments belong basically in the places, or the topical tradition, developing not out of Aristotle's work on *Categoriæ* (or *Predicamenta*) but out of his *Topica,* although their treatment at the hands of Ramus and Milton and other Ramists included material from Aristotle's *Categoriæ* as well as others of the works grouped in the Aristotelian *Organon.*

It should be further noted that places to which one can fruitfully have resort no matter what subject is under consideration—such as, for example, efficient cause, effect, or related things—are in the strict sense styled *"common*places" (*loci communes*) if they are of common value to all fields of inquiry or knowledge. Causes, effects, similitudes are commonplaces in this sense: No matter what subject one wants to treat, they could well furnish arguments. Other places are of value only in a particular field such as physics or medicine or law or theology. These latter places relevant only to a particular field are in strict use called "private places" (*idia topika* in Aristotle). It is doubtful, however, whether such strict usage was ever truly current in ancient Greece or anywhere else. By and large, the term "commonplace" (*locus communis*) was widely used to refer to "private" places as well as to places that were "common" in the strict sense. Any number of treatises can be found listing medical commonplaces (instead of medical places), legal commonplaces (instead of legal places), and so on.

The first part of Ramist logic, although it is styled invention or discovery, in fact says nothing about the process of discovery as such. It describes what the items are that one "discovers," that is to say, what contraries are, how privatives are negative contraries, how the argument of "name" argues, how "notation" argues, and so on. This part of logic called invention thus is in fact a classificatory description of the various kinds of arguments (that is, of concepts utilizable as middle terms) and of their interrelationships, a catalogue of what invention can discover, of all the possible kinds of terms, rather than a treatment of how to do the discovering. Such a treatment would in the last analysis be superfluous, for how to do the discovering was clearly implied and transparently simple: one merely ran through all the possibilities for proof laid out in the Ramist catalogue and availed oneself of those that worked. Because these were laid out, as will be seen, in binary classes as on a computer flow chart, the mind went through selective operations like those of a digital computer retrieving a desired item or items.

In formal logic—as against topical logics, which treat probable argumentation—the topics were developed by Boethius (480?–524?)

in his work *On Topical Differences (De Differentiis Topicis),* not as a means of discovering a middle term but rather as a means of accounting for the probative force of each of the different topics. Boethius's work, developed ultimately out of Aristotle's *Topica* with considerable influence from Cicero, became the standard *auctoritas* for the Middle Ages, from Abelard on, and the source of the medieval theory of consequences in formal logic.[72] Investigation of the probative force of the different topics generates the various "maxims" that govern the way in which consequences flow variously from each topic. The maxim, in the formal sense this term enjoys in Peter of Spain (1210/20–77) and later, is an abstract statement of the way in which consequences follow from the use of one or another topic or locus or place. Thus, for example, Boethius takes the following syllogism: "An animal is an animate sensible substance. A tree is not an animate sensible substance. Therefore, a tree is not an animal." The middle term is a definition, and hence the topic or place that furnished it is that of definition. The *prima et maxima propositio* (or simply *maxima* in Latin, yielding "maxim" in English) that governs this kind of consequence is, "That to which the definition of a genus does not apply is not a species of that of which the definition is given." This maxim is simplified or further formalized by the time of Abelard, who gives it in this form: "From whatever the definition is removed, the item defined is also removed." [73] William of Ockham (1300?–49?), who further recasts some of the maxims, styles them not maxims but rules.[74] Although, with much else in medieval logic, formalization of the topics was largely dropped in the Renaissance, Ramus and Milton both develop out of their discussion of the arguments (i.e., topics) rules that are redolent of the Boethian and medieval maxim. In Book I, chapter xxx, "On Definition," for example here, Milton, following Ramus, states (p. 310 below), "And just as definition argues or explains what is defined, so conversely it can be argued from what is defined." Or again, in Book I, chapter xx, "On the Less," Milton states (p. 280 below), "But if those cases which signify subordination are applied to what is argued, they are indeed signs of the lesser, but the argument is from the greater because

---

[72] For a brief but highly informative account of this much neglected relationship between the topics (*loci,* places) and formal logic, see Otto Bird, "The Formalizing of the Topics in Mediaeval Logic," *NDJFL,* I (1960), 138–49, and "Topic and Consequence in Ockham's Logic," *NDJFL,* II (1961), 65–78.

[73] Bird, "Formalizing Topics in Mediaeval Logic," pp. 138–39.

[74] Bird, "Topic and Consequence in Ockham's Logic," p. 69.

what is argued is the lesser." It appears that equal formalization was not achieved or even attempted for all the topics. Topics such as "the similar" and "the dissimilar" are obviously much more loose and less manageable than is that of "definition," and maxims or rules to cover their operations could smother in their own elaborations.

There is little evidence that formalization of the topics developed in formal logic a concern for using the topics actually to discover arguments, that is, for *inventio,* as this figures in topical logics such as Ramus's and Milton's. Formal logic is descriptive rather than prescriptive or heuristic. Discovery of arguments for given cases or problems, in pre-Ramist tradition generally, was relegated to dialectic (in the sense of disputation logic as against fully formal logic) and even more to rhetoric. In rhetoric particularly there is abundant evidence that speechmakers or writers were taught to run through certain sets of loci systematically to start up whatever arguments might be productive and to organize discourse in strings of loci.[75] The process was often quite exhaustive. Thus, in praising or vituperating a person, one could do so in terms of his procreating causes (his parents—admirable persons or despicable in every way), his material cause (his body and its constituents—his head, shoulders, arms, etc., his food, etc.), his formal cause (his soul, with its virtues or vices), his final cause (he was patently designed to do good or, like Richard III, to do evil), and so on, with divisions and subdivisions ad infinitum. The Ramist classifications of arguments could be used this way (those just mentioned are from Milton's *Logic*), but since Ramism allocated all invention to logic, such effusive rhetorical performance was discouraged in fact if not absolutely in theory. This effusiveness is a mark rather of non-Ramist virtuosi, who set up structures of loci or places not only in logic but separate ones in rhetoric as well.

Ramus's assignment of all invention to logic as a matter of fact established in his art of logic much that is not formal logic at all. In reviewing each of the arguments in the first "part" of logic, Milton, like Ramus and his other editors and commentators, brings in what is really a great deal of metaphysics and Aristotelian or scholastic "physics." As running through all the loci means running through the mind's entire repertory of concepts in a summary way, this first part of logic becomes in effect a general introduction to philosophy.

In another way, too, Ramist logic weakened true logical formalism. By developing rigorous classifications in the lists of places,

[75] See Howell, *Logic and Rhetoric,* pp. 138–45, etc.

both rhetoric and logic had the effect of formalizing noetic materials more and more throughout what we have called the ages of rhetoric and logic; that is, they had the effect of making for "straight" or "hard" thinking such as fostered scientific and related procedures. But rhetoric and logic were not equally hard. Because logic represented relatively more formalized or "harder" thinking than did rhetoric, Ramus's assignment of all loci to logic represented a drive toward more and more formalization. But the achievement was specious. Superficially strengthening logic by decreeing that all noetic activity was equally logical in the formal sense—poetry was for a Ramist subject to the same inexorable rules of logic as was mathematics—Ramus in fact produced a relatively crude, oversimplified logic. He rhetoricized logic as much as he logicized rhetoric. Although Renaissance logics by and large abandoned many of the formal advances the science had made in the Middle Ages, few in fact abandoned as much as Ramism did.[76]

The arguments in Ramus and Milton are classified in neat, dichotomized fashion. The first division is into artificial and inartificial. Artificial arguments "argue" of themselves, "by an innate and proper force." Since they are situated within the "art" of logic, their power derives from within this art, though Milton asserts (Book I, chapter ii, p. 221 below) that these arguments are not discovered by art any more than inartificial arguments are. Artificial arguments are those found under cause, effect, disparates, and indeed all arguments except those derived from testimony, under which fall all the inartificial arguments; for to argue from what someone says about a matter is to step outside the art of logic into actual history. The arrangement of the arguments can be gathered readily from Milton's table of contents. A graphic representation of their dichotomized organization is often provided in other Ramist logic books in a branching diagram,[77] but there is no such diagram in Milton's work.

(B) Disposition, including Method.

From antiquity the second part of dialectic or logic had commonly been styled judgment (*iudicium*) and the corresponding second part of rhetoric disposition or arrangement (*dispositio*). When Ramus merged the first two parts of rhetoric with the corresponding

[76] See Ashworth, "Syllogistic in the Sixteenth and Seventeenth Centuries," pp. 17–33.

[77] Some are reproduced in Ong, *Ramus, Method, and Decay of Dialogue,* pp. 202, 317, etc.

parts of logic, he had to decide between the two competing terms, *iudicium* and *dispositio,* as the name for the second part. He opted for *iudicium* but noted explicitly in his 1572 text (Book II, chapter i) that *dispositio* means the same thing.

Milton differs explicitly with Ramus in choosing the term *dispositio* for the second part of logic. The doctrine of judgment (*iudicium*), as he explains in Book I, chapter ii, and Book II, chapter i (pp. 323–24 below), teaches how to judge well and is an effect of both parts of logic, whereas arrangement (*dispositio*) teaches how to dispose or arrange the arguments found in the first part of logic. That is to say, disposition teaches how to put together, first, propositions and then syllogisms and finally the longer assemblages of discourse governed by what Ramus and Milton and Ramus's many other followers call "method."

Disposition or arrangement of arguments is divided by Ramus and Milton into two kinds, axiomatic and dianoetic. The first of these, axiomatic disposition, treats the various kinds of propositions, which Ramus and Milton style *axiomata* or axioms. An axiom in this sense is defined as "an arrangement of one argument with another by which a thing is shown to be or not to be" (Book II, chapter ii, p. 325 below)—from which it is clear that "argument" for Ramus and Milton refers not only to a term used as a middle term but to any term at all, for the "one argument" and "another" that Ramus speaks of here are simply the subject and predicate terms in a proposition, either of which or neither of which might prove to be a middle term in a syllogism. Under axiomatic disposition, Ramus and Milton treat affirmation and negation, truth and falsehood, and the various kinds of "axioms" (propositions), simple and compound (with various kinds of this last).

Dianoetic disposition is again divided into two kinds, syllogism and method. Ramus's and Milton's treatment of the various kinds of syllogism and of their properties is simple and scientifically uneventful, for the one discovery often credited to Ramus, the syllogism constituted of singular terms, had been known at least since Ockham, two-and-a-half centuries earlier.[78] But Ramus's introduction and Milton's retention of this syllogism is unusual, and their logic elsewhere does exhibit some other moderately peculiar features. Its terminology is often idiosyncratic, even when it has some kind of classical precedent, as it commonly does. Ramus and Milton call the major and minor of a syllogism respectively the proposition (*propositio*) and assumption (*assumptio*), for example,

---

[78] Bocheński, *History of Formal Logic,* p. 232.

and use the term "species" (*species*) for the more usual "figure" (*figura*), although they retain the usual concomitant term "mode" or "mood" (*modus*).

In his 1546, coyly pseudonymous *Three Dialectical Commentaries Published with Omer Talon as Author*,[79] which appeared while he himself was forbidden to teach philosophy, Ramus had introduced two invalid modes of the conditional syllogism ("connected syllogism," *syllogismus connexus,* in Ramus's and Milton's terminology). This he had finally disavowed in his 1566 revision,[80] quietly inserting his own lengthy explanation of his mistake into the commentary by Omer Talon (which had been appearing regularly with his text), though Talon had died four years earlier (1562). Milton comments on these two invalid modes as paralogisms, without identifying Ramus by name as having been among the "some" who taught them as valid: Ramus's revised 1572 *Dialectic,* on which Milton's *Logic* is based, of course showed them no longer and had been published without any commentary at all.[81]

In discussing paralogisms and their refutations here and elsewhere (see Milton's Appendix to Book II, chapter ix, pp. 353–57 below), Milton follows Downame and other Ramists and departs from Ramus himself, who had steadfastly refused to consider in his logic the matter of fallacies, which logic had commonly treated since Aristotle's work *On Refutations of the Sophists*. Ramus had thought of and described each art, including of course logic, the paradigm of all the arts, the "art of arts," as a closed field, with explicit invocation of "Solon's Law" for delimitating real estate in Athens,[82] maintaining that proper surveillance of boundaries assured the integrity of every art and kept out all error.

Method, the second part of dianoetic disposition, is the most distinctive feature of Ramist logic and of the whole Ramist economy of thought. It marks a new stage in the management of knowledge in the West because it breaks clearly with the rhetorical tradition that had hitherto dominated knowledge storage and retrieval in the academic world. Method prescribes for what we might call the transsyllogistic organization of statements ("axioms"). The syllo-

---

[79] *Dialecticæ Commentarii Tres Authore Audomaro Talæo Editi* (Paris: Ludovicus Grandinus, 1546). This work is certainly by Ramus, not by Talæus (Talon). See Ong, *Ramus and Talon Inventory*, pp. 49–50.

[80] Ramus, *Dialecticæ Libri Duo, Audomari Talæi Prælectionibus Illustrati* (Paris: A. Wechelus, 1566), pp. 351–55. See pp. 379–80 below.

[81] See note to Book II, chap. xiv, below.

[82] Ramus, *Scholæ Rhetoricæ,* Lib. I, in *Scholæ in Liberales Artes,* cols. 237–38; Lib. III, cols. 255–56; etc.

gism is normally a relatively short bit of discourse. And although Ramists commonly believed that even long treatises or poems could be reduced to a syllogism or a few syllogisms, there was still the question: How is protracted discourse about a given subject (reducible to syllogisms though it may be) to be organized? The Ramist answer is simple: by proceeding from the general to the particular or "special." This procedure is "method." The answer appears annoyingly *simpliste,* but in a rough way it describes the typical modern encyclopedia article. And it represented a new approach in teaching; for, generally speaking, from classical antiquity through the Renaissance the only form of longer discourse taught as such in the academic world had been the oration, with its two to seven (commonly four) parts, or related genres (the disputation or the letter, which was commonly designed with more or less the same parts as the oration). Ramist method marks a major move away from the old oratorical, oral world.

The details of method can be gleaned readily from Ramus and Milton—Book II, chapter xvii, pp. 390–95 below—and no further explanation need be added here. But two features of method might be pointed out. First, when faced with recalcitrant audiences or readers, one could on occasion put method into reverse by proceeding from particulars or "specials" to the general. This reverse procedure was called "cryptic method."

Secondly, the paradigms that Ramus and Milton offer for method are curriculum subjects themselves, such as grammar or logic. Milton's *Logic* not only contains method as one of its parts but in its total, overall organization exemplifies method, for it is a "methodized" logic, as all Ramist logics are, proceeding from the most general to the particular (definition of logic, division into its "parts," definition of the first part, that is of invention, division of invention into its parts, definition of the first part of invention and treatment of this and the successive parts and parts of parts all the way down to the ultimate parts, which are the particular arguments; then back to the second part of invention, which is treated the same way; and so on). Ramists held that all academic subjects were to be taught this way. But method reached beyond the classroom. This model treatment of an academic art becomes for Ramus the paradigm for all discourse of any and all sorts, for all discourse is to be methodized. Ramism is academicism with a vengeance. An oration is to be organized like the art of grammar.[83]

[83] See Milton's Book II, chap. xvii, below. Milton much curtails Ramus's voluble explanation of the way grammar is methodized.

The reduction of knowledge to this general-to-special art form Ramists style "technology" (*technologia*), and the knowledge so organized they call "technological"—from the Greek word for art, *technē,* the equivalent of the Latin *ars*. "Methodical" (*methodica*) is a synonym for "technological." Thus one can have—and indeed should have—technological or methodical grammar, technological arithmetic, technological rhetoric, and so on. Technological or methodical knowledge is knowledge in a closed field, for, as has been seen, each Ramist art is complete in itself and separated, like a plot of real estate, from other knowledge. For a Ramist, in fact, the closed noetic field is doubly closed. Applied to any art, method establishes the art in a closed field. Among the arts that method so closes is logic. But method, as already noted, is itself *part* of logic! The recipe for establishing closed fields is found in a closed field, indeed in the most closed of all closed fields, logic itself. It is a tribute to the intensity, if not the truth, of Ramus's vision here that two centuries later Kant still believed that that is what logic is.[84]

IV. THE TEXT

(A) The History of the Text.

The textual problems for an edition of Milton's *Logic* are minimal. No manuscript is known, and in Milton's lifetime there was only one printing, more or less supervised by Milton himself. The work was published in London in 1672 by Spencer Hickman, printer to the Royal Society, a small volume in 12mo. Later the 1672 title page was removed from some sheets and a cancel title page substituted, from a new setting of type with some minor variations in punctuation but exactly the same wording except for the imprint, which lists the publisher simply as "S.H." and the bookseller as "R. Boulter," giving the latter's address and the new date of 1673.[85] The list of errata in the 1672 issue is included in the 1673 issue, which, except for the cancel title page, is from exactly the same setting of type and most likely from the same press run. The new title page was simply bound in with the sheets previously printed. The one stop-press correction, which Allan H. Gilbert found, on page 6, line 10, and which he reports in Columbia, XI, 519, 524, does not distinguish the 1672 and 1673 issues, for the Saint Louis University copy of the 1672 issue and the Dr.

---

[84] Bocheński, *History of Formal Logic,* p. 6, where the relevant passage from Kant is quoted.

[85] See the 1672 and 1673 title pages reproduced in facsimile pp. 206–07 below.

Williams's Library copy of the 1673 issue both read "causæ" for the corrected "causa." [86]

The collation of the volume, based on the Bibliothèque nationale copy (R10913), with notes in brackets based on the Saint Louis University Library copy and other copies, is: A^{12} (de facto this gathering includes as its last two leaves those falsely signed B1 and [B2]—see below), B^{12} (but with original B1 and B2 cut out, leaving stubs, as in Saint Louis University copy and some other copies, or no visible remnant at all as in Bibliothèque nationale copy—without these two cut-out leaves and with the last two leaves of gathering A bearing the faked signatures B1 and [B2], the collational formula falsely appears to be A^{10}, B^{12}), $C–K^{12}$, L^6. Page size is 8.1 × 14.4 cm. in the Bibliothèque nationale copy, 8.2 × 13.6 cm. in the Saint Louis University copy, and close to these sizes in all other copies I have examined. The pagination: [20] unnumbered pages followed by 228 numbered pages. The present leaf B2 lacks the signature, and the following pages are misnumbered (the number in parentheses is the incorrect number appearing in the volume): 48 (46), 74 (76), 75 (77), 78 (80), 79 (81), 82 (84), 83 (85), 86 (88), 87 (89), 90 (92), 91 (93), 94 (96), 95 (97), 98 (68), 228 (223).

Contents (of Bibliothèque nationale copy—the only copy I know containing leaf [A1]): [A1] blank [in Bibliothèque nationale copy with Milton portrait offset on recto]; [A2^r] blank [but also in Bibliothèque nationale copy with Milton portrait offset]; [A2^v] portrait of Milton from metal engraving; [A3^r] title; [A3^v] blank; A4–[A9^r] *Præfatio;* [A9^v] blank; [A10^r] *Typographi errata;* [A10^v] blank; [A11–A12], falsely signed B1–[B2] (see explanation below), *J. MILTONI* Angli, / Artis Logicæ Plenior Institutio, *&c.* (reprinted first four pages of the text proper of the work); [original] B1–B2, cut out of all copies I know, but, as indicated above, represented by stubs in the Saint Louis University copy and many other copies though not in the Bibliothèque nationale copy, original first four pages, now cut out except for stubs, of the text proper of the work; [B3]–[L6^v] the rest of the text proper of the work.

The stubs of the two leaves mentioned above here were noted by Professor Gilbert (Columbia, XI, 521–22), who found them between pages 4 and 5 (leaves [B2] and B3) in a number of copies. I have examined sixteen copies (mostly in London and Cambridge, where Christ's College has six, one of them, as noted earlier, signed

[86] See *N&Q,* CLXV (1933), 56, as cited by Gilbert, Columbia, XI, 519, for establishment of the fact that the 1672 and 1673 issues are from the same press run except for the title pages.

on the title page "W. Wordsworth") and have found four of them
with stubs where Professor Gilbert indicates; one copy (Cambridge
University Library, Ven. 8.67.3) with one stub between pages 2
and 3 and another stub between pages 4 and 5, and one copy (of
the 1673 issue, Dr. Williams's Library, London, 564.D.3) with one
quite different stub (part of, because continuous with the title-page
leaf) between the errata leaf and page 1 (the present false B1—this
different stub is explained below). Many of the sixteen copies lacking stubs, though not all of them, have been rebound. Despite the
excision of the pages of which the stubs are the remnants, Milton's
text is complete, as Gilbert notes: the cut-out pages, as can be seen
from those stubs wide enough for edges of the printed text to show
(as in the Saint Louis University copy and some others), corresponded to the present pages 1 through 4 in their numbering and
text, although the positioning of the text on the present pages differs
slightly from that on the original pages 1–4. Clearly, the printer
simply reprinted pages 1–4 and cut out the original pages 1–4 in
some sort of maneuver whereby he reconstituted the makeup of
the first two gatherings in the book.

Why did Hickman reprint pages 1–4 and reconstitute these gatherings? With the help of the foregoing data, we can reconstruct
something of what must have happened and make some conjectures
about other things. When he printed the opening of the text proper
of the *Logic*, which began on the original B1^r, Hickman had probably estimated or "cast off" preliminary matter (title, *Præfatio,
Errata*), which as usual was to be printed after all the rest of the
book, as just right for filling a gathering to consist of eight leaves.
Then something seems to have occurred that made him want to
reprint the first two leaves of his original gathering B.

What this was we simply cannot be sure. It may have been some
revision on Milton's part. But there is no positive evidence of any
such revision either internal to Milton's thought or expression here
or internal to the printed text. The present first four pages develop
Ramus's logic in a fairly routine way—which does not indicate that
Milton changed anything in his text any more than it indicates he
did not change anything: He could have written a routine text from
the beginning, or he could have changed from one routine Ramist
treatment to another routine Ramist treatment. As has been noted
above, in no copy I have examined where the stubs show bits of
words or ornament next to the gutter margins is there any indication
of a change in text. The bits of words beginning or ending lines,
together with edges or ornaments, on the stubs represent exactly

the same words or ornament edges at the gutter margins of the present falsely signed B1 and [B2], although what Gilbert had noted about a copy he had examined is true also of other copies: The lines of print (and/or the ornament edges) are spaced differently at times, higher or lower, on the stubs than on the false B1 and [B2]. But in the copies I have examined (as apparently in Gilbert's copies) the stubs show the edges of only a very few of the lines on the four pages: there is no way to tell whether other parts of the text were changed or not. Examination of all known extant copies, of which Parker locates eighty-four,[87] might turn up one or another with wider stubs, though my own experience with those I have examined makes the likeliness of this appear to me small: many have no stubs at all, and most stubs show no print whatsoever. Of course, it is even possible that a copy might turn up with the original B1 and B2 complete. Let us hope so but not count on it.

If Milton did not revise his text, any number of occurrences might have prompted the reprinting of the first two leaves of the text proper of the *Logic*. Some serious typographical errors might have been discovered that Milton or the printer himself felt had to be corrected. Or in the stack of printed sheets in the shop the part carrying B1 and B2 might have been damaged somehow. One could imagine other reasons. We simply do not know what the reason was.

But we can conjecture about some of the adjustments that the reprinting of the original B1 and B2 as the false B1 and [B2] entailed, and in particular about the relationship of the reprinting to the portrait of Milton at the beginning of the *Logic*.

The portrait itself presents a curious problem. The plate does not fit the book, for it is much too large. In all copies of the *Logic* in which the portrait appears, copies trimmed quite normally with regard to the text, the engraving invariably bleeds off the page at the outer margins: there is no room on the trimmed page for some three-eighths of an inch of the oval frame enclosing Milton's bust.

The portrait is printed from the engraved plate that in 1671 William Dolle had copied from William Faithorne's 1670 engraving.[88] The Dolle engraving had never been used before, as far as is known, when Hickman elected to insert it in the *Logic*, even though it did not quite fit in size—it does fit, as Parker notes, the

---

[87] Parker, *Milton,* p. 1143. The present explanation of Hickman's operations is taken, in a few places verbatim, from the present author's "Printer's Legerdemain in Milton's *Artis Logicæ Plenior Institutio,*" *TCBS,* VI, pt. 3 (1974), 167–74.

[88] Parker, *Milton,* pp. 615, 1139.

1674 edition of *Paradise Lost* (printed by S. Simmons), in which it often appears, and would have fitted the 1671 edition of *Paradise Regained* (printed for J.M. by John Starkey), for which it may have been done but in which it had not been used. How Hickman got hold of the Dolle engraving, no one knows—or at least Parker does not know, which is about the same thing—but his use of the portrait may connect with his decision to cancel and reprint the original leaves B1 and B2. The portrait gave him something that would not only enhance the book but also facilitate his shift from an 8vo gathering to a 12mo: the cancel false B1 and [B2] would use up two of the four additional leaves, the portrait would take care of one other, [A2], and he could let the first leaf of the book, [A1], remain blank—a common enough practice.

One might suspect that perhaps the book's reorganization might somehow have been further complicated by the substitution of what has been identified as the cancel title page in the 1673 issue for the original 1672 title page. But the cancel title page was only that: it entailed only substitution of a single leaf in the original 1672 printing. This fact has been noted earlier and can be ascertained by close comparison of the printed pages in the two issues, but it is otherwise conspicuous in the 1673 copy in Dr. Williams's Library (564.D.3). As I have mentioned above, in this copy between the errata leaf and page 1 there is a stub. Fortunately, the binding in this copy is quite loose, so that it can be seen that this stub has nothing to do with the stubs of the original leaves B1–2 (pp. 1–4) discussed above and that it is in fact the same leaf of paper as the cancel title page itself, providing the hold for stitching the cancel into the volume. The cancel is thus entirely distinct from the rest of the book.

Some further details may offer additional suggestions for those who may wish to delve deeper into this bibliographical sandbox. The leaf with Milton's portrait is missing from almost half the copies of the *Logic* (1672 and 1673 issues indiscriminately) that I know of. But even in copies from which this leaf is missing, as well as in those in which it is present, the portrait is almost always offset (usually quite distinctly, sometimes exceedingly faintly) on the title page, which the portrait faces. There are two exceptions, however: in one Cambridge University Library copy (Ven. 8.67.3), the portrait is missing and is not offset at all; in the Bibliothèque nationale copy (R10913) it is present but not offset on the title page, whereas it is offset on [A1^r] and on [A2^r]—the other side of the leaf on which the portrait is actually printed. Without quite knowing exactly what happened, I suspect some reasons for these phenomena trace to Hickman's problems in handling sheets bearing both intaglio engraving and letterpress printing.

Since 1673 Milton's *Logic* has never appeared except in editions of collected works of Milton.[89] All editions after 1673 depend on the 1672 (1673) printing exclusively and hence have no textual authority in themselves at all. They are, however, useful for suggesting possible emendations when these may be called for in Milton's 1672 text and have been used well for this purpose by Gilbert, as noted below.

(B) Milton's Textual Sources for the *Logic* Proper.

The text of Ramus that Milton incorporates into his own work and on which he builds is that of Ramus's final revision, which had appeared certainly by May of 1572,[90] well before Ramus's murder on August 26 of the same year in the Saint Bartholomew's Day Massacre. No edition before this corresponds with Milton's text in chapter headings or terminology (for example, the use of *axioma* for what Ramus before 1572 had styled *enunciatum*). Milton's book and chapter numbers correspond exactly to Ramus's (and to Downame's) except that the last four chapters of Ramus's Book II (xvii–xx) are abridged by Milton and combined into one (xvii). Ramus's last revision of his *Dialectic* before his final 1572 revision was in his *Dialectica Audomari Talæi Prælectionibus Illustrata* (Basel: E. Episcopius et Nicolai fratris hæredes, 1569). Milton sometimes varies Ramus's 1572 text somewhat, transposing words, abridging or extending quotations, and so on, not, however, so far as my samplings indicate, by returning to Ramus's 1569 text or earlier texts.

Milton reproduces almost all of Ramus's 1572 text—roughly, I estimate, around 85 percent of it—including Ramus's own quotations from classical authors. Mme. Lusignan shows (pp. 156–60) that in Milton's Book I approximately 25 percent of the text and in Book II approximately 22 percent of the text is from Ramus, the rest of Milton's text being largely commentary. She shows also (pp. 182, 187–91) that, while Milton in most cases probably takes his text of Ramus from that reproduced in Downame, at other

---

[89] Twelve of the editions, 1698 to 1935, are listed in Ong, *Ramus and Talon Inventory*, nos. 460, 462–72. Since publication of this work, I have located five more editions of Milton's works that include the *Logic*. All editions except Columbia and the present one are of course in the original Latin.

[90] See Ong, *Ramus and Talon Inventory*, pp. 192–93, with illustration between these two pages.

times he resorts directly to the *Dialecticæ Libri Duo* (Paris, 1572, or one of the reprints of this edition). But it is by no means always possible to tell directly from Milton's text itself what is from Ramus and what is not. The problem hinges on Milton's use of italics in the *Logic*. In general, he uses italics for what present-day editorial practice would enclose in quotation marks (which he never employs in the *Logic*), such as verbatim quotations from other authors, including Ramus's text itself (which from the end of Book I, chapter xxi, is most often set also in larger italic type), or for individual words or groups of words being attended to as such, including sample syllogisms and the like, as well as for titles of works (most of the time, but not always), or occasionally for authors' names. In verbatim quotations the principle Milton generally follows is to identify the source of the quotation in every case except where the quotation is simply Ramus's text itself, in which case it is simply italicized without any attribution, or from Downame, in which case it is normally neither put in italics nor identified as Downame's in any way at all. Milton, in other words, simply appropriates much of Downame's text as though it were his own.

These practices leave the reader in constant uncertainty, even where they are consistently applied. Does a quotation from a classical author come from Ramus's text, or is it Milton's own selection? It would appear in italics in either case. Thus there is no way to tell except by direct collation with the 1572 edition of Ramus. Is a sample syllogism from Ramus, or is it Milton's own? Again, there is no way to tell from Milton's text, for in either case it would be in italics.

Moreover, Milton is by no means always consistent. Often sizable excerpts from Ramus that Milton's policy demands be put in italics are simply not in italics. Less often, a line or two in italics with no attribution to a specific author turns out to be not from Ramus after all, for Milton once in a while used italics just for emphasis.

This use of italics for emphasis is the strongest of many indications that Milton himself rather than the printer is controlling the punctuation. His famous insert, "Here let the theologians take notice," in Book I, chapter vii (below, p. 233), is an instance in point. The italicizing of this one sentence, Milton's own interpolation in what is an almost word-for-word excerpt from Downame set in roman type, makes it quite clear that the author is in charge. How Milton implemented his control—he had been blind over twenty years when the *Logic* was published—remains a question. The book is a clumsy piece of printing but fairly well proofread, except for the title page, where "Annalytica" (1672 and 1673) is a misspelling and where in the 1673 cancel the title-page punctuation is vagrant, even by seventeenth-century standards.

Other authors besides Ramus are quoted from or echoed in Milton's text, almost always without acknowledgment except in the case of classical authors. Downame's *Commentarii in P. Rami . . . Dialecticam,* in one of its five continental editions (1601, 1605, 1606, 1610, 1616), not in its one and only and belated British edition (1669), as mentioned earlier, is Milton's chief source after Ramus himself. Milton borrows from Downame liberally and often verbatim and, as noted above, without any acknowledgment whatsoever, though, as Mme. Lusignan notes (p. 200) he regularly drops all references or quotations in Downame that are postclassical. However, on rare occasions Milton will introduce on his own, independently of Downame, references to contemporaries, as in Book I, chapter vii (below, p. 233), a reference to Scaliger. Milton's Preface itself (below, pp. 208–15) often paraphrases or duplicates Downame's wording,[91] and so does the text of the *Logic* itself. Mme. Lusignan's careful statistical study (pp. 166–91) shows that in Milton's Book I approximately 82 percent of Milton's text and in Book II approximately 73 percent are from Downame's text (understanding by Downame's text not only what is original with him but also his reproduction of Ramus and of others). Milton at times even forgets to change Downame's *dialectica* into his own preferred surrogate, *logica* (Lusignan, p. 203).

Milton uses almost all of Ramus's examples and some of Downame's. He uses particularly Downame's examples from poets and orators, and he makes his own many of the numerous quotations from Aristotle that give Downame's commentary a characteristic coloring somewhat different from Ramus's text and Talon's commentary, for Ramus and, to a lesser extent, Talon are chary of the Stagirite although not entirely neglectful of him. Downame himself comments on examples from Ramus's own text and takes other examples from Talon's commentary (*prœlectiones*) as this appears in the 1569 Basel edition of Ramus's *Dialectica* or one of its reprintings. These *Prœlectiones* of Talon derive partly from Ramus's own earlier *Remarks on Aristotle (Aristotelicœ Animadversiones),* later entitled *Lectures on Dialectic.* This can be seen, for example, by comparing Talon's and Downame's commentaries

---

[91] Some passages are given in Thomas S. K. Scott-Craig, "The Craftsmanship and Theological Significance of Milton's *Art of Logic,*" *HLQ,* XVII (1953), 6–8. See also Lusignan, "*L'Artis Logicœ.*"

with Ramus's text in Book I, chapter v. But Downame does not use all of Talon's examples and introduces many not in Ramus and Talon—whether from other secondary sources I do not know. It must be remembered, too, that Talon's *prælectiones* have not only multiple sources but a long history of their own. In 1550 there had appeared his *prælectiones* or explanatory lectures on Ramus's *Institutionum Dialecticarum Libri Tres,* the work out of which Ramus's *Dialectica* emerged. From its first Latin edition in 1556, this *Dialectica* was also equipped with *prælectiones* by Talon, more or less related to the earlier redaction. As noted above (p. 168) these *prælectiones* were subsequently revised in places by Ramus himself for the new edition of his *Dialectica* appearing in Paris in 1566, four years after Talon's death. Here Ramus's acknowledgment of his own hand in "Talon's" commentary is expressed so enigmatically and discretely that unless the reader was aware of the fact of Ramus's revision from some other source he could hardly know what Ramus was talking about.[92]

Although there is this sharing of examples, in spot-checking I do not find Downame's commentary or Milton's own *Logic* copying Talon's commentary at any length apart from the examples. Ramus, Talon, Downame, and Milton all work in the usual tradition of the *loci communes,* which runs from antiquity through the Middle Ages and the Renaissance: no one hesitated to use lines of thought or even quite specific wordings from another person without crediting the other person, for these were all taken to be— and most often were—part of the common tradition. The author from whom you got them had almost certainly taken them from another author who in turn had them from someone else. This tradition is no longer openly honored today, but in philological circles at least it is not dead. For passages from classical authors cited by Ramus and Milton are very often exactly the same passages cited in today's dictionaries to give context and meaning to the Latin or Greek words in the passages.[93] Like his contemporaries, and like Shakespeare and Chaucer and Boethius and Cicero and everyone else before him, Milton was working in a conspicuously traditional intellectual culture, where deviationism was possible only if it, too, could be backed by authority. The culture was a residually oral one, not yet adjusted to a typographic noetic economy. Nevertheless, ingenuity was not entirely absent by any

[92] See Ong, *Ramus and Talon Inventory,* p. 189.

[93] As noted in the following section, the present editors have not identified all the examples in Milton's *Logic* which have a long history of use in the Western philosophical tradition, but they have discussed some puzzling examples.

means. Ramus's use of examples from contemporary French poets in his French *Dialectique* (1555) and the Ramist Abraham Fraunce's use of examples from Sir Philip Sidney in *The Arcadian Rhetorike* (1588) and from Edmund Spenser in *The Sheapheardes Logike* [94] show a remarkable ability to identify logical constructs or the semblance of logical constructs on one's own—an ability in which boys were rigorously schooled. My impression is that both Ramus and Talon probably located a good many of their examples themselves. Milton did so only rarely if at all: Ramism was almost a century old when he wrote his *Logic* in the 1640s, and there were already more than enough examples at hand.

About Milton's use of Ramus and Downame a few additional observations can be made. The poetry Milton quotes is virtually all from Ramus's own text. Other references and quotations, especially from Aristotle, are often out of Downame, who, as has been seen, quotes Aristotle more liberally than Ramus does. Milton commonly uses but abridges Downame's references to Aristotle's *Physics* and to contemporaries or near contemporaries, such as the Scalingers or Mornæus (Philippe de Mornay-Duplessis). Book I, chapter v (pp. 226–29 below), gives a good sampling of the state of affairs. Brian Weiss has discussed Milton's differences with Downame regarding the relationship of physics to logic. [95] Unlike Downame, Milton normally avoids all reference to postclassical authors, but he does at times cite some contemporaries or near contemporaries, such as Francis Bacon (Book I, chapter ii—below, p. 220), Julius Caesar Scaliger (Book I, chap. vii), and Keckermann (Book II, chap. iii). Mme. Lusignan discovers, however, no true contemporary direct "source" for Milton other than Ramus and Downame: Whatever material in Milton matches Keckermann, for example, can be found also elsewhere.

(C) The Present Text.

In dealing with this potpourri the present editors had first thought of identifying (by differing type faces such as italic and boldface) what in the work is Ramus's text and what is Downame's text, thus disengaging Milton's own part. This policy, however, would be impossibly confusing, for Downame weaves Ramus's text

---

[94] British Museum Addit. MS 34361; now edited by Sister Mary Martin McCormick, "A Critical Edition of Abraham Fraunce's 'The Sheapheardes Logike' and 'Twooe General Discourses' " (Ph.D. diss., Saint Louis University, 1967).

[95] Brian Weiss, "Milton's Use of Ramist Method in His Scholarly Writings" (Ph.D. diss., City University of New York, 1974).

into his own commentary in snippets, sometimes slightly reworded to fit his own constructions, and Milton weaves Downame's text and often Ramus's text into his, sometimes taking Ramus's text in adjusted form from Downame, sometimes from Ramus's own *Dialecticæ Libri Duo* (Paris, 1572, or a reprint of this edition). Moreover, an English translation inevitably interposes a screen between the reader and the original Latin that further blurs the interrelationship of individual bits and pieces of text. Readers interested in knowing the patterns of Milton's dependence on Downame and of Downame's incorporation of Ramus can consult Mme. Lusignan's invaluable chapter-by-chapter tabulations (pp. 156–59, 177–80, 183–86). For more detailed comparisons, the only practicable tactic would appear to be on-the-spot collation of juxtaposed texts of Ramus, Downame, and Milton—a tactic not at all difficult to implement by photocopying, where necessary.

In view of the textual interrelationships just described, the present editors have adopted the following policy. Milton's use of roman and italic type is retained except in these cases: (1) quotations from authors whom Milton identifies by name and/or title of work, if set off by Milton from his text, have been set off similarly here but put in roman type instead of Milton's italics, in accordance with present practice; if not set off by Milton but included in his own text, they have been set in roman type here and enclosed in quotation marks (in each case such quotations have been verified, and Milton's often casual references completed and, where necessary, corrected by the present editors, abbreviations of titles being those given in the *Oxford Classical Dictionary,* 2nd ed., 1970); (2) citation of names of persons and of titles has been regularized, names of persons in roman and titles in italic type (Milton sometimes reverses this, his ordinary practice); (3) in the few instances when a Latin term from Milton is retained in this translation or added in parentheses after its English equivalent for clarification, it is italicized, as being a foreign word in an English-language context, even if it is not italicized in Milton; (4) where, by obvious oversight, Milton prints in roman type a lemma taken from a text he has just printed in italics, his oversight is corrected and the lemma italicized.

The present editors' added bracketed references to Greek and Latin authors quoted by Milton are given with the standard book, chapter, and line numbers found in all modern editions, unless otherwise noted. The English translation of quotations from classical authors are usually not taken from modern published translations but are the present editors' own, rendered in ways that will let emerge as clearly as possible the points intended by Milton when he gives the quotations. In some cases, Milton's allusions to classical authors are so imprecise that the editors were able to supply references that may only approximately correspond to the allusions. Many of the examples (e.g., of definitions, arguments, etc.) cited by Milton have a long history of use in the Western philosophical and logical tradition. The editors have not attempted to trace the history of all such examples but have sketched the history of some whose terminology would puzzle most modern readers.

In volume XI of the Columbia edition, Allan H. Gilbert has admirably edited the Latin text of Milton's *Logic* and we have, except where noted (e.g., p. 90, line 22; p. 92, line 14; p. 260, line 5, in Columbia; p. 247, line 27; p. 248, line 3; p. 310, line 5, in this present edition), followed his text and emendations, which are minor and with almost no exceptions merely typographical and indisputable. The emendations indicated in the errata listed in the original 1672 (and 1673) edition Gilbert incorporated without comment into his Latin text, which does not reproduce the page of errata itself, as we do not here.

The Greek words in Milton's text, which are few, are often typographically manhandled: accents are omitted at times, wrong letters used. Typographical mistakes have been silently corrected in the Greek here. Moreover, to adjust to English usage, when a single word is cited, the dictionary form of the word is normally used (e.g., the nominative case for nouns, even where Milton uses an oblique case to fit the Greek into his Latin sentence structure).

(D) The "Analytic Exercise" from Downame.

Ramus and his followers made a great deal of *usus,* of exercise, that is, of putting into practice what one learned. In this they were like most humanist educators, who felt that abstract mastery of all the "parts" of an art—which meant, in effect, the ability to recall them in proper order—was inadequate. The art had to be related to activity, which could be either *genesis* (also called *synthesis*) or *analysis.*[96] Genesis or synthesis, Ramus says, is the making of a new work—"composition" we would call it today. Analysis means

---

[96] For genesis, see [Ramus], *Dialecticæ Commentarii Tres Authore Audomaro Talæo Editi* (Paris: Ludovicus Grandinus, 1546), p. 110; also Lib. III of the subsequent three-book editions of Ramus's *Institutiones Dialecticæ* (Paris: Ludovicus Grandinus, 1547; etc.), and Ramus's *Ciceronianus* (Paris: A. Wechelus, 1557). For analysis, Ramus's *Scholæ Dialecticæ,* Lib. II, cap. viii, in *Scholæ in Liberales Artes,* col. 54; Lib. III of *Institutiones Dialecticæ,* just mentioned, where it is treated with genesis.

breaking down passages of discourse to show the "laws" of the various arts operating in them—grammatical, rhetorical, logical, arithmetical, and so on. Logical analysis would be subdivided by some Ramists, such as Johann Bisterfeld (Bisterfeldius) into thematic, topical, axiomatic, syllogistic, and methodic analysis.[97] One examined a text and identified its themes, topics (arguments), axioms (propositions), and so on, classifying them under whatever part of the "art" of logic they belonged to. Milton's "Analytic Exercise" from Downame is basically a topical analysis, detailing what kind of arguments (in non-Ramist terms, *topoi* or *loci*) figure in given passages. It mentions some logical elements other than arguments, such as syllogistic (as in the first paragraph after the first passage presented for analysis, from Ovid), but its focus is on arguments and, indeed, on quite specific ones, the efficient, procreative, and conserving causes. For the "Analytic Exercise," which Milton simply excerpts verbatim from Downame's text (with variations that are infrequent and insignificant), forms part of Downame's commentary on Ramus's Book I, chapters iii and iv, which treat these causes. In Downame the exercise is run in with the rest of his commentary, without any heading of "praxis" or anything else.

Outside as well as inside Ramist circles, the sort of academic exercise that Milton here calls an "analytic exercise in logic" (*praxis logicæ analytica*) was common enough in sixteenth- and seventeenth-century education and later, as perusal of the marginalia in used schoolbooks can show. The practice would distress most academic persons today as insensitive and wooden. But, however abrasively, it drove the student into close contact with texts, with thought, and with expression, and it is one of the major causes behind the great literature of the sixteenth and seventeenth centuries not only in the British Isles but also on the Continent. The presence of this exercise in Milton shows that he endorsed it.

(E) Milton's Abridgment of Freige's "Life of Peter Ramus."

The life of Ramus that Milton published with his *Logic* is pretty much what Milton indicates in its title, that is, Freigius's life of Ramus with the "digressions" omitted. The resulting abridgment is about one-sixth the length of Freige's original work.

---

[97] Ioannes Bisterfeldius, "Usus Lexici," V–X, in *Bisterfeldus Redivivus* (1661), II, pt. II, pp. 57–64.

Johannes Thomas Freige (or Freig or Frey, Latinized as Freigius) was born, the son of a jurist, in Freiburg-im-Breisgau in 1543.[98] Freige matriculated at the University of Freiburg in 1554, at the age of eleven, and received his bachelor's degree in arts in 1557 and his master of arts degree in 1559 at the age of sixteen—an age not exceedingly precocious for the times, when most education was what today would be called "lock-step." In 1567, unwilling to take the oaths demanded after the Council of Trent, Freige took up residence in Basel, where he taught rhetoric and studied law, receiving the doctor of laws degree in 1568. Freige got to know Ramus when the latter visited Basel in 1569 and 1570 and took up Ramism with ardor, eventually styling himself "Ramus's heir" after he published Ramus's *Life* in the 1575 posthumous Basel edition of Ramus's *Prælectiones in Ciceronis Orationes Octo Consulares*.[99] Freige's works, all in Latin, as was normal for academic works, are virtually all either adaptations of Ramus's own publications or works processing various subjects by Ramist "analysis." They include epitomes of grammar (Latin and Greek) and of rhetoric, poetic, and logic, a catechetical edition of Ramus's logic, an adaptation of Ramus's logic for the use of lawyers (1582, the first of several such adaptations, antedating by six years the publication of Abraham Fraunce's English language adaptation), a beginners' book on jurisprudence, legal commentaries, an outline of history, lectures on plane and solid geometry and on economics, politics, and physics, a *Ciceronianus,* which Freige says is complementary to the *Ciceronianus* of Erasmus and that of Ramus and which

[98] In the absence of a detailed modern study of Freige, information on him here is taken, besides from my own examination of Freige's works and of contemporary references to him, from standard biobibliographical sources, notably from Christian Gottlieb Jöcher, *Allgemeines Gelehrten-Lexicon* (Leipzig: Johann Friedrich Gleditschens, 1750–51), II, cols. 737–38 (art. "Freige, Johann Thomas"), and *Allgemeine Deutsche Biographie,* VII (Leipzig: Verlag von Duncker und Humblot, 1878), 341–43 (art. "Freigius. Ioannes Thomas").

[99] *Petri Rami Vita,* pp. 5–46, in Petrus Ramus, *Prælectiones in Ciceronis Orationes Octo Consulares Una cum Ipsius [P. Rami] Vita per Ioannem Thomam Freigium Collecta . . .* (Basileæ: Petrus Perna, 1575—copy in Library of Emmanuel College, Cambridge, autographed "Georgius Downamus"). All subsequent references here are to this edition. I know of two other editions of Freige's *Petri Rami Vita* before Milton's: (1) in Petrus Ramus, *Prælectiones in Ciceronis Orationes Octo Consulares Una cum Ipsius [P. Rami] Vita per Ioannem Thomam Freigium Collecta . . .* (Basileæ: Petrus Perna, 1580), a collection somewhat enlarged and otherwise slightly varied from the 1575 work of the same title; (2) in Petrus Ramus and Audomarus Talæus, *Collectaneæ Præfationes, Epistolæ, Orationes: Quibus Adiunctæ Sunt P. Rami Vita cum Testamento . . .* [ed. Ioannes Hartmann] (Marpurgi: Paulus Egenolphus, 1599).

includes a Ramist dichotomized outline of Cicero's career, an edition of Quintus Smyrnæus's fourteen books adding to the Homeric account of the Trojan War, a book called *Pædagogus,* which is a 366-page Ramist assemblage of all the "arts" (some twenty of them, from grammar—Latin, Greek, and Hebrew—through logic, mechanics, geography, and medicine to jurisprudence and theology), and, finally, Freige's famous *Petri Rami Professio Regia,* a collection of the seven liberal arts as taught by Ramus and outlined in Ramist charts by Freige—grammar, rhetoric, dialectic or logic, arithmetic, geometry, physics, and ethics (it will be noted that these seven subjects, which represent actual curricula, do not correspond to the partly mythological seven liberal arts mentioned by Martianus Capella and to this day often treated as representing actual curricula). Freige's works are as long on rigid diagrammatic organization of miscellaneous detail as they are short on imagination or insight. They are often turgescent and boring where they are not owlishly ludicrous (in the *Pædagogus* he includes Ramist dichotomized analyses of the Hebrew alphabet and of the bubonic plague). In 1575 he was deprived of his professorship in Basel for teaching Ramus instead of Aristotle and moved to Altdorf, where he became rector of the school. He died in 1583 in Basel.

This was the man whose biographical account of Ramus Milton elected to publish in abridged form. Milton could have used either one or two or all three of the editions of Freige's Latin *Life of Peter Ramus* (1575, 1580, and 1599—see n. 99 above) and could have produced his abridgment of Freige either when the *Logic* proper was got up, probably in or around 1645–47, or at any time later up to 1672. Milton's blindness might not have been disabling for this work.

Milton omits Freige's account of why he wrote his life of Ramus. Freige gives several reasons: [100] Ramus's fame, the absence of any other life of Ramus, Ramus's kindness to Freige himself in Basel and his subsequent correspondence with Freige, Freige's own desire to bring Ramus to the attention of those interested in "true and Socratic philosophy," and his desire to encourage publication of Ramus's as yet unpublished works. Freige says his sources are two: Ramus's own books (which indeed do contain occasional rather lengthy autobiographical data and reflections) and the knowledge about Ramus in common circulation ("quæ . . . communi de illo fama cognita essent"). Freige quotes Ramus's own works at length, for example, a letter from Ramus to Jakob Schegk (Schegkius, also

[100] *Petri Rami Vita,* p. 5.

known as Jakob Degen) and Ramus's own lengthy account of how he came to reform logic and learning.[101] Neither Ramus nor anyone else is given as a source by Freige, however, when Freige states that Ramus at his *inceptio* for his master's degree defended the *problema* or thesis, *Quæcumque ab Aristotele dicta essent commentitia esse* ("Everything that Aristotle said is a fabrication").[102] In view of the astonishing silence about any such thesis on the part of Ramus himself and of Ramus's major biographer, Nicolas de Nancel (Nancelius), who had been Ramus's student, confidant, and amanuensis, as well as in view of Freige's failure to mention a source (Had he got it from fanciful hearsay?—"quæ . . . communi de illo fama cognita essent?"), it remains questionable whether Ramus did in fact defend such a thesis at all.[103] Assertions that he did, repeated still today in biographical notes, all appear to derive directly or indirectly from Freige. Milton of course includes Freige's assertion that Ramus defended this *problema*. Elsewhere, too, Milton follows Freige uncritically, erroneously assigning Ramus's autobiographical passage (which Freige quotes at great length but Milton merely mentions) to Book V instead of Book IV of Ramus's *Scholæ Dialecticæ*.[104]

In a recent study reporting in detail just what Milton did to Freigius's *Petri Rami Vita*,[105] Leo Miller has shown that Milton put little of himself into the work but simply stripped Freige to the bare facts, producing a "strictly utilitarian" biographical account. Milton omits the German writer's quotations from Virgil, his quotations from Ramus himself and from Ramus's literary lieutenant Omer Talon, as well as various illustrative comparisons and parables. He retains some trivial personal anecdotes about Ramus, omits others. He does not rewrite Freigius, whose sentences are often reproduced verbatim and whose sequence of narration is followed.

Freigius's, and hence Milton's, organization of his account follows a typical pattern of the formulary rhetoric inherited by the Renaissance from antiquity and the Middle Ages as part of the commonplace tradition deriving ultimately from the world of oral

---

[101] Ibid., pp. 7–8, 10–13.

[102] Ibid., p. 10. For a discussion of the meaning of *commentitia* and of this *problema*, see Ong, *Ramus, Method, and Decay of Dialogue*, pp. 36–47.

[103] Ong, *Ramus, Method, and Decay of Dialogue*, pp. 37–41.

[104] Ibid., p. 38.

[105] *Ren&R*, VIII (1972), 112–14.

performance. He explicitly announces the pattern at the beginning: (1) Ramus's *natura* (literally, birth, including gifts of mind and body), then (2) his learning (*doctrina*), and finally (3) the results of his life and work.

For today's scholars, perhaps the greatest loss in Milton's abridgment is his omission of the names of many of Ramus's contemporaries, of whom Milton in general retains only the best known. Among those whose names Milton drops are Erasmus Oswald Schreckenfuchs of Freiburg, Freigius's father-in-law—perhaps, Miller suggests, out of Milton's feeling of antagonism for his own father-in-law. When he blue-penciled Schreckenfuchs, Milton also lopped out the next item in Freige, which is mention of Ramus's visit to Basel—a curious enough omission indeed on Milton's part. Miller plausibly conjectures that the excision of Basel was a mistake: Milton's excision of Schreckenfuchs was so vigorous that it overextended itself.

Miller cautiously advances the suggestion that Milton's omission of Freige's account of Ramus's bout with ophthalmia may be an argument that the *Life,* like the *Logic* it accompanies, was got up not later than 1648, when the onset of Milton's own eye troubles would have made it likely that he would have preserved mention of Ramus's. Miller further suggests that Milton's tendency to mitigate Freigius's anti-Aristotelian and antischolastic tendentiousness may mean that Milton just before publication somewhat revised the work in the direction of restraint and caution. This may be, but it may also be that Freigius's contentiousness sounded not dangerous but merely quaint to Milton because it engaged issues no longer burning in Milton's milieu. Milton could hardly share the wild (though at the same time curiously ambiguous) anti-Aristotelianism of earlier Ramists.

(F) This Translation.

This is the second translation of Milton's *Artis Logicæ Plenior Institutio* into English. The first was made by Allan H. Gilbert and published as volume XI of Columbia. The present translation is a completely new translation. But any translator with his wits about him is indebted to earlier translators, and the present translators are most indebted to and grateful to Professor Gilbert. To a much lesser extent they are indebted to the several English translations (often much adapted) of Ramus's *Dialectic* or *Logic* done in the sixteenth and seventeenth centuries by Roland MacIlmaine (1574), Dudley Fenner (1584), Abraham Fraunce (1588), Thomas

Granger (1620), Anthony Wotton (1626), Thomas Spencer (1628), and R[obert] F[age] (1632)—who are also variously indebted to one another.

The present version is mostly the work of Charles J. Ermatinger, who translated the body of the *Logic* proper, the "Analytic Exercise" from Downame, and Milton's abridgment of Freige's "Life of Peter Ramus." Walter J. Ong translated Milton's Preface. But both have worked over each other's translations together and accept joint responsibility for the final results. They have collaborated in the editorial work.

In general, an effort has been made to translate into currently meaningful idiom, not into the idiom of the sixteenth- and seventeenth-century translations of Ramus or of other Latin texts. In these earlier centuries, as noted earlier here, there was as yet no established way of talking or writing in English or other vernaculars about technical matters of the sort met with in the school curriculum, which in principle and generally in fact used only Latin for instruction (Greek was taught in Latin; English was not taught, and its use was ancillary to Latin and Greek, in principle at least). Hence English terminology was chaotic.

Milton's Latin in his *Logic* belongs to the scholastic tradition and to the humanist tradition as well. As its subject demands, his writing is technical and spare, yet it maintains a rapport with nontechnical writing that gives it an urbane ease. Although it is often trim, somewhat in the scholastic fashion, it is never "gnarled"—a favorite humanist charge against scholastic writers, particularly logicians, who had their eyes on complex accuracy and nothing else. Technical writing is at times condemned as being somewhat gnarled to those not interested in the subject. But it can also be quite urbane and more, exploiting the fuller resources of a language in a way that is scientifically creative. Milton's Latin is not of this sort. Probably it could not have been without the gnomic and nuanced irony, the two-edged dialectical tactics of a Plato or a Sir Thomas Browne or a Baltasar Gracián. But the gnomic language of paradox was not Milton's forte any more than it was the forte of Ramus, whose motto was the grim antiaphorism *Labor omnia vincit*. Ramist logic, even when it is called dialectic, is at the opposite pole from Plato's dialectical thinking. In Milton, as in Ramus, want of wit and of sly aphoristic subtlety is supplied for by indignation. For Milton's Latin style in the *Logic* is not without emotion, which is chiefly aroused when he feels that others are wrong, as in his Preface or in the "Here let the theologians take notice" in Book I, chapter vii (below, p. 233), referred to above (p. 185). In general, it can be said that his Latin here has a supple, humanistic texture, Ciceronian in a large sense, but no great distinction. A good sample of his style might be the long passage in Book I, chapter xxvii (below, p. 303) on individuals as ultimate species, which is remarkable for graceful and unaffected flow of expression but leaves much to be desired in the way of philosophical insight—the insight that can be obtained by full response in depth to the meaning of the terms one seizes on.

In the present translation, as this is a technical work more or less in the late scholastic tradition, the currently meaningful idiom has at times to be the idiom of present-day scholarship dealing with scholastic philosophy. But an effort has been made to be minimally technical in vocabulary. And, to a great extent, Ramist logic explains itself as it goes along, with its explicit definitions and divisions.

For authors quoted by Milton, often we give our own translations because the standard translations can frequently obscure the very point Milton is making. Reference to the Latin or Greek texts will make it possible for the reader to check the originals.

V. THE RELATION OF MILTON'S *LOGIC* TO HIS OTHER WORKS

Did Milton's interest in logic, which led to the composition of his *Artis Logicæ Plenior Institutio,* have any discernible effect on his other works? This is a large question, involving the ways in which an express concern with logic can affect an entire life style. Milton's endorsement of logic was pretty sweeping. His use of logic as a principle of curriculum design, noted above, results from the persuasion that everything in existence should be made as "logical" as possible, a persuasion widespread in Milton's age for far-reaching historical reasons dealt with above. A survey of Milton's other works indicates that logic certainly had its effects on them, some effects clearly calculated and others unconsciously enforced. Recently, a good many studies have made this point clear—although it should be noted that not every work whose title points to "logic" or the "logical" in Milton has anything to do with his *Logic:* many simply infer that Milton's work is coherent by present-day standards or that he is willing to bring reason into relationship with divine revelation, as millions of other persons in the tradition of Christian humanism had done. We are here interested in more specific connections with his *Logic* and the tradition it represents.

(A) Prose Works.

The most obvious effect of logic in Milton's prose works is the *Logic* itself, which, as has been seen, is not merely concerned with logic as its subject matter but also on principle uses logic to organize its presentation of logic in logical, "methodical" fashion, according to the prescriptions of "method" that Ramist logic itself contains.

Next to the *Logic* itself, the works most clearly evincing the conscious effects of applied logic and rhetoric are probably Milton's *Prolusiones* ("preludes," or "try-outs"), the academic exercises—in Latin, of course—dating from his years at Cambridge, 1625–32, which he published in 1674, the year of his death.[106] These are highly oratorical platform performances such as the curriculum regularly called for, got up in a style that deliberately rhetoricizes in humanist fashion in order to poke fun at the inanities of scholasticism: one of the *Prolusiones* is "Against Scholastic Philosophy" (a favorite commonplace). Rhetoric and logic both proceed by antitheses, and Milton's *Prolusiones* are highly antithetical, opting for one or another of two opposed positions: "Whether Day or Night Is the More Excellent" (day is, Milton says) and "Partial Forms Are Not Found in an Animal beside Its Whole Form" are two more of the titles. But logical antitheses are more forthright and nonnegotiable than rhetorical antitheses are, and Milton's performances, despite the humanist rhetorical show, are in fact more logical in spirit than rhetorical, more like scholastic dispute than Ciceronian or Erasmian dialogue. The style at Cambridge would have called for this, for Cambridge University education remained through the seventeenth century highly scholastic.[107]

What Milton learned regarding the importance of logic from Saint Paul's and Cambridge and from his extraacademic participation in the intellectual currents of his time he carried into his later prose works, too. These works generally make use of logic in ways that are at times probably automatic but at other times, and often, are quite self-conscious and designedly conspicuous.[108]

---

[106] See Sister Mary H. Cavanaugh, S.S.J., "John Milton's Prolusions Considered in the Light of His Rhetorical and Dialectical Education at St. Paul's Grammar School and Cambridge University" (Ph.D. diss., Fordham University, 1968); *DAI*, XXIX (1969), 2668A–69A.

[107] See William T. Costello, *The Scholastic Curriculum at Early Seventeenth-Century Cambridge* (Cambridge: Harvard University Press, 1958).

[108] See Franklin Irwin, "Ramistic Logic in Milton's Prose Works" (Ph.D. diss., Princeton University, 1941); Wilbur E. Gilman, *Milton's Rhetoric: Studies in His Defense of Liberty,* University of Missouri Studies, vol. XIV, no. 3 (Columbia: University of Missouri Press, 1939), which includes discussion of Milton's use of

Milton's Preface to his *De Doctrina Christiana,* in words (*institutio, methodica*) that echo the full title of his *Logic* itself, states that the work undertakes to reduce Christian teaching to "method." [109] With no hesitation, he brings logic to the analysis of Scripture. [110] In his controversial works, defects in logic on the part of his opponents are censored by Milton mercilessly. Thus, in his *Animadversions upon the Remonstrants Defense against Smectymnuus* (1641), Milton packs his protestations with logical terms:

> take up your Logick else and see. . . . Bishop *Downam* in his *Dialecticks* will tell you it is a generall axiome. . . . The inference is undeniable, *a thesi ad hypothesin,* or from the general to the particular, an evincing argument in Logick. [111]

Bishop Hall has committed the capital sin against logic, neglect of method:

> Y'are too quick; this last place is to bee understood by the former, as the Law of Method, which beares cheife sway in the Art of teaching, requires, that clearest and plainest expressions bee set formost, to the end they may enlighten any following obscurity. [112]

Milton is more cautious than Ramus in that the English poet restricts the claims of "method" to teaching procedures. [113] But here its claims are paramount. Such instances of Milton's outspoken resort to logic for proving or confuting can be multiplied by the hundreds in Milton's controversies. His more designedly expository works, if anything, are even more patently "logical," not only in their vocabulary but also in their plan. His *De Doctrina Christiana* is organized in strict Ramist method and admits of being outlined neatly in the common Ramist dichotomized tabular form, which a modern scholar has carefully worked out. [114]

The self-conscious logic that Milton's prose often advertises does not mean, however, that his prose is always in fact tightly reasoned.

---

logical proof, though without full realization of the Ramist logic-rhetoric disjunction; Weiss, "Milton's Use of Ramist Method."

[109] "Aliquam doctrinæ christianæ methodicam institutionem, aut saltem disquisitionem, quæ subvenire fidei, vel memoriæ, vel utrique possit." Columbia, XIV, 6.

[110] See Theodore Long Huguelet, "Milton's Hermeneutics" (Ph.D. diss., University of North Carolina, 1959), pp. 213, 206–15, 261–66, etc.

[111] *Complete Prose,* I, 672.

[112] Ibid., pp. 709–10.

[113] See Milton, *Logic,* Book II, chap. xvii, below, pp. 391–92 and n. 5 there.

[114] Irwin, "Ramistic Logic," table between pp. 68 and 69.

Logical terms and concepts can themselves be used for rhetorical purposes—to show one's intellectual muscle or to cow one's opponents, and even to distract from the real issues—and Milton, like many of his contemporaries, often so uses the available logical equipment. K. G. Hamilton and Stanley Fish have shown that often Milton's imagery swamps logical meaning,[115] and Fish has further shown that this was at times clearly Milton's intention, as in *The Reason of Church-Government*, where Milton often refuses to argue at all, maintaining that what he asserts is "for the plainness thereof a matter of eye sight." [116] "Plainness" was an ideal, a posture, and sometimes even an achievement fostered by Ramist logic.[117] But not always. Ramist logic in fact lent itself to rhetorical and even paralogical use more than most logics, as its opponents delighted in pointing out. For in professing to govern everything in discourse and indeed life itself by the same inexorable logical "laws," it had to make these laws—particularly the laws of method—too expansible to meet strictly formal logical standards.

(B) The Poetry.

A good case might be made that Milton's poetry is, by and large, more "logical" than most of his prose. The poems are, somewhat paradoxically, generally less impassioned and more carefully composed than his prose, their feeling, however high, under more rational control. Milton treats the core of a poem as a series of propositions rationally connected with one another.[118] In his three major poems he seldom mentions logic or dialectic explicitly, but his frequent references to "reasoning" are all to logic.[119] In their

[115] K. G. Hamilton and Stanley Fish, "The Structure of Milton's Prose," in Ronald D. Emma and John T. Shawcross, eds., *Language and Style in Milton* (New York: Frederick Ungar, 1967), p. 324.

[116] Stanley Fish, "Reasons That Imply Themselves: Imagery, Argument, and the Reader in Milton's *Reason of Church Government*," in Earl Miner, ed., *Seventeenth-Century Imagery: Essays on Uses of Figurative Language from Donne to Farquhar* (Berkeley and Los Angeles: University of California Press, 1971), pp. 83–102.

[117] See Walter J. Ong, "Peter Ramus and the Naming of Methodism," *JHI*, XIV (1953), 235–48.

[118] See William A. Scott, "Ramism and Milton's Concept of Poetic Fancy," *PQ*, XLII (1963), 183–89.

[119] Harry Lee Frissell, "Milton's *Art of Logic* and Ramist Logic in the Major Poems" (Ph.D. diss., University of Michigan, 1951), p. 188. See also Christopher Grose, "Milton on Ramist Similitude," in Miner, *Seventeenth-Century Imagery*, pp. 103–16, and the same author's *Milton's Epic Process: "Paradise Lost" and Its Miltonic Background* (New Haven and London: Yale University Press, 1973), pp. 123–39.

larger features the poems reveal conscious logical preoccupations. The temptation theme, which Milton so often deals with, of itself feeds the pro-and-con movement of disputation and oratory.[120] The announced purpose of *Paradise Lost,* "to justifie the wayes of God to men," is realizable in the Ramist noetic economy only by resort to logic (not rhetoric).[121]

Particular details of the poems show further preoccupation with logical structures. In *Paradise Lost* and *Paradise Regained,* and less conspicuously in *Samson Agonistes,* Milton reveals his acquaintanceship with theologians such as Johann Wolleb, William Ames, and Zacharias Ursinus, who employ the full armory of "logical" terms such as external cause, internal cause, principal cause, assisting cause, immediate and proximate cause, instrumental cause, and the like to analyze the origins and consequences of Adam's sin and of other actions. How fully Milton's characterization—so often achieved through characters' speeches—derives from conspicuous relation or lack of relation to logical structures has been detailed by John M. Steadman. Satan, for example, reveals his duplicity by his conspicuous misuse of "consentany" and "dissentany" arguments.[122]

Milton's shorter poems reveal equal preoccupation with logical design, especially in his feeling for "reciprocal relationships," although often "direct logical representation was avoided."[123] The neatly opposed "L'Allegro" and "Il Penseroso" are the most obvious

[120] See Dan S. Collins, "Rhetoric and Logic in Milton's English Poems" (Ph.D. diss., University of North Carolina, 1961). See also J. M. Broadbent, "Milton's Rhetoric," *MP,* LVI (1959), 224–42.

[121] See Leon Howard, " 'The Invention' of Milton's 'Great Argument': A Study of the Logic of God's Ways to Man," *HLQ,* IX (1945–46), 149–73; and more generally, Lee A. Jacobus, *Sudden Apprehension: Aspects of Knowledge in "Paradise Lost,"* (The Hague: Mouton, 1976). Because its title might suggest some special relevance here, it should be noted that Dennis H. Burden's *The Logical Epic: A Study of the Argument of "Paradise Lost"* (Cambridge: Harvard University Press, 1967) does not treat Milton's *Logic* at all or any of the logical tradition as such out of which Milton was operating; the "logical" in the title apparently refers simply to general intellectual consistency.

[122] John M. Steadman, *Milton's Epic Characters: Image and Idol* (Chapel Hill: University of North Carolina Press, 1968), p. 264; for other instances of the relation of logic to character, see many logical terms in the book's index. See also Richard B. Lewis, "Milton's Use of Logic and Rhetoric in *Paradise Lost* to Develop the Character of Satan," (Ph.D. diss., Stanford University, 1948); Ross C. Brackney, " 'By Fallacy Surpris'd': Logic and the Miltonic Hero" (Ph.D. diss., Stanford University, 1969); *DAI,* XXX (1970), 5400A–1A.

[123] See Bernard Shroder Adams, "Milton and Metaphor: The *Artis Logicæ* and the Imagery of the Shorter English Poems" (Ph.D. diss., University of Pittsburgh, 1964), pp. 248–49.

examples. Contrasts such as this derive from a historical tradition
that is both logical (or dialectical) and rhetorical, but again, in the
Ramist noetic economy, they belong as contrastive arguments in
principle to logic. Other poems, such as "On the Morning of Christ's
Nativity" and "At a Vacation Exercise," turn on hinges of "for's"
and "but's" that make plain their argumentative structure. Even
in so programmatically fanciful a piece as "A Maske Presented at
Ludlow Castle" such structures show, advertised not only by the
dialogic movement of thought between the interlocutors but also
by the frequent labeling of logical furniture:

> *La*[dy] . . . this Jugler
> Would think to charm my judgement, as mine eyes,
> Obtruding false rules pranckt in reasons garb.
> I hate when vice can bolt her arguments
>
> . . . .
>
> Enjoy your deer Wit, and gay Rhetorick
>
> . . . .
>
> Thou art not fit to hear thy self convinc't.
>
> [lines 757–60, 790, 792]

This is a climate of controversy, which, to a Ramist, signals logic.

(C) Specific Effects of Ramism.

What has been said above in discussing the relationship of Ramist logic and rhetoric to the pre-Ramist tradition suggests ways
in which one must approach the question as to how distinctively
Ramist were the logical elements that everywhere make themselves
evident in Milton's works.[124] As has been seen, Ramus made no
new discoveries in formal logic. No more did Milton. What is
distinctive of Ramist logic can be subsumed conveniently with
reference to Milton under two headings. First, because Ramus
appropriated to logic all the heuristic and discursive procedures
formerly distributed between logic and/or dialectic and rhetoric,
eliminating all "soft" or probable argumentation in favor of pur-
portedly universal "hard" thinking, he made of logic an extraordinarily assertive and autocratic art, all the more so because of the
Ramist postulate that all arts were closed fields, complete in themselves. Possibly all thought that vaunts its claims to logic is imperious, but no logic encourages single-minded conviction of one's
own rightness more than Ramism. Whatever there is in Milton of
unbending persuasion of the rightness of his own opinion no doubt

---

[124] One of the earliest discussions of this question is that in P. Albert Duhamel,
"Milton's Alleged Ramism," *PMLA,* LXVII (1953), 1035–53. See also Peter J.
Fisher, "Milton's Logic," *JHI,* XXIII (1962), 37–60, esp. p. 60.

owes much to Ramism, although it is hard to say what is cause and what is effect here. Milton's mind may have had an affinity to Ramism before he came into contact with it.

Secondly, Ramism stood for what Frances Yates has deftly labeled "inner iconoclasm." [125] Eliminating the parts of the oration and the elaborate iconographic memory systems associated with these parts and with rhetoric, Ramus had substituted his "method," which was nicely abstract and which lent itself to diagramming by means of charts displaying words rather than iconographic symbols in spatial arrangements. This, Miss Yates shows, goes far to explain the appeal of Ramism to the iconoclastic Calvinist mind. Milton of course does not eschew iconographic symbols in his poetry although he downgrades their religious utility in his prose. It has, however, been convincingly argued by Isabel MacCaffrey that, although *Paradise Lost* deals with symbols in a genuinely "mythical" manner, it does so with considerable reservation. Milton's images, even the dark and mystifying images of evil, do not quite live a life of their own, as they do, for example, in Shakespeare or other Elizabethan and Jacobean dramatists, but are strictly reined by reason. [126] It is not too much to see here a relationship to Ramist "inner iconoclasm," although again it is not certain whether Milton needed Ramist logic to arrive at this poetic economy. His predisposition to this poetic economy may be reflected in his liking for Ramist logic. Along similar lines, Jackson I. Cope has argued that Milton's preoccupation with space, particularly in *Paradise Lost,* has in it much of the Ramist proclivity to project knowledge itself in spatial patterns, [127] a proclivity associated with disinterest in an iconography that lives its own life independently of conscious rational control. Miss Yates has shown how concern with space is integral to memory systems and to the noetic shifts that were taking place after the invention of print. [128]

At any rate, Milton did not go the whole way with Ramist logic, which in theory and actuality is about as unpropitious for poetry as any noetic theory could well be. [129] Ramist poets are few and far between. Milton's wide reading guaranteed in his sensibility and

[125] Yates, *Art of Memory,* pp. 234–35.

[126] Isabel MacCaffrey, *Paradise Lost as "Myth"* (Cambridge: Harvard University Press, 1959).

[127] Jackson I. Cope, *The Metaphoric Structure of Paradise Lost* (Baltimore: Johns Hopkins University Press, 1962).

[128] Yates, *Art of Memory,* p. 231 ff.

[129] See Ong, *Ramus, Method, and Decay of Dialogue,* pp. 33, 253, 281–83, 287.

in his works a strong reserve of Ciceronian,[130] rationally controlled rotundity, basically oratorical in cast, which is to say rhetorical in the traditional, non-Ramist sense. Milton had more feeling for sound than the typographically styled Ramist noetic and poetic allowed for. And his *Commonplace Book* reveals a preoccupation with proverbial and anecdotal wisdom uncongenial to the obsessively analytic Ramist mind. Nevertheless, Milton remains, through his *Logic* and its relationship to his other work, linked to Ramism more clearly than any other poet of much stature. For even Spenser and Sidney, although they moved in Puritan circles that were more or less Ramist and although Abraham Fraunce exploited their works in his Ramist *Sheapheardes Logike* and *Arcadian Rhetorike,* can hardly be said to have been involved in Ramism as deliberately as Milton was.

Milton's deep-seated, if largely inarticulate, reserve about Ramist logic as it touched, or professed to touch, the more persuasive and fictive uses of language shows in the closing words of his *Logic.* He has condensed Ramus's last four chapters, which treat method, into one and has made unambiguously clear—more unambiguously than Ramus certainly—that Ramist method applies only to handing on or teaching already processed knowledge (knowledge typically organized in a "methodized" Ramist art, which moves relentlessly from general to particular or special). At the very end of the *Logic,* with Ramus, he treats "cryptic" method, which is used by poets or orators confronted by recalcitrant audiences and which is really not method at all but reverse method or antimethod, as it does not strictly follow general-to-special order but, as Ramus had elsewhere explained,[131] even reverses this order. Milton reproduces part of Ramus's text on this cryptic method and adds only this comment of his own to close the issue and the *Logic:* "But to the orators and poets should be left their own account of method, or at least to those who teach the art of oratory and poetry." This completely overturns the Ramist cart. Ramus had insisted that all method of any kind belonged not to rhetoric or to poetry but to logic and to nothing else. It appears that Milton is not so sure.

---

[130] See Collins, "Rhetoric and Logic," passim.

[131] E.g., *Dialectique* (Paris: A. Wechel, 1555; BM), pp. 128–29, where cryptic method is styled an "ambush" *(executer l'embusche); Dialectica Audomari Talœi Prœlectionibus Illustrata* (Basel: E. Episcopius et Nicolai fratris hæredes, 1569), pp. 576–78.

For help in assembling bibliographical material for this edition, thanks are due to Mr. James M. Bell, Mr. Robert E. Kelly, Jr., Dr. Ralph L. Mastriani, Dr. John D. Schaeffer, and Dr. Thomas M. Walsh, who worked generously and intelligently on this project while they were graduate students at Saint Louis University. Permission to reproduce the title pages has been granted by Christ's College Library, Cambridge University, for the 1672 edition, and by Dr. Williams's Library, London, for the 1673 edition.

JOANNIS MILTONI

Angli,

Artis Logicæ

Plenior Inſtitutio,

AD

PETRI RAMI

Methodum concinnata,

Adjecta eſt Praxis Annalytica & *Petri Rami* vita.   Libris duobus.

LONDINI,

Impenſis *Spencer Hickman,* So-
cietatis Regalis Typographi, ad
inſigne *Roſæ* in *Cæmeterio,*
D. Pauli. 1672.

JOANNIS MILTONI

Angli,

Artis Logicæ

Plenior Institutio,

AD

PETRI RAMI

Methodum concinnata.

Adjecta est Praxis Analytica &
Petri Rami vita; Libris duobus.

LONDINI,
Impensis *S. H.* Prostant pro *R. Boulter*
ad Insigne Capitis *Turcæ* exadversum
Mercatorio Regali in Vico vulgò
Cornhill dicto, 1673.

PREFACE[1]

ALTHOUGH many of the philosophers, confident of their own native ability, are said to have despised logic, among those of them who have thought that logic was worthwhile, either for themselves or for others less sharp and alert, and who have thought that they ought carefully to cultivate it, the most deserving, in my opinion as in the opinion of our good Sidney,[2] is Peter Ramus. The rest irresponsibly confuse physics, ethics, and theology [3] with logical matters. But our author has tried too hard for brevity, and while he is lucid, he fails to be lucid enough, for in teaching an art

---

[1] Milton omits Ramus's own introductory letter to the reader. Much of Milton's Preface here is taken, sometimes verbatim, from Downame's *Prolegomena*. For some parallel passages in English translation, see Thomas S. K. Scott-Craig, "The Craftsmanship and Theological Significance of Milton's *Art of Logic*," *HLQ*, XVII (1953), 6–8.

[2] Sidney's advocacy of Ramist logic and his association with the Cambridge Ramists Abraham Fraunce, Gabriel Harvey, and William Temple are well known. See John Buxton, *Sir Philip Sidney and the English Renaissance* (London: Macmillan, 1954), pp. 45–50. Sidney had paid for the Cambridge education of Fraunce, who repaid him posthumously with *The Arcadian Rhetorike* (1588), a Ramist rhetoric in which Fraunce takes all his examples of rhetorical usage from Sidney's *Arcadia*. In *The Lawiers Logike* (1588), fol. A1r, Fraunce states that he and Sidney found themselves drawn "to a greater liking of, and my selfe to a further travayling in, the easie explanation of Ramus his Logike." The French Protestant pastor Théophile de Banos (Theophilus Banosius), at the end of his *Petri Rami Vita* in his posthumous edition of Ramus's *Commentariorum de Religione Christiana Libri Quatuor* (Frankfurt: A. Wechelus, 1576), fol. 4r, comments on Sidney's devotion to Ramus: "You have not only loved [him] as a parent while he was alive, but also esteem and honor him after his death" (*qui parentem superstitem non tantum amaveris, sed mortuum colis et observas*). Milton may here have had either of these passages or others in mind, or may simply have been referring to what was common knowledge about Sidney's Ramism.

[3] Further on in this Preface (p. 211), Milton inveighs more explicitly about the intrusion of theology into logic. Unlike many logicians, including not a few Ramists, Ramus himself had made no reference in the text of his *Dialectica* to specifically Christian theological matters, although he does not avoid all theology, giving "divine testimony" as one of the "arguments." But even in treating divine testimony, as elsewhere in the *Dialectica,* he takes his examples from pagan sources—oracles and the like. Milton uses almost exclusively pagan sources for his examples, too, but occasionally permits one from the Bible, as in Book I, chap. xvi, where he cites Rom. 9:25 (itself a quotation from Hosea). His own theological persuasions also occasionally assert themselves as vigorous asides, for example, in his famous *Evigilent hic Theologi* in Book I, chap. vii, and in a long

one should not be sparing of light but generous [A4ʳ] with it. The many commentaries on him testify to this. Hence I have come to the conclusion that material from Ramus' own *Lectures on Dialectic* [4] and from the commentaries by others [5] necessary for the fuller understanding of the precepts of the art must be transferred

---

excursion in Book II, chaps. iii and iv. Other theological references occur in Book I, chaps. iv, v, vii, xi, xvi, xviii, Book II, chap. iii. See also below, Book I, chap. xxxii, and n. 2, p. 319. But Milton is, generally speaking, not a theologizing logician. A prime example of a theologizing Ramist logic would be *The Logike of . . . P. Ramus . . . newly translated and in divers places corrected after the mynde of the author per M[agistrum] Roll[andum] Makylmenœum Scotum . . .* (London: Thomas Vautrollier, 1574), recently edited by Catherine M. Dunn, Renaissance Editions, no. 3 (Northridge, Calif.: San Fernando Valley State College, 1969). In this English version, though not in his Latin edition of the same work of Ramus's published the same year, 1574, MacIlmaine substitutes scriptural examples for a good many of Ramus's secular ones and thereby slips in highly programmed theological doctrine. So does Dudley Fenner in *The Artes of Logike and Rethorike* [sic] *Plainlie Set Foorth . . .* ([Middelburg: R. Schilders], 1584; another ed., 1588), a work bearing neither Fenner's nor Ramus's nor Talon's name (the *Rethorike* was later erroneously attributed to Thomas Hobbes), although it is nothing more than an abridged adaptation of Ramus's *Dialectica* and of Talon's Ramist *Rhetorica*. Theologizing Ramist logics appeared also on the continent, for example, Johannes Piscator's *In P. Rami Dialecticam Animadversiones* (Francofurti: A. Wechelus, 1580), an edition of Ramus with a commentary that illustrates logic from Holy Writ. Among non-Ramist works following similar practices might be cited *The Art of Logick* (London: Robert White for George Calvert, 1654), a work identified on its title page as "by Zachary Coke" but in fact apparently by Henry Ainsworth—see "Advertisement to the Reader" in 2nd ed., 1657, and also, for full discussion, James S. Measell, "The Authorship of *The Art of Logick* (1654)," *Journal of the History of Philosophy*, XV (1977), 321–24. Ainsworth ("Coke") sees eye to eye with Ramus and the latter's followers in his view that formal logical structures can be discerned with no trouble at all in any kind of discourse. The introduction of physics and ethics into logic was less widespread and less programmed, but proceeded also chiefly by way of examples.

    [4] *Scholarum Dialecticarum Libri XX,* first published under this title in the collection *P. Rami Scholœ in Liberales Artes* (Basileæ: E. Episcopius et Nicolai fratris hæredes, 1569) and subsequently in other editions. The work is a revision of Ramus's earlier *Aristotelicæ Animadversiones* (1543, etc.). See Walter J. Ong, *Ramus and Talon Inventory* (Cambridge: Harvard University Press, 1958), pp. 56–66, 431–37. Milton appears to have made only indirect use of this work of Ramus's. Parts of it were embedded in Talon's commentary (*Prælectiones*) published with many editions of Ramus's *Dialectic*. Downame incorporates a good deal of Talon's commentary into his own, where Milton would have found it. See n. 5 below.

    [5] Notably George Downame or Downham. See Introduction, pp. 168, 184–88, above.

to the body of the art [6] proper and woven in there, except where I disagree with what these commentaries say. For what is the use of achieving brevity if this means we must go elsewhere for clarification? It is better to produce a longish treatment of an art which achieves clarity all in the course of one work than to explicate a too brief work through a separate commentary, which results in less clarity. This is evident because the latter is what has hitherto been done, with more trouble and less convenience than if the art itself were made to explain itself out of its own resources. Indeed, learning from greater experience, Ramus himself adopted a more diffuse procedure of teaching an art in his *Arithmetic* and *Geometry,* which he published somewhat later,[7] explaining the rules himself in a brief running commentary instead of leaving them to others to explain. Many of these commentators, perhaps carried away by an irresistible desire to comment, some of them oblivious of all orderly procedure (*methodus*)—an astonishing fact in their case[8]—mix everything together, insisting on putting last things first, introducing axioms, syllogisms, and the rules for these things [A4^{v}] in the chapters on simple arguments, and in this way necessarily surrounding their pupils with darkness rather than light. I have therefore thought that I should be careful to take nothing for granted, to presuppose nothing as already taught and understood, to take up nothing except in its proper place. In this I should have no fear that I might appear perhaps too narrow in my explanation of the precepts while I was trying to set them forth by means of what depends on them rather than by merely running through them.[9] Yet I should not readily agree with those who hold

[6] Ramist doctrine called for a skeletal "art" of grammar, rhetoric, logic, physics, etc., and even Christian doctrine, which contained the totality of each of these subjects—consisting largely of definitions and divisions—as in a closed field and which was supplemented or "defended" by "commentaries."

[7] This statement is somewhat misleading, for Ramus's 1572 edition of the *Dialectic,* his final revision, published only a few months before his death and used by Milton for his basic text here, is one of the most compact and brief of all the editions, even the commentary being omitted. See Ong, *Ramus and Talon Inventory,* pp. 191–93. The *Arithmetic* was published as early as the *Dialectic* (1555), but later editions were indeed fuller. Editors and publishers alternately abridge and expand Ramus's *Dialectic,* solemnly justifying whichever activity they are engaged in as being for the convenience of students—see the entries in Ong, *Ramus and Talon Inventory.*

[8] Orderly presentation in teaching, the notion that controlled, if it did not always entirely limit, the concept of *methodus,* was the particular business of logicians according to Ramists and the post-Johann Sturm world generally.

[9] *Per pendenda magis quam percurrenda*—a play on words in the Latin. In speaking of what "depends on" or, in the basic meaning of the Latin, "hangs

against Ramus his paucity of rules,[10] since a great number of the rules garnered out of Aristotle by others, not to mention rules which these others have themselves thrown onto the heap, are either uncertain or useless and thus impede the learner and burden him instead of helping him. And if they are of any use or show any acumen, it is of the kind which anyone could come by more easily through his native ability than through a lot of memorized rules. I have even more decidedly made up my mind not to stuff in random rules which come from theologians rather than from logic; [11] for theologians produce rules about God, about divine substances, and about sacraments right out of the middle of logic as though these rules had been provided simply for their own use, although nothing is more foreign to logic, or indeed to reason itself, than the grounds for these rules as formulated by them.[12] [A5^r]

But before I enter upon the work itself, since the art of logic is the first of all arts and its bounds the widest, I shall prefix here some general remarks on art and the division and interrelation of the arts. Next, I shall treat the art of logic itself. Finally, I shall provide some examples of analysis, or of the use of the art for the sake of practice on the part of those who have need and inclination for this sort of thing. I say for those who have need, for I do not propose that those whose native ability is active and strong torture themselves in this analytic procedure with too much labor and agony.[13] For art is employed to help nature, not to hinder it. If it is used too feverishly and too finically, especially when there is no need of this, it blunts rather than sharpens a sensibility already keen enough in itself, just as in the case of medicine the use of too

---

down from" the precepts, Milton is perhaps influenced by the picture of one of the bracketed outline tables in which Ramists specialized and which diagrammatically represented the division of concepts as a kind of ramification, in which each term had two other terms branching out or "hanging down" from it, each of these two two more, and so on.

[10] Ramus, Milton, and most of their contemporaries looked on logic as prescriptive rather than descriptive. It tells how one ought to think rather than how one does think.

[11] See no. 3, p. 208 above.

[12] Milton himself brings "rules about God," buttressed by sacred Scripture, into the present work, all the same. See Milton's text and n. 3. above.

[13] Many schoolmasters certainly demanded endless exercises in "logical analyses" of everything from physics and theology and law to orations and poetry. This is evident from the glosses in printed texts and from occasional appearances of such exercises in print, as in Abraham Fraunce's *The Lawiers Logicke* (1588). The Ramist Johannes Piscator (1546–1625) published logical analyses of many of the books of the Bible, though he failed to cover them all.

great or of unnecessary remedies debilitates rather than strengthens one's health. As for adding the authority of Aristotle and of other older writers to practically every rule of logic, this would be superfluous in teaching the art were it not that the suspicion of novelty, which has up to now been especially attached to Peter Ramus, must be quieted by the testimony of these older writers.[14] [A5ᵛ]

The body (*corpus*) and full expanse of all the arts is called in Greek ἐγκυκλοπαιδεία, that is, a kind of circle of knowledge closed in on itself and thus in itself complete and perfect, or it is also called philosophy.[15]

This latter term properly signifies zeal for wisdom, but popularly either the teaching or the knowledge of all the arts: teaching, when it hands on the precepts of the arts; knowledge, when the art, which is a kind of permanent possession (*habitus*) of the mind, is laid hold of and as it were possessed by means of these precepts. In the same way, the meaning of art is distinguished: when it signifies a teaching (*doctrina*), about which we are especially concerned here, it is the orderly assemblage of precepts and examples,[16] or the method (*methodus*), by which anything is usefully taught.

The precepts are the material of an art.[17] Of what sort these

[14] Almost all of his many citations of older writers are taken by Milton from Ramus and George Downame. See Introduction, above, p. 186.

[15] Although the notion of "encyclopedia" is certainly Greek, Milton's identification of "philosophy" with a round of curriculum subjects bears the mark of the medieval university tradition, in which "philsophy" became more or less the round of subjects purveyed by the "arts" faculty. Milton registers here also the Ramist tendency to regard knowledge as existing in closed fields. See Walter J. Ong, *Ramus, Method, and the Decay of Dialogue* (Cambridge: Harvard University Press, 1958), pp. 121, 225–30, 280–81.

[16] Milton thinks not only of what one does in purveying logic or other "arts" to others as teaching, but also of what one teaches—the "content" of the course—as a "teaching" or "doctrine" (*doctrina*). Almost all his predecessors and contemporaries have this same frame of mind, because of the fact that historically knowledge is at first thought of in terms of speech and communication (teacher to pupil) and only late in the evolution of human thought, after the Copernican and Newtonian revolutions exalt space and sight at the expense of sound and speech, comes to be more commonly considered as "content," independent of speech (as, of course, it never entirely is). Milton's view of knowledge, evident enough in the Socratic tradition, was given a special currency and plausibility in the medieval milieu dominated by the teachers' unions or universities. For a fuller discussion, see Ong, *Ramus, Method, and Decay of Dialogue*, pp. 159–67, etc.

[17] What constituted the "material" of an art was a matter of dispute between Ramists and others, and among Ramists themselves. Milton follows the view of William Temple (the elder), who held for the precepts in his *Epistola de Dialectica P. Rami* (Francofurti, 1590), pp. 6–7, against Johannes Piscator, who held that the arguments were the material of dialectic and disposition the form in his *In P. Rami Dialecticam Animadversiones* (Francofurti: A. Wechelus, 1580), p. 14.

precepts should be, it is the business of the art of logic, which we are now teaching, to set forth in the proper place.

The form or rationale (*ratio*) of the art is not so much the methodical arrangement of these precepts as it is the teaching of some useful matter, for an art is what it is by reason of what it teaches rather than by the order of its teaching.[18] [A6ʳ] This is seen from the definition of any art, as will be shown below.

There are three kinds of precepts of an art. The two principal ones are definitions and distributions, both of which logic itself explains in due course. The third, less basic, is called a consectary. It is the explanation of some property, usually deduced from a definition.

Examples are those things by which the truth of precepts is demonstrated and their use shown. As Plato [*Tht.* 202 E] nicely observes, they are guarantees, so to speak, of our assertions, for what is taught with regard to the genus by the precept is confirmed with regard to the species by the example.

I am supposing that no one doubts that the primary efficient source of an art is God, the author of all wisdom. Even the ancient philosophers were aware of this.

The ministerial causes were the talented and divinely instructed men who in the past discovered the various arts. Their way of discovery was much like the procedure in painting. [A6ᵛ] For, just as in a picture there are two things, the subject or primary model and the art of painting, so in the discovery of an art, the natural use [19] and the example of skilled men corresponds to the primary model, and logic corresponds to the art of the painter—natural logic, at least, for this is the faculty itself of reason in the human mind, according to the common saying that art imitates nature.

Reason or logic—first natural reason or logic, and then artificially trained reason or logic—makes use, so to speak, of four helpers, as Aristotle notes in the *Metaphysics* i.1 [i.1.980a22–982a3], sense, observation, induction, and experience. For, since the pre-

---

[18] In its basic conceptualization the matter-form or hylomorphic analysis of (material) being is based on intuition into the situation where wood (ὕλη) is given shape (μορφή) by a sculptor. The resulting elemental matter-form dyad applies in a bewildering variety of ways to an art (as to many other things besides). Deciding which was the most basic application—what was "matter" and what "form"—could be a crucial tactical and theoretical decision, as it implied views of the nature of the mind, of communication, of man, and of being itself.

[19] *Natura sive usus*. Cf. Ramus, *Dialecticœ Institutiones* (1543), fols. 5–6, where *natura* refers not to the "nature" of dialectic but to dialectic in its original or, as we should today say, unreflective state. See Ong, *Ramus, Method, and Decay of Dialogue*, pp. 176–78.

cepts of the arts are general formulations, they can be gathered only from singular instances, and singular instances can be gathered only from sensation. And sensation is useless without observation, which commits to memory the isolated singular instances; observation useless without induction, which from as many singulars as possible sets up a general rule by an induction; and induction useless without experience, which judges the common agreement and, so to speak, consent of all the singular instances.

Hence Polus rightly remarks in Plato's *Gorgias* [448 C], "Experience gave birth to art, inexperience to fortune," that is, to haphazard and to that extent unreliable statements. And [A7ʳ] Aristotle says in the *Prior Analytics* i.30 [*An. Pr.* i.30.46a17–20], "It is the business of experience to provide the principles of anything; thus experience in astrology supplies the principles of that science." And Manilius says [*Astronomicon* i.61–62]:

> By varied use experience wrought art,
> Example showing the way . . .

And Cicero [*De or.* i.42.187–88]: "All the things now enclosed within the arts were once lying loose and scattered until this art was made use of to fasten together and confine within the bounds of reason disconnected and dispersed items." He means the art of logic, whether this be the natural logic born in us or that artificial logic which we soon learn, for this latter discovers and teaches the precepts of the arts. So much for the efficient causes of the arts.

The form of an art, as I have said above, is not so much the arrangement of the precepts as the actual laying down of the precepts for doing something useful. The end of an art is the same. For just as the form and end of logic is not so much the orderly arrangement as it is simply discoursing well,[20] so form and the end as well of an art in general is not only the arrangement of the precepts, [A7ᵛ] but the actual prescribing for doing something useful. Moreover, everyone agrees that what is taught should be useful in man's life, or as the Greeks say, βιωφελές, and that whatever does not aim at some good or utility in man's life which is at the same time morally commendable, does not deserve the name of art, since to such good or utility all precepts of an art are referred. Therefore it necessarily follows that the form of an art is the laying down of precepts for something useful, through which the art is evidently what it is. But natural ability without art is considered

---

[20] *Bene disserere*—this formula is from Ramus and Cicero. See Introduction, p. 155, and Book I, chap. i, pp. 217–18.

to go further than art without natural ability, although neither can go so far as it should unless supplemented by practice. Hence Ovid's observation [*Ars am.* ii.676]:

All that makes a skilled workman is practice.

There are two kinds of practice: analysis and genesis. The former occurs when the examples of an art are, so to speak, resolved into their principles, as they are weighed in their various parts against the norm, that is, against the precepts [A8ʳ] of the art; the latter, when we produce or put together something according to the prescriptions of the art.

So much for the causes of the arts; next, the species. Arts are either general or special. The general arts are those of which the subject matter is general. This matter belongs either to the one skilled in the art or to the art itself. The general matter belonging to the one skilled in the art is common to all the general arts,[21] whereas the general matter belonging to the art is proper to each of the separate arts. For the general matter belonging to the one skilled in the art is the totality of what really exists or is feigned to exist, and the general matter belonging to the art is that which each of the separate arts effects upon this totality. All this is embraced either by reason or by speech, and thus the general matter of the general arts is either reason or speech. For these arts are employed either in refining reason in order to argue well,[22] or in refining speech, and this either in order to speak well,[23] as in the case of grammar, or in order to express oneself well,[24] as in the

---

[21] Aristotle had noted in his *Rhetoric* i.1 (1354a) that rhetoric and dialectic have to do with matters of common knowledge, that is, that their subject matter is not restricted in the way in which the subject matter of physics or grammar is restricted (physics does not deal with grammar, nor grammar with physics, but rhetorical and dialectical argumentation can have to do with matter from physics or grammar or anything else at all).

[22] *Ad bene ratiocinandum.* Ramus had defined dialectic or logic as *ars disserendi.* See Introduction, p. 155.

[23] *Ad bene loquendum.* Cf. Ramus's definition of grammar as *ars bene loquendi,* "the art of speaking well," to which he adds at times *beneque scribendi,* "and of writing well." See Ong, *Ramus, Method, and Decay of Dialogue,* pp. 246, 363, n. 56.

[24] *Ad dicendum bene.* Cf. Ramus's definition of rhetoric as *ars bene dicendi,* discussed in Ong, *Ramus, Method, and Decay of Dialogue,* pp. 271–72. Originally *loquendi* referred to "framing one's speech in suitable words," *dicendi* to (oral) delivery, for rhetoric was originally the art of oratory. As, by mostly unacknowledged and indeed unwitting adjustment, it came to refer more and more to writing, *dicendi* loosened its connections with oral delivery and referred more and more to stylistics. See Introduction, pp. 157–59.

case of rhetoric. But of all the arts the first and most general is logic, next grammar, and finally rhetoric, since reason can be used, and even used extensively, without speech,[25] but speech cannot be used at all without logic. We give the second place to grammar [A8^v] because speech can be faultless even when it is unadorned, but it cannot easily be adorned unless it first be faultless.[26]

Special arts are those which have special matter, namely nature itself or human conduct. However, this is not the place for a more accurate classification of these arts. [A9^r]

[25] Milton appears to take the view, common enough in his time and still common today, that thinking goes on independently of language, which is thus taken to be something added to thought, the words somehow being considered to be attached to the completed thought afterward when one wishes to manifest it to someone else. This view does not deal with certain truths about language today widely discussed in phenomenological treatments, such as the fact that human thought typically occurs in a context of words, so that, although when we "think" we certainly engage in activities, conscious and unconscious, that are not explicitly verbal, still our thought moves toward verbal formulation and matures or fully finds itself as thought when it is verbally formulated, that is, stated at least to oneself in explicit concepts. Such concepts are verbally grounded, so that there is no way to formulate or state a truth to oneself without at the same time making it statable to others. Human thought is verbalized not by ex post facto arrangement but somehow in its very constitution. Furthermore, Milton's text hardly makes it clear whether by "speech" he is referring to imaginary, internal speech or to audible speech: the relationship of rhetoric to the oral and the imagined or the written is quite confused.

[26] As words and grammar are added to thought, so ornament (the tropes and figures) is added to words, in Milton's view. This persuasion that phenomena such as metaphor are decorations added to speech, rather than the normal stuff of speech, which can be eliminated only with the greatest difficulty and perhaps never entirely, represents the most common misunderstanding of speech coming down from classical antiquity through arts scholasticism and the Renaissance to later ages. It admits of varying degrees of sophistication but in the hands of Ramus and Ramists generally is pretty gross. See Ong, *Ramus, Method, and Decay of Dialogue,* pp. 277–79.

A FULLER COURSE &c.
IN THE ART OF LOGIC

BY JOHN MILTON THE ENGLISHMAN

BOOK THE FIRST

CHAPTER I

WHAT IS LOGIC?

L OGIC is the art of reasoning well.[1] And in the same sense it is often called Dialectic.

Now logic, namely, the rational art, is so named from λόγος,[2] a Greek word meaning reason;[3] and the object of logic is to refine reason.

To reason is to use the faculty of reason; as the definition adds, to use it well—that is, correctly, skillfully and promptly—in order to distinguish the perfection proper to the art of logic from the imperfection of the faculty of reason in its natural state.

Rather than use the term dialectic, as Peter Ramus does, I have used the term logic,[4] because by the latter term the whole of the rational art is most aptly signified; whereas dialectic, [1] derived

[1] Milton's *ars bene ratiocinandi* alters Ramus's *ars bene disserendi* (the art of discoursing well). See Introduction, pp. 154–55.

[2] We follow the usual practice for citing Greek nouns in English, putting them in the nominative case. Milton works the case of λόγος into the Latin sentence structure with the Latin preposition *a: a λογῳ*. Gilbert (Columbia, XI, 19) translates "from λόγῳ." This corresponds to earlier Latin, but not present English practice.

[3] Milton's Latin term *ratio* ranges in its various senses far more widely than the English "reason" but here is very close to this English term.

[4] Milton defines logic and then assimilates dialectic to it; Ramus had defined dialectic and then assimilated logic to dialectic: "Dialectic is the art of discoursing well, and in the same sense is called logic." Which term was paramount was hotly disputed. Donald L. Clark, *John Milton at St. Paul's School* (New York: Co-

from the Greek word διαλέγεσθαι, means rather the art of questioning and answering, that is, of debating, as we learn from the *Cratylus* of Plato [390 C], from the teachings of the Peripatetics and Stoics, from Fabius [Quint. *Inst.* ii.21.13, xii.2.13], Suidas [5] and others. Yet Plato, in the first book of the *Alcibiades* [129 C], insists that τὸ διαλέγεσθαι means the same as to use one's reason. The first meaning is too narrow to signify the use of reason, while the second, if authors do not agree on it, is too uncertain.[6]

In the definition I say the art of *reasoning* rather than that of discoursing, because *to reason,* used no less broadly than *reason* itself, properly means the same thing as *to use the reason;* whereas *to discourse (disserere),* besides being an expression used here in a transferred and not a proper sense, generally has no wider sense than *to discuss (disputare).*[7]

In the definition some persons add a reference to the subject of dialectic, namely, that it is the art of reasoning well about any subject whatsoever. But since, as we saw in the Preface, dialectic has this in common with grammar and rhetoric, it need not be repeated here.

---

lumbia University Press, 1948), pp. 65–77, suggests that Milton's preference for *logica* possibly reflects the influence of his boyhood teacher, Alexander Gill (or Gil), Sr., author of *Logonomia Anglica,* but it also follows the general drift in the sixteenth, seventeenth, and eighteenth centuries away from a social treatment and toward a solipsistic treatment of thought.

[5] *Suidæ Lexicon,* ed. Ada Adler, vol. I, pts. i–iv, of *Lexicographi græci* (Editio stereotypa editionis primæ 1929–38; Stutgardiæ: In Ædibus B. G. Teubneri, 1967), pt. ii, p. 62. "Suidas" (or *Suda*) designates the work and is not the name of an author; see *Oxford Classical Dictionary,* ed. N. G. L. Hammond and H. H. Scullard, 2nd ed. (Oxford: Clarendon Press, 1970), pp. 1019–20.

[6] There is a whole history here of the detachment of thought from discourse and of the individual from society: Earlier ages tended to associate thought with discourse, later ages to dissociate the two.

[7] *Disserere* ranges in meaning from "examine, argue, discuss" to "speak, discourse"; *disputare* signifies "reckon, calculate; treat of, discuss; state; dispute."

CHAPTER II

ON THE PARTS OF LOGIC
AND KINDS OF ARGUMENT

ALL reasoning is carried out by means of reasons either considered alone and by themselves or arranged with respect
to each other. These reasons are more often called arguments
(*argumenta*). [2]

There are thus two parts to logic: the invention of reasons or
arguments, and their disposition.[1]

Following the ancients—Aristotle, Cicero and Fabius—Ramus
divides dialectic into invention and judgment.[2] Nevertheless, not
invention, which however taken is too broad a term, but the invention of arguments should be called the first part of logic. Why
the disposition of arguments, rather than judgment, is the second
part will be explained at the beginning of the second book. But
meanwhile our own division does not want for authorities, whether
those already mentioned or others. For Plato, in the *Phædrus*
[236 A], adds disposition to invention; Aristotle, *Topics* 8.1
[viii.1.155b3–4], adds τάξις, which is the same; and Cicero, *De
oratore* [i.e., *Orat.* 13.43–44], admits that discovery and disposition
belong not to oratory but to reasoning.

Indeed to what things other than arguments should we relate
invention and disposition?

Thus in Greek the invention of arguments is called *topica*, because it involves τόποι,[3] that is, places from which arguments are
taken, and teaches the way and method of discovering arguments

---

[1] Present meanings of "invention" often suggest contrivance, manufacture, production, rather than finding or coming upon something—thus a machine is invented whereas a country or an idea is not invented but discovered or found.
Because "discovery" applies usually to something previously unknown—a new
country, a new idea—and because the "arguments" one used were often very well
known from previous use, the term "discovery" does not render *inventio* very
well either. The most apt English word would be simply "finding." But in logic
and rhetoric, the established technical term has long been "invention," and for
this reason the term is used here throughout for Milton's *inventio*.

[2] It appears that the sources specified later in this paragraph are the ones Milton
has in mind in this sentence. Not mentioned later is Fabius Quintilianus, whose
Inst. v.14.27–29 Milton may well have in mind.

[3] The places (or commonplaces), loci (*loci* or *loci communes* in Latin).

effectively [*bene*], once these have indeed been placed in their proper order. Whence, whether they are displayed as to their origin or examined in analysis, *topica* shows at the same time the force and the utility of the arguments discovered.

An argument is that which is suited to the arguing of something, i.e., that which has a relevance to arguing; or, as Cicero says in the *Topics* [2.8], that which is relevant to something of which there is question; or again, as Boethius [*Comm. on Cic. Top. (PL* lxiv.1057D–1058A)] explains it, that which bears on or stands in some relation to that of which there is question. [3]

If this relevance is removed, there is no argument; if it is changed, the argument is not the same but is itself changed.

The definition specifies "to the arguing of something," that is, with a view to showing, explaining or proving something. Thus according to the well-known quotation, "Fear argues degenerate souls," *Æneid* 4 [iv.13], and according to the one from Ovid [*Tr.* iv.3.80], "Virtue is made manifest and argued by afflictions." But the proper and primary strength of even a simple argument is that it explains and proves on what grounds it is first judged that one thing follows or does not follow from another, i.e., that, one thing being posited, something else is or is not posited. This is something which our compatriot Bacon, *De augmentis scientiarum* 5.4,[4] very correctly suggests concerning induction, that "by one and the same operation of the mind the object of a query be both discovered and judged." But this is no less true of individual simple arguments.

From this it also follows that judgment is not the second part of logic [5] but more like an effect common to both parts and to be derived from both: to be derived quite evidently indeed, but only secondarily from the use of the syllogism, especially when the syllogism resolves a doubtful matter; but many teach the contrary.[6]

The *something* mentioned in the definition is anything whatsoever that is being argued, for the subject of logic is whatever exists or is claimed to exist, as was shown above. But an argument, properly speaking, is neither a word nor a thing, but a certain relevance of a thing to arguing; it can be called a *reason,* as above.

[4] Francis Bacon, *The Works of Francis Bacon,* collected and edited by James Spedding et al. (Cambridge: Printed at the Riverside Press, 1863), II, 395.

[5] The second part of logic was often denominated *iudicium* or judgment rather than *dispositio,* disposition or arrangement. Milton differs from Ramus and Downham here: see Book II, chap. i. The history of these terms is complicated. See Introduction, pp. 156–57.

[6] The sense of the Latin is somewhat puzzling: there may possibly be some error in Milton's printed text.

Logic therefore treats neither of words nor of things. Although it is possible to reason without words, nevertheless logic seems quite justified, by the very convention of speech, in requiring that whenever words must be used they be distinct and thus unambiguous, and not inappropriate. Things themselves [4] logic leaves to their several arts, considering only the relevance or *ratio* to arguing which they have among themselves.

Ratio, borrowed from the mathematicians, is a word by which is signified a certain relation of terms proportional to each other.

An argument is either artificial or inartificial. Thus Aristotle, *Rhetoric* 1.2 [i.2.1355b35–36], followed by Fabius, Book 5, chapter 1 [Quint. *Inst.* v.1.1.]. Cicero [*Top.* 18.69] divides arguments into *innate* and *assumptive.* But an argument is called artificial not because it is discovered by art more than is the inartificial, but because it argues by itself, that is, by an innate and proper force.

An artificial argument is either primary or derived from a primary one. A primary argument is one which is of its own origin, that is, its relevance to arguing it has not only in itself, but also from within itself. This will appear more clearly below, when it is explained what is meant by *derived from a primary argument.*

A primary argument is either simple or comparative.

A simple argument is one which is considered simply and absolutely, that is, it has a simple relevance to arguing that which is being argued, without being compared with the latter either in quantity or in quality.

A simple argument is either one of agreement or one of disagreement.

For things considered without comparison necessarily either agree among themselves or disagree.

An argument of agreement is one which agrees with the thing which it argues. That is, it posits, or affirms, the existence of the thing which it argues.

And an argument of agreement is such either absolutely or in a certain respect. Absolutely means perfectly, for to make absolute is to perfect. This division is also made by Aristotle [e.g., *Metaph.* x.3.1054b1–13]. But of those things which agree absolutely, one is understood to exist in virtue of the other; and thus cause and effect agree. So these are the general divisions of arguments based on the differences in their relevance to arguing; [5] and now they are to be treated individually in their proper order. But the first of all arguments is *cause,* as anyone can know for himself.

CHAPTER III

ON THE EFFICIENT CAUSE,
THE PROCREATIVE AND THE CONSERVING

A CAUSE is that by the power of which a thing exists. Or if there is need to repeat from a preceding chapter what can be understood and remembered, a cause is an artificial argument, primary, simple, of absolute agreement, by the power or ability of which a thing, that is, an effect, is argued to be or to exist. A cause is not badly defined as that which gives existence to a thing.

By the power or ability *of which,* means that the thing by which, from which, through which or on account of which a thing is, is called a cause. And the word *thing,* just as the word *something* in the definition of an argument, is used in a general sense to signify that there is a cause, just as there are other arguments, for all things that exist or are imagined to exist; for things which really exist have true causes, and fictitious things have fictitious causes.

From this it will be understood that a *causa sine qua non,* as it is commonly called, is improperly and as it were arbitrarily named a cause, as when the loss of something is called the cause of its recovery; even though the loss necessarily precedes the recovery. For cause, as Cicero, *De fato* [15.34], teaches, should not so be understood that what precedes anything be called its cause, but what efficiently precedes something; [6] in such a way, namely, that the thing exists by the power of it. Hence a cause properly so called is also termed a *principium* by Cicero, *De natura deorum* 1 [i.1.1], and more frequently among the Greeks.

But a cause is that by the power of which a thing not only is, but also was or will be. For just as the precepts of logic are to be understood with reference to all things, so the precepts of all the arts with reference to all time; whence they are called eternal and of an eternal truth.

From the definition of cause there emerges as a consequence that third precept of art about which we spoke in the Preface: this first locus of invention is the source of all knowledge; and in the last analysis a thing is considered really to be known when its cause is grasped.

That oft-repeated demonstration of Aristotle is nothing other than one by which an effect is argued, proved, known and posited from a cause which has been posited, whatever genus of cause it may prove to be, as when a thing's ability to laugh is proved from its being rational: to wit, every man is able to laugh because he is rational. And the more certain, proximate and important the cause, the more clear will be the demonstration.

A cause is efficient-and-matter, or form-and-end. Why cause should be thus divided into two nameless genera will be more easily understood below in our remarks on division.

We assert that there are as many species of cause as there are ways in which a thing exists by the power of something. But in four ways does a thing exist by the power of something, as Aristotle, *Physics* 2.7 [ii.7.198a14–24], rightly says and we said above; for a thing is correctly said to exist by the power of that by which, from which, through which or on account of which, it exists. These ways, and no more, are found, nor can there be fewer; cause is therefore correctly divided into cause by which, from which, through which and on account of which, namely, efficient and [7] matter, as well as form and end.

The efficient cause is the cause by which a thing is or is brought about. For the beginning of motion is from the efficient cause; yet the cause itself is not within its effect.

By Cicero every cause is called efficient; for he writes thus in *Topics* [14.58]: "The first place is that of efficient things, which are called causes"; and in *De fato* [15.34]: "A cause is that which brings about that of which it is cause." This is why the thing caused, although resulting from all its causes, is called simply an effect; what is meant is merely that the efficient cause is the principal and primary cause, but that every cause in some way effects.

Although no true genera or species of the efficient cause suggest themselves to us, its great variety is distinguished in several ways.

First, that which procreates or maintains is an efficient cause.

Thus, a father and mother procreate, and a nurse maintains. Here are also to be counted all inventors of things, authors, founders and preservers. Procreating and maintaining are therefore two of the ways in which one and the same thing will often function as efficient cause, procreating that which does not yet exist, and conserving that which already exists so that it may continue to exist.

CHAPTER IV

ON THE EFFICIENT CAUSE OPERATING ALONE
AND WITH OTHER CAUSES

SECONDLY, an efficient cause works either by itself or along with other efficient causes, and of all these often one will be the principal cause, while another is less principal, or an assisting and helping cause. Such a cause Cicero, in *De partitione oratoria* [26.93–94], calls the co-efficient cause; [8] and the power of this type, he says, is various, being often greater or less, so that the one having the greatest power is often the only one called cause. Thus, in *Æneid* 9 [ix.424–30] Nysus transfers from his comrade Euryalus to himself the blame and punishment for the slaughter that was perpetrated, as if he himself were its single author, because he was the chief one. And a solitary cause with many principal and associated ones is variously displayed in *Pro Marcello* [e.g., 6–7]. But see these two examples in the exercise in logical analysis following the present work.

A cause which is less principal (as some like to call it) is either an impelling cause, one which impels or moves the principal one, or it is an instrumental cause.

There are two types of impelling cause, called in names derived from the Greek respectively *proegumenic* or the *procatarctic*.[1] The first moves the principal cause from within, and the second from without; and if it is real it is called an *occasion,* but if feigned a *pretext*.

Thus the proegumenic cause which from within moved the infidels to persecute the Christians (for here we shall use traditional examples)[2] was their ignorance or perhaps their impiety, while the procatarctic cause was the nocturnal meetings of the Christians, or rather their strength when holding a meeting. The proegumenic cause of the killing of Christ was the ignorant zeal of the Jews, while the procatarctic cause was the alleged violation of the Sab-

---

[1] The Greek originals mean, respectively, predisposing or basic and immediate or inciting.

[2] Milton programmatically and usually follows Ramus in excluding theological references from his logic; hence this apology here. See above, Milton's Preface and n. 3.

bath and seditious speeches. But it is to be noted that where there is no proegumenic, or internal, cause, the procatarctic or external cause is inoperative. It appears that what was above called the *causa sine qua non,* if it is to be numbered among the causes at all, must often be considered a procatarctic cause, if it can in any way be said to move externally the principal cause.

Instruments are also counted among the helping causes. Such an argument was used by Epicurus, according to Cicero, *De natura deorum,* Book I [i.8.18–20], to maintain that the world has never been made.[3] This example, too, we have put in the exercise in logical analysis. [9] Properly speaking, instruments do not act, but are rather acted upon or help. And anyone who has only instruments as helping cause can correctly be called a solitary cause, however broad the admitted meaning of "instrument" may be, as when Aristotle, *Politics* I.3 [i.2.1253b27–28], says that "instruments are either animate or inanimate." In this sense almost all helping and ministering causes can be called instrumental.

To this place or locus it seems we can very conveniently refer that order of causes in which one cause is called *primary,* and this either absolutely (as with God) or in its genus (as with the sun or anything else of this sort); and others *secondary,* and so on, each depending on the primary or on prior causes and each like an effect. One cause may also be called *remote,* another *proximate,* in accordance with the saying that whatever is cause of the cause is also cause of what is caused. This rule holds for causes in so far as they are necessarily ordered among themselves. But these divisions of causes are not to be observed too rigorously in logic, since the whole force of an argument is contained in the proximate cause; and only to this cause does the general definition of cause apply.

[3] That is, God would have needed instruments to create things, but before he created anything there would have been no instruments. See the reference in Milton's text below, p. 398.

CHAPTER V

ON THE EFFICIENT CAUSE
PER SE AND PER ACCIDENS

THIRDLY, an efficient cause is such either *per se* or *per accidens*. This is the third pair of the modes of efficient causality, noted also by Aristotle and the ancients.

A *per se* efficient cause is one which causes efficiently through its own power, that is, one which produces an effect from an intrinsic principle. [10]

Such are the things which operate through their own nature or through deliberation. Elements, minerals, plants and animals are things which operate through their own nature. An example of operation through deliberation is Cicero's confession to Caesar [*Lig.* 3.7]: "Compelled by no force, of my own judgment and volition, I helped in the war which had been undertaken against you."

Some include appetitive tendency with nature, and art with deliberation, but they think of appetitive tendency either as natural or toward nature or toward a vice of nature. Art can without difficulty be referred to deliberation, for to the extent that things are efficiently caused through art and deliberation, art does not seem to originate only from understanding and deliberation only from will, but each from both sources. For art is usually not involuntary, at least not in any strict sense; and the prudent and knowing man exercises deliberation. These four modes of *per se* efficient causation sometimes combine to produce one and the same effect; as when someone speaks, it is through his natural capacity, and he says this or that both by deliberation and appetitive tendency, and he does so elegantly through art.

It seems, too, that this is the place to which we should refer the impelling cause, whether proegumenic or procatarctic, of which we spoke in the chapter above; these are not so much causes associated with or ministering to the principal cause as they are modes of efficient cause by which someone, impelled by some emotion or because the occasion is offered, under the guidance of deliberation does this or that, as can be understood from the examples there adduced.

Causes which act through nature do so out of necessity, while those which act through deliberation do so freely. That cause acts out of necessity which cannot act otherwise than as it does but is determined to the doing of some one thing and does only this thing through a propensity which is called a necessity of nature—*ex hypothesi,* to be sure—unless God wills something else or some external force impels in some other direction, as a stone upward. An efficient cause does freely not just some one thing, like a natural agent, but it does this or that out of choice, and either absolutely or *ex hypothesi.* [11] Only God does all things with absolute freedom, that is, He does whatever He wills; and He can act or not act. This is attested to throughout Sacred Scripture.[1] Only those causes act freely *ex hypothesi* which do things through reason and deliberation, as angels and men—on the hypothesis, to be sure, of the divine will, which in the beginning gave them the power to act freely. For freedom is the power to do or not do this or that, unless of course God wills otherwise or some other force violently interferes.

A *per accidens* efficient cause is one which causes through an external power, that is, one not its own, when the source of the effect is outside the efficient cause and is an external principle as opposed to the internal; for thus the efficient cause acts not through itself but through something else. For this reason it is truly said that every effect of a *per accidens* cause can be reduced to a *per se* cause.

This is the case in those things which come about through coercion or by fortune, for these two factors are external principles opposed to the internal ones, namely, nature and will or deliberation. Thus Aristotle, *Rhetoric* 1.10 [i.10.1368b33–35], when he says that some things men do not of themselves and others of themselves, adds: "Of those things they do not of themselves, some are done by fortune, some out of necessity." But "necessity" is too broad a term, as will be clear from what was said above about natural efficient cause.

Something comes about through coercion when the efficient cause is compelled by some force to produce an effect, as when a stone is hurled upward or horizontally, whereas by its nature it is borne downward. This is called necessity of coercion and can sometimes happen even to free causes. Thus it is necessary for a merchant in a storm to throw his cargo overboard if he wishes to be safe, so that this necessity produces certain mixed actions, ones which a man does willingly but with an unwilling heart, as they say. [12]

---

[1] See above, Milton's Preface and n. 3.

Something comes about by fortune, or fortuitously, when it happens outside the intention of an efficient cause. For not fortune, but the efficient cause acting by fortune, or fortuitously, is properly the *per accidens* cause of fortuitous things, because their source—that hidden cause which we call fortune—is outside the efficient cause; but fortune is the source, albeit the hidden one, of these events, not *per accidens,* however, but *per se.* So that among the ancients fortune was considered either a name without an object which men used, as Hippocrates testifies somewhere [*De arte* vi. 13–18], when they did not know the secondary causes of contingent things; or fortune is the latent cause itself, as Cicero says in the *Topics* [16.63]: "for since nothing comes to be without a cause, here is what fortune is: the obscure cause of an event, one which operates under cover." Aristotle, *Physics* 2.6 [ii.6.197a36–198a13], and Plutarch, *De placitis philosophorum* [pseudo-Plutarch *Epit.* i.29.3] and *De fato* [572 E], see a difference between fortune (*fortuna*) and chance (*casus*), to the effect that chance extends more widely than fortune: fortune is found only in those beings who use reason, whereas chance obtains in all things, animate as well as inanimate. But ordinary usage also includes chance under the name of fortune, whenever anything happens outside the intention or the end of an efficient cause. "Thus by a fortuitous chance," says Tully, *De natura deorum* 3 [iii.28.70], "Jason of Pherae was helped by an enemy who with his sword opened up a boil which the physicians had been unable to heal."

In this genus of causes imprudence is usually included. Thus Aristotle, *Ethics* 3.1 [iii.1.1109b35–1110a1], says: "Those things seem not to be voluntary which are done through force or ignorance." And Ovid, *Tristia* 2 [ii.103–8], writes:

> Why did I see anything? Why make my sight guilty?
> Why did I unwittingly become privy to someone's fault?
> Unintended was Actaeon's view of Diana unclothed:
> None the less he became the prey of his dogs. [13]
> So among deities even ill fortune has its penalty,
> Nor is chance an excuse for an offense against a god.

The poet complains that this is harsh, for under other circumstances such an event is ordinarily taken as an occasion for begging forgiveness, and sometimes even an excuse can be granted in such cases. An example of begging for forgiveness is found in Cicero, *Pro Ligario* [30]: "Pardon, father; he erred, he slipped, he did not think." And a little later he says [30]: "I have erred, I have acted rashly; I repent and appeal to your mercy."

But the name "fortune," as was said above, grew out of ignorance of causes; for when something occurs which is unplanned and unexpected, this is commonly called fortune. Whence Cicero, according to Lactantius *Institutiones* 3.29 [*Div. Inst.* iii.29.18], said that "ignorance of things and causes produced the name 'fortune.' " Nor was the remark by Juvenal [*Sat.* x.365–66] inappropriate:

> Divinity is not absent if there is prudence:
> But you, O Fortune, we make into a goddess and
>   we place you in heaven.

For fortune surely is to be placed in heaven, but its name should be changed and it should be called "divine providence." Whence Aristotle, *Physics* 2.4 [ii.4.196b5–7], says: "There are some to whom fortune appears to be a cause, but unknown to human intelligence and as something divine." And Cicero, *Academic Questions* 1 [i.7.29], writes: "The providence of God which pertains to men they sometimes call fortune, since it brings about many things which we do not anticipate or think about because of the obscurity of the causes and our ignorance of them." But providence is the first cause of all things, whether their secondary causes are known or unknown: and if necessity is added to providence, it is called fate. But certainly theology will discuss providence better than logic will. But in passing let this much be said: fate or divine decree does not force anyone to do evil, [14] and on the hypothesis of divine foreknowledge all things are certain, to be sure, but not necessary. So Cicero *Pro Ligario* [17–18], is not to be excused when he says: "Some fatal calamity seems to have befallen and occupied the unforeseeing minds of men; so that no one should be surprised that human counsels are countermanded by divine necessity." Elsewhere he says much more correctly: "Necessity is indeed allowed for—but a necessity which goes counter to the purpose of the efficient cause and to the will." [2]

---

[2] Milton is here very likely referring to *De officiis* 1.16.56, where Cicero quotes Aristotle to the effect that one can understand how a people under siege will, against their own desires, pay exorbitant prices for a bit of water, if one "makes allowance for their actions on the score of necessity" (*veniam necessitati dare*— Milton's text here corresponds closely: *datur quidem venia necessitati*). In Milton's text everything here represented by the English "Necessity is . . . to the will" appears in italics, but (see pp. 185–86 above) Milton's italics do not always signal direct quotations even when he pinpoints his references more than he does here.

CHAPTER VI

ON MATTER

M_ATTER is the cause out of which a thing is._ In the order of nature matter follows the efficient cause and is a kind of _effect of the efficient cause;_ for the efficient cause prepares matter so that it will be ready to receive a form. Inasmuch as the efficient cause is that which first moves and matter is correspondingly that which is first moved, the efficient is called the active principle and matter the passive principle. This definition of matter is virtually the same among all writers. The definition says that matter is a _cause;_ for an effect exists by the influence of its matter. This influence is signified by the phrase _out of which,_ although the phrase commonly denotes not only matter, but sometimes the efficient cause (as in "out of the blow came a wound"), sometimes the parts (as in "man is made out of soul and body") and sometimes any kind of change (as in "it turns black out of white"). By _thing_ we mean the thing which the matter makes evident, that is, the materialized effect; so that we think of matter as common to all beings and non-beings, and not peculiar just to sensible and corporeal things. But of whatever sort the things themselves may be, [15] such, too, should be their matter: sensible matter for sensible things, eternal matter for eternal things, and so on. Thus the matter of the arts is their precepts. The definition specifies out of which a thing _is,_ that is, out of which it is caused or of which it consists: whence Cicero, _Academic Questions_ 1 [i.6.24], says that "matter is the cause which offers itself to the efficient cause as that out of which the effect not only may come to be, but also of which the effect, once existing, may consist." Forming fictionally an argument of this sort, Ovid, _Metamorphoses_ 2 [ii.1–4], says that the house of the sun is composed of gold, bronze, ivory and silver: "The palace of the sun was," etc. Thus Caesar, _Civil War_ 1 [i.54], describes the material of ships: "The keel and ribs of the ship were made of light material," etc.

Matter is commonly divided into primary and secondary, the secondary into proximate and remote. This distinction is, to be sure, more relevant to physics, for all the logician considers in matter is that a thing be composed out of it, and especially that it be proximately composed out of it; for proximate matter argues most forcefully.

CHAPTER VII

ON FORM

SUCH *is the first genus of cause consisting of efficient cause and matter; the second, consisting of form and end,* follows, namely because it is later in time. For the efficient cause and matter are contained in the earlier genus because they precede in the production of an effect; form and end are contained in a later genus because they come after the efficient cause and matter and accompany the effect itself. For once the efficient cause and matter are given, the form and the end do not follow at once, for the efficient cause, even though adequate to the matter, is sometimes frustrated with respect to its form and its end. If the form and the end are present, [16] then the efficient cause and the matter must have existed. But the order of causes which is observed in practice should also be observed in presentation. Yet this order of causes does not really establish the genera of causes, but establishes rather some other genus which lacks a name. Hence one may with good reason regard as not sufficiently accurate the division of causes—commonly attributed to Aristotle [e.g., *Phys.* ii.3.194b16–195b30]—into those which precede the effects as efficient cause and matter, and those which exist simultaneously with the effect, as form and end. For although this division preserves the order of causes, it does not distinguish their nature; indeed, it is not suitable for causes and is not proper to them. It is not suitable because a cause, as cause, does not precede but is simultaneous with its effect. In one way or another the efficient cause and the matter precede the effect either in the order of nature or in the order of time. If in the order of nature, then these causes have this in common with the other causes and with all subjects. If in the order of time, then this is not common to every efficient cause and to all matter (for some of these occur only simultaneously with their effect), nor is it proper to them alone, for many subjects are prior in time to their attributes. Nor is Aristotle [e.g., *Phys.* ii.3.194b16–195b30] [1] any more successful in dividing causes into extrinsic (efficient cause and end)

[1] This and the preceding reference are intended only to indicate a place where a good discussion by Aristotle of his theory of causes can be found; they are not intended to document unequivocally what Milton reports about the division of causes into the prior and the simultaneous, the intrinsic and the extrinsic. These divisions are suggested more or less clearly by Aristotle's theory of causes, but

and intrinsic (matter and form); for this division, although it can be of some use, is less appropriate to the laws of art, since to be extrinsic or intrinsic is not proper to causes, but is common to effects and to attributes. Then matter and form, since they are within the effect, are not so much causes as parts of the effect. Why? Because the end, which is a perfection of a thing and its special aptitude for use, would more aptly be called an intrinsic cause. Finally, this division disturbs the order of causes, and therefore also the rules of art, for the efficient cause is the principle of movement and [17] the first of the causes, and the end is the last. Therefore if the intrinsic is put before the extrinsic, then matter and form, which are in some sense the effects of the efficient cause, will be put before the efficient cause. If the extrinsic is put before the intrinsic, then the end will be adjoined to the efficient cause, that is, the last will be adjoined to the first, and it will be put before the intermediate ones, namely, matter and form. So Ramus more cautiously and more in a manner and form. So Ramus more cautiously and more in a manner befitting the art leaves the genera of causes nameless. To show this we, with your permission, digressed at some length; now let us return to the other genus of causes, namely, form and end. The first place is to be given to form, since the end is nothing other than a certain result of the form.

The form is the cause through which a thing is what it is. This definition combines the Platonic and the Aristotelian, for Plato defines a form as a cause through which, and Aristotle as the what-is-being.[2] Just as matter, so also form is a certain effect of the efficient cause. For the efficient cause both produces a form not yet existing and introduces it into matter. But the form is also the cause of its effect, and indeed the principal one, and it alone establishes the effect, which exists chiefly by reason of its form. For

---

by themselves they are misleading simplifications, though long popular in textbook presentations. Milton could have encountered these divisions in any number of sources. For example, on the division into intrinsic and extrinsic causes, see Bartholomæus Keckermannus, *Systematis Logici Plenioris Pars Altera,* cap. iv, 12–13, in his *Operum Omnium quæ Extant Tomus Primus* [*-secundus*] (Geneva: Petrus Aubertus, 1614; PML), I, cols. 853–56.

[2] Milton's Latin "quod quid est esse" is one of the standard elliptic Latin renditions of Aristotle's own crucial and compressed definition, "τὸ τί ἦν εἶναι," literally, "the *what* being (really, enduringly) *is*"—the emphasis "really . . . *is*" is given in the Greek by the use of the imperfect ἦν rather than the present or aorist. For a thorough discussion of Aristotle's meaning, see Joseph Owens, *The Doctrine of Being in the Aristotelian "Metaphysics,"* 2nd ed. rev. (Toronto: Pontifical Institute of Mediaeval Studies, 1963), pp. 180–88.

the efficient cause can be frustrated with respect to the form, but not the form with respect to its effect. So the phrase *through which* in the definition signifies that cause and that force which informs and constitutes the thing or the effect. For there is no thing which does not have its form, although the form may be unknown to us.

Singular things, or individuals, as they are commonly called, have their own singular and proper forms; certainly they differ in number among themselves, which no one denies. But what does it mean for things to differ among themselves, if not to differ by reason of their singular forms? [3] For number, as Scaliger correctly says,[4] is a property consequent upon essence. Therefore, things which differ in number also differ in essence, [18] and never do things differ in number without also differing in essence. *Here let the Theologians take notice.*[5] Because if all things which differ in number also differ in essence, but not by reason of their matter, then they necessarily differ by reason of their forms. But this is

[3] This passage makes it clear that, with Ramus, Milton was an essentialist rather than an existentialist, in the scholastic tradition in which his philosophy moves. The problem, as Milton's words reflect it, had been advanced far beyond its Aristotelian formulation. For the existentialist Saint Thomas Aquinas the *principle* of individuation is matter, and actual individuation is effected by its *existence* in determined matter, not by its form, which determines *what* Socrates is (a man), not who he is. For a discussion of the complex tradition from which Milton, with Ramus, emerges here, see Etienne Gilson, *Being and Some Philosophers,* 2nd ed. (Toronto: Pontifical Institute of Mediaeval Studies, 1952).

[4] Milton has here given an "essentialist" twist to Scaliger's "existentialist" argument for individuation through form. See Julius Caesar Scaliger, *Exotericarum Exercitationum Liber XI, de Subtilitate, ad Hieronymum Cardanum* (Paris: Michael Vascosanus, 1557; PML), p. 401 (Exercitatio cccvii, 17): "Individuum, cum sit substantia, necesse est ut sit hoc quod est per id per quod est. Est autem per animam (de homine loquimur). Ergo erit individuum per animam. Anima igitur erit principium eius quod est: quam nostri Barbari scitissima voce individuationem appellarunt. . . . Dicunt distingui animas numero. Crassissimum iudicunt. *Numerus enim est res quædam consequens existentiam,* & vagans per collectionem unitatum. Non quia numerantur animæ dicemus eas numero distingui, sed numerari quia sunt diversæ, hoc est separatæ unitates." The passage apparently referred to by Milton has been italicized.

[5] Milton's italics here are for emphasis: The italicized sentence is not from Ramus. Milton here cannot resist violating his own rule in his Preface, p. 211 above, against bringing theology into logic, though his violation here is certainly minimal in extent. See also n. 2 to chap. iv above. He apparently means to imply that since the Father, Son, and Holy Spirit differ in "number"—in the words of the Athanasian Creed, each Person is "other," or one is not the other—they cannot all be one God in essence. Milton's objection here is hardly startling but is simply one version of possibly the oldest of all objections against Trinitarian doctrine and the one to which Trinitarian doctrine at its very center has always addressed itself, as the Athanasian Creed and patristic theology generally make clear. See

not by reason of common forms; hence it is by reason of proper forms. Thus the rational soul is the form of man generically; the soul of Socrates is the proper form of Socrates. The definition states: *through which a thing is what it is,* that is, which gives a thing its proper existence. For since the essence of any thing is partly common and partly proper, matter constitutes the common essence and form the proper. And a thing can indeed be said to *be* through other causes, but only through form to *be that which it is.*

Therefore by its form a thing is distinguished from all other things, that is, by a distinction which they call essential. From form alone comes the essential difference. Indeed, things which differ among themselves in any way differ also in their forms. And form is the source of all difference; nor do things differ one from another by any evidences without first differing in their forms. This in fact is the first consequence of the definition; another follows.

The form is generated within a thing simultaneously with the thing itself. Whence this truest of maxims: *if the form is posited, the thing itself is posited, and if the form is taken away the thing is taken away.* Let us now consider some examples. The rational soul is the form of man, because through it a man is a man and is distinguished from all other natures. The form of geometrical figures consists in their being triangles and quadrangles. The form of physical things consists in its being the form of a heavenly body, of earth, of trees, or of fishes.

Therefore, just as there is a proper nature of things, so will there be an explanation of them, if the nature can be discovered. This is the third consequence of the definition. Hence, what was said above about cause in general, namely that it is the source of all knowledge, is understood to apply especially to form. [19] For the cause which most properly constitutes the essence will, if it is known, make for the best knowledge. But to know the intrinsic form of anything, a form which is often most remote from the senses, is especially difficult. But in artificial things the form, being external and exposed to the senses, is more easily observed; as in Caesar, *Gallic War* 7 [vii.23]: "All of the Gallic walls are of about

---

Scott-Craig, "Craftsmanship," pp. 1–16; William B. Hunter, Jr., "Some Problems in John Milton's Theological Vocabulary," *HTR,* LVII (1964), 353–65; and Michael Lieb, "Milton and the Kenotic Christology: Its Literary Bearing," *ELH,* XXXVII (1970), 342–59; also Maurice Kelley's introduction and notes in his edition of Milton's *De Doctrina Christiana* in *Complete Prose,* VI—Hunter and Kelley disagree. See above, Milton's Preface, n. 3.

this form," etc. Thus the form of the port in Virgil, *Æneid* 1 [i.159], is explained: "There is a place within a spacious recess," etc.

There is no true division of forms. For the division into intrinsic and extrinsic held by some does not apply to all things but only to corporeal things; and the extrinsic form is no less essential to each artificial thing than the intrinsic to each natural thing.

CHAPTER VIII

ON THE END

THE end is the cause for the sake of which a thing is. Thus also Aristotle, *Metaphysics* l.3 [i.3.983a31–32] states: "The fourth cause is the good of anything; for this is the end of all generation." For when the efficient cause has achieved its end it comes to rest in it and it imposes an end to its action. So the end is the last of the causes. Yet, as Aristotle correctly says in *Physics* 2.2 [ii.2.194a32–33], "Not everything which is last is final cause, but only that which is best." For the end signifies the terminus of a thing or the good of a thing, just as there is a terminus of duration, of magnitude, or of a figure. But the final cause is only something good, and in the same [20] sense it is called an end and a good— whether a real good or an apparent one is of no importance to its force as a cause. Thus also Aristotle in the *Physics* 2.3 [ii.3.195a23–26], and in various places in the *Ethics* [e.g., ii.3.1104b30–34], says that the avoidance of evil has the nature of good. Some distinguish between the end and the final cause, saying that the end is the use of a thing while the final cause is consideration of its use. Nevertheless, not consideration but the thing— that is, the very end of the effect—is the real final cause, for there is also prior consideration of matter and of form, but without this distinction. There is also consideration of the impelling cause, and it moves the efficient cause, and yet it cannot be called a final cause, since the efficient cause is not appetitively inclined toward it but is more often opposed to it, as when emotion or some perverse habit impels toward the pursuit of some apparent good. Again, the end is first in the mind of the efficient cause, but last in the action and in the effect. But while it is still only in the mind of the efficient cause and has not been achieved, it does not yet truly exist; and since it does not yet exist, how can it be a cause? So while it is commonly said that the end, inasmuch as it moves the efficient cause—persuasively, as it were—to prepare matter and induce a form in it, is the cause not only of the effect but of the causes themselves and is the best of the causes, this is said improperly and out of a certain preconception. But although in action and use the end is often last, nevertheless in its suitability for use—unless it be considered as simultaneous in time and nature with form—

it will be posterior to the effect already constituted by a form, and it will be an attribute of the effect rather than its cause. Thus not actual occupation, but rather the suitability for occupation which is simultaneous in time and nature with the induced form, is to be considered the proper end of a house, and this suitability is a perfection of the thing and a result of the form. For this reason the Greeks not only derive the verb τελέω (I perfect) from τέλος (end), but they also [21] name a thing τέλειον (perfect) from the end, according to Aristotle, *Metaphysics* 4.24 [v.24.1023a34].

The proper grounds for distinguishing the final cause from other causes are expressed in the words *for the sake of which,* and by other expressions as well, namely, *because of which, toward, because of, for, on account of, by reason of, for which purpose,* and the like. But *lest* is a sign of that end which concerns the avoidance of some evil. End is spoken of not only in the case of those beings which set their own end, that is, rational efficient causes, but in the case of any things whatsoever which are referred to an end, that is, all effects. Thus man is set as the end of physical things, and God as the end of man. Aristotle was aware of this in *Physics* 2.2 [ii.2.194a34–35]: "We use things," he says, "as if all things were for our sake: for we too are in a way an end." The wise Hebrew teaches that God is the end of all things in Proverbs 16.4: "The Lord hath made all things for Himself." Of all arts there is some supreme and ultimate end, which is also their form: of grammar, to use words well; [1] of rhetoric, to deliver a speech well; [2] of logic, to reason well. [3]

That a form can also be an end Aristotle testifies more than once in *Metaphysics* 4.24 [v.24.1023a34], *Physics* 2.7.8 [ii.7.198a25–26, 8.199a30–32]. And Plato in the *Philebus* [54 B–C] establishes the essence or form of a thing as the end of generation; whence Aristotle in *De partibus animalium* 1.1 [i.1.640a18–19] says the same thing.

Just as of form so also of end there is no true division. The ones commonly mentioned are not divisions of the end of logic but distinctions of special ends for a variety of effects. Aristotle in *De anima* 2.4 [ii.4.415b2–3] distinguishes the *end of which* and the *end for which.* The end of which is the end of the action or of the operation. The end for which is the end of the thing done or made. For example, in the building of a house, the end of which, or the

---

[1] *Bene loqui.*

[2] *Bene dicere.*

[3] *Bene ratiocinari.* As at the opening of this work, Milton here alters Ramus's view that the end of dialectic (or logic) is to discourse well (*bene disserere*). See Introduction, above, pp. 154–55.

end of the action, is the house; the end for which, or of the thing made—namely of the house that [22] has been built—is its suitability for occupation.

There are mentioned also other divisions of the end which pertain to the end for which, as in Aristotle, *Magna moralia* 1.2 [i.2.1184a7–8]: "One end is perfect, the other imperfect"; or, what comes to the same thing, in others: "An end is either supreme or subordinate." The supreme end is what is desired for its own sake, and it is either universal, that is, common to all things, or special, being proper and peculiar to each species. But a subordinate end is not so much an end as it is something intended for an end; and to be supreme or subordinate, universal or special, belongs to other arguments as well as to end. Finally, the rule of division requires that the members of a division be opposites: and between the supreme and the subordinate there is no opposition. For an understanding of all the ends of all things a single definition suffices, that an end be that for the sake of which a thing is. But whether the end be supreme or subordinate, universal or special, logic does not consider, but leaves to various inferior disciplines.

A N *effect is that which exists by reason of its causes.* Although an effect exists by reason of all its causes, it is named an effect from its principal cause, namely, the efficient. But since an effect is, properly speaking, brought about only by its efficient cause, and yet exists by reason of all its causes, it is therefore not defined by being named that which is brought about by its causes, but rather, through reference [23] to the common force of causes, as that which is or exists by reason of its causes. Now is the time to stress what we stressed in chapter ii when we explained cause, namely, that an effect is an argument in an absolute sense, with a cause or in agreement with a cause, that is, it argues a cause absolutely; so that just as when a cause is posited an effect is posited, so when an effect is posited a cause is posited. For just as causes give existence to the effect, so the effect has its existence from its causes, that is, it exists as from the agent, out of matter, through its form and on account of its end. An effect therefore argues causes and is in turn argued by them, but not in the same way, for an effect argues the present or prior existence of a cause (in Greek ὅτι), while a cause demonstrates why the effect exists (in Greek διότι). Causes are prior and better known; the effect, as posterior, argues less forcefully. Thus silver as the material of a cup more forcefully argues and reveals the nature of the cup, than the cup does the nature of silver. But sometimes the effects, not by reason of themselves but because they are better known to us, more clearly argue their causes than they are argued by their causes. Thus also Aristotle, *Posterior Analytics* 1.10 [i.13.78a28–29], says: "There is no reason why, of those things which mutually argue one another," such as cause and effect, "the one which is not cause should not sometimes be better known."

If, therefore, anything is produced or destroyed, or moved in any way, this movement and the thing made by the movement is called an effect. Just as there were indeed modes of causes, so now by these words certain modes of effects are revealed. The modes of effects are either general or special. The general modes are either movement of any sort, which is called *operation* and *action,* or the things made by the movement, which are *products.* Special modes

or special examples are *generation, corruption,* and the like, taken
from physics. For the corrupting cause is the cause which produces
corruption. But it should be noted [24] here that a thing, not just
as moved, but as made by the movement, is called an effect, for
only a moved thing which is made to be is an effect of a mover;
a corrupted thing is contrary to the thing corrupting it.

In this place belong praise and blame, of which the sacred and
profane books are full. For it is especially for his deeds that anyone
is praised or blamed.

Here also belong things spoken and things written, as well as
counsels and deliberations, even when they are not carried out.
For not only deeds, but also things considered and reflected on are
to be classed as effects.

There are also effects of virtues and vices. Horace [*Epist.* i.5.16]
describes in this way the effects of drunkenness:

> What does drunkenness not reveal? It uncovers hidden things, etc.

Here most interpreters of Ramus hold that the doctrine of movement, concerning as it does a general fact, belongs to logic; but
not rightly. For what can logic say about movement that is not
natural and physical? "Knowledge," they say from Aristotle in
Physics 8.3 [viii.3.253a35–b1], "and opinions all use movement."
They use it, indeed, but as physics teaches, by deriving it from
nature. Thus logic uses reason, yet does not teach the nature of
reason but the art of reasoning. Every cause does indeed move,
and an effect is moved, but the logician does not consider what
moves or is moved, but what argues or is argued. But *arguing or
being argued* in itself belongs to logic not because it is movement
or something made by movement, but because, by presenting argument, it helps the power of reasoning or teaches the art.

Two common rules of cause and effect, which should be treated
in physics rather than in logic—like many other things which the
Aristotelians [25] are in the habit of lumping together here—but
which often turn up and are fallacious, can for this reason be
conveniently touched upon here, along with the precautions to be
taken in using them, in the form of a brief appendix. The first is:
the thing caused is like the cause, from Aristotle in *Topics* 2.9
[ii.9.114a29–31]. This is not true, first, in *per accidens* causes. For
example, from "This shoemaker is a good man" one cannot infer
that "He makes good shoes"; for he may not be a good shoemaker.
Second, it is not true in universal causes; for example, "The sun

warms all things," but not "Therefore, the sun is warm."[1] Third, it is not true in voluntary causes, unless they act voluntarily. Fourth, it is not true if the thing in which the effect is to be produced is by nature not able to receive the effect.

The second rule is, *That on account of which a thing is of a certain sort is itself even more of that sort,* from Aristotle, *Posterior Analytics* 1.2 [i.2.72a29–30]. This, namely, is also false, first, in causes *per se*. For example, from "This man is drunk" one cannot infer that "Wine is drunker." Second, it is false if that from which things are denominated as such and such is itself intrinsic to each thing; as "Wax gets soft from the sun," but not "Therefore, the sun is softer." Thirdly, it is not true in the case of a cause which is capable of degrees of more and less; it does not follow that "If the son is a man because of his father, the father is for this reason more a man." But the above mentioned rule does hold especially in final causes, as "He devotes effort to his studies for the sake of gain; therefore, he is more concerned about gain."

[1] In *Paradise Lost* X.652–64, the sun and moon are planets "like the other five," and there is no suggestion that the sun is hot any more than the others. This is in accord with the usual cosmology.

CHAPTER X

ON THE SUBJECT

N EXT comes the argument which in some sense is one of
agreement, as instanced in subject and adjunct. For the
absolute agreement of cause and effect properly precedes
this modified agreement of subject and adjunct. [26] Those things
are said to agree in a modified way with the thing they argue,
which agree only slightly and extrinsically, that is, apart from any
consideration of essence; for a subject does not give existence to
an adjunct as a cause does to its effect, nor does an adjunct receive
its essence from its subject. The subject should be treated first, for
a subject is by nature prior to all of its adjuncts and in a certain
way is related to its adjunct as a cause to its effect.

A subject is that to which something is adjoined. This argument
Cicero calls the subject thing, since it certainly is the subject of
something. That thing is said to serve as a subject, to which, once
it is constituted by its causes, there is joined something as a kind
of addition over and above the thing's causes; so that there is joined
something which, extrinsically and over and above essence, is
added to another thing, namely, to the subject already perfected
and constituted by its causes. A subject, therefore, is that which
is relevant to the arguing of something added to it over and above
the essence which it has from its causes.

Just as a cause, so a subject has its various modes. A thing is
said to serve as a subject either by receiving its adjuncts or by
appropriating them. Whence subject can be divided into *receiving*
subject, which the Greeks call δεκτικόν, and *appropriating* subject,
which is commonly called *object* because in it the adjuncts are
appropriated.[1] The receiving subject receives its attributes either
into itself or toward itself; the subject receiving its attributes into
itself either sustains and as it were supports them, so that they are
called *implanted* or *inhering,* or it contains them, as a place contains what is placed within it.

---

[1] Note that the typical present-day opposition of subjective-objective does not
concern Milton (or his age generally). For a brief discussion of the shift (in effect,
a reversal) from pre-Newtonian senses of subject and object, see Walter J. Ong,
The Presence of the Word (New Haven and London: Yale University Press, 1967),
pp. 222–31.

The first mode, therefore, obtains when a subject receives its implanted or inhering attributes. In this manner the soul is the subject of knowledge, ignorance, virtue and vice, because these are all joined to the soul, that is, are added to it over and above its essence; and the body is the subject of health, sickness, strength, [27] infirmity, beauty and deformity, because they are indeed within the body, but over and above its essence.

The second mode is that of the subject which contains its attributes within itself, that is, the mode of place. In this manner a place is the subject of the thing placed in it or in which the placed thing is contained. Thus the philosophers ascribe a place to divine things, though these lack parts and magnitude. And in this manner the geometricians assign place and differences of place to geometric entities. And the physicians consider place much more diligently in physical things—in the world, in the simple elements, in composite things. Hence some dialecticians in their zeal for increasing the scope of their art contend that the doctrine of place as well as that of motion should be treated in logic. But since place is an external property of some nature or other, whether corporeal or incorporeal, I wonder what persuaded them—especially the disciples of Ramus—to decide that, although they teach that arguments (i.e., not things, but reasons) are the subject matter of logic, things or properties of natural things—movement, place, time—should nevertheless be treated in logic. Place, they say, is common to absolutely all things. Therefore, I say, it belongs to some art dealing not only with bodies but with all natural things, that is, to physics, a universal art, and not to logic, which considers not what place is—whether space or the surface of a surrounding body—but how it argues a placed thing, exactly as a subject argues an attribute.

The third mode is that of a subject receiving attributes into or about itself, which latter are therefore called adjacent properties or circumstances. Thus, man is the subject of riches, poverty, honor, infamy, clothing, companionship, and generally of those things which are called antecedents, concomitants, and consequents, [28] if they have among themselves any relationship at all that is not necessary. This relationship is usually at least an argument of the causes and effects which arise from these attributes. So much for the recipient subject.

The fourth mode is that of the appropriating subject, in which the attribute is truly appropriated and engaged; and so this (subject) is properly called an object. Thus, sensible things are in this way called the subjects of the senses, and things attached to virtues and vices the subjects of the vices and virtues. Color is the subject of sight, and sound the subject of hearing; because these senses are appropriated and engaged by these sensible things. The virtues and the vices are explained in ethics by this sort of argument: temperance and intemperance by pleasure, fortitude [2] and cowardice by perils, liberality and avarice by riches. In this way a thing as numerable is the subject of arithmetic, and a thing as measurable, so to speak, the subject of geometry. By subject understood in this sense Cicero in *Agrarian Law* 2 [ii.33.91] argues that among the Campani there is no discord, because there is no honor. "They are not borne by any desire for glory," he says, "for where there is no public honor, there can be no desire for glory."

[2] Milton has *fortitudo* for Ramus's *magnanimitas*.

CHAPTER XI

ON THE ADJUNCT

AN *adjunct is that of which something is the subject,* or that which is relevant to the arguing of a subject. The doctrine of adjuncts corresponds in all points to the doctrine of subjects. Cicero [*Top.* 3.11–9.50] calls this argument that of adjunct and conjunct. It is called by Aristotle [e.g., *Top.* i.5.102b4–26] an accident, [29] and not inappropriately, for whatever happens extrinsically to any subject, whether fortuitously or not, is that subject's adjunct. What are called the goods and evils of the spirit, of the body and of the whole man are adjuncts of the spirit, the body and the man.

Since therefore an adjunct is added to a subject over and above the latter's essence, the essence of the subject is not changed by the addition or removal of the adjunct, nor does the subject thereby become something else, but it merely exists according to a different mode. Whence what are called modes are also to be counted among the adjuncts. Thus in the case of causes, procreating and conserving are modes (as stated above) or adjuncts, either of the efficient cause or of the thing to be caused.

Although this argument is of less weight than that of subject, it is nevertheless more copious and more frequent. It is of less weight than an argument of subject because a subject is prior and in some way the cause of its adjuncts. This is not held to be true of any and all adjuncts. Hence Aristotle in *Metaphysics* 6.1 [vii.1.1028a31–33] says that "an adjunct is posterior to its subject in the order of definition, time, knowledge and nature." And this is true of every adjunct, except in the order of time. For logic does not consider the existence of an adjunct, but the mutual relation it has with its subject, a relation which is simultaneous for both, so that a subject is no more prior in time to its adjunct than the adjunct is to its subject. Therefore, if the subject is removed, so is the adjunct, as in "A dead man *is* not, therefore a dead man is not miserable." Hence it is rattled out in the schools that "from *is* in a proposition of the second adject to *is* in a proposition of the third adject, there is a valid consequence, if both propositions are

negated." [1] And if the adjunct is posited, then the subject is necessarily posited, as in "If a dead man is miserable, then necessarily
a dead man *is*." This is stammered out in the schools as follows:
"From *is* in a proposition of the third adject to *is* in a proposition
of the second adject there is a valid consequence if both propositions
are affirmed." But the argument of adjunct is more copious and
more frequent than that of subject because [30] there can be many
adjuncts of one and the same subject. So concerning signs of this
sort Ovid, *De remediis* 2 [419–20] says:

> Perhaps someone will call these things small (for so they are)
> But things which singly are of little use, help in numbers.

So here are classed the signs which should rather be related to
effects; and they have as much force of arguing something as their
causes are certain and known. Thus a swelling of the womb is the
sign of a pregnant woman, but an uncertain one because there can
be other causes of the swelling; milk in the breast is a much more
certain sign, because the cause is more certain and better known.
Of the same sort are the signs of physiognomy,[2] and the prognostics
of the astrologers and physicians. So just as causes and effects
produce knowledge, so subjects and adjuncts for the most part
produce conjecture. With this sort of argument Cicero in *Pro Ro-
scio Comœdo* [7.20] mocks Fannius Chaerea, and from his bodily
characteristics infers signs of malice: "Do not that head and those
eyebrows so carefully shaved seem to smack of malice and to proclaim cunning? Does he not seem from top to toe (if the concealed
shape of the body allows such a conjecture) to be made up of fraud,
fallacies, lies?" In this manner Martial, Book 2 [*Epigr.* xii.54],
makes sport of Zoilus:

> Red-haired, black-mouthed, short-footed, one-eyed;
> Zoilus, if you are good, you manage a great performance.

To the modes of subject correspond further the modes of adjunct.
Therefore, just as a subject is either a recipient one or an appropriating one, so an adjunct is either received or appropriated. A
received adjunct is received either into a subject or toward a sub-

---

[1] "Man is" is a proposition of the "first adject": One word, "is," has been added
to the noun substantive. "Man is mortal" is a proposition of the second adject:
Two words have been added. This use of "adject" (*adjectum*) is part of the
semantic history of the term "adjective."

[2] In Milton's day perhaps the best known of the works on physiognomy was
De Humana Physiognomia Libri Quatuor (Vico di Sorrento: J. Cacchius, 1586—
with many subsequent editions), by the Neapolitan mathematician Giovanni
Battista della Porta (1535?–1615).

ject: one received into a subject is either sustained by it, or [31] contained or located in it; and one that is sustained is an implanted or inhering adjunct.

The first mode, therefore, is that of inhering or implanted adjuncts. Qualities (a quality is that by which a thing is said to be such and such) [3] are adjoined to their subjects wholly over and above the latters' causes, that is, over and above external forms (which are also counted among qualities); and this holds true whether the qualities are proper, belonging to every one of their subjects and solely to them, such as laughter to men, whinnying to horses, barking to dogs; or common, being any which are not in this way proper. But adjuncts are called proper usually in four ways: proper solely to their subjects but not to every one of them, as being a mathematician is proper to man, but not to every one; proper to every one of their subjects but not solely to them, in the way being a biped is proper to man; proper to every one of their subjects and solely to them, but not always, in the way growing gray in old age is proper to man; and proper to every one of their subjects, solely to them and always, in the way the ability to laugh is proper to man. The last mentioned sort of adjunct is truly proper and reciprocal, so that every man is capable of laughter, and everything capable of laughter in any proper sense is a man. And thus a proper adjunct, although posterior in nature to its subject and of lesser weight as well, is nevertheless simultaneous with its subject and better known to us. And if a proper adjunct is posited, its subject is posited, and conversely, for a subject is in some way essential to its proper [4] adjunct, and this adjunct originates from the form of its subject; the adjunct therefore gets from the form of its subject, and not from its own nature, the force of positing and removing its subject.

A common quality is either separable or inseparable: as the cold of water is a separable quality and wetness an inseparable one, while both are common. And these distinctions of qualities—common and proper, separable and inseparable—are most useful for forming judgments, as we shall easily ascertain in the second book. [32] Referred to this mode is also quantity, by which things are called large or small, many or few; and passion, by which a thing is said to undergo something; and movement as well, if referred to the thing moved, belongs here. So much for the adjunct which is sustained in its subject.

[3] Latin, *qualis,* such.

[4] The *proprie* of Milton's text, unaltered in Columbia, is here emended to *proprio*. Otherwise, no clear meaning appears.

The second mode is that of adjuncts which are contained in their subject, like a placed thing in its place. And here too belongs the situation of placed things,[5] unless it seems to someone that this should be referred rather to the first mode, since situation is a certain passion of a located thing and thus pertains to the first mode. And so much for adjuncts which are received into their subject.

The third mode is that of adjuncts which are received toward their subject. These are commonly called circumstances because they are outside their subject. Here belongs time, namely, the past, present and future duration of things. Thus also God is called He who is, was and will be (Apocalypse 1.4 and 4.8).[6] Yet to God is usually attributed *ævum* or eternity, and not time. But what properly is *ævum* if not perpetual duration, in Greek αἰών—as it were, ἀεὶ ὤν, or ever existing? But now the same thing should be recommended concerning time as in the preceding chapters concerning movement and place: that it does not belong to logic to philosophize about what time is, but about the genus of argument in which it is to be placed—here, namely, among the adjuncts. Here also are referred riches, poverty, honor, infamy, clothing, companionship, and anything of this sort which can be said to be present, to be adjacent to, to be a circumstance of, or without causal force to precede, accompany, or follow, as we said above concerning subject; or, as Cicero says in the *Topics* [12.51], "Whatever happens before a thing, with a thing, or after a thing, as long as it does so nonnecessarily." [33]

By means of circumstances of this sort Dido departing for the hunt is magnificently described in Æneid 4 [iv.129–31]:

> Meanwhile Aurora rising left the sea.
> By early light the chosen youths went out the gates:
> Wide-meshed nets, snares, broadheaded spears, etc.

In this example *Dido* is the subject with respect to whom the adjacent adjuncts or various circumstances are here enumerated: (1) the *time,* "Meanwhile," etc.; (2) the *companions,* doubtless the "chosen youths," the "horsemen," the "Phoenician" leaders; (3) the associated instruments (which as such are referred to their possessor), of which sort are certainly the "wide-meshed nets," the "snares," the "spears," the "dogs," the "charger"; (4) belongings

---

[5] We have taken the "locorum" (of places) in Milton's Latin text to be a typographical error for "locatorum" (of placed things), which the sense demands; there is no equivalent to this passage in Ramus or Downame.

[6] See above, Milton's Preface and n. 3.

(*habitus*) or clothing, such as the "Sidonian cloak," the "purple dress," etc. So much for the received adjuncts.

The fourth mode is that of the appropriated adjunct. For *the utility of the adjuncts with respect to the subjects by which they are appropriated is likewise great.*

By an argument of this sort Plato [*Resp.* iii.404E–405D] feels that "those states are wretched which need a multitude of physicians and judges, because necessarily much intemperance and injustice will be practiced in such a state," namely because physicians, in curing the effects of intemperance, and judges, in redressing the effects of injustice, are engaged like appropriated adjuncts by the subject which appropriates them.

But the category (*categoria*) [7] or locus of arguments of agreement is of the sort that from it anything agreeing with something can be called either identical or one with it; and all modes of unity and, so to speak, of identity are to be referred here as to their primary and simple sources.

These final words are added to explain the use of arguments of agreement in comparisons. For just [34] as the modes of every agreement of two things in a third are to be sought here, so also are the modes of unity. By as many ways as several things are said to agree among themselves, they are also said to be one or identical: namely, either absolutely, or in a certain way. They are absolutely one and identical by cause and effect, and in a certain way one and identical in subject and adjunct. If it is by cause, then either by efficient cause or matter or form or end. Thus many statues [8] are identical in their efficient cause, if by the same artist; in their matter if out of the same matter, such as gold or ivory; in their form if likenesses of the same man, such as Alexander or Caesar; in their end if intended to honor the same man. Similarly two or more adjuncts in the same subject are identical in subject; and many subjects to which the same attribute is adjoined are identical in adjunct, as two or more white or black things are identical in whiteness or blackness.

[7] The assimilation of the Aristotelian κατηγορίαι (*prædicamenta,* predicaments, "accusations") to the loci of dialectic is a characteristic of Ramism. See Ong, *Ramus, Method, and Decay of Dialogue,* pp. 104–12, 183.

[8] In a work that Milton could well have known—there are many copies in England—the Ramist physician (a rare bird, for doctors of medicine were from the start Ramus's most active opponents) Theodor Zwinger (1533–88) gives a Ramist logical analysis of the Coleoni equestrian statue in Venice according to the four causes and the accidents (adjuncts). See Theodor Zwinger (Zwingerus), *Methodus Apodemica* (Basel: Eusebius Episcopius, 1577), p. 398.

Chapter XII

ON THE DISAGREEING

THE *argument of agreement has been treated* in terms of cause and effect, subject and adjunct.

There follows another species of artificial, primary and simple argument, namely, that of disagreement. And it ought to follow, for just as affirmation is prior to negation, so agreement to disagreement, but prior not only by nature, but also in use and dignity. For from affirmation and agreement all art and teaching, like all science, is derived. [35]

An argument of disagreement is one which disagrees with the thing it argues, namely with another argument of disagreement of the same kind and name. For in this kind of arguments, those arguments which are relevant to each other are expressed by the same name and therefore by the same plural name, and they are explained by the same definition and teaching.

Arguments which disagree with each other are equally manifest: and each is argued equally by the other; yet by their disagreement they show forth more clearly.

These are the two common properties of arguments of disagreement. For first in arguments of agreement, causes were prior to, better known than, stronger than and more excellent than their effects, and subjects than their adjuncts. In arguments of disagreement one is not prior to or better known than the other, but they are by nature simultaneous, namely, in their very disagreement, and equally well known and equally strong among themselves, as is necessary since they are considered under the same name and definition.

Also the second property, which Aristotle [e.g., *Rh.* iii.2.1405a 11–13] associates with contraries, is common to all arguments of disagreement, namely, that *in their disagreement they show forth more clearly.* If this were not the case, arguments of disagreement would be of no use. For every argument ought to be relevant to the arguing or elucidating of something. But of those things which have the property of being equally known and unknown, one cannot be argued or elucidated by another. This second property is therefore subordinate to the first, for although arguments of disagreement be equally manifest among themselves, so that one cannot be argued from another as better known, nevertheless from their disagreement—or, as others say, by their juxtaposition—they do show forth more clearly. Thus the advantages of good health are made more manifest by the disadvantages of poor health, and the praise of virtue is elucidated by the censure of the contrary vice. [36]

So these loci of disagreements, as attested by Aristotle in *Topics* 3.4 [iii.6.119a32–38] are useful not only for arguing and elucidating, but also for urging and refuting. For just as the loci of agreements have force especially for arguing, proving, and confirming, so loci of disagreements for disproving, urging, and refuting: so that one who refuses to be taught by an argument of agreement is reduced by the absurd consequence of an argument of disagreement to the point where, even though unwilling, he cannot but assent to the truth. Hence Aristotle in *Rhetoric* 3.17 [iii.17.1418b1–4] places refuting arguments before demonstrative ones.

Arguments of disagreement are diverse or opposed.

Arguments of disagreement which are diverse are those which disagree only in relation to something. This name seems most suitable for designating this very slight sort of disagreement, for by this expression are signified those things which, though they seem to have a certain agreement among themselves and can by themselves and by their nature belong simultaneously to the same subject, are nevertheless not identical nor do they belong to the subject in relation to which they are said to disagree. But things that disagree with the same third thing also disagree among themselves.

They disagree, therefore, only in relation to something, because they do not disagree by themselves and in their nature, but only in some relation of attribution, that is, in relation to and with respect to some subject, to which they are not simultaneously attributed. So the distinction of arguments of disagreement on the basis of their disagreement is rightly made: for just as one agreement is stricter and absolute, another looser and imperfect (whence arguments of agreement are divided into those which agree absolutely or in a limited sense), so every disagreement is either of the looser type, as in the distinction [37] or separation of diverse things, or of the stricter type, as in the disjunction of opposites. Therefore, arguments of disagreement disagree either in relation to something and in a certain sense, such as in the case of diverse things, or they disagree in themselves and absolutely, as opposites. And the objection that could also have been made regarding arguments of agreement, that a genus must be equally communicated to its species (for let it be permitted sometimes to anticipate, with apology to method,[1] these expressions which are understood also from common use prior to any art), can be answered by saying that just as arguments of agreement, whether absolute or in a certain sense, were equally ones of agreement but did not equally agree, so the diverse and the opposite are equally arguments of disagreement but do not equally disagree. There is disagreement in the diverse as well as in opposites, but not as much, as Cicero, *De finibus* 4 [iv.27.75], writes concerning a similar matter: "It happens equally to all lyres that they get out of tune, but not necessarily that they are equally out of tune." But the diverse are treated first because on account of their very slight disagreement they seem to exhibit a certain affinity with arguments of agreement. But though the doctrine about the diverse is omitted by all logicians except Ramus, yet it is certain that in the doctrine of arguments some place must also be given to the diverse, since arguments are to be distinguished by their varying relevance to arguing, but the relevance of disagreement in the diverse is, as we said, slighter, and in opposites more marked. The reason why logicians have so far omitted the diverse seems to be that they refer all arguments to one syllogism, in which the diverse have no place, as will be shown in Book 2.[2]

The signs of diverse arguments are most often *not this . . . but that, although . . . nevertheless,* as in *Pro Pompeio* [Cic. *Leg. Man.* 3.8]: "They did not bring back the victory, but the tokens of victory." Victory and the tokens of victory [38] are quite closely related and they can and should belong to the same commander, but if you consider Sulla and Murena, who triumphed but brought back no victory, they are arguments of disagreement and are distinguished, and one is affirmed while the other is denied. Thus Ovid, *Ars amatoria* 2 [ii.123]:

Ulysses was not fair but he was eloquent.

And in *Æneid* 2 [ii.533–34]:

Although Priamus was already held in the midst of death
Yet he did not abstain.

Just as victory and the tokens of victory in the case of Sulla and Murena, so being fair and being eloquent in the case of Ulysses, and being held in the midst of death and not abstaining from reproaches in the case of Priam, are examples of the diverse and

[1] See Book II, chap. xvii.
[2] See Book II, chap. vii.

are moreover disagreements. It is little otherwise in the *Eunuchus* [Ter. *Eun.* v.2.865–66]:

> For if I am most deserving of this contumely,
> Yet you are unworthy to inflict it.

But this is the same as if it had been said: although I am worthy, yet you are unworthy to inflict this contumely upon me. Thais affirms that she is indeed worthy of insult, but that she is worthy of it from Chaera she denies. Cicero, *Tusculan Disputations* 5 [v.33.95–96], says: "Although they are judged by a bodily sense, they are nevertheless referred to the mind." Once this is affirmed, the negation "not to the body" is understood.

Also, examples of another type appear in *Pro Ligario* [17]: "Do you call that a crime, Tubero? Why? The matter has so far wanted for such a name: for some call it an error, others fear; some, more severely, hope, cupidity, hatred, obstinacy; the severest, rashness; a crime, so far none but you." In this type of examples something is conceded so that another similar thing [39] may be denied: of this sort is the saying that truth can be concealed but it cannot be extinguished, and the like.

And so there are these modes of the diverse: those in which it often happens that things which by their nature are opposites, are nevertheless in relation to some certain subject only diverse, as in the above example error, fear, hope, cupidity, obstinacy, crime. Thus, gold, silver, and brass are opposites, as will appear below,[3] but by a relation of attribution to this or that subject which has one or some of them, but lacks the other or the rest (whereas it could have them all at once), they are diverse.

---

[3] Book I, chap. xiii, where, however, Milton does not mention gold, silver, and brass specifically as examples.

CHAPTER XIII

ON DISPARATES

T HOSE arguments of disagreement are opposite which disagree in themselves and in their relations. Opposites correspond in name to what are called ἀντικείμενα by
Aristotle; but in themselves and in their meaning they extend further. For to Aristotle (who does not touch on disparates) ἀντικείμενα
are nothing other than *contraries* [e.g., *Top.* v.6.135b8–17].[1] They
can also be called *incompatibles,* if indeed those things are said to
be incompatible which are such that they cannot cohere; for Cicero
says in the *Topics* [12.53] that opposites are of this sort. But *in
themselves* and *in their relation* means not only in relation to some
certain subject which, when attributed to it, they do not simultaneously fit, but also in their very reality, that is, by themselves
and among themselves they disagree by their nature, even when
not attributed to any subject. And if they are attributed to a subject,
they not only do not fit it, but, in view of the law of opposites,
which follows, [40] they cannot fit it. That law, which follows from
the definition itself, and is common to all opposites (and not, as
Aristotle teaches [e.g., *Top.* ii.7.113a20–23],[2] proper to contraries),
is as follows: *Opposites cannot be attributed to one and the same
thing by reason of the same thing, with reference to the same thing
and at the same time. To one and the same thing,* that is, to a thing
or subject one in number. *By reason of the same thing,* that is, by

[1] This reference is to one of many places where Aristotle discusses opposites
(ἀντικείμενα). Only later in the paragraph do we learn how Milton can identify
Aristotle's opposites as nothing more than contraries, even though for Aristotle
himself contraries are only one of several types of opposites. For Milton, opposites
may disagree "by themselves and among themselves . . . even when not attributed
to any subject," and this "essentialist" or idealist meaning of "opposite" is quite
alien to Aristotle's theory of ἀντικείμενα, whose various types (contraries, contradictories, relatives, privatives) all involve subjects taken singly or pairwise.
It is this subject-dependence that Milton sees as proper to contraries. For more
on Aristotle's own theory of opposites, see, e.g., *Metaph.* x.3.1054b32–8.1058a17;
xi.5.1061b34–6.1063b35.

[2] This reference to Aristotle makes sense only if we think of opposites and
contraries in the special senses Milton is giving to them, as explained in the
preceding footnote. The law enunciated by Milton was formulated by Aristotle
as applying to all opposites in *his* sense; see, e.g., *Metaph.* iv.3.1005a19–8.1012b32;
v.10.1018a20–25.

reason of the same part. *With reference to the same thing,* that is, in the same respect. For example, *the sun is both greater than the earth and smaller;* but not in the same respect; in itself it is indeed greater, but as it appears to us it is smaller. Aside from these conditions, opposites can be attributed to one and the same subject. *Thus Socrates cannot be black and white by reason of the same thing, that is, in the same part; nor father and son of the same,* or as related to the same person; *nor healthy and ill at the same time. But he can be white in one part and black in another; the father of one and the son of another; healthy today and ill tomorrow.*

So if one opposite is affirmed, the other is denied.

From this it easily appears what the difference is between the diverse and the opposite. For in the former *one is affirmed* and the other is negated; in the latter, *because one is affirmed* the other is negated: that is, from the affirmation of the one there necessarily follows the negation of the other. Thus, taking an example of the diverse, "they brought back not victory but the signs of victory" [Cic. *Leg. Man.* 3.8]: here the signs of victory are affirmed and victory is negated; not because the signs are affirmed is the victory negated. But in opposites, in view of the aforementioned law, Socrates is a man, therefore he is not a horse, in accordance with the dictum that *opposites eliminate each other.*

But *opposites are either disparate or contrary.* [41]

Disparates are opposites of which one is equally opposed to many.

The opposition of disparates seems therefore to be more diffuse, that of contraries sharper. Disparates are also called by Boethius [*De hypotheticis syllogismis (PL* lxiv.834D)] "those things which are merely diverse from each other, not incompatible by reason of contrariety"; such as clothing and fire. But according to Cicero, *De inventione* 1 [i.28.42], and Fabius, Book 5, Chapter 10 [Quint. *Inst.* v.11.31], disparates mean things which are contradictory. Forced by scarcity of terms, we follow Boethius. *To many,* namely, without any certain law or number of opposition; for an almost infinite number of things can be mutually opposed in this way: and thus the word opposed is to be understood, in accordance with the dictum: *Terms in the arts signify inherent capacity.* Thus, clothing and fire, although two things, are mutually disparate, in that they can be opposed to many things. *Equally:* that is, for an equally like reason, by the same mode of disagreement. For in order to be disparate they should be opposed not only to many, but equally so. White is opposed to black, yellow, and red, as one to many; but not to each one of them as a disparate, because not equally, for to black it is opposed as a contrary, to the others as a disparate.

Green, gray, and red are intermediates between white and black, and are individually disparate with respect to the extremes and among themselves. Thus, liberality and avarice are mutually disparate. Thus, man, tree, stone, and infinite things of this sort are mutually disparate; nor can the same thing be a man, a tree, and a stone. Virgil, *Æneid* 1 [i.327–28], debates by means of this argument:

> What shall I call you, O maiden? Surely your face is not mortal,
> Nor does your voice have a human sound. Truly you are a goddess! [42]

CHAPTER XIV

ON RELATIVES

CONTRARIES *are opposites, of which one is opposed to one only.*
But it is understood that one thing is opposed to one thing in the same genus of contraries, as of relatives one to one only, and so on in the rest; for in some species of contraries, several items can as contraries be opposed to one and the same concrete thing. Thus, to *one who sees* there can be opposed *one who does not see,* and *one who is blind;* to *movement,* a *contrary movement* and *rest;* and to *servant,* lord and *freeman.*

What Aristotle [e.g., *Cat.* 10, *Top.* v.6, *Metaph.* v.10] calls ἀντιθέμενα and ἀντικείμενα, Cicero (whom Ramus follows) in the *Topics* [11.47–49] calls contraries: and into the same four species into which Aristotle divides ἀντικείμενα, Cicero divides *contraries.*

But before we come to the distinction of contraries into species, there should be inserted a certain distinction useful both for a clearer understanding of the things we said in the preceding chapter and for differentiating between what in the second book will be called necessary and contingent disjunctions. It was said in the preceding chapter that green, gray, and red are intermediates between white and black and that they are individually disparate with respect to the extremes and among themselves. So it should be known that contraries are in a sense such that some have extremes, others an intermediate, while others lack an intermediate: the intermediate is one either of negation or participation. This is from Aristotle, *Topics* 4.3 [iv.3.123b13–28], and *Metaphysics* 3.7 [iv.7.1011b30–32]. An intermediate [43] of negation is anything between two contraries that can be said to be neither one of them: for example, between teacher and pupil, one who is neither teacher nor pupil. An intermediate of participation is something that participates in the nature of each extreme, such as green between white and black, tepid between hot and cold. Of those contraries, therefore, which have an intermediate, it is not necessary that either one be affirmed, for the intermediate can be affirmed; but of those which lack an intermediate, it is necessary that one be affirmed. Which contraries have an intermediate and which do not can be gathered from what Gellius, *Noctes Atticæ* 16.8 [xvi.8.13–14], relates. Those contraries whose contradictories are also contrary when attributed to a subject to which they can properly be attributed, do not have an intermediate. Healthy and sick are contraries: their contradictories, not-healthy and not-sick, if you attribute them to an animal (the only sort of thing to which they can be attributed), you will find also to be contrary. For not-healthy is sick, and not-sick, healthy; healthy and sick therefore lack an intermediate. Thus, night and day, not-night and not-day, are equally mutually contrary; for not-night is day and not-day is night. They therefore lack an intermediate. Similarly, being endowed with sight and being blind, if you attribute them to man. But those whose contradictories are not contrary have an intermediate, such as teacher and pupil; for not-teacher is not pupil, nor is not-pupil teacher; and thus there can be some third or intermediate thing. Likewise with white and black: for not-white and not-black can be said of any intermediate color. Let us now come to the division of contraries.

Contraries are either affirmative or negative. [44]

They are affirmatives when each one affirms, namely, affirms a thing, real or feigned; or when each of their names posits and signifies a definite thing; and when one is opposed to the other as one thing to another, as a father to his son, or heat to cold. And so affirmative contraries, as should be noted and distinguished here, are those of which each one affirms a thing but is not affirmed of the same thing or subject, for this would be plainly counter to the above mentioned rule of opposites, according to which from the affirmation of one results the negation of the other. If it affirms a thing or denies it, an affirmation or denial is called topical; one by which a thing is affirmed or denied of something else is called axiomatic, and Book 2 will treat of this.

Affirming contraries are either relative or adverse.

Relatives are such that one exists from the mutual relation of the other.

And this indeed in such a way that from their mutual relation arises the contrariety itself, as will be shown below. Does this mean that relatives are therefore now in agreement, now in disagreement? Not at all, as relatives; but those things which are related can serve as subjects to various other genera of arguments; but meanwhile the genera themselves of the arguments remain non-confused and distinct. Thus, cause and effect, which in arguing mutually are related, and are to that extent in disagreement and equally manifest, nevertheless retain their own force of arguing by which they are also in agreement and the cause prior to and better known than its effect. That relatives are contraries is clear from the definition and consequences of contraries; for those things are opposites, of which one is opposed to one only, [45] such as father and son. But, you say, one can be opposed to many, a father to his children, a brother to his brothers, a teacher to his pupils, a master to his servants. The answer is that a parent is opposed to his child as a relative, and nothing other than a child to a parent and a parent to a child, and so on; but that this particular parent and this child, this teacher and this pupil, and so on, are not relatives but disparates; nor does one of them exist from the mutual relation of the other; nor are they simultaneous in nature, and one can exist without the other. So primary substances, or individual and singular things, as Aristotle says in *Categories* 5 [7.8a13–18], "are not relatives." And in *Categories* 6 [8.11a23–24] he says that "many genera are relatives, but no singular things." But I do not see why relatives, just like other arguments, cannot be considered also in singular things, for almost all examples are singular things. Nor do I any more see why in one singular relative there cannot be a multiple relation to many things, provided that there be numerically only one relation between two things and that it be considered as many times as there are relatives; the relation of father certainly as many times as there are children; of child as there are parents, namely, father and mother; of brother as there are brothers and sisters. For unless whatever is commonly said about relatives in general is also truly said of singular relatives, it can also not be said truly of relatives in general. If you reply from Aristotle in *Metaphysics* 6 [vii.1.1028a20–25] that related things do not signify existence, then neither do the other arguments signify that, but only a mutual relevance. They are *affirmative,* that is, just as there are two expressions, so there are two mutually opposed things, as father and son. But for one thing to exist from a mutual relevance of another thing means that they have no other essence, as relatives, apart from that mutual [46] relevance of one to the other and of the other to it. And the reason why they are called relatives is that they are mutually referred to each other and their whole nature consists in their relation. Thus, to be a father is to have a child, and to be a child is to have a father. Hence, the saying that all relatives are convertible: a father is the father of a child, and a child is the child of a father. By reason of this mutual relevance relatives are mutual causes of each other and mutual effects, for that someone is a father he has from his child, and that someone is a child he has from his father; and yet by reason of this mutual relevance they are opposed to each other in such a way that neither the one can be affirmed of the other nor both of a third. For example, Aeneas is the father of Ascanius and therefore not the son of Ascanius; Ascanius is the son of Aeneas and therefore not the father of Aeneas. But since, of relatives, one exists from the mutual relevance of the other, and they are mutually causes of each other, and effects, therefore this consequence follows.

Relatives are simultaneous in nature, so that whoever knows one perfectly also knows the other.

Even the old logicians, Aristotle [e.g., *Top.* vi.4.142a22–34], Damascenus [1] and others, teach that relatives are simultaneous in nature and that relatives mutually infer and remove each other, as when a father is posited, a child is posited; and if the father is removed so is the child: for even though he remains who was the child, he does not remain as child. And not only is it impossible for one to exist without the other, but one cannot even be understood without the other. It is therefore necessary, as Aristotle in *Topics* 6.4 [vi.4.142a31–32] also is mindful, *that one be included in the definition of the other;* and that whoever knows one perfectly, that is, by its definition, immediately knows·the definition of the other, which, like their essence, is reciprocal. And so [47] Ramus defined subject as that *to which something is adjoined,* not as *that which serves as subject to something else,* as others preferred, even though in these words not only the essence of subject but also its etymology seems to be contained. Then he defined attribute as *that with respect to which something serves as subject,* and not as that which is adjoined to something else, since subject and attribute are relatives; and a subject of an attribute and an attribute of a subject are each to be defined by that mutual relevance of the one by which the other exists, which is their essence. Let us now come to some examples.

Pro Marcello [3–4]: "By which you truly understand how much praise there is in the benefit given, since in its acceptance there is such glory." Here giving and receiving are relative, concerning which Cicero says that the consequent of one is understood from the consequent of the other. Martial, *In Sosibianum,* book 1 [*Epigr.* i.82], writes:

> You know you were born a slave, and you fondly admit it
> When you, Sosibianus, call your master father.

Sosibianus argues that he was born a servant, while he seems to deny it, because his master he calls father. Thus in Quintilian,

---

[1] John Damascene, *Dialectica,* version of Robert Grosseteste, ed. Owen A. Colligan (St. Bonaventure, N.Y.: Franciscan Institute, 1953), pp. 33–34, lines 31–40.

book 5, chapter 10 [*Inst.* v.10.78–79]: "If it is honest for the Rho-
dians to farm out the right to collect duties, so is it for Hermacrion
to buy the right to collect them." In the same manner Cicero writes
in *De oratore perfecto* [*Orat.* 42.145–46]: "Is there any danger," he
says, "that someone will think it base to teach others, in a great
and glorious art, that which it would be honorable for him himself
to learn?" In Ovid, *Metamorphoses* 1 [i.144–48], in the description
of the iron age, various examples of relatives are presented:

> Guest is not safe from host,
> Not father-in-law from son-in-law; and brotherly love is rare.
> The man watches for his wife's death, and she for his. [48]
> Fearsome stepmothers mix ghastly poisons,
> And the son wonders too soon about his father's years.

*So an argument of such a relation has no contrary; rather, it argues
mutual causes:* thus, I am your father, and you are therefore my
son. *But when I say,* I am your father, and am therefore not your
son, *then we have contraries;* and they result from this mutual
relation itself.

CHAPTER XV

ON THE ADVERSE

T*HE adverse are affirmative contraries which are directly opposed to each other absolutely.*
      Thus they are also called by Cicero in the *Topics* [11.47–48]. *They are contraries* because one of them is opposed to one only; as the honorable to the base; for only two things can be directly opposed to each other. *They are affirmatives,* because one is opposed to one as a thing to a thing, as was demonstrated above and will appear more clearly below. But with these words *are directly opposed to each other* is understood nothing other than direct opposition, and the greatest; such as that between two points in the diameter of one and the same circle. By these words the adverse are distinguished from their intermediates, which are disparate from each other and from their extremes. *Absolutely,* that is, in every way, perfectly; as in arguments of agreement which agree absolutely. Ramus said *continuously:* but I agree with others who prefer the word *absolutely,* [49] for to be opposed continuously is common to all opposites, even relatives, insofar as they are opposed, that is, disagree in their relations and in themselves. But *absolutely* is added so that by this particle the adverse can be distinguished from relatives, in which there is a certain agreement, inasmuch as one exists from the mutual relevance of the other, of which there is nothing of the sort here. Thus whiteness and blackness, heat and cold, are opposed.

      Aristotle defines contraries (for so he called *the adverse* in *Categories* 6 [6.6a17–18] "as those things which are at the greatest distance within the same genus"; and again in *Categories* 8 [11.14a14–15] he says that "contraries are either in the same species or in the same genus." Cicero follows him in the *Topics* [11.47–49] and Galen in *De optima secta.*[1] But in truth the adverse, as Aristotle teaches in his chapter on contraries, not only differ most widely in the same genus, as do white and black, but also in contrary genera, as do justice and injustice; or the genera themselves, as

---

[1] *De Optima Secta ad Thrasybulum,* in *Medicorum Græcorum Opera quæ Extant* (Editionem curavit D. Carolus Gottlob Kühn; Lipsiæ: Officina Libraria Car. Cnoblochii, 1821), I, 215.

good and evil, virtue and vice. To differ in the same genus seems to be common to the adverse along with relatives; hence instead of *in the same genus,* it is more correct to put *directly* in the definition, as Cicero [*Top.* 11.47] explains.

In *Aeneid* 11 [xi.362]:

> There is no safety through war; we all ask for peace.

Liberty and servitude in Tibullus, Book 2 [*Eleg.* ii.4.1–2]:

> Thus for myself I see servitude, a ready mistress;
> Farewell to you, my paternal liberty.

Thus, counsel and chance; *Pro Marcello* [7]: "For temerity is never mingled with wisdom, nor is chance admitted to counsel." And in *Paradox 1, contra Epicureos* [14]: "That they hold closely and diligently defend the principle that pleasure is the supreme good: all of which seems to me to be the voice of swine and not of men." [50] Cicero opposes swine and men as adverse: pleasure is the good of swine, and therefore not of men. For the use of this argument occurs not only in qualities, as is commonly thought, but also in substances and quantities, and indeed in all things: something which Aristotle does not deny when he says in *Metaphysics* 10.3 [xi.3.1061a10–15] that "Contraries are assigned also to the primary differences of being"; and again [*Top.* vi.6.143b1–3] that "There is contrariety in every genus." Contrariety, then, is acknowledged by all to be a logical argument. Nothing therefore prevents it from pertaining to all genera of things. Some genera are even forms or, especially, substances; but that all specific forms are mutually adverse is most commonly admitted by all: indeed there seems to be greater contrariety of forms than of qualities, for qualities can easily be mixed together, forms hardly ever. Therefore, what Aristotle elsewhere [*Cat.* 5.3b25–26, 6.5b11] teaches, namely, that nothing is contrary to substance and quantity, is refuted not only by reason but also by his own testimony cited above; but the contention that there is no contrariety of substances, although not a matter of physics, is nevertheless a matter of logic, as long as from the affirmation of one singular substance another is denied. [51]

CHAPTER XVI

ON CONTRADICTORIES

NEGATIVE *contraries are such that one of them affirms and the other negates the same thing.* They are so named from the one that negates; for in pure negatives, as they say, there is no exercise of reason. And so from this it at last becomes more clear what affirmative contraries are: when these have been sufficiently discussed so have the negatives.

They are either contradictory or privative.

Contradictories are negative contraries of which one totally negates: such as just, not-just; animal, not-animal; is, is-not.

Contradictories are contraries, since one negation is opposed to one affirmation, and conversely; and indeed without an intermediate. Thus also Aristotle, *Posterior Analytics* 1.2 [i.2.72a13–14], says that "Contradiction is an opposition in which there is of itself no intermediate." *Of which one totally negates;* that is, with respect to any thing whatsoever; for, to negate totally applies to any case in which what has been affirmed is not asserted. For example, a thing of which *it sees* is not affirmed is one of which *it does not see* is affirmed. Whence the common saying that "all things are contradictories," and the words of Aristotle, *Posterior Analytics* 1.2 [i.1.71a13–14], that "One can truly either affirm or deny anything; but it is impossible truly to affirm and deny at the same time." And in *Topics* 6.3 [vi.6.143b15–16] he says that "of any thing either an affirmation or negation is truly asserted." One thing is said always to deny either expressly or implicitly; expressly, as above, with [52] a negating particle; implicitly when in fact it is no less contradictory and repugnant to another thing than if it negated verbally, as an infinite body or a special property which is common. It is commonly called a contradiction in adject,[1] since it adjoins to a subject that which clearly removes the subject; and thus it implies a contradiction. And thence it is that contradictories lack an intermediate not only of participation but also of negation, since it is necessary that one of them affirm or negate something about the other. Thus also Boethius writes in the *Topics* [*Comm.*

---

[1] "Adject" here means the term next to or joined to another. See Book I, chap. xi. The *OED* fails to note this technical logical meaning in the examples it cites.

on Cic. Top. i (*PL* lxiv.1054C)]: "Between affirmation and negation
there is no intermediate." Here now are some examples of contradictories. In the defense of *Murena* [31.65] there is contradiction
in the opinions of Cato and Cicero, the former a Stoic, the latter
an Academic. The dialogue goes this way: "You will forgive nothing: that is to say, something, but not all things. You will do
nothing to gain favor; that is to say, do not refuse to gain favor
when office and duty require. Do not be moved by mercy, not even
in mitigating severity; but there is still something to say for kindness. Hold fast to your opinion; yes indeed, unless another better
opinion wins out." In this example there is a fourfold contradiction:
you will forgive nothing, you will forgive something; you will do
nothing to please, you will do something to please, etc. Martial
writes in Book 1 [*Epigr.* i.64]:

> You are beautiful, we know; you are a maiden, true;
> And rich; for who can deny it?
> But when you praise yourself too much, Fabulla,
> You are neither rich nor beautiful nor a maiden.

Cicero in the *Tusculan Disputations* [i.6.12] by this argument
forces Atticus the Epicurean to admit that the dead are not unhappy
if they do not exist at all, as the Epicureans believed: "The same
one whose existence you deny you say exists: for when you say that
he is unhappy, [53] then one who does not exist you say exists."
Thus in Terence [*Eun.* iv.4.714], Phaedria disparages the speech
of Dorius the eunuch, because first he affirmed what he later denied: "Now he affirms, now he denies."

There are those who hold that there is no contradiction but the
axiomatic,[2] about which Book 2 will treat. But certainly if there
is a topical affirmation and negation, as we demonstrated above,
there must also be a topical contradiction, such as the one in Romans 9 [9:25]: "I will call them my people who are not-my-people;
and her beloved who is not-beloved."[3] In distinctions also the use
of this sort of contradiction is most frequent; especially when one
member of a distinction cannot be expressed by an apt term. For
example, the matter of dialectic is being and non-being; law is
written or unwritten. Thus Socrates says to Crito [*Cri.* 44 A]: "You
seem to have failed conveniently to awaken me." In these examples
there is no axiomatic contradiction: just as in what was quoted

---

[2] I.e., propositional.
[3] See above, Milton's Preface and n. 3.

above in this chapter from Martial: "You are beautiful, we know, and maiden, etc." For not the verb "is," or the connection, is denied, but the parts. Fabulla is beautiful and a maiden and rich; Fabulla is not-beautiful and not-maiden and not-rich. For an axiomatic contradiction would be of this sort: Fabulla is not beautiful and a maiden and rich: which will be understood more clearly in Book 2. [54]

CHAPTER XVII

ON PRIVATIVES

PRIVATIVES *are negative contraries, one of which negates only in that subject to which the affirmative by its very nature belongs.* And here what is affirmed is called *habitus,* by which someone possesses something, but the negative is called privation, by which someone is deprived of or lacks that something: examples are sight and blindness, or movement and rest in those things which are preserved by movement. They are contraries because one thing is opposed to one thing, *habitus* to privation, in view of which they are also called negatives: for here also to the affirmation of something is opposed the negation of the same thing, that is, to being non-being, for privation, as Aristotle says in *Physics* 1.8 [i.8.191b16], "is in itself non-being." And Plutarch *De primo frigido* [*Mor.* xii.946B], writes: "Privation is the negation of essence, and is opposed to *habitus,* not as a nature or an essence existing in itself, but as its corruption and removal." One which negates only in that subject to which, etc. By these words is expressed the form of privatives by which they are distinguished from contradictories. For in contradictories negation is infinite, negating its affirmative everywhere, that is, in any thing whatsoever; for example, whatever is not just is not-just. But in privatives the negation is finite, negating the affirmative or the *habitus* only in that subject to which the affirmative by its very nature belongs, or can belong, as Aristotle says in the *Categories* [10.12a26–31]. Thus blindness is the negation of sight, not everywhere and in any thing whatsoever, but only in the thing to which sight by nature should belong; for [55] a thing is said to be deprived only when it lacks what it naturally has: not everything, therefore, which does not see, is properly called blind. In contradictories, then, the negative denies by contradicting and is pure negation, as seeing and not-seeing; in privatives it negates by depriving, nor is it solely negation, but a depriving negation and the removal of some *habitus* which by nature should or can belong to a subject, as seeing and blind. Hence those properties of privation in Plutarch, *De primo frigido* [*Mor.* xii.946B, D], are not without use: "Privation is inert and incapable of acting: it is not susceptible to degrees of more and less"; for neither would anyone say that this man is more blind

than that one; or that a silent person is more or less silent; or that
a deceased person is more or less dead: for there can be degrees
of *habitus* but not of non-being. But the property assigned by
Aristotle [*Cat*. 10.13a31–33] is less certain: "From privation back
to *habitus* there is no return"; for since the *habitus* by which someone is said to have something is of two types, namely, potency and
act, the purely natural recovery from a privation of a potency or
a faculty is what is denied. In short, contradictories lack an intermediate not only of participation but also of negation: but privatives do indeed lack an intermediate of participation, for there is
no mixture of habit with privation; but they do not lack an intermediate of negation (for there are many things which do not see
and yet are not blind, such as a stone, a tree, etc.) except when
they are attributed to a subject to which they should by nature
belong, for then they also lack an intermediate of negation; indeed,
every man is seeing or blind, knowing or ignorant. Examples of
privatives are rich and poor, as in Martial, book 5 [*Epigr*. v.81]:

> If you are poor, Emilian, you will always be poor:
> Resources are given to none but the rich. [56]

Another example is life and death, as in *Pro Milone* [Cic. *Mil*.
29.79]: "Sit still, avengers of the death of this man, whose life, if
you thought it could be restored by you, you would not want."
Likewise, speaking and being silent, as in the first *Oration against
Catiline* [i.8.20–21]: "Why do you wait for the authority of a
speaker whose preference for remaining silent you perceive?" The
other examples which Ramus gives are less suitable, such as drunk
and sober, mortal and immortal, which are rather adverse. For
neither does the prefix "in" in compounds always signify privation,
but often an adverse *habitus;* hence, I would also not call sin a
privation; because if this or that is a sin or a vice it is not a privation.
And so these are species of contraries. But here it is customary to
ask which of them are mutually contrary in the highest degree.
Aristotle [e.g., *Metaph*. x.4.1055a4–b29] ascribes the greatest contrariety sometimes to adverse things, sometimes to contradictories.
But the greatest disagreement seems to be that between privatives,
next that between adverse things, less between contradictories, and
the least between relatives; for relatives, because of their mutual
relevance, are partly in agreement. Contradictories are indeed completely negative contraries, but nevertheless because of their infinite negation they are frequently taken for intermediates and
disparates. For example, not-hot is not as strongly opposed to hot
as cold is; because what is not-hot can be lukewarm. Thus, not-

good can be a sort of intermediate and indifferent, and not-white can be said or understood of something red. Adverse things are indeed oppositely adverse, but not in such a way that they cannot be mingled; but privatives admit of no mixture, and privation is usually the removal and elimination, or at least deficiency, of *habitus*. And *habitus* is being, privation non-being; but to being, nothing and non-being are equally contrary. [57]

But the category of arguments of disagreement is such that anything whatsoever can differ from something else in any way.[1]

For although the cause of every essential difference is originally form, and of the other differences the other arguments of agreement—so that things are said to disagree in as many ways as they agree, namely, in cause or effect, or in subject or attribute—nevertheless all the ways in which things differ among themselves either in their relation or in themselves are treated only among the arguments of disagreement, or if they are compared, among the comparatives. Hence to differ in genus or species is nothing other than to differ in common or proper form, of which they are symbols, as will be said below.

[1] Privatives are the last of the arguments from disagreement. Milton returns to mention the larger classification as he moves on from it to its counterpart, agreement, in the ensuing chap. xviii.

Chapter XVIII

ON EQUALS

*S*IMPLE *arguments therefore, as we have seen, consist in ar-guments of agreement and arguments of disagreement.*

Comparatives are primary arguments which are compared among themselves.

The simple relevance of things has had to be treated before the comparison among them: for if you abstract from comparison, then all comparatives are either arguments of agreement or ones of disagreement. The teaching of Plato and that of Xenophon are the respective attributes of both separately before becoming compar-atives. *They are primary arguments* and not derived, because the derived, as will appear below, have the same relevance as the primary from which they are derived; comparatives, even though they were first simple, do not have the relevance of simple argu-ments. [58] *Compared among themselves:* certainly those which are of the same genus; and division will presently inform us concerning the genera. Next to be discussed are the properties of comparatives.

Although by the very nature of comparison comparatives are equally well known, nevertheless one of them must be better known and more evident to some one than the other.

Here it should be noted that it is not by their own nature but by the nature of comparison that comparatives are said to be equally well known. So also, you will say, are relatives in virtue of their relation, and indeed all arguments which also are related. But, I say, relation and comparison are not the same; and the other arguments, even though as logically related equally well known, are nevertheless by their own respective natures either equally or not equally manifest: arguments of disagreement equally, argu-ments of agreement not equally, as was already said above. But to one with whom we debate, a comparative used as an argument should, by its nature and before the comparison is made, be better known and more evident than that which is argued; for something equally obscure would argue nothing. From this the remarkable utility of comparatives becomes clear; by their use it comes about that an unequal knowledge of things is made equal by virtue of a comparison. Thus, arguments of agreement are most suitable for proving, those of disagreement for refuting, and comparatives for elucidating.

But comparatives are often more briefly indicated by signs; sometimes they are more fully distinguished by their parts, which are called proposition (propositio) *and reddition* (redditio). [59]

The form of comparison is therefore twofold: one contracted, the other explicated. The contracted form is one concluded in one word, as below in chapter 21. The explicated form is one which is distinguished by its parts; and these parts are called proposition and reddition. The proposition often precedes, and is the argument; the reddition often follows and is that which is argued; if it occurs otherwise, then there is inversion. But every contracted form of comparison can be explicated by its parts.

And so in every respect even fictitious comparatives argue and produce conviction.

They argue, to be sure, a real object; in this respect they are more excellent than the other arguments, which, if fictitious, argue only a fictitious object: for example, fictitious material argues a fictitious house of the sun. But comparatives, even fictitious ones, not indeed by their own nature, but in virtue of the comparison, do argue real objects and produce conviction.

Comparison occurs either in quantity or quality.

Quantity is that by which compared things are said to be so much or so many.

And it refers to things which are alike or unlike in quantity. We do not speak here merely of mathematical quantity, which belongs to magnitude or number, but of logical quantity, which is any reference or relation by which any things compared among themselves can be said to be quantified, that is, equal or unequal, matching or nonmatching in quantity.

Equals are things which have one quantity. [60]

So they are defined also by Aristotle in *Metaphysics* 4.15 [v.15.1021a12]. This is the same as saying, whose ratio is equal. *One:* that is, the same or equal, so that in the plural they are explained by the same name and definition.

An argument from the equal therefore occurs when equal is illustrated by equal.

Let us come to some examples, and first to those which in contracted form, as we said, are indicated rather briefly by signs. Chief among these signs are *like, equal, to equate,* as in the following. *Æneid* 2 [ii.794]:

Like the light wind.

Here the lightness of the shade of Creusa is compared with the lightness of the wind. *Æneid* 3 [iii.491]:

And now should grow in equal age with thee.

Æneid 6 [vi.781–82]:

Behold, you born under these auspices, celebrated Rome
Will make its empire equal to earth and men's spirits equal with
  Olympus.

Other signs similar to these are *likewise, just as, equality, equally, in like manner as if,* and others of that sort.[1]

The explicated form follows, in which there are distinguished the proposition and the reddition, which in the contracted form were implicit. But in this full form equal quantity is either indicated openly by signs or is apprehended by the mind and reason without signs. These signs are either proper to equals or are the negations of unequals; proper signs of equals are *the same . . . as, as well . . . as, as much . . . as, as many . . . as.* In each of these pairs of signs the first concerns the reddition and the second the proposition. *Against Catiline* 4 [iv.10.21]: [61] "Whose deeds and virtues are contained within the same boundaries and limits as the course of the sun." *Æneid* 4 [iv.188]:

As well one holding to the false and
  perverse, as a messenger of the truth.

Catullus 4 [*Carm.* 49]:

As much the worst of all poets
As you are the best of all patrons.

Ovid, *Tristia* 4 [v.2.23–27]:

As the shores have shells, the pleasant rose-gardens flowers
And the sleep-inducing poppy seeds,
By as many misfortunes am I pressed.

Negations of unequals, either of greater and less separately, or of both at once, are *not more, not less. Philippics* 9 [ix.5.10–11]: "For neither was he more learned in the law than in justice, etc. Nor did he any more prefer to institute litigation than to remove controversies." Ovid, *Ars amatoria* 2 [ii.13]:

It is no less a virtue to keep a share than to seek it.

A negation of both at once, as in *Pro Murena* [7.15]: "I recognize these to be equal in Lucius Murena, and so equal, that neither can

---

[1] This sentence is derived from Ramus's text here but is abridged and otherwise altered.

he be surpassed in dignity nor be superior in dignity to you." But it should be noted that the negation of the greater or the lesser, separately, is not always a sign of equals; for it is not the case that if the slave is not greater than the master he is therefore equal, nor that if the master is not smaller than the slave he is therefore equal.

So much for examples with signs; now without signs these following. And especially in this type of examples without signs there appears the same force of arguing for either part; so much so that if one thing is, then so is the other, and if one is not, neither is the other. So that if one of them is affirmed, the other is affirmed, and if one is negated, the other is negated, as in *Philippics* 2 [ii.29.72]: [62] "Why not a common prey for those whose crime is common?" Terence in the *Adelphi* [v.3.803]:

> Since I do not care for yours, do not care for mine.

To this locus, namely of equals without signs, belong those consequences which, though indeed following from contraries, are handled by a comparing of equals, as these from adverses. Cicero says in *Pro Sulla* [17.48]: "Nor truly can I understand why you are angry with me. If because I defend the person whom you accuse, why am I not also enraged at you who accuse the person whom I defend? I accuse my enemy, you say: and I say I defend my friend." Similarly in *Tusculan Disputations* 5 [v.17.50]: "Since they admit that there is sufficiently great power in vice for an unhappy life, should it not be admitted that there is the same power in virtue for a happy life? For contraries are the consequences of contraries."

But this rule is not universally true unless, first, there be a comparing of real equals: it does not follow that if evil works damn, good works therefore justify, for evil works are entirely evil and good works imperfectly good; the former are our own, the latter are not wholly ours.[2] But, secondly, the rule is true only in those

---

[2] Here again, Milton introduces Christian theological material into his logic. See above, Milton's Preface and n. 3. The root of what he says is scriptural (see, for example, 2 Cor. 3:5, Rom. 7:13–23, etc.), but his statement, far neater than anything in the Bible, registers not the biblical text itself directly so much as subsequent reflection on biblical passages by the Church. Milton's statement appears to echo that of the Second Council of Orange (A.D. 529), quoting Prosper and Augustine: "Men do their own will when they do what displeases God, but when they do what they will in order to follow the divine will, even though they do what they do willingly, they nevertheless do the will of Him by whom what they do is prepared and commanded"—Henricus Denziger et al., eds., *Enchiridion Symbolorum, Definitionum et Declarationum de Rebus Fidei et Morum,* 31st ed. (Barcelona: Herder, 1950), p. 90 (no. 196), editor's translation from the Latin.

equals which are taken from the locus of contraries and whose
statement is convertible, something which does indeed very frequently happen in relatives, as in Martial [*Epigr.* i.82]:

> You know you were born a slave, and you fondly admit it
> When you, Sosibianus, call your master father.[3]

The father is the son's master and the son's master is the father:
equally, therefore, the son is the father's servant. Similarly in adverses: *the good is to be desired, and equally, therefore, evil is to
be avoided,* namely, because, properly and also [63] convertibly,
everything which is to be desired is good. And in privatives, as in
Ovid, *Fasti* 1 [i.217–18]:

> There is worth in worth, property bestows honors,
> It bestows friendships: the poor man is always despised.[4]

The rich man has worth, and whoever has worth is rich; therefore, all poor men are despised.

Whenever the proposition of comparison is not convertible, or
whenever to one of the equals there is attributed as proper to it
something which is common to both, their consequences are not
contrary but often the same.[5] This, then, involving relatives, is
fallacious: *The father is rich, and the son is therefore poor:* because
the proposition is not convertible, for not every rich man is a father.
And this, involving adverses, is also fallacious: *Man is endowed
with sense; a beast therefore lacks sense. Man is mortal; a beast
is therefore immortal.* Certainly, neither is it proper to man to be
endowed with sense, nor is it proper to man to be mortal; but it
is common to both contraries, both to man and to beast. This,
involving contradictories, is also fallacious: *Man is an animal;
therefore, not-man is not-animal.* And lastly this, involving privatives: *The seeing man lives; therefore the blind man is dead:* for,
to live is common to the seeing man and to the blind man. *For it
is not that the same thing cannot not be asserted of the same thing:
rather, what receives one of the contraries receives the other; and
what does not receive one does not receive the other.* For example:
*In the thing in which there is love there can also be hate. To those
without rights no injury can be done.*

---

[3] This example, with the next, occurs in Ramus's text before the one from
Cicero, *Pro Sulla,* above.

[4] See immediately preceding note.

[5] Though italicized in Milton's text as if part of Ramus's text, this sentence is
not.

There is also another mode of equals without signs, in which sometimes when provoked we return like for like. Of this sort is Virgil's *Third Eclogue* [iii.104], where the altercation of the shepherds is repeated: "Tell in what place," etc. Of the same sort is also Matthew 21.23 [21:23–25], etc.: "By what [64] authority do you do these things, etc.? I will also ask you something: Whence was the baptism of John?" Akin to this is the passage in Cicero, *De officiis* 2 [ii.25.89]: "Cato, when he was asked, 'What of usury?' replied, 'What of murder?' "

But fictitious equals, whose property we said above was to argue a real thing, are those in Cicero, *De inventione* 1 [i.31.51–52], from Aeschines the Socratic, where Aspasia is brought in speaking as follows with the wife of Xenophon and with Xenophon himself: " 'Tell me, pray, wife of Xenophon, if your neighbor has better gold than you have, whether you would rather have hers or yours.' 'Hers,' she said. 'And if better clothes?' 'Hers, to be sure,' she replied. 'Well, then, if she had a better husband, would you rather have hers?' Here the woman blushed." [6] The comparison is like this: If you would rather have the better gold and clothes of your neighbor than your own, you argue that you also prefer your neighbor's better husband. She does not say that the neighbor has better gold or clothing, but she pretends or supposes it, and if the wife of Xenophon should prefer them, it is argued that she also prefers the neighbor's husband, if he is better.

[6] Milton here adapts Ramus's text and, as often, abridges his quotation.

CHAPTER XIX

ON THE GREATER

U *NEQUALS are things which have not one quantity.*
        Not one, that is, not the same; whose ratio is not equal:
        for the ratio of contraries is contrary.
The unequal is either greater or less.
The greater is that whose quantity exceeds. [65]

But greater or smaller quantity is estimated from the elevation
or subordination of things which are compared, as Cicero says in
the *Topics* [18.68, 71], that is, from excess or deficiency, which are
either indicated by signs or, if signs are lacking, are understood
by other expressions which signify excess or deficiency. But from
what we said above about logical quantity, it is to be understood
that that also is logically greater of which not only the magnitude,
measure, or number, but also the authority, power, distinction,
probability, difficulty or anything of this sort is greater; or, more
briefly, what in any way exceeds is greater, and this not only in
the nature of the thing but also in the opinion of the person discoursing. The greater is therefore that whose quantity exceeds that
which is less, for the greater is here adduced to argue the lesser.

Just as of equals, so of an argument from the greater, one form
is contracted and is more briefly indicated by signs, while another
is explicated and is distinguished more fully by its parts.

Of the more contracted form the signs are either comparative
and superlative terms governing their respective cases, or certain
verbs; and in either case not only those which signify excess—such
as *greater, better, worse; to excel, to surpass, to conquer, to exceed,*
to be preferred—when referred to what argues, but also those terms
and verbs which signify a deficiency, such as *less, inferior, esteem*
less, yield, be conquered, be overcome, if they are referred to what
is argued.

The explicated form occurs sometimes with signs, sometimes
without signs. The signs are *not only . . . but also, not so*
much . . . as,[1] and comparisons, and those verbs, as above, signifying not only superiority with [66] the particle *than,* if this particle is assigned always to what is argued, but also those which

---

[1] Milton adapts Ramus's text here.

signify subordination, if only the particle *than* refers to what argues. For example, *it is less to strike a friend than one's father.* But this example argues rather from the less how serious an offense it is to strike one's father than from the greater that it is not so serious to strike a friend. The same thing is to be said of other examples of this sort.

An example of the first mentioned sign is Cicero, *Pro Murena* [14.30]: "Removed is not only this verbose pretence of prudence, but also that queen of all things, wisdom. Rejected is not only the orator whose speech is annoying or who is loquacious, but also the good one." In examples of this sort, *but also* is the proposition which, as the greater, argues the apodosis *not only* as the lesser.

A sign akin to this is *indeed,* or *nay more.* Of this sort is the passage in Terence [*Eun.* iii.1.391–94]:

Thraso.	Does Thais really give me great thanks?
Gnatho.	Enormous.
Thraso.	Do you mean it? Is she glad?
Gnatho.	Not so much for the gift itself as that it was given by you: for that she is quite earnestly jubilant.

Easily understood here are "enormous indeed" and "for that she is indeed earnestly jubilant." Enormous thanks argue great thanks; and to be jubilant argues that she is glad. Thus in *Against Catiline* 1 [i.1.2]: "Yet this person lives. He lives? Nay more, he comes into the senate." And in *In Verrem* 3 [II.i.3.9]: "Not a thief but a ravisher; not an adulterer but a violator of chastity," etc.

An example of the second sign, namely, of comparatives and of verbs with the particle *than,* is from Cicero, *Pro Marcello* [26]: "About to gain more admiration than glory." But it is ambiguous: for either more admiration argues less glory, and thus the argument is from the greater; or less glory, if it is great, argues the greatest admiration. [67]

An example of verbs signifying superiority with the particle *than* will be this: *It is better to beg than to steal.* Here begging, though dishonorable, nevertheless as something more to be done and preferably, argues that much less should one steal.

Thus, I *wish that more,* namely, what argues, *than this,* namely what is argued, as in Juvenal's eighth *Satire* [viii.269–71] against the pretentious noble:

> I wish more that Thersites be your father, as long as you
> Are like Aeacides, and that you wield Vulcanian arms,
> Than that Achilles should beget you in the image of Thersites.

From the fact that he prefers an ignoble courageous man, something nevertheless not so desirable, he argues and shows from the greater or the stronger how very much less he wants a noble coward. Caesar [*B. Gall.* vii.52]: "In a soldier I prefer modesty to valor." Modesty, in Caesar's opinion, being greater and more distinguished, argues that valor and fortitude are less to be required in a soldier than modesty: or rather from the lesser he exalts the mark of modesty in a soldier before the mark of valor.

Now follows a treatment of the greater without signs.

And in this genus alone that is greater whose probability or difficulty is greater. Here also the logicians customarily teach the rules of consequences (*consequentiæ*), not merely by negating—in accordance with Aristotle, *Rhetoric* 2.23 [ii.23.1397b12–18]—but also by affirming, for the varying function and consideration of quantity, in diverse examples: for of any given example there is only one procedure. If the greater is more probable, then only negation applies, in this way: *what does not hold in the greater, will not hold in the lesser.* If the greater is more difficult or [68] more incredible, only affirmation applies: *what holds in the greater thing, holds in the lesser,* as Cicero says in the *Topics* [4.23]. An example of this is *Æneid* 1 [i.198–99]:

> O partners (for we were not ignorant of these evils before)
> O you who have suffered graver things! God will end these, too.

If God has made an end to more serious evils, He will certainly end these. Thus Cicero in *Pro Murena* [iv.9–10]: "Do not be so unjust that, while your fountains lie open to your enemies, you feel your rivers should be closed even to your friends."

Fictitious greater things have the same value in refuting or proving their consequences.

An example of refuting is in Terence, *Heautontimorumenos* [iii.1.452–54]:

> If a satrap became a lover he would never be able to endure its expense;
> much less could you.

It is as if he said, pretend you are a satrap. And in *Æneid* 5 [v.17–22]:

> Noble Aeneas, not if Jupiter pledged his support
> Would I hope to reach Italy under this sky.
> The winds, now shifted, roar across our course, surging
> In from the dark west, and the air is pressed into cloud.
> To oppose or contend with so much we are not able.

That is, much less now, since Jupiter is not supporting us. [69]

CHAPTER XX

ON THE LESS

THE greater and the lesser are mutually relevant and related: to the point that whoever knows the definition of one knows that of the other. Just, therefore, as the greater is that whose quantity exceeds, *so the lesser is that whose quantity is exceeded.* Just as the quantity of the greater consisted of any superiority or excess of things, so now that of the lesser consists of any subordination or deficiency of things. For the lesser probability or difficulty of opinions has no place except in the explicated form of the lesser, as can be understood also from the explicated form of the greater. For a lesser is that whose quantity is exceeded by a greater: an argument from the lesser is thus one in which what is lesser is used to argue what is greater.

The lesser, too, are either indicated more briefly by signs or are distinguished more fully by their parts. Of each such form there are proper signs of the lesser or negations of equals.

The proper signs of the more contracted form are, first, the comparative expressions of grammar, nouns as well as verbs, both signifying superiority if only they are assigned to what is argued. Ovid, *Tristia* 3 [iii.11.39]: "You are more fierce than the harsh Busiris." [1] Here the lesser ferocity of Busiris argues the greater ferocity of the person against whom the poet inveighs. *Wisdom is better than riches. More fierce* and *is better than* signify superiority and are signs of the greater; but since they are assigned to what is argued, [70] the argument in both cases is from the lesser. And this must be carefully noted, so that you can distinguish an argument from the greater from one from the lesser, for the greater and the lesser, especially in the contracted form, generally exhibit the same signs; and the same example can argue in either sense either from the greater or from the lesser: as in "You are more fierce than the harsh Busiris." If this is said to stress the ferocity of someone, as here, then it is from the lesser, but if to disparage Busiris, then it is from the greater. If, therefore, those cases which signify superiority are applied to what is argued, then they are

---

[1] This and the following twelve examples are given by Milton in a quite different order from that in Ramus's text.

indeed signs of the greater, but the argument is from the lesser; because the greater of which they are the signs, is what is argued. But if those cases which signify subordination are applied to what is argued, they are indeed signs of the lesser, but the argument is from the greater because what is argued is the lesser.

Secondly, the signs of the more contracted form are comparisons of grammar and verbs signifying subordination, such as *lesser, inferior,* etc., and *esteem less, put after, yield, to be conquered, to be overcome,* etc., if only the reference is to what argues, as in *Let arms yield to the toga.* Here the dignity of the toga is argued from the lesser dignity of arms, which yields.

And these are the affirming signs of the contracted form, with which are to be numbered also these expressions formed by the negation of equals. *Philippics* 9 [ix.5.10]: "All those of every age who in this city have had an understanding of law, if brought together in one place, are not to be compared with Servius Sulpitius." That is, they are not to be equated with him, which was a sign of equals. So much for the contracted form.

The explicated form occurs either with signs or without signs. Proper signs are first *not only not . . .* [71] *but not even.* Cicero, *Against Catiline* 2 [ii.4.8]: "Not only in Rome, but not in any corner of all Italy, there was no one burdened with debt whom he did not admit into the incredible league of crime." Here the later sign "but not" belongs to the proposition and is a sign of the lesser; and it argues "not only not," which belongs to the reddition and is a sign of the greater, which is argued. Not in any corner of Italy did he not do what was less useful to himself; not only not in Rome, therefore, did he not do—much more, he *did* do—what was greater or more useful to himself. *Pro Fonteio* [17.40]: "Not only did they make known no crime by this man, but they did not even reprehend any word of his." They did not even do the lesser thing of reprehending anything he said: this is the proposition; and it argues *not only not the greater thing,* that is, therefore they did not do the greater thing of making known a crime: and this is the reddition and the thing argued.

To be sure, in examples of this sign, the sign of the proposition, *but not even,* is sometimes omitted. *Ad Lentulum* [*Fam.* i.ix.21]: "Not the least word of mine, and not only not my actions, have interceded for Caesar," that is, not only no action, but not even a word. Akin to this sign is the expression, *so far from this, that not even that.* *Pro Marcello* [25]: "You are so far from the perfection of truly great works that the foundations which you contemplate you have not yet laid." You have not even done the lesser, and you are therefore a long way from that which is greater.

Signs of the second sort are grammatical comparisons and certain verbs with the particle *than,* which signify either superiority, such as *rather this than that, I want this more than that,* or subordination, such as *less, inferior,* so that in either case *than* is applied to what is argued. *Against Catiline*1 [i.10.27]: "So that you can as an exile rather tempt than as a consul annoy the republic." When Cicero would rather that an exile tempt the republic than that a consul annoy it, [72] the former as the lesser evil argues that the latter is the greater. Here the grammatical comparison *rather* is applied to what argues, namely, to the lesser evil; the particle *than* is applied to what is argued, namely, to the greater evil. *Thus Metellus preferred to be removed rather from the republic than from his opinion.* Here *preferred,* a verb of superiority, is applied to what argues, namely, to the lesser evil, in the judgment of Metellus, of removal from the republic; the particle *than* is applied to what is argued to be the greater evil, namely, to be removed from his opinion. Thus, in the signs which signify subordination the particle *than* is always applied to the greater thing which is argued, just as in those which signify superiority, as in *it is less to receive than to give, Caesar is lower than Scipio.*

Akin to these signs is *before,* that is, *rather than.* Pro Milone [38.103–4]: "Would that Clodius were dictator rather than that I should behold this spectacle."

The third sign is *if . . . then surely,* as in *De lege agraria 2* [ii.2.5]: "If it is for all a difficult and great doctrine, then surely for me above the others."

There follow negations of equals in this explicated form: *not so much . . . as. Against Catiline 2* [ii.7.16]: "Although those who keep repeating that Catiline has gone to Massilia do not so much complain of it as fear it." Similarly *not so many . . . as,* as in *Pro Murena* [17.35]: "For what channel, what Euripus do you think has so many movements, so many and such varied disturbances of its waters as the reason of assemblies has disquiet and anxiety?" In this example, the question more strongly negates the equals.

Let us now take up examples of the form explicated without signs. Cicero, *De officiis 1* [i.31.114]: "So will an actor see this on stage, and a wise man not see it in life?" And from this the consequences are obtained not only by affirming [73] and proving, as Aristotle claims in *Rhetoric 2.23* [ii.23.1397b12–18] and Cicero in the *Topics* [4.23], but also by negating and refuting, if indeed this is understood of an example not the same; but if of the same, then the correct procedure is either only by affirming or only by negating. An example of affirming is Ovid, *De remediis* 1 [229–31]:

> To redeem your body you suffer sword and fire, etc.
> To save your soul will you refuse to bear anything?

If for the sake of the body, much more for the sake of the soul you will bear anything, for the soul is more worthy. Likewise in *Pro Archia* [8.19]: "Wild beasts are often tamed by singing; should we not then be moved by the words of the poets?" Similar is the passage in Matthew 6:23: "God cares for sparrows; much more therefore for men." But by denying, no consequence is deduced from these examples: it does not therefore follow that *if for the sake of the body you do not endure anything, therefore neither for the sake of the soul;* and so on. Rightly, therefore, if Aristotle is understood in this way, the procedure from the lesser to the greater is only by affirming. To be sure, examples are not lacking in which the argument is from the lesser by negating alone; of this sort is the example cited above in *Pro Marcello* [25]: "You have not yet laid the foundations; certainly therefore you have not perfected the work." But it is not the same by affirming; *you have laid the foundation; therefore you have finished the work.* Here one should avoid positing a negation which is equivalent to an affirmation: thus, *God does not neglect the sparrows* is the same as *He cares for them.* For in this way, for each consequence the same example can be given according as the same thought is varied by affirming or negating, as in *If thieves are to be punished, much more the sacrilegious,* and *If thieves are not to be spared, much less the sacrilegious.* Here *to punish* and *not to spare* are the same, and *less* can be considered [74] the sign of the greater. Not signs, therefore, but the superiority or the subordination of things causes the greater or the lesser. So much for the consequences of the lesser without signs.

The same consequences, to be sure, are deduced from the explicated form, which occurs also with signs, as you can see from the examples given above. It is in this explicated form without signs that there occurs a certain gradation of the lesser, as in *In Verrem* 7 [II.v.66.170]: "It is wicked to put a Roman citizen in chains, a crime to flog him, almost high treason to kill him; what shall I say it is to crucify him?"

There is also the fictitious lesser, as in Virgil, *Eclogues* 1 [i.59–63]:

Sooner therefore will fleet stags be feeding in the air
Than his face slip from by my bosom.

Philippics 2 [ii.25.63]: "If this had happened to you at dinner time in the midst of your revels, who would not consider it base? But in the assembly of the Romans while conducting public business, as chief of the cavalry," etc.

Chapter XXI

ON THE SIMILAR[1]

So far, comparison has been in quantity. There follows *comparison in quality, by which things compared are said to be of this or that sort.*

For logical quality is not only a *habitus,* or disposition, or a natural potency or impotency, or, finally, a shape or external form, which for Aristotle [*Cat.* 8.8b25–10a27] are species of quality and are to be treated in other arts, but it is any relevance or basis [75] for saying of things compared with each other that they are of this or that sort, namely, similar or dissimilar. But there is nothing which, if compared with another thing in quality, will not be similar to it or dissimilar.

Similar things are those whose quality is the same.

Aristotle, *Metaphysics* 4.15 [v.15.1021a12], also defines them in this way, and Boethius, *On the Topics of Cicero,* Book 2 [*PL* lxiv.1065C], says: "Similarity is a unity of quality." An argument of similarity, therefore, occurs when the similar is explained by the similar. There is indeed a great affinity of equal things with similar things; to be sure, as can be seen from their definitions, they differ most markedly in this, that equal things do not admit of superiority or subordination, while similar things do: for even the most highly similar things can be greater or lesser, while equal things cannot.

Similarity is called proportion, in Greek usually *analogia;* and similar things are called proportional, in Greek, *analoga.* But a proportion is simply a similarity of two relations: but a relation is a comparison of two terms or things with each other. *It [2] should be kept in mind, however, that similar things, whether of the contracted form or of the explicated, should not be pushed beyond that quality which the person making the comparison intended to show to be the same in both things: thus a magistrate is likened to a dog, certainly, only in the fidelity of his custodianship. Whence

---

[1] See Christopher Grose, "Milton on Ramistic Similitude," in Earl Miner, ed., *Seventeenth-Century Imagery* (Berkeley and Los Angeles: University of California Press, 1971), pp. 103–16.

[2] With this asterisk Milton cues in a later cross-reference, from p. 288 here.

the saying [3] in the schools: *nothing similar is identical, the similar thing does not run on four feet, every similarity limps.*

Similar things are sometimes indicated more briefly by signs, and are sometimes distinguished more fully by their parts; for this is common to all compared things. The contracted signs of similarity compressed into a single word are either proper signs of similar things or negations of dissimilar things. [76] Proper signs of similar things are either nouns such as *resemblance, effigy, image, in the fashion of, after the manner of, like to, the way;* adverbs such as *such as, just as, as if, just as if;* or verbs such as *imitate, refer to,* etc.[4] *Æneid* 1 [i.589]: "In face and shoulders like a god." *Philippics* 9 [ix.5.12]: "Although Servius Sulpitius could leave no more illustrious monument than his son, the image of his manners, virtue, constancy, piety, wit." *Tristia* 1 [i.1.99–100]:

> For no one, or only he who caused my wounds,
> Can like Achilles take them away.

In Pisonem [22.52]: "Like immortality to me was that one day on which I returned to my country." *Divinatio in Verrem* [*Div. Cæc.* 17.57]: "Suddenly from the likeness of a man, as if by some Circean cup, he became a boar." *Pro lege Manilia* [14.41] [5]: "And so all who are now in these places regard Cnaeius Pompeius in amazement as one not sent forth from the city, but fallen from heaven." Negations of dissimilar things are *not otherwise, not differently, not unlike,* etc. *Æneid* 3 [iii.236]: "They do not otherwise than as commanded." Terence in *Phormio* [iii.2.530]: "In no way am I or have I been otherwise than he."

To the contracted form of similarity belongs also the metaphor: for the metaphor, as the rhetoricians teach, is a similarity reduced to a single word, where the signs are lacking but nevertheless understood. *Pro Sestio* [69.144]: "Whose father I consider a god and the parent of my fortune and my name," that is, *as a god.*

The parts of a similarity are explicated successively, and that disjunctively or continuously.

A disjunctive similarity occurs when four terms or things are really distinguished, that is, when [77] two terms or distinct things in the proposition are compared with two terms or distinct things

---

[3] See Bartholomæus Keckermannus, *Systema Logicæ Minus*, Lib. III, cap. xii, in his *Operum Omnium quæ Extant Tomus Primus* [-*Secundus*], I, col. 303.

[4] Milton varies Ramus's samples in this sentence.

[5] *Pro Lege Manilia*] Ramus *Pro Pompeio.* The reference is to the same oration: the Manilian Law authorized Pompey's command.

in the reddition.[6] But this form occurs both with signs and without signs. The signs are *such as . . . so,* the former belonging to the proposition, the latter to the reddition. Likewise, signs belonging to the proposition are *in whatever way, as, just as,* to which correspond, respectively, *so, in the same way, similarly* in the reddition. *Eclogues* 5 [v.45–46]:

> Such your verses to us, divine poet,
> As sleep to the weary upon the grass.

The verses are to the listener as sleep to the weary; the four terms are distinct. *Ad fratrem* 1 [*QFr.* i.1.5]: "Just as the best helmsmen frequently cannot master the force of a storm, so the wisest men frequently cannot master the thrust of fortune." Here again there are four terms; as the helmsman is to the storm, so the wise man to fortune. *Tristia* 1 [i.5.25–26]:

> As tawny gold, namely, is examined in fire,
> So in difficult times is faith put to the test.

Cicero, *Philippics* 2 [ii.45.115]: "But, to be sure, just as some because of illness and dulled senses do not notice the good flavor of food, so the lustful, greedy and wicked have no taste for true praise." In the *Life* of Virgil [7]

> I made these little verses, another reaped the reward;
> So you, birds, build nests not for yourselves,
> So you, bees, store honey not for yourselves, etc.

In this example, the reddition precedes without a sign. But the particle *so,* which is usually a sign belonging to the reddition, is here assigned to the proposition. [78]
Sometimes there is no sign at all. Virgil, *Eclogues* 2 [ii.17–18]:

> O handsome lad, trust not too much your hue,
> The white privets fall, the black whortleberries are gathered.

A continuous similarity occurs when as the first term is to the second, so the second is to the third. De legibus 3 [iii.1.2]: "As laws govern the magistrates, so the magistrates govern the people." Here

---

[6] Milton here opposes the term "proposition" (*propositio*) to the term "reddition" (*redditio*) in the way his text here describes; in Book II, chap. ix, below, he uses the same term "proposition" (*propositio*) to refer to what is ordinarily called the major premise of a syllogism, as opposed to the minor premise, which he calls the "assumption" (*assumptio*).

[7] Ramus, *P. Virgilii Maronis Bucolica, P. Rami . . . Prælectionibus Exposita, quibus Poetæ Vita Præposita Est . . .* (Paris: A. Wechelus, 1558; CAM), p. 19.

the terms are three: the law, the magistrates, the people. But the middle term is applied twice and is continued in every continuous proportion; and it is the second term of the proposition and the first term of the reddition. For in every proportion the terms should number at least four. The order here is as follows: just as the laws govern the magistrates, so the magistrates govern the people.

But although similar things are suited more for illustrating than for proving, and Plato says in the *Phaedo* [92 D], "Discourses which use demonstrations from similar things I have well known to be arranged with a view to display, and unless one is on guard against them they easily deceive," nevertheless, as regards the rules of consequences (*consequentiæ*), it can be seen from the definition of the similar that similar things are similar in nature, and that similar things therefore allow valid consequences both affirmative and negative. Whence Aristotle in *Topics* 2.10 [ii.10.114b29–31]: "In similar things, what holds for one will also hold for the others, and what does not hold for one will also not hold for the others."

But since similarity involves not only the proposition and the reddition, but also the terms in relation to each other, it follows that if certain things are similar they will also be inversely similar, and vice versa. And they will be inversely similar in two ways: by inversion of the proposition and the reddition, which inversion is common also to the other comparatives; [79] or by inversion of terms, which seems proper to the similar. For example, as the helmsman is to the storm, so is the wise man to fortune; and inversely, therefore, as the wise man is to fortune, so the helmsman to the storm. This is an inversion of the proposition and the reddition. Again, as the storm is to the helmsman, so fortune to the wise man; this is an inversion of terms. Alternation occurs when the antecedent of the proposition is compared with the antecedent of the reddition, and the consequent of the one with the consequent of the other. The rule here is that if certain things are similar they will also be alternately similar. As the helmsman is to the storm, so the wise man to fortune: therefore, alternately, as the helmsman is to the wise man, so the storm to fortune. The most extensive use of inversions and alternations of this sort occurs in mathematical proportions. But proportion, not only mathematical but also logical, is, as we said above, common to all things; its rules could therefore not be omitted here.

A fictitious similarity has the same force as those mentioned above, and in this explicated similarity the fables of Aesop especially excell.

Horace, *Epistles* 1 [i.1.70–75]:

> If the Roman people should happen to ask me
> Why I enjoy neither tribunal nor trials,
> Nor pursue or flee what they love or hate,
> I will repeat what the sly fox once said to the ailing lion,
> That I am deterred by the footprints
> All pointing toward you and none coming back.

Here belongs also what is commonly called the Socratic parable, which is an induction of similar things, consisting almost entirely of questions. [80] But that, Fabius [Quint. *Inst.* v.11.3] says, "has this force, that after Socrates had asked many things which his adversary had to admit, he would infer, concerning the subject of inquiry, a conclusion to which his adversary had already conceded something similar." See above, p. 284 [8] at *.

---

[8] In Milton's original Latin text the page reference here is to his p. 76.

CHAPTER XXII

ON THE DISSIMILAR[1]

So much for similar things, whose quality is the same. Dissimilar things are comparatives whose quality is diverse.

For contraries are treated in one and the same science. And in the *Topics* [11.46] Cicero says that "It belongs to the same science to discover the dissimilar and the similar." Dissimilar things differ from diverse in this, that dissimilarity is a comparative difference, and is not attributed to one and the same thing, at least at the same time, but usually to diverse things. And so with diverse things, if one is negated the other is affirmed; but dissimilar things, whether diverse or opposite, can be affirmed or negated at the same time. But a diverse quality is one which is not the same, whether it is diverse or opposite; you might say that the nature of dissimilar things is dissimilar. Therefore, an argument of dissimilarity occurs when the dissimilar is argued from the dissimilar.

Signs of the contracted [2] form of dissimilarity are *dissimilar, unlike, different, other, otherwise*. *Pro Plancio* [28.68]: "The owing of money and of thanks is dissimilar." *Ennius* [i.e., Cic. *Off.* 1.39.139]: [3] "O ancient house, alas, to rule by a lord so much unlike you." But unlike is not unequal, but dissimilar. Caesar, *Gallic War* 1 [i.1]: "All these differ from each other in language, institutions, and laws." *De lege agraria* 2 [ii.5.13]: "He planned to be of another countenance, another [81] tone of voice, another gait." Cicero, *De natura deorum* 2 [ii.9.23]: "Because I began to act otherwise than as I had promised in the beginning."

Signs of dissimilarity are also obtained by the negation of similar things, such as *not similar, not such, not the same, not just as,*

---

[1] The title of this chapter in Milton's Latin text reads, by typographical error, *De Similibus* instead of the obviously intended *De Dissimilibus*.

[2] *Contractæ*] Ramus *proprie*.

[3] The little quotation attributed by Milton to Ennius is included in the "Ex incertis incertorum fabulis" by Otto Ribbeck, *Tragicorum Latinorum Reliquiæ* (Leipzig: Teubner, 1852), p. 224, lines 184–85, whose source is the text of Cicero that we have indicated. The quotation is not included in *Ennianæ Poesis Reliquiæ*, ed. Iohannes Vahlen (Leipzig: Teubner, 1928). Cicero leaves the quotation anonymous, but since he is a main source of Ennius fragments it is possible that the quotation was therefore attributed to Ennius in some earlier collection of fragments seen by Milton.

etc. *De oratore* 3 [iii.21.79]: "Philosophy is not similar to the other arts." *Æneid* 2 [ii.540–41]:

> Not he, by whom you falsely claim to be engendered, not Achilles
> Was such an enemy to Priam.

Horace, *Epistles* 1 [i.1.4]: "Not the same is the age, not the same the mind." *Ad fratrem* 1 [*QFr.* i.1.13]: "Let your ring be not only as an ornament but just as you yourself." By this argument the shepherd admits his error, in the first *Eclogue* [i.19–20]:

> The city (which they call Rome), Meliboeus, I
>   thought, foolishly, similar to ours here.

And then [i.22–23]:

> Thus I had allowed pups to be similar to dogs and kids to dams
> And thus I used to put the great together with the small.

As neither puppies are similar to dogs, nor kids to dams, so Mantua is not similar to Rome. In this example the admission of error amounts to a negation of similarity.

An explicated dissimilarity likewise occurs with signs or without signs; among the signs here are also counted negations of similarities. *Philippics* 3 [iii.1.2]: "A certain fixed day is customarily expected to be one not so much of deliberation as of sacrifice."

Generally there is no sign when the dissimilarity is more fully explicated.

Quintilian, book 5, chapter 11 [*Inst.* v.11.7]: "Brutus killed his children as they were attempting treason. Manlius punished by death the virtue of his son." [82] Catullus [*Carm.* 5.4–6]:

> Suns may set and rise again:
> For us, when once the brief light fails,
> There is a perpetual night of slumber.

The dissimilarity is that between a day and our life. The reddition is that life once lost is not restored. It is illustrated by something dissimilar, namely, the proposition that suns may set and rise again.

CHAPTER XXIII

ON CONJUGATES

So far, primary arguments have been treated, of which the three genera were arguments of agreement, those of disagreement, and comparatives.

There follow *those arguments derived from the primary ones and related to what they argue just as the primary ones from which they are derived: such as conjugates and notation, distribution and definition.*[1]

So in themselves they have a force of arguing just as artificial arguments, and the same force as the arguments from which they are derived; but they do not have this force of themselves, because they are not primary, as has already been said in the second chapter. But they scarcely require any definition other than their name itself, which by itself sufficiently explains their nature. Hence we have this consequence, *that derived arguments are related in the same way to what they argue as are the primary arguments whence they are derived.* [83]

These four species of derived arguments are divided into two genera—albeit nameless ones[2]—as well because of the interest in dichotomy as because conjugates and notation are contained under the same genus on account of the close connection existing between them. So Cicero in the *Topics* [9.38] says that the locus from conjugates resembles notation. And in many examples conjugates differ not at all or only slightly from notation and name. The connection between them is twofold: first, because they are arguments which are nominal, or derived from a name. But they differ in this—as Boethius has it in *On the Topics of Cicero* 4 [*PL* lxiv.1112D]—that notation is accomplished by the exposition of a name, but conjugation by the similarity of a word and by derivation. But they do not for this reason belong to grammar, for to derive arguments from the force of names is the business of the logician, not of the grammarian. The second connection is that they are both simple derivatives: for their individual examples are derived not from several primary arguments conjoined at the same

---

[1] Milton's text varies somewhat from Ramus's here.

[2] Ramus calls the first genus (conjugates and notation) "names" but assigns no name to the second genus (distribution and definition).

time, but from some one primary argument, except in the case of compound names, for of compound names the notation is sometimes composed of several arguments. But distribution and definition are real arguments, that is, they are usually employed in the explanation of things, and compound, that is, they originate from several primary arguments conjoined at the same time. If, therefore, the genera of derived arguments, which we said are nameless, are to be distinguished by names, the derived arguments will be either nominal and simple (conjugates and notation), or real and compound (distribution and definition), unless we perhaps make the exception that definition can sometimes consist of a single primary argument, that is, of form alone. Of these two genera, we should first treat the one in which are contained conjugates and notation, since it is usually the more simple. [84] And in this genus conjugates claim first place, because they are derived only from arguments of agreement, while notation is obtained from any primary argument. Fabius, 5.10 [Quint. *Inst.* v.10.85], makes conjugates of no importance, but Aristotle and Cicero [3.11] in their *Topics* judge otherwise. Aristotle, 3.4 and 7.2 [iii.6.119a37–39; vii.3.153a26–27, b25–26], says that loci from disagreements, conjugates, and cases are of great value and useful for a great many arguments.

Conjugates are names variously derived from the same root, such as justice, just, justly. Aristotle and Cicero define conjugates, the former [*Top.* ii.9.114a37–39] as names of the same conjugation, the latter [*Top.* 3.12] as those of the same derivation. But neither does the latter [3] exclude from the class of conjugates the "yoke" concept *(jugum)* itself, as it were, of conjugates, nor the former [4] the derivation, nor Ramus the root itself, that is, the origin and stem. But conjugates are not only all substantive and adjective names, but also verbs and adverbs (which Aristotle [*Top.* ii.9.114a35–37] calls cases—*casus*), both paronyms—i.e., derivatives—and stems, providing the following conditions are observed: (1) if, when they sound the same, they also signify the same; (2) if their manner of signification is the same, for if one signifies potency or capacity or *habitus,* while the other signifies act, and from the potency or *habitus* the act is argued, or conversely, a fallacy results; (3) if they betoken arguments of agreement, that is, if they are derived from agreements, whose force and relevance in arguing they represent by other, conjugate names, and by whose

---

[3] Latin text has "former" *(ille),* apparently by error.
[4] Latin text has "latter" *(hic),* apparently by error.

evidence we are led to the discovery of this nominal conjugation. And thus it is clear that the use of this locus is not to be disparaged, especially in definitions. [85]

There follow some examples, such as justice, just, justly. In examples of this sort it should be noted that what they call the abstract is the cause of the concrete, and the concrete is the cause of the adverb. For example, justice is the cause of someone's being just; and because he is just, he acts justly. But this is not everywhere true: for what is healthy, that is, what produces or preserves health, is the cause of health; the concrete, namely, is cause of the abstract, as Aristotle observes in *Topics* 2.3 [ii.2.110a19–22]. Propertius, book 2 [*Eleg.* ii.23.23–24]:

> Because liberty remains for no one who loves,
> No one will be free if he wishes to love.

Here, because liberty, the cause of your being free, does not remain, therefore no one, etc. Cicero, *De natura deorum* 3 [iii.34.84], when speaking of Dionysius the tyrant: "Now he ordered that there be removed from all the temples the silver table on which, by the custom of ancient Greece, there was inscribed 'Of the good gods,' saying he wanted to use their goodness: the gods are good, so their goodness should be used." Here it is argued from effects to causes, according to Ramus: but as it seems to me, from causes to effects. Terence [*Heaut.* i.1.77]: "I am a man, I consider nothing human foreign to me." From the subject it is argued to the attribute. *In Pisonem* [9.19]: "Since the whole matter was consular and senatorial, I needed the help both of consuls and of a senate." From the attributes it is argued to the subject. *Philippics* 2 [ii.5.10]: "I will not treat him as a consul, lest he treat me also as of consular rank." This is from the effect to the cause, for being a consul is the cause of someone's then being of consular rank. Whence it is argued thus: he does not recognize in me the effect, so therefore I shall not recognize in him the cause. It should be noted that some words are conjugates only in meaning, not in sound, such as *nap, a sleeper; sickness, an invalid.* [86]

CHAPTER XXIV

ON NOTATION

N *OTATION* (notatio) *is the interpretation of a name,* that is,
a reason given why a thing is named as it is. Now this
definition is from Boethius, *On the Topics of Cicero* 1 [*PL*
lxiv.1062C]. "Notation," says Cicero in the *Topics* [8.35], "is called
by the Greeks etymology, which means, in its own derivation, true-
speaking: but we, avoiding the novelty of a word not sufficiently
fitting, call this genus notation, since words are the signs *(notæ)*
of things." Thus Cicero. From what has been said above, therefore,
it can be understood that notation is a derived argument and to
that extent representative of a primary argument; and that it is a
nominal argument, that is, as Cicero says, one elicited from the
force of a name.

*Certainly names are the signs of things, and every name, whether
derived or compound, if the name was indeed bestowed by means
of a true notation, can be accounted for from some primary
argument.*[1]

For example, homo (man) from humus (earth).[2] Here the notation
is from the matter. But languages, both the first one which Adam
received in Eden, and those various ones, perhaps derived from
the first, which the builders of the tower of Babel suddenly received, were without doubt divinely given; hence it is not strange
if the meaning of primitive words is not known. But as for words
which are derived or compound, either their origins are to be sought
in other ancient and now obsolete languages, or [87] because of
their age or the usually corrupt pronunciation of the lower classes
they are so changed and from the practice of incorrect writing [3]
are as it were so far obliterated that a true notation of words is
very rarely to be had. Therefore, an argument from notation, unless
the latter happens to be very obvious, is quite fallacious and often
ludicrous.

---

[1] Milton varies Ramus's text in this sentence.

[2] This etymology is basically correct.

[3] Milton shares the notion common in his age, and still common today, that
it is a function of correct writing to preserve a language from "corruption."

Now let us see the remaining examples. Ovid, *Fasti* 6 [vi.299]:

> The earth stands by its own force; standing
>   by force (*vi stando*) it is called Vesta.

The earth is called *Vesta* from its natural effect, since it stands by its own force (*vi sua stat*).[4]

> But the hearth (*focus*) is so called from the
>   flames and because it warms (*fovet*) everything.

The notation is from the effects. Likewise the *Oration against Verres*, 4 [II.ii.21.52]: "O distinguished sweepings (*Verrea*)! For what place did you ever approach without bringing this day with you? What house, what city did you approach, and even what holy place, which you did not leave plundered and stripped clean? Wherefore these things may indeed be called sweepings, since they are caused not by your name but by your habits and your nature." Here likewise the notation is from the effects. Ovid, *Fasti* 1 [vi.101]:

> This first day is for you, Carna, goddess of the hinge (*cardo*),
> By her divine command she opens the closed, closes the open.

This notation is from the subject, namely, from the hinge, for this goddess is concerned with the turning of hinges. Hence that ridiculing of Antonius the son-in-law [Cic. *Phil.* iii.6.16]: "The father of your wife, a good woman and certainly rich, was a certain Bambalio, no man at all—nothing more contemptible than he—who because of his stammering speech and dullness of spirit bore his surname as by insult." This notation of *Bambalio* is from the attributes, because the man was [88] a stammerer (*balbus*) and slow-witted. But from disagreements are those in Quintilian, book 1, chapter 6 [*Inst.* i.6.34]: "A grove (*lucus*) because, being dark with shade, it shows little light (*parum luceat*); and a school (*ludus*), because it is very far from play (*lusus*); and Dis, because he is not rich at all (*dives*)." And from comparatives is the notation of red bronze (*pyropus* [Greek, *fiery-eyed*]) because at times it presents an appearance of fire.

So much for notation: now something should be added about names. *For just as there is a relevance of a notation to its name, so in turn of name to a notation.* This means that just as notation

---

[4] Reconstruction of etymologies for the most part demanded far more knowledge than Milton's age, and, a fortiori, Ovid's, had been able to accumulate. *Vesta* traces to Indo-European root *wes*, to delay, dwell, stay the night, with derived meaning of "to be"—the same root as for the English "was." The correctness or incorrectness of Milton's other etymologies here is not noted further, since his point is clear despite their inaccuracies.

argues a name, so in turn a name argues a notation. For example: full of spirit, therefore spirited; and, conversely, spirited, therefore full of spirit. For a name, too, is a derived argument, but from what source it is derived, the notation explains. But this brief appendix on name has been added because, while all the other mutually relevant arguments which are not included under the same term and definition have their separate chapters, there would be so little to say about name, and it did not seem that for this a new chapter should be made. In this chapter, therefore, are contained two loci of invention, that of notation and that of name; and if a comparison is to be made between them, the stronger locus would seem to be that of name. Whence this whole category is called by Aristotle [*Rh*. ii.23.1400b16–25] the *locus from name*. An argument is derived more often and more firmly from name than from notation: for example, he is a man (*homo*), therefore he is from earth (*humus*); it is a hearth (*focus*), therefore it warms (*fovet*). But not with the same force is an argument derived from notation: for example, he is from earth, therefore he is a man; it warms everything, therefore it is a hearth. [89]

CHAPTER XXV

ON DISTRIBUTION

O F the derived arguments there remains the argument of distribution and definition.

In each of these there is a relation of reciprocity, one of all parts with the whole in the first, and one of the definition with what is defined in the second.

The reciprocity meant here is one by which absolutely the same thing and, one might say, the same essence is signified on both sides: for all the parts taken at once, that is, properly combined, are the same as the whole, and the definition is the same as what is defined. This is something that can be claimed for no other genus of arguments. From this arises the rule, common to both arguments, that in definition and distribution there should be nothing lacking and no redundancy: for where there is reciprocity there must also be equality. It is from this that there developed that exceptional quality of distribution and definition, namely, that they are the chief elements in the rules of the arts.[1] For since all the precepts of the arts should consist of reciprocal arguments, and reciprocity is found only between form (which is itself usually included in definitions) and what is formed, or between subject and proper attributes, it follows that all precepts are either definitions, distributions or certain rules or consequences [90] which are called explanations of properties.

Distribution occurs when the whole is distributed into its parts.

The whole is that which has parts.

A part is that which is contained by the whole.

Logically, and in general, that is called a whole which is in any way distributed and contains parts; a part is that which is in any way contained by a whole.

And just as the division of the whole into its parts is called distribution, so the collection of the parts to make up the whole is called induction.

Now between this induction and distribution there is no difference except that distribution proceeds from the whole to the parts,

---

[1] Thus the present *Art of Logic* is organized entirely by definition and distribution: logic is defined and divided into two parts, each of which is in turn defined and divided into two parts, and so on till there is no more to say: A Ramist art is a cut-up closed field.

while induction proceeds from the parts to the whole.[2] For this reason, just as name was related above to notation, so here induction is to be related to distribution; and not to syllogisms, as many have it, since in no other way do we argue from induction than from distribution: because the road from Thebes to Athens is the same as from Athens to Thebes. Aristotle [*Metaph*. i.6.987b1–4] recognized Socrates as the originator of induction, and testified that the necessity of induction was so great that, while science is of universals, we cannot know universals except through induction. By means of induction, therefore, the precepts of the arts have been discovered, as we suggested in the preface.

Distribution is derived from arguments which are in agreement with the whole but in disagreement among themselves. [91]

But the disagreement is not a disagreement of distribution (for there is never a distribution of a disagreement into a disagreement) but rather of the distributed parts.

So the greater the agreement of the parts with the whole and their mutual disagreement the more accurate the distribution.

From this it results that the most accurate distribution is one into two parts, and this is called *dichotomy:* for the disagreement between two things is the greatest, and in contraries one thing is opposed to only one thing. Hence the rule of Plato [*Pol.* 262 B]: "It is best to divide number in the closest possible way." Because if we cannot find a dichotomy—for it is difficult always to find one—it is better to posit two pairs of species, as though under two genera, though nameless ones, rather than four species under one genus.[3] For this form of distribution, though not the best, is nevertheless next to the best. For this reason in chapter 3 above Ramus [4] divided causes into two nameless genera, namely, efficient and material, form and end. But where dichotomy can in no way be conveniently applied, *a thing should be divided by many successive specific differences,* as Aristotle [*Part. An.* i.643b24–25] advises. For there should also not be any mutilation, complication or confusion of distribution due to a striving for dichotomy. [92]

---

[2] Ramism generally ignores the fact that induction is not simply the reverse of deduction: it proceeds from some—not all—of the "parts" to a whole. The nature of induction has always been a live philosophical question.

[3] Needless to say, any number of items, odd or even, can thus be rendered binary. If one must divide into three, one should make one item a "genus" with no "species" and put the other two under a nameless genus or one assigned an ad hoc name. See Introduction, above, for the relation between Ramist dichotomies and computer flow charts, p. 158.

[4] Ramus, *P. Rami . . . Dialecticæ Libri Duo* (Lutetia [Paris]: A. Wechelus, 1572; YUL), p. 6: "Causa est efficiens & materia, aut forma & finis."

CHAPTER XXVI

ON DISTRIBUTION FROM CAUSES

THE *primary distribution is by means of things absolutely in agreement, namely, causes and effects. A distribution by means of causes occurs when the parts are causes of the whole.*

Here distribution of the integral whole into its members is especially noteworthy.

The integral whole is one to which the parts are essential, that is, one constituted by the parts making up its whole essence; and it is therefore indicative of an effect existing from matter through form.

A member is part of an integral whole.

It is truly a part essential to its integral whole. Or, according to Aristotle, *Metaphysics* 4.25 [v.25.1023b20–23], "Members are those things of which an integral whole is composed." And members are indications of essential causes, certainly of matter and form, of which the whole essence of the integral whole consists: for the individual members contain the matter, and taken together also the form itself. *Thus grammar is divided into etymology and syntax, rhetoric into elocution and action, and logic into the invention and arrangement of arguments.*[1] *For of these parts those arts consist,* not as of causes but as of indications of causes. For since the essence of dialectic is partly a common one (namely, matter, that is, the precepts, and also form, [93] namely, the methodical arrangement of those precepts) and partly a proper one, which consists of discoursing well, this whole essence of dialectic is comprised in invention and arrangement. But these parts are not the matter itself, that is, the precepts, nor the common form itself, that is, the methodical arrangement of the precepts, nor the proper form, that is, the faculty itself of discoursing; but they are made up of the precepts methodically arranged, and the faculty of discoursing itself is contained within the ends of invention and arrangement.

The two examples in our author which follow here, one from Virgil, *Georgics* 1 [i.1–5], and the other from Cicero, *Pro Murena*

---

[1] Ramus and Ramists generally favor curriculum subjects as paradigms for definition and division. Cf. below, Book I, chap. xxx; Book II, chap. xvii.

[5.11], are each distinguished by their objects and not by causes, and therefore belong to chapter xxviii, namely, distribution from subjects, to which belongs also the preceding remark on use.[2]

Rather, this genus of argument is handled otherwise, either from the parts to the whole, or from the whole to the parts.

Concerning this matter Aristotle, *Topics* 6.6 [vi.13.150a22–36], gives certain rules. First, from the parts: "If all the parts are affirmed, so is the whole"; and conversely, "If all the parts are removed so is the whole." Likewise from one part: "If one part is removed, so is the whole." Secondly, from the whole to the parts: "If the whole is affirmed so are the parts." Certainly all of these are well enough understood from the rule of reciprocity given at the beginning of the chapter above. For in reciprocal things, one in turn and necessarily is concluded affirmatively and negatively from the other. But, as Aristotle [*Top*. vi.13.150a35–36] also notes, this does not follow: if the integral whole is taken away, so are its parts. [94]

Of each type (namely, of affirmation and negation from the parts to the whole) we have an example in Catullus [*Carm*. 86]:

> Quintia to many seems beautiful: to me she is fair, tall, straight: all of
>   these things I singly admit:
> But that the whole is beautiful, I deny. For there is no appeal in that
>   grand body, not a grain of salt.
> Lesbia is beautiful: her whole being is exquisite, so that she alone has
>   stolen all the individual charms from all others.

There is also another distribution from causes, one properly called less perfect, since the distribution is not so much one of the thing itself as of its causes: for example, from the efficient cause, when the testimony is divine or human. Thus some ancient statues were made by Phidias [Milton's text spells "Phydias"], others by Polyclitus, etc. Distribution of this sort is sometimes of the whole into the parts, where, however, not so much the parts are given as, instead, their efficient causes by which they are mutually distinguished. Thus, some statues were gold, others silver, others bronze, others ivory, etc. Here the distribution is from the matter. Other distributions are made according to the likeness of men, others according to that of brute animals; this is a distribution from an external form. Others are made for a religious use, others for a civil one; this is a distribution from the end. [95]

---

[2] See Milton's Book I, chap. xxviii, below.

Chapter XXVII

ON DISTRIBUTION FROM EFFECTS, INCLUDING
GENUS AND SPECIES

D*ISTRIBUTION from effects occurs when the parts are effects.
Distribution of genus into species is here most important.*
Some, following Cicero [*Top.* 6.30–7.30], call distribution of an integral whole into members *partition,* and that of genus into species *division.* And not without reason, for members are usually joined together and species disjoined.

Genus is a whole which is essential to its parts.

In this it is contrary to the integral whole, for with the integral whole the parts are essential to the whole, but with genus the whole is essential to the parts: whence it is certain that the former is rightly called a distribution from causes, the latter a distribution from effects. Now *genus is a whole essential to its parts,* because in its signification it includes that essence, namely matter and form, which is equally common to all species; or, more briefly, because it is a sign of the common essence. For genus does not properly speaking communicate essence to species (since in itself and apart from its species it is really nothing), but only signifies their essence. For the notion of what is essential and common to all species is called *genus,* and by the Greeks often *idea,* not indeed one separated from things, as they would hold [1] the Platonic ideas to be— which are nonsense according to Aristotle, *Metaphysics* 1.7 and 12.5 [i.9.991a21–23, xiii.5.1079b25–27]—but something which in thought [96] and reason is one and the same thing common to many species in which in fact and by nature it occurs individually, as Plato says in the *Meno* [75 A]. The Stoics, too, as Plutarch reports, *De placitis philosophorum* 1.10 [pseudo-Plutarch *Epit.* i.10.5], said that the ideas were our own notions.

A species is part of a genus.

Thus also Aristotle, *Metaphysics* 4.25 [v.25.1023b19]. And Cicero, *De inventione* 1 [i.22.32, 28.42]: "A part which falls under a genus." Now from the definition of genus we understand that species is the sort of part whose common essence is contained in

---

[1] The nonword *velunt* of Milton's text, unaltered in Columbia, is here emended to *velint.*

the signification of genus. But its proper essence, through which it is what it is, the species has from its proper form, which is not at all contained in the signification of genus. Thus also Aristotle, *Metaphysics* 7.12 [vii.12.1037b18–21]: "Genus does not seem to share the differences: for then the same thing would share contraries, for differences are contraries." Hence the saying that there is more in species than in genus, and the words of Porphyry [*Isag.* 11.1]: "Difference is that by which species exceeds genus." The total essence of a genus is therefore equally present in its species, but the total essence of a species is not in its genus, except potentially, as Porphyry [*Isag.* 15.15 ff.] says. Hence just as species is a part of genus, so genus seems in some way to be part of its species, something which Plato, too, notes in his *Politicus* [263 B]. Thus we say that animal is the genus of man and beast. For animal is a whole whose essence—namely, corporeal, animated, sentient—belongs in common to man and beast. Thus we say that man and beast are species of animal, because with respect to animal they are subjective parts which have the common essence of animal.

A genus is supreme or subaltern. [97]

A species is subaltern or ultimate.

A supreme genus is one of which there is no higher genus.

For example, in logical invention argument is the supreme genus of artificial and inartificial arguments.

A subaltern genus, as also a subaltern species, is that which is species in one respect but genus in another.

That is, it is something which is now genus, now species: genus with respect to species under it, species with respect to its genus.

Thus, cause is genus of matter and form, but it is a species with respect to argument absolutely in agreement. Thus man is either a subaltern genus or a subaltern species: species with respect to animal, genus with respect to individual men.

An ultimate species is one which is indivisible into other species.

For example, the matter and form of any individual thing. Thus, individual men are the ultimate species of man, and individual lions of lion.[2]

---

[2] The Ramist stand, which Milton here adopts, that individuals are "species" met with great resistance from non-Ramists generally. See Ong, *Ramus, Method, and Decay of Dialogue,* pp. 203, 348–49. The stand appears to imply at least two different but related positions. First, it implies that singular terms are names of classes, as universal terms are, only of classes with only one member each, unit-classes. Thereby it opens the way to syllogisms that allow singular propositions not merely as minor premises (as Aristotle had of course done) but also as major premises, as in Book II, chap. x, below. The syllogism with a singular major

Most logicians call man an ultimate species, and men individuals, not species. But just as animal is a whole whose common essence—namely, corporeal, animate, sentient—belongs commonly to man and beast, so man is a whole whose common rational essence belongs commonly to individual men: and just as man and beast are species of animal because with respect to animal they are subjective parts which have the common essence of animal, so [98] individual men are species of man because with respect to man they are subjective parts which have the common essence of man. Therefore, man is no less the genus of individual men than animal of man, and individual men are no less species of man than man of animal. For individual men differ by their proper form; but things that differ by their proper form also differ in species, according to Aristotle, *Physics* 1.7 [i.7.190a16–17]. Moreover, what-

---

premise has often been credited to Ramus as his own invention; in fact, it was treated by Ockham 250 years earlier. See I. M. Bocheński, *A History of Formal Logic,* trans. and ed. Ivo Thomas (Notre Dame, Ind.: University of Notre Dame Press, 1961), p. 232. Secondly, the Ramist stand clearly indicates that the relationship of the individual to the *infima species* or class just above the individual is exactly the same as that of this class to the class that includes it. Provided that the individual is considered as a unit-class, this position is quite intelligible. But if by the individual is meant a singular existent, problems abound that are not answered if they are even noticed, apparently, by Ramus and his followers generally, including Milton. If some specific difference distinguishes Peter from John, and every one of the billions of existent human beings from every other, just as "rational" distinguished the human animal from other animals, what does each of these billions of differences consist in logically? The name given to an individual does not *really* distinguish him from others. Any number of persons can have the same name. Milton here, following the usual Ramist explanation, simply says that this difference "cannot be known by us except through certain effects and accidents." The "specific" difference of the individual as individual thus eludes formal logic. The difficulty is that formal logic does not have to do with existence as existence, which is always singular: When formal logic treats the singular, it treats it as a member of a class or as itself a unit-class, that is, as a division of something larger, or as something itself divisible but only by one. But existence is not being-a-unit-class. I am not a unit-class. The world of formal logical structure and the existential world are not interchangeable, although they are related. But for a Ramist—and, it must be owned, even for many if not most of Ramus's opponents as well—the world of formal logical structure and the existential world were pretty much equated or amalgamated. Or, better, the world of formal logical structure was projected largely unconsciously and uncritically onto the existential world. Since logic was for Ramists a closed field—as indeed were each of the arts—the implications for one's cosmological view here were tremendous. The world was an oyster. Milton's rationalism, his confidence that he could "justifie the wayes of God to men" and that, after the fall, Adam could find "a Paradise within," find nourishment here.

ever differs, differs in genus or in species, again according to Aristotle, *Metaphysics* 10.3 [x.3.1054b28–29]. But no one would say that individual men differ in genus. Therefore, they differ in species. For the claim that man is the species of individual men is clearly absurd, for a species is a part of that of which it is species, as is plain from its definition. Further, since genus and species are relatives, genus will certainly be the genus of a species and species will be the species of genus. If, therefore, man, as they commonly claim, is the species of individual men, individual men will be the genus of man—something altogether absurd. But, they say, individual men differ only in number, not in form. But that things which differ in number differ also in form we have already adequately shown above in the chapter on form, although the difference of the proper form of a thing cannot be known by us except through certain effects and accidents, as they are called. Furthermore, individual men are mutually disparate and therefore opposed; but there cannot be one and the same form of things which are mutually opposed: they differ therefore in form and not only in number. And so according to Laertius, *In Zenone* [Diog. Laert. vii.61], the Stoics teach that Socrates is an ultimate species. What is more, Aristotle, *De partibus animalium* 1.4 [i.4.644a25], calls Socrates and Coriscus lowest species. Thus, jurists call man a genus and Stichus and Pamphilus species. [99]

Genus and species are signs of causes and effects.

For in an animal there is corporeal essence, which is the matter belonging commonly to the species; and there is the capacity for life and sense, a form likewise pertaining in common to the species. Therefore, *genus contains the causes which belong in common to its species; and conversely the species contains the effects of its genus.*

Hence genus is notable and preeminent because it manifests the cause.

Aristotle says the same thing in *Posterior Analytics* 1.24 [i.24.85b24–28, 31.88a5–6].

Distribution of genus into species is important indeed but is difficult and rarely found.

It is important because anything in the arts which is derived from causes and effects is almost totally included in the notions of genus and species. It is difficult because forms, from which species originate, are likewise difficult to find, and also because of the scarcity of terms by which genera and species can be designated.

Yet for the sake of illustration and example we shall provide what we can. Ovid, *Metamorphoses* 1 [i.72–73], divides animal into five species, namely, celestial bodies, birds, beasts, fishes, and men. He endows celestial bodies with souls, as do also certain philosophers.

> So that no region should be without its animate things,
> Only the divine and forms of the gods occupy the celestial bodies, etc.

Thus, Cicero in *De officiis* 1 [i.5.15] divides virtue into four species, namely, prudence, justice, fortitude and temperance; which, however, are not themselves posited in distribution, but— what amounts to the same thing—their forms: "But everything honorable comes from one of four [100] sources: for it expresses itself either in perfect knowledge of what is true and in ingenuity; in the defence of the fellowship of men, the allotment to each man of his due and the faithful observance of contracts; in the greatness and strength of a lofty and invincible spirit; or in an order and form in all things done or said, in which modesty and temperance prevail."

Now this, as I have said, is *a distribution of genus into the forms of its species,* which is just like a distribution into the species themselves, *because forms together with the genus constitute their species.*

Genus and species are treated not only in this simple formula of division, but also separately one from the other.

This means that what is affirmed of the whole genus is also correctly affirmed of all its species. Thus Cicero in *Pro Archia* [1.2], comparing the poetic art with eloquence, which are both species of art, says that they are mutually related, because the same thing is affirmed of the arts in general, especially the more humane ones: "Truly all arts, which pertain to humanity, have a certain common bond, and as if in a certain kinship they contain one another."

Conversely, a genus is treated through its species.

This means that what is affirmed of all species is also correctly affirmed of their genus. Thus Ovid, *Tristia* 4 [iv.3.75–80], proves that virtue is more evident in adversity, by an induction of species: namely, because the capacity of a soldier, sailor and physician is observed in adversity: [101]

> Who would know Hector if Troy were fortunate?
> The way virtue becomes public is through adversities:
> Your art, Tiphys, lies neglected if there are no waves on the sea;
> If men are healthy, your art, Phoebus, is despised.
> Lying hidden and unknown when times are good,
> Virtue appears and is proven when they are bad.

And thus, since genus is treated also through its species, as we are informed by the rule above, and the special examples are species of those things of which they are examples, it follows that *special examples appropriate to their genus are also to be included here,* whether only one is presented, or several through induction. And I say special examples, for examples are either similar which argue similar things, or special which argue their genus, such as those that have been taken from the poets and orators in the various classes of arguments.[3] Now the use of special arguments is clearly necessary not only in discovering and teaching the arts (for by induction from examples the precepts are inferred and by the use of examples the precepts are illustrated), but also in all discourse whenever something requires clarification. Of such sort is the passage from Cicero, *Ad Atticum* [vii.11.3]: "You would leave the city? So too if the Gauls came. The republic, he says, does not consist in walls but in altars and homes. Themistocles did the same thing, for one city could not withstand the onslaught of all the barbarians. But Pericles, almost fifty years later, did not do the same thing when he held nothing besides the fortifications. And once our own citizens, when the rest of the city had been taken, nevertheless kept the stronghold." Here from a special example both alternatives are discussed. Themistocles deserted Athens; therefore it is licit to desert the city. Pericles did not desert Athens, nor did the Romans desert Rome at the approach of the Gauls; therefore the city should not be deserted. [102] If one argued to the effect that since Themistocles left the city, so can I, then the argument would be from the similar, for examples, when they are appropriate to other special ones, are either similar or dissimilar. But here belong also those examples which are appropriate to their genus.

There is another less perfect distribution from effects when the parts are not properly speaking the effects of the whole but of the parts themselves. For example, Cicero, *De senectute* [6.17]: "Some sailors climb the masts, others run up and down the gangways, and others empty out the bilge-water; but the helmsman holds the rudder in the stern." In the example the whole is sailor, which is the genus of individual sailors; the parts are the climbing of masts, the running up and down, etc. Yet these latter are not parts or species of sailor as of a whole or genus, but rather as of a species, that is, they are the effects or the duties of the individual sailors

---

[3] Milton has in mind commonplace books, such as his own, which collect examples under headings of the virtues, vices, and other useful classifications.

by which the species themselves, that is, the individual sailors, are mutually distinguished. Actually, just as this distribution is relatively imperfect, so it is relatively common. But its chief use is to compensate for the rarity of a more perfect distribution, since the distribution of genus into species, as remarked above, is so difficult to find. [103]

Chapter XXVIII

ON DISTRIBUTION FROM SUBJECTS

THE remaining distribution is in a certain sense concerned with arguments of agreement, as with subjects and adjuncts. A distribution from subjects occurs when the parts are subjects, that is, when the true parts, though understood, are distinguished and suggested by their subjects.

For example, in Catullus [*Carm.* 62]:

> Your virginity is not all yours: it is partly from your parents.
> A third of it was given by your mother, a third by your father;
> Only a third of it is yours. Do not fight the two
> Who to their son-in-law gave rights along with the dowry.

The girl's virginity, or rather the right of virginity, is divided into three parts distinguished by their subjects—the mother, the father, and the girl herself. Another example, transferred here from chapter twenty-six, is Virgil, *Georgics* 1 [i.1–5], where he begins his work by a division into four parts distinguished by their appropriating subjects, namely fields, trees, livestock and bees: [104]

> What makes fields fruitful, in what season one should till the soil,
> Maecenas, and join the vines to the elms; how to care for oxen, how to
> manage livestock, and how much experience there is in the thrifty bees,
> I now begin to relate.

A third example, transferred here from the same chapter, is Cicero in *Pro Murena* [5.11]: "I understand, judges, that there were three parts to the accusation, one concerned with a censure of his life, another with a striving for dignity, the third with crimes of illegal office-seeking." Here the whole accusation is divided into three members distinguished by their preoccupying subjects, and in these three examples the whole is an integral whole. A fourth example is of distribution of genus into species, from Cicero, *Tusculan Disputations* 5 [v.27.76]: "There are indeed those three genera of goods. While those of the body and the external ones lie close to earth, and may be called goods only because they have to be employed, the others, however, the divine ones, are esteemed far and wide, and touch heaven." Here Cicero divides goods into three species, which he calls genera, distinguished by their subjects; they are goods of the spirit, of the body and of fortune. [105]

CHAPTER XXIX

ON DISTRIBUTION FROM ADJUNCTS

D*ISTRIBUTION from attributes occurs when the parts are adjuncts.*
 For example, some men are healthy, some sick; some are rich, some poor.

Thus Virgil, *Georgics* 1 [i.233–34], divides the world into five parts: a middle torrid part, two frigid extremes, and the remaining two temperate:

> Five zones the heavens hold, one always red
> From the flaming sun, burning hot from fire, etc.

Caesar, *Gallic War* 1 [i.1]: "The whole of Gaul is divided into three parts, one of which the Belgae inhabit, another the Aquitani, and the third those who in their own language are called Celts, in ours Gauls."

In imperfect distributions of this sort one should give attention to that which appears to be distributed. For if it is of the nature of a whole, either integral or generic, there is distribution; if it does not have the nature of a whole, but is some simple argument, such as cause, effect, subject or attribute, there is no distribution but rather an enumeration, one either of several causes of the same effect, several effects of the same cause, several subjects of the same attribute, or finally several attributes of the same subject. By this imperfect type of distribution [106] arguments whose true species do not appear at all are often distinguished by certain modes; but we have established the modes above in the section on attributes. Thus, in causes *procreating* and *conserving* are called *modes* of efficient cause, not species: because they do not differ from each other as species through opposite differences, but in such a way that they can belong to one and the same efficient cause, since the same cause that procreates usually also preserves, and it can be an efficient cause of the same thing either alone or with other causes, and of some things either *per se* or *per accidens*.

CHAPTER XXX

ON DEFINITION

IN teaching the arts definition is prior in use to distribution (for
any given thing is defined before it is distributed), but by nature
and in order of invention it comes later: for genus—without
which (if one is available) no definition can be formed—borrows
from distribution, which [1] is the proper locus of genus.

Definition occurs when it is explained what a thing is.

It is called definition because it defines the essence of a given
thing and circumscribes it as if by its limits.[2]

And just as definition argues or explains what is defined, so
conversely it can be argued from what is defined. Although this
[107] property of arguing and, conversely, being argued mutually
is common to all arguments, nevertheless here the thing defined
is mentioned for the same reason for which name was mentioned
in the chapter on notation: namely, lest the thing defined appear
to be excluded from the class of arguments, since it does not have
the same name as the definition which it argues, and does not have
a special chapter of its own, as do other pairs of arguments which
do not have the same name. As regards reciprocity, which is common to definition and distribution, that of the definition and the
thing defined is most evident: for logic is the art of reasoning well,
and conversely the art of reasoning well is logic. So in this way
every definition, as some rightly advise, should be examined by
means of conversion: whence Boethius, *Topics* 5 [i.e., *De differentiis topicis* iii (*PL* lxiv.1196C)], says that "every definition is
made equivalent to the thing it defines."

*A definition is either perfect or imperfect: the former is properly
called a definition, the latter a description.*

*A perfect definition is one which consists solely of causes con-
stituting essence.* Whatever is posited beyond this is therefore redundant in a perfect definition.

Now such causes are comprised of genus and form.

---

[1] The *qui* of Milton's text, unaltered in Columbia, is here emended to *quæ.*
Otherwise, no clear meaning appears.

[2] Latin *finis*, limit, boundary; *de-finire*, to de-limit; *de-finitio*, de-limitation.

For genus and form (which are as it were the body and soul of definition) constitute the whole essence of a thing. But the necessity of a genus in a perfect definition is not so great that a definition will not be perfect if it has no genus. For, first, of supreme genera, such as argument in logical invention, there is no genus; rather, their whole essence is contained within the form itself, which also includes their [108] appropriate matter. Secondly, it can happen that the causes themselves present themselves more readily than the genus which represents them. So if the definition consists of the causes themselves it will be perfect; if it consists of the genus, it will merely be more succinct. Now the proximate genus, and not a remote one, should always be posited in a definition, for whoever posits the proximate genus has also posited the remotest ones, unless perhaps the proximate genus is nameless, for then (and also whenever the genus, whether nameless or not, has been mentioned a short time before) the genus can be lacking in the definition and be correctly understood at the same time. For example, in our definition of definition, the remote genus, namely, that of derived argument, as well as the proximate one, namely, that of real and compound argument, are understood at the same time. Now what we here call form in a definition, many call difference. But difference is the result of form and does not appear except in a comparison of things, of which there is none in a definition; and form is that from which the best explanation of things is obtained and it therefore has a preeminent place in definition.

So in this way man is defined as a rational animal: that is, by the genus *animal* we understand, as stated above, a corporeal essence replete with life and sense, which is the matter of man and part of the form: if to this you add *rational* you include the whole form of man by the capacity for life, sense, and reason.

And so a perfect definition is nothing other than a universal representation of the causes which constitute the essence and the nature of a thing. [109]

Such are the definitions of the arts.[3] Grammar is the art of using words well, rhetoric the art of delivering a speech well, logic the art of reasoning well, arithmetic the art of numbering well, geometry the art of measuring well. For by the genus *art* we understand a set of precepts [4] arranged in order, which is the matter of an art and part of its form, or the common form, and if to this you

---

[3] On Ramist use of curriculum subjects as paradigms, see n. 1, Book I, chap. xxvi above.

[4] Note that an art is here assumed to be totally articulated or rationalized.

add the proper form of a given art (a form which also includes the end, as was said in chapter 8) you have the whole essence of the art explicated, which is a perfect definition.[5]

As for the rules of consequence, namely, going from the definition to what is defined, and conversely, whether affirmatively or negatively, these have all been explained clearly enough in their proper place in the section on reciprocity, which also belongs to distribution.

---

[5] It is typical of Ramist logic that, in its entirety, it applies perfectly to only one kind of thing: a curriculum subject as organized by Ramist logic. For everything else it proves a Procrustean Bed. See Walter J. Ong, "Ramist Classroom Procedure and the Nature of Reality," *SEL*, I (1961), 31–47.

CHAPTER XXXI

ON DESCRIPTION

B ECAUSE of the obscurity of causes and especially of forms, perfect definitions are hard to find; to compensate for their rarity, therefore, *description* has been devised.

A description is an imperfect definition, defining a thing through other arguments, that is, explaining a thing in some way through any other available things. [110]

So when the form cannot be had (for genera are commonly better known) a property should be taken in place of the form or the difference. For example, *an angel is an incorporeal substance; a horse is an animal that whinnies,* etc. Attributes, or accidents, as they are called (because substances alone, as Aristotle says in *Metaphysics* 6.5 [vii.4.1030b5–7], are defined primarily, accidents only secondarily), when they are proper, are defined by genus, by subject, and by proximate cause, either efficient or final or both. By genus and subject alone, as *snubness is curvature of the nose.* By subject and efficient cause, as *thunder is the sound of a cloud breaking because of compressed fire,* and *continuous quantity is an attribute of a body from the extension of matter.* By final cause, as *sense is a natural faculty in an animal for judging singular things.* Or by both efficient and final cause, as *respiration is the reciprocal attraction and expulsion of air carried out by the lungs for the cooling of the heart.* The subject is often omitted in the definition of proper attributes, certainly because it is understood from its genus or its cause, as *memory is an internal sense conserving images of things known.* It is not said to be *an internal sense of an animal,* namely by adding the subject, because the latter is understood at the mention of *sense.* Natural powers are defined by their action and their efficient cause, as *risibility is a faculty for laughing, deriving from the rational soul.* Habits are defined by their end or object, which often coincide; by the end, as in *logic is the art of reasoning well,* and by the object, as in *physics is the science of natural things.* Sensible qualities are defined by their subject and their efficient cause, as in *color is a quality of a mixed body resulting from the proper mixture of the bright and the dark.* Actions are generally defined by their subject, efficient cause and end. Relations are defined by the mutually related things and by their foundation or cause, as in *fatherhood* [111] *is the relation of father to child resulting from procreation.*

Common attributes are defined by object, efficient cause, final cause, or by as many of these as are useful: for example, *whiteness is a color resulting from the bright overcoming the dark.*

Now generally in descriptions one should avoid taking cause for the genus, as when doubt is described as an equality of reasons, health as a balance of humors, pain as a dissolution of the continuous,[1] an eclipse of the moon as the interposition of the earth;[2] or the subject for the genus, as when wind is described as air in motion, justice as a constant will, a wound as a torn part of flesh, original sin as nature corrupted, and the like.

For the rest, fixed rules cannot be given in these matters. For sometimes a description is given from a remote contrary alone, as [Hor. *Epist.* i.1.41]:

It is virtue to flee from vice, and wisdom first to have lost folly.

---

[1] Milton is drawing on a very old tradition for some of these instances of what he considers to be incorrectly formulated descriptions. For example, the description of pain as a dissolution of the continuous goes at least as far back as Claudius Galen (131–201). See, e.g., *Hippocratis De Acutorum Morborum Victu Liber et Galeni Commentarius II,* in *Medicorum Græcorum Opera quæ Extant,* (ed. Carolus Gottlob Kühn (Leipzig: Car. Cnoblochius, 1828), XV, 515: "ἡ ὀδύνη γίγνεται . . . τῆς συνεχείας λυομένης" ("pain occurs . . . when the continuum is dissolved"). The Latin version given by Milton was familiar to medieval medical doctors, partly through the translations of Galen by Gerard of Cremona (c.1114–87); see, e.g., Galen's *Ars Medica* (τέχνη ἰατρική, called variously *Ars parva, Tegni, Microtegni,* etc., in the Middle Ages), in Ugo Benzi (d. 1439), *Expositio Super Libros Tegni Galeni* (Venice: Heredes Octaviani Scoti ac sociorum, 1518; NLM), fol. 56r: "Dolores vero secundum quem incumbunt locum aut continuitatis solutionem aut alterationes subitas ostendunt." Wounds of various types were also defined as instances of *solutio continuitatis;* see Gerard of Cremona's translation of Avicenna (980–1037), *Canon,* Lib. I, Fen 2, Doctrina 1, c. 4, in *Avicennæ . . . Libri in Re Medica Omnes, qui Hactenus ad Nos Pervenere* (Venice: Vincentius Valgrisius, 1564; PML), p. 83: "Solutionis vero continuitatis ægritudo plerunque accidit cuti, & vocatur excoriatio aut scarificatio. Et plerunque accidit carni quæ est ei propinqua, in qua nondum factum est pus, & vocatur plaga." This general definition of *plaga* (wound) introduces an elaborate discussion of wounds in Guy de Chauliac (d. c.1368), *La Grande Chirurgie . . .,* ed. E. Nicaise (Paris: Germer Baillière, 1890), p. 196: "Playe est solution de continuité récente, sanglante, sans pourriture, faite en parties molles." Something closely akin to Guy's definition can still be found in modern dictionaries; see, e.g., the entry for "plaie" (from the Latin *plaga*) in *Nouveau Larousse Classique* (Paris: Larousse, 1958), p. 914: "Solution de continuité dans les parties molles du corps."

[2] This description of eclipse is one of Aristotle's favorite examples in his discussion of definition and its relation to demonstration; see *An. Post.* ii.2.90a3–24 and passim.

Sometimes description is clearly arbitrary.

Hence, although there is only one definition of a thing, there can be many descriptions.

Now just as definition can be argued by the thing defined, as we advised above, so also description can in turn be argued from the thing described. But not only this mutual relation obtains between description and the thing described, but also reciprocity, in accordance with the common rule of distribution and definition [112] given above in chapter 25, according to which a description too should be proper to the thing described and reciprocal. For although in descriptions often many things are combined of which some may be of greater extension than what is described, these things in combination are nevertheless equivalent to the thing described and make the description a proper one; but if they are of lesser extension, then the description is to be considered defective and useless. For example, *man is a mortal animal, capable of being instructed.* Here with a certain cause (namely, matter and the common form contained under the genus animal) there are combined two circumstances or attributes, one common, that is, *mortal,* and one proper, that is, *capable of being instructed.* But, you may ask, why the term *mortal,* since there is no animal which is not mortal? Because Aristotle, whose description this is (*Topics* 5.1 [v.1.128b34–36]), says that certain animals are immortal (*Topics* 4.2 [iv.2.122b13–15]),[3] and in the same chapter [iv.2.122b12–13] he calls God himself ζῷον ἀθάνατον, that is, an *immortal animal.*

But this succinct brevity[4] *does not always obtain in this species, which often calls for a more lucid and more detailed explanation.*

Succinct descriptions which emulate perfect definitions are useful especially in teaching the arts and in disputations. The longer ones, being better adapted to the ears of ordinary people, are found more frequently in the orators and poets.

Thus fame is described in *Pro Milone* [35.97–98]: "Yet of all the rewards of virtue, if rewards were to be calculated, the most ample is fame: which alone comforts the brevity of our life with the thought of remembrance in posterity; which makes us be present when we are absent, and to be living when we are dead; by whose steps, in short, even men seem to ascend into heaven." [113] This description of fame consists of a genus, namely, *reward of virtue;*

---

[3] This and the immediately preceding reference to the *Topics* Milton got from Downame, who in turn found them in Talon's *Prælectiones* on Ramus's *Dialectic* (Basel: Eusebius, 1569), p. 245.

[4] The brevity called for in definition, as explained in Book I, chap. xxx, above.

its amplitude is specified by increase from the lesser to the effect that it is the most ample of all; and then four of its effects are added.

In *Æneid* 4 [iv.173–88] rumor is thus described

> From the temple of Libia rumor travels through the great cities, something evil; nothing else more quickly thrives by its mobility, and it gains strength as it travels, etc.

Rumor is described (1) by its genus, as *an evil thing,* (2) by specification of its speed, which is illustrated by a negation of the greater, "nothing else more quickly," and by a double effect unlike that of other things, because it

> thrives by its mobility, and it gains strength as it travels.

Rumor is described (3) by specifying its variation, as shown from the other attributes, to the effect that it is first *small,* and this is argued by its cause, namely, *fear,* and by the circumstance of time, namely, *at first;* and then it suddenly becomes greater, in an incredibly short period of time, and this is shown by three effects individually illustrated by their subjects:

> Soon it lifts itself to the winds: it goes forth alone and conceals its head among the clouds.

It is described (4) from the procreating cause, "earth brought her forth,"—that is, the mother of giants—and by its mode of working, namely, by counsel or by natural force, "irritated by the anger of the gods," who had killed the giants; but the common procreating cause is illustrated by a specification of time and by common testimony: [114]

> begot her as the youngest sister, as they say, of Caeus and Enceladus;

We have her further illustrated by attributes, as

> swift of foot, with agile wings,
> a dreadful monster, enormous.

Then there is a description from the parts of her body and her members, which turn out to match one another in number:

> and for every feather on her body there is a watchful eye underneath,
> amazing to say, and a tongue, a sounding mouth, an erect ear.

Then she is described from her nocturnal effects, these being partly affirmed and illustrated by the places in which they occur:

> at night she flies through the heavens,
> hissing about in the shadow of the earth,

and partly denied:

> nor does she close her eyes in sweet repose.

And there is a description from her day-time effects, these being illustrated from the places in which they occur and from the site where she sits:

> when it is light she sits watchfully on the ridge of the highest roof or upon lofty towers, and terrifies great cities.

Finally she is described from her mutually corresponding adjuncts:

> as well one holding to the false and perverse, as a messenger of the truth.

Such are the descriptions of plants and animals by natural philosophers; of rivers, mountains and cities by geographers and historians; and finally of persons by poets and orators. [115]

CHAPTER XXXII

ON DIVINE TESTIMONY

HAVING *treated the artificial argument, we follow with the inartificial. An inartificial argument is one which argues not by its own nature but by a force derived from some artificial argument.*

This is designated by the single term, testimony [1]; namely, as Cicero says in the *Topics* [19.73], "something taken from an external thing to produce conviction."

But it is called inartificial not because it is not discovered through the power and assistance of art (since its discovery, as Cicero says in *De partitione* [14.48], is taught in the art), but because of itself and by its nature it has no part in this art and in the ability to argue. It can also be called an assumptive argument, because it argues by an assumed force and not by its own. For an inartificial argument does not reach the nature of a thing, and much less does it argue the nature as an artificial argument usually does; nor is it a relevance of the thing to arguing, as is an artificial argument. Rather, it is the bare attestation of someone concerning a thing, or an affirmation or denial of the person attesting. But neither do things exist because of an affirmation nor fail to exist because of a denial: testimony, therefore, does not argue anything of itself and by its nature *but rather by the assumed force of some artificial argument.* But this force is the authority of the person giving testimony, on which the reliability of the testimony totally depends. Now authority consists of a variety of arguments, but it is discernible especially in the effects and attributes of the one giving testimony. [116]

So when the exact truth or nature of things is more carefully investigated, testimony has a very meager probative force.

Hence Cicero in *De natura deorum* 1 [i.5.10]: "In disputation one should seek not so much authorities as weight of reasons."

But in civil and human affairs, when an action is the object of inquiry, *this argument commonly produces special conviction in view of the moral character of the person arguing, if prudence, honesty, and benevolence are present.*

---

[1] These words occur somewhat later in Ramus's text.

If one of these is lacking, then either through the imprudence of the witness, or through his dishonesty, or because of enmity or excessive indulgence, something false is uttered as testimony.

Testimony is either divine or human.

And it is rightly divided into species distinguished by their efficient causes. For it is chiefly from its efficient causes that testimony derives its force. Thus it is an effect with respect to the one giving testimony, and it is testimony with respect to the thing testified. Now I do not see why anyone should be offended that in an investigation of the exact truth and nature of things very meager probative force is commonly attributed to testimony, and that this appears to apply to divine testimony as well as to human. For testimony, whether it be divine or human, equally has all its force from its author and none in itself. And divine testimony does indeed affirm or deny that a thing is so, [117] and it makes me believe; it does not prove, it does not teach, it does not make me know or understand why it is so, unless it also adds reasons.

Divine testimony is that which has God as its author.[2]

Among divine testimonies are numbered not only the oracles of the gods, but also the responses of the seers and soothsayers.

Whether these are true or fictitious, or from a true divine command or a false one, the logician does not consider, but only what force of arguing any given one has. And so also in civil and human affairs divine testimony has just as much probative force as its author is a true or false god.

Of this sort are the testimonies in *Against Catiline* 3 [iii.8.18]: "For, that I should omit those things, the meteors seen by night in the west, the blazing heat of the sky; the thrusts of lightning, the earthquakes, and the other things which did so plentifully occur while I was consul, so that the things which now take place the immortal gods seemed to proclaim." [118]

---

[2] This definition is found in Downame. No definition at all is given by Ramus, who says nothing here or elsewhere in his *Dialectic* about Judaeo-Christian revelation, which Milton also bypasses here. See above, Milton's Preface and n. 3. Ramus's division of testimony into divine and human is taken from Cicero's *Partitiones Oratoriæ* 2.6, quoted in Talon's commentary (*prælectiones*) in Ramus, *Dialecticæ Libri Duo A. Talæi Prælectionibus Illustrati* (Basel: Episcopius, 1569; UBB), p. 258. Talon says here that testimony has no true logical divisions, since the same testimony can be divine and human, and that Ramus's division by efficient cause is a kind of distribution to provide some sort of description—ibid., pp. 258, 252.

Chapter XXXIII

ON HUMAN TESTIMONY

HUMAN testimony is that which has a man as its author.[1]
And it is common or proper.
This distribution is suggested not as an accurate division
(for it is not proper to testimony) but as a sort of distinction of
subaltern species, to which inferior species of testimony examples
can also be referred. And, just as with the above distinction into
divine and human, human testimony is also determined from the
efficient cause, who may be a public or common person, or a proper
or private one.

Common testimony is like a law or an aphorism.

For these two are examples rather than species, and to them
may be added *common report,* which Cicero in the *Topics* [20.76]
calls a certain testimony of the multitude, and which others call
a consensus of the citizenry and a public testimony.

Now there is a testimony of both unwritten and written law, as
in *Pro Milone* [4.10–11]: "For there is, Judges, a law which is not
written but natural, which we have not learned, accepted, or read,
but which from nature itself we have taken, drawn into ourselves,
and expressed, for which we are not taught but made, not instructed but naturally endowed: for example, if our life should be
threatened by treachery, or by force or arms either of robbers [119]
or enemies, we should resort to all honorable means to ensure our
safety." And in the same work [3.9]: "If the Twelve Tables stipulated that a thief in the night be killed under any circumstances,
but that one coming by day be killed with impunity if he used a
weapon in his own defense, who is there who, etc."

There remains the aphorism: proverbs are things of this sort.
Examples are: Like seeks like. You were born in Sparta, so adorn
that city. Then there are the sayings of wise men, such as: Know
thyself. Nothing in excess. Make a vow, danger is near. For although these sayings have perhaps each been derived from individual authors, nevertheless, since they are in the mouths of all,
they become as it were the property of all and are rightly classed
as common testimony.

[1] Ramus's text does not have this or any definition of human testimony. Milton
takes the definition from Downame. See n. 2, Book I, chap. xxxii, above.

Proper testimony is like that of Plato in *Ad Quintum fratrem* I [i.1.10]: "And indeed that prince of genius and learning, Plato, thought that republics would at long last be happy when either learned and wise men began to rule them or those who ruled them devoted all their effort to learning and wisdom."

Such testimonies occur in the poets. *Æneid* 6 [vi.620]:

> Learn justice, you who have been admonished; and do not despise the gods.

Likewise in these Homeric verses [Il. ii.557–58]:

> Αἴας δ' ἐκ Σαλαμῖνος ἄγεν δυοκαίδεκα νῆας
> Στῆσε δ' ἄγων ἵν' 'Αθηναίων ἵσταντο φάλαγγες.
> But Ajax led twelve ships out of Salamis
> And ordered them stationed where the Athenian lines were drawn.

The Megarians were vanquished in the contest with the Athenians over the island of Salamis, [120] which was equally close to both cities.

And these were testimonies of ancient men and of absent ones, and generally of dead persons, which in principle are cited most forcefully.

The testimonies of men living and present, which in practice are most often called upon, occur not only *when there is an inquiry about farm property, about a murder, or about some matter of this sort, but there are also testimonies regarding obligation, confession, and oath.*

An example of obligation is in *Philippics* 5 [v.18.51]: "I promise, guarantee, and pledge that Caesar will always be the kind of citizen he is today and the kind we ought most to wish and desire him to be."

A wager is also a kind of obligation, as in Virgil, *Eclogues* 3 [iii.28–31]:

> Do you wish, then, that we prove to each other what each in turn can do? I'll wager this heifer (lest you refuse it, it has been milked twice and now suckles two calves). Now you tell me with what wager you match me.

A confession is either free, in which a man's testimony is considered quite unimportant on his behalf but very serious against him; or it is extracted by torture and is in this case properly called interrogation (quæstio).

Such was the argument against Milo, which was ridiculed by Cicero [22.60]: since torture exposes and extorts truth no more often than it does falsehood. "But come, what or of what sort was the interrogation? Listen, where was Roscius? Where was Casca? Has Clodius planned treachery for Milo? If the answer is yes, then the cross for him. If the answer is no, then liberty as hoped."

Here also can be classed the argument we use when we propose to an adversary the proof and experience of what we affirm. [121]

In Verrem 4 [ii.10.26]: "Would anyone have given Volcatius a farthing if he had come of his own accord? Let him come now and find out; no one will receive him in his house."

Terence, *Eunuchus* [iii.2.476–78]:

> Make a trial in letters, in rhetoric, in music. I shall give you one skilled
> in everything it is fitting for a young freeman to know.

Tristia 3 [iii.11.73–74]:

> So that it may be more evident, and that I not be thought to pretend
> it,
> I should like that you feel my punishment.

An oath is also a testimony, as in *Æneid* 6 [vi.459–60]:

> By the gods above, and by whatever is true within the earth, unwillingly,
> O Queen, have I left your shore.

Now although in oaths divine testimony is in some way invoked, the reliability of the oath still depends on the authority and moral character of the one making the oath.

Reciprocation is here rather obscure with respect to the thing testified, and for this reason the other argument is here relevant, namely, that because the thing testified is true, the one giving testimony is truthful.

But just as it is not the testimony by its own force but the authority of the one giving testimony that argues the thing testified, so in turn the thing testified argues not the testimony itself but the authority of the one giving testimony. [122]

THE ART OF LOGIC

conformed to the method of Peter Ramus

BY JOHN MILTON THE ENGLISHMAN

BOOK THE SECOND

The Disposition of Arguments

CHAPTER I

WHAT IS THE DISPOSITION OF ARGUMENTS?

U P to this point, the first part of the art of logic was concerned with the invention of arguments. There follows the second part, concerned with their disposition.

Just as the first part of grammar is about single words and the second part about their syntax, so the first part of logic was about the invention of arguments and the second is about their disposition, that is, it is the part which teaches how to arrange arguments correctly. [123] Thus, disposition is as it were a certain syntax of arguments, but not merely with a view to judging [1] well, as Ramus holds, for this is too narrow, but with a view to reasoning well, which is the general end of logic, to which single end all the precepts of the art are to be ordered. So I do not agree with those who claim that judgment is the second part of logic, since in their opinion judgment is the end and result of this second part, namely, of disposition, whereas it is impossible for one and the same thing to be the end and that of which it is the end, or the result caused and the cause of that result, which is disposition. But, they say, judgment as an object of instruction is a part of logic, while as the habit of judging well it is an end. I say, on the contrary, that instruction

[1] For the history of the competing terms "judgment" (*iudicium*) and "arrangement" (*dispositio*), see Introduction, above, pp. 175–76.

in disposition works not only toward judging well, but toward reasoning well, but I would not with Ramus take judgment and disposition to be the same. For if, as Ramus himself says, everything is judged by a definite rule of arrangement, then certainly if disposition and judgment are the same the rule and that of which it is the rule will be the same. Moreover, instruction in judgment teaches nothing other than to judge well, while instruction in disposition, by its function of arranging, teaches also how to reason well, whether it be understanding, judging, disputing, or remembering. For by a definite rule of disposition any function of reasoning is improved.

So while at the beginning I stated that the simple relation of arguments among themselves does of itself contribute to judgment and right reasoning, I now state that the disposition of arguments accomplishes the same thing to a considerably higher degree and more clearly as well.

But before we come to the parts of disposition, a certain general property of disposition, [124] called *crypsis,* must be touched upon, as something which pertains in common to all species of disposition. Now this crypsis, or concealment, is threefold, namely, a deficiency, a redundancy, or an inversion of arranged parts. So it should be pointed out here once and for all that if because of these crypses a doubt arises, then the parts lacking should be filled in, the redundant ones should be eliminated, and every part should be restored to its place.

CHAPTER II

ON THE AFFIRMATION AND NEGATION OF AN AXIOM

D*ISPOSITION is either axiomatic or dianoetic.
    An axiom is disposition of one argument with another
    by which something is shown to be or not to be.*
    For Aristotle [e.g., *Metaph.* iv.3.1005a19–b34] an axiom often
means a proposition or affirmation which is so clear that it is as
it were worthy [1] of being assented to for its own sake. Otherwise
he considers an axiom and a proposition or affirmation of any sort
to be the same, and rightly, for just as *affirmation* is derived from
I affirm, that is, *I estimate* or *I am of the opinion*, so *axiom* is
derived from the Greek word meaning the same thing. And that
this general meaning of the term was accepted among the ancient
dialecticians is evident from Cicero [e.g., *Acad. Pr.* 29.95], Plutarch
[e.g., *Mor.* xiii.1011 E], Laertius [Diog. Laert. vii.65], Galen [*Inst.
log.* i.5] and Gellius, 16.8 [*NA* xvi.8.2–8].

In Latin axiom is *enuntiatum, enuntiatio, pronuntiatum, pronuntiatio, effatum,* and in Varro, according to Gellius, Book 16
[*NA* xvi.8.2], it is *profatum* and *proloquium,* that is, a judgment
in which nothing is lacking. From the Greek it is also called *oratio*
and *propositio.* [125]

Why, then, you ask, has a word of Greek origin, and this one
rather than others, seemed best? Because, I say, it is most appropriate. For *oratio* and *sententia* are more general words, and for
this reason the Greeks who call it λόγος or reason usually add *first,
shortest* or *enuntiative.* And then *propositio* is an ambiguous word,
for it signifies sometimes the first part of a full comparison, sometimes the first part of a syllogism. But the Latin words *enuntiatum,
enuntiatio,* etc., seem to belong more to external speech than to
internal reasoning, whereas our logical disposition is entirely a
matter of reasoning, mentally conceived as well as vocal, and just
as words are the symbols and signs of simple notions, so *enuntiatum*
seems to be a symbol of an axiom mentally conceived. So we can
still retain the Latin words *enuntiatum, enuntiatio,* etc., if with
Aristotle [*Int.* 1.16a1–10] we divide speech into the exterior, which
is uttered vocally, and interior, which is only mentally conceived.

---

[1] 'Αξιόω in Greek, whence ἀξίωμα, means to deem worthy, to value.

Now the genus of axiom is rightly determined to be disposition, and not judgment, which, as I indicated above, is an effect of disposition and here in particular is that by which something is judged to be or not to be.

By the phrase "argument with argument" is meant that which argues, along with that which is argued.[2]

The end of disposition is that through it something may be shown to be or not to be, or that something may be said or not said of something else. Hence Aristotle, *Metaphysics* 8.10 [ix.10.1051b11–13]: "To be is to be organized and to be one, but not to be is not to be organized but to be many." And simple arguments considered alone do indeed signify something, but not that it is or is not, unless they are arranged. Now only in the indicative mode is it indicated that something is or is not, and not in the other modes unless they are reduced to the indicative, as in *Go away,* [126] which reduces to *I order you to go away. Thy will be done* reduces to *We pray that it be done. Would that I might be destroyed* reduces to *I desire to be destroyed. What is dialectic?* reduces to *I ask what it is.*

Now when in an axiom one argument is arranged with another, one of these must precede and the other follow; hence the parts of an axiom (Aristotle [*An. Pr.* i.1.24b17–19] calls them *terms*) are two, the antecedent and the consequent. The first one is commonly called the minor term or the subject, and the second one the major term or the predicate, because it contains what is predicated or said of the subject. Really, the latter names are more narrow than the former, as will appear below.

The common condition of an axiom is that threefold crypsis about which, and about whose threefold remedy, we spoke in the preceding chapter. There is deficiency when some part is missing, as in *departed, burst forth, escaped,* that is, Catiline did, or some one else did; or in *rains, thunders,* that is, God or heaven does. There is redundancy, which is also called amplification, when an argument and its synonym are used; or when to illustrate the argument some other thing is given. An example of the former is *Logic or dialectic is the art of reasoning well.* An example of the latter is

    Envy, the sluggard's vice, does not pass into a noble disposition.

---

    [2] This appears clearly to be the meaning of Milton's sentence. Downame's expansion shows that he took it this way. The emendation in Columbia, XI, 301 (and cf. p. 532), thus appears uncalled for.

Inversion occurs when the consequent is put in place of the antecedent, as in *A great gain is piety with a mind contented with its lot,* that is, piety with a mind contented with its lot is a great gain.

There are two remaining characteristics of an axiom, one of them arising from its disposition, the other pertaining to judgment. For the intellect, when it arranges [127] arguments, either combines them or divides them: but such combining and dividing are nothing other than affirmation and negation. But when it makes a judgment about this disposition, it judges it either to be true or to be false. But just as disposition is prior to judgment, so to be or not to be is something prior to and simpler than affirmation and negation, and both are prior to and simpler than judging to be true or false.

An axiom, therefore, is something affirmed or denied.

This is a twofold mode of enunciating, and there are not two species of what is enunciated, or of the axiom; for by contradiction the same axiom is affirmed and negated, but affirmation and negation are two species of enunciation—that is, of enunciating—and not of the thing enunciated. For both affirmation and negation can be called an enunciation, but never what is enunciated. Each of them is therefore a characteristic of an axiom, but not an axiom.

An axiom is affirmed when its connective is affirmed, and negated when the connective is negated. For the connective is the form of the axiom. In virtue of the connective the matter of the axiom is arranged and as it were animated; when the connective is affirmed or negated, the axiom itself is affirmed or negated. So affirmation and negation are characteristics of the connective and hence of the axiom and its species. But the connective is either a verb or a grammatical conjunction, as will appear later when the axiom is divided into its species.

Now this affirmation and negation, as we said above, is nothing other than a combining and dividing, for an axiom is affirmed when its consequent, by affirmation of the connective, is combined with its antecedent; and it is negated when, through negation of its connective, its consequent is divided from its antecedent. [128] Axiomatic negation is therefore not non-being, as topical negation was, but is only a division of being from being.

From this is derived the contradiction of axioms, when the same axiom is affirmed and negated.

CHAPTER III

ON THE TRUE AND THE FALSE

AN *axiom, then, is either true or false.*

This judgment is of course based on affirmation and negation, for when those things are affirmed which should be affirmed, and those negated which should be negated, the axioms are judged to be true, and conversely. Whence Aristotle, *De interpretatione* 1 [1.16a13]: "The true or false are in combining and dividing." But the false is not taught this way in art, but is judged, for a false enunciation is no less an axiom than a true one is, since there is the same disposition in both cases. The same cannot be said of the syllogism or of method.

An axiom is true when it enunciates as the thing is, and false otherwise.

Thus Plato in the *Cratylus* [385 B]. So for the forming of a judgment not only the teachings of art are required but also a knowledge of things themselves, because the thing itself is the norm and measure of truth.

A true axiom is either contingent or necessary. It is contingent when it is true in such a way that it can sometimes be false. For example: Fortune favors the bold.

So the judgment of this contingent truth is called opinion. A man's opinion of past and present things [129] can be certain, but of future things it cannot through nature alone be so certain. But even though not all times are present to God, as is commonly believed, for He can change the present though not the past, opinion nevertheless does not belong to God, since He knows all things equally through their causes.

But concerning contingent things, both past and present, human judgment is indeed called a firm opinion, but not knowledge, for knowledge comes from arguments which are immutably relevant, and arguments of this sort are not arranged in a contingent axiom. Nor is opinion regarding past and present things not had for the simple reason that these are manifest; rather, it is especially under these circumstances that we are said to have an opinion regarding contingent things; for if the things are doubtful, whether they be contingent or necessary, we have no opinion at all, but are in doubt; and even though they are necessary and most certain, if we do not know their cause, even of them we have only an opinion.

But, you will say, past and present things are not contingent, but necessary, because they are immutable; for what is done cannot be undone, and whatever is, as long as it is, necessarily is. The answer is that it is indeed necessary that what has been will have been, and what now is, is; but it does not follow that what has been or is is properly speaking necessary. For in a contingent axiom, either of the past or of the present, the necessity which appears is not absolute, nor does it depend upon the nature of the arranged things, but only upon their condition and upon the law of contradiction: for as long as something is, it cannot not be, nor as long as it is true can it be false, and yet what is now true can turn out sometimes to have been or to be about to be false. The same thing is to be said of future things; if something is certainly about to be, it is necessarily about to be true (for every axiom [130] is either true or false), but not necessary. If this is not admitted, then every future contingent will be necessary, which implies a contradiction. It should also be noted that future things themselves are neither true nor false, neither contingent nor necessary, for they do not yet exist, but only their affirmation or negation with respect to the future; and the same sort of view should be held concerning past things.

An axiom is necessary when it is always true and cannot be false. The closing phrase here is not superfluous, for something contingent, too, can always be true; but something necessary is not only always true, but it cannot be false. Thus also Aristotle in the *Posterior Analytics* 1.26 [i.33.88b32–33].

Conversely, what is always false and cannot be true is called an impossible axiom. Thus also Aristotle in *Metaphysics* 4.12 [v.12.1019b23–26].

Now this immutability of truth in the necessary and of falsity in the impossible depends on the complete agreement or the permanently irreconcilable disagreement of the arguments which are arranged in them. Likewise the mutability of the true or the false in the contingent and possible is seen in the slight agreement or disagreement of the arguments which are arranged in them.

From this it readily appears how useless was Aristotle's introduction [*Int.* 12.21a34–38] of that doctrine of the four modal formulas, *it is necessary, it is impossible, it is possible, it is contingent.* Examples are *It is necessary that a man be an animal, It is impossible that a man be a horse, It is possible that Socrates be rich, It is contingent that Socrates be learned.* These four modals do in some way affect the arrangement of pure enunciations. The pure is *Every man is an animal*, the modal *It is necessary that every*

man be an animal. Here *that every man be an animal,* although
in inverse order,[1] [131] is the subject of the modal enunciation, and
the mode *necessary* is the predicate. Indeed, of what use is it to
express by signs or modes the way in which the parts of an axiom
are related, when this can be more correctly judged from the very
arguments which are arranged in them, and to these modes there
can no less usefully be added many others, such as *easy, difficult,
honorable, base?*

Indeed, I should consider as more important than these primary
modals those secondary ones, as they are called, by which enunciations are commonly divided into *exclusives,* whose signs are
alone, only, merely, etc., as in *Faith alone justifies;* [2] *exceptives,*
whose signs are *except, besides, unless,* etc., as in *No one except
you knows;* and *restrictives,* whose signs are *as, to the extent that,
as far as, according as,* etc., as in *Man, as animal, senses.* And an
exclusive is such either in its subject or in its predicate: in its subject
when, by a prefixed exclusive sign, it excludes all other subjects
from the predicate. But reason would dictate this rule in vain if
it is permitted to certain modern logicians, and particularly to
Keckermann, suddenly to destroy it by a rule invented for this
purpose. "An exclusive," he says, "does not exclude the concomitants of the subject, as in *The Father alone is true God.* Here,"
he says, "there is not excluded the concomitant, namely, the Son
and the Holy Spirit." [3] But who does not see that this rule is
intended to ridicule that perfectly clear text in John 17.3? [4] No
more useful is that rule of the restrictive enunciation which he
gives in book 2, chapter 4 (a restrictive enunciation is one which
shows to what extent the subject agrees with the predicate): "A
contradictory predicate," he says, "is not by any limitation made
to agree with its subject," [5] from Aristotle, *Topics* 2 [ii.11.115a13–14],

---

[1] "Inverse order" because, in Milton's original Latin as in the present translation, "that every man be an animal," though the subject, is placed after the
predicate, "is necessary."

[2] Another instance of Milton's introduction of his theological doctrine. See
above, Milton's Preface and n. 3.

[3] A still further instance (see immediately preceding note) of Milton's theologizing. Bartholomæus Keckermannus, *Systema Logicæ Tribus Libris Adornatum
Pleniore Præceptorum Methodo et Commentariis,* Lib. I, cap. iv, in his *Operum
Omnium quæ Extant Tomus Primus* [-*Secundus*], I, col. 706: "*Exclusiva subiecti
non excludit concomitantia.* Ut: Solus pater est verus Deus, hîc non excluditur
concomitans filius et spiritus sanctus . . ."

[4] "And this is life eternal, that they might know thee, the only true God, and
Jesus Christ whom thou hast sent."

[5] Keckermannus, *Systema Logicæ,* col. 709.

the last chapter, section 4. What can be said that is more evident? And [132] yet there are those who, by interposing certain little distinctions, claim that *an accident can exist without its subject* (something inconsistent) *in the Lord's supper;* and then those who, by making up similar little distinctions, commit an equal contradiction by arguing *the human nature of Christ and thus even his body are infinite.*[6] But leaving aside the paradoxes of the theologians, let us return to the precepts of logic.

A necessary affirmative axiom is called κατὰ παντός, *or true of all* (de omni).

That is, when the consequent of the axiom, or the predicate, as they call it, is always true of every instance and of the whole antecedent or subject. Thus also Aristotle in the *Prior Analytics* 1.1 [i.1.24b28–32] and in the *Posterior Analytics* 1.4 [i.4.73b26–29], and he sometimes also calls this καθόλου, that is, *of the whole* (*Posterior Analytics* 2.13 [ii.13 passim]).

The axioms of the arts ought to be κατὰ παντός *in this way.*

That is, they ought to be true of every instance and of the whole, not false; necessary, not fortuitous, for otherwise they would not produce knowledge but opinion; lastly, they should be affirmed, not negated, for what is affirmed is firm, certain, and succinct, but what is negated is unsteady, uncertain, undefined, and teaches nothing. For example, if someone defined logic as not being the art of speaking well, he would not teach what logic is but what it is not, and that definition would fit all the other arts, except grammar, as well as logic. From this law some add that the axioms of the arts ought to be general. But this rule is not only of every instance but of the whole, and in the arts there are many precepts about special things, as in theology about Christ, in astronomy about the sun and the moon and the other planets; and in the other arts [133] other things of this sort which, since they are special, even though they cannot be called κατὰ παντός, they can nevertheless be called καθόλου, which suffices. For this reason, if someone objects that in general matters the precepts of the arts cannot be κατὰ παντός because of the multitude of exceptions, as is observed in grammar, the answer is that anomaly joined to analogy is the same as κατὰ παντός.[7]

---

[6] For Milton's rejection of ubiquitarianism in *Christian Doctrine,* see *Complete Prose,* VI, 442–43.

[7] That is, if you note the exceptions (anomalies) together with the rules, you have covered everything.

But the precepts of the arts should also be homogeneous and reciprocal.[8]

An axiom is homogeneous when its parts are essential to each other.

That is, either absolutely, as a form to the thing formed, a genus to a species, members to an integral whole, a definition to the thing defined; or relatively, as a subject to its proper attribute.

This is called καθ' αὐτό, *or per se.*

Another reason why the parts of an axiom should be essential to each other is so that a precept of art can be productive of knowledge, for of accidents, as Aristotle testifies [*An. Post.* i.6.75a18–20], there is no knowledge. There is no knowledge except through essence and cause. Aristotle, *Posterior Analytics* 1.4 [i.4.73b8–10], opposes τὰ καθ' αὐτό and τὰ συμβεβηκότα, that is, accidents. So it is not enough that the parts be in agreement with each other, but they must be essential. Since this comes about from the complete agreement of the arguments among themselves, from which we said above that a necessary axiom also comes about, I do not see what of great moment is added by this rule of καθ' αὐτό to the one above of κατὰ παντός, since no axiom can be necessary unless its parts are also essential to each other. Nor do I think that it is here prescribed that nothing heterogeneous or alien [134] be taught in an art, for here there is no question of the arrangement of precept with precept but only of argument with argument, which is the doctrine of the axiom and is understood from the very definition of the homogeneous and its examples.

An axiom is reciprocal when its consequent is always true of the antecedent, not only of every one and per se, but also reciprocally.

For example, *Man is a rational animal, a number is either even or odd, a wolf is born to howl.* This is called καθόλου πρῶτον, first of the whole, namely, because it is said of nothing else prior, and is therefore proximate and immediate, proper and equal—in a word, reciprocal. An example is risible of man, for every man is risible, and reciprocally everything risible is a man. Unless this rule is observed, it is not possible to avoid tautology in the arts. For an axiom fails to be reciprocal when the antecedent is not equal to the consequent, or conversely, but either something special is attributed to some genus or something general to some species; but the general is not said first of a species, for it is said in a prior way of the genus. But when what belongs to a genus is attributed

---

[8] Milton substitutes *reciproca* for Ramus's *catholica* here. See his discussion above.

to a species, then in the remaining species it is necessary to repeat the same thing that should have been said once and for all of the genus. So to this rule belongs that noble precept of art, γενικὰ γενικῶς, that *general* things are to be taught *generally* and once for all. This law is in the interests of brevity, and brevity is in the interests of intelligence and memory.

And these are the three laws of proper proofs in the arts. The first, κατὰ παντός, is the law of truth, because it demands from the relationship of agreement among the parts the necessary truth of the affirmed axiom. The second, καθ᾽ αὐτό, is the law [135] of justice, because it requires justice in the essential relationship of the parts. Therefore, they sin against this law who divide rhetoric into invention, arrangement, memory, etc., because they attribute to rhetoric parts which are proper to dialectic.[9] The third, καθόλου πρῶτον, can properly be called the law of wisdom, both because its judgment is the truest knowledge, as will be said later, and because it prohibits the vices contrary to wisdom, inequality or lack of agreement of the antecedent with the consequent, and tautology.

You will say that the first two laws are included in the third, and this must indeed be admitted. But just as a tetragon includes a triangle and a pentagon includes a tetragon, and these do not for this reason fail to be distinct figures, so these laws, even though any one of the later includes the earlier, had to be distinguished for the sake of clarity.

So the judgment of such axioms reciprocal in this way is the truest and the primary knowledge. It is primary because it is of principles which are per se indemonstrable and most evident in their own light and do not require the light of a syllogism or of any clearer argument for producing knowledge. It is therefore necessarily also true. [136]

---

[9] See Introduction, above, pp. 155–59.

CHAPTER IV

ON THE SIMPLE AXIOM

S*O much for the common features of an axiom. The species now follow.*
   An axiom is either simple or compound.

Thus also Aristotle in *De interpretatione* 1.5 [5.17a9–10, 20–22].
In the same sense propositions are commonly divided into categorical and hypothetical. But the categorical includes only the affirmed simple proposition which κατηγορεῖται, that is, is predicated, of a subject.

A simple axiom is one which is held together by a verbal
connective.

For since the connective, as we said above, is the form and as
it were the soul of an axiom, it follows that just as there are two
species of connectives, the verb and the conjunction (the former
of a simple axiom, the latter of a compound one), so the axiom,
too, on the basis of this division is divided into opposite forms or
species. But the connective of a simple axiom is not only a substantive verb, as it is called, but any verb signifying action or
passion contains within itself the force of a connective, and is either
the whole consequent or part of the consequent, as in *Socrates*
writes. For the opinion of some, that every verb should be resolved
into substantive and participle, so that by this means a substantive
verb may appear as the connective (to wit, *Socrates is writing*),
is often found to be quite unsuitable. Suppose someone should
resolve the statement *Socrates* [137] *docetur* (Socrates is being
taught) into *Socrates est doctus* ¹ (Socrates is learned); the latter
is a far different statement. Also, a substantive verb sometimes
includes both the connective and the whole consequent, as in
Socrates is, the dead are not, that is, they do not exist. But if
several verbs occur in one simple axiom—as in *Unequals are com-*
paratives whose quantity is not the same—it should be noted that
the verb which the grammarians call the principal one is the connective of the axiom.

   ¹ There is no present passive participial form in Latin, so a perfect passive
participle, as the nearest equivalent, is here used. The example is actually specious, appearing valid only because of the limits of Latin inflection and not really
telling against the contested opinion.

If the principal verb is affirmed, the simple axiom is affirmed;
if it is negated, the simple axiom is negated.[2]

But it is negated if the sign of negation precedes the principal
verb, for if it follows then the axiom is not negated but affirmed.
For example, in the statement *Socrates is a lion not necessarily*,
it is affirmed because the note of negation follows the verb; nor is
the whole consequent denied, but only the mode.

Now the signs of negation are not only the negative adverbs, but
also the exclusive particles (like *only* and *solely*) and verbs signifying disagreement or difference, like *to differ, to be opposed*, etc.

Let us now look at some examples. *Fire burns, fire is hot, fire
is not water.* Here *fire* is the antecedent, *burns* the consequent.

*And here is the primary arrangement of invented things, of cause
with effect, as in the first example; of subject with attribute, as in
the second; of things that disagree, as in the third example.*

*In this way any arguments mutually related can be enunciated,
those that agree by affirming, those that disagree by negating.* Exceptions are the full comparisons, in which there are two plainly
distinct axioms, the proposition and the reddition. For distributions, [138] which even Ramus considers an exception—such as *An
argument is either artificial or inartificial*—can be enunciated in
a simple axiom, as will be explained below. And so can diverse
things (which others consider an exception) if you enunciate them
in the form *Some eloquent man is not handsome*, and contraries,
as in *Virtue is not vice*, etc.

A simple axiom is either general or special.

This division is one of the simple axiom on the basis of an
associated quantity, which constitutes modes, not species. But in
a compound axiom no account is taken of quantity, but only of
the connective, as we shall explain below.

*An axiom is general when a common consequent is attributed in
a general way to a common antecedent.*

It is usually called *universal*. Now a consequent is attributed in
a general way to an antecedent when it is attributed to every and
to the whole or universal antecedent and to all those things which
are contained within its signification. For a general axiom, therefore, these three things are required: a general consequent and
antecedent, and an attribution in a general way. For a general
axiom was not to be defined from a universal mark or sign, since
very frequently the mark is not present, and when it is present it

---

[2] Despite Milton's italics, suggesting this is Ramus's text, it differs from
Ramus's.

is not the cause but only the sign that the axiom is general. In-
definites, therefore, as they are commonly called, even though they
have no general sign, are nevertheless general; as in the case of
definitions and the other precepts of the arts, which no one will
deny to be general, and which nevertheless do not have a general
sign prefixed. The signs of a general axiom, an affirmed one as
well as a negated one, are these: *every, none, always, never, everywhere, nowhere,* etc. [139]

*And so here contradiction does not always divide the true and
the false; but both parts of a contingent axiom can be false.* For
example:

*Every place in the city surpasses the delights of Bajae. No place
in the city surpasses the delights of Bajae.*

The same is true of noncontingent axioms.

For example, *Every animal is rational, no animal is rational.*
For these are not contingent, but rather absurd, because a special
consequent is attributed in a general way to a general antecedent.
Therefore, both parts of a general contradiction can be false, but
not both true, because falsehood is indeed multiple, while the true
is one.

*An axiom is special when the consequent is not attributed to
every antecedent.*

It is called special because it is enunciated of some species. And
so just as in a general axiom the consequent is attributed in a
general way, or to every instance and to the whole of the antecedent, so in a special axiom it is attributed in a special way, or not
to every instance.

In this axiom contradiction always divides the true and the false.

That is, one part of a special contradiction is always true, and
the other part always false.

A special axiom is particular or proper.

*It is particular when a common consequent is attributed to the
antecedent in a particular way.* [140]

It is a special axiom because it is enunciated of some species,
although the latter is uncertain and indefinite: but a consequent
is attributed in a particular way when it is attributed not to the
whole antecedent but to some part of it. The marks or signs of
particular attribution are *some, someone, sometimes, somewhere;*
and negations of general signs, such as *not none, not never, not
always, not every,* etc., which are equivalent to a particular. But
the consequent must be common, in accordance with the rule that
the consequent is never less than the antecedent but always either

greater or at least equal. Whence Aristotle, *Prior Analytics* 1.28 [i.27.43a40], denies that a singular is predicated of anything else.

What follows concerns the contradiction of particulars.

The contradiction to this axiom [i.e., the "particular" axiom] is something general.

Something is to be pardoned, nothing is to be pardoned; Some clemency is not to be praised, every clemency should be praised. Here to an affirmed particular a negated general axiom is opposed, and to a negated particular an affirmed general one. But if both parts are particulars, not only is there no contradiction of axioms, but no opposition at all. For example, *Some man is learned, some man is not learned.* For they are not attributed to the same subject, as required by the law of opposites. Therefore, both parts may be true, as is also the case when both parts are affirmed or negated, as in *Every man is rational, some man is rational,* or *No man is irrational, some man is not irrational.* In these not only is there no contradiction, but there is complete agreement, namely, of genus and species. [141]

A proper axiom (which others call a singular one) *occurs when a consequent is attributed to its proper antecedent.* Now, an antecedent is called proper in a logical sense when it designates a singular thing or person, whether it is expressed by a proper name or not. Such are demonstratives, as *this man.* Such also are singulars named by synecdoche of a genus, as the Poet for Homer or Virgil, the Philosopher for Aristotle or Plato, and the like.[3] But as for the consequent of this axiom, it can be either common or proper.

There is a contradiction of a proper axiom when both parts are proper, in which respect it differs from the particular, of which only one part has to be particular; but it agrees with the general axiom, both of whose parts are general, as in *Fabulla is beautiful,* whose negation and contradiction is *Fabulla is not beautiful.* So much for the simple axiom. [142]

---

[3] Milton is following Downame here, in great part verbatim, as commonly— a typical instance.

APPENDIX[4]

To these characteristics of the simple axiom the Aristotelians add equipollence and conversion.

Equipollence is defined as *an agreement in fact and in sense of enunciations which are verbally dissimilar;* thus, *Some man is [not]* [5] *learned* and *Not every man is learned* have the same value, and so for similar cases, as was said above in connection with signs. So equipollence, since it is constituted only verbally and not in fact, should be relegated to grammar or to rhetoric and vocabulary.

Conversion is the transposition of the predicate of one enunciation into the place of the subject with a view to proving another enunciation which results from that transposition or conversion. Three types of conversion are practiced: simple, *per accidens,* and by contraposition. There is simple conversion when the quantity and quality of the enunciation remain the same, and this occurs in three ways: in a universal negative, as in *No man is a stone, therefore no stone is a man;* in a particular affirmative, as in *Some man is white, therefore some white thing is a man;* and finally in a universal and necessary affirmative, as in *Every man is risible, therefore every risible thing is a man.* And this one is the truest of all conversions, and is also called *reciprocation,* namely, of a property with its subject, of the thing defined with its definition.

Conversion *per accidens* changes the quantity of the enunciation, namely, a universal affirmative [143] into a particular, as in *Every man is an animal, therefore some animal is a man.* They insist that this be called conversion *per accidens* because something else follows first, namely, *Some man is an animal,* from which there then follows by simple conversion the statement that *Therefore some animal is a man.*

Conversion by contraposition changes the quality of the enunciation, namely, a universal affirmative into a negative; it is a conversion in which in place of the subject and predicate is put the contradiction of each one's converse, as in *Every man is rational, therefore whatever is not rational is not a man; Everything*

---

[4] This Appendix is not in Ramus, nor is it in Downame, who only states here very briefly (p. 560) that equipollence belongs to grammar, if it is of any worth at all, not to logic, and that conversion has no use or result.

[5] Milton's text and the Columbia translation omit this negative, which the sense seems to require.

mortal has been begotten, therefore what has not been begotten is not mortal; They are to be admitted to the sacraments who have penitence and faith, therefore those who do not have them are not to be admitted. These three modes of conversion they derive from Aristotle, the first two from *Prior Analytics* 1.2 [i.2.25a6–10], the third from the *Topics* 2.1 [ii.4.111b22–24], and they were invented by him for the purpose of syllogistic reduction, whose usefulness will be shown below.

So that we are not perhaps deceived by this conversion—for it is not the most trustworthy—certain precautions are customarily taken. The first is that the terms should not be figurative, as in *Bread is the Body of Christ.*[6] The second is that nothing should be mutilated, as in *Someone sees the blind man, therefore the blind man sees someone,* for here *the blind man* is not the whole predicate, but rather *sees the blind man;* and as in *Every old man has been a boy, therefore some[7] boy has been an old man,* for here not *boy* but rather *has been a boy* is the whole predicate, and it should therefore be converted as *Someone who has been a boy is an old man.* The third precaution is that cases which are made oblique by the conversion be made direct again, as in *Some tree is in the field, therefore something in the field is a tree,* and not *therefore some field is in the tree.* [144]

But, leaving aside all these precautions, the more expeditious way is to reject any conversion, if it is doubtful, as a sophism of *petitio principii,* as something trying to prove a doubtful thing without a middle term; concerning this sophism we shall give some advice below. [145]

[6] Another instance of Milton's injection of theological matters into logic, despite his protest against doing so. See above, Milton's Preface and n. 3.

[7] The *quidem* of Milton's text, unaltered in Columbia, is here emended to *quidam.*

CHAPTER V

ON THE COPULATED AXIOM

A compound axiom is one which is held together by a conjunction.

This genus of axiom Aristotle entirely passes over. It is commonly called a *hypothetical proposition*, that is, a conditional, but too narrowly so, since this expression does not fit all compounds, as will appear in its proper place. Now, it is called compound since it is a multiple statement which can be divided into several simple ones. But it should not be said that it is composed of simple axioms, but rather of arguments which, put together by means of the connective conjunction, make a multiple statement. The reason why an axiom is a compound one is that the arguments joined in it agree and call for composition with each other. But no account is taken here of its quantity—that is, whether it is general or special—but only of its being compound. Now just as the verb was the connective of a simple axiom, so the conjunction is the connective of the compound one, and therefore is its form and as it were its soul.

And so from an affirmed or negated conjunction the axiom is affirmed or negated. If the conjunction is not negated, the axiom will not be negated, even when all of its parts are negated.

And of a contradiction one part is true, the other false. About this the common run of logicians is silent.

A compound enunciation [1] *is, according to its conjunction, either congregative or segregative.* [146]

A congregative axiom is one whose parts are grouped together by its conjunction as simultaneously true, that is, not only by the grammatical conjunction but also by any relation at all of statements. But although this relation, whether grammatical or logical, is multiple—namely, of essence, consequence or cause, quantity, quality, time, place—the relation of essence (whose signs are *he who, that which*) and of place (whose signs are *where, there*) is to be referred to simple axioms. The rest will be treated in their place.

A congregative axiom enunciates all agreeing things by affirming and all disagreeing things by negating. That is, if one of the agreeing

[1] *Enunciatum* in the Latin, apparently by oversight for *axiōma*. Despite Milton's italics, suggesting that this sentence is in Ramus's text, it is not.

things is attributed to a subject, so is the other, and conversely if one is negated so is the other; if one of the disagreeing things is affirmed of a subject, the other is negated, and conversely. Thus, agreeing things must here always be affirmed or negated at the same time, but disagreeing things not at the same time.

A congregative axiom is either copulated or connected. A copulated axiom is one whose conjunction is copulative, as in *Æneid* 1 [i.85–86]:

> Together flow the east and south winds,
> And the stormy southwest wind.

Here, then, there will be negation and contradiction, if the conjunction is negated: *Not together flow the east and south winds,* etc. *Socrates was both learned and handsome: Socrates was not both learned and handsome.* If the negation went *Socrates was neither learned nor handsome* (which mode of contradiction should be applied when all the parts are false), then the contradiction would not be axiomatic, for not the connective but the parts would be negated; for copulation signifies [147] that both are true at the same time and its negation that not both are true. But the second negation signifies that neither is true, as if it were said that *Socrates was both not learned and not handsome.* Then, too, in a compound axiom one part of a contradiction is true and the other false; but here both are false. Therefore the axiom *Socrates was neither learned nor handsome* is rather an affirmed copulated axiom whose parts are negated. But the negation of a copulated axiom can also be made by a separate axiom, when not all its parts are false, as will be apparent below. Finally, the conjunction in these cases is often not present but is understood.

A true judgment of a copulated axiom depends on the truth of all the parts, a false judgment on at least one false part. That is, a copulated axiom is judged to be true if all the parts are true at the same time, and false if even one part is false. Gellius, 16.8 [*NA* xvi.8.11], teaches the same thing. For in a copulated axiom, the truth of all the parts is intended, since all the parts are enunciated absolutely as true at the same time.

Akin to this genus is the axiom of related quality, whose conjunction is more logical than grammatical, namely, *relation itself.*

Now a related quality is a complete similarity, as its very signs testify: *as . . . such, just as . . . so. Eclogue* 3 [5.45–46]:

> Such your verses to us, divine poet,
> As sleep to the weary upon the grass.

Here the copulated judgment would be like saying that *Sleep is pleasing to the weary, and in the same way your verses are pleasing to us.* The negation of this is *Not in the same way your verses . . . as sleep,* etc. [148]

To this locus belongs also the relation of quantity in full comparisons, whose signs are, in comparisons from an equal, *the same . . . as, as much . . . as, by as much . . . as, as many . . . as, by that . . . by which;* from the greater, *not only . . . but also;* from the lesser, *not only not . . . but not even* (the sign of an affirmed copulated axiom whose parts are negated), and *both . . . and.* But this relation, both of quality and quantity, if enunciated hypothetically and not absolutely, is to be classed rather as a connected axiom.

But relations of place are more properly classed as simple axioms, as was said above. For not even in an example of the sort *Where there are friends there are resources* is there a copulated judgment, but a simple and indeed a general one, to the effect that *Every rich man has friends.*

CHAPTER VI

ON THE CONNECTED AXIOM

A *connected axiom is a congregative one whose conjunction is connexive.*
For example, *if* and *unless* when used affirmatively. For *unless* has the same value as *if not,* by which not the whole axiom but only its antecedent is negated. For example, in *Æneid 2* [ii.79–80]:

> If Fortune made Sinon wretched,
> Then, wicked, she will make him vain and a liar. [149]

The negation of this, by negation of the conjunction, is *It is not the case that if Fortune made Sinon wretched, then, wicked, she will make him vain and a liar.*

Sometimes also this conjunction is more clearly negated by negating the consequence. For example, not necessarily, not immediately, not for that reason, not therefore, for by these expressions it is not the consequent of the axiom that is more clearly negated— for this would not produce a contradiction—but rather the very consequence of the parts, which is the logical conjunction, as in *Pro Amerino* [33.94]: "Not necessarily am I a murderer if I associate with murderers." And in *De fato* [12.28]: "Nor if every enunciation is true or false does it immediately follow that causes are immutable."

For affirmation signifies that if the antecedent occurs then so also does the consequent. So negation and contradiction establish that if the antecedent occurs the consequent does not for that reason occur.

A connected axiom can also be contradicted by a separate axiom, as in *Although every enunciation is either true or false, causes are nevertheless not immutable.* This will appear in the following chapter.

But when you judge a connected axiom to be absolutely true, that is, per se and by its nature, *you also judge it to be necessary: and you understand this necessity to result from the necessary connection of the parts, which can occur even when the parts are false.*

For example, *If man is a lion, then he is also a quadruped* is a necessary connected axiom, because the connection of the argu-

ments which are here connected—namely, lion and quadruped—
is necessary, being one of species with genus. Whence there is
produced an axiom which is generally true and therefore necessary;
the fact that *Every lion is a quadruped* is an indication of absolute
truth in the connected axiom. Thus, *If Socrates is a man, then he
is also an animal* is absolutely true and necessary, since every man
[150] is an animal, and the consequent of this connected axiom
cannot be false unless the antecedent is also false, which is another
sign of absolute truth.

But if the consequent is false, then the antecedent is also false.
If that, then this; if not this, then also not that. And so, as we
have already demonstrated, if the connection is absolutely true, it
will also be necessary; but if it is true conditionally and by a
convention without which the connected axiom would not be true
per se and by its nature, it will be only contingent.

*But if the connection is contingent and is proposed only in view
of its probability, then a judgment concerning it will be only an
opinion.*

For example, Terence in *Andria* [ii.1.322]:

Pamphilus, if you do that, you see the last of me today.

That is, if you take Philumena as your wife, I shall die today;
which no one would consider to follow except on the assumption
that Charinus, who says this, is hopelessly in love with Philumena.
For there is no necessary connection, per se, between the marriage
of Pamphilus and the death of Charinus. But if someone, out of
the violence of his love, thinks there is, then his judgment will not
be knowledge but opinion.

Now in order that we can judge which connection is absolutely
true and which not, we should ascertain whether the arguments
which are connected in the axiom mutually agree or not, and in
what way. For example, *If it is day, then there is light* is a necessary
connected axiom, since day or the sunrise is the cause of light. *If
it is day, then Dion walks* is either a false or a contingent connected
axiom, since there is no relation of absolute agreement between
day and Dion. [151]

Akin to the connected axiom is the relation of consequence,
which by some is called the *relation of cause* and which produces
an axiom which the Stoics call *causal,* according to Laertius, *In
Zenone* [Diog. Laert. vii.72], namely, because the antecedent is
cause of the consequent and, moreover, its connective a causal
conjunction like *since, because, whereas,* to which correspond
therefore or *certainly,* as in *Since Tully is an orator, he is certainly*

expert at speaking. But although these relatives are akin to connected axioms, they are still somewhat different, for in the antecedent of a connected axiom there is a certain condition, but in this sort of relative none; and a true connected axiom can consist of false parts, while this sort of relative or causal axiom cannot be true unless its antecedent is true, as in *Since it is day, the sun is above the horizon.*

Akin to the connected axiom is also the relation of time, as Ramus himself says in chapter 13 below.

Now the relation of time has the signs *then . . . when, as long as, while, as long as . . . so long.* For example, in the *Epistles* of Ovid [*Her.* v.29–30]:

> When Paris can leave Oenone and still breathe,
> The waters of Xanthus will return to their source.

Thus, *As long as you are fortunate you will count many friends.*

A connected axiom can also be enunciated not only without any sign of relation but also without one of connection, as in *If the cause is given, so is the effect given. Do this and you will live.* And Ovid in his *Epistles* [*Her.* xv.23]: "Take the lyre and the quiver, and you will be recognized, Apollo." Sometimes with two negatives, as in Cicero, *Pro Milone* [31.84]: "This fragile human body is not ruled by the mind, and the universal body of the world is not ruled by a mind." [152]

CHAPTER VII

ON THE DISCRETE AXIOM

A segregative axiom is one whose conjunction is segregative. Therefore it enunciates arguments which disagree.
A segregative axiom is either discrete or disjunct.

A discrete axiom is one whose conjunction is discretive. It is called discrete because by the segregative conjunction there are distinguished and segregated especially those things which disagree slightly and by reason only.

So from among arguments which disagree it enunciates especially those which are diverse.

Especially, because the signs of diverse arguments, such as *not this . . . but that,* as was said in the preceding book, in the section on the diverse, are sometimes applied to opposites. But just as the doctrine of the diverse, so also that of the discrete axiom is suitable only for distinctions and not for conclusions, and is therefore omitted by the other dialecticians, who relate everything to the syllogism. But no activity of reason should be passed over in logic. For example, in *Tusculan Disputations* 5 [v.33.95–96]: "Although they are judged by the senses of the body, they should nevertheless be referred to the spirit." The negation and contradiction of this is *It is not the case that although they are judged by the senses of the body, they should nevertheless be referred to the spirit,* or *Although they are judged by the senses of the body, they should nevertheless not be referred to the spirit.* For *nevertheless* is here the main conjunction. But just as a discrete axiom can be the negation and contradiction of a copulated and a connected axiom, so in turn a copulated and connected axiom can be the negation and contradiction of a discrete axiom, [153] as in *Although he is without fault, he is nevertheless not free of suspicion,* whose contradiction through a copulated axiom is *He is without fault and free of suspicion,* through a connected axiom, *If he is without fault he is free of suspicion.*

A discrete axiom is judged to be true and legitimate if its parts are not only true but also discrete; otherwise it is false or ridiculous.

For example, *Although Ulysses was handsome he was nevertheless not ineloquent* is false because its antecedent is false. But as long as the consequent is true, the axiom will be true even though the antecedent is only conceded to be true. But this—*Although Menelaus was handsome, he was nevertheless eloquent*—is not discrete, and indeed not even segregative, for of any segregative axiom the parts are segregated as not simultaneously true, whereas here they are grouped together as simultaneously true. *Although Ulysses was eloquent he was nevertheless not ineloquent* is ridiculous, because the parts are not discrete but opposite. [154]

Chapter VIII

ON THE DISJUNCT AXIOM

A *disjunct axiom is a segregative axiom whose conjunction is disjunctive.*

For example, *Either it is day or it is night. This enunciation is either true or false.* For when from Cicero [*Acad.* ii.29.95] there is cited the example, *Every enunciation is either true or false,* it appears to be a distribution rather than a disjunction.[1] But a distribution, in so far as the parts are enunciated of a divided whole, is a simple and general axiom, and so neither compound nor disjunct. For neither do the parts of a distribution, even though they are mutually opposed, produce any opposition or disjunction, but they are subjects with respect to one and the same whole, and in the consequent of one and the same simple axiom agree, through the verbal copula, with the whole which is the antecedent; but apart from a distribution, where they are enunciated not of a whole but of some part or species of the whole, they do finally produce a disjunct axiom, as the one proposed above, *This enunciation is either true or false.*

Here what is expressed is that only one of the disjuncts is true.

Namely, because here only opposites should be arranged. And that is always indicated by the person discoursing, although [155] it sometimes happens that more than one of the disjuncts or none at all is true. The negation and contradiction will therefore be *It is not either day or night.*

And by contradiction is signified that not necessarily is either one of the disjuncts true.

For if the disjunction is absolutely true it is also necessary; and the disjunct parts are opposites without any intermediate. On these matters see the chapter on contradictories in the preceding book.

But although an absolutely true disjunction is also necessary, there is no necessity that its parts taken separately be necessary.

For example, *Tomorrow either it will rain or it will not rain,* is a necessary disjunction because it consists of contradictories which are contraries without an intermediate; and yet *Tomorrow it will rain* and *Tomorrow it will not rain* are both contingent axioms. So also with *The man is either good or he is not good,* etc.

---

[1] Milton is differing with Ramus here.

For the necessity of a disjunction depends on the necessary op-position and disjunction of its parts and not on their necessary truth.

Hence there is a solution of that argument of Chrysippus the Stoic and other ancients in Cicero's *De fato* [10.20–21] by which they tried to prove that all future things are necessary and as it were fated, since it is necessary that they be either true or false. The disjunction is indeed true, as we said, but each part of the disjunction will be just like its cause, either necessary or contingent, that is, free or fortuitous. [156]

So much for the necessary disjunction, the judgment of which is knowledge.

But a disjunction is often conditional.

As when it is asked whether Cleon will come or Socrates, because it has been agreed that only one or the other will come.

So if a disjunction is contingent (it is contingent if its parts have an intermediate) *it is not absolutely true but only an object of opinion.*

This kind is frequent in the practice of men, as when Caesar [Plut. *Vit. Cæs.* 7.3] says to his mother: "Today you will see me either pontifex or exile." Ovid in the *Epistle of Leander* [*Her.* xviii. 195–96]:

> Either a successful venture will leave me safe
> Or there will be death, the end of troubled love.

Chapter IX

ON THE SYLLOGISM AND ITS PARTS

A ND so of the sort just described is the axiomatic or noetic arrangement of the axiom which is manifest *per se;* there follows the dianoetic arrangement.

There is a dianoetic arrangement when one axiom is deduced from another.

The Greek word διάνοια signifies a discourse of mind and reason, which occurs chiefly when [157] one statement is by reasoning deduced from another.

A dianoetic arrangement is a syllogism or method.

A syllogism is a dianoetic arrangement by which a question is so arranged with its argument that if the antecedent is given the question is necessarily concluded.

It is *dianoia:* it is therefore a discourse of the mind and reason by which one thing is by reasoning gathered from another; the very term syllogism signifies this gathering, as it were, by the person reasoning. Indeed, this gathering or deducing has arisen from the weakness of the human intellect, which weakness, being unable by an immediate intuition to see in an axiom the truth and falsity of things, turns to the syllogism, in which it can judge whether they follow or do not follow.

And so when an axiom is doubtful it becomes a question, and to achieve conviction regarding it there is need of a third argument arranged in proper order with the question.

The parts of a question are commonly called its terms; and the antecedent is called the minor term, the consequent the major term, because the consequent is generally broader than the antecedent. The third argument is called by Aristotle [*An. Pr.* i.4.25b36–37] the *middle* and the *middle term*. Not because the middle term in the syllogism is always placed between the two terms of the question, but because like an arbiter it decides and judges concerning the mutual agreement or disagreement of the two terms. And these are the three arguments out of which alone every syllogism is constructed, namely two in the question, and a third argument; and they are commonly called *the three terms*. But these three terms are not always simple words, but sometimes rather long expressions, nor are they always expressed in direct cases, [158] but sometimes in oblique.

The parts of a syllogism are two, the antecedent and the consequent. The antecedent of a syllogism is the part in which the question is arranged with the argument.

The antecedent of a syllogism has two parts, the proposition [1] *and the assumption,* which are commonly called the *premises.*

The proposition is the first part of the antecedent, by which at least the consequent of the question is arranged with the argument.

At least; because sometimes the *whole* question is arranged with the argument in the proposition, as will appear below.

The proposition is commonly called the *major,* either because it has greater force (for it is as it were the basis and foundation of the argumentation), or because the major term, that is, the consequent of the question, is put in the proposition.

The assumption is the second part of the antecedent, which is taken from the proposition.

For from the proposition is taken either the third argument or the whole assumption, as will be clear below. So the third argument or the middle term is recognized by its being posited twice prior to the conclusion. The assumption is commonly called the minor proposition, either because it has less force, being plainly deduced from the proposition, or because the minor term, that is, the antecedent of the question, is often arranged in it, but not always, as we shall see below.

But the consequent is the part of the syllogism which combines the parts of the question and concludes the question. Whence it is called the combination and the conclusion.

From this it follows that the conclusion, both in its words and in the order of its terms, must clearly be the same as [159] the proposed question; and that otherwise the conviction regarding the syllogism is weak and fails, as it were, to return what was deposited in it. From this is understood, secondly, the rule that *the third argument or the middle term never enters the conclusion.* The reason is that the middle is not what is concluded and not that of which anything is concluded, but is rather that by whose presence the question is concluded, or its two terms are judged to be mutually in agreement or disagreement. So if the middle term or any part of it is in the conclusion, it vitiates the syllogism. This is most easily detected if not only the proposed question but also something that was repeated twice in the premises enters into the conclusion.

But since in every syllogism, as is certain from its definition, a question is so arranged with an argument that, by positing the

---

[1] See n. 6, Book I, chap. xxi, above, concerning another use of the term "proposition" (*propositio*) in Milton's text.

antecedent, that is, by conceding the premises, the question is necessarily concluded (which necessity is one not of the consequent but of the consequence, not of the matter but of the form), it is obvious that in the form of the syllogism there is no difference between the contingent and the necessary, but that every syllogism concludes necessarily (as is testified also by Aristotle in the *Prior Analytics* 1.33 [i.32.47a33–36, 33.47b15–17]); and that this necessity depends on the proper arrangement of the question with the third argument and not on any necessary truth of the parts arranged in the antecedent. This refutes those who commonly divide the syllogism into the dialectical and apodictic, namely, the probable and the demonstrative or necessary, both because that distinction is one of axioms and because a syllogistic consequence is just as necessary in the contingent and even the false as in the true and necessary; indeed, from false premises a conclusion follows necessarily, sometimes a true one, sometimes a false one, as in *Every lion is a quadruped,* [160] *Socrates is a lion, therefore Socrates is a quadruped.* In this respect a syllogism is somewhat like a connected axiom, from which it perhaps takes its origin, for just as a connected axiom with false parts can be necessary, as long as the connection itself is true, as in *If a lion is a quadruped, and Socrates a lion, then Socrates is necessarily a quadruped,* so a syllogism concludes necessarily, from true parts indeed only the true, but from false parts both the false and the true, as long as the arrangement itself is proper.

The Aristotelians divide the syllogism into the true and the false or apparent; and the true, whose matter is true, they divide into the dialectical or probable, whose matter is contingent, and the apodictic or the demonstrative and necessary. And the last they divide into the perfect, which [2] is called διότι or *a priori,* in which an accident is affirmed of a subject through a posited efficient or final cause, but is negated if the cause is removed; and the imperfect, called τοῦ ὅτι or *a posteriori,* in which an accident is proved of a subject through its effect. But this division, of whatever kind it is, since it is proper to the axiom and in no way concerns either the form of the syllogism, as in the dialectic and apodictic, or in general the art of logic, as in the false or sophistical, is better rejected. [161]

---

[2] The present translation takes Milton's *quæ* as an error for *quod;* otherwise apparently no sense can be made of his text.

APPENDIX ON PARALOGISMS WHICH ARE
REFUTED BY THIS GENERAL DOCTRINE OF THE SYLLOGISM[3]

AND this was the general doctrine of the syllogism. Now just as the straight is indicative both of itself and of the oblique, so the doctrine of truth, when rightly presented, indicates through itself all error and refutes it. But since not every man's perspicacity or allotted share of talent is such that he can either by the rules themselves notice all the devices of an adversary or always have in mind all the rules of the art, it will not be out of place to give here separately some advice concerning the main fallacies which are customarily committed against this general doctrine of the syllogism.

So since we are taught by the general doctrine of the syllogism that only three arguments or three terms should be arranged in a syllogism, it is easily seen that every syllogism in which more or fewer than three terms are arranged sins against this general doctrine. But the terms are not so much the words as the meanings and significations of the words.

The fallacy of too many terms is either obvious or hidden. It is obvious (to pass over trifles regarding accent, figure of speech, so-called multiple interrogations, and the like) when three terms are distinctly counted in the proposition, as in *Whoever is good and a dialectician is a good dialectician, Cleanthes is good and is a dialectician, therefore* [162] *he is a good dialectician.* This is called fallacy of composition, because it wrongly compounds things that are divided. Conversely, *Whoever is a good dialectician is good and is a dialectician, Cleanthes,* etc. This is fallacy of division because it wrongly divides things that are compound, or because it proposes compound things but concludes them divided. The same fallacy is committed also without a conjunction, as in *A good cithara singer is good, Nero is a good cithara singer, therefore he is good.* Here good is arranged with *cithara singer* in the proposition in a double meaning; there are therefore four terms. So also when with different words one thing is clearly in the proposition while another is in the assumption, as in *The right hand of God is ev-*

---

[3] This Appendix is not in Ramus nor in Talon's commentary. But in this same place Downame has inserted a section on exactly this same subject, which Milton here appropriates and expands. Downame has another one-page section entitled "Refutation of Sophisms" at the end of Book II, chap. xvi, where Milton has no such thing.

erywhere, the humanity of Christ sits at the right hand of God, therefore the humanity of Christ is everywhere.

The hidden fallacy of too many terms occurs either through *homonymy* or *amphiboly.*

Homonymy or equivocation occurs, first, when a twofold meaning is given for a simple expression or a single term, as in *Leo* [Latin, a lion] *is a beast, Leo is pope, therefore a pope is a beast.* Secondly, it occurs when an argument is put in its proper sense in one part and figuratively in another, or in one part for the thing itself and in another for some artificial notion of the thing. Of the latter sort are the expressions of the arts, such as *Potent is an adjective, the king is potent, therefore the king is an adjective. Animal is a genus, a man is an animal, therefore a man is a genus.*

Amphiboly or ambiguity occurs either in syntax or in the thing itself. In syntax, as in *Money that is Caesar's is possessed by Caesar, this money is Caesar's,*[4] *therefore it is possessed by Caesar.* Ambiguity in the thing itself, which is also called *improper exposition,* occurs when the attribute of a thing in the assumption is not the same as the one in the proposition, whereas if the attribute is changed the argument is changed, as in *You have eaten the meat you bought, you bought raw meat, therefore you have eaten raw meat.* Here the proposition speaks of [163] meat and the substance of meat, while the assumption speaks of its quality; the proposition should therefore have been . . . *the sort of meat you bought.* The same fallacy occurs when that which is proposed *in the abstract,* as they say, is assumed in the concrete, as in *Whiteness tends to dilate the sight, a wall is white, therefore a wall tends to dilate the sight.*[5] Also when in the copula itself there is a concealed fourth

---

[4] I.e., in the sense of Matt. 22:21, this money is imperial coinage, stamped with Caesar's image.

[5] The terminology in this example goes back to Plato, *Timaeus* 67 D–E (cf. 45 C ff.), where there is developed a theory of sight and color based on a particle theory of light. According to the theory, seeing takes place when light particles streaming from the eyes encounter light particles streaming from external objects. Object-emitted particles that are of the same size as particles in the visual stream are perceived as the transparent medium, and the larger object-emitted particles contract or compress the visual stream whereas the smaller ones dilate or penetrate it: "Τὰ μὲν οὖν ἴσα ἀναίσθητα, ἃ δὴ καὶ διαφανῆ λέγομεν, τὰ δὲ μείζω καὶ ἐλάττω, τὰ μὲν συγκρίνοντα, τὰ δὲ διακρίνοντα αὐτήν [ὄψιν]." The dilative or penetrative particles produce the sensation of white, and the contractive or compressive ones produce the sensation of black: "Οὕτως οὖν αὐτὰ προσρητέον, τὸ μὲν διακριτικὸν τῆς ὄψεως λευκόν, τὸ δ' ἐναντίον αὐτοῦ [συγκριτικὸν] μέλαν . . ." Aristotle uses Plato's terminology (but without explicit mention of the particle theory of light) to give an example of differences constitutive of contrary species within a genus: "Οἷον εἰ τὸ λευκὸν καὶ μέλαν ἐναντία, ἔστι δὲ τὸ μὲν

term, as in *Fortitude is not clemency, of a prince is fortitude,*[6] *therefore of a prince is not clemency.* Here the verb *is* in the major signifies *to be,* but in the minor it signifies *to have,* and it brings about a change of direct cases into oblique ones, which indicate that there are four terms. *No boy has lived long, Nestor was a boy, therefore Nestor has not lived long.* Here the major speaks of one who is a boy and the minor of one who was a boy, and these are two terms. There are, then, four terms when there is more in the conclusion than in the premises.

But the terms are fewer than three when the third argument is lacking. This occurs whenever something identical in meaning or something equally obscure is taken as an argument (for an identical thing is not a third thing and something equally obscure is not an argument), which is called a begging of the question or of what was in the question, since the question itself is postulated so that it may be conceded gratuitously, that is, without an argument, as in *Every glaive is sharp, every sword is a glaive, therefore every sword is sharp.* Or *What every man is, individual men are; every man is just; therefore individual men are just.* Here I class that much debated syllogism: *What you have not lost you have, you have not lost your horns, therefore you have horns.* To have and to lose are privatives and as such without intermediate; therefore *not to lose* and *to have* are the same; so there is here no middle term, but it is as though [164] you said *What you have, you have; you have horns; therefore you have them.*[7] Of this type is the case in which an incomplete third argument is assumed from the proposition, as in *All the apostles are twelve, Peter and John are apostles; therefore Peter and John are twelve.* Here *all,* taken collectively, is part of the third argument and should have been taken *in toto*

διακριτικὸν χρῶμα τὸ δὲ συγκριτικὸν χρῶμα, αὗται αἱ διαφοραὶ τὸ διακριτικὸν καὶ συγκριτικὸν πρότεραι" (*Metaph.* x.7.1057b8–11; cf. *Top.*
1.15.107b26–33; iii.5.119a30–33). The expressions διακριτικόν and συγκριτικόν
were translated as *disgregativum* and *congregativum* in the medieval Latin versions of Aristotle. See, e.g., Thomas Aquinas, *In Metaphysicam Aristotelis Com-
mentaria,* ed. M.-R. Cathala (Turin: Marietti, 1935), p. 594, for a Latin version
of the passage just quoted from the *Metaphysics:* "Ut si album et nigrum contraria:
est autem hic quidem disgregativus color, ille vero congregativus color: hæ
differentiæ congregativum et disgregativum priores."

[6] Word-for-word rendition of the Latin, *principis est fortitudo,* which in the
Latin means "The prince has fortitude."

[7] This solution would not be admitted by many, who find rather four terms
here: In the proposition the first term is really *what you have possessed and have
not lost.*

in the assumption. With this sophism are to be classed, then, all conversions of enunciations whenever they purport to prove a doubtful matter not by an argument or a middle term but by conversion alone, about which we warned above. And usually in these ways do offenses against the general form of the syllogism occur.

The matter of a syllogism is defective whenever one part or both parts of the antecedent are false, and this occurs according to as many modes as there are types of arguments. Although both the truth and the falsity of the arguments are judged in an axiom, nevertheless, because the arguments themselves are arranged in a syllogism, we shall here touch briefly on those modes in particular which by the dialecticians are called defective either in their matter alone or partly in their matter and partly in their form.

The first defective mode concerns matter alone and is called that of *non-cause as cause.* Now the term cause is here used for any argument whatsoever, even that of non-effect as effect, non-subject as subject, and so on. The definition of the individual arguments easily refutes this fallacy.

The second defective mode is the so-called fallacy *of accident,* or, what is the same thing, a proceeding from something said in a relative sense to something said in an absolute sense, or, conversely, from something said in an absolute sense to something said in a relative sense. This happens whenever what belongs to an adjunct is affirmed of its subject, or conversely, when what belongs to a subject is attributed to its adjunct. For example, *Things which should not be restored to an insane master should not be restored to a master,* [165] *arms should not be restored to an insane master, therefore not to a master.* Or conversely, *Things which should be restored to a master should be restored also to an insane master, arms should be restored to a master, therefore to an insane master.* In these the proposition is always false.

The third defective mode is *ignoratio elenchi* (*elenchus* being any refutation, whether true or false), occurring when the laws of opposition are not observed for the numerically same thing, according to the same thing, in relation to the same thing, and at the same time, as in *The blind see, those who lack sight are blind, therefore those who lack sight see.* The proposition has to be distinguished in this sense, that *Those who were blind now see.* Again, *If anyone does not see, he is blind, a sleeping person does not see, therefore he is blind.* This is not in relation to the same thing, for the proposition speaks of the power of sight, the assumption of the act of seeing; or there are four terms, and it can be called a defective exposition. According to others *ignoratio elenchi* occurs when the state of a controversy is clearly changed or distorted, or the conclusion of an adversary is not directly opposed to our thesis according to the canons of a proper opposition.

The fourth defective mode is the fallacy *of the consequent,* or of comparatives which are indeed derived from contraries but handled by relating equals, when it is argued that contraries are the consequents of contraries, a rule whose falsity was abundantly shown in book 1, chapter 18. An example is *Things equal to the same thing are equal to each other, therefore things unequal to the same thing are unequal to each other;* as in *Two and two are both unequal to five, therefore they are unequal to each other;* and *Two sides of a square are not symmetrical with the diagonal, therefore they are not symmetrical with each other.* [166]

CHAPTER X

ON THE SIMPLE CONTRACTED SYLLOGISM

A *syllogism is either simple or compound.*
It is simple when the part which is the consequent of the question is arranged in the proposition, and the part which is the antecedent is arranged in the assumption.

Just as the general form of the syllogism was the arrangement of the question with the argument, so a special form is the arrangement of the question with an argument of any given species. For example, *Man is an animal, Socrates is a man, therefore Socrates is an animal.* From this it is easily seen that if the major term of the question is not arranged in the major proposition and the minor term in the minor proposition, then there is no proper syllogism. But if it sometimes happens in practice that the antecedent of the question appears to be arranged in the proposition and the consequent in the assumption, we must understand that the parts of the syllogism are being inverted, as in *Socrates is a man, man is an animal, therefore Socrates is an animal.*

Now follows the division of the simple syllogism into its proper modes which arise from the relationship of its parts, that is, its axioms.

A simple syllogism is affirmed when all of its parts are affirmed. It is negated when one part of the antecedent is negated with the conclusion, and not when all parts are—as it is affirmed when all parts are affirmed—for unless a third argument agrees with one part of the question, it proves nothing. [167]

But in order that the whole nature of the syllogism may be understood (which I think can be done most conveniently at this point) it is necessary to know that it is founded principally on two laws, one taken from the locus about equals, the other from genus. From the locus about equals: *Things that agree in some third thing agree with each other;* and, conversely, *Things that do not agree in one third thing do not agree with each other.* From the locus on genus: *Whatever is attributed generally to a genus is also attributed to all the species contained under that genus.* The latter rule is called in the schools the *dictum of every and none.* The former was first discovered by the geometers, and readily, with sensory perception leading the way, and it is taught by Aristotle in the *Prior Analytics* 1.1 [i.1.24b27–31]: "For just as in the case of a measure, if it agrees with two lines equally it demonstrates that those two lines agree mutually, or are equal"; clearly in the same way if the middle term agrees with the two terms of the conclusion it demonstrates like a measure that those two terms agree mutually; and conversely. So if a question is to be affirmed one must through all the loci of invention seek the argument which agrees with both parts; if the question is to be negated, then one must seek an argument which agrees with one and disagrees with the other; for if it disagrees with both it cannot be a third argument, for it will prove nothing. For example, it is asked *whether Socrates is an animal.* If this question is to be affirmed, then for the two arguments in the question—*Socrates* and *animal*—there must be sought some third argument which agrees with both parts of the question. *Man* is an argument of this sort, for *man* agrees with *animal* as a species with its genus, and with *Socrates* as a genus with its species; therefore, *Socrates* and *animal* do mutually agree, and so *Socrates is an animal.* But if the question is to be negated, as *Socrates is not a brute beast,* there must be sought [168] a third argument which disagrees with only one of the parts. *Man* is an argument of this sort, for a *man* is not a *brute beast,* but *Socrates* is a *man;* therefore, Socrates is not a beast. But if the middle term agrees with neither term of the question it can be the measure of neither one, nor does it show whether they mutually agree or not; it affirms neither *of all* nor *of none* and so neither proves nor refutes anything. Hence the rule of Aristotle, *Prior Analytics* 1.24 [i.24.41b6–7], that "if both premises are negated nothing is concluded," as in *No stone is an animal, no man is a stone, therefore no man is an animal.* But an exception to this rule occurs if the middle term is negated, or there is double negation in the major, as in *What does not sense is not an animal, a plant does not sense, therefore a plant is not an animal.* For here the major, which appears to be negative, is equivalent to an affirmative and is the same as if it were said that *Everything that senses is an animal;* and these negations are more topical [1] and infinite than axiomatic, and negations of the parts rather than of the whole axiom, a mode of enunciating more like *What is non-sentient is non-animal,* and this is clearly an affirmative axiom. But on this matter we shall say more below in chapter 12 in connection with the second species of the explicated syllogism. But the reason why the conclusion has

---

[1] I.e., have to do with the terms as such in the axiom.

to be negated when one part of the antecedent is negated is given by the well-known rule that *the conclusion follows the weaker part,* and the negative is weaker than the affirmative, the particular than the general, the contingent than the necessary. The reason for the rule is that the conclusion is as it were an effect of the premises, but no effect is in any case more excellent or stronger than its cause. The following paralogism is therefore fallacious: *Whoever does not differ from a brute differs from the son of Sophroniscus, Socrates does not differ from the son of Sophroniscus, therefore he does not differ from a brute.* This conclusion does not follow, [169] as it should, the negative assumption, but rather the affirmative proposition, for *does not differ from a brute* is not the negation of the whole proposition but only of its antecedent, and is equivalent to the affirmative *whoever is the same as a brute.* But the conclusion or the consequent follows the negative part of the antecedent and not the affirmative, because if the parts of the conclusion do not agree in the third argument then they do not mutually agree; the conclusion follows the special part and not the general one, because the genus includes the species but not the species the genus, in accordance with the above mentioned *dictum of every and none.*

A *simple syllogism* (that is to say, one consisting of simple axioms) *is either general, special, or proper.*

A *general syllogism consists of a general proposition and a general assumption.*

But it does not consist also of a general conclusion, as will appear below.

A *special syllogism is one whose proposition alone or assumption alone is general.*

For the following rule is also absolutely invariable: *If both premises are particular nothing is concluded.* For the *dictum of every and none* requires that at least one part of the antecedent be general; moreover, in two particular premises there are four terms, for since so-called *vague* individuals make particular propositions, it comes about that the major applies to one subject and the minor commonly to another. For example, *Some animal is a man, some animal is a brute, therefore some brute is a man. Some men are rich, some men are learned, therefore some learned men are rich.*

A *proper syllogism consists of a proper proposition and a proper assumption.* [170]

Now the reason why there is a syllogism when both are proper, while there is none when both are particular, is because the proper are definite and said of the same thing, while the particular are vague, as was said above.

From this it is clear why the special syllogism cannot be divided into the particular and the proper, as the special axiom was, since the proper syllogism is not a species of the special syllogism.[2] But why not all the parts are proper, that is, proper axioms, will also appear below. And indeed the proper syllogism, although neglected by Aristotle and rejected by others, is nevertheless very frequently used.

A simple syllogism is either contracted in its parts or explicated.

Aristotle [*An. Pr.* i.4.25b32–35, 5.26b34–36, 6.28a10–12] divides the syllogism into three figures, the first, the second and the third. But the facts themselves will show that the present twofold division of Ramus is more convenient and corresponds better with the order of nature.[3]

A syllogism is contracted when in place of an argument an example serves as subject to a particular question in such a way that it is understood to serve as antecedent with respect to both parts of the question and to be affirmed by the assumption.

For example: *Some confidence is a virtue, such as constancy. Some confidence is not a virtue, such as audacity.*

In these, as we see, first only a particular question is proposed; for the general, as Aristotle says in *Prior Analytics* 1.6 and 2.7 [i.6.29a17–19, ii.7.59a1–2], cannot be concluded in this species, which is the third Aristotelian figure. Nor, I add, can the proper be concluded; and this is the reason why neither the general syllogism is defined as one whose arguments are all [171] general, nor the proper syllogism as one whose arguments are all proper, since in this species the consequent or conclusion must always be particular, even when both parts of the antecedent are general or proper. From this it follows that only particular questions are concluded in this species. Then, too, in place of an argument a special example serves as subject or is subjoined, such as *constancy*.

This syllogism will be seen to have this special arrangement if we explicate the contracted syllogism (although it almost never occurs in practice except as contracted) so that the example or the third argument will first of all be the antecedent with respect to each part of the question occurring in the so-called premises, or will be the subject of each premise.

Now here the argument or the example is understood to be the antecedent with respect to each part of the question because each

---

[2] See n. 2, to Book I, chap. xxvii, above.

[3] There is considerable literature on the proposed fourth figure of the syllogism.

part of the question is attributed to the argument or example, that is, is affirmed of it or denied of it; just as if it were explicitly said *that constancy is a virtue and is confidence, and that therefore some confidence is a virtue;* or again *that audacity is not a virtue but is nevertheless confidence, and that therefore some confidence is not a virtue.* Therefore, even though the example or the third argument in a contracted syllogism serves as subject with respect to the question, it will nevertheless, if you explicate the contracted syllogism, be found to be the antecedent or the subject of the proposition and the assumption. Now the contracted syllogism is a certain species of enthymeme which, when explicated, is resolved into a certain distinctive form of syllogism, and for this reason required special treatment. Second, the arrangement of this syllogism requires that the assumption always be affirmed. For since the third argument is a special example and is moreover a species of the antecedent or minor [172] term of the question which is always arranged in the assumption, and the antecedent is thus the genus of the third argument, it is necessary that the genus always be affirmed of the species.

And this exposition of a question through an example serving as subject is made by Aristotle, Prior Analytics 1.6 [i.6.28a23–24], etc., *the basis of the syllogism explicated in its parts, as though in itself clearer and more evident than the full judgment of the syllogism.*

The contracted syllogism is therefore prior in order to the explicated, both because it is clearer and because it is simpler. It is so clear that the mind perceives it, contracted as it is, before it can be explicated in its parts, and therefore the practice of discoursing, content with this contracted form, will very rarely employ the explicated form. But its great clarity is seen also in the fact that since there are only two sophisms in this species, the contracted form of this syllogism more easily reveals their emptiness than does the explicated form, *as will be shown below.*

So to remove doubt, the parts of the syllogism should not be supplied here, as they are in the enthymeme, but rather contracted; the contracted form is here definitely more explicit than the explicated, and from a judgment of the syllogism there should be here as it were an appeal and a return to the clearer judgment of the axiom.

As for the modes of this species, if we consider only the contracted form, there is no need for more than two, one affirmative, the other negative, because it does not matter whether the example is a subordinate species or an ultimate one. But if we consider this species in its explicated form, then it has more modes than do the other species. There are four affirmative ones and as many negative ones; two of them are general, four special, and two proper. [173] Now there are four special modes in this species, but only two in the others, because in this species the proposition can be either general or particular, whereas in the others it is never particular. Here are some examples.

The first mode is general affirmative, as in *Constancy is a virtue, constancy is confidence, therefore some confidence is a virtue.*

The second mode is a general negative, as in *Audacity is not a virtue, audacity is confidence, therefore some confidence is not a virtue.*

The special affirmative is twofold; these are the third and fourth modes. The third is one whose proposition is particular, as in *Some wise man is rich, every wise man is praiseworthy, therefore some praiseworthy man is rich.*

The fourth mode is one whose proposition is general, as in *Every wise man is praiseworthy, some wise man is poor, therefore some poor man is praiseworthy.*

The special negative is again twofold, making the fifth and sixth modes. The fifth is one whose proposition is particular, as in *Some fool is not fortunate, every fool is despised, therefore some despised man is not fortunate.*

The sixth mode is one whose proposition is general, as in *A fool is not happy, some fool is fortunate, therefore some fortunate man is not happy.*

The two remaining modes are proper,[4] since the example is an ultimate species or individual. The affirmative one is *Socrates is a philosopher, Socrates is a man, therefore some man is a philosopher.* The negative one is *Thersites is not a philosopher, Thersites is a man, therefore some man is not a philosopher.*

Of the contracted syllogism there are two vices or sophisms which are guarded against by the definition. One of them occurs if [174] the question or conclusion is not particular, as in *Every man is rational, every man is an animal, therefore every animal is rational.* This is a sophism because what is not attributed gen-

---

[4] Non-Ramists insisted that these two modes are exactly the same as the first and second above in this same chapter (general affirmative and general negative), for the individual functions as a class that simply has one member (a unit-class). The syllogisms are thus examples of *baralipton* and *felapton* in the mnemonics in William of Shyreswood and other medieval logicians.

erally in the assumption (for not every animal is a man) cannot be a general subject of the conclusion. The other sophism occurs when the assumption is negated, as in *A man is an animal, a man is not a beast, therefore a beast is not an animal.* These two sophisms are, as I said above, more easily revealed in the contracted form of this syllogism and are at once, by an immediate intuition, seen to be ridiculous, as with *Every animal is rational, like man; some beast is not an animal, such as man.*

CHAPTER XI

ON THE FIRST SPECIES OF THE SIMPLE
EXPLICATED SYLLOGISM

A N EXPLICATED syllogism needs no definition other than its name. It is called explicated, not because it always occurs explicated in all its parts—for scarcely one syllogism in a thousand occurs this way—but because not only in its complete form but also in its enthymeme it always has its parts distinct.

In the explicated syllogism the proposition is either general or proper, and the conclusion is similar to the antecedent or the weaker part.

Similar, namely, in quality and quantity. And *to the antecedent,* that is, to each of its parts, the proposition [175] and the assumption, if they are mutually similar, whether affirmative or general or proper; but if they are dissimilar, then to the weaker part, as above.

There are two species of the explicated syllogism. The first is where the argument always follows, negated in one of the parts.

This first species of the explicated syllogism is called by Aristotle [*An. Pr.* i.5.26b34–36] *the second figure.* But this species is produced first, because its arrangement is simpler, as we may discover by comparing it with the other species. Now the argument always follows both parts of the question, its consequent in the proposition and its antecedent in the assumption, whence it is said by Aristotle, *Prior Analytics* 1.5 [i.5.26b36–37], to be *predicated of both.* But the argument is said to be negated in one of the parts because one of the parts, either the proposition or the assumption, is always negated. Whence, since the conclusion must also always be negated, it follows that all modes of this species are negated and that only negative questions can be concluded in this species, which is concerned entirely with refutations.

The modes of this syllogism are six, all of them, as we said, negated: there are two general, two special, and two proper.

The first general mode is one whose proposition is negated: *The confused man does not use his reason well, the wise man uses his reason well, therefore the wise man is not confused.* This example in its crypsis occurs thus in Cicero, *Tusculan Disputations* [iii.7.15]:

"Just as when the eye is troubled it is not well disposed to carry out its function, and the remaining parts of the body, and the whole body when moved from its stability, fails its office and function, so a troubled mind is not well disposed to carrying out its function. [176] But the function of the mind is to use its reason, and the mind of the wise man is always so disposed that he uses his reason in the best way; his mind is therefore never troubled." Here the crypsis is in a single redundance, for the order of the parts is right, nor is any part lacking; there is one prosyllogism [1] of the proposition, for the proposition is illustrated by a full comparison, whose apodosis is the statement of the proposition itself.

The second general mode is one whose assumption is negated, as in *A mortal thing is composite, the spirit is not composite, therefore the spirit is not mortal.* This syllogism, concealed in a crypsis, occurs in Cicero, *Tusculan Disputations* 1 [i.29.71], where he judges that the spirit is immortal: "Now in knowledge concerning the soul," he says, "we cannot be in doubt, unless we are ignorant concerning natural things, that there is nothing admixed with souls, nothing grown together with them, nothing joined with them, nothing doubled with them. Since this is so, certainly the soul cannot be taken apart, divided, dismembered; nor can it, therefore, perish, for perishing is as it were a parting and separating and division of those parts which before the perishing were held in a certain bond." In this example the order of the parts is inverted, for in the last place is put the statement of the proposition, namely, that compound things are perishable; the assumption occurs first: "Now in knowledge concerning the soul," etc. And it is embellished with synonyms; the conclusion is intermediate and is explained by its cause: "cannot be taken apart . . . nor can it, therefore, perish."

The first special mode is one whose proposition is negated, as in *The envious man is not magnanimous, Maximus is magnanimous, therefore Maximus is not envious.* With this judgment Ovid, *Epistles from Pontus,* 3.3 [iii.3.101–8], concludes: [177]

> Envy, a slothful vice, does not ascend into high minds:
> And like a hidden viper it creeps low upon the ground.
> Your lofty mind rises above its ancestry.
> Nor is there a name for you more sublime than your nature.
> So let others in their wretchedness harm and choose to be feared,
> And bear arrows dipped in biting venom.
> But your house is wont to help the suppliant,
> Among whose number pray let me now be.

[1] An argumentation with more than two premises and a conclusion; Ramus, *Dialectica Audomari Talæi prælectionibus illustrata,* p. 346 (Lib. II, cap. vii).

Of this example, too, the crypsis is merely redundance; the proposition has its prosyllogisms, and envy is put in place of the envious man, or the attribute in place of its subject, and is illustrated by a contrary mean quality and again by something similar, a *viper.* The assumption, that is, the magnanimity of Maximus, is illustrated partly by the lesser magnanimity of the whole race, partly by a notation of his name, that is, Maximus, to which he shows the magnanimity of his mind to be equal. The conclusion denies that Maximus is envious, partly because he is unlike the envious, whom Ovid describes by their effects—"So let others . . . work harm," etc.—and partly because he does the things a magnanimous person, who differs from an envious one, customarily does: "But your house . . . the suppliant."

The second special mode is one whose assumption is negated: *A dancer is lustful, Murena is not lustful, therefore Murena is not a dancer.* Cicero says in *Pro Murena* [6.13–14]: "For almost no man dances while he is sober, unless perhaps he is insane: neither in solitude nor at a moderate and honorable banquet. The excesses of dancing are the companion of a riotous banquet, a pleasant place, and many luxuries. You seize from me that which must be the worst of all vices; and you leave those without which this vice cannot be at all: no disgraceful banquet, no love, no gluttony, no sensual desire, no prodigality is shown. And since [178] there are not found those things which bear the name of pleasure and are vicious, do you think that in one in whom you cannot find lust itself you will find the shadow of lust?" The parts of this syllogism, too, are embellished with prosyllogisms. The statement of the proposition is contained in the words "The excesses of dancing," etc., illustrated in the preceding prosyllogism by contraries: "For almost no man dances while he is sober," etc. The assumption is explained through its parts, "no disgraceful banquet," etc., and is illustrated by certain lesser items; its prosyllogism precedes, namely, the rebuking of Cato for postulating the consequent even though the antecedent was not proved. In the last place is put the conclusion which denies that Murena is a dancer by repeating certain things which preceded in the assumption and by denying all the more emphatically through an interrogation.

By this mode of judgment Ovid, *Tristia* 1.1 [i.1.39–46], concludes in a threefold manner as he presents the apology for his verses:

> Verses succeed when composed while the soul is at peace;
> Our times are darkened by unexpected evils.
> Verses require retirement and leisure for their writer;

The sea, the winds, the fierce winter torment me.
All fear is out of place in verses; I, wretched,
Believe a sword will directly hang fast on my throat.
So what I here make a fair judge will admire;
And what is written he will read with some indulgence.

There are three syllogisms here which can be reduced to one as follows: *For anyone to be able to write good verses he must be happy, at leisure, and secure; I am neither happy, at leisure, nor secure; therefore I do not write good verses.* In place of assumptions there are put prosyllogisms from disagreeing things and from impeding causes. [179] Then follows the conclusion, not indeed the conclusion itself but its logical consequence: that it is surprising if they are good, but that they should rather be read with indulgence, since they are not good.

The first proper mode [2] is one whose proposition is negated, as in *Agesilaus was not painted by Apelles; Alexander was painted by Apelles; therefore Alexander is not Agesilaus.*

The second proper mode is one whose assumption is negated, as in *Caesar oppressed his country; Tully did not oppress his country; therefore Tully is not Caesar.*

In this connection there are two sophisms, one of which is common to both species of the explicated syllogism, the other proper to the first species. The common one occurs when the proposition is particular, which in accordance with the common rule for explicated syllogisms ought to be general or proper.

The sophism proper to the first species occurs when the third argument is not negated in the second part of the antecedent as the definition of the first species prescribes; hence the common saying *that from two affirmed premises in the second figure nothing is concluded.* But an exception must be made if the proposition happens to be a reciprocal axiom, as in *Man is a rational animal, Socrates is a rational animal, therefore Socrates is a man.* But here one should rather understand [3] an inversion of the parts of the proposition: *A rational animal is a man.* In this way it is related to the following species of syllogism. [180]

---

[2] These "proper modes" correspond again to the first two above in this same chapter (general affirmative and general negative).

[3] That is, with the natural logic that underlies the art of logic.

CHAPTER XII

ON THE SECOND SPECIES OF THE SIMPLE
EXPLICATED SYLLOGISM

T*HE second species of the explicated syllogism occurs when the argument is the antecedent in the proposition and follows affirmatively in the assumption.*

This species is called by Aristotle [*An. Pr.* i.4.25b32–35] the *first figure,* but in the order of nature it is last. For while in the other species the arrangement of the question with the third argument is simple and of one sort, in this species it is twofold; for in the proposition the argument as more specific is the antecedent with respect to the consequent of the question, and in the assumption it follows the antecedent of the question, as more general. Hence perhaps only in this figure is the middle term properly so called. But that the proposition is never particular, and that the conclusion is always similar to the antecedent or to the weaker part, the second species has in common with the first explicated species; and with the contracted species it has in common that it is affirmed in the assumption, except that in the contracted species the antecedent of the question, as more general, is affirmed of the argument, while in this species the argument is affirmed of the antecedent of the question.

It is chiefly this figure that is founded on the *dictum of every and none.* For the antecedent or the subject of the proposition contains the genus and is therefore always general, while the subject of the assumption contains the species [181] which is affirmed of that genus. So the assumption must always be affirmed. From this it follows that whatever is said of the genus in the proposition is in the conclusion rightly concluded of that which in the assumption is affirmed to be the species of that genus. But if that genus, namely, the subject of the proposition, is expressed by a negative infinite term or topically by a contradictory term, the assumption is not to be considered immediately as negated, although it may appear so, for it merely takes from the proposition the genus expressed by that term which is only topically contradictory and does not itself axiomatically deny anything. For example, *Whoever does not believe is damned, a certain Jew does*

not believe, therefore a certain Jew is damned. Here the subject
of the proposition is the genus *whoever does not believe,* that is,
every nonbeliever or infidel. A Jew is in the class or species of
nonbelievers, which the assumption does not deny but affirms exactly as if it said *a certain Jew is a nonbeliever.*

Now from this affirmation it follows that no argument disagreeing with the antecedent of the question has any place in this
second species. Besides, this species is not restricted to particular
questions, as the contracted species is, nor to negated ones, as the
first species of the explicated syllogism is, but is properly employed
for concluding all types of questions.

There remain the modes of this species, which, though partly
affirmed and partly negated, are nevertheless not more numerous
than those in the other species, where all modes were only negated.
The reason for the equality is that the affirmation of the assumption
and thereupon the negation only of the proposition reduces the
number of negated modes. The modes of this species are therefore
again six in number, three [182] affirmed and three negated; and
again both are general, special, and proper.

The first mode is general affirmative, as in *Every just thing is
useful, every honorable thing is just, therefore every honorable
thing is useful.* Cicero, *De officiis* 2 [ii.3.10], concludes this as
follows: "Whatever is just they consider useful, and again whatever
is honorable, just; from which it is brought about that whatever
is honorable is useful." The prosyllogism of the proposition from
the testimony of the Stoics is put first, and then all the parts of the
syllogism follow in order. The parts of this syllogism are axioms
of related essence, which have the force of simple axioms.

The second mode is general negative: *A fearful man is not free,
a miser is fearful, therefore a miser is not free.* This is concluded
and judged by Horace, *Epistles* 1.16 [i.16.63–66], as follows:

> How better than a slave, or freer, a miser can be,
> When he stoops for a farthing espied in the street,
> I do not see. For he who desires also fears; further,
> He who lives in fear seems to me to be free never.

In this example there is a twofold crypsis, an inversion of parts,
and a prosyllogism. First is put the conclusion, illustrated by two
prosyllogisms, first by an equal, to the effect that *a miser* is not
freer than a slave, and secondly by the effects, that he "stoops for
a farthing." Then is put the assumption, "he who desires also
fears." The proposition is put last:

> He who lives in fear seems to me to be free never. [183]

Terence in the *Eunuchus* [i.1.57–63] concludes and judges as follows: *What lacks counsel cannot be ruled by counsel, love lacks counsel, therefore it cannot be ruled by counsel.* The syllogism follows in these words:

> Master, that thing which has in itself neither counsel
> Nor any measure you cannot rule by counsel.
> In love there are all these vices: injuries,
> Suspicions, enmities, truces, war, peace again.
> If you demand that all these uncertain things be done by
> Certain reason, you do no more than if you
> Worked hard at being mad with reason.

In this example the proposition is in its proper place: " . . . that thing which has in itself," etc. In place of the assumption is put its prosyllogism of the various attributes of love which impede counsel; love lacks counsel because "In love there are all these vices," etc. The conclusion follows: "If you demand," etc. The statement of the conclusion is comprised in a comparison of equals: therefore if you wish to rule love by counsel, "you do no more than," etc.

The third mode is special affirmative: *Consuls appointed because of their virtue should carefully guard the state, Cicero was appointed consul because of his virtue, therefore Cicero should carefully guard the state.* Thus the orator concludes and judges his diligence, *On the Agrarian Law* 2 [ii.36.100, 37.100]: "For not only all the consuls should exercise care and diligence in guarding the state, but especially those who were made consuls not in the cradle but in the field of battle. None of our elders pledged to the Roman people that I am to be trusted; you should ask of me that which I must do, you should make your demands on me. Just as, when I was petitioning, none of our ancestors commended me to you, so if I neglect anything no ancestors will intercede with you on my behalf. [184] So provided I live (though I am one who can defend my life from their wickedness and treachery) I promise this to you, Quirites, that you in good faith have committed the state to a vigilant man, not a timid one, to a diligent man, not an idle one." The parts of this syllogism are embellished with prosyllogisms. The proposition is illustrated by the lesser; the statement of the proposition is the apodosis of a comparison, illustrated by diverse things: "For not only all the consuls . . . but especially those"; the diverse things are "not in the cradle but in the field of battle." The assumption follows, "None of our elders pledged to the Roman people," etc.; it again is illustrated by the same diverse things and by something similar: by my own merits, not by those of our ancestors;

in the field of battle, not in the cradle. A similarity is contained in the words "Just as, when I was petitioning," etc. Then follows the statement of the conclusion, illustrated first by the testimony of a promise with the force of an obligation—"I promise," etc.— and then by the diverse and the disparate: "So provided," etc. Therefore Cicero will be vigilant and not timid, diligent and not idle.

Here is another example: *That a thing longed for should come back is pleasing, the longed-for Lesbia has come back to Catullus, therefore she is pleasing* [Catull. *Carm.* 107].

> If anything has ever come back to one desiring and longing for it
> And yet not expecting it, this is especially pleasing to the soul.
> Wherefore this is pleasing and dearer to us than gold,
> That you come back, Lesbia, to me who longed.
> You come back to one longing and yet not expecting. You yourself
> Return to us; O day of brightest quality!
> Who that lives is happier than I, or that there is more
> To be wished for in this life who can claim?

In this example the proposition appears to be compound, but it is nevertheless simple, and the syllogism is simple, [185] since the arrangement of the argument with the parts of the question is simple. There is a twofold crypsis here, inversion and redundance. In the first position is the proposition, "If anything has ever come back to one desiring," etc., that is, whatever has come back, for *if* is not always the sign of a connected expression. The assumption is in the fourth and fifth verse, to the effect that the longed-for Lesbia has returned to Catullus. The conclusion in the third verse is illustrated by the lesser, "Wherefore this is pleasing and dearer . . . than gold." In the last three verses the statement of the conclusion is repeated, first by the attribute of *time*—"O day . . ." —and then by something equal, to the effect that no one is happier than I: "or that there is more to be wished for in this," etc.

The fourth mode is special negative: *The deceiver of a loving girl is not to be praised, Demophoon is the deceiver of a loving girl, therefore Demophoon is not to be praised.* In Ovid [*Her.* ii.63–66], Phyllis judges in the following way that Demophoon is not to be praised:

> To lead a trusting girl astray is no great glory:
> Ingenuousness deserved consideration.
> I have been deceived, both as a lover and as a woman, by your words;
> May the gods make this to be your most important claim to praise!

The proposition has its place with the prosyllogism of adjoined ingenuousness, as the reason why the deceiver is not to be praised.

The assumption follows, "I have been deceived," etc. The statement of the conclusion is contained in the imprecation, "May the gods make," etc.

The fifth mode [1] is proper affirmative, as in *Octavius is the heir of Caesar, I am Octavius, therefore I am the heir of Caesar.*

The sixth mode is proper negative, as in *Antonius is not the son of Caesar, you are Antonius, therefore you are not the son of Caesar.*
[186]

So the chief feature of this mode, compared with the others, is that it concludes all genera of questions, namely, general, special, or proper, and these either affirmatively or negatively. Most important, it concludes general affirmative questions, which is chiefly why Aristotle put this species before the others—because its first mode, the general affirmative, is in the highest degree productive of knowledge, *Posterior Analytics* 1.11 [i.14.79a17–33], since it alone demonstrates the precepts of art—and why he so laboriously and subtly worked out [*An. Pr.* i.5–7] the reduction of other figures to this one. But this species is not so much better than the other two that reduction to this species should therefore have been worked out with such alphabetical [2] annoyance as does actually occur, since the other species are not imperfect and do not conclude

---

[1] Again, the fifth and sixth, "proper" modes, reduce to the first and second given in this same chapter.

[2] Milton seems to be referring here to the *Prior Analytics* i.5–7, where Aristotle uses letters of the alphabet as subjects and predicates ("A belongs to all B," etc.), but he may also be referring obliquely to the mnemonic verses for the valid moods of the syllogism that appear first in the *Introductiones in Logicam* or *Summulæ* of William of Sherwood or Shyreswood (fl. 1254–67) and were well known through the Middle Ages and long past the Renaissance:

> Barbara celarent darii ferio baralipton
> Celantes dabitis fapesmo frisesomorum;
> Cesare campestres festino baroco; darapti
> Felapton disamis datisi bocardo ferison.

The meter is classical dactylic hexameter, the words a mixture of genuine Latin words and some fabrications, worked out so that the vowels and consonants provide the proper mixture of long and short syllables for the verse while encoding a vast number of formal logical laws and rules. See William and Martha Kneale, *The Development of Logic* (Oxford: Clarendon Press, 1962), pp. 232–33, where the following explanation is given: "Here each word is to be taken as the formula of a valid mood and interpreted according to the following rules: the first three vowels indicate the quantity and quality of the three propositions which go to make up a syllogism, *a* standing for the universal affirmative, *e* for the universal negative, *i* for the particular affirmative, and *o* for the particular negative [these code letters from "*A*ffirmo" and "*ne*go," I affirm and I deny]; the initial consonant of each formula after the first four indicates that the mood is to be reduced to that mood among the first four which has the same initial; *s* appearing immediately

less necessarily—this is common to all species of the syllogism—
and finally because they sometimes conclude the questions correctly
referred to their judgment more aptly than is possible in this second
species. So Galen, *De placitis Hippocratis et Platonis* 2 [ii.224],
following Antipater and Chrysippus, properly explodes this reduction and all its alphabetical equipment as an empty and futile
doctrine of the vainest subtlety. And Keckermann himself,[3] who
is usually rather unfair to Ramus, nevertheless admits that he has
retained the so-called reduction *per impossible*—invented solely for
the purpose of refuting those absurd and quite rarely encountered
people who deny the conclusion when both premises are conceded—more because of the custom of the schools than because
of any great utility it might have. But certainly the custom of
talking nonsense should rather have been removed from the schools
than retained. [187]

Three paralogisms are to be refuted here, two of which are
common to both explicated species, namely, the particular proposition and the conclusion of a part other than the weaker one.
This can serve as an example of both: *Some animal is rational, a
beast is an animal, therefore a beast is rational.* Moreover, the
whole middle, namely, *some animal,* is not assumed.

---

after a vowel indicates that the corresponding proposition is to be converted
simply during reduction, while *p* in the same position indicates that the proposition
is to be converted partially or *per accidens,* and *m* between the first two vowels
of a formula indicates that the premisses are to be transposed; *c* appearing after
one of the first two vowels indicates that the corresponding premiss is to be
replaced by the negative of the conclusion for the purpose of a reduction *per
impossibile.*" The rather ferocious hostility of Ramists to these extraordinarily
ingenious and quite harmless schemata, obviously the product of a culture both
chirographically skilled and yet highly oral in its ways of storing and retrieving
knowledge, is one of the many indications of the fact that Ramism projects a
basically typographic noetic economy, which automatically rejects as retrogressive
such oral recall devices (the mnemonics use a chirographic phenomenon, the
alphabet, but subject to metrical—that is, oral—management). Metrics might be
all right for poetry but no longer for practical knowledge storage and retrieval,
which was to be managed by indexes and diagrams.

[3] Bartholomæus Keckermannus, *Systema Logicæ Tribus Libris Adornatum
Pleniore Præceptorum Methodo et Commentariis,* Lib. III, cap. vii, in his *Operum
Omnium quæ Extant Tomus Primus* [-*Secundus*], I, col. 756: "Hæc est doctrina
reductionis *per impossibile* . . . quam quidem nos propter scholarum consuetu-
dinem retinuimus, fatentes alias ultro eius usum magnum non esse, tum quia
tantum habet locum in duobus modis [sc. baroco, bocardo]; tum quia non fit
facile, ut adversarius utramque præmissarum concedat, & conclusionem neget."

A paralogism peculiar to this species is the negation of the argument in the assumption, as in *Every man is an animal, a horse is not a man, therefore a horse is not an animal.*

Here also *only* and *single* are to be taken as particles of negation; they likewise render the assumption sophistical, as in *Whatever is in my house is in the town, a single fountain is in my house, therefore a single fountain is in the town.* And this: *Whatever is risible is an animal, only man is risible, therefore only man is an animal.* For both these particles, and a negation in the minor, show that the major is not reciprocal, and that therefore the conclusion from the major through the minor, or the general from the proper, does not follow.

Next to be considered here are some words of definition, which signify not so much the assumption itself as the argument affirmed in the assumption. For when the antecedent of the proposition (which is the third argument) is expressed by an infinite negation which is only topical, the consequent of the assumption (which is also the third argument) must retain the same negation; otherwise there would not follow an argument affirmed in the assumption, but rather one removed by contradiction. Now this negation should not be called a negation of the assumption or of the argument, but rather [188] an affirmation of an infinite argument: for the argument is negated in the assumption only when its negation is opposed to the affirmation of the proposition. For example, *Whoever is not rich is despised, Posthumus is not rich, therefore Posthumus is despised.* The affirmation of the conclusion proves here that the assumption is not negated, but it is just as if it were argued in this way: *Every man who is not rich is despised, Posthumus is a man who is not rich, therefore Posthumus is despised;* or in this way: *Everyone not rich is despised, Posthumus is one not rich, therefore he is despised.* But from the things said above in connection with the definition of this species I judge that the present matters are not obscure.

Further, in certain examples whose proposition is reciprocal it sometimes appears that this syllogism has a negated assumption; whereas it should be said instead that the parts of the proposition are inverted and that if they are put back in order the syllogism will be in the first species of explicated syllogism, as in John 8.47, *He who is of God hears the words of God, you are not of God, therefore you do not hear the words of God.* The proposition should be inverted: *He who hears the words of God is of God, you are not of God, therefore you do not hear the words of God.* [189]

Chapter XIII

ON THE FIRST CONNECTED SYLLOGISM

So far the simple syllogism has been treated.
The compound syllogism is a syllogism in which the whole question is one part of an affirmed compound proposition, and the argument is the other part.

Aristotle denies that there is any species of syllogism besides the three figures; and nevertheless he himself often uses a compound one which can be classed with none of the three figures. But practice, the best teacher, shows that in the common speech of men and in disputations, compound syllogisms are more often used than simple ones because they rather conveniently arrange many questions and many arguments which the simple syllogism does not accommodate. Even Theophrastus and Eudemus, disciples of Aristotle, as well as the Stoics and after them Cicero and Boethius, following practice as their teacher, did not omit the compound syllogisms. Now the compound syllogism is so called not because it consists of compound axioms, for a simple syllogism can also consist of compound and even related axioms, but because of a compound arrangement of the whole question with the third argument in the proposition, whence the whole assumption is also taken; and the conclusion is not deduced partly from the proposition and partly from the assumption, [190] but entirely from the proposition. For since the proposition is compound, it comprises the two remaining parts of the syllogism (which are simple axioms) conjoined by a connective of conjunction; the part which contains the argument makes up the assumption and the other the conclusion. But the proposition must be affirmed, since if it were negated it would cease to be compound, for the compound is dissolved by negation. But a proposition is made negative, as was said above in connection with the compound axiom, not by the negation of the parts but by that of the conjunction. For example, *If he is not an animal, he is not a man;* this proposition, though consisting of all negated parts, is affirmative, whence it is therefore rightly assumed and concluded, *But he is not an animal, therefore not a man either.* But if I should speak this way, *It is not the case that if he is not an animal he is therefore not a man,* then from this negative proposition nothing at all could be deduced or concluded.

So in compound syllogisms the assumption and conclusion are deduced by the very force of the conjunction. For of the two expressions which are conjoined in the proposition, either one is assumed so that the other may be concluded, or one is removed so that the other can be removed.

But to remove in a compound syllogism is not to negate but to posit a special contradiction.

Now a special contradiction, as we said in connection with the simple axiom, is either particular or proper. Therefore, to remove a part of the proposition in the assumption or in the conclusion is to posit its particular or proper contradiction. But in connection with the simple axiom we also learned that the particular is contradicted generally and the general is contradicted particularly. We shall in its proper place make the matter clear with examples. [191]

There follows now the distribution of the compound syllogism. Its genera result from the composition of propositions, and propositions are always compound axioms. Now of the four genera of compound axioms, the copulated, if it is affirmed, has no place in the compound syllogism, but if it is negated it is sometimes equivalent to a disjoined axiom. The discrete axiom has no place in the syllogism because the diverse expressions of which it consists do not clearly agree and yet so easily disagree that even when one is posited or removed it still does not follow that the other is posited or removed; or it has the force of a connected axiom.

So a compound syllogism is either connected or disjoined.

A connected syllogism is a compound syllogism with a connected proposition, or one whose proposition is a connected axiom.

But since a relative axiom of time is akin to a connected axiom, as we showed there [chapter 6], a connected syllogism's proposition can also be a relative one of time: for relative propositions of quantity, quality and place have a role in simple syllogisms, because in these propositions only the consequent of the question is arranged with the argument. But then a relative axiom of consequence, discussed in chapter 6 above, is not suitable for syllogisms.

There are two modes of the connected syllogism.

The first mode of the connected syllogism is one which assumes the antecedent and concludes the consequent. [192]

It is by this mode that Cicero judges and concludes in *De divinatione* 2 [ii.17.41]: "If there are gods, then there is divination; but there are gods; therefore, there is divination."

Another example occurs in *De officiis* 3 [iii.6.27–28]: "And if also nature prescribes that a man desire consideration of the interests of another man, whoever he may be and because of the very fact that he is a man, then it is necessary according to this same nature that the interests of all men be common. But if this is so, then we are all bound together by the same law of nature. And if this latter is so, then certainly we are forbidden by the law of nature to violate the other man. But the first is true, and so therefore is the last."

The proposition of this is a sorites (to be treated below) of three degrees: "And if also nature prescribes that," etc.

Frequently here not the same thing but something greater is assumed.

For example, in *Against Catiline* 1 [i.7.17]: "If your parents hated you, you would depart; now your country (which is the common parent of us all) hates you; therefore all the more will you depart." [1] But the expression *all the more* can easily be contained in a proposition in this way: If you would depart because of the hate of your parents, then all the more because of the hate of your country. *But the former is true, therefore all the more the latter.*

By a similar method is concluded also the greater or the lesser, as in Cicero, *Pro Quinto:* [2] "Even though he had forfeited his recognizances, you should still not have invoked the extremest laws." But he did not forfeit, therefore much less should you, or much more should you not.

The mode of concluding, as we said above, *is here the same when the proposition is a relative of time.* [193]

For example, *When Paris abandons Oenone, Xanthus will return; Paris has abandoned Oenone; therefore, Xanthus will return.*

But nevertheless the relatives of time, and the other compound axioms, as we indicated above, will belong to the simple syllogism whenever not the whole question is arranged in the proposition, which does indeed always happen when there is question of a certain and definite time. For example, if it is asked whether at this time it is summer, the syllogism will be as follows: *If the sun is in Cancer it is summer; but at this time the sun is in Cancer; therefore, at this time it is summer.* [194]

---

[1] Milton abridges this quotation from Cicero, altering the text as given by Ramus.

[2] This quotation could not be traced, but it does summarize an argument used by Cicero, *Pro Quinctio:* "Et etiamsi desertum vadimonium esset, tamen in ista postulatione et proscriptione bonorum improbissimus reperiebare" (18.56), and "et, si maxime deberetur, commissum nihil esset, quare ad istam rationem perveniretur" (18.60).

CHAPTER XIV

ON THE SECOND CONNECTED SYLLOGISM

T*HE second mode of the connected syllogism removes the consequent so that it may remove the antecedent.*

For the force of the connected axiom consists in this, that if the consequent is not, the antecedent is not. Thus Cicero, *De finibus* 4 [iv.19.55]: "The dialecticians," he says, "teach us, etc. If that is true, then this is true; but this is not true, therefore neither is that."

Examples follow: *If a wise man ever assents to anything, then he will sometimes have an opinion; but he will never have an opinion; therefore, he will assent to nothing.* Here the consequent is removed by a special contradiction in the assumption, *sometimes . . . never;* and the conclusion specially contradicts the antecedent, *anything . . . nothing.*

By the same syllogism Ovid, *Tristia* 2 [ii.13–16], judges his folly:

> If I were wise I would justly hate those learned sisters,
> Deities harmful to their worshipper.
> But now (such is the madness that accompanies my sickness)
> Knowing the stones I've struck, I bang my foot against them once more.

The proposition is *If I were wise, I would hate the Muses,* whose prosyllogism is from the attributed harm. The assumption is *but I have not hated;* it is expressed by something similar, "But now . . . I knowingly," etc. *Therefore I am not wise* is the conclusion whose statement is given in the parentheses: "Such [195] is the madness," etc. And in this example there is a proper contradiction.

These two species of syllogism are the most frequently used of all.

For not only are those arguments which cannot be arranged in simple and disjoined syllogisms easily arranged in connected syllogisms, but also from among those which can be concluded in the other forms many are concluded in these species more easily and more promptly; indeed, no argument at all which is used in a syllogism fails to fit into these species of the connected syllogism.

Besides these two modes of connected syllogism, some persons add two others,[1] the first of which removes the antecedent so that

---

[1] On these two invalid modes, finally disavowed by Ramus after he had taught them for over twenty years, see Introduction, above p. 177.

it removes the consequent, while the second assumes the consequent in order to conclude the antecedent. Though common speech and sometimes even good authors fall into these modes, nevertheless, since in the syllogism not the truth of the parts but the necessity of the consequentiality (*consequentia*) is considered, one must hold those modes to be vicious which from true premises can conclude the true along with the false. Therefore here the first mode which removes the antecedent is the paralogism of the earlier legitimate mode, akin to the negated assumption in the second species of the explicated syllogism, as in *If man is a lion, then he senses; he is not a lion; therefore he does not sense.* And here is an example: *If Dio is a horse, then he is an animal; but he is not a horse; therefore, he is not an animal. If he is an orator, he is a man; he is not an orator; therefore neither is he a man.* If you resolve this into the second species of the explicated syllogism—*Every orator is a man*—the fallacy will be evident. Indeed, even without this reduction it is evident by itself, for it removes the antecedent, which is lesser, in order to remove the consequent, which is greater; but from the lesser to the greater there is no consequence of this sort. [196]

The second mode, which assumes the consequent in order to conclude the antecedent, is the fallacious form of the second legitimate mode, akin to the paralogism of all premises affirmed in the first species of the explicated syllogism, as in *If man is a lion, then he senses; but he does sense; therefore he is a lion.* Both of these paralogisms Aristotle calls the fallacy of the consequent, which occurs whenever the proposition is not reciprocal.

But there is still another sophism of the second mode, when the assumption does not remove by a special contradiction, that is, when it generally contradicts a general consequent or particularly contradicts a particular consequent. An example of a general contradiction is *If every animal is irrational, then every man is irrational; but no man is irrational; therefore no animal is irrational.* An example of a particular contradiction is *If man is rational, then some animal is rational; but some animal is not rational; therefore neither is man.* [197]

CHAPTER XV

ON THE FIRST DISJOINED SYLLOGISM

A disjoined syllogism is a compound syllogism with a disjoined proposition.

There are two modes. Thus also Cicero in the *Topics* [14.56–57], and the Stoics according to Laertius [Diog. Laert. vii.81].

The first removes one expression and concludes the other.

For example, *It is either day or night; but it is not day; therefore it is night.* Or *It is not night; therefore it is day.*

Cicero's judgment in *Pro Cluentio* [14.42] is as follows: "But when this condition had been proposed to him, that he either accuse justly and equitably or die painfully and disgracefully, he preferred to accuse in whatever way he could rather than die in that way." The disjunction will be clearer this way: *There must be either accusation or death; there is not to be death; therefore there is to be accusation.* In this example, as it occurs in Cicero, there is an inversion of the parts, and the whole syllogism is concealed under a relative axiom of consequence. The proposition is not absolutely true, but conditionally. The assumption and conclusion are established through a comparison of the lesser in such a way that the conclusion precedes.

The same reasoning occurs in the second *Philippic* [ii.12.30–13.31]: "Will you never understand that you must determine whether those who have done this thing are homicides or protectors of liberty? But note, etc. I deny that there is any intermediate. I admit that they are, if not liberators of the Roman people and preservers [198] of the state, more than assassins, more than homicides, more than parricides; if indeed it is more horrible that a father of the country, etc. If they are parricides, then why have they always been addressed by you out of respect both in this order and among the Roman people? Why, etc. And these things were done by you. They are therefore not homicides. It follows that by your judgment they are liberators, since there can be no third." Here at the beginning is proposed a question about Caesar's killers: "whether those," etc. The proposition is put by means of a connected axiom:

"I admit that they are, if not," etc., which is equivalent to the disjunct, *Either they are protectors of liberty or more than homicides;* for that part of the disjunction is illustrated by the greater, and there precedes a prosyllogism by which it is shown that this disjunction is without intermediate and therefore necessary. The assumption follows: "They are therefore not homicides," and this is confirmed by a prosyllogism from the testimony and deeds of Antony himself. The prosyllogism is concluded in the second connected axiom, "If they are parricides, then why, etc. And these things were done by you. They are therefore not homicides." Then follows the conclusion to the effect that *they were liberators,* and this is confirmed by a repetition of the prosyllogism of the proposition, "since there can be no third," or intermediate.

If the parts of a disjoined proposition are more than two, the method of judging and concluding will be the same.

Now although the parts of a disjunction can often be more than two, as happens in disparates, there are nevertheless only two parts of the proposition itself, of which one is the question, the other the argument. In this mode where the question is always concluded, the third argument [199] comprises several opposites, which must all be removed in the assumption in order for the question to be concluded; for it is not possible for several opposites to be affirmed at the same time, but several can be negated at the same time.

Thus Cicero judges that Rabirius should have been with the consuls. *For he was either with the consuls or with the seditious persons or he was hidden. But he was neither with the seditious persons nor was he hiding. Therefore, he was with the consuls. Pro Rabirio* [8.24]: "Indeed we see," he says, "these three things to have been in the nature of the affair, that he would be either with Saturninus or with the good or that he should be hiding. But to be hiding was like the basest death, to be with Saturninus like insanity and wickedness; virtue, honor and decency demanded that he be with the consuls." The proposition is clear in itself. The parts of the assumption are illustrated by prosyllogisms, first by the similar, then by attributes. The conclusion is illustrated by a prosyllogism from the efficient cause.

It should be observed that in this mode a special contradiction is not so much needed as in the others, for in this mode it does not pertain to the necessity of the consequence, as in the others, but to the truth of the assumption alone. If, therefore, the assumption can bear a general contradiction, one can use it through the consequence, for it suffices for the method of the consequence that one expression be removed, in whatever way, in order for the other one to be concluded, and the conclusion will be the same, whether there occurred a special or a general contradiction in the assumption, but in the other mode, where the contradiction falls in the conclusion itself, it will be otherwise. [200]

CHAPTER XVI

ON THE SECOND DISJOINED SYLLOGISM

T*HE second disjoined syllogism from a proposition affirmative in all its parts assumes one and removes the other.*
It becomes the *second* because it is less general than the first, being restricted by certain properties to which the first one was indifferent. The properties are these: (1) the affirmation of all parts of the proposition and not only of the whole proposition, for this is common to all compound syllogisms, and a proposition can indeed be affirmed even when all of its parts are negated; (2) the assumption is affirmed, since it has been affirmed in the proposition; (3) in the conclusion there is always a negation, and it is a special contradiction; in the first disjoined syllogism the conclusion is indeed sometimes negated, but this occurs when the part of the proposition which is concluded has been negated. For example: *Either it is day or it is night; it is day, therefore, it is not night.*

A syllogism of this sort is produced frcm a negated copulated proposition, which is called a negated combination—or, what is the same thing in Greek, a negated copulation—*and gains the force of an affirmed disjunction.*[1] [201]

---

[1] An "affirmed disjunction" of what? If we let Milton's "negated copulated proposition" or "negated combination" be represented by "not (P and Q)," then the possibilities for a corresponding "affirmed disjunction" are "P or Q," and the three others obtained by first letting just P, then just Q, then both be negated; in all four cases the disjunction as a whole would be affirmed. Milton's vagueness about the relations among conjunction, disjunction, and negation stands in sharp contrast to the way in which these relations were formulated by some of the late medieval logicians, for whom "not (P and Q)" is equivalent precisely to "not P or not Q." See, for example, Walter Burleigh (c.1275–c.1346), *De Puritate Artis Logicæ . . .,* ed. Philotheus Boehner (St. Bonaventure, N.Y.: Franciscan Institute, 1955), p. 209: "Dicendum pro regula, quod contradictorium copulativæ valet unam disiunctivam habentem partes contradicentes partibus copulativæ. Verbi gratia, contradictoria huius copulativæ, 'Sortes currit et Plato currit,' valet istam, 'Sortes non currit vel Plato non currit.' " Underlying this approach to conjunction-disjunction-negation relations is in part the use of "or" just to indicate that at least one of the statements joined by it is true. With this in mind, the reader can verify that an equivalence of the sort formulated by Burleigh provides a schema by which Milton's "second disjoined syllogism" can be explained as having either a negated conjunction (Milton's way) or a disjunction of negations as one of its premises. Of considerable historical interest is the fact that the late medieval

It is not both day and night; but it is day; therefore it is not night. On this negated copulation Cicero says in the *Topics* [14.57]: "Not both this and that; but this; therefore not that."

Now only to this second mode does the negated copulation belong, for, since in this sort of proposition any opposites can be arranged, when one of them is negated—except in those opposites which lack an intermediate—the other is not necessarily affirmed and concluded, as occurs in the first mode, but when one is affirmed the other is negated, which is the common rule of all opposites and which occurs only in this second mode.

Regarding sophisms associated with these modes, there is none for the first. Those associated with the second are refuted by the definition. The first sophism occurs if some part of the proposition is negated, as in *A lion is either an animal or it is not a man; but it is not a man; therefore, neither is it an animal.* The second occurs if the assumption is negated, as in the example above. The third occurs if there will not be a special contradiction in the conclusion, as in *Either a man is an animal or every animal is irrational; but a man is an animal; therefore, no animal is irrational.* [202]

---

treatment of the relations among conjunction, disjunction, and negation is found reformulated in modern systems of logic in a set of rules called De Morgan's Laws, after the nineteenth-century logician who independently rediscovered them. See Augustus de Morgan, *Formal Logic* (1847), ed. A. E. Taylor (London: Open Court Co., 1926), pp. 133–36.

APPENDIX ON THE ENTHYMEME, DILEMMA AND SORITES[2]

AFTER the exposition of all the species of the simple and the compound syllogism, there follows the common characteristic of the axiom and the syllogism, or rather the anomaly of which we spoke before, the crypsis. It is so frequent in every practice of speech and type of writing, and generally for the sake of brevity, that almost no one utters or writes complete syllogisms without some crypsis.

But since crypsis and its threefold mode affect all species of syllogisms, there was therefore no place for speaking of the crypses of the syllogism before all the species of the syllogism had been discussed.

If any part of a syllogism is lacking this is called an enthymeme.[3]

This appears from an example: *Themistocles was allowed to leave the city, therefore I am allowed to do so.* The proposition may be added: *What was allowable for Themistocles was allowable also for me.* It appears also from the induction: *Invention and disposition have to do with arguments; therefore, so does the whole of logic.* The assumption may be added: *The whole of logic is the invention and disposition of arguments.*

Also to be constantly observed is this, that if the predicate of the conclusion is lacking, the major proposition is lacking; if the subject is lacking, the minor proposition is lacking; if both are lacking, the major proposition of a compound syllogism is lacking, or rather the antecedent of the major, which is arranged with the whole question as with a consequent. This indicates that the full syllogism will be compound, and the antecedent part [203] of the enthymeme will be the antecedent of the major, and the whole

---

[2] This Appendix is not in Ramus's text (1572). In 1569 Ramus had elsewhere mentioned the enthymeme in the common (but not Aristotelian) sense of a syllogism with one of its premises understood, and Talon's commentary treats the enthymeme at length, though without ever quite comprehending Aristotle's meaning for the term (generally neglected from Boethius on); P. Ramus, *Dialecticæ Libri Duo Audomari Talæi Prælectionibus Illustrati,* pp. 346, 357–65 (Lib. II, cap. viii). At this point, the end of Book II, chap. xvi, in Downame, there is a one-page section on "Refutation of Sophisms" but no appendix or anything else on the enthymeme, dilemma, or sorites. Downame does treat the enthymeme in commenting on Book II, chap. ix (pp. 617–25 in 1631 Frankfurt edition).

[3] This definition of enthymeme, common from Boethius (480?–524?) through the present, is not Aristotle's. By enthymeme Aristotle means an argument from probable premises to a probable conclusion, the typical rhetorical syllogism.

enthymeme will be converted into the major proposition of a connected syllogism. For example: *Virtue makes men happy; therefore,*
vice makes them unhappy. In the antecedent of this enthymeme
appears neither the antecedent nor the consequent of the question;
therefore, convert the whole into a connected or disjoined axiom,
and you will know that the full syllogism is compound, as in: *If*
virtue makes men happy, then vice makes them unhappy; but the
former is true; therefore, so is the latter. It is not night, therefore
it is day. Convert this whole into a disjoined axiom, and you will
supply the major and produce a full disjoined syllogism: *Either it*
is day or it is night; it is not night; therefore it is day.

If anything is added to those three parts of the syllogism, it is
called a prosyllogism, for it is an added proof for some part of the
syllogism.

Often, too, the order of the parts is confused. Both of these occur
in the dilemma and in the sorites.

A dilemma is a certain special crypsis not of a syllogism but of
syllogisms, so called from a twofold proposition which the Stoics
call a lemma, and which is commonly called a *disjunctive, biform*
and *horned syllogism,* as though striking with its horns; its force,
in two connected axioms with the form of a syllogism, is clear
enough. For example, in Martial [*Epigr.* ii.91.7–8]:

> If I have displeased, these will be our consolation;
> And these will be our reward, if I have pleased.

And there is that passage in the Gospel [John 18:23]: "If I have
spoken well, why do you beat me? and if evil, give evidence of
evil." Then there is that notable reciprocal dilemma of Protagoras
the teacher to Euathlus the student, in *Gellius* 5.10 and 11 [*NA*
v.10–11]: "If judgment is passed against you, the reward will be
due me for that reason, [204] since I win; but if the judgment is
in your favor, the reward will be due me by agreement, since you
win." To whom Euathlus replied, "But I also, good teacher, win
either way," etc. Of this sort is also the passage in Aristotle *Rhetoric*
2.23 [ii.23.1399a23–25]: "One should not deal with the people,
since if you speak justly you will be hateful to men, and if unjustly,
to God. On the other hand, one should deal with the people, for
if you speak unjustly you will be pleasing to men, and if justly,
to God."

Now this crypsis is explicated by means of a disjoined axiom,
and then by as many connected or even categorical syllogisms as
there were members of the disjoined axiom, as in the advice of
Bias on not marrying: *You will marry either a beautiful woman or*

an ugly one; if a beautiful one, she will be a harlot, and if an ugly one, she will be an affliction; but neither is good; therefore one should not marry. Or categorically thus: *A harlot should not be married, a beautiful woman will be a harlot, therefore,* etc. Or again, *An affliction should not be married, an ugly woman will be an affliction, therefore,* etc. But that disjoined axiom does not enumerate all the disjoined parts, for there is an intermediate sort of woman who is neither beautiful nor ugly; and the consequent of neither connected syllogism is true, for it can happen that a beautiful woman will not be a harlot nor an ugly woman an affliction.

A sorites is a cryptic syllogism of many propositions proceeding in a continuous series in such a way that the predicate of the preceding proposition is invariably the subject of the following, until finally the consequent of the last proposition is concluded of the antecedent of the first, as in *A man is an animal, an animal is a sentient body, a sentient body is living, a living thing is a substance, therefore man is a substance.* It is called in Greek a sorites and by Cicero in Latin a heaping (*acervalis*), because it adds bit by bit and as it were produces a kind of heap (*acervus*). [205]

It is generally used either to attribute a supreme genus to an ultimate species or to attribute a primary cause, though remote, to its effect; and the former is done through intermediate genera, as in the example above, the latter through intermediate causes, as in the following example: *Those whom God has foreknown He has predestined; those whom He has predestined He has called; those whom He has called He has justified; those whom God has justified He has glorified; therefore, those whom He has foreknown He has glorified.*[4]

Now the sorites uses both intermediate genera and subordinate causes as so many middle terms to prove a conclusion; namely, as many of them as there are terms between the subject of the first proposition and the predicate of the conclusion; but there are as many syllogisms as there are middle terms.

So it is an enthymematic progression containing one syllogism less than its propositions. The principal syllogism has as its major the proposition nearest the conclusion; as the minor term of its minor, the subject of the conclusion; and as the major term of its minor, the subject of the major proposition. For example: *Those whom He has justified He has glorified; those whom He has foreknown He has justified; therefore, those whom He has foreknown*

---

[4] Rom. 8:29–30.

He has glorified. The remaining syllogisms are prosyllogisms of the minor, and each preceding one is the proof of the following one.

From this is understood the threefold crypsis of the sorites: deficiency, redundance, and inversion. If therefore of the parts, whether they are species or causes, there is not a correct subordination and a firm connection, the sorites will not be sound. For example, *From evil customs come good laws; from good laws the well being of the state; from the well being of the state all good things; therefore from evil customs come all good things.* Here causes *per se* are improperly subordinated to a cause *per accidens.* [206]

This is also fallacious: *If there were no time there would be no night; if there were no night there would be day; if there were day, there would be time; therefore, if there were no time there would be time.* For if there were no time, certainly there would also be no day; it is therefore fallacious in the second proposition, which is not truly connected, but posits an effect after the cause has been removed. The sorites has the rest of the vices in common with the other species of the syllogism. [207]

ON METHOD[2]

M ETHOD *is a dianoetic disposition [3] of various homogeneous axioms ordered according to the clarity of their
nature, from which the mutual agreement of all of them
is judged and embraced by the memory.*

Method is used extensively in every walk of life, and therefore
deserves high commendation. Plato in the *Philebus* [16 C] says it
is "a gift divinely given to men." Aristotle [e.g., *Metaph.*
xii.10.1075a11–13] also counts "order among the greatest goods."
And there is Fabius [Quint. *Inst.* vii.proem.3]: "Nor do they," says
he, "appear to me to be mistaken who feel that the very nature of
things consists in an order; if this order is disturbed all things will
perish."

Now *method is a disposition of various homogeneous axioms,*
that is, of those which pertain to the same matter and are related
to the same end. If they were not homogeneous, they could not be
subordinated with respect to each other and therefore not ordered
at all. So in geometry method excludes arithmetic, and in arithmetic
geometry, as something heterogeneous and foreign.[4] All axioms are
to be ordered for the clarity of their nature according as they
comprise prior, better known, and more evident arguments. It
matters little whether the prime arguments or ones derived from
them precede, since both have the same sort of relevance.

[1] Milton combines Ramus's chaps. xvii–xx into this one chapter, abridging
them somewhat. We are indebted to William B. Hunter, Jr., for calling attention
to the fact that Milton's telescoping of Ramus's last four chapters into one makes
the total number of chapters in each book of his *Logic* the same as in each book
of the *Christian Doctrine:* thirty-three for Book I and seventeen for Book II, for
a total of fifty chapters in each work. Whether calculated or accidental, this
correspondence results in Milton's own doing, for Downame's edition of Ramus
retains Ramus's original number of chapters, thirty-three and twenty. The editors
do not know what to make of the correspondence.

[2] Ramus's title is more programmatic: "On Method, Which according to Aristotle Is Strictly One" (*unica*).

[3] "Dispositio dianoëtica" in Milton's Latin; Ramus's text reads "dianoia" (dianoia, discursive thought).

[4] Ramist method, designed for all discourse, actually is modeled on the purported ideal organization of a curriculum subject. See Ong, "Ramist Classroom
Procedure and the Nature of Reality," *SEL,* I (1961), pp. 31–47.

So just as truth and falsity are considered in an axiom, and consequence or inconsequence in a syllogism, so in method care is taken that whatever is clearer in itself precedes and the more ob- scure follows, and in general there is a judging about order and [208] *confusion. Thus, from among the homogeneous axioms the one which is first by absolute knowledge will be arranged in first place, the second one in the second, the third one in the third, and so on.*

Now, of the prior just as of the posterior we speak in five ways. We speak of the prior in time, as an old man with respect to a youth; of the prior by nature, as a cause with respect to an effect, or a genus with respect to a species; and then of whatever is prior in the order of existing, that is, what is given when something else is given; and of that which when it is given the other is not given, as unity with respect to any pair; and sometimes, where the order is reciprocal, of what is simultaneous in time but prior by nature, as the sun with respect to its light. The prior by nature is also spoken of in two ways; there is the prior in generation, as parts with respect to a whole, the simple with respect to the compound, the means with respect to an end; and the prior in intention, as the whole with respect to its parts, the compound with respect to the simple, the end with respect to the means. That is called prior in arrangement or in place which is nearer the beginning, as in speaking the narration is prior to the confirmation. We speak of the prior in dignity, as a magistrate with respect to a citizen, gold with respect to silver, virtue with respect to gold. Finally, that is prior in knowledge which it is easier to know, whether in itself or for us: in itself because it is prior in nature, or for us because it is posterior and an object of the senses, the former being the more perfect knowledge and the latter the less perfect.

Therefore, method invariably proceeds from universals, as con- taining causes, to singulars, and, what is more, from antecedents which are generally and absolutely better known, to the clarifi- cation of unknown consequents.

From this it is understood that it is here a question of method of handing on (*tradendi*) or teaching, rightly called analytic, and not one of invention.[5] For the method of invention, which by Plato is called synthetic, proceeds from singulars, which are prior in time

[5] Milton is more guarded than Ramus in advocacy of the general-to-special procedure as the one and only method for thought. He restricts its use to handing on knowledge or to teaching and omits the unqualified statement in Ramus's text that there is a "one and only" method. Milton echoes Downame's more prolix commentary.

and present themselves first to the senses, and by whose induction general notions are gathered. But the method of teaching, or [209] of arranging invented and judged things, which is here in question, proceeds by the contrary way—as Aristotle, *Metaphysics* 1.1 and 2 [i.1.981a5–28; 2.982a21–b4], also teaches—from universals which are prior and better known by nature; not because they are known in a prior way or more easily, but because once they are known they are as much prior in the nature and clarity of their conception as they are more removed from the senses. Thus the general species of things (as the writers on optics also teach) present themselves to the senses more quickly, as when I judge an approaching thing to be an animal before I judge it to be a man, and a man before Socrates. And this is the only method that Aristotle taught throughout his works.

But [6] *the unity of method is especially demonstrated and especially assured by examples from bodies of teachings and from the arts.*

Although in these all rules are general and universal, nevertheless degrees in these rules are distinguished; and the more general any one of them is, the closer to the beginning it will lie.

The most general one will be first in place and order, since it is first in clarity and knowledge.

The subordinate ones will follow, since they are next in clarity; and just as from among these the ones better known by nature will be put first, so those less well known will be put under them.

Finally the most highly specialized ones will be put down.

So the most general definition will be first, for it contains the causes. To the definition will be subjoined the logical consequents, or the explanations of the properties, if there are any and if they are not of themselves clear from the definition. The division will follow.

If the division is manifold, a partition into integral parts will precede, and a division into species will follow. And the parts themselves and the species are again [210] *to be treated and defined in the same order in which they were divided.*

And if a rather long explanation intervenes between them, they are to be joined together by connecting transitions, for this restores and refreshes the listener.

Now a transition is either perfect or imperfect. A perfect one shows briefly both what has been said and what follows, as the

---

[6] This sentence begins Ramus's chap. xviii, "On the First Illustration of Method by Examples of the Arts."

one at the beginning of this second book: "Up to this point, the first part of the art of logic," etc. An imperfect transition is one which shows only one of these, either what has been said or what follows, such as the one in book 1, chapter 18: "Simple arguments, therefore, as we have seen," etc.

Let grammar serve as an example.[7] Its definition, as the most general rule, will by the law of method be established in the first place, namely, that it is the art of using words well. In second place will be the partition of grammar into etymology and syntax. Then etymology, which treats of words, will be defined; and then will follow the parts of a word in letters and syllables, and the species in words with number and without number; and the transitions after the various endings will be put in their proper places. And thus of all parts of etymology the definitions, the divisions, the connections, and finally the most specialized examples in single instances, will be arranged; and the same thing will be done in syntax. This is the way that all the arts have set for themselves.

Certain modern writers [8] have instituted a two-fold method, one which is *synthetic* and *analytic,* the former being more suited to the teaching of the theoretical sciences, such as physics or mathematics. By the synthetic method the parts of a science are so arranged that one proceeds from a universal subject of speculation to particulars, from simple things to compound. Thus physics begins with the definition of a natural body, and then proceeds to its causes or parts and its general properties, and finally to its species. The analytic method [211] they define as one by which the parts of a practical science are so arranged that from a notion of the end one proceeds to knowledge of the principles or means for the attainment of that end. Thus in ethics one proceeds from the end, namely beatitude, to the means, namely, the virtues. But since both of these methods proceed in one and the same way, namely, from the most general definition—whether this contain the subject

[7] On Ramist use of curriculum subjects as paradigms, see n. 1, Book I, chap. xxvi above. Milton here much curtails Ramus's voluble explanation. With no mention of Ramus, Milton in his own *Accedence Commenc't Grammar* presents a two-part Latin grammar in accordance with Ramus's prescriptions (for Ramists all arts had two parts): (1) etymology (forms of individual words including declensions and conjugations) and (2) syntax (how to put words together in utterances). Milton's preface "To the Reader" states that he believes no one has ever before presented a two-part Latin grammar in English. "Grammar" commonly referred to syntax only, to the exclusion of accidence (declensions and conjugations).

[8] This discussion of competing views is not in Ramus or in Downame. Opponents of Ramus's "one and only method" were numerous and vociferous. See Ong, *Ramus and Talon Inventory,* pp. 498–500, 506–10.

or the general end—to the less general, from the better known to the less well known, from simple things to compound, in either case always by dividing, it does not seem that because in the general definition there is a different sort of reference—to a subject there and to an end here—there should be constituted a twofold method, but rather that for the arts which are to be taught there is one method and that it should be called analytic.

Indeed,[9] *method is applied not only in the subject matter of the arts and doctrines, but in all things which we wish to teach easily and clearly.*

Therefore, poets, orators, and all writers of whatever sort, whenever they propose to teach a listener, want to follow this way, although they do not always enter into it and persist in it.

Thus Virgil in the *Georgics* divides his proposed subject matter into four parts, as was said before; in the first book he deals with general matters, such as astrology and meteorology, and he treats of crops and their cultivation, which is the first part of his work. And then at the beginning of the second book [ii.1] there is a transition:

Thus far the cultivation of fields, etc.

Then he writes in a general way about trees, and then specifically about vines. Thus in the whole work, [212] he endeavors to put the most general matter in the first position, the subordinate things in an intermediate position, and the most specialized things last.

In the *Fasti* Ovid follows the same convenient arrangement. At the beginning he proposes a summary of his work [i.1]:

The periods counted throughout the Latin year, and their causes, etc.

Having implored for help, he establishes the division of the year. Then having explained the common differences between days on which business was transacted and days on which no business was transacted, he at length describes each month in its proper place, and in the preface indicates his particular concern for this order from general things to special [*Fast.* i.61–62]:

These things, firmly established for the whole calendar,
I shall say once for all lest I be obliged to interrupt the sequence of things.

[9] This sentence begins Ramus's chap. xix, "On the Second Illustration of Method, from Poets, Orators, and Historians."

In their introduction, narration, confirmation, and conclusion, orators strive for this order, calling it the order of nature, art, and subject matter, all the while following it quite assiduously.

For example, in the *Oration against Verres* [i.12.34], Cicero first proposes and then divides: "Quaestor," he says, "you have been for fourteen years since Cnaeus Papyrius was consul, and the things you have done from that day to this I call to judgment," etc. Here the proposition is also the definition of the chief matter, as the one most general in this judgment. The division follows: "These are the years, etc. Wherefore this will also be the fourfold division of my whole accusation." These four parts and the smaller parts of these parts he then treats, each in its order and place, and joins them with transitions, the first three in the third book, and so on. [213]

This [10] then will be the method in the various homogeneous axioms known either by an immediate judgment or through the judgment of a syllogism, whenever a matter is to be taught clearly.

But when the listener is to be influenced through pleasure or some stronger impulse by an orator or a poet, as is commonly the chief concern of some, a crypsis of method will usually be employed; some homogeneous axioms will be suppressed, such as the clarifying definitions, divisions, and transitions. Certain heterogeneous ones will be appropriated, such as digressions from the point and dwelling on a point. And especially will the order of things be inverted.

But to orators and poets should be left their own account of method, or at least to those who teach the art of oratory and poetry. [214]

---

[10] This sentence begins Ramus's chap. xx, "On Concealment of Method."

AN ANALYTIC EXERCISE IN LOGIC
FROM DOWNAME[1] ON THE THIRD CHAPTER OF
THE DIALECTIC OF RAMUS

T**HE** *first example is one of the procreating and conserving cause, from Ovid, De remediis* 1 [135–40]:

Therefore when you have appeared to be curable by our art,
Act according to my advice and avoid idleness first.
This is what makes you love, this defends whatever you do;
This is the cause of your being pleasure-bent, and it feeds the evil.
If you remove idleness, Cupid's bow is undone,
And his torches lie despised and hidden.

In the individual examples which are adduced to illustrate the doctrine of efficient cause, three things should be considered, the efficient cause, the effect, and the mode of efficiency. In this example love is the effect and idleness is the efficient cause which causes love by a twofold mode, both by procreating and by conserving, as [215] the poet teaches in the second distich. Now the disposition of this example (to give a rather complete analysis of it) is syllogistic. The question which the poet proposes as one to be concluded is this: Idleness should be avoided by one who wishes to be immune from love. And it is concluded in two syllogisms, in the first of which the third argument is drawn from the effects of idleness, certainly, but really from the procreating and conserving cause of love, in this way: *The procreating and conserving cause of love should be avoided by one who wishes to be free from love itself; but idleness is the procreating and conserving cause of love; therefore, idleness should be shunned by one who wishes to be free from love.* The proposition is lacking. The assumption is in the second distich first proposed simply, and then its second part concerning the conserving cause is illustrated by a similarity with feeding. The conclusion precedes in the first distich. The second proof is a logical consequence deduced from the assumption of the first syllogism: *Idleness is the procreating and conserving cause of love; therefore, if idleness is removed, then love is removed.* Its proposition and foundation is the logical axiom that *if the cause is removed the effect is removed,* and if this proposition is added the syllogism will be complete.

---

[1] Milton simply pieces together here two verbatim excerpts from Downame's commentary, the first from Book I, chap. iii, the second from Book I, chap. iv.

The second example there is from *Æneid* 4 [iv.365–67]:

No goddess bore you nor is Dardanus your progenitor,
Faithless one: but from its hard rocks did fearsome
Caucasus beget you. And Hyrcanian tigers suckled you.

Here the effect is Aeneas. The efficient causes are mother, father, and nurse; but the mode of efficiency is not one, for the parents cause children by procreating, but a nurse by conserving. [216] Now this example is arranged with a discrete axiom. Anchises and Venus are not the parents of Aeneas, so Dido feels, but the fearsome Caucasus and its hard rocks, while Hyrcanian tigers suckled him as nurses.

The third example is one of solitary cause as in chapter 4, from *Æneid* 9 [ix.427–29]:

Me, me; here I am, the one who did this; against me turn the sword,
O Rutuli. The deceit is all mine; this man ventured nothing, nor could
    he.

In this example the effect is the slaughter of the Rutuli. Its efficient cause is Nysus. But as to the mode of efficient causation, he himself, as he says, caused alone. Now the arrangement of this example is syllogistic. He who alone is the cause of the slaughter should alone be killed. *But I,* he says, *am the sole cause of the slaughter; therefore,* etc. The proposition is lacking, but the assumption is contained in verse two: "The deceit," that is, the blame, "is all mine." He proves the assumption by removal of an associated cause: "this man ventured nothing," etc. The conclusion is in verse one: "Me, me," that is, *kill* me; ". . . against me turn the sword," etc.

Another example of the same sort of cause is in Cicero's oration *Pro Marcello* [6–7]: "For warlike qualities some are wont to disparage with words and to take away from their leaders and share them with many, lest they be qualities proper to their commanders. And certainly in war the strength of the soldiers, the advantages of positions, the help of comrades, the forces, and supplies help much. But the greatest role fortune, as it were by her own right, claims for herself, and whatever is successfully accomplished she considers almost all hers. But in this glory, Caesar, which you [217] acquired a short while ago, you have no companion: all of this, however great it is, and it is certainly the very greatest, all, I say, is yours. There is no centurion, no commander, no cohort, no troop to take away from you any of this quality; not even Fortune, the mistress of human affairs herself, enters into partnership in this glory; she makes way for you, admitting it is all

your own." This example contains a full comparison from the lesser
to the greater for the purpose of amplifying Caesar's quality of
clemency. In the protasis there is an example of causes which work
with others. The effect is victory and the efficient cause is the
emperor, not indeed alone but with other causes, one of which,
fortune, is the principal one and as it were the companion of the
emperor, while the others are helping and ministering causes, of
which sort five are listed: the strength of the soldiers, the advantages of positions, the help of comrades, the forces, and supplies.
In the apodosis we have an example of a solitary cause; the effect
is the clemency shown toward Marcellus. Of this the one and only
cause is Caesar himself, and it is illustrated by the removal of
helping causes. Cicero's purpose is to show that he deserves more
praise because of his clemency than because of his deeds, and he
shows this from a comparison among themselves of the modes of
efficiency, because certainly Caesar was not the sole author of his
deeds but was the sole author of the clemency shown. Now certainly an efficient cause which does something alone deserves more
praise or blame, while one which does something with other causes
deserves less. So this proof can be concluded as follows: That of
which Caesar is the sole author deserves more praise than that of
which he is not the sole author. He is not the sole author of deeds
done in war, but he is the sole author of the clemency shown
toward Marcellus. Therefore Caesar's clemency deserves more
praise than the deeds done in war. [218] Of this syllogism only the
assumption is given in the example above, and its first part is
illustrated by an enumeration of the helping causes, and the second
by their removal.

In the same chapter there is an example of instrumental cause
from *De natura deorum* 1 [i.8.19]: "By what eyes of the mind could
your Plato contemplate that making of so great a work by which
he assumes that the world is constructed and built by God? What
effort, what instruments, what levers, what engines, what assistants were there for such a work?" The syllogism is like this: *One
who did not have instruments did not create the world; God did
not have instruments; therefore,* etc. The wholly false proposition
of this syllogism is lacking; the conclusion precedes and the assumption follows, illustrated by a certain induction of species. Both
the assumption and the conclusion are negated with great force [2]
through interrogation. [219]

---

[2] Milton uses the Greek word here, ἐμφατικωτερον.

THE LIFE OF PETER RAMUS
TAKEN FROM
JOHN THOMAS FREIGE[1]
WITH DIGRESSIONS OMITTED[2]

PETER RAMUS was born in the year 1515. His grandfather, as he himself relates in the preface of his *Professio regia,* was originally of a distinguished family in the district of Liège, but when his fatherland was captured and burned by Charles, Duke of Burgundy, he fled to the territory of the Vermandois and, being stripped of his property, was forced to make charcoal. Hence Ramus was taunted with having had a charcoal-burner for a father but his father was a farmer. As a boy scarcely out of the cradle, as he himself relates in the epilogue to his *Defense against Jakob Schegk,* he twice suffered serious illness. As a youth, with fortune unfavorable and in every way adverse, he came to Paris eager to learn the liberal arts. He was of tall and noble stature, with a very gentle face, the most blameless habits, [220] firm and robust health, which by continuous abstinence and continence and by steady work he rendered still firmer. When about to receive the title of Master at the University of Paris, he defended this thesis: *Whatever has been said by Aristotle is fabrication.*[3] Stunned by the novelty and strangeness of the thesis, the examiners and masters for an entire day, but in vain, opposed the incepting master, as they call him. Following this surprising success, he seized the opportunity to take

[1] On Freige, see Introduction, above, pp. 191–95. For the relationship of this abridgment of Milton's to Freige's full text, see Leo Miller, "Milton Edits Freigius' 'Life of Ramus,' " *Ren&R,* VIII (1972), 112–14.

[2] I.e., Freige's digressions. See Introduction, above, pp. 191, 193–95

[3] "Quæcumque ab Aristotele dicta essent, commentitia esse." *Commentitia* in this account of Freige's has often been rendered "false," but it means, rather, "fabricated," "unnaturally put together"—"false" in this quite special sense. See Ong, *Ramus, Method, and Decay of Dialogue,* pp. 45–47. The statements, still recurrent in biographical sketches and elsewhere, that Ramus defended such a thesis all trace back, generally through Freige, to Freige's verbatim source, Theodor Zwinger (Zwingerus), *Theatrum Vitæ Humanæ* (1571), and to no other independent contemporary evidence: Other contemporary primary sources more informed than Freige conspicuously omit all reference to such a thesis. See also Walter J. Ong, review of Peter Ramus, *The Logike of the Most Excellent Philosopher P. Ramus Martyr,* trans. Roland MacIlmaine (1574), ed. Catherine M. Dunne (Northridge, Calif.: San Fernando Valley State College, 1969), in *RenQ,* XXIX (1971), 89–90. Unless further evidence surfaces, Ramus's purported defense of such a thesis must remain at best an uncertainty.

issue with and to inquire seriously and freely into Aristotle. He decided first to improve logic as the instrument of the other arts (as he himself explains at length in the epilogue to Book 5 of his *Training in Dialectic*), but he had begun to work at these things in his twenty-first year. Seven years later he published at the University of Paris what is considered his first *Dialectic* and his *Remarks on Aristotle*,[4] and in the following year his Latin Euclid,[5] which he embellished with a preface. From that time he aroused many adversaries[6] against himself, especially two men whom Talon in his *Academia,* while relating the whole quarrel, nevertheless fails to name. Hardly, he says, had the *Remarks on Aristotle* been read, when a group of men, alleging falsely that they were acting in the name of the University, suddenly dragged Peter Ramus away to a capital trial at the tribunal of the provost and accused him of a novel crime, namely, that by opposing Aristotle he was weakening the arts; for by this oration of theirs the litigation over Aristotle was touched off. From there, harassed by the cries of the Aristotelians, he was taken to the highest commission of the Parliament of Paris. When this did not come off the way his adversaries planned, they used new tactics to refer the matter from the Parliament of Paris to the jurisdiction of the king; five judges were appointed; two were named by each side [221] and the fifth by the king. Ramus was ordered to plead his case for the individual chapters of the *Remarks on Aristotle,* and though he considered three of the judges thoroughly hostile, nevertheless, in order to comply with the royal command, he was present on the appointed

[4] These two works are, respectively, (1) Ramus's *Dialecticæ Partitiones* (Paris: Iacobus Bogardus, 1543), in later editions entitled *Dialecticæ Institutiones, Dialecticæ Commentarii Tres,* or *Institutionum Dialecticarum Libri Tres,* and (2) his *Aristotelicæ Animadversiones* (Paris: Iacobus Bogardus, 1543), in later editions called *Scholarum Dialecticarum Libri Viginti.*

[5] A Latin rendition of Euclid's *Elements,* known to us in only the one Bibliothèque nationale copy, in which leaves ai–aii, and thus the title page, are missing, was published in Paris by Ludovicus Grandinus in 1545, presumably with the same prefatory letter by Ramus to Charles of Lorraine, archbishop of Rheims, dated 5 cal. feb. 1544, on the missing pages as that which appears in the edition published in Paris by Thomas Richardus in 1549 under the simple title *Euclides.* This Latin translation, which in his *Proœmium Mathematicum* (Paris: A. Wechelus, 1567) Ramus simply says he used "twenty-five years ago" and commended with his prefatory letter, proves to be by Bartolomeo Zamberti. See Peter Sharratt, "La Ramée's Early Mathematical Teaching," *BHR,* XXVIII (1966), 605–14; also Ong, *Ramus and Talon Inventory,* pp. 68–69, where the translation itself is erroneously ascribed to Ramus.

[6] See Ong, *Ramus, Method, and Decay of Dialogue,* pp. 214–24 and passim; Ong, *Ramus and Talon Inventory,* pp. 492–533.

day. One scribe was on hand to take down the arguments of Ramus and the opinions of the judges. For two days they engaged in a heated debate on the definition and division of the art of dialectic, which are not in the books of the *Organon of Logic*. On the first day the three Aristotelian judges, contrary to all the laws of a well presented art, judged that for the perfection of the art of logic there was no need for a definition. The two judges chosen by Ramus were of the contrary opinion. On the next day the Aristotelian judges, much upset, agreed with the matter of division, and adjourned the case to another day. But for fear that Ramus might fail to be condemned, they devised a new plan to renew the whole debate from the beginning and to void what had been decided the day before. Ramus appealed this inconstancy of the judges, but in vain, for a judgment without appeal was given by the three judges, and that sentence of the three condemned not only the *Remarks on Aristotle* but also the *Training in Dialectic*. The author was forbidden in the future to touch upon any part of philosophy either by teaching or by writing. Plays, even some with elaborate stage apparatus, were presented in which Ramus and Ramist dialectic were held up to ridicule. From these difficulties one man alone, Charles of Lorraine,[7] freed Ramus, for he persuaded King Henry that philosophy should always be free. Having thus regained his previous liberty to teach and write, for four years he applied himself to his studies in complete peace. In his thirty-first year he gave an oration in favor of joining the studies of philosophy [222] and eloquence. With his brother Talon [8] (so he always called him) he divided the parts of his teaching so that Talon would teach philosophy in the morning and he himself eloquence in the afternoon; in explaining the poets, orators, philosophers, and authors of all types he demonstrated the use of dialectic. The accusation was later leveled against him that in philosophical studies he did not explain the philosophers, but, contrary to the laws of the University, the poets instead; Ramus cleared himself and asked that his Collège de Presles be inspected by honest and learned men.[9]

[7] Charles de Lorraine, archbishop of Rheims (1538) and cardinal (1547), known first as the cardinal of Guise and later, on the death of his uncle John, as the cardinal of Lorraine, had been a fellow student of Ramus at the Collège of Navarre at the University of Paris.

[8] Omer Talon (Latin, Audomarus Talæus, c.1510–62); see Ong, *Ramus, Method, and Decay of Dialogue*, pp. 22–28.

[9] For some account of this dispute, see Charles Waddington, *Ramus (Pierre de la Ramée): Sa Vie, Ses Écrits, et Ses Opinions* (Paris: Ch. Meyrueis, 1855), pp. 73–78. Waddington's account will be seen to be tendentious, sharing some of the acrimony of the original dispute.

But a specially assigned judge, a youth of noble birth, condemned the pupils of Ramus without a hearing, enjoined them from use of public lecture halls, the seals and the registers, and then excluded them from the functions and privileges of the University. The pupils of Ramus appealed this unusual judgment before an assembly of philosophers at Saint Julian's, and they were acquitted on condition that their teacher affirm under oath that he had lectured on the books prescribed by the laws of the University. Ramus affirmed this; but a little later not the pupils, as before, but their masters were attacked by the same youthful judge. Ramus was enjoined to renounce and abjure his teachings in the public lecture halls. A second time he appealed to the higher authorities of the University, but when, to avoid a riot, he defended himself *in absentia* by a written statement, that young judge, although overruled by two appeals, judged and condemned him a third time. Ramus appealed a fourth time; when the accuser advanced the day of the appeal, Ramus was forced to appear suddenly in the senate. Here again Charles of Lorraine was his only defense. He heard a very serious accusation by someone who called Ramus a professor [223] who had doubts about human and divine laws, who set before his listeners ambiguous passages of Saint Augustine, interpreting them in favor of unrestrained and impious liberty, and who, in order more easily to take advantage of unguarded minds, dispensed with all logical disputations. Ramus easily defended himself against these calumnies. So it was decided in the senate to restore Ramus and his pupils fully to their former status. In his thirty-sixth year, after Charles of Lorraine had reported to King Henry at Blois on the teachings of Ramus, Ramus was elected to the number and rank of the regius professors through royal letters honorably addressed to him. So he publicly gave thanks to King Henry and to Charles of Lorraine, and was convinced that he had been placed by the king in the most distinguished position in the state and that it was therefore up to him to work day and night with the greatest diligence, lest he fail in so great an office as Professor of both Eloquence and Philosophy.[10] Hence he enkindled in the minds of young men such a desire to get ahead with their educations that

[10] Eloquence represented the ideal of Renaissance humanism, philosophy the traditional ideal of the Arts Faculty, the largest by far of the four university faculties. Ramus's chair thus was representative of the tensions of the age, in one way those between the active life (rhetoric, ordered to decision making) and the contemplative (philosophy). For discussion of the issues, see Jerrold E. Seigel, *Rhetoric and Philosophy in Renaissance Humanism* (Princeton, N.J.: Princeton University Press, 1968).

the royal lecture hall, although ample for an ordinary audience, was nevertheless often quite unable to hold the crowd of students who assembled there. His supreme perseverance withstood the petulance of his adversaries, and his motto was *Work conquers all.* In the year 1552, when in the College of Cambrai he began to lecture on his *Dialectic* before a very large audience, undisturbed in the midst of loud noises, shouts and whistles, he persevered remarkably, speaking on through the intervals in the shouting, and concluded. His enemies, losing confidence in the face of this drive of his, thereafter caused him less annoyance. Also in the University of Heidelberg, where he was brought to teach by the authority of the prince, he endured without flinching the similar loud shouting of his rivals. [224] He observed like silence toward certain learned men,[11] Gouvea,[12] Galland,[13] Périon,[14] Turnèbe,[15] Melanchthon.[16] For twenty years he was quite abstemious, until the physicians persuaded him to use wine for the sake of his health; for he had developed a distaste for wine, having as a child slipped into the wine cellar without his parents' knowledge and drunk so immoderately that he was found lying on the ground as though dead. Until his old age he used straw as a bed. He remained celibate all his life. He was content in the work of the Collège de Presles (work which had been entrusted to him without any public stipend). The payments offered to him by his pupils, though due him, he did not accept. In the year 1556 he published the *Ciceronianus* on the best method of instructing youth. He was one of the foremost advocates of correcting the pronunciation of the Latin language, which at that time at the University of Paris was very corrupt. To be sure, there were loud objections by the Sorbonists, who were such stubborn defenders of all bad practices that they contended that a

---

[11] For Ramus's disputes with Gouveia, Galland, Périon, Turnèbe, and others, see Ong, *Ramus and Talon Inventory,* pp. 492–510.

[12] Antonio de Gouveia, in Latin Antonius Goveanus (1505–66), Tunisian-born logician and jurist at the University of Paris, defended Aristotle against Ramus.

[13] Pierre Galland, in Latin Gallandius (1510–59), Regius Professor of Latin Eloquence at Paris, defended Aristotle against Ramus.

[14] Joachim de Périon, (1499–1559), a Benedictine monk and an extreme hellenist, who opposed Meigret's and Ramus's and others' reforms in French orthography, attacked Ramus's anti-Aristotelianism and anti-Ciceronianism.

[15] Adrien Turnèbe, in Latin Turnebus (1512–65), classical scholar, took issue with Ramus's tendency to reduce the philosophical question of fate to a matter of logic and with Ramus's captiousness as a commentator.

[16] Philip Melanchthon, in German Schwartzerd (1497–1560), German humanist and Reformer, who had published a reorganized *Dialectic* competing with Ramus's.

certain priest, who was charged before the Parliament of Paris with using the revised pronunciation, should because of this grammatical heresy, as they called it, be deprived of his very large ecclesiastical revenues. And his superiors did indeed appear to be about to give up the contest, when Peter Ramus and other regius professors hurriedly converged on the court and dissuaded it from pronouncing so strange and extravagant a judgment. Indeed so gross was the ignorance of that time that it is related in printed books how there were doctors in that university who obstinately maintained that the syntax of *ego amat* was as proper as that of *ego amo*,[17] and how there was need for public authority to repress their obstinacy. What Ramus accomplished in mathematics is attested by his *Lectures on Mathematics* and by other works of his. The calamity of civil war interrupted him while he was preparing these works; [225] upon receipt of letters from the king, he proceeded to the royal library at Fontainebleau and completely rewrote his mathematical lectures in fuller and richer form. Then he thought of going to Italy, where the University of Bologna had respectfully invited him, or at least to Germany, but fear of death, which threatened on all the roads, and a report that his Collège de Presles had been pillaged and the library plundered kept him near the royal city of Vincennes. But some other impulse urged him even more strongly to flee by impassable roads from Vincennes and to lie hidden from time to time in various places; yet in flight and in hiding he found leisure and most devoted hosts. And during this leisure he wrote his *Lectures on Physics,* or rather began this work. He took refuge in the camp of the nobles when the civil war broke out again. When after six months this tumult had been put down, he returned and found in his library nothing but empty cabinets. Resner [18] (who remained in Paris) had opportunely

---

[17] The "ego amat" question is a highly technical one generated out of logical and semiotic problems, not, as the text here implies, out of unfamiliarity with grammar. It has to do with questions of the sort treated today in terms of morphemic variation and semiotic redundancy (in the normal "ego amo," the pronoun "I" is signaled both by the pronoun and by the normal verb ending). As everyone who has read medieval and Renaissance academic Latin knows, such Latin is completely "correct" in the sense given this word in prescriptive grammar, though in a very few places its idiom varies somewhat from the classical. The implication that Paris scholars did not know or care about the conjugations is utterly false. See Ong, *Ramus, Method, and Decay of Dialogue,* p. 75.

[18] Friedrich Risner (Resner, Reisner, Fridericus Resnerus or Risnerus), d. 1580. Born at Herzfeld in Hesse, he became Ramus's assistant in mathematics and later himself professor of mathematics in Paris. The full title of Risner's *Opticæ Libri Quatuor (Four Books of Optics)* states that Risner wrote the work "in accord with

snatched away from the plunderers only his mathematical commentaries.[19] With civil war threatening now for the third time, he
obtained from King Charles a commission for one year to visit
foreign universities as a free ambassador. On the borders of the
kingdom he would hardly have escaped the hands of certain soldiers
except for the royal warrant. Three times released, three times
taken again, he finally arrived in a great hurry at a place where
a free man was not at the mercy of assassins. His arrival in Germany was greeted with singular kindness and joy by all good and
learned men. At Strasbourg, Johann Sturm,[20] the founder and
rector of its university, received him most lovingly. Then the whole
university, together with certain counts and barons who lent their
prestige to the festivities, treated him most generously; [226] and
then, on a day when a most magnificent marriage was celebrated
there, the highest magistrate of the city led him with Sturm to the
city hall for a public expression of good will. Passing by Bern, he
only viewed the city, but he did not leave without the respectful
generosity of Consul Steger [21] and the friendly well-wishing of
Haller,[22] Aretius [23] and other learned men. In Zurich Henry Bullinger [24] was the first one present to greet Ramus as soon as he
entered the city, and he prepared for him a banquet made most
pleasant by the learned conversation of the guests Josias Simler,[25]

---

the last wishes" of Peter Ramus (*ex voto Petri Rami novissimo . . . conscripti*),
but the work was published only posthumously, edited by Nicolaus Crugius
(Cassell: Wilhelmus Wesselius, 1606).

[19] Ramus's library was again pillaged at the time of his murder, but one volume
from it has recently surfaced and has been presented to the Pius XII Memorial
Library at Saint Louis University. See John F. Daly, "Ramus: Recently Discovered Unpublished Edition of His Mathematical Works," *Manuscripta,* XVII
(1973), 80–90. Concerning another recently discovered volume very likely from
Ramus's library and now also at Saint Louis University, see Walter J. Ong, "A
Ramist Translation of Euripides," *Manuscripta,* VIII (1964), 18–28.

[20] Works written and edited by Johann Sturm, in Latin Sturmius (1507–89),
the humanist and publisher, figure in the early Renaissance history of "method"
eventuating in Ramist "method."

[21] Johannes Steiger (1519–62), prominent member of the city council of Bern
and founder of a distinguished family dynasty.

[22] Johann Haller the Younger (d. 1575), Reformation clergyman, established
in Bern from 1548 until his death.

[23] Benedicht Marti, in Latin Aretius (1505?–74), Reformation preacher and
successively professor of logic, philosophy, Greek and Hebrew, and theology.

[24] Johann Heinrich Bullinger (1504–75), Swiss theologian and clergyman, successor to Zwingli as leader of the Reformation in Zurich.

[25] Josias Simmler or Simler (1530–76), Reform theologian and voluminous historian in Zurich.

Rudolph Gualter,[26] and Louis Lavater.[27] On the following day, when he was taken by Bullinger to the public square, he wondered why the great gathering of citizens of all ranks had assembled there, and he inquired of Bullinger whether there, as in Strasbourg, a splendid wedding was being celebrated. To this Bullinger replied: "Our citizenry is celebrating this wedding for you." Heidelberg brought him as friends Ursinus [28] and Olivianus,[29] and as his host Immanuel Tremellius [30] and then as patron the Palatine Elector [31] himself, who presented a golden image of himself to the departing Ramus. Going from there to Frankfurt, he was honorably received by some of the leading citizens; then he proceeded to Nürnberg to the outstanding artisans and mechanics and other learned men and especially Joachim Camerarius,[32] and here the lawyers' guild was commissioned by the senate to arrange a banquet for Peter Ramus in the official name of the city. From there he proceeded to Augsburg, where the chief magistrate of the city treated him most courteously, while present as guests at a banquet were persons learned in various fields of knowledge, but especially Jerome Wolf [33] and Tycho Brahe.[34] With the latter Ramus was taken after the meal to the suburban home of the chief magistrate and had several [227] conversations on mathematical studies. Called back by a report that peace had finally been restored, he hastened to Lausanne, and here at the request of some learned men he presented for several days to a great gathering a series of lectures on logic. At Geneva he was deeply engaged in talks with various highly learned men

[26] Rudolph Gualter or, in German, Walther, (1519–86), Swiss Reform theologian, classical scholar, and clergyman.

[27] Ludovicus Lavater (1527–86), Protestant clergyman and theologian, author of many books of biblical commentaries.

[28] Zacharias Ursin or, in Latin, Ursinus (1534–83), Reform theologian, with Caspar Olevianus one of the two principal authors of the mildly Calvinistic Heidelberg Catechism (commissioned 1562 by the elector Friedrich III, adopted 1563 by a synod convened at Heidelberg).

[29] Caspar Olevian or, in Latin, Olevianus (1536–87), Reform theologian; see preceding note on Ursin.

[30] Immanuel Tremellius (1510–80), an Italian-born Jewish convert to Protestantism, was a Hebrew scholar, theologian, and translator of the Old Testament from Hebrew into Latin.

[31] Frederick III, "the Pious" (1515–76), who had commissioned the Heidelberg Catechism, of which the principal authors were Zacharias Ursin and Caspar Olevian.

[32] Joachim Camerarius or, in German, Kammermeister (1500–74), German classical scholar and Lutheran theologian.

[33] Hieronymus Wolf (1516–80), German humanist and schoolmaster.

[34] Tycho Brahe (1546–1601), the Danish astronomer, studied at Augsburg.

on other liberal studies as well as logic, especially with Franciscus Portus the Cretan [35] and Andrew Melville, a Scot.[36] Earlier he had through letters cultivated friendship with many other highly erudite men, with Commandino [37] and Papio [38] in Italy, with Dee [39] and Acontius [40] in England, with Chytraeus [41] in Germany, and with a host of others. Noble and famous cities sought to attract him with large and honorable payments, even with a proposed stipend of six hundred crowns. John the elected king of Hungary proposed that he direct the University of Stuhlweissenburg, with a large salary. He was invited on most generous terms to Cracow, and even to Bologna in Italy at a stipend of a thousand ducats, but did not want to abandon his homeland. So while Ramus in his own country was the target of calumnies from all sides and of the malicious attacks of the envious, Charles IX not only sustained him with his powerful support, but also strengthened and dignified him with honors and granted him leave from his labors. At last in the year 1572, in that massacre of Christians and citizens at Paris, he lost his life in a most lamentable way. The cause of his murder some attribute to his rivals, and many think the cause was the same as that for which others were slaughtered on that night.[42] In his will he left a splendid annual legacy for a professor of mathematics at the University of Paris. [228]

[35] Franciscus Portus (1511–81) came from his native Crete to study in Padua and Venice. He taught Greek in Italy and, after embracing the Reform, in Geneva. His numerous works, in Latin, are concerned, many of them, with classical Greek literature and rhetoric.

[36] Andrew Melville (1545–1622), Scottish scholar and Reformer, had studied under Ramus at Paris and, after Ramus's death, introduced Ramist doctrines and procedures into the Scottish universities of Glasgow, Aberdeen, and Saint Andrew's.

[37] Federico Commandino (1509–74), Italian mathematician who produced an important Italian translation of Euclid.

[38] Apparently Bernardus Papio (fl. mid-1500s), a Spaniard from Catalonia, author of *Tractatus de Reformatione Populi et de Ornatu Loquendi.* I find no record of his being in Italy—but his biographical notices are skimpy.

[39] John Dee (1527–1608), English mathematician, astrologer, alchemist, and necromancer.

[40] Jacopo Acontio (also Aconcio or Concio) or, in Latin, Acontius (1492–1566?), Italian engineer and religious reformer, after 1559 a refugee in England, who favored minimizing Christian dogma and was in disfavor with Protestants as well as with Catholics.

[41] David Chytræus, or, in German, Kochhafe (1531–1600), German Lutheran classical scholar, theologian, and polymath educational reformer.

[42] The massacre of Saint Bartholomew's Day, August 24, 1572, in which some three thousand Protestants were killed by order of Charles IX at the instigation of his mother, Catherine de Médicis. The massacre actually continued into August 26.

OF TRUE RELIGION, HÆRESIE, SCHISM, TOLERATION

March or April 1673

PREFACE AND NOTES BY KEITH W. F. STAVELY

Of True Religion was written and published sometime before May 6, 1673, the date of licensing of the Easter 1673 term catalogue in which it was advertised.[1] William Haller thought the tract was probably issued "in the early months of 1673." Parker was "inclined to think" it appeared soon after the "no Popery" Parliament adjourned on March 29, although he also states that this judgment is not based on internal evidence.[2] Before the date of publication can be investigated more carefully, it will be necessary briefly to review the government's ecclesiastical policy since the Restoration and describe in some detail the actions Parliament took during its session of February 4–March 29, 1673, in response to the king's Declaration of Indulgence of March 15, 1672. Insufficient attention paid to possible connections between the specific actions of this Parliament and specific arguments used by Milton is one of the sources of Masson's invidious comparisons between *Of True Religion* and *A Treatise of Civil Power*.[3]

On the basis of Charles II's Declaration of Breda of April 4, 1660, most Puritan factions were hopeful that the Restoration would not restore Laudian ecclesiastical policies:[4]

> And because the Passion and Uncharitableness of the Times have produced several Opinions in Religion by which men are engaged in Parties and Animosities against each other, which, when they shall hereafter unite in a Freedom of conversation, will be composed, or better under-

---

[1] Edward Arber, ed., *The Term Catalogues*, 3 vols. (London, 1903–6), I, 135. A work that shows a remarkable and contemptuous familiarity with Milton's writings in both prose and poetry is listed on the same page: Richard Leigh(?), *The Transproser Rehears'd* (Oxford, 1673; HCL). Parker, *Milton*, p. 629, counts seventeen references to Milton in this book. One of them is a glancing thrust at *Of True Religion*. See below, p. 428 and n. 45.

[2] Columbia, VI, 368; Parker, *Milton*, p. 1144.

[3] Masson, *Life*, VI, 696–99.

[4] The following passage from the Declaration of Breda is quoted in Frank Bate, *The Declaration of Indulgence, 1672* (Liverpool, 1908), pp. 5–6. Except where

stood; we do declare a liberty to tender Consciences; and that no man
shall be disquieted or called in question, for Differences of Opinion in
Matters of Religion which do not disturb the Peace of the Kingdom; and
that we shall be ready to consent to such an Act of Parliament, as, upon
mature Deliberation, shall be offered to us, for the full granting that
Indulgence.

Even assuming the sincerity of this and other such pronouncements, Charles's chronic dependence on Parliament for money and
supplies ensured the dominance of that largely Cavalier body in
making ecclesiastical policy. On December 20, 1661, it passed the
Corporation Act, the first of a series of ecclesiastical statutes later
known as the Clarendon Code. This law struck at the strongholds
of Puritanism by requiring all officeholders in corporations to swear
to the unlawfulness of taking up arms against the king and to
abjure all obligations arising from the Solemn League and Covenant. All officeholders elected after passage of the act were to be
required to take the sacrament according to the rites of the Church
of England. On May 19, 1662, the Act of Uniformity became law.
This required all ministers and schoolmasters to take the same
oaths required of corporation officers by the Corporation Act. It
also demanded "unfeigned assent and consent to all and everything
contained and prescribed in the book intituled 'The Book of Common Prayer.' " The penalty for those failing to comply was expulsion from their livings. On Saint Bartholomew's Day, August
24, 1662, approximately 1,800 ministers were so expelled. Two
years later on May 17, 1664, lay Nonconformity was suppressed
by the Conventicles Act, which forbade religious meetings of more
than four persons, over and above the members of the household,
and stipulated fines and prison terms, of increasing severity for
second, third, and later offenses. This act expired in 1667 but was
renewed in 1670, with added penalties for officials who failed to
enforce it rigorously enough. Finally, the Five-Mile Act of 1665
required all Nonconformist ministers to take the Oxford Oath,
which restated the unlawfulness of taking up arms against the king
and disallowed "any alteration of government either in church or
state." Those refusing to take the oath were forbidden to come
within five miles of any city, corporate town, or borough returning
burgesses to Parliament, or in which they had preached since the
Act of Oblivion. They were also forbidden to teach in schools.

In sum, a large proportion of Englishmen were restrained from
conscientious worship and their leaders were prevented from earn-

---

otherwise noted, the substance of the next three paragraphs is drawn from pp.
1–105 of this study.

ing a livelihood. Although the Clarendon Code was not rigorously enforced always and everywhere, its effect was severe enough to move one historian to call these years the period of "The Great Persecution." [5] Enforcement was neglected most systematically during the period between the dismissal of Clarendon in 1667 and the renewal of the Conventicles Act in 1670, and these years also saw the most voluminous "stream of pamphlets" on toleration and related issues to appear at any time between the Restoration and the toleration briefly established in 1672–73. [6] Charles was temperamentally disinclined to persecute, but except for such periods of de facto relief, he could do little to mitigate the harshly punitive code after the failure of his Declaration of Indulgence of December 26, 1662. His principal aim was of course an indulgence for Roman Catholics, and he connived throughout this period to prevent prosecution of papist recusants. Such efforts were redoubled after the secret Treaty of Dover concluded with Louis XIV in 1670, by which Charles received substantial payments from Louis in return for his agreement to support Louis against the Dutch, eventually to announce his own conversion, and to work toward the reestablishment of Roman Catholicism in England.

The financial independence of Parliament he thus achieved was probably the immediate reason Charles issued the Declaration of Indulgence on March 15, 1672, two days before the start of the Second Anglo-Dutch War. Lamenting "the sad experience of twelve years," which showed "that there is very little fruit of all these forcible courses," the declaration suspended all penal laws in ecclesiastical matters and invited Protestant Nonconformists to apply for licenses permitting public worship. Roman Catholics were allowed to worship "in their private houses only." [7] Immediately upon its publication, a "no Popery" agitation commenced in pulpit and pamphlet, in part engineered by the archbishop of Canterbury and the bishop of London. [8] Samuel Parker made several indirect but clearly critical references to the declaration, ref-

[5] Gerald R. Cragg, *Puritanism in the Period of the Great Persecution, 1660–1688* (Cambridge: Cambridge University Press, 1957).

[6] A. A. Seaton, *The Theory of Toleration under the Later Stuarts* (Cambridge, 1911), p. 134. Those in Parliament opposed to the Clarendon Code also became more numerous and vocal at this time.

[7] The text of the declaration is given in full in Bate, *Declaration*, pp. 76–78, and in William Cobbett, *A Parliamentary History of England*, 36 vols. (London, 1806–20), IV, 515–16.

[8] This agitation could not have been unexpected. In great part aroused by suspicions of Charles and his court, fears of popery had grown throughout the 1660s and had crystallized in the widespread belief that papists were responsible

erences that Marvell was quick to make more explicit.[9] Papists were advised "by a private exercise of your Worship, and a peaceable Demeanour to provide for the coming of a Parliament, as by Repentance men do for Death." [10] The response of Protestant Nonconformists was generally positive, and there were numerous applications for licenses to preach and worship in public. Reservations were expressed, however, because the declaration countenanced popery [11] and was felt to be constitutionally dubious, and because it was feared that Parliament would be in a vengeful mood at its next meeting. These hesitations were sufficiently widespread to provoke a series of pamphlets, aimed at an audience of Protestant Nonconformists of varying persuasions, arguing both sides of the question of whether or not such Nonconformists should avail themselves of the freedoms granted by the declaration.[12]

When Parliament met on February 4, 1673, it heard the king say in his opening speech, "I shall take it very ill to receive contradiction in what I have done. And I will deal plainly with you; I am resolved to stick to my Declaration." [13] The Commons nevertheless resolved on February 10 by a vote of 168 to 116 "that penal statutes, in matters ecclesiastical, cannot be suspended but by Act of Parliament." This was in effect the end of the declaration, although it was not officially withdrawn until March 8. When the Address to the King consequent upon the vote of February 10 was debated on February 14, the question of some measure "for ease

---

for the London Fire of 1666. See Michael McKeon, *Politics and Poetry in Restoration England* (Cambridge: Harvard University Press, 1975), pp. 132–47.

[9] Samuel Parker, *A Preface Shewing what Grounds there are of Fears and Jealousies of Popery,* prefixed to John Bramhall, *Bishop Bramhall's Vindication of Himself* (London, 1672; HCL), d4, e4; Andrew Marvell, *The Rehearsal Transpros'd* (London, 1672; HCL), pp. 13, 93.

[10] *A Letter to Mr. S. a Romish Priest* (London, May 19, 1672; HCL), p. 3.

[11] As Masson notices (*Life,* VI, 698), Quakers are not included in Milton's discussion (below, pp. 423–26) of the various Protestant groups that should be tolerated. A reason for this may be that the Quakers altogether refused to participate in the "no Popery" agitation provoked by the declaration.

[12] Against utilizing the declaration: *Toleration not to be Abused by the Independents* (London, 1672; UTSL); Francis Fullwood, *Toleration not to be Abused* (London, 1672; HCL), addressed to Presbyterians. In favor of utilizing the declaration: *Indulgence not to be Refused, Comprehension Humbly Desired* (London, 1672; HCL); *Short Reflections upon a Pamphlet Entituled Toleration not to be Abused* (London, 1672; UTSL); Richard Baxter, *Sacrilegious Desertion of the Holy Ministery Rebuked* (London, 1672; HCL); John Salkeld, *The Resurrection of Lazarus* (London, 1673; UTSL), a sermon actually preached on April 23, 1672.

[13] The following discussion of parliamentary actions relies on Bate, *Declaration,* pp. 106–29; and Cobbett, *Parliamentary History,* IV, 501–85.

of tender consciences" was immediately raised and was intermittently considered until March 19, when a bill "for the Ease of his majesty's Protestant subjects that are Dissenters in matters of Religion from the Church of England" passed the Commons. In the Lords the bill was saddled with amendments unacceptable to the Commons, and when Parliament adjourned on March 29, it had therefore not been enacted. As presented to the Commons on February 27 and as passed on March 19, the bill covered all Protestants who would subscribe to the doctrinal articles of the Church of England and take the Oaths of Allegiance and Supremacy. Such Protestants would no longer be penalized for not attending the parish church, would no longer be subject to the "assent and consent" clause of the Act of Uniformity, and would be allowed freedom of public worship, provided that every minister gave notice of where he intended to hold his meetings and took the required oaths. Such a law would have included Presbyterians, Independents, and some Baptists. Meanwhile, on February 28, the Commons began the debates that eventually produced the Test Act. The substance of the act is contained in the Commons' Address to the King of March 7, which also called upon the king to issue a proclamation expelling all priests and Jesuits and enforcing the penal laws against all other papist recusants. The king complied with these latter demands with his Proclamation of March 13. Officially called "An Act for preventing dangers that may happen by Popish Recusants," the Test Act was passed by the Commons on March 12 and became law on March 29. It required all holders of public office to take the Oaths of Allegiance and Supremacy, to receive the sacrament according to the rites of the Church of England, and to renounce the doctrine of transubstantiation.

Milton was probably informed of the proceedings in Parliament by Marvell and others, and there can be no doubt that he became intensely interested when he learned on February 14 or shortly thereafter that some form of toleration for Protestant Dissenters was under consideration. *Of True Religion* contains no references direct or indirect to the bill "for ease" that was moved in the Commons on February 27 and passed on March 19. An allusion to the matters eventually legislated in the Test Act would date the writing of the tract after February 28, but if I am correct in finding the language of the Royal Proclamation of March 13 reproduced in Milton's title,[14] *Of True Religion* was written and published sometime between March 13 and May 6, 1673.

[14] See below, pp. 417, 430, and nn. 1, 2, and 55.

This does not solve the problem of whether it was written before or after Parliament adjourned on March 29. In view of the silence Milton carefully maintained for thirteen years, I suspect Parker is correct in supposing that Milton kept quiet until it became clear, as it did not until adjournment, that the bill for ease would not be enacted at this session of Parliament.[15] As far as Milton knew, however, the bill's chances of passage at the next session were good. In Parker's words, "Milton thought the time auspicious for an attack on Popery in England and a terse argument for toleration among all English Protestants. . . . It was important to keep the issues simple and clear, and to link the case for toleration as closely as possible to the universal 'No Popery' agitation." [16] This accounts for the differences between *Of True Religion* and *Of Civil Power* that troubled Masson. In a sense, Milton has excised most of the arguments for toleration used in the earlier pamphlet, including his most cherished arguments from Christian liberty,[17] and has replaced them with an expanded polemic against popery,[18] leaving only the narrower, purely Protestant arguments for toleration that are the most appropriate to the immediate situation. In organizing his pamphlet so as to confront papist intrigues and superstitions with principles common to all Protestants, Milton approves Parliament's determined opposition to the Declaration of Indulgence and its passage of the Test Act and implies that these actions make logically necessary the enactment of the bill for ease of tender Protestant consciences. The bill almost passed in the session of Parliament that had just adjourned was not entirely satisfactory, however, for its requirement of accepting the Anglican doctrinal articles would have excluded antitrinitarians. In an attempt to rally support for a broader law, Milton fills his pamphlet with explicit references to official Anglican documents and with silent quotations of the best-known works of moderate or latitudinarian Anglicans, including one that says that an antitrinitarian is not necessarily a heretic, may indeed be a fellow Christian.[19]

[15] Milton's silence on constitutional questions remained undisturbed by the present pamphlet, and this is one of the many signs of its rhetorical prudence and restraint: The notorious defender of regicide keeps to himself his reaction to the spectacle of a Cavalier Parliament successfully resisting a Stuart king's attempt to assert his royal prerogative.

[16] Parker, *Milton,* pp. 624, 628.

[17] *Complete Prose,* VII, 262–65.

[18] On the basic contours and continuity of Milton's hostility to Roman Catholicism, see ibid., II, 178–81.

[19] See below, pp. 422–23, nn. 24, 27, and others. Aside from the hostile one documented below, p. 428 and n. 45, only one contemporary reaction to *Of True*

The present text is based on a facsimile of the copy of the 1673 edition in the library of the Andover-Harvard Divinity School, designated "A" in the textual notes below. A few minor variations and three major ones have been discovered as a result of collation with the following copies: B, New York Public Library; C, McAlpin Collection of the Union Theological Seminary Library; D, Beinecke Library of Yale University; E, Houghton Library of Harvard University. Copies A, B, and C agree with each other on all points but one; copies D and E agree with each other entirely. There are thus two distinct groups of texts. The most significant variants are at p. 12, lines 12–13 and 30–31, and p. 16, line 4. Lesser variants at p. 12, line 24, and p. 16, lines 7 and 8, appear to have been necessitated by the major ones. Milton must have been made aware of the printed contents before the impression was completed and must have corrected the readings of D and E to those found in A, B, and C.[20] The printer then made minor adjustments to maintain pagination. All copies share the following features: p. 12 mispaginated as 13 and p. 13 mispaginated as 12; the bottom of p. 15 and all of p. 16 set in much smaller type; a title page that identifies the author only as "J.M." and that does

---

Religion has been recorded. See the anonymous letter of 1675 printed in *CSPD, 1675–1676,* p. 89: "J. Milton has said more for [toleration] in two elegant sheets of true religion, heresy, and schism than all the prelates can refute in seven years." The writer goes on to associate Milton with William Penn and Jeremy Taylor. Also quoted in Parker, *Milton,* p. 628, and *Milton's Contemporary Reputation* (Columbus, Ohio, 1940), p. 50. Milton's conciliatory gestures toward Anglicans convinced a later commentator of his orthodoxy. Thomas Burgess's 1826 edition of the pamphlet, part of his campaign to prove that Milton was not the author of *Christian Doctrine,* contains the following remarks in the preface, p. xxv: "He does not scruple in this quiet evening of his life, to quote the Articles of the Church of England, and to appeal to her authority; and again identifies himself with the members of the Church of England in contrasting it with the Church of Rome. 'The papal Antichristian Church permits not her Laity to read the Bible in their own language. *Our Church,* on the contrary, hath proposed it to all men, and to this end translated it into English.' " Burgess attempts to construe the syntax of the account of antitrinitarian opinions (below, pp. 424–25) in a way that would support his theory of Milton's antipathy to antitrinitarianism. See also Nathaniel H. Henry, "Milton's Last Pamphlet: Theocracy and Intolerance," in *A Tribute to George Coffin Taylor,* ed. Arnold Williams (Chapel Hill, N.C., 1952), p. 205 n.

[20] Of the later editions I have examined, all follow D and E on the three major points except for the following: John Mitford, ed., *The Works of John Milton in Verse and Prose,* 8 vols. (London, 1851), V, 406–19; Frank A. Patterson, ed., *The Student's Milton* (New York, 1930), pp. 914–19; and Columbia, VI, 165–80, which is based on B.

not identify the printer. Collation: 4°: B–C⁴; pp. 16. Contents: p. [1], title; p. [2], blank; pp. 3–16, text.

Variants within this first edition [21] are as follows:

Page	Line	
6	24–25	*Heretick I will*]*Heretick will* (B)
9	1	enjoyns]enjoyes (D,E)
9	28	*6th*]*6th*, (D,E)
12	8	them? The]them The (A,B,C)
12	12–13	And the common]And [in several places of the Gospel,] The common (D,E)
12	17	They]they (D,E)
12	24	*Jerem.*] *Jeremiah* (D,E)
12	25	2.]2 (A,B,C)
12	30–31	expresly, [in several places of the Gospel,] But]expresly, But (D,E)
16	4	Clergy in prohibiting the Scripture. At]Clergy. At (D,E)
16	5	Latin which]Latin, which (D,E)
16	7	sold &]sold and (D,E)
16	8	Arminians, &]Arminians, and (D,E)
16	22	abounding:]abounding. (D,E,)
16	24	soul: the]soul, the (D,E)
16	31	*Agnus Dei's,*] *Agnus, Dei's* (D,E)
16	33	heart]hea t (D,E)
16	40	hainous]hanious (D,E)
16	49	penitency we]penitency qe (D,E)

This edition could not have been completed without the kind assistance of the staffs of the New York Public Library and the libraries of the Union Theological Seminary, Yale University, Boston University, Harvard University, and the Andover-Harvard Divinity School. I am indebted to my friend Michael McKeon for indispensable guidance on basic sources in Restoration history. The British Museum generously has granted permission to reproduce the 1673 title page found on p. 416.

[21] Later editions are: (1) F. Maseres, ed., *Occasional Essays on Various Subjects Chiefly Political and Historical* (London, 1809), pp. 416–30. (2) B. Flower, ed., *Thoughts on True Religion, Heresy, Schism, and Toleration . . . to which are Added Remarks on Essentials in Religion, Charitableness and Uncharitableness, Extracted from the Writings of Isaac Watts* (London, 1811). (3) Thomas Burgess, ed., *Protestant Union. A Treatise of True Religion, . . . to which is Prefixed a Preface on Milton's Religious Principles and Unimpeachable Sincerity* (London, 1826). (4) The tract is included in all complete collections of Milton's works or prose works, from the anonymously edited *The Works of Mr. John Milton* (London, 1697), pp. 428–34; and *A Complete Collection of the . . . Works of John Milton* (Amsterdam, 1698), pp. 807–12; to Columbia, VI, 165–80.

OF

True Religion,

HÆRESIE,

SCHISM,

TOLERATION,

And what beſt means may be
uſ'd againſt the growth of

POPERY

The Author *J. M.*

LONDON
Printed in the Year, 1673.

OF

True RELIGION,[1]
HÆRESIE, SCHISM,
and TOLERATION.

IT is unknown to no man, who knows ought of concernment among us, that the increase of Popery [2] is at this day no small trouble and offence to greatest part of the Nation; [3] and the rejoycing of all good men that it is so; the more their rejoycing, that God hath giv'n a heart to the people to remember still their great and happy deliverance from Popish Thraldom, and to esteem so highly the precious benefit of his Gospel, so freely and so peaceably injoy'd among them. Since therefore some have already in Publick with many considerable Arguments exhorted the people to beware the growth of this Romish Weed; [4] I thought it no less

[1] In the Royal Proclamation dated March 13, 1673, issued in response to the Parliamentary Address of March 7 calling for expulsion of priests and enforcement of penal laws against papists, Charles praised Parliament's demonstrated concern "for the preservation of the True Religion Established in this Kingdom."

[2] This phrase and the one used on the title page both echo the language of the proclamation cited above. Charles states that he is acting in response to a parliamentary petition representing "their fears and apprehensions of the Growth and Increase of the Popish Religion in these Our Dominions." Parker, *Milton*, p. 1144, notes that "growth and increase" is the language used in both the term catalogue advertisement and the listing of the pamphlet in Robert Clavel, comp., *The General Catalogue of Books Printed in England* [1666–74] (1675), p. 47.

[3] One of the participants in the Commons debate of February 14 reported that papist "insolence is the complaint in every street. This has filled the minds of the people with apprehensions." Cobbett, *Parliamentary History*, IV, 533. See also Robert Wild, *A Letter from Dr. Robert Wild* (London, 1672; HCL), p. 11: "I cannot deny to you, but that there was some *grumbling* of the *Gizard*, both amongst *Prelatists* and *Puritans*, that these cunning and cruel *Papists*, as we call them, and their croaking *Priests* and *Jesuits* should be exempted from *Penalties*." This letter is dated March 22, 1672, one week after the Declaration of Indulgence was promulgated.

[4] Andrew Marvell, who thoroughly approved of the Declaration of Indulgence and considered fears of popery to be groundless, had this to say about the "many considerable Arguments" deployed in antipapist exhortations: "[The Bishops]

then a common duty to lend my hand, how unable soever, to so
good a Purpose. I will not now enter into the Labyrinth of Councels
and Fathers, an intangl'd wood which the Papist loves to fight in,[5]
not with hope of Victory, but to obscure the shame of an open
overthrow: which yet in that kind of Combate, many heretofore,
and one of late,[6] hath eminently giv'n them. And such manner of
dispute [3] with them, to Learned Men, is useful and very com-

---

upon the publishing the Declaration gave the word, and deliver'd Orders through
their Ecclesiastical Camp to beat up the Pulpit Drums against Popery . . . though
for so many years, those your Superiors had forgot there was any such thing in
the Nation as a Popish Recusant, . . . all on a sudden (as if the 15*th* of *March*
had been the 5*th* of *November*) happy was he that could climb up first to get
down one of the old Cuirasses, or an Habergeon that had been worn in the dayes
of Queen *Elizabeth*. Great variety there was, and an heavy doo. Some clapp'd
it on all rusty as it was, others fell of oyling and furbishing their armour: . . .
Some by mistake catched up a Socinian or Arminian Argument, and some a
Papist to fight a Papist." *The Rehearsal Transpros'd* (London, 1672; HCL), pp.
268–69.

    [5] *Of Reformation, Complete Prose,* I, 569: "But I trust they for whom *God* hath
reserv'd the honour of Reforming this Church will easily perceive their adversaries
drift in thus calling for Antiquity, they feare the plain field of the Scriptures, the
chase is too hot; they seek the dark, the bushie, the tangled Forrest"; *The Likeliest
Means,* ibid., VII, 317: "To persue them further through the obscure and intangld
wood of antiquitie, fathers and councels fighting one against another, is needles,
endles, not requisite in a minister, and refus'd by the first reformers of our
religion." The fact that Milton is about to approve a kind of debate he had
previously condemned is the first of the tract's many conciliatory gestures toward
moderate Anglicans. See below, nn. 6 and 7.

    [6] There seems little doubt that this refers to Edward Stillingfleet, *A Discourse
concerning the Idolatry Practised in the Church of Rome* (London, 1671; HCL),
which was published three times by 1673 (a fourth edition appeared in 1676) and
which provoked at least eleven replies in the period 1671–73. Milton refers to
one of these replies three times (see below, nn. 63, 65, 66). In *Fanaticism Fanatically Imputed to the Catholick Church by Doctour Stillingfleet* (Douay(?),
1672; UTSL), "To the Reader," and pp. 50 ff., 88 ff., Hugh P. Cressy sneers at
Stillingfleet's "Latitudinarian conscience" and associates him with radical sectar-
ians and rebels. The "many heretofore" of Milton's text would include among
others various antipapist treatises of the 1660s written by Anglicans generally
regarded as moderate or latitudinarian. See, for example, Thomas Pierce, *The
Primitive Rule of Reformation* (London, 1663; HCL); Daniel Whitby, *Romish
Doctrines Not from the Beginning* (London, 1664; HCL); Jeremy Taylor, *A Dissuasive from Popery* (Dublin and London, 1664; HCL); and *The Second Part of
the Dissuasive from Popery* (London, 1667; HCL); Henry More, *A Modest Enquiry
into the Mystery of Iniquity* (London, 1664; HCL); *An Antidote against Idolatry*
(London, 1669; UTSL); and *A Brief Reply to a Late Answer* (London, 1672;
UTSL). Stillingfleet and his predecessors all argue on the basis of "Councels and
Fathers," though not exclusively or primarily.

mendable: [7] But I shall insist now on what is plainer to Common apprehension, and what I have to say, without longer introduction.

True Religion is the true Worship and Service of God, learnt and believed from the Word of God only.[8] No Man or Angel can know how God would be worshipt and serv'd unless God reveal it: He hath Reveal'd and taught it us in the holy Scriptures by inspir'd Ministers, and in the Gospel by his own Son and his Apostles, with strictest command to reject all other traditions or additions whatsoever. According to that of St. *Paul, Though wee or an Angel from Heaven preach any other Gospel unto you, than that which wee have preacht unto you, let him be Anathema, or accurst.*[9] And *Deut.* 4.2. *Ye shall not add to the word which I command you, neither shall you diminish ought from it.* Rev. 22.18, 19. *If any man shall add,* &c. *If any man shall take away from the Words,* &c. With good and Religious Reason therefore all Protestant Churches with one consent,[10] and particularly the Church of *England* in Her thirty nine Articles, Artic. 6*th,* 19*th,* 20*th,* 21*st,*[11]

[7] As noted above (n. 5), this contrasts sharply with Milton's comments in earlier pamphlets on the uselessness or sinfulness of arguments from antiquity. The latitudinarian view of tradition and antiquity, to which Milton's statement may allude, is outlined in Simon Patrick, *A Brief Account of the New Sect Called Latitude-Men* (London, 1662; YUL), p. 9: "in interpreting [Scripture], they carefully attend to the sense of the ancient Church, by which they conceive the modern ought to be guided: and therefore they are very conversant in all the genuine Monuments of the ancient Fathers, those especially of the first and purest ages, not to gather out fine phrases and quaint sentences, but that they may discern between the modern corruptions, and ancient simplicity of the Church; to distinguish between the Doctrines received in these latter ages, and those which the primitive Christians received from Christ and his Apostles: for those opinions in Religion, how specious soever, are justly to be suspected, whereof there are no footsteps to be discerned in that golden age of Christianity, that was tryed and purifyed in the fire of persecution: we are not so secure of the succeeding silver age of peace and prosperity, but that there might be some drossy mixture, inferior to the golden, but better than the brazen that trode upon its heels."

[8] *Christian Doctrine, Complete Prose,* VI, 132: "No one, however, can form correct ideas about God guided by nature or reason alone, without the word or message of God"; *Of Civil Power,* ibid., VII, 242: "we of these ages, having no other divine rule or autoritie from without us warrantable to one another as a common ground but the holy scripture."

[9] Gal. 1:8.

[10] *Of Civil Power, Complete Prose,* VII, 243: "With good cause therfore it is the general consent of all sound protestant writers, that neither traditions, councels nor canons of any visible church, much less edicts of any magistrate or civil session, but the scripture only can be the final judge or rule in matters of religion, and that only in the conscience of every Christian to himself."

[11] This is the most explicit of the pamphlet's attempts to persuade Anglicans. For Article 6, see below, p. 429. Articles 19 and 21 state that particular churches

and elsewhere,[12] maintain these two points, as the main Principles of true Religion: that the Rule of true Religion is the Word of God only: and that their Faith ought not to be an implicit faith,[13] that is, to believe, though as the Church believes, against or without express authority of Scripture. And if all Protestants as universally as they hold these two Principles, so attentively and Religiously would observe them, they would avoid and cut off many Debates and Contentions, Schisms and Persecutions, which too oft have been among them,[14] [4] and more firmly unite against the common adversary.[15] For hence it directly follows, that no true Protestant

---

and General Councils have erred. Article 21 concludes as follows: "Wherefore things ordained by [General Councils] as necessary to salvation, have neither strength nor authority, unless it may be declared that they be taken out of holy Scripture." Article 20 states that church ordinances may not contradict scripture and concludes as follows: "Wherefore, although the Church be a witness and a keeper of holy Writ, yet, as it ought not to decree any thing against the same, so besides the same ought it not to enforce any thing to be believed for necessity of salvation."

[12] Article 8 affirms the agreement with scripture of the Nicene, Athanasian, and Apostles' Creeds. Articles 22, 24, and 28 deny various Roman Catholic doctrines that are "plainly repugnant to the Word of God." Article 34 allows for diversity and mutability in ecclesiastical customs so long as "nothing be ordained against God's word." The substance of this article is not favorable to toleration and is debated below, pp. 427–29. See also "A Fruitfull Exhortation to the Reading and Knowledge of Holy Scripture," in *Certaine Sermons or Homilies Appointed to be Read in Churches in the Time of the Late Queen Elizabeth of Famous Memory* (London, 1623; HCL), p. 2: "Let us diligently search for the Well of Life in the bookes of the New and Old Testament, and not runne to the stinking puddles of mens traditions (devised by mens imagination) for our justification and salvation. For in holy Scripture is fully contayned what we ought to doe, and what to eschew; what to beleeve, what to love, and what to looke for at GODS hands at length."

[13] Among Milton's many references to this concept, the best known is in *Areopagitica, Complete Prose,* II, 543–44: "There be, who knows not that there be of Protestants and professors who live and dye in as arrant an implicit faith, as any lay Papist of Loretto."

[14] The language is much stronger in *Of Civil Power,* ibid., VII, 253: "How many persecutions then, imprisonments, banishments, penalties and stripes; how much bloodshed have the forcers of conscience to answer for, and protestants rather then papists!"

[15] Several speakers in the Commons debate of February 14 thought that the projected bill "for ease of tender consciences" should instead be called a bill "for Uniting Protestant subjects." Cobbett, *Parliamentary History,* IV, 527–29. See also Sir Charles Wolseley, *Liberty of Conscience the Magistrates Interest* (London, 1668; HCL), p. 13: "Liberty of Conscience will breed men up with an irreconcileable dislike to all imposition in Religion and Conscience, and so unite them in a general abhorrence of Popery, as the Grandmother and Author of it."

can persecute, or not tolerate his fellow Protestant, though dissenting from him in som opinions, but he must flatly deny and Renounce these two his own main Principles, whereon true Religion is founded; [16] while he compels his Brother from that which he believes as the manifest word of God, to an implicit faith (which he himself condemns) to the endangering of his Brothers soul,[17] whether by rash belief, or outward Conformity: for *whatsoever is not of Faith, is Sin.*[18]

I will now as briefly show what is false Religion or Heresie, which will be done as easily: for of contraries the definitions must needs be contrary. Heresie therefore is a Religion taken up and believ'd from the traditions of men and additions to the word of God. Whence also it follows clearly, that of all known Sects or pretended Religions at this day in Christendom, Popery is the only or the greatest Heresie: and he who is so forward to brand all others for Hereticks, the obstinate Papist, the only Heretick.[19] Hence one of their own famous Writers found just cause to stile the Romish Church *Mother of Error, School of Heresie.*[20] And

[16] This argument is made more succinctly and pointedly in Wolseley, *Liberty of Conscience the Magistrates Interest,* p. 6: "to instruct men in Protestant Principles, and then put a yoke of Uniformity upon them, has no more proportion in it, than to educate a man at *Geneva,* that is to live at *Rome,* and to breed him a *Calvinist* whom you intend for a *Papist.*" Several times in *Of Civil Power,* Milton makes similar accusations of the incipient popery involved in ecclesiastical coercion. See *Complete Prose,* VII, 245, 253–55. That he refrains from doing so here is further evidence that his rhetorical strategy is to avoid attacking Anglicans, certainly to avoid linking them with papists, at a time when they appear prepared to grant a limited toleration on grounds of Protestant unity against popery.

[17] *Of Civil Power, Complete Prose,* VII, 266: "It concerns the magistrate then to take heed how he forces in religion conscientious men: least by compelling them to do that wherof they cannot be perswaded, that wherin they cannot finde themselves justified, but by thir own consciences condemnd, instead of aiming at thir spiritual good, he force them to do evil." See also John Owen, *A Peace-Offering* (London, 1667; YUL), p. 37: "but as to our Minds and Consciences in the things of [God's] Worship and Service, he hath reserved the Soveraignty of them unto himself, to him must we give an account of them at the great Day; nor can we forego the care of preserving them intire for him, and loyal unto him, without a renunciation of all hopes of acceptance with him, and so render our selves of all men the most miserable."

[18] Rom. 14:23.

[19] *Of Civil Power, Complete Prose,* VII, 249: "concluding, that no man in religion is properly a heretic at this day, but he who maintains traditions or opinions not probable by scripture; who, for aught I know, is the papist only; he the only heretic, who counts all heretics but himself."

[20] This appears to be inaccurately recollected from Petrarch, Sonnet 107, line 2: "scola d'errori e templo d'eresia." Numbered 108, a translation of the latter portion of this sonnet is quoted in *Of Reformation, Complete Prose,* I, 559. Two

whereas the Papist boasts himself to be a Roman Catholick, it is a meer contradiction, one of the Popes Bulls, as if he should say, universal particular a Catholic Schismatic. For Catholic in Greek signifies universal: and the Christian Church was so call'd, as consisting of all Nations to whom the Gospel was to be preach't, in contradistinction to the Jewish Church, which consisted for the most part of Jews only. [5]

Sects may be in a [21] true Church as well as in a false, when men follow the Doctrin too much for the Teachers sake, whom they think almost infallible; and this becomes, through Infirmity, implicit Faith; and the name Sectary, pertains to such a Disciple. [22]

Schism is a rent or division in the Church, when it comes to the separating of Congregations; and may also happen to a true Church, as well as to a false; yet in the true needs not tend to the breaking of Communion; if they can agree in the right administration of that wherein they Communicate, keeping their other Opinions to themselves, not being destructive [23] to Faith. [24] The Pharisees and Saduces were two Sects, yet both met together in

---

other approving references to Petrarch's denunciations of papal corruptions appear in Milton's prose writings: *Of Reformation,* ibid., p. 577; and *Familiar Letters,* ibid., II, 764.

[21] in a]1673 a in

[22] The only acknowledgment in Milton's works of any inherent dangers in sectarianism, this may be another bow in the direction of the latitudinarians. See Henry Fowler, *The Principles and Practices of Certain Moderate Divines* (London, 1670; HCL), p. 297: "And upon the same grounds, that all Protestants complain of that Corrupted [Roman] Church; these Persons greatly blame those, whose practice is in this particular, like to theirs: and that while they inveigh against the Pope, make Popes of themselves, or of the Masters of their several Sects; and so intrench, as he doth, upon God's Authority."

[23] destructive]1673 destuctive

[24] Perhaps a reference to one of the latitudinarian classics: John Hales, *A Tract concerning Schisme and Schismatiques* (London, 1642; YUL). This tract became increasingly popular after the Restoration, particularly among Nonconformists. Marvell quotes extensively from it toward the end of *The Rehearsal Transpros'd.* From Milton's point of view it is of special interest because both in the present passage and in the one to which Milton more definitely alludes (see below, n. 27), Hales clearly implies comprehension or toleration of antitrinitarians. See p. 10: "I do not see that . . . men of different opinions in Christian Religion, may not hold communion in *Sacris,* and both go to one Church, why may I not go, if occasion require, to an *Arian* Church, so there be no Arianism exprest in their Liturgy, and were Lyturgies and Publique formes of Service so framed, as that they admitted not of particular and private fancies, but contained only such things, as in which all Christians do agree; *Schismes* on opinion were utterly vanished."

their common worship of God at *Jerusalem*.[25] But here the Papist will angrily demand, what! Are Lutherans, Calvinists, Anabaptists, Socinians, Arminians, no Hereticks? [26] I answer, all these may have some errors, but are no Hereticks. Heresie is in the Will and choice profestly against Scripture; error is against the Will, in misunderstanding the Scripture after all sincere endeavours to understand it rightly: Hence it was said well by one of the Ancients, *Err I may, but a Heretick I will not be*.[27] It is a humane frailty to err, and no man is infallible here on earth. But so long as all these profess to set the Word of God only before them as the Rule of faith and obedience; and use all diligence and sincerity of heart, by reading, by learning, by study, by prayer for Illumination of the holy Spirit, to understand the Rule and obey it, they have done

---

[25] This is mentioned in innumerable contemporary pamphlets. See, for example, *Persecution Inconsistent with Christianity* (London, 1670; HCL), pp. 24–25; *A Letter to a Member of this Present Parliament for Liberty of Conscience* (London, 1668; UTSL), p. 6; John Owen, *Indulgence and Toleration Considered* (London, 1667; HCL), p. 11. It was sufficiently commonplace to be used in the Commons debate of March 19 as a subsidiary argument in support of the bill granting relief to Protestant Dissenters. See Cobbett, *Parliamentary History*, IV, 573.

[26] It is of course in keeping with Milton's strategy to pretend that only "the Papist" would consider any of these groups heretical. No Anglican errors are listed in the ensuing discussion.

[27] In a discussion remarkably similar to Milton's, Hales (*A Tract concerning Schisme*, p. 9) attributes this dictum to Augustine. Hales goes on to suggest that Arius was not a heretic: "for *Heresie* is an act of the will, not of the reason, and is indeed a lye and not a mistake, else how could that of *Austen* go for true, *Errare possum, Haereticus esse nolo: . . .* but can any man avouch that *Arius* and *Nestorius,* and others that taught erroneously concerning the Trinity, and the person of our SAVIOUR, did maliciously invent what they taught, and not rather fall upon it by error and mistake? till that be done, and upon good evidence, we will think no worse of all parties than needs we must, and take these Rents in the Church to be at the worst but *Schisms,* upon matter of opinion." See also another latitudinarian masterpiece, Jeremy Taylor, *A Discourse of the Liberty of Prophesying* (London, 1647; YUL), pp. 23, 28: "For heresy is not an errour of the understanding, but an errour of the will . . . yet if [a man's] errour be not voluntary, and part of an ill life, then because he lives a good life, he is a good man, and therefore no Heretick. No man is a Heretick against his will." Nathaniel H. Henry, "Milton's Last Pamphlet," pp. 203–4, is correct in disputing Masson's claim (*Life,* VI, 696–97) that this definition of heresy is more conservative than the basic one given in *Of Civil Power.* See *Complete Prose,* VII, 247: "In apostolic times therfore ere the scripture was written, heresie was a doctrin maintaind against the doctrin by them deliverd: which in these times can be no otherwise defin'd then a doctrin maintaind against the light, which we now only have, of the scripture." A similar statement is made in *Christian Doctrine,* ibid., VI, 123. The difference between these definitions and the one given in the present pamphlet is rather that Milton forges an alliance with the latitudinarians by plagiarizing their distinction between error and heresy.

what man can do: God will assuredly pardon them, as he did the friends [6] of *Job,* good and pious men, though much mistaken, as there it appears, in some Points of Doctrin.[28] But some will say, with Christians it is otherwise, whom God hath promis'd by his Spirit to teach all things. True, all things absolutely necessary to salvation: But the hottest disputes among Protestants calmly and charitably enquir'd into, will be found less then such. The Lutheran holds Consubstantiation; an error indeed, but not mortal.[29] The Calvinist is taxt with Predestination, and to make God the Author of sin; not with any dishonourable thought of God, but it may be over zealously asserting his absolute power, not without plea of Scripture.[30] The Anabaptist is accus'd of Denying Infants their right to Baptism; again they say, they deny nothing but what the Scripture denies them.[31] The Arian and Socinian are charg'd to dispute against the Trinity:[32] they affirm to believe the Father, Son, and Holy Ghost, according to Scripture, and the Apostolic Creed;[33] as for terms of Trinity, Triniunity, Coessentiality, Tri-

[28] Job 42:7–10.

[29] *Christian Doctrine, Complete Prose,* VI, 554–55: "Consubstantiation and particularly transubstantiation and papal ἀνθρωποφάγια or cannibalism are utterly alien to reason, common sense and human behavior. What is more, they are irreconcilable with sacred doctrine, with the nature and the fruit of a sacrament, with the analogy of baptism, with the normal use of words, with the human nature of Christ and with the heavenly state of glory in which he is to remain until the day of judgment." This virtual equation of the Lutheran doctrine with popery is particularly interesting in view of Milton's comment below, pp. 431–32, that transubstantiation amounts to flat idolatry. But in the interests of Protestant unity, consubstantiation is here only "an error indeed, but not mortal." See also Henry More, *An Exposition of the Seven Epistles to the Seven Churches* (London, 1669; UTSL), p. 112: "yet a great part of this *Sardian* Church, I mean the *Lutherans,* rack their own Wits, and disturb the rest of Reformed Christendome, to maintain that odd Paradox of *Consubstantiation,* that so man may eat and drink that grosse Flesh and Bloud of *Christ* that was crucify'd upon the Crosse in the Celebration of their Eucharists."

[30] Discussed at length in *Christian Doctrine, Complete Prose,* VI, 153–202. The Calvinist "is taxt" with making God responsible for sin several times in this discussion, for instance at pp. 164–65: "To conclude, we should feel certain that God has not decreed that everything must happen inevitably. Otherwise we should make him responsible for all the sins ever committed, and should make demons and wicked men blameless." For similar comments by a latitudinarian, see Fowler, *Principles and Practices,* pp. 199–200.

[31] Milton agrees with "the Anabaptist" on this question. See *Christian Doctrine, Complete Prose,* VI, 544–50.

[32] For Milton's own "dispute against the Trinity," see ibid., pp. 203–98.

[33] For another statement of antitrinitarian acceptance of the Apostles' Creed, see ibid., pp. 278–79 and n. In *A Letter to a Member of this Present Parliament,* p. 10, as part of a discussion of the difficulty of agreeing on a formula for

personality, and the like, they reject them as Scholastic Notions, not to be found in Scripture,[34] which by a general Protestant Maxim is plain and perspicuous abundantly to explain its own meaning in the properest words, belonging to so high a Matter and so necessary to be known; [35] a mystery indeed in their Sophistic Subtilties, but in Scripture a plain Doctrin.[36] Their other Opinions are of less Moment. They dispute the satisfaction of Christ,[37] or rather the word *Satisfaction,* as not Scriptural: but they acknowledge him both God and their Saviour. The *Arminian* lastly is condemn'd for set- [7] ting up free will against free grace; [38] but that Imputation he disclaims in all his writings, and grounds himself largely upon

---

comprehension, the author remarks on "how little doth the dubious Creed of the Apostles conduce to the deciding among Protestants and *Socinians.*"

[34] For another denial that the Trinity is biblical, see *Christian Doctrine, Complete Prose,* VI, 420.

[35] Ibid., p. 214: "Let us look first at the gospel. This should provide the clearest evidence, for here we find the plain and exhaustive doctrine of the one God which Christ expounded to his apostles and they to their followers. It is very unlikely that the gospel should be ambiguous or obscure on this point."

[36] Ibid., p. 218: "But it is amazing what nauseating subtlety, not to say trickery, some people have employed in their attempts to evade the plain meaning of these scriptural texts. They have left no stone unturned; they have followed every red herring they could find; they have tried everything. Indeed they have made it apparent that, instead of preaching the plain, straightforward truth of the gospel to poor and simple men, they are engaged in maintaining an extremely absurd paradox with the maximum of obstinacy and argumentativeness. To save this paradox from utter collapse they have availed themselves of the specious assistance of certain strange terms and sophistries borrowed from the stupidity of the schools."

[37] This opinion is perhaps "of less Moment" because Milton disagrees with it, although he goes on to express even stronger disagreement with trinitarians. See ibid., p. 444: "Those who maintain that Christ sought death not in our place and for the sake of redemption, but only for our good and in order to set an example, try in vain to evade the evidence of these texts. Moreover I confess that I cannot see how those who hold that the Son is of the same essence as the Father manage to explain either his incarnation or his satisfaction."

[38] Ibid., pp. 189–90: "Many people decry this theory and violently attack it. They say that, since repentance and faith have been foreseen already, predestination is made subsequent to man's works. Thus, they say, this predestination depends upon human will. They say this deprives God of some of the glory of our salvation. They say that man is thus swollen with pride, that Christian consolation in life and death is shaken, and that gratuitous justification is denied. None of these objections can be allowed. On the contrary, this theory makes the method and consequently the glory not only of divine grace, but also of divine wisdom and justice considerably more apparent, and to show this was God's principal aim in predestination."

Scripture only.[39] It cannot be deny'd that the Authors or late Revivers of all these Sects or Opinions, were Learned, Worthy, Zealous, and Religious Men, as appears by their lives written,[40] and the same of their many Eminent and Learned followers, perfect and powerful in the Scriptures, holy and unblameable in their lives: and it cannot be imagin'd that God would desert such painful and zealous labourers in his Church, and ofttimes great sufferers for their Conscience, to damnable Errors & a Reprobate sense, who had so often implor'd the assistance of his Spirit; but rather, having made no man Infallible, that he hath pardon'd their errors, and accepts their Pious endeavours, sincerely searching all things according to the rule of Scripture, with such guidance and direction as they can obtain of God by Prayer.[41] What Protestant then who himself maintains the same Principles, and disavowes all implicit Faith, would persecute, and not rather charitably tolerate such men as these, unless he mean to abjure the Principles of his own Religion? [42] If it be askt how far they should be tolerated? I answer doubtless equally, as being all Protestants; that is on all occasions to give account of their Faith, either by Arguing, Preaching in their several Assemblies, Publick writing, and the freedom of Printing. For if the *French* and *Polonian* Protestants injoy all this liberty among Papists, much more may a Protestant justly expect it among

[39] Discussed at length in ibid., pp. 153–202. Although Milton's own Arminianism would have been evident to attentive contemporary readers of *Paradise Lost,* this passage may also function as another appeasing gesture in the direction of the Anglican establishment, which was frequently accused of Arminian deviance by orthodox Nonconformists. See John Owen, *A Discourse concerning Evangelical Love* (London, 1672; HCL), pp. 165–66; and *Short Reflections upon a Pamphlet,* pp. 21, 24–25.

[40] A recent and pertinent example was *The Life and Death of James Arminius and Simon Episcopius* (London, 1672; HCL).

[41] *Christian Doctrine, Complete Prose,* VI, 166: "There are some people, however, who, struggling to oppose this doctrine through thick and thin, do not hesitate to assert that God is, in himself, the cause and author of sin. If I did not believe that they said such a thing from error rather than wickedness, I should consider them of all blasphemers the most utterly damned." For similar comments in latitudinarian writings, see Fowler, *Principles and Practices,* p. 314: "They are so perswaded of the graciousness of the Divine Nature, that they verily believe that *simple* Errors shall be destructive to none, I mean, *those* which men have not contracted by their own default; and that where mistakes proceed not from evil affections, and an erring *judgment* from a corrupt *heart,* through the goodness of God, they shall not prove damnable. But that he will allow, and make abatements for the weakness of Mens Parts, their Complections, Educations, and other ill Circumstances, whereby they may be even *fatally* inclined to certain false Perswasions." See also Taylor, *Liberty of Prophesying,* pp. 42–43.

[42] See above, p. 421 and n. 16.

Protestants; [43] and yet some times here among us, the one persecutes the other upon every slight Pretence. [8]

But he is wont to say he enjoyns only things indifferent.[44] Let

[43] Both countries were often cited in tolerationist pamphlets, though usually without Milton's emphasis on the incongruity of papists tolerating and Protestants persecuting. See Owen, *Indulgence and Toleration Considered*, pp. 29–30. The relevant laws were for Poland the Confederation of Warsaw of 1573, and for France the Edict of Nantes of 1598. Both were being seriously undermined at the date of Milton's writing. In Poland the antitrinitarian community had been expelled in 1658, and in 1669 a law was passed prohibiting conversions of Roman Catholics to Protestantism, upon pain of death or exile. In France Louis XIV was well embarked on the policies that would lead to the Revocation of the Edict of Nantes in 1685. On Poland, see *Complete Prose*, VI, 61–65; and Count Valerian Krasinski, *Historical Sketch of the Rise, Progress, and Decline of the Reformation in Poland* (London, 1840), pp. 12, 290, 389–403, 411. On France, see Henry M. Baird, *The Huguenots and the Revocation of the Edict of Nantes*, 2 vols. (London, 1895), I, 419–566. On Milton's specific claim of "Publick writing, and the freedom of Printing" for French Protestants, see *A Brief Relation of the Persecution and Sufferings of the Reformed Churches of France* (London, 1668; HCL), p. 9: "Another [Act] hath restrained the Liberty of Printing any Books in favour of our Religion, by imposing upon us a necessity of obtaining Licences from the King's Council: Which any may well know they will never grant." A marginal note gives January 19, 1663 (1664), as the date of this law.

[44] The Anglican doctrine of indifferency, stemming from Article 34 (see above, n. 12) and various passages in Hooker (for example, *Ecclesiastical Polity*, V, x), is summarized in Edward Stillingfleet, *Irenicum: A Weapon Salve for the Churches Wounds* (London, 1661; HCL), p. 70: "So that whatsoever is left indifferent, obedience to the Magistrate in things indifferent is not: And if wee are not bound to obey in things undetermined by the word, I would fain know wherein we are bound to obey them? or what distinct power of obligation belongs to the authority the Magistrate hath over men? For all other things we are bound to already by former Laws; therefore either there must be a distinct authority without power to oblige, or else wee are effectually bound to whatsoever the Magistrate doth determine in lawful things." See also Richard Perrinchief, *A Discourse of Toleration* (London, 1668; UTSL), p. 38. In *Of Civil Power*, *Complete Prose*, VII, 263, Milton refers to arguments of this sort more directly and contemptuously: "They who would seem more knowing, confess that these things are indifferent, but for that very cause by the magistrate may be commanded." The most recent latitudinarian statement on this question, in Fowler, *Principles and Practices*, p. 305, differs only in emphasis: "we are bound by no means to oppose the Determinations of [the Church's] Governors and Representatives in disputable Matters; nor do they . . . require our internal Assent to their Articles, but enjoyn our submission to them, as to an Instrument of Peace onely. And what wise and good man can think, though he should suppose them (not only subject to error, but likewise) to have actually erred in some of them, that Contention about them can by any means make amends for the loss of the Churches Peace." For the orthodox Nonconformist view, see Owen, *Discourse concerning Evangelical Love*, p. 178: "And the Judgement which the Rulers of the Church are to make for the whole, or to go before it, is, in what is commanded, or not so, by Jesus Christ, not in what is fit to be added thereunto by themselves."

them be so still; who gave him authority to change their nature by injoyning them? If by his own Principles, as is prov'd, he ought to tolerate controverted points of Doctrine not slightly grounded on Scripture, much more ought he not impose things indifferent without Scripture. In Religion nothing is indifferent, but, if it come once to be Impos'd, is either a command or a Prohibition, and so consequently an addition to the word of God,[45] which he professes to disallow. Besides, how unequal, how uncharitable must it needs be, to Impose that which his conscience cannot urge him to impose, upon him whose conscience forbids him to obey? What can it be but love of contention for things not necessary to be done, to molest the conscience of his Brother, who holds them necessary to be not done? [46] To conclude, let such a one but call to mind his own Principles above mention'd, and he must necessarily grant, that neither he can impose, nor the other believe or obey ought in Religion, but from the Word of God only. More amply to understand this, may be read the 14*th.* and 15*th.* Chapters to the Romans, and the Contents of the 14*th,* set forth no doubt but with full authority of the Church of *England;* the Gloss is this. *Men may*

[45] The author of *The Transproser Rehears'd,* who repeatedly demonstrates his familiarity with Milton's writings, appears to refer to this passage, p. 110: "to avoid this Rock, you split upon a worse, concurring rather with your *Dear Friend* Mr. *Milton:* who says, that the only true Religion if commanded by the Civil Magistrate, becomes Unchristian, Inhuman, and Barbarous." See Preface, above, n. 1. Samuel Parker himself (if he is not the author of *The Transproser*) sneers copiously at this argument in *A Discourse of Ecclesiastical Politie* (London, 1670; HCL), pp. 175–98. A more moderate statement of Milton's view is given in Owen, *Discourse concerning Evangelical Love,* p. 180: "Moreover, suppose . . . that the things mentioned, though in their own nature indifferent, do become *unlawful* unto them to observe when imposed as necessary conditions of all Church-Communion, contrary to the command and appointment of Christ? . . . it is . . . unreasonable, that things *confessedly indifferent* should not be left so, but be rendred necessary unto practise, though useless in it, by arbitrary commands."

[46] Cf. Sir Charles Wolseley, *Liberty of Conscience upon Its True and Proper Grounds Asserted and Vindicated* (London, 1668; HCL), p. 42: "A Magistrate imposeth Uniformity in Religion, acknowledgeth himself not infallible, but that he may be under mistakes; acknowledgeth likewise that no man is bound to obey him actually in any thing sinful; acknowledgeth that the Judgment of what is sinful lies in every mans own Conscience, as to his particular actings, and that every mans Conscience, though erroneous, is to be followed till better informed. Take the coherence of these things, which are all granted Truths amongst us, and the result will be two-fold; First, That a man that cannot in Conscience conform to such an imposed Uniformity, as thinking it sinful, is punished for doing what is acknowledged to be his duty. Secondly, There can never be any other end in forcing Uniformity, where such Principles are taken for granted, but to bring such men into suffering, who resolve to keep their integrity."

not contemn, or condemn one the other for things indifferent.[47] And in the 6*th* Article above mentioned,[48] *whatsoever is not read in Holy Scripture, nor may be proved thereby, is not to be required of any man as an article of Faith, or necessary to salvation.* And certainly what is not so, is not to be required at all; as being an addition to the Word of God expressly forbidden. [9]

Thus this long and hot Contest, whether Protestants ought to tolerate one another, if men will be but Rational and not Partial, may be ended without need of more words to compose it.

Let us now enquire whether Popery be tolerable or no. Popery is a double thing to deal with, and claims a twofold Power, Ecclesiastical, and Political, both usurpt, and the one supporting the other.

But Ecclesiastical is ever pretended to Political.[49] The Pope by this mixt faculty, pretends right to Kingdoms and States, and especially to this of *England,* Thrones and Unthrones Kings, and absolves the people from their obedience to them; [50] sometimes interdicts to whole Nations the Publick worship of God, shutting up their Churches: [51] and was wont to dreign away greatest part of the wealth of this then miserable Land, as part of his Patrimony, to maintain the Pride and Luxury of his Court and Prelates: [52] and

[47] The full gloss on Rom. 14 in the 1611 edition of the Authorized Version is as follows: "3 Men may not contemn nor condemn one the other for things indifferent: 13 But take heed that they give no offence in them: 15 For that the Apostle proveth unlawfull by many reasons."

[48] See above, p. 419.

[49] See, among other parallel comments, *Areopagitica, Complete Prose,* II, 565. Virtually all participants in ecclesiastical debates since the sixteenth century had descanted on the political dangers of popery. See Richard Perrinchief, *Samaritanism Revised and Enlarged* (London, 1669; UTSL), p. 113 ff.; and John Humfrey, *A Proposition for the Safety and Happiness of King and Kingdom* (London, 1667; UTSL), p. 63: "The *Interest of State* consists not with the *Jesuite,* as the King's Supremacy does not with the *Pope.*"

[50] In a dispute over selection of the Archbishop of Canterbury, Innocent III excommunicated King John in 1209 and threatened him with deposition in 1212. John capitulated in 1213, recognizing the pope as his feudal overlord. Pius V's bull of 1569, *Regnans in Excelsis,* excommunicated Elizabeth and declared the queen's subjects "absolved from the oath of allegiance, and every other thing due unto her whatsoever; and those which from henceforth obey her are innodated with the anathema." Quoted in W. K. Jordan, *The Development of Religious Toleration in England,* 4 vols. (Cambridge, Mass., and London, 1932–40), I, 118 n.

[51] One of Innocent III's weapons in his struggle with John was his placing England under Interdiction from 1208 to 1214.

[52] Papal taxation was systematized toward the end of the twelfth century. Tax collectors, usually foreigners, came "armed with the full spiritual powers of coer-

now since, through the infinite mercy and favour of God, we have shaken off his *Babylonish* Yoke, hath not ceas'd by his Spyes and Agents, Bulls and Emissaries, once to destroy both King and Parliament; [53] perpetually to seduce, corrupt, and pervert as many as they can of the People.[54] Whether therefore it be fit or reasonable, to tolerate men thus principl'd in Religion towards the State, I submit it to the consideration of all Magistrates, who are best able to provide for their own and the publick safety.[55] As for tolerating the exercise of their Religion, supposing their State activities not to be dangerous, I answer, that Toleration is either public or private; and the exercise of their Religion, as far as it is Idolatrous, can be tolerated neither way: [56] [10] not publicly, without grievous and unsufferable scandal giv'n to all consciencious Beholders; not privately, without great offence to God, declar'd against all kind of Idolatry, though secret.[57] *Ezekiel* 8.7, 8. *And he brought me to*

---

cion" and were resented as "essentially extortionate. . . . beyond the actual financial sacrifice there was a not unjustified fear of what might come next from a papacy that advanced with relentless logic from tax to tax, progressing steadily in financial efficiency, and using for its purposes the spiritual sanctions of excommunication and suspension. Feelings of grievance were aggravated in the fourteenth century by the knowledge that wealth was passing out of England into hands that were now regarded as bound in sympathy with the national foe [i.e., France]." David Knowles, writing in *Medieval England,* ed. Austin Lane Poole, 2 vols. (Oxford: Clarendon Press, 1958), II, 418–20. John received his kingdoms back from Innocent III in return for a payment of tribute, but it was not long before this obligation was disregarded.

[53] A reference to the Gunpowder Plot.

[54] For a discussion of papal missionary activities at the court of Charles I, see Jordan, *Development,* II, 186–96. See also Cobbett, *Parliamentary History, IV,* 531: "These [Jesuits], out of an excellent good intention, commit high treason every day, going to jails to convert people condemned; they get into our houses, perverting people every day; surely his majesty's good intentions are abused."

[55] This expression of confidence in the magistrate, and the fact that Milton sees no need to make his own recommendations, indicates that the pamphlet was written and published after the Commons first discussed on February 28 what later became the Test Act on March 29.

[56] Disloyalty and idolatry were the two reasons most frequently adduced for not tolerating Roman Catholics. See, among others, Edward Bagshaw, Jr., *A Brief Enquiry into the Grounds and Reasons Whereupon the Infallibility of the Pope and Church of Rome is Founded* (London, 1662; HCL), Preface, B3; Humfrey, *Proposition for the Safety,* pp. 62–63; and *Short Reflections upon a Pamphlet,* pp. 4, 25.

[57] Masson (*Life,* VI, 697) laments the contrast between this and the statement on the same issue in *Of Civil Power, Complete Prose,* VII, 254–55: "Lastly, for idolatrie, who knows it not to be evidently against all scripture both of the Old and New Testament, and therfore a true heresie, or rather an impietie; wherin

the door of the Court, and when I looked, behold a hole in the Wall. Then said he unto me, Son of Man, digg now in the wall; and when I had digged, behold a Door, and he said unto me, go in, and behold the wicked Abominations that they do here. And verse 12. *Then said he unto me, Son of Man, hast thou seen what the Antients of the house of* Israel *do in the dark?* &c. And it appears by the whole Chapter, that God was no less offended with these secret Idolatries, then with those in public; and no less provokt, then to bring on and hasten his Judgements on the whole Land for these also.

Having shown thus, that Popery, as being Idolatrous, is not to be tolerated either in Public or in Private; it must be now thought how to remove it and hinder the growth thereof, I mean in our Natives, and not Forreigners, Privileg'd by the Law of Nations.[58] Are we to punish them by corporal punishment, or fines in their Estates, upon account of their Religion? I suppose it stands not with the Clemency of the Gospel, more then what appertains to the security of the State: [59] But first we must remove their Idolatry, and all the furniture thereof, whether Idols, or the Mass wherein

---

a right conscience can have naught to do; and the works therof so manifest, that a magistrate can hardly err in prohibiting and quite removing at least the publick and scandalous use therof." The contrasting emphasis in the present pamphlet on suppressing the private as well as the public worship of Roman Catholics is to be ascribed not to a change in Milton's convictions but to the rhetorical needs of the moment. The Declaration of Indulgence had permitted only private worship by Catholics. By a vote of February 10, the Commons had effectively destroyed the declaration, which was formally withdrawn on March 8. Meanwhile, the Commons continued to debate a limited toleration for nonconforming Protestants. Milton thus obliquely approves the forced withdrawal of the declaration in the hope that Parliament will regard him and other Nonconformists as allies deserving of relief.

[58] Cobbett, *Parliamentary History*, IV, 523: "You cannot hinder [Merchant-strangers], by law of nations." But for an account of the fears and disorders occasioned by the clerical retinue of Charles I's Catholic queen and by services at the queen's chapel as well as at churches affiliated with the embassies of Catholic countries, see Jordan, *Development*, II, 182–84.

[59] After quoting this sentence, Masson (*Life*, VI, 699) wonders "how there could have been a policy of suppression without fines and imprisonment." But while disavowing coercion of Roman Catholics "upon account of their Religion," Milton sees no objection to fining and imprisoning them for their subversive politics. The penal laws against Roman Catholics had been officially justified in exactly this manner ever since they were first enacted in 1570 in response to the bull cited above, n. 50. See Jordan, *Development*, I, 119–31, 163–77.

they adore their God under Bread and Wine: [60] for the Commandment forbids to adore, not only *any Graven Image, but the likeness of anything in Heaven above, or in the Earth beneath, or in the Water under the Earth, thou shalt not bow down to them nor worship them, for I the Lord thy God* [11] *am a Jealous God.*[61] If they say that by removing their Idols we violate their Consciences, we have no warrant to regard Conscience which is not grounded on Scripture: [62] and they themselves confess in their late defences, that they hold not their Images necessary to salvation, but only as they are enjoyn'd them by tradition.[63]

Shall we condescend to dispute with them? The Scripture is our only Principle in Religion; and by that only they will not be Judg'd, but will add other Principles of their own, which, forbidden by the Word of God, we cannot assent to. And the common Maxim also in *Logic* is, *against them who deny Principles, we are not to dispute.*[64] Let them bound their disputations on the Scripture only, and an ordinary Protestant, well read in the Bible, may turn and wind their Doctors. They will not go about to prove their Idolatries by the Word of God, but run to shifts and evasions, and frivolous

[60] That transubstantiation entails idolatry is argued in Stillingfleet, *Discourse concerning the Idolatry,* pp. 96–120; More, *Antidote against Idolatry,* pp. 40–52; and Taylor, *Dissuasive from Popery,* pp. 137–38.

[61] Exod. 20:5.

[62] *Of Civil Power, Complete Prose,* VII, 254: "Besides, of an implicit faith, which they profess, the conscience also becoms implicit; and so by voluntarie servitude to mans law, forfets her Christian libertie. Who then can plead for such a conscience, as being implicitly enthrald to man instead of God, almost becoms no conscience, as the will not free, becoms no will."

[63] Statements to this effect, not presented as confessions, are made in John Vincent Canes, *An Account of Dr. Stillingfleet's Late Book against the Church of Rome* (n.p., 1672; UTSL), pp. 18–21. Canes reprinted this tract with the same pagination as the first of the three letters in his ΤΩ ΚΑΘΟΛΙΚΩ *Stillingfleeton* (Bruges, 1672; UTSL).

[64] Aristotle, *Physics,* I.ii, in *The Basic Works of Aristotle,* ed. Richard McKeon (New York, 1941), p. 219: "For just as the geometer has nothing more to say to one who denies the principles of his science . . . so a man investigating *principles* cannot argue with one who denies their existence." See also *Eikonoklastes, Complete Prose,* III, 547: "But he who neither by his own Letters and Commissions under hand and Seale, nor by his own actions held as in a Mirror before his face, will be convinc'd to see his faults, can much less be won upon by any force of words, neither he, nor any that take after him; who in that respect are no more to be disputed with, then they who deny Principles"; and Patrick, *Brief Account of the New Sect,* p. 24: "How shall the Clergy . . . encounter with the witts (as they are called) of the age, that assault Religion with new kind of weapons? will they acquiesce in the authority of *Aristotle* or St. *Thomas?* or be put off with a *Contra negantem principia?*"

distinctions: Idols they say are *Laymens* Books, and a great means to stir up pious thoughts and Devotion in the Learnedst.[65] I say they are no means of Gods appointing, but plainly the contrary: Let them hear the Prophets; *Jerem.* 10.8. *The stock is a Doctrin of Vanities.* Habakkuk 2.18. *What profiteth the graven Image that the maker thereof hath graven it: The Molten Image and a teacher of Lyes?* But they alleadge in their late answers, that the Laws of *Moses* giv'n only to the Jews, concern not us under the Gospel: [66] and remember not that Idolatry is forbidden as expresly, [in several places of the Gospel,] [67] But with these wiles and fallacies *compassing Sea and Land, like the Pharisees of old, to make* [12] *one Proselite,* they lead away privily many simple and ignorant Souls, men or women, *and make them twofold more the Children of Hell then themselves,* Matt. 23.15. But the Apostle hath well warn'd us, I may say, from such Deceivers as these, for their Mystery was then working. *I beseech you Brethren,* saith he, *mark them which cause divisions and offences, contrary to the doctrin which ye have learned, and avoid them; for they that are such serve not our Lord Jesus Christ, but their own belly, and by good words and fair speeches deceive the heart of the simple,* Rom. 16.17, 18.

The next means to hinder the growth of Popery will be to read duly and diligently the Holy Scriptures, which as St. *Paul* saith to *Timothy,* who had known them from a child, *are able to make wise unto salvation.*[68] And to the whole Church of *Colossi; Let the*

---

[65] *Christian Doctrine, Complete Prose,* VI, 693: "So the Papists are mistaken when they call idols the layman's books." A recent statement of this doctrine appears in Canes, *Account,* pp. 16–17: "the same is without words painted unto us by these compendious hieroglyphicks, serving more speedily then words can do, to fasten us into a strict recollection in our prayers by one short glance about us, and to a fear and awfulness of Gods presence . . . and also to a dissipation of any worldly thoughts, . . . All this benefit we have by our Pictures, when we have haply no book to look upon, or know not by our ignorance to read."

[66] See Canes, *Account,* p. 41: "I add yet withal, over and above what is yet said, that neither the law of Moses, nor any of his Ten Commandments, nor any other of his precepts either ceremonial judicial or moral, does any way oblige Christians at all, as it comes from Moses, who is not our Lawmaker or master, but ruler and leader of the Jews." See also Stillingfleet, *Discourse concerning the Idolatry,* pp. 80–81: "This [survey of patristic evidence] I have the more largely insisted upon, to shew, . . . that the command against *Image-worship* was no Ceremonial *Law,* respecting mearly the *Jews,* but that the reason of it doth extend to all *Ages* and Nations, and especially to us who live under the *Gospel.*"

[67] Acts 14:14–15, 17:29–30; 1 Cor. 12:2, 10:14, 20 ff.; 2 Cor. 6:14, 16; Gal. 5:20; Rev. 21:8; and 1 John 5:20 are all cited in this connection in More, *Modest Enquiry,* p. 5. The brackets are not editorial insertions but part of the 1673 text.

[68] 2 Tim. 3:15.

word of Christ dwell in you plentifully, with all wisdome, Coloss.
3.16. The Papal Antichristian Church permits not her Laity to read
the Bible in their own tongue: Our Church on the contrary hath
proposd it to all men, and to this end translated it into English,
with profitable Notes on what is met with obscure,[69] though what
is most necessary to be known be still plainest: [70] that all sorts and
degrees of men, not understanding the Original, may read it in
their Mother Tongue.[71] Neither let the Countryman, the Trades-
man, the Lawyer, the Physician, the Statesman, excuse himself by
his much business from the studious reading thereof. Our Saviour
saith, Luke 10.41, 42. *Thou art careful and troubled about many
things, but one thing is needful.* If they were ask't, they would be
loath to set earthly things, wealth, [13] or honour before the wisdom
of salvation. Yet most men in the course and practice of their lives
are found to do so; and through unwillingness to take the pains of
understanding their Religion by their own diligent study, would
fain be sav'd by a Deputy.[72] Hence comes implicit faith, ever
learning and never taught,[73] much hearing and small proficience,
till want of Fundamental knowledg easily turns to superstition or

[69] *Likeliest Means, Complete Prose,* VII, 304: "To these I might add other
helps, which we enjoy now, to make more easie the attainment of Christian
religion by the meanest: the entire scripture translated into English with plenty
of notes." But see *Apology,* ibid., I, 932, where Milton attacks the guides of "our
Church" for failing to do exactly what he commends them for doing here: "For
while none thinke the people so void of knowledge as the Prelats think them,
none are so backward and malignant as they to bestow knowledge upon them;
both by suppressing the frequency of Sermons, and the printed explanations of
the English Bible."

[70] *Christian Doctrine,* ibid., VI, 578–79: "Thus the scriptures are, both in
themselves and through God's illumination absolutely clear. If studied carefully
and regularly, they are an ideal instrument for educating even unlearned readers
in those matters which have most to do with salvation."

[71] Ibid., p. 577: "It is clear from all these texts that no one should be forbidden
to read the scriptures. On the contrary, it is very proper that all sorts and conditions of men should read them or hear them read regularly."

[72] Cf. the "Character" of the conforming "heretick in the truth" who finds "som
factor, to whose care and credit he may commit the whole managing of his
religious affairs." *Areopagitica,* ibid., II, 544.

[73] *Likeliest Means,* ibid., VII, 302, 320: "1 *Tim.* 3.7. *ever learning and never
attaining;* yet not so much through thir own fault, as through the unskilful and
immethodical teaching of thir pastor, . . . But while Protestants, to avoid the due
labor of understanding thir own religion are content to lodge it in the breast or
rather in the books of a clergie man, and to take it thence by scraps and mammocks
as he dispences it in his sundays dole, they will be alwaies learning and never
knowing, alwaies infants."

Popery: Therefore the Apostle admonishes, Eccles. 4.14.[74] *That we henceforth be no more children tossed to and fro and carryed about with every wind of Doctrine, by the sleight of men, and cunning craftiness whereby they lye in wait to deceive.*[75] Every member of the Church, at least of any breeding or capacity, so well ought to be grounded in spiritual knowledg, as, if need be, to examine their Teachers themselves, Acts. 17.11. *They searched the Scriptures dayly, whether those things were so.* Rev. 2.2. *Thou hast tryed them which say they are Apostles, and are not.* How should any private Christian try his Teachers unless he be well grounded himself in the Rule of Scripture, by which he is taught.[76] As therefore among Papists, their ignorance in Scripture cheifly upholds Popery; so among Protestant People, the frequent and serious reading thereof will soonest pull Popery down.[77]

Another means to abate Popery arises from the constant reading of Scripture, wherein Beleivers who agree in the main, are every where exhorted to mutual forbearance and charity one towards the other, though dissenting in some opinions. It is written that the Coat of our Saviour was without seame:[78] whence some would infer that there should be no [14] division in the Church of Christ.[79] It should be so indeed; Yet seams in the same cloath, neither hurt

[74] The quotation that follows is from Eph. 4:14.

[75] This text was often cited by Roman Catholics as evidence of the need for an infallible church. See Cressy, *Fanaticism Fanatically Imputed to the Catholick Church,* p. 102.

[76] *Christian Doctrine, Complete Prose,* VI, 600: "They should be able, through the scriptures and the Spirit, to put any teacher to the test, or even the whole body of teachers at once, though these may try to pass themselves off under the title of the church." See also *Apology,* ibid., I, 931–32.

[77] Cf. Wolseley, *Liberty of Conscience the Magistrates Interest,* p. 13. This argument was also used by those who supported the Declaration of Indulgence and discounted popery as a serious threat. The passage cited above (n. 3) from *A Letter from Dr. Robert Wild* continues as follows: "Let but the *King* . . . allow us our *Bibles,* and we have 100000 *Shop-keepers* and *Farmers* (and let our *Ministers* stand by and keep our *Gole,* and strike never a stroke) that dare meet as many of their *Fryers* and *Monks* at a *Disputation,* and let any *point* (for which formerly they made *Smithfield* smoak) that they will chuse, be the *Foot-ball.* My friends, fear not *Anti-Christ,* nor his Masters *cloven foot.* Let but us love the *Truth,* and the *Truth* will make us free, and keep us so."

[78] John 19:23.

[79] Such inferences are made by the licenser of *Paradise Lost,* Thomas Tomkins, in *The Inconveniencies of Toleration* (London, 1667; HCL), p. 6: "Uniformity if it were carefully maintained, and diligently looked after, would in a few years recall our Ancient Unity; The People would quickly forget all these Fantasies, if it were not for these small *Levites* which are perpetually buzzing them into their ears; We should quickly see, that the People would come to the Churches,

the garment, nor misbecome it; and not only seams, but Schisms will be while men are fallible: [80] But if they who dissent in matters not essential to belief, while the common adversary is in the field, shall stand jarring and pelting at one another, they will be soon routed and subdued. The Papist with open mouth makes much advantage of our several opinions; [81] not that he is able to confute the worst of them, but that we by our continual jangle among our selves make them worse then they are indeed. To save our selves therefore, and resist the common enemy, it concerns us mainly to agree within our selves, that with joynt forces we may not only hold our own, but get ground; and why should we not? The Gospel commands us to tolerate one another, though of various opinions, and hath promised a good and happy event thereof, *Phil.* 3.15. *Let us therefore as many as be perfect be thus minded; and if in any thing ye be otherwise minded, God shall reveal even this unto you.* And we are bid, 1 *Thess.* 5.21. *Prove all things, hold fast that which is good.* St. *Paul* judg'd that not only to tolerate, but to examine and prove all things, was no danger to our holding fast of that which is good. How shall we prove all things, which includes all opinions at least founded on Scripture, unless we not only tolerate them, but patiently hear them, and seriously read them? If he who thinks himself in the truth professes to have learnt it, not by implicit faith, but by attentive study of the Scriptures & full perswasion of heart, with what equity can he refuse to hear or read him, who demonstrates to have gained his knowledge by the same

---

if there were not so many Conventicles to keep them thence; and if they were but used for a little while to come thither, they would not find the Liturgy to be such a fearful Idol, as they have been often told of."

[80] Cf. John Hales, *Golden Remains* (London, 1673; HCL), p. 50: "for since it is impossible, where Scripture is ambiguous, that all conceits should run alike, it remains, that we seek out a way, not so much to establish an unity of opinion in the minds of all, which I take to be a thing likewise impossible, as to provide, that multiplicity of conceit, trouble not the Churches peace." This collection was first published in 1659. See also Owen, *Discourse concerning Evangelical Love*, p. 102: "For the *Unity of Faith* did never consist in the same precise Conceptions of all revealed Objects: Neither the nature of Man, nor the means of Revelation, will allow such a Unity to be morally Possible."

[81] Usually while arguing the insufficiency of scripture as the sole rule of faith. See, for example, Edward Worsley, *Protestancy without Principles* (Antwerp, 1668; HCL), p. 99: "Unity in Doctrin (most known and remarkable in the Catholick Church) they have none, witnes those innumerable Sects which now swarm amongst them, and this new Faith hath produced of *Arminians, Zwinglians, Brownists, Independents* &c. And now our late *Quakers* are sprouted out of it, the last spring, perhaps, (though no body knows) of this Reformed Gospel."

way? is it a fair course to assert truth by arrogating to himself the only freedome of speech, and stopping the [15] mouths of others equally gifted? This is the direct way to bring in that Papistical implicit faith which we all disclaim. They pretend it would unsettle the weaker sort: [82] the same groundless fear is pretended by the Romish Clergy in prohibiting the Scripture.[83] At least then let them have leave to write in Latin which the common people understand not; that what they hold may be discust among the Learned only.[84] We suffer the Idolatrous books of Papists, without this fear, to be sold & read as common as our own. Why not much rather of Anabaptists, Arians, Arminians, & Socinians? There is no Learned man but will confess he hath much profited by reading Controversies, his Senses awakt, his Judgement sharpn'd, and the truth

[82] This may refer to such commonplaces as the following in Parker, *Discourse of Ecclesiastical Politie,* p. 7: "Most mens minds or Consciences are weak, silly, and ignorant things, acted by fond and absurd principles, and imposed upon by their vices and their passions; so that were they entirely left to their own conduct, in what mischiefs and confusions must they involve all Societies." But in view of the earlier allusions to Hales, and especially in view of the fact that Milton immediately concedes something to this position (see below, n. 84), it is more likely that he was thinking of Hales's sermon on Rom. 14:1, "Him that is weak in the faith receive, but not to doubtful disputations," in *Golden Remains,* pp. 47–48: "For as for the Unlearned, in private, nothing more usual with them then to take offence at our dissentions, and to become more uncertain and unjoynted upon the hearing of any question discust: It is their usual voice and question to us, Is it possible that we should be at one in these points in which your selves do disagree? thus cast they off on our backs the burthen of their backsliding and neutrality; wherefore to acquaint them with Disputation in Religion, were as it were to blast them in their infancy, and bring upon them some improsperous Disease to hinder their growth in Christ. . . . A third reason is the marvellous violence of the weaker sort in maintaining their conceits, if once they begin to be Opinionative. For one thing there is that wonderfully prevails against the reclaiming of them, and that is, The natural jealousie they have of all that is said unto them by men of better wits, stand it with reason never so good, if it sound not as they would have it. A jealousie founded in the sense of their weakness, arising out of this, that they suspect all to be done for no other end but to circumvent and abuse them. And therefore when they see themselves to be too weak in reasoning, they easily turn them to violence."

[83] This view is briefly stated in another of the replies to Stillingfleet's *Discourse:* Abraham Woodhead, *The Roman-Church's Devotions Vindicated* (London, 1672; UTSL), p. 68: "But [the Holy Scriptures], mean while, (as sad experience shews,) are better withheld from all such, who seem self-wise, disobedient, not well-contented and resigned, in all matters difficult, and controverted there, to submit to the Churche's judgment."

[84] As suggested above (n. 82), this concession to Hales's analysis of "the weaker sort" is in keeping with the pamphlet's general strategy. No doubt Milton hoped that the enactment of some form of toleration for Protestant Nonconformists would allow him to publish *Christian Doctrine.* See Parker, *Milton,* p. 627.

which he holds more firmly establish't.[85] If then it be profitable for him to read; why should it not at least be tolerable and free for his Adversary to write? In *Logic* they teach, that contraries laid together more evidently appear: [86] it follows then that all controversies being permitted, falshood will appear more false, and truth the more true: which must needs conduce much, not only to the confounding of Popery, but to the general confirmation of unimplicit truth.

The last means to avoid Popery, is to amend our lives: it is a general complaint that this Nation of late years, is grown more numerously and excessively vitious then heretofore; Pride, Luxury, Drunkenness, Whoredom, Cursing, Swearing, bold and open Atheism every where abounding: [87] Where these grow, no wonder if

[85] *Areopagitica, Complete Prose,* II, 516–17: "Since therefore the knowledge and survay of vice is in this world so necessary to the constituting of human vertue, and the scanning of error to the confirmation of truth, how can we more safely, and with lesse danger scout into the regions of sin and falsity then by reading all manner of tractats, and hearing all manner of reason? And this is the benefit which may be had of books promiscuously read." As noted in James H. Elson, *John Hales of Eton* (New York, 1948), p. 39, Milton and the latitudinarians part company on this point. Milton's emphasis on vigorous and unrestrained debate is askew from the latitudinarian longing for "the Churches peace" and resembles instead the position taken by even a conservative Independent in Owen, *Discourse concerning Evangelical Love,* p. 103: "Neither is there any thing implyed in the means of preserving the *Unity of Faith,* that should hinder us from explaining, confirming and vindicating, *any Truth* that we have received, wherein others differ from us; provided that what we do, be done with a spirit of meekness and love; Yea, our so doing is one principal means of *ministring nourishment* unto the Body, whereby the whole is increased as with the increase of God."

[86] *Art of Logic,* above, p. 250: "for although arguments of disagreement be equally manifest among themselves, so that one cannot be argued from another as better known, nevertheless from their disagreement—or, as others say, by their juxtaposition—they do show forth more clearly. Thus the advantages of good health are made more manifest by the disadvantages of poor health, and the praise of virtue is elucidated by the censure of the contrary vice."

[87] Such a complaint is part of the meaning of *Paradise Lost,* VII, 32–38. See also Nicholas Lockyer, *Some Seasonable and Serious Queries* (London, 1670; HCL), p. 12: "Whether it had not been more prudential, and better becoming the Wisdom and Gravity of the State, and the true Ordinance of Magistracy, that bears not the Sword in vain, to have made some vigorous Act to have inforc'd that first wholsome Proclamation to suppress Health Drinking, swinish Drunkenness, prophane Swearing, and abominable Whoredoms, that so fearfully abound, and are wink'd at, tolerated, and encouraged in the Land; and to suppress Stage Plays, those Nurseries of all manner of Vice and Wickedness, so numberless, and to which there are such great assembling and flocking of all sorts?" The argument is that suppressing all this would have been far better than the renewal of the Conventicles Act.

Popery also grow a pace. There is no man so wicked, but at somtimes his conscience will wring him with thoughts of another world, & the Peril of his soul: the trouble and melancholy which he conceives of true Repentance and amendment he endures not; but enclines rather to some carnal Superstition, which may pacify and lull his Conscience with some more pleasing Doctrin. None more ready and officious to offer her self then the *Romish,* and opens wide her Office, with all her faculties to receive him; easy Confession, easy Absolution, Pardons, Indulgences, Masses for him both quick and dead, *Agnus Dei's,* Reliques, and the like: and he, instead of *Working out his salvation with fear and trembling,*[88] strait thinks in his heart (like another kind of fool then he in the Psalmes) [89] to bribe God as a corrupt judge; and by his Proctor, some Priest or Fryer, to buy out his Peace with money, which he cannot with his repentance.[90] For God, when men sin outragiously, and will not be admonisht, gives over chastizing them, perhaps by Pestilence, Fire, Sword, or Famin,[91] which may all turn to their good, and takes up his severest punishments, hardness, besottedness of heart, and Idolatry, to their final perdition. Idolatry brought the Heathen

---

[88] Phil. 2:12.

[89] Ps. 14:1: "The fool hath said in his heart, There is no God."

[90] Cf. Richard Baxter, *Fair-Warning: Or XXV Reasons against Toleration and Indulgence of Popery* (London, 1663; HCL), p. 13: "They debauch poor souls with Licenciousness, that when they are troubled in conscience, and upon their death-bed, know not how to be saved: they may in dispair throw themselves into *Popery* for that pardon and indulgence which no other Religion can afford them." Even though Baxter had been one of those ejected the previous Saint Bartholomew's Day, he issued this tract in opposition to the Declaration of Indulgence of December 26, 1662.

[91] The London Plague of 1665, the London Fire of 1666, and the defeats suffered in the Dutch Wars were often cited as divine judgments, visited on England for reasons that varied with the grievance of the writer. Refraining from attacks on anyone but papists, Milton ascribes God's wrath to the most general of causes, outrageous sinning, and removes whatever political impact there might be in this interpretation by declining to blame the court of "the Merry Monarch" for England's moral collapse. There were others who professed to discern in these events the divine displeasure with the Clarendon Code. See *A Few Sober Queries* (London, 1668; HCL), p. 4: "And whereas God never left following the Nation, with some severe Judgments since that Law [against Conventicles] was first made, until the execution of it was relaxed; hath not the Nation sufficiently felt the evil Consequences of this, with the other Laws against *Nonconformists*? for what Publick Judgments have we been under, ever since some of them were made? Shall we forget the *Plague, Fire,* and late *War*?" See also Humfrey, *Proposition for the Safety,* p. 5.

to hainous Transgressions, *Romans 2 d.*[92] And hainous Transgressions oft times bring the slight professors of true Religion, to gross Idolatry: 1 Thess. 2.11, 12.[93] *For this cause, God shall send them strong delusion that they should believe a lye, that they all might be damnd who believe not the truth, but had pleasure in unrighteousness.* And Isaiah 44.18. Speaking of Idolaters, *They have not known nor understood, for he hath shut their Eyes that they cannot see, and their hearts that they cannot understand.* Let us therefore using this last means, last here spoken of, but first to be done, amend our lives with all speed; least through impenitency we run into that stupidly, which we now seek all means so warily to avoid, the worst of superstitions, and the heaviest of all Gods Judgements, Popery.

FINIS

[92] This enigmatic reference is emended in most editions to "Romans ii." Milton appears to be thinking, however, of Rom. 1:21–32.

[93] The ensuing quotation is actually 2 Thess. 2:11–12.

A DECLARATION, OR LETTERS PATENTS OF THE ELECTION OF THIS PRESENT KING OF POLAND JOHN THE THIRD

July 1674(?)

PREFACE AND NOTES BY MAURICE KELLEY

A translation of a Latin *Diploma Electionis S.R.M. Poloniæ* promulgated by the Poles in 1674, *A Declaration, or Letters Patents* is the last and rarest of Milton's prose works. Published in London by Brabazon Aylmer, probably in July or a little later in 1674,[1] the pamphlet is preserved, to my knowledge, in only six copies: British Museum; Christ's College, Cambridge; Harvard; Indiana; Texas; and Yale.[2] Textually, these differ significantly in only two instances: British Museum, Christ's College, Harvard, and Indiana read "strategam" and "interriegn" where Texas and Yale have "stratagem" and "Inter-reign."[3] Milton's name is not printed on the pamphlet, but five of the known copies have on their title pages an added manuscript attribution—all in the same printed hand— reading "by Iohn Milton," while the sixth, Harvard, bears on its title page the inscription "John Phillips J.M. 1674."[4] The pamphlet is furthermore assigned to Milton in Edward Phillips's list of his uncle's works[5] and printed in the 1698 edition of Milton's prose.[6]

---

[1] Masson's date (*Life,* VI, 725), and generally accepted by later scholars.

[2] Collating, according to Parker (*Milton,* p. 1151), 4°: A–B⁴, pp. [ii], 12, [2]. The contents: pp. [i–ii], blank; p. [1], title; p. [2], blank; pp. 3–12, text; pp. [13–14], blank.

[3] Below, p. 448, n. 7, and p. 451, n. 16.

[4] Reported by Parker, *Milton,* p. 1151, as missing since 1947 but recovered by Miss Carolyn E. Jakeman in 1972 and now in the Houghton Library.

[5] *Letters of State Written by Mr. John Milton* (London, 1694), p. [liii].

[6] *A Collection of Historical, Political, and Miscellaneous Works of John Milton,* 3 vols. (Amsterdam [London], 1698; PUL), I, 44, and II, 839–43.

Of the circumstances leading to publication we know nothing.[7] Did, for instance, Aylmer bring the Latin document to Milton for translation, or did Milton bring the translation to Aylmer for publication? Was Milton merely translating the Latin document for a translator's fee, or had Milton been following contemporary events in Poland and wished that that nation's election of a strong king be made known to the English people? As French has rightly observed, "No satisfactory explanation for his [Milton's] having performed this unusual task at this period in his age has been offered." [8]

Even though Milton possibly was not familiar with current Polish events, a comprehension of the history lying behind the *Diploma Electionis* is useful in understanding Milton's *A Declaration*. Slightly larger than Texas, the commonwealth of Poland consisted primarily of Great and Little Poland and the Grand Duchy of Lithuania.[9] These were divided into palatinates ruled by Palatines; and the palatinates were in turn divided into castellanies ruled by Castellans. An elected king, sometimes a foreigner, served as head of state. Assisting him as a somewhat large privy council was the Senate, made up of high ecclesiastics and great nobles; and complementing this body was the Diet, a general assembly of representatives chosen by the provincial diets of the palatinates.[10]

The noble elected to succeed the dead King Michael was the forty-five-year-old Crown General Jan Sobieski. He was descended from an old and distinguished Polish family; and in spite of a weak and pitiable king and an intestinely troubled kingdom, he had gained a series of brilliant military victories against superior forces of Turks, Tartars, and Cossacks. In 1674, Sobieski was indeed man of the hour. But his election was not won without foreign competition and domestic opposition. These, however, his supporters overcame by intrigue, bribery, and the cleverness of his extraordinary wife, Maria Kazimiera; and on May 22, 1674, Sobieski was elected to the crown. The Latin *Diploma Electionis*,

[7] For assumptions and suggestions, however, see Masson, *Life*, VI, 725–27; Parker, *Milton*, p. 638; and Christopher Hill, *Milton and the Puritan Revolution* (New York: Viking Press, 1978), pp. 219–20.

[8] French, *Life Records*, V, 83–84.

[9] Gathered around and united with these three were the other territories enumerated below, p. 451.

[10] For more on the political structure of Poland, see Earl Morse Wilbur, *A History of Unitarianism: Socinianism and Its Antecedents* (Cambridge: Harvard University Press, 1945), pp. 268–69, and *The Cambridge History of Poland from Its Origins to Sobieski*, ed. W. F. Reddaway et al. (Cambridge: Cambridge University Press, 1950), pp. 417–40.

which Milton translated, was the official announcement of Sobieski's ascent to the throne.[11]

In translating the *Diploma*, Milton has introduced paragraphs into the body of the document, which in its original form is set solid in italic type. A more important change is his omission of the long lists of names and titles of the Poles attending the election. He thus reduces the eleven-page *Diploma* by some four and one-half pages and rids it of data that are historically important but of little, if any, interest to his prospective English reader.

I wish to thank the Beinecke Library at Yale University for permission to use the title page reproduced on the following page.

[11] *Cambridge History of Poland*, pp. 532–39. A nineteenth-century account of Sobieski is Alicia T. Palmer, *Authentic Memoirs of John Sobieski, King of Poland* (London, 1815); a recent biography is Otto Forst-Battaglia, *Jan Sobieski, König von Polen* (Zurich: Benziger & Co., 1956).

A

DECLARATION,

OR

Letters Patents of the Election
of this present

King of POLAND

JOHN the Third,

Elected on the 22ᵈ of *May* laſt paſt,
Anno Dom. 1674.

Containing the Reaſons of this Election, the
great Vertues and Merits of the ſaid Serene Elect, His eminent Services in War, e-
ſpecially in his laſt great Victory againſt the
𝕿urks and 𝕿artars, whereof many Particulars are here related, not publiſhed before.

Now faithfully tranſlated from the Latin Copy.

By John Milton

LONDON,
Printed for *Brabazon Aylmer,* at the Three Pigeons in
Cornhil, 1674.

LETTERS PATENTS[1] OF THE ELECTION OF THE MOST SERENE KING OF POLAND.

In the name of the most holy and Individual [2] Trinity, the Father, Son, and Holy Spirit.

WE ANDREW TREZEBICKI, Bishop of *Cracovia,* Duke of *Severia,* JOHN GEMBICKI of *Uladislau* and *Pomerania,* &c. Bishops to the number of Ten.[3]

STANISLAUS WARSZYCKI, Castellon of *Cracovia;* ALEXANDER MICHAEL LUBOMIRSKI of *Cracovia,* &c. Palatines to the number of Twenty Three.

CHRISTOPHERUS GRZYMALTOUSKI of *Posnania,* ALEXANDER GRATUS de *Tarnow* of *Sandimer:* Castellons to the number of Twenty Four.

HILAREUS POLUBINSKI, High Marshal of the great Dukedom of *Lituania,* CHRISTOPHERUS PAC, High-Chancelor of the great Dukedom of *Lituania,* Senators and Great Officers, to the number of Seventy five.

WE Declare by these our present Letters unto all and single Persons whom it may concern: Our Commonwealth being again left Widowed,[4] by the unseasonable death of that famous MICHAEL late King of *Poland,* who having scarce reigned

---

[1] Plural (after Latin *Litteræ Patentes*) with singular meaning: "an open letter or document, usually," according to *NED,* "from a sovereign or person in authority, issued for various purposes, e.g., to put on record some agreement or contract."

[2] *NED,* A, 1: "one in substance or essence, forming an indivisible entity," translating *Individuæ.*

[3] By such summaries here and at the ends of the three following paragraphs, Milton disposes of some three and a half pages of names and titles significant to the Latin *Diploma* but not to the English reader.

[4] A trope to be repeated some three centuries later: "France is a widow"— President Pompidou announcing the death of Charles de Gaulle (*New York Times,* Nov. 11, 1970, 1:8). The Latin is *Viduata iterum Respublica Nostra.*

full five years, on the tenth day of *November* of the year last past, at *Leopolis,* changed his fading Crown for one Immortal; in the sence of so [3] mournful a Funeral and fresh Calamity, yet with an undaunted Courage, mindful of her self in the midst of Dangers, forbore not to seek Remedies, that the World may understand she grows in the midst of her losses; it pleased her to begin her Counsels of preserving her Country, and delivering it from the utmost chances of an Interreign,[5] from the Divine Deity, (as it were by the only motion of whose finger) it is easie that Kingdoms be transferred from Nation to Nation, and Kings from the lowest state to Thrones; And therefore the business was begun according to our Countrey-Laws and Ancestors Institutions. After the Convocation of all the States of the Kingdom ended, in the month of *February* at *Warsaw,* by the common consent of all those States on the day decreed for the Election the 20th of *April;* At the report of this famous Act, as though a Trumpet had been sounded, and a Trophy of Vertue erected, the wishes and desires of Forreign Princes came forth of their own accord into the Field of the *Polonian* Liberty, in a famous strife of Merits and good-will towards the Commonwealth, every one bringing their Ornaments, advantages and Gifts to the Commonwealth: But the Commonwealth becoming more diligent by the prodigal ambition used in the last Interreign, and Factions, and disagreeings of minds, nor careless of the future, considered with her self whether firm or doubtful things were promised, and whether she should seem from the present state to transfer both the old and new honours of *Poland* into the possession of strangers, or the military glory, and their late unheard-of Victory over the *Turks,* and blood spilt in the war, upon the purple of some unwarlike Prince; as if any one could so soon put on the love of the Country, and that *Poland* was not so much an enemy to her own Nation and Fame, as to favour strangers more than her own; and valour being found in her, should suffer a Guest of new Power to wax proud in her; therefore she thenceforth turned her [4] thoughts upon some one in her own Nation, and at length abolished (as she began in the former Election) that reproach cast upon her, under pretence of a secret Maxime, *That none can be elected King of* Poland *but such as are born out of Poland;* neither did she seek long among her Citizens whom she should prefer above the rest (for this was no uncertain or suspended Election, there was no

[5] Interregnum. *NED,* 1, lists no use of the term after Speed, 1611. Owing to the elective nature of the kingship, Polish interreigns were not infrequent. Translating *Interregni.*

place for delay;) for although in the equality of our Nobles many might be elected, yet the vertue of a Hero appeared above his equals, therefore the eyes and minds of all men were willingly and by a certain divine instinct turned upon the High Marshal of the Kingdom, Captain of the Army *John Sobietski*. The admirable vertue of the Man, the High Power of Marshal in the Court, with his supreme command in Arms, Senatorial Honour, with his civil Modesty, the extraordinary Splendor of his Birth and Fortune, with open Courtesie, Piety towards God, love to his Fellow-Citizens in words and deeds; Constancy, Faithfulness, and Clemency towards his very enemies, and what noble things soever can be said of a Hero, did lay such Golden Chains on the Minds and Tongues of all, that the Senate and People of *Poland* and of the great Dukedome of *Lituania;* with Suffrages and agreeing Voices named and chose him their KING; not with his seeking nor precipitate counsel, but with mature Deliberations continued and extended till the third day.

Certainly it conduced much for the honour of the most serene Elect, the Confirmation of a free Election, and the eternal praise of the People electing, that the great business of an Age was not transacted in one day, or in the Shadow of the night, or by one casuul heat [6]: for it was not right that a Hero of the Age, should in a moment of time (and as it were by the cast of a Die) be made a King, when as Antiquity by an ancient Proverb has delivered, that *Hercules* was not begot [5] in one night; and it hath taught that Election should shine openly under a clear Sky, in the open Light.

The most serene Elect took it modestly that his Nomination should be deferred till the third day, plainly shewing to endeavour, lest his sudden facility of assent being suspected, might detract from their Judgment, and the World might be enforced to believe by a more certain Argument, that he that was so chosen was elected without his own Ambition, or the envy of corrupted Liberty: or was it by the appointed Counsel of God that this debate continued three whole days, from *Saturday* till *Munday,* as if the *Cotimian* Victory (begun on the Saturday, and at length on the third day after accomplished, after the taking of the *Cotimian* Castle) had been a lucky presage of his Royal Reward; or, as if with an auspicious *Omen,* the third day of Election had alluded to the Regal name of *JOHN* the Third.

---

[6] *NED*, 9: "a single intense effort or bout of action; one continuous operation." The Latin is *nec uno fortuito impetu.*

The famous Glory of War paved his way to the Crown, and confirmed the favour of Suffrages to his most serene Elect. He the first of all the *Polonians* shewed that the *Scythian* swiftness (troublesome heretofore to all the Monarchies of the World) might be repressed by a standing Fight, and the terrible main Battalion of the *Turk,* might be broken and routed at one stroke. That we may pass by in silence the ancient Rudiments of Warfare which he stoutly and gloriously managed under the Conduct and Authority of another, against the *Swedes, Muscovites, Borussians, Transylvanians* and *Cossacks;* though about sixty Cities taken by him from the *Cossacks* be less noised in the mouth of fame; yet these often and prosperous Battels, were a *Prelude* to greatest Victories in the memory of man. Miriads of *Tartars* had overrun within this six years with their plundering Troops the coast of *Podolia;* when a small force and some shattered Legions were not sufficient against the hostile assault, yet our General knowing [6] not to yeeld, shut himself up (by a new stratagem [7] of War) in *Podhajecy,* a strait Castle, and fortified in haste, whereby he might exclude the cruel destruction which was hastening into the bowels of the Kingdom, by which means the Barbarian deluded and routed, took Conditions of Peace; as if he had made his inroad for this only purpose, that he might bring to the most serene Elect, matter of Glory, Victory.

For these Four last years the famous Victories of *Sobietski* have Signalized every year of his Warlike Command on the *Cossacks,* and *Tartarians,* both joyned together; the most strong Province of *Braclavia,* as far as it lyes betwen *Hypanis* and *Tyral,* with their Cities and Warlike people, were won from the *Cossack* enemy.

And those things are beyond belief which two years ago the most serene Elect, after the taking of *Camenick,* (being undaunted by the Seige of *Laopolis,*) performed to a Miracle by the hardness and fortitude of the *Polonian* Army, scarce consisting of three thousand men, in the continual course of five days and nights, sustaining life without any food, except wild herbs; setting upon the *Tartarians,* he made famous the names of *Narulum, Niemicrovia, Konarnum, Kalussia,* obscure Towns before, by a great overthrow of the Barbarians. He slew three Sultans of the *Crim-Tartars,* descended of the royal *Gietian* family, and so trampled on that great force of the *Scythians,* that in these latter years they could not regain their Courage or recollect the Forces. But the felicity of this last Autumn exceeded all his Victories; when-as the fortifications at *Chocimum,*

---

[7] BM, CCC, H, I, strategam.

famous of old, were possessed and fortified by above forty thousand Turks, in which three and forty [8] years ago the *Polonians* had sustained and repressed the Forces of the *Ottoman* Family, drawn together out of *Asia, Africa,* and *Europe,* fell to the ground within a few hours; by the only (under God) Imperatorious Valour and Prudence, [7] of *Sobietski;* for he counted it his chief part to go about the Watches, order the Stations, and personally to inspect the preparations of Warlike Ordinance, to encourage the Soldiers with voice, hands, and countenance, wearied with hunger, badness of weather, and three days standing in arms; and he (which is most to be admired) on Foot at the head of the foot-forces made thorough and forced his way to the Battery, hazarding his life devoted to God and his Countrey; and thereupon made a cruel slaughter within the Camp and Fortifications of the Enemy; while the desperation of the *Turks* whetted their valour, and he performed the part of a most provident and valiant Captain; at which time three *Bashaw's* [9] were slain, the fourth scarce passed with difficulty the swift river of *Tyras;* eight thousand *Janizaries,* twenty thousand chosen *Spachies,* [10] besides the more Common Souldiers, were cut off; the whole Camp with all their Ammunition, and great Ordinance: besides the *Assyrian* and *Phrygian* wealth of luxurious *Asia,* were taken and pillaged, the famous Castle of *Cotimia,* and the Bridg over *Tyras,* strong Fortresses, equal to Castles on each side the River, were additions to the Victory. Why therefore should not such renown'd Heroick Valour be crowned with the legal reward of a Diadem? All *Christendom* have gone before us in example, which being arrived to the recovery of *Jerusalem* under the conduct of *Godfrey of Bullion,* on their own accord gave him that Kingdom, for that he first scaled the walls of that City. Our most serene Elect is not inferior, for he first also Ascended two main Fortresses of the Enemy.

The moment of time adorns this Victory unheard-of in many ages, the most serene King *Michael* dying the day before, as it were signifying thereby that he gave way to so great valour, as if it were by his command and favour, that this Conqueror might so much the more gloriously suceed [8] from the Helmet to the Crown, from the Commanders Staff to the Scepter, from his lying in the Field to the Regal Throne.

---

[8] "Three and forty" is incorrect. The Latin reads *tres & quinquaginta.*
[9] An earlier form of Pasha.
[10] Obsolete form of Spahi: a Turkish cavalryman.

The Commonwealth recalled the grateful, and never to be forgotten memory of his Renowned Father, the most Illustrious and Excellent *James Sobietski,* Castellion of *Cracovia,* a Man to be written of with sedulous care, who by his Golden Eloquence in the publick Counsels, and by his Hand in the Scene of War, had so often amplified the State of the Commonwealth, and defended it with the Arms of his Family. Neither can we believe it happened without Divine Providence, that in the same place wherein forty years ago his Renowned Father Embassador of the *Polonian-*Commonwealth, had made Peace and Covenants with *Cimanus* [11] the Turkish General, his great Son should Revenge with his Sword the Peace broke, (Heaven it self upbraiding the perfidious Enemy). The rest of his Grandsires and Great-Grandsires, and innumerable Names of Famous Senators and great Officers have as it were brought forth light to the serene Elect by the emulous Greatness and Glory of his Mothers descent, especially *Stanislaus Zelkievius,* High Chancellor of the Kingdom, and General of the Army, at whose Grave in the Neighbouring fields, in which by the *Turkish* rage in the year 1620 [12] he died, his victorious Nephew took full revenge by so remarkable an overthrow of the Enemy: The immortal valour and fatal fall of his most noble Uncle *Stanislaus Danilovitius* in the year 1635, Palatine of *Russia,* doubled the Glory of his Ancestors; whom desirous of honour and not induring that sluggish Peace wherein *Poland* then slept secure, valour and youthful heat accited [13] at his own expence and private forces, into the Taurick fields; that by his footing [14] and the ancient Warlike Polonian discipline, he might lead and point the way to these merits of *Sobietski,* and being slain by *Canti-* [9] *miz* the Tartarian Cham, in revenge of his Son by him slain, he might by his Noble blood give lustre to this Regal Purple; neither hath the people of *Poland* forgot the most illustrious *Marcus Sobietski* elder Brother of our most serene Elect, who when the Polonian Army at *Batto* was routed by the Barbarians, although occasion was offer'd him of escape, yet chose rather to die in the overthrow of such valiant men, a Sacrifice for his Countrey, than to buy his life with a dishonourable retreat; perhaps the divine Judgment so disposing, whose order is that persons pass away and fail, and causes and

[11] The Latin is *Osmano.*

[12] Milton has corrected the "1920" of the *Diploma.*

[13] *NED,* 1: "to summon, to call, to cite," with Milton's use here cited as the last. The Latin is *propulerat.*

[14] *NED,* 2: "a footprint, or footprints collectively; a trace, track, trail," translating *per vestigia sua.*

events happen again the same; that by the repeated fate of the *Huniades,* the elder Brother of great hopes removed by a lamented slaughter, might leave to his younger Brother surviving the readier passage to the Throne. That therefore which we pray may be happy, Auspicious and fortunate to our Orthodox Commonwealth, and to all Christendome, with free and unanimous Votes, none opposing, all consenting and applauding, by the right of our free Election, notwithstanding the Absence of those which have been called and not Appeared, We being led by no private respect, but having only before our eyes the Glory of God, the increase of the ancient Catholick Church, the safety of the Commonwealth, and the dignity of the *Polish* Nation and Name, have thought fit to elect, create,[15] and name, *JOHN in Zolkiew and Zloczew Sobietski,* Supreme Marshal General of the Kingdom General of the Armies, Governour of *Neva, Bara, Strya, Loporovient,* and *Kalussien,* most eminently adorned with so high endowments, merits and splendor, to be *KING* of *Poland,* Grand-Duke of *Lituania, Russia, Prussia, Mazovia, Samogitia, Kyovia, Volhinnia, Padlachia, Podolia, Livonia, Smolensko, Severia,* and *Czerniechovia,* as we have Elected Created Declared and Named Him; I the afore said Bishop of *Cracovia* (the Archiepiscopal See being vacant) exercising the Office and Authority of Primate and [10] by consent of all the States thrice demanded, opposed by none, by all and every one approved, conclude the Election: Promising faithfully that we will always perform to the same most serene and potent Elect Prince, Lord *John the third,* our King, the same Faith, Subjection, Obedience and Loyalty according to our Rights and Liberties, as we have performed to his blessed Ancestor, as also that we will crown the same most serene Elect in the next Assembly at *Cracovia,* to that end ordained, as our true King and Lord, with the Regal Diadem, with which the Kings of *Poland* were wont to be crown'd, and after the manner which the *Roman* Catholick Church before-time hath observed in Anointing and Inaugurating Kings, We will anoint and inaugurate him; Yet so as he shall hold fast and observe first of all the Rights, Immunities both Ecclesiastical and Secular, granted and given to us by his Ancestor of Blessed memory; as also these Law's which we our Selves, in the time of this present and former Inter-reign,[16] according to the Right of our Liberty, and better preservation of the Commonwealth have established. And if moreover the most Serene Elect will bind himself by an Oath,

[15] *NED,* 3: "to invest with rank, title," translating *creandum.*
[16] BM, CCC, H, I, interriegn.

to perform the conditions concluded with those persons sent by his Majesty, before the exhibition of this present Decree of Election, and will provide in best manner for the performance of them by his authenick Letters; which Decree of Election we by Divine aid, desirous to put in execution, do send by common consent, to deliver it into the hands of the most Serene Elect, the most illustrious and reverend Lord Bishop of *Cracovia,* together with some Senators and chief Officers, and the illustrious and magnificent *benedictus Sapieha,* Treasurer of the Court of the Great Dukedom of *Lituania,* Marshal of the *Equestrian* Order; commiting to them the same Decree of intimating [17] an Oath, upon the aforesaid premises, and receiving his Subscription; and at length to give and deliver [11] the same Decree into the hands of the said Elect, and to act and perform all other things which this affair requires, in assurance whereof the Seals of the Lords Senators, and those of the *Equestrian* Order deputed to sign, are here affixed.

Given by the hands of the most illustrious and reverend Father in Christ, the Lord *Andrew Olszonski,* Bishop of *Culma* and *Pomisania,* High Chancellor of the Kingdom, in the general ordinary Assembly of the Kingdom, and great Dukedom of *Lituania,* for the Election of the new King. *Warsaw* the 22th day of May, in the year of our Lord 1674.

In the presence of *Franciscus Praszmouski,* provost of *Guesna,* Abbot of *Sieciethovia,* chief Secretary of the Kingdom; *Joannes Malachowski,* Abbot of *Mogila,* Referendary [18] of the Kingdom, &c. with other great Officers of the Kingdom and Clergy, to the number of fourescore and two.[19] And the rest, very many great Officers, Captains, Secretaries, Courtiers, and Inhabitants of the Kingdom, and great Dukedom of *Lituania,* gathered together at *Warsaw,* to the present Assembly of the Election of the Kingdom and great Dukedom of *Lituania.*

Assistants at the solemn Oath taken of his sacred Majesty on the 5th day of the Month of *June,* in the Palace at *Warsaw,* after the Letters Patents delivered upon the Covenants, and Agree-

[17] *NED,* 1: "to make known formally, to notify, announce, state," translating *intimandi.*

[18] *NED* defines as "a title given at various times to certain officials in the papal, imperial, and some royal courts, charged with the duty of examining and reporting upon petitions, requests, use of the seal, and similar matters." The Latin is *Referendariis.*

[19] Thus again Milton disposes of a list of names and titles occupying virtually a page of the *Diploma.*

ments, or Capitulations,[20] the most Reverend and Excellent Lord *Francisco Bonvisi,* Archbishop of *Thessalonica,* Apostolick Nuntio; Count *Christopherus a scaffgotsch, Cæcareus*[21] *Tussanus de Forbin, de Jason* [22] Bishop of *Marseilles* in *France, Joannes* free-barron *Hoverbeck,* from the Marquess of *Brandenburg,* Embassadors; and other Envoyes and Ministers of State.

FINIS. [12]

---

[20] *NED,* 3: "the making of terms, stipulations, conditions," translating *Capitulationem.*

[21] A typographical error? The Latin text reads *Cæsareus.*

[22] The Latin text reads *Janson.*

A BRIEF HISTORY OF MOSCOVIA

1682

PREFACE AND NOTES BY GEORGE B. PARKS

I. FIRST ANNOTATED EDITION

The *Moscovia* was published in 1682, eight years after Milton's death. According to the publisher's Advertisement, it was "writ by the Authour's own hand, before he lost his sight. And sometime before his death dispos'd of it to be printed." "The Authour's Preface," written presumably when he brought out the old manuscript to the printer, declares that he compiled the book "many years since . . . at a vacant time" and left it unfinished to turn to another task.

The book was therefore done well before 1652, when the poet's blindness became total. In the early 1670s the author wrote a preface, perhaps made some revisions, and brought his manuscript to the printer. The publisher hoped for another Milton work to add in order to make out a book of some size and delayed printing. At length he brought it out by itself in 1682.

Given by the printer the title *A Brief History of Moscovia,* the printed book ran to 109 printed pages of text in octavo (15½ cm.), and may contain some 14,000 words. Forty-six copies are recorded as extant.[1] The book has been regularly reprinted in the collected editions of Milton's prose works, beginning in 1698. It has been separately reprinted twice, in 1929 and in 1941, and it was translated into Russian in 1874. The *Moscovia* has not, however, been annotated. All the place-names have been identified in Gilbert's *Geographical Dictionary of Milton,*[2] but Milton's choice of them

I am grateful to the Huntington Library for a grant in aid of the research for this edition of the *Moscovia,* and I thank Professor J. Max Patrick for criticism of the draft of this preface. The title page of the 1682 edition (below, p. 473) is from a copy in the New York Public Library, Rare Book Division, and is reproduced by permission of the Library.

[1] Parker, *Milton,* p. 1210.

[2] Allan H. Gilbert, *A Geographical Dictionary of Milton* (New Haven, 1919; rpt., New York: Russell & Russell, 1968).

and the view of Russia they create have been asserted rather than explained. The present edition gives annotations and quotes most of Milton's source passages at length.

The *Moscovia* has at times been too respectfully viewed, as by James Holly Hanford, when he called it "a small masterpiece of expository narrative," [3] or by a reviewer who compared it with the *Germania* of Tacitus. [4] It has been appropriately praised by Robert R. Cawley for its able and forceful style, achieved by vigorous condensation of the often diffuse language of its sources in the travel narratives. [5] On the other hand, it was severely criticized for its inadequacy by its Russian translator, as is explained below in Appendix D, pp. 605–09, on the book's fortune in Russia. The most recent judgment, by John B. Gleason, notes the book's scanty coverage of Russia and its ignoring of much necessary material, deficiencies that clearly demonstrate its fragmentary and unfinished nature. [6] It is of course obvious that the book is unfinished, and indeed one may prefer not to think of it as a book at all. It is in fact a collection of notes on Russia, condensed and often tightened in statement, but all copied out of two books. Milton claimed no more for it than as notes that need not be collected again. Nonetheless, the choice of material may be original and should indicate Milton's ideas of what is important in geography.

II. PLAN AND MAKING

If the *terminus ad quem* of the compiling of the *Moscovia* is 1652, the *terminus a quo* has been placed as early as the years at Horton, 1633–38. [7] Lloyd E. Berry has recently declared again for the Horton period on the ground that the book echoes the tone and the animosity toward Russia shown in Giles Fletcher's book *Of the Russe Common Wealth* (1591), which Milton must have known at

---

[3] James Holly Hanford, reviewing Robert R. Cawley, *Milton's Literary Craftsmanship,* in *Library Quarterly,* XII (1942), 327.

[4] *TLS,* 5 December 1929, p. 1024. The possibility that the *Germania* may have been Milton's model was suggested by Alfred Stern, *Milton und seine Zeit,* 2 vols. (Leipzig, 1877–79), II, 177–78.

[5] In the introduction to his edition, entitled *Milton's Literary Craftsmanship* (Princeton, 1941), passim.

[6] "The Nature of Milton's *Moscovia,*" *SP,* LXI (1964), 640–49. Professor John B. Gleason has kindly agreed to survey the Russian commentaries in Appendix D, below, pp. 605–09.

[7] As, for example, by D. S. Mirsky, in the introduction to his edition of the *Moscovia* (London: Blackamore Press, 1929), p. 14: "early in the sixteen-thirties." He gives no evidence for the dating, assuming that the work was an early experiment.

an early date, since he knew and was influenced directly by other works of Giles Fletcher and his son Phineas published in 1633.[8] Or he might, I add, have been reminded of it by the republication of Fletcher's book in 1643 as *The History of Russia.*

Several scholars have linked the composition of *Moscovia* with that of *The History of Britain,* considering it a companion piece of Milton's scholarship. Masson dated the *Moscovia* between 1649 and 1652, as a new start after the completion in March 1649 of the first four books of the *Britain;* [9] but he also allowed the alternative of assigning it "possibly to his days of private study and pedagogy," that is, after 1639 (if the word "pedagogy" is decisive). Hanford originally followed Masson's first choice in placing the composition "at some interval of leisure during the Commonwealth or early Protectorate," [10] but he later added the alternative "possibly even as early as the Horton period." [11] Joseph A. Bryant, Jr., has on the other hand thought the *Moscovia* an early experiment in historiography, done "to sharpen his pen before beginning a historical work on England," that is, between 1639 and 1641.[12] Parker also thought that it was undertaken before the *History of Britain* but as late as 1648.[13]

So the conjectures have dated the book variously from 1633 to 1650. If we turn for guidance to the *Commonplace Book,* we should suppose with Hanford that at Horton Milton was studying classical and medieval history and Italian literature, rather than modern history.[14] It was after his return from Italy in 1639, it is to be inferred, that he read later history: The English historians and Jovius, Sleidanus, Thuanus, Sarpi, Herberstein were on his list.[15] With history naturally went geography, not only in his reading but in his new task as teacher. That is, he assigned geographical works to his students: maps of both the ancient and the modern world;

[8] Lloyd E. Berry, "Giles Fletcher, the Elder, and Milton's *A Brief History of Moscovia,*" *RES,* XI (1960), 150–56.

[9] Masson, *Life,* VI, 812–13.

[10] James Holly Hanford, *A Milton Handbook* (New York: F. S. Crofts & Co., 1926), p. 101.

[11] In the 1939 edition and in subsequent editions to 1961 (ibid., p. 129).

[12] Joseph A. Bryant, Jr., "Milton and the Art of History: A Study of Two Influences on *A Brief History of Moscovia,*" *PQ,* XXIX (1950), 15–30, the conclusion on pp. 29–30. The two influences are those of Polybius and Bacon.

[13] Parker, *Milton,* p. 325.

[14] James Holly Hanford, "The Chronology of Milton's Private Studies," *PMLA,* XXXVI (1921), 251–314; reprinted in his *John Milton: Poet and Humanist* (Cleveland, Ohio: Western Reserve University Press, 1966), pp. 106–8.

[15] Hanford, "Milton's Private Studies," pp. 288–97; confirmed by Ruth Mohl in her edition of the *Commonplace Book, Complete Prose,* I, 348.

Pierre Avity in French (1614), a current large-scale geography; Dionysius Periegetes in Greek, a verse survey of the ancient world.[16] He also made use of globes.[17] So we suppose that in the early 1640s Milton was reading modern history with its naturally accompanying geography; he was also reading geography as such with his pupils and possibly giving thought to its method as well as its content.

"The Authour's Preface" is not very precise in noting the occasion of the actual undertaking of the book. Milton remembered that he was displeased by the treatment of cultural geography in the textbooks, which gave either too scanty or too voluminous and inconsequential attention to the topic of "Manners, Religion, Government and such like." Any teacher will recognize this kind of displeasure with a textbook, and it may well have been classroom experience that provoked the intent to do a better book. Since we know that he used Avity,[18] it is easiest to think that it was that geographical work that annoyed him. It is difficult to accuse Avity of disproportion, however, and the same is true of Heylyn, which author Milton was to be using in 1656 and whose works he probably knew earlier.[19] On the other hand, Milton might have taken umbrage at the popular *Introductio in Universam Geographiam* of Philippus Cluverius (1624 et seq.), which consisted largely of a listing of provinces and cities with many individual maps, which he might have thought "too brief and deficient." It would be interesting to know what he thought of Giovanni Botero, whose *Le Relationi Universali* (1591) was expansively political geography.[20] We cannot tell, however, which books displeased Milton, because he does not say.

[16] The books are named by Edward Phillips, Milton's nephew and pupil, in his *Life of Milton* (1694), ed. Helen Darbishire, in *The Early Lives of Milton* (London, 1932), pp. 60–61. Milton's *Of Education* (1644) proposed these studies. See *Complete Prose*, II, 389, 391, 395.

[17] Mentioned by John Aubrey, "Minutes," ed. Darbishire, in *Early Lives,* p. 12.

[18] Pierre Avity, *The Estates, Empires, and Principallities of the World,* trans. Edward Grimstone (1615), pp. 685–99. See Allan H. Gilbert, "Pierre Davity: His 'Geography' and Its Use by Milton," *Geographical Review,* VII (1919), 322–36.

[19] Peter Heylyn, *Microcosmos: A Little Description of the Great World* (Oxford, 1621, et seq., 8 eds. to 1639), enlarged as *Cosmographie in four bookes* (London, 1652, et seq., 9 eds. to 1703). For Milton's use of Heylyn, see Robert R. Cawley, *Milton and the Literature of Travel* (Princeton: Princeton University Press, 1951), especially chaps. i, ii, v.

[20] Botero was translated by Robert Johnson as *The Travellers Breviat; or, An Historicall description of the most famous kingdomes in the World* (1601), much expanded under different titles in six further editions to 1630.

At any rate, he decided, "at a vacant time," to try a description of one sample country. He chose Russia, he remembered, because it was the northernmost country of Europe (Cluverius called it *Ultima Europæ regio*), which was not a very good reason, and also because it had been opened to western Europe by the English, which was. The best information about Russia was to be found in the reports of English travelers to Russia from 1553: first in Richard Hakluyt's *Principal Navigations, Voyages, Traffiques, and Discoveries of the English Nation* (3 vols., 1598–1600), especially in its first volume, and then in its sequel, Samuel Purchas's *Purchas His Pilgrimes* (4 vols., 1625), its material on Russia being in the third volume. In that volume was reprinted the best work on Russia hitherto, Giles Fletcher's *Of the Russe Common Wealth* (originally 1591), which Milton could not expect to surpass. It was in those volumes, I conjecture, that Milton discovered his own individual approach to geography, that is, extracting from the travel narratives the details that would add up to a picture of a country, to make an inductively developed geography. This has always of course been the method of the geographer, who is largely a compiler of other persons' reports, if he does more than copy previous geographers. Even if a Herodotus or a Strabo or a Fletcher could himself observe some of the countries he described, he was still largely dependent on other observers, preferably eyewitnesses, as Milton called them.

This seems to me as close as we can come to Milton's approach to his project, that is, to try a country on which much material was available. At any rate, he combed Hakluyt and Purchas for the details he wanted. His preface considerably exaggerates his pains. "What was scatter'd in many Volumes" was actually scattered in only two. It is true that the Russian material in Hakluyt occupies some eight hundred pages in the modern octavo edition, and the Purchas material is close to four hundred like pages. Our compiler would presumably read through, then go back and mark items to be copied in a given order or under given heads, then copy and condense in the copying. The task was one of compilation only; and, allowing for false starts and redirections, it need not have taken more than a few months' "vacant time."

We still cannot be certain when Milton took up the project. His *Commonplace Book* twice refers to his reading Purchas at a time thought by Hanford to be probably before 1644; [21] but neither entry refers to Russia or to volume III of Purchas, which contains

[21] Hanford, *Milton: Poet and Humanist*, p. 95.

the Russia material. Milton also read, or knew of, Herberstein, author of the first significant account of Russia,[22] to whom he found reference in Thuanus. The Herberstein passage is, however, a brief one on divorce in Russia and therefore has little relation to a survey of that country; Hanford dates its appearance in the *Commonplace Book* as probably after 1643. This notebook does not mention Hakluyt at all among the books that Milton read and informs us in sum only that Milton had read in Purchas and at least knew of Herberstein.

One piece of evidence on the project has recently appeared. In July of 1648, Samuel Hartlib, the educator to whom Milton had addressed the essay *Of Education,* noted in his diary:

> Milton is not only writing a Vniv. History of Engl. but also an Epitome of all Purcha's Volumes. Haack.[23]

Haack was Theodore Haak, scholar and translator, of the Hartlib circle. Hartlib's marginal note with this item reads:

> Milton. Histi· Anglic' Purchas.

One would like to suppose this note to say that by July of 1648 Milton had finished his compiling from Hakluyt and was now compiling from Purchas, and consequently would soon finish the *Moscovia.* Or it might mean that he was thinking of doing the compiling, or that he had done it and put it away. As we know of the uncertainties arising from conversations about a third person, we can be sure of no more than that Milton spoke of working on Purchas. The project was singularly appropriate in that setting because it happens that Purchas was not unknown in the Hartlib circle of scientists and educators. In the same month in which

[22] Ibid., p. 97.

[23] Cited by G. H. Turnbull, *Hartlib, Dury, and Comenius* (Liverpool, 1947), pp. 40–41; reprinted in French, *Life Records,* II, 214. French erroneously dated the entry in the diary as "supposed 1648," but the date is certain. The diary (Ephemerides) of Hartlib is a multivolume manuscript owned by Lord Delamere and left by him on deposit at the Sheffield University Library. Miss J. L. Gilham, Sub-Librarian of that library, kindly informs me that, in the volume labeled 1648, the year occasionally forms part of a date of entry: specifically on p. N 8 ("15 of May 1648"); on p. O 1, and p. P 1; on p. T 1 appears the date "5 July" without the year. Eight pages later, a second S 1 (following a T section) contains the Milton entry, undated. On p. V 1 the date "5 August" is appended to a report of the death of Lord Herbert of Cherbury, who died in 1648, though not until August 22. The Milton entry, therefore, occurs between July 5 and August 5, 1648, in what Miss Gilham assures me is a continuous series of entries without interpolation; the Milton entry is therefore of July 1648. I am grateful to Miss Gilham for her help, and to Lord Delamere for permitting access to his possession.

Milton's interest was reported, a member of the circle, Benjamin Worsley, wrote to Hartlib to commend a digesting, as he called it, of the observations by Purchas's travelers of natural phenomena: [24]

> J have often wished, that as he [Purchas] him selfe digested all the discourses of manners, policy & Religion, into one which he calls his Pilgrimage: And as others have digested some other parts of his discourses, of the norwest passage of Chymæ [*sic*] & of other parts, according to their particular fancies; That some would collect all his Naturall History, without abbreviating or Epitomizing it. for this would spoyle [it], which had J not beene prevented, J had long agoe undertaken.

The letter goes on to recommend the collection of information about climate as a part of natural science, and in the words we recognize the idiom of the new scientific movement we now call Baconian. Milton must have heard this idiom in the talk of his scientist friends, and it may have encouraged him in the collection of the items of his survey of Russian geography. The idiom of his preface is, to be sure, pre-Baconian, suggesting only the traditional scholarly aim of proper proportions and no childish exotics. (Worsley's letter at one point said to a contrary effect: "Neyther is it matter if some things sound fabulous, for so wee have esteemed many Truths unknowne to us.")

For the actual date of the *Moscovia* enterprise, we now have somewhat narrowed the choice. The nature of the enterprise, a summary collection from existing books on Russia, sounds like the project of a man casting about for a scholarly topic: that is, the Milton student and teacher of the years from 1639 to 1645. A large part of his time then was, however, taken up with the writing of his tracts, and it is hard to see when he could have worked in the *Moscovia* note taking. However, the *Commonplace Book* attests his looking up Purchas and perhaps Herberstein, whence he may have derived the idea of the Russia project. We might try 1643 or 1644 for the compilation, but we would find more convincing the time after 1645, when the tracts ceased for a while and Milton planned such arduous scholarship as the *History of Britain*. More-

---

[24] Turnbull, *Hartlib, Dury, and Comenius,* reprinted in French, *Life Records,* II, 214–15. Worsley's letter is copied into Hartlib's letterbook with the date "27 July 1648 Amsterdam"; the reference is Hartlib 42/1/1ᵛ, and I am again indebted to Miss Gilham for a photocopy of this item as well as the diary page containing the Milton allusion. Worsley's reference to Purchas points to his compilation of the history of religion, which he called *Purchas His Pilgrimage* (1613 et seq.) and which is distinct from the collection of travels he called *Purchas His Pilgrimes* (1625, 4 vols.).

over, we may guess that he stretched the time of his reading by taking only a few Russian narratives at a time, so that it was presently 1648 when he was still reading Purchas and arousing the comment of friends. Presently it was the end of 1648, and it was time, during the king's trial and execution, to return to public affairs with *The Tenure of Kings and Magistrates,* published in early February of 1649, and then assuredly "other occasions diverted" him.

One more question suggests itself. It does not necessarily follow that 1648–49 marked the end of Milton's interest in his compilation. Did the *Moscovia* indeed drop completely out of sight for two decades after that date? It is hard to think so, because on several occasions the work might have served a useful public purpose. That is to say, a crisis in the diplomatic relations of Great Britain and Russia occurred in 1649, and the country that had evoked the purely scholarly interest of Milton may soon have come to the attention of the secretary for foreign tongues.

Specifically, Czar Alexis was moved by wrath over the execution of Charles I to deprive the English merchant colony in his country of most of their trading privileges, which went back to 1555, and to banish them from Moscow and elsewhere to Archangel, their port of entry. His action was taken on July 1, 1649, though it seems not to have been known in England until late September. On December 2 the Council ordered a letter of protest to be written, and after further moves in the House and the Council, Colonel William Hawley was appointed, on January 23, 1649/50, a special envoy to carry the approved letter of protest. As it happened, Hawley did not go.[25]

Whether or not Milton wrote the official letter of protest and the instructions to the envoy, we do not know, and these documents are not extant. Milton may well have known of the moves, however, and being certain that his notes would make a useful guide for a diplomat bound for Russia, he might have brought them to

[25] Inna Lubimenko, "Anglo-Russian Relations during the First English Revolution," *Transactions of the Royal Historical Society,* 4th ser. XI (1928), 39–59, describes the missions both of the Commonwealth and of Charles II in exile. The documents are in the *State Papers Domestic;* in John Thurloe, *A Collection of State Papers,* vols. I–III (1742); and in *The Writings and Speeches of Oliver Cromwell,* ed Wilbur C. Abbott, 4 vols. (Cambridge: Harvard University Press, 1937–47), vols. II–IV. Dr. Lubimenko had access also to the English Archives of the Foreign Office in Moscow.

Hawley's attention. Indeed, I once ventured to believe that this was his sole purpose in making the compilation. Before the publication of the Hartlib diary note on Milton's activity, I conjectured that the *Moscovia* was most plausibly composed precisely for the guidance of the Hawley mission and that it was done in the "vacant time" between October 6, 1649, when his *Eikonoklastes* was published, and January 8, 1650, when he was commissioned to write the answer to Salmasius.[26] The editor of the *Life Records of John Milton* accepted this conjecture and entered it under these dates (II, 267–68). No evidence connecting Milton with the Hawley mission has, however, been found, and I recommend that the entry in the *Life Records* be withdrawn.

It is still reasonable to believe that Milton brought his notes on Russia into the open and may even have added to them the chapters iv and v, which were especially relevant to diplomatic missions. Certainly no aide-mémoire would have been more suitable for an envoy to take with him to tell him what he should know about Russia. He would have plenty of time to read up on the subject in the month or two months aboard ship to Archangel, and he might conceivably take along the volume I of Hakluyt and volume III of Purchas. He needed not, however, since the *Moscovia* had arranged the essential information, to which he might join Fletcher's treatise with its full political detail. The *Moscovia* began uniquely with the view of Russia from Archangel rather than from Moscow, the capital, and described the river routes that the English followed to Moscow, to Novgorod, to Astracan on the Caspian. The two chapters on the journeys to Siberia would not be important, though an envoy should know about them as indicating the Russian expansion. Most important, the capsule history of Russia and the history of the reception of the English at the Russian court would be essential, and we can hardly think of Milton not wanting to exhibit them.

It might be said, and has been said,[27] that the chapters on Russian history and on the reception of English diplomats are natural parts of geographical treatises and that their presence here proves nothing about a special aim of the compilation. I question the statement. The history of a country, the subject of the fourth chapter, was not a normal part of a geographical treatise: there is no such history in Jovius's *Moschovia,* in Fletcher's *Russia,* in Avity's

[26] "The Occasion of Milton's *Moscovia,*" *SP,* XL (1943), 399–404.
[27] Bryant, *PQ,* XXIX (1950), 23.

chapter on Muscovie, in Botero, in Heylyn. As for the matter of
the fifth chapter, a history of ambassadorial receptions, the subject
is virtually unknown in both geographical treatise and in history.
Diplomatic travelers of course reported on their own reception but
not on that of others. Even the histories available in England of
countries with which England had long diplomatic relations do not
do more than describe the pattern, not the individual records. The
authoritative history of Turkey was the compilation by Richard
Knolles, first published in 1603, republished through the century,
continued by Sir Paul Rycaut, himself ambassador to Turkey, in
1687–1700. Neither work gives any account of English relations.

The *Moscovia* remains, in sum, unique in content, more akin
to a foreign-office briefing than to a book. Hawley may have been
shown it; but since he did not go, Milton's preface could hardly
say that his book had been useful. A second envoy, William Pri-
deaux, was appointed in 1654. He sailed to Archangel, was officially detained there until winter, when he was finally permitted
to go on to Moscow, and altogether spent more than a year in
negotiations in Russia. Again, despite numerous letters and reports
of his mission, we do not possess his credentials or his instructions
and cannot know whether Milton had dealings with him. If he was
shown the *Moscovia* or took it with him, Milton would have mentioned the fact, and we draw a blank here.

The third envoy was Richard Bradshaw, British Resident in
Hamburg, who was appointed to a Russian mission in 1657. Here
we do have evidence of Milton's concern, since he drew up the
official letter from Cromwell to the czar [28] and also the instructions
to Bradshaw.[29] The envoy was on the continent at the time and
may not have seen Milton or Milton's notes on Russia. Actually
he was detained at Riga by Russian unwillingness to receive him
and never reached Russia.

The possible public use of Milton's notes remains then a matter
of mere conjecture, and we know only that he kept them by him
for twenty-odd years. It has been suggested [30] that his friend Andrew Marvell may have added to the notes on returning from the
Carlisle mission to Russia in 1664–65, and indeed the published
report of the mission by Guy Miège contained lively up-to-date

---

[28] [10] April 1657; in *Literæ Pseudo-Senatus* (1676), p. 163; translated in *Complete Prose,* IV, 788–89.

[29] Columbia MS. #98; *Complete Prose,* IV, 786–87.

[30] Stern, *Milton und seine Zeit,* II, 178.

detail on Russia.[31] Because all the material in Milton's *Moscovia* was taken from Hakluyt and Purchas, and so noted in the margins, nothing could have been added by or from Marvell. Moreover, the publisher declared that the manuscript was written in Milton's hand, and in 1665 the poet was obliged to rely on amanuenses. At most, Marvell might have corrected or urged deletions here and there, but there is no evidence.

III. CONTENTS AND ACCOMPLISHMENTS

Milton's own title for his notes was undoubtedly that on page 1: *Moscovia: Or, Relations of Moscovia, As far as hath been discover'd by English Voyages.* In other words, this was not a book, but a collection of material for a book. What the book was to include that was not already available and well arranged in Fletcher or Avity it is difficult to say. The remark in the preface that points to Jovius as a forerunner in the description of a single country must not be allowed to be more than merely casual. For what Jovius did in his descriptions had little in common, either in method or content, with what Milton seemed to be aiming at. Paulus Jovius, a distinguished modern historian, had written not one or two but three such descriptions: one each on Russia, Britain, and the Turks—as Milton may not have known. The *Moschovia* (1525) was the result of a series of interviews in Rome with a Russian churchman on a diplomatic mission and contained much information about Russian provinces and cities and people, as well as about neighboring Tartar tribes, and something about Russian products and the face of the country; but its material on the government and social system was scanty. I think Milton would not have approved of it if he had gone back to it. Nor did he, I believe, remember very well the *Britannia* (1548), which was more ambitious in plan than anything Milton seemed to have in mind. Jovius's dedication notes his intent to report "the kingdoms and regions of the entire known world, the resources of their rulers, their abilities, history, the manners of their peoples, their heroes in war and their illustrious writers, the wealth of the lands, and the miracles reported." [32] For this largely political geography Jo-

---

[31] [Guy Miège], *The Earl of Carlisle's Relation of Three Embassies . . . to the Duke of Muscovy, the King of Sweden, and the King of Denmark, in 1663 and 1664* (London, 1669).

[32] "Igitur totius cogniti orbis imperia, & regiones, Regum opes, ingenia, res gestæ, gentium item mores, viri, bellica virtute, aut literis clari, terrarumque demum dotes, atque miracula illustri enarrata ordine nomine tuo dicabuntur"; *Descriptio Britanniæ, Scotiæ, Hyberniæ, & Orchadum*, in *Descriptiones*, 2nd

vius could make use of Polydore Vergil's history of Britain and also of the collaboration of George Lily, English exile and eyewitness. Jovius was of course drawing the long bow in writing as he did in this sweeping fashion at the end of a long life (1483–1552) with his major work, the *Historia sui temporis,* nearly ready and precluding any overambitious geography. In fact, none of his three treatises could be called concise or probably well proportioned, but his intended scope was far more ambitious than Milton's or even Fletcher's.

We come to the *Moscovia* itself. Of its five chapters, the first describes Russia as the English eyewitnesses saw it. Milton followed their routes: via the Arctic Ocean to their successive White Sea bases at St. Nicholas, Rose Island, and Archangel; up the Dvina River to Vologda; and overland to Moscow, altogether 1,500 miles from the port. (This was twice the north-south length of Great Britain, though Milton did not make the comparison.) Thence the English had gone from Moscow to the Volga and downstream to its mouths at Astracan on the Caspian Sea. Again from Archangel by rivers and lakes their routes led southeast to Novgorod, whence an approach to the Baltic countries (not yet under Russian dominion) and to the cities of Pskov and Smolensk on the western frontier (most of the Ukraine and the Crimea were not yet Russian); from Archangel again eastward to the Petzora region, both by sea and overland. Not every traveler in Hakluyt had given full itineraries, and Milton was obliged to skip from one to another and back to fill in missing distances and ignored towns and regions. He was able to preface the chapter by listing the boundaries of Russia as taken from Fletcher; he did not try to fill in the whole list of the nineteen provinces he would have had to take from Avity; nor did he draw or suggest a map which would give an idea of Russia as a whole. As the beginning of a guide to Russia, however, the starting point of Archangel and the pattern of the river routes radiating from that port provided an ingenious substitute for a map.

The second half of the first chapter, ten and a half pages, gives a succinct account of the people of Russia, noting government, law, revenues of the emperor, army, religion, customs of marriage and burial, manners and character, means of travel. Avity and Fletcher gave more detail, but the basic matter is here. We re-

---

ed. (Basel, 1561), p. 3. Jovius's *Moschovia* is contained in the same volume, separately paged, its preface again on p. 3.

member that this was to be the main content of the notes, "Manners, Religion, Government, and such like," here shrunk to but a small part of the whole. One wonders if Milton remembered, when he wrote his preface, just how little remained of what he thought had been his original aim.

The second and third chapters take thirteen pages to describe the mostly Russian, though occasionally English, itineraries in northern Siberia going well beyond the Yenisei River, and then the first reported Russian journey in 1619 from Tomsk in central Siberia to Cathay and its capital White City. Milton's Siberia is slight and sketchy, a country of immense rivers dotted with the names of new Russian military posts, which would assert domination over peaceable tribes. He added an account of the ingenious Samoed nomads. This material came from a new Dutch geographer, Isaac Massa, though Milton's footnotes refer not to the author but the publisher Gerrits; his *Beschryvinghe* was published in Amsterdam in 1612 and was followed by maps of Russia. Milton found the narratives in Purchas and presumably did not proceed to study the Dutch and German collections marked *Rerum Moscoviticarum Auctores Varii* (Frankfurt, 1600) or the much later *Russia seu Moscovia itemque Tartaria* (an Elzevir product, Leiden, 1630) or *Respublica Moscoviae et Urbes* (Leiden, 1630).[33]

One question suggested by this material has been answered: Why did Milton leave Russia to describe the routes to Cathay? His preface has conveyed one answer, that the travelers "with some delight drew me after them, from the eastern Bounds of Russia, to the Walls of Cathay"; he was fascinated by the approach to the East. (Incidentally, it would be clever of an ambassador seeing these notes to know of new developments in the country he was assigned to.) The other question is why Milton stopped with 1619. The immediate answer is that he was drawing upon a book published in 1625. The larger answer is that there were no later published sources, and if the Muscovy Company had later unpublished reports from its agents such as Purchas had printed, we cannot know, for the company records were destroyed in the London fire.

---

[33] See George V. Lantzeff, *Siberia in the Seventeenth Century,* and Raymond H. Fisher, *The Russian Fur Trade, 1550–1700,* both in University of California Publications in History, no. 30 (1943); Robert J. Kerner, *The Urge to the Sea: The Course of Russian History* (Berkeley: University of California Press, 1946); George V. Lantzeff and Richard A. Pierce, *Eastward to Empire: Exploration and Conquest on the Russian Open Frontier to 1750* (Montreal: McGill-Queen's University Press, 1973).

The second and third chapters thus remain tastes of the unknown and contain presumably all that was available at the time. For content, the chapters stress in turn the nomad life of the reindeer-drawn Samoeds and the opulence of Cathay.

We are one-third of the way through the book. The fourth chapter is not geography at all, but a précis of Russian dynastic history from 573 to 1613, especially treating the period from 1584, the date of the death of Ivan IV (not yet known as the Terrible), through the usurpation of Boris Goudonov to the time of troubles and the establishment of the settled Romanov dynasty in 1613. All is taken from Hakluyt and Purchas, sometimes from English observers. The emphasis of the much condensed history is on the behavior of tyrants, which led to pretenders to the throne, civil war and foreign intervention, and the ultimate triumph of order brought about by honest commoners. Dramatic violence is the clear subject of the chapter.

The last and longest chapter is an eyewitness chronicle of the English discovery of Russia and the reception of successive English diplomatic missions to Moscow from 1553 to 1604. It is not in the least diplomatic history, since Milton does not concern himself with the achievements of the envoys and does not even mention the enterprising further missions of Anthony Jenkinson and others from 1557 to 1572, which brought English envoys to the far court of Persia and beyond even to Bokhara. It collects instead the accounts of Russian court ceremonies and pageantry involved in the receptions of the English envoys and is therefore a record of one aspect of Russian court protocol. The chapter is in a sense a filling in of pictorial background behind the names and dates, and an account as well of the thorny paths of the ambassadors.

Altogether the *Moscovia* is a summary in bare précis form of the English knowledge of Russia, including an outline list of its rulers. It ignores, however, the whole substance of the Anglo-Russian relations, that is, trade and its conditions, which Milton depreciated at the beginning of the last chapter as due merely to "the excessive love of Gain and Traffick." Perhaps for the same reason Milton does not even mention the natural products of Russia, except for the furs that motivated the expansion to Siberia. At the same time he cannot refrain from mentioning the mere curiosities of the wolverine, which gives birth by squeezing between two stakes, or the morse (walrus) that uses its teeth (tusks) in climbing, or the whale that gives a "pittiful cry" when sucked into the maelstrom. Fletcher on the other hand lists fourteen commodities, from fur to iron, noting as of special value wax, tallow, hides, train oil (from seals), and "Ickary or Cavary" (caviare).[34]

We may regret Milton's inattention to economic matters of this sort and wish that he had otherwise followed Fletcher's lead not only in matters of fact but also in matters of geographical thought. To illustrate winter cold, for example, Milton did select two striking details: one of the log in flames but dripping moisture; one of the sailors coming on deck only to drop as if "stifl'd" by the Arctic air inhaled. Fletcher is equally vivid, but he also works out a variety of effects of cold:

> When you passe out of a warme roome into a cold, you shall sensibly feele your breath to waxe starke, and even stifeling with the cold, as you draw it in and out. Divers not only that travell abroad, but in the very Markets, and streets of their Townes, are mortally pinched and killed withall: so that you shall see many drop downe in the Streets, many Travellers brought into the Townes sitting dead and stiffe in their Sleds. . . . And yet in the Summer time you shall see such a new hew and face of a Country, the Woods (for the most part which are all of Firre and Birch) so fresh and so sweet, the Pastures and Meadowes so greene and well growne, (and that upon the sudden), such varietie of Flowers, such noyse of Birds, (specially of Nightingales, that seeme to be more loud and of a more variable note then in other Countries) that a man shall not lightly travell in a more pleasant Countrey.
>
> And this fresh and speedy growth of the Spring there, seemeth to proceed from the benefit of the Snow, which all the Winter time being spred over the whole Countrey as a white robe, and keeping it warme from the rigour of the Frost, in the Spring time . . . doth so throughly drench and soake the ground, . . . that it draweth Hearbs and Plants forth in great plentie and varietie, in a very short time.[35]

Or one might wish that Milton had seized on such a historical generalization, if not a geographical, as can be found in one of the universal geographers whom he affected to scorn. I cite the following from Giovanni Botero in a part translation of 1601:

> Some will haue it, that in times past the countrey [Russia] was better replenished with people, and that afterwards it became desolate for three causes: the first was the plague (a newe disease in Moscouie) which gleaned away many thousand people: the second the tyrannie of their Emperors, who haue put infinite numbers to death, especially of the nobilitie: the third, the incursions and robberies of the Tartars Precopie, and Negaians, which neuer cease vexing their bordering neighbors. These Tartars harrie not onely the countrey, but leading away captiue

[34] *Purchas His Pilgrimes*, III, 416–17.
[35] Ibid., p. 415.

whole cities, selling them to Turks and other nations. These inrodes
have laid waste many and far remooued prouinces.[36]

We may not, however, ask more of the *Moscovia* than was
intended; that is, a brief extract of the English experience. Commentators have noted some characteristic Miltonic ideas in the
unfinished work. Two recent studies make much of the acrid distaste for Russia and the Russians that the *Moscovia* generally displays. Berry has noted the contempt for Russian tyranny, oppression,
and ignorance throughout the work as it appears equally in the
Fletcher treatise.[37] Szenczi finds in the work a pervading conde-
scension to Russia as a tyrannical government, with an unworthy
clergy, a wretched and ignorant populace.[38] In addition, Patrick
remarks the unfailing animus toward the clergy, which must be
linked with ignorance and depravity whenever it is mentioned.[39]
I must point out, however, that this was not a specifically English
view of Russia. Cluverius, a German settled in Holland, found it
sufficient to say "gens ipsa rudis, perfida, servituti supra modum
addicta." [40] Avity described at length the Russian "barbarousnesse,
treacherie, subtilitie, loosenesse, and venal justice." [41] By comparison Milton is seen to be relatively restrained in expressing the
common Western view.

It remains to praise the eloquent language of Milton's notes. We
must without dissent admire the concision, the frequent master
hand shown by the turn of a phrase, the many rewarding moments
of sudden insight. We note specially the poetry of place-names and
remark the dozen of them carried over into *Paradise Lost* and
elsewhere: Astracan, Cambaluc (for Peking), Caspian, Cathay,
Lapland, Mosco, Nagay, Ob, Pechora, Russian, Samoedia, Tartaria.[42] Some echoes of more than names in Milton's verse have

[36] Cited from an early edition of the translation, 1601, here entitled *The Worlde,
or, An historicall description of the most famous Kingdomes and Commonweales
therein,* pp. 131–32. The Italian original was published in 1591.

[37] See n. 8, above.

[38] Miklos Szenczi, "Milton on Russia," in the Alekseev *Festschrift* (1966); see
Gleason on the Russian commentaries, below, p. 609, n. 10. Professor Szenczi
has kindly shown me the English version of his article, which constitutes a full
critique of the *Moscovia.*

[39] J. Max Patrick, ed., *The Prose of John Milton* (Garden City, N.Y.: Doubleday, 1967), p. 575.

[40] Philippus Cluverius, *Introductio in Universam Geographiam* (1624; in enlarged ed., Wolfenbuttel, 1661), p. 492.

[41] Avity, *Estates,* p. 625.

[42] I take the names from the list and commentary of Gilbert, *Geographical
Dictionary.*

been pointed out by Cawley [43] but actually fewer than can be traced to Heylyn's *Cosmographie,* which Milton must have had at hand when dictating *Paradise Lost.* But the *Moscovia* is interesting not only for what Milton borrowed from it later. It has its own striking moments, as of the Russian soldier lying in winter on the bare earth; of the hunters imagining ships with square sails and artillery on a distant Arctic river; of the horse-drawn sleds of the Russians and the reindeer-drawn sleds of the Samoeds speeding over frozen wastes; and, for a colorful moment, of the scene close to the Arctic Circle of "Rose Island, full of damask and red Roses, Violets, and wild Rosemary." [44]

Finally, to return from telling detail to the larger intent and content, we are indebted to Bryant for observing in the work the spirit of Bacon. [45] In Bacon's scheme of history we note:

> Another kind of Mixed History is the History of Cosmography, which is indeed mixed of many things: of Natural History, in respect of the regions themselves, their sites and products; Of History Civil, in respect of the habitations, governments, and manners of the people; and of Mathematics, in respect of the climates and configurations of the heavens, beneath which the regions of the world lie. In which kind of history or science we may congratulate our own age. For this great building of the world has in our age been wonderfully opened up. . . . And this proficience in navigation and discovery may plant also great expectation of the further proficience and augmentation of the sciences. [46]

If it cannot be said that Milton's notes on Russia rise to the heights imagined by Bacon, it is nonetheless clear that they derive from the scientific thought that Bacon reflects and that was most cogently named by Hakluyt "the search and discovery of the world." The *Moscovia* makes but a small eddy in this stream; or, to speak without metaphor, it is no more than the beginning of a neat and useful handbook and guide to the Russia the English had come to know.

[43] Cawley, *Milton and the Literature of Travel,* chap. 3, largely concerns the *Moscovia.*

[44] Patrick, *Prose of Milton,* p. 574.

[45] *PQ,* XXIX (1950), the Baconian influence noted on pp. 27–29. I am not able to follow Bryant in his assertion of the influence of Polybius on either the *Moscovia* or the *History of Britain.*

[46] Bryant cites the passage from *The Advancement of Learning* (1605); I quote from the *De Augmentis Scientiarum* (1623), as translated by James Spedding and printed in *The Philosophical Works,* ed. J. M. Robertson (London, 1905), p. 437, though there is no material difference between the English and Latin texts at this point.

IV. BIBLIOGRAPHY AND FOOTNOTING

A Brief History of Moscovia, etc. (see facsimile of title page, below, p. 473), London, 1682.

Entered in February, 1682, in *The Term Catalogues, 1608–1709,* ed. Edward Arber (London, 1903), I, 472. Not entered in the Stationers' Register. Wing M-2096.

Forty-six copies now recorded.

Collation of the British Museum copy: 8vo (15½ cm.); A^4, B–G^8, H^7; 59 leaves; pp. [8]. 1–109. Contents: [A 1], title page (verso blank); A 2–[A 4], Preface; [A 4^v], Advertisement [by the printer]; B 1–[H 6], the work; [H 6^v–H 7], Names of the Authours [of the relations cited from Hakluyt and Purchas]; [H 7^v], blank.

Reprinted in *A Complete Collection,* vol. II, 1698; *A Complete Collection,* ed. Thomas Birch, vol. II, 1738, reprinted 1753; *Prose Works,* ed. Charles Symmons, vol. IV, 1806; *The Prose Works,* ed. Robert Fletcher, 1833, reprinted 1858; *Prose Works,* ed. R. W. Griswold, vol. II, Philadelphia, 1847; *The Works,* ed. John Mitford, vol. VIII, London and Boston, 1851; *Prose Works,* ed. John A. St. John, vol. V, London, Bohn's Library, 1853; *The Works,* Columbia ed., vol. X, New York, 1932.

Reedited separately, D. S. Mirsky, London, 1929; R. R. Cawley, in *Milton's Literary Craftsmanship,* Princeton, 1941, reprinted Brooklyn, 1965. Translated into Russian by IUrii Tolstoi in *Chteniiya* of Moscow University, Society for Russian History and Antiquities, vol. III, 1874.

Many footnotes to my text of the *Moscovia* begin with Milton's own marginal note, here indicated by (M.). For example, my footnote 5 of chapter I begins: "(M) The North and East, *Hack.* 251.]" My editorial footnote follows the]. In the text of chapter I the supralinear 5 precedes "The" of the text and indicates that Milton's note is in the margin just to the left of "The":

The North	The north parts of this Country
and East,	are so barren, that the inhabitants
Hack. 251.	fetch their Corn . . .

I follow this practice for all Milton notes appearing on even-numbered pages of the *Moscovia,* which are the versos of the leaves constituting the book. For Milton's notes on the odd-numbered pages, rectos of the leaves, the supralinear footnote number (here

10) follows the nearest word (*"Rose"*) and locates Milton's note as follows:

| over against the Abby is *Rose* | *Rose Island,* |
| *Island* . . . | *Hack.* 365. |

Thus the footnote number linked to a Milton marginal note is placed either before or after the word nearest to the first line of Milton's marginal note. Numbers of footnotes not pointing to a Milton note are in customary locations.

Page references in the footnotes to Hakluyt's *Principal Navigations* (vol. I, 1598) and to *Purchas His Pilgrimes* (vol. III, 1625) are to the original editions. The more accessible modern octavo editions of the Hakluyt Society (Edinburgh, 1903–5 and 1905, respectively) indicate throughout by marginal notes the original pagination; so there is no need to refer to modern pagination as well as to the original. Milton's sources are in vols. II–III of the modern Hakluyt edition and in vols. XI–XIV of the modern Purchas edition.

My text of the *Moscovia* is that of the first edition of 1682. It therefore preserves certain typographical conventions of that time, such as the printing in italics of names of persons and places, as also the frequent capitalization of the first letter of important nouns. I note also the changed ending of past participles from "-ed" to "-'d", as in the word "congeal'd". I have let these patterns stand.

In my citation of passages from Milton's sources, the works of Hakluyt and Purchas, I have modernized some earlier fashions of spelling in accordance with present-day scholarly editing practice. To do so, I have reversed the printing of u/v, changing "riuer" and "ouer" to "river" and "over", and "vnto" to "unto"; likewise with i/j, changing "Iosias" to "Josias", and "Ienkinson" to "Jenkinson". I have let stand one archaism. Beginning with Milton's page 46, we find references to Russian emperors (not yet known as czars) as Juan Vasilivich, Pheodor Iuanowick, and Demetrius Euanowich. These names we now recognize as Ivan and Ivanowitch. Milton and his readers may or may not have recognized them in his text as sixteenth-century i/j spellings, and to modernize them might conceal a misunderstanding. It has seemed best to let his spelling stand.

In quoting from Purchas, I have followed the 1625 edition's typographical practice of employing roman type, with names of persons and places italicized. In quoting from Hakluyt, where the 1598 edition's text is in black-letter with names of persons and places in roman, I use roman throughout.

· A Brief

HISTORY

OF

MOSCOVIA:

AND

Of other less-known Coun-
tries lying eastward of *Russia* as
far as *Cathay*.

Gather'd from the Writings of several Eye-witnesses.

By *JOHN MILTON*.

LONDON,
Printed by M. *Flesher*, for *Brabazon Ayl-
mer* at the *Three Pigeons* against the
Royal Exchange. 1682.

THE AUTHOUR'S PREFACE.

THE *study of Geography is both profitable and delightfull; but the Writers thereof, though some of them exact enough in setting down Longitudes and Latitudes, yet in those other relations of Manners, Religion, Government and such like, accounted Geographical, have for the most part miss'd their proportions.* [A2ʳ] *Some too brief and deficient satisfy not; others too voluminous and impertinent cloy and weary out the Reader; while they tell long Stories of absurd Superstitions, Ceremonies, quaint Habits, and other petty Circumstances little to the purpose. Whereby that which is usefull, and onely worth observation, in such a wood of words, is either overslip't, or soon forgotten: which perhaps brought into the mind of some men, more learned and judicious, who had not the leisure or purpose to write an entire Geography, yet at least to assay something in the descrip-* [A2ᵛ] *tion of one or two Countreys, which might be as a Pattern or Example, to render others more cautious hereafter, who intended the whole work. And this perhaps induc'd* Paulus Jovius *to describe onely* Muscovy *and* Britain.[1] *Some such thoughts, many years since, led me at a vacant time to attempt the like argument; and*

---

[1] Jovius (Paolo Giovio, 1483–1552) wrote as his principal work a history of his own time (*Historiarum sui temporis libri XLV*, published Florence, 1551–53). His (separate) *Moschovia* was first published in Rome in 1525 as *Libellus de legatione Basilii magni Principis Moschoviae ad Clementem VII;* it was frequently reprinted, notably in editions of Herberstein's *Commentarii* (on his two missions to Russia, first published in Vienna in 1549), and again with the *Britannia* and other works in *Pauli Jovii Descriptiones regionum atque locorum* (Basel, 1561). It was translated into English by Richard Eden in the latter's *Decades of the newe worlde* (1555; reprinted 1577).

Jovius's *Britannia* was published in Venice in 1548, together with George Lily's *Elogia* of certain English humanists, his *Chronicon* or annals of British history, and an excellent map of Britain. The dedication indicated Jovius's intent to describe "totius cogniti orbis imperia, & regiones," and not merely these two countries. For comment, see the introduction above, section 3.

Jovius's *Moschovia* is an essay of some eight thousand words, or perhaps ten thousand in English. About one-fifth is devoted to the Russian embassy to Rome, one-half to physical geography (neighboring peoples, regions, products), one-third to people and manners, especially religious organizations and practices. It certainly does not tell "long Stories . . . little to the purpose," and except that its map-picture remains vague, it is not too brief to satisfy.

Jovius also wrote a *Commentario delle Cose de' Turchi* (Venice, 1531), which was twice translated into English before 1550.

I began with Muscovy, *as being the most northern Region of* Europe *reputed civil; and the more northern Parts thereof, first discovered by* English *Voiages. Wherein I saw I had by much the advantage of* Jovius. *What was scatter'd in many Vo-* [A3ʳ] *lumes, and observ'd at several times by Eye-witnesses, with no cursory pains I laid together,[2] to save the Reader a far longer travaile of wandring through so many desert Authours; who yet with some delight drew me after them, from the eastern Bounds of* Russia, *to the Walls of* Cathay, *in several late Journeys made thither overland by* Russians, *who describe the Countreys in their way far otherwise than our common Geographers. From proceeding further other occasions diverted me. This Essay, such as it is, was thought by some, who knew of it, not* [A3ᵛ] *amiss to be published; that so many things remarkable, dispers'd before, now brought under one view, might not hazard to be otherwise lost, nor the labour lost of collecting them.*

J.M.   [A4ʳ]

ADVERTISEMENT.

This book was writ by the Authour's own hand, before he lost his sight. And sometime before his death dispos'd of it to be printed. But it being small, the Bookseller hop'd to have procured some other suitable Piece of the same Authour's to have joyn'd with it, or else it had been publish'd 'ere now.

[A4ᵛ]

---

[2] Actually, as Milton's marginal notes fully indicate, he did all his searching in two volumes: the first volume of Richard Hakluyt, *Principal Navigations* (expanded edition, 1598), and the third volume of Samuel Purchas, *Purchas His Pilgrimes* (1625). It was they who had "laid together" chronologically "what was scatter'd in many volumes," though often in manuscript reports by English travelers; but Milton was obliged to skip about in the two volumes to find his geographical material.

MOSCOVIA:
OR,
Relations of *Moscovia*,
As far as hath been discover'd by
English *VOYAGES;*

Gather'd from the Writings of several Eye-witnesses:[3] And of other less-known Countries lying Eastward of *Russia* as far as *Cathay,* lately discovered at several times by *Russians.*

[3] Recourse to first-hand reports by eyewitnesses was an English tradition established by Hakluyt and followed by Purchas. Hakluyt found his precedent in Ramusio's *Navigationi et Viaggi* (Venice, 1550–59) and went beyond him to the Greeks, quoting "Ptolemies assertion, that *Peregrinationis historia,* and not those wearie volumes bearing the titles of universall Cosmographie which some men that I could name have published as their owne, beyng in deed most untruly and unprofitablie ramassed and hurled together, is that which must bring us to the certayne and full discoverie of the world" (*Principall Navigations,* 1589 ed., sig. *3 verso).

Chap. I.

A brief Description.

THE Empire of *Moscovia*, or as others call it, *Russia*, is bounded on the North with *Lapland* and the Ocean; [1] Southward by the *Crim Tartar;* on the West by *Lituania*, *Livonia* and *Poland;* on the East by the River *Ob*, or *Oby*, and the *Nagayan Tartars* on the *Volga*, as far as *Astracan.*[4]

[5]The north parts of this Country are so barren, that the Inhabitants fetch their Corn a 1000 miles, and so cold in Winter that the very Sap of their Wood-fewel burning on the fire, freezes at the Brands end where it drops.[6] The Mariners which were left a shipboard in the first English Voyage [7]thither, in going up onely from their Cabins to the Hatches, had their breath so congeal'd by the cold, that they fell down as it were stifl'd. The Bay of Saint [8]*Nicholas*, where they first put in, lyeth in 64 degrees; call'd so from the Abby there built of Wood; wherein are 20 Monks; unlearned, as then they found them, and great Drunkards: [2] their Church is fair, full of Images, and Tapers. There are besides but

---

[4] The paragraph is close to Giles Fletcher, *Of the Russe Common Wealth*, 1591, as reprinted in Hakluyt, I, 475: "It is bounded northward by the *Lappes* & the North *Ocean*. On the Southside by the *Tartars* called *Crimmes*. Eastward they have the *Nagaian Tartar*, that possesseth all the countrey on the East side of Volga towards the *Caspian* sea. On the West and Southwest border lieth *Lituania*, *Livonia* and *Polonia*."

[5] (M) The North and East, *Hack*. 251.] From Hakluyt, I, 251 (Clement Adams, report of the voyage of Richard Chancellor to Archangel and thence journey to Moscow, 1553): "The people come a thousand miles to Mosco, to buy that corne, and then cary it away upon sled: and these are those people that dwell in the North parts, where the colde is so terrible that no corne doth growe there."

[6] Hakluyt, I, 248 (the same narrative): "The north parts of the Countrey are reported to be so cold, that the very ice or water which distilleth out of the moist wood which they lay upon the fire is presently congealed and frozen: the diversitie growing suddenly to be so great, that in one and the selfe same firebrand, a man shall see both fire and ice."

[7] (M) *Hack*. vo. I. 248.] "Our mariners which we left in the ship in the meane time to keepe it, in their going up onely from their cabbins to the hatches, had their breath oftentimes so suddenly taken away, that they eftsoones fell downe as men very neere dead, so great is the sharpenesse of that colde climate."

[8] (M) Saint *Nicholas, Hack*. 376.] (Thomas Randolfe, mission to Moscow, 1568): "S. Nicholas standeth Northeast: the elevation of the pole 64 degrees." (St. Nicholas was southwest of Archangel, then called St. Michael, on the Gulf of Archangel off the White Sea. Archangel is in latitude 64°33'.)

6 Houses, whereof one built by the English.[9] In the Bay over against the Abby is *Rose*[10] *Island,* full of damask and red Roses, Violets, and wild Rosemary; the Isle is in circuit 7 or 8 miles: about the midst of *May* the snow there is clear'd, having two months been melting; then the ground in 14 daies is dry, and Grass knee-deep within a month: after *September* Frost returns, and Snow a yard high: it hath a House built by the English near to a fresh fair Spring. North-east of the Abby on the other side of *Duina* is the Castle of *Archangel;* where the English[11] have another House. The River *Duina* beginning about 700 miles[12] within the Country, having first receiv'd *Pinega* falls here into the Sea, very large and swift, but shallow. It runneth pleasantly [3] between Hills on either side; beset like a Wilderness with high Firre, and other Trees: their Boats of Timber without any Iron in them, are either to sail, or to be drawn up with Ropes against the stream.[13]

[9] Ibid.: "At S. Nicholas . . . there standeth an abbey of Monks (to the number of twentie) built all of wood: the apparell of the Monks is superstitious, in blacke hoods, as ours have bene. Their Church is faire, but full of painted images, tapers, and candles. Their owne houses are low, and small roomes. They lie apart, they eat together, and are much given to drunkennesse, unlearned, write they can, preach they doe never, ceremonious in their Church, and long in their prayers. . . . Towne or habitation at S. Nicholas there is none more then about foure houses neere the abbey, and another built by the English Company for their owne use."

[10] (M) *Rose Island, Hack.* 365.] Hakluyt, I, 365 (Arthur Edwards, voyage of 1567): "Rose Island in S. Nicholas Baie is full of Roses damaske and red, of violets and wild Rosemarie: This Island is neere 7. or 8. miles about, and good pasture, and hath the name of the roses. The snow here about the midst of May is cleared, having bin two moneths in melting, then the ground is made dry within 14. dayes after, and then the grasse is knee high within a moneth. Then after September the frost commeth in, the snow is a yard deepe upon plaine ground. The Island hath Firre and Birch, and a faire fresh spring neere the house built there by the English." The Rose Island house replaced the first house at St. Nicholas; then the English moved to Archangel.

[11] (M) *Archangel.*] The first mention I have found in Hakluyt of the English house at Archangel is in 1596 (I, 507); but Archangel was "the new castle" in 1586 (Hakluyt, I, 470) and in 1591 was the port town (I, 502, which has Hakluyt's marginal note: "This is a new port").

[12] (M) *Duina. Pinega.*] Hakluyt, I, 376 (Randolfe, 1568): "The river that runneth there [at St. Nicholas] into the sea is called Dwina, very large, but shallow. This river taketh his beginning about 700 miles within the countrey. . . . The river pleasant betweene hie hils of either side inwardly inhabited, and in a maner a wildernesse of hie firre trees, and other wood." Pinega is mentioned elsewhere, among other places by Jenkinson in his 1557 journey (Hakluyt, I, 312), on the same page with the next item.

[13] Hakluyt, I, 312: "These vessels called Nassades, are very long builded, broade made, and close above, flatte bottomed, and draw not above foure foote

North-east beyond *Archangel* [14]standeth *Lampas,* where twice a year is kept a great Fair of *Russes, Tartars* and *Samoeds:* and to the Land-ward *Mezen,* and *Slobotca* two Towns of traffick between the River *Pechora,* or *Petzora,* and *Duina;* To Seaward [15]lies the Cape of *Candinos,* and the Island of *Colgoieve* about 30 leagues from the Bar of *Pechora* in 69 degrees.

The River *Pechora* or *Petzora* holding his course through *Siberia,* how far, the *Russians* thereabouts know not, runneth into the Sea at 72. mouths,[16] full of Ice: abounding with Swans, Ducks, Geese and Partridge, [4] which they take in *July,* sell the Feathers, and salt the Bodies for Winter Provision.[17] On this River spreading

---

water, and will carrie two hundred tunnes: they have none iron appertaining to them but all of timber, and when the winde serveth, they are made to sayle. Otherwise they have many men, some to hale and drawe by the neckes with long small ropes made fast to the sayd boats, and some set with long poles."

[14] (M) *Lampas,* 284.] Hakluyt, I, 284 (Richard Johnson, reporting in 1556): "And East Northeast of Russia lieth Lampas, which is a place where the Russes, Tartars and Samoeds meete twise a yeere, and make the faire to barter wares for wares." "Mizemske Sloboda, where the Samoeds keep their Mart," is mentioned (Hakluyt, I, 364, as of 1567) as close to Lampas, and 230 versts (some 250 miles) from St. Nicholas.

[15] (M) *Candinos, Colgoieve, Pur.* par. 3. 533.] Purchas, III, 533 (William Gourdon, voyage along the Arctic coast to Pechora, 1611): before arriving at Colgoieve, Gourdon reached (p. 531) "the Cape of *Callinos.*" Richard Finch, reporting the same voyage, called it *"Candinos"* (III, 538). The Hondius map of the Arctic regions, which Purchas printed in this volume (p. 625), calls the name also *"Candinos."* Gourdon continues: "of *Colgoiene* Iland . . . the latitude . . . was 69. degrees. 20. minutes. . . . This Ile of *Colgoiene* is but thirtie leagues from the Barre of *Pechora.*"

[16] Purchas, III, 533: "the river *Pechora* . . . they say, runneth through *Siberia;* and how much farther they themselves know not. . . . By report of the Inhabitants the River hath two and seventie mouthes." The English travel relations from 1556 on all say Pechora. Petzora is the name given the province in Avity, English version (pp. 688, 690); The Massa map has Petzora. Purchas, III, 534 (Finch, the same voyage): "wee came to the mouth of the River of *Pechora.* . . . And being entred into the aforesaid Harbour, it was full of Ice, and hard to finde. . . . After our getting over the Barre . . . and that we were come to an anchor, we rode in great danger by the abundance of Ice".

[17] Purchas, III, 533 (Gourdon): "one of the principall men of the Towne [of Pustozera] . . . lay there [on the river] at this time [15 July], to take Duckes, Swannes, Geese, and other Fowles: for then was the time of the yeere. Their feathers they sell, and their bodies they salt for winter provision. . . . [On the 25th] having one of their Boats full with feathers, wee departed from the Towne." This note is repeated by Richard Finch, with prices, III, 536. Finch also notes the winter trade in sables and other furs. Gourdon's record notes: "we came to the Towne of *Pustozera,* which standeth upon a Lake."

to a Lake stands the Town of *Pustozera* in 68 degrees,[18] having some 80, or 100 Houses, where certain Merchants of *Hull* winter'd in the year 1611. The Town *Pechora* small and poor hath 3 Churches.[19] They traded there up the River 4 daies journey to *Oustzilma* a small Town [20] of 60 Houses. The *Russians* that have travail'd, say that this River springs out of the Mountains of *Jougoria* and runs through *Permia*.[21] Not far from the Mouth thereof are the Straits of *Vaigats,* of which hereafter: more eastward is the Point of *Naramzy,*[22] and next to that, the River *Ob.* Beyond which, the *Muscovites* have extended lately their dominion. Touching the *Riphæan* Mountains [23] whence *Tanais* was anciently thought to

---

[18] (M) *Pustozera, ibid. Purc.*] Purchas, III, 544 (marginal note of relation of Josias Logan, wintering in Pustozera): "*Pustozera* in 68. degrees 30. or 35. minutes."

Ibid., III, 541 (same relation): "we arrived at the Towne of *Pustozera* . . . the number of houses there . . . are betwixt fourescore and an hundred, being of wood."

[19] Purchas, III, 536 (Finch, same voyage): "The Towne of *Pechora* is small, having three Churches in it: and the most part of the people are poore," being engaged in hunting birds.

[20] (M) *Purc.* 549.] Purchas, III, 544 (Logan, 1611): "the sixe and twentieth [of May] . . . I departed from *Pustozer,* to goe to *Ust-zilma,* where I arrived the thirtieth day instant. . . . *Ust-zilma,* is a Village of some thirtie or fortie houses."

Ibid., III, 549 (William Pursglove, the same voyage): "The sixe and twentieth, *Iosias Logan* with our Hoast the *Polonian,* hired a Boate and went toward *Oustzilma,* carrying with him certayne Cloath and Copper Kettles, in hope to sell them well there. . . . *Oust-zilma* is a pretie Towne of some sixtie Houses: and is three or foure dayes sayling with a faire wind against the streame from *Pustozer.*"

[21] Purchas, III, 552 (Pursglove, 1613, apparently reporting Russian information): "The River of *Pechora,* runneth through great *Permia;* and the head thereof is five Weekes from *Pustozera.*"

Ibid., III, 525 (A Description of . . . the East and Northeast, 1612): "Out of the same Mountaines [of Jugoria] issueth the River *Petsora.*"

[22] (M) 545, 551.] Purchas, III, 543 (Logan, 1612): "I had conference with a *Russe* . . . And he told me, that their course from *Medenskoy Zavorot,* at the mouth of *Pechora* to the Eastward" adds up to five days and six nights sailing to the Strait of Vaygats, and ten or twelve days more to the River of Ob. A marginal note sums up: "From *Medemskoy Zavorot* to Ob is 16. dayes sayling."

Ibid., III, 55 (Pursglove, the same voyage): "From *Medenskoie Zavorot* to the Isle of *Vaygats,* is two dayes sayling with a Russe Lodia. From *Vaygats* to the River *Ob,* is foure dayes sayling."

Ibid., III, 544 (Logan, the same voyage): "I was told by a *Permack,* having some speech with him concerning the Vaygats, that from Medniskoy Zavorot to the Vaygats, is one day and a nights sayle with a faire wind . . . [and four days to Naromzia]."

[23] (M) *Riphæan* Mountains.] The text now returns without notice to the first account of Russia in Hakluyt, I, 248 (Clement Adams's report of Chancellor's voyage, 1553): "Touching the Riphæan mountaines, whereupon the snow lieth

spring, our men [5] could hear nothing; but rather that the whole Country is Champain, and in the northmost part huge and desert Woods of Firre, abounding with Black Wolves, Bears, Buffs, and another Beast call'd Rossomakka,[24] whose Female bringeth forth by passing through some narrow place, as between two Stakes; and so presseth her Womb to a disburthening. [25]Travailing southward they found the Country more pleasant, fair and better inhabited, Corn, Pasture, Meadows and huge Woods. [26]*Arkania* (if it be not the same with *Archangel*) is a place of English trade, from whence a days journey distant, but from Saint [27]*Nicholas* a 100

continually, and where hence in times past it was thought Tanais the river [Don] did spring, and that the rest of the wonders of nature, which the Grecians fained and invented of olde, were there to be seene: our men which lately came from thence, neither sawe them, nor yet have brought home any perfect relation of them, although they remained there for the space of three moneths, and had gotten in that time some intelligence of the language of Moscovie. The whole Countrey is plaine and champion, and few hils in it: and towards the North it hath very large and spacious woods, wherein is great store of Firre trees, a wood very necessarie, and fit for the building of houses: there are also wilde beastes bred in those woods, as Buffes, Beares, and blacke Wolves, and another kinde of beast unknowen to us, but called by them Rossomakka: and the nature of the same is very rare and wonderfull: for when it is great with yong, and ready to bring foorth, it seeketh out some narrow place betweene two stakes, and so going through them, presseth it selfe, and by that meanes is eased of her burden, which otherwise could not be done." (The Hyperborei Montes ran from east to west across the top of the map of Europe until well into the sixteenth century. They were redirected to north-south in Jenkinson's map of 1562 [published in the Ortelius atlas, *Theatrum Orbis,* 1570] and later became the Ural Mountains.)

[24] The story of the wolverine (Russian rosomakha) must have been collected during the three months' stay at St. Nicholas; the animal had been identified as the "wolvering" when the fur was shipped home (1559: Hakluyt, I, 306) after a skinner had been sent out (I, 298). See further Harris Fletcher, "A Note on Two Words in Milton's *History of Moscovia,*" *PQ,* XX (1941), 501–11.

[25] (M) From Saint *Nicholas* to *Mosco.*] Milton seems to have added the words "they found the Country more pleasant," as Randolfe wrote (Hakluyt, I, 376, dated 1568): "many prety villages, well situated for pasture, arable land, wood, and water. The river pleasant betweene hie hils of either side inwardly inhabited, and in a maner a wildernesse of hie firre trees, and other wood."

[26] (M) *Arkania,* 546, 542.] The word is not in Hakluyt. In Josias Logan's voyage east of the White Sea, 1611, he told the people on the Pechora (Purchas, III, 542): "what a trade is now at *Arkania,*" clearly meaning Archangel, the base of English trade in the north. Again, returning from this voyage (Purchas, III, 546): "wee arrived at *Arkania,* where wee landed our Oyle . . . [the next day] wee arrived at Colmogro."

[27] (M) *Colmogro, Hack.* 376.] Hakluyt, I, 376 (Randolfe, 1568): "Colmogro being 100 versts, which we account for three quarters of a mile every verst, . . . is a great towne, builded all of wood, not walled, but scattered house from house. The people are rude in maners, and in apparell homely. . . . In this towne

versts, *Colmogro* stands on the *Duina:* a great Town not wall'd, but scatter'd. The English have here Lands of their own, given them by the Emperour, and fair Houses; not far beyond, *Pinega* running be- [6] tween Rocks of Alabaster and great Woods, meets with *Duina*. From *Colmogro* to *Ustiug* are 500[28] versts or little miles, an ancient City upon the Confluence of *Juga,* and *Sucana* into *Duina* which[29] there first receives his name. Thence continuing by water to[30] *Wologda;* a great City so nam'd of the River which passes through the midst; it hath a Castle wall'd about with Brick and Stone, and many wooden Churches, two for every Parish, the one in Winter to be heated, the other us'd in Summer;[31] this is a Town of much Traffick a 1000 miles from Saint *Nicholas.* All this way by water no lodging is to be had but under open Sky by the River side, and other provision onely what they bring with them. From *Wologda* by *Sled* they go to *Yeraslave*[32] on the *Volga,* whose breadth is there at least a mile over; and thence runs 2700 versts

---

the English men have lands of their owne, given them by the Emperour, and faire houses, with offices for their commodity, very many."

[28] (M) *Ustiug.*] Hakluyt, I, 312 (Anthony Jenkinson, 1557): "I departed in a little boate up the great river of Dwina, . . . and the selfe same day passed by the mouth of a river called Pinego. . . . On both sides of the mouth of this river Pinego is high land, great rockes of Alablaster, great woods, and Pineapple trees lying along within the ground. . . . I came into a town called Yemps, an hundred verstes from Colmogro. . . . From thence I came to a place called Ustiug, an ancient citie. . . . At this citie meete two rivers: the one called Jug, and the other Sucana, both which fall into the aforesaid river of Dwina. . . . I came unto Vologhda, which is a great citie."

[29] (M) *Hack.* 312.]

[30] (M) *Wologda.*] Hakluyt, I, 376–77 (Randolfe, 1568): "Vologda standeth upon the river of Vologda, which commeth into Dwina. The towne is great and long, built all of wood, as all their townes are. In this towne the Emperor hath built a castle invironed with a wall of stone, and bricke, the walles faire and hie, round about."

[31] Hakluyt, I, 312 (Jenkinson, 1557): "Their Churches are all of wood, two for every parish, one to be heated for Winter, and the other for Summer. . . . there dwell many marchants, and they occupie the said boates with carying of salte from the sea side. . . . from Colmogro, 1000 verstes.

"All the way I never came in house, but lodged in the wildernesse, by the rivers side, and caried provision for the way. . . . I departed from Vologhda in poste in a sled, as the maner is in Winter."

[32] (M) *Yeraslave.*] Hakluyt, I, 377: "At Yeraslave we passed the river of Volga, more then a mile over. This river taketh his beginning at Beal Ozera, & descendeth into Mare Caspium."

Ibid., I, 364 (Edwards, 1567): "To the Caspian sea are 2700. versts from Yeraslave."

to the *Ca-* [7] [33]*spian* Sea, having his head Spring out of *Bealozera,* which is a Lake, [34]amidst whereof is built a strong Tower wherein the Kings of *Moscovy* reserve their Treasure in time of War. From this Town to *Rostove,* then to *Peraslave* a great Town situate on a fair Lake; thence to *Mosco.*[35]

Between *Yeraslave* and *Mosco* which is 200 miles, the Country is so fertile, so populous and full of Villages, that in a forenoon 7 or [36]800 *Sleds* are usually seen coming with Salt Fish, or laden back [37]with Corn.

[38]*Mosco* the chief City, lying in 55 degrees, distant from Saint *Nicholas* 1500 miles, is reputed to be greater than *London* with [39]the Suburbs, but rudely built, their Houses and Churches most of Timber, few of Stone, their Streets unpav'd; it hath a fair Castle four-square, upon a Hill, two miles about, with Brick [8] Walls very high, and some say 18 foot thick, 16 Gates, and as many Bulwarks; in the Castle are kept the chief Markets, and in Winter on the River being then firm Ice. This River *Moscua* on the southwest side encloses the Castle, wherein are nine fair Churches with round gilded Towers, and the Emperour's Palace; which neither

---

[33] (M) *Hack.* 377.]

[34] (M) 248.] Hakluyt, I, 248 (Chancellor, 1553, reported by Adams): "the chiefest and most principall [lake] is called Bealozera, which is very famous by reason of a very strong towre built in it, wherein the kings of Moscovie reserve and repose their treasure in all time of warre and danger."

[35] Hakluyt, I, 312 (Jenkinson, 1557): "so to Rostove, 50 verstes, then to Rogarin 30 verstes, so to Peraslave 10 verstes, which is a great towne, standing hard by a faire lake."

[36] (M) 251.] Hakluyt, I, 251 (Chancellor, 1553): "this Yeraslave is distant from Mosco, about two hundred miles: and betwixt them are many populous villages. Their fields yeeld such store of corne, that in convaying it towards Mosco, sometimes in a forenoone, a man shall see seven hundred or eight hundred sleds, going and comming, laden with corne and salt fish."

[37] (M) 335.] Hakluyt, I, 335 (Jenkinson, 1559): "Mosco in Deg. 55. Min. 10."

[38] (M) *Mosco.*] Hakluyt, I, 248 (Chancellor, 1553): "Of Mosco the chiefe Citie of the kingdome. . ."

Ibid., I, 363 (Edwards, 1567): "The way from Saint Nicholas Baie to Mosco . . . [to Vologhda] 1100 versts . . . To Mosko . . . 440 versts." (Milton should have written 1,540 versts, not 1,500 miles.)

[39] (M) 313.] Hakluyt, I, 248–49 (Chancellor, 1553): "Our men say, that in bignesse it is as great as the Citie of London, with the suburbes thereof. There are many and great buildings in it, but for beautie and fairenesse, nothing comparable to ours. . . . their streetes and wayes are not paved with stone as ours are: the walles of their houses are of wood: the roofes for the most part are covered with shingle boords. There is hard by the Citie a very faire Castle, strong and furnished with artillerie . . . the walles also of the Castle are built with bricke, and are in breadth or thicknesse eighteene foote."

within, nor without is equal for state to the King's Houses in *England* but rather like our Buildings of old fashion with small Windows, some of Glass, some with Latices, or Iron Bars.

They who travail from *Mosco*[40] to the *Caspian*, go by Water down the *Moscua* to the River *Occa;* then by certain Castles to *Rezan*, a famous City now ruinate; the 10*th* day to *Nysnovogrod* where *Occa* falls into *Volga*, which the *Tartars* call *Edel.*[41] From thence the 11*th* day to *Ca-* [9] *zan* a *Tartan* [*sic*] City of great wealth heretofore, now under the *Russian;* wall'd at first with Timber and Earth, but since by the Emperour *Vasiliwich* with free Stone.[42] From *Cazan* to the River *Cama* falling into *Volga* from the Province of *Permia*, the People dwelling on the left side are *Gentiles*, and live in Woods without [43]Houses: beyond them to *Astracan*, *Tartars*

Ibid., I, 313 (Jenkinson, 1558): "The Emperors lodging is in a faire and large castle, walled foure square of bricke, high, and thicke, situated upon a hill, 2 miles about, and the river on the Southwest side of it, and it hath 16 gates in the walles, and as many bulwarks. . . . In his palace are Churches [Chancellor had said nine churches], some of stone and some of wood, with round towers fairely gilded. In the Church doores and within the Churches are images of golde: the chiefe markets for all things, are within the sayd Castle. . . . And in the winter there is a great market without the castle, upon the river being frozen."

Ibid., I, 249 (Chancellor, 1553): "As for the kings Court and Palace, it is not of the neatest, onely in forme it is foure square, and of lowe building, much surpassed and excelled by the beautie and elegancie of the houses of the kings of England. The windowes are very narrowly built, and some of them by glasse, some other by lettisses admit the light."

[40] (M) South-east. *Hack.* 325.] Hakluyt, I, 324 (Jenkinson to the Caspian and Bokhara, 1558): "I departed from Mosco by water. . . . we came [in 5 days] unto a river called Occa, into which the river Mosco falleth. . . . we came unto a castle called Terrevettisko. . . . we came unto the place where olde Rezan was situate, being now most of it ruined and overgrowen. . . . the 11. day [of May, actually 19 days from Moscow, which he left on April 23], we came unto another faire town & castle called Nyse Novogrod, situated at the falling of the foresaid river Occa into the worthie river of Volga."

[41] Hakluyt, I, 334 (the same relation, but this item occurs later in the account of the return journey): [the Volga] "called in the Tartar tongue Edell."

[42] Hakluyt, I, 324 (the same relation): "the 29. [of May, 37 days from Moscow] came unto an Island one league from the citie of Cazan. . . . Cazan is a faire town after the Russe or Tartar fashion, with a strong castle, situated upon a high hill, and was walled round about with timber & earth, but now the Emperour of Russia hath given order to plucke downe the old walles, and to builde them againe of free stone."

[43] (M) 334.] This page number is erroneous, as it refers to Jenkinson's return voyage on the Caspian Sea. It should be 325, referring still to Jenkinson's voyage down the Volga. This passage continues his story as follows: "we passed by a goodly river called Cama. . . . This river falleth out of the countrey of Permia

of *Mangat,* and *Nagay;* on the right side those of *Crimme.* From *Mosco* to *Astracan* is about 600 leagues.[44] The Town is situate in an Island on a Hill-side wall'd with Earth, but the Castle with Earth and Timber; the Houses except that of the Governour's, and some few others, poor and simple; the Ground utterly barren, and without Wood: they live there on Fish, and Sturgeon especially; which hanging up to dry in the Streets and Houses brings whole [10] swarms of Flies, and infection to the Aire, and oft great Pestilence. This Island in length 12 leagues, 3 in breadth is the *Russian* limit toward the *Caspian,* which he keeps with a strong Garrison; being 20 leagues from that Sea into which *Volga* falls at 70 mouths. From Saint *Nicholas,* or from *Mosco* to the *Caspian* they pass in 46 daies and nights, most part by Water.[45]

---

into the river of Volga, and is from Cazan 15. leagues: and. . . . on the left hand of Volga. . . . the inhabitants be Gentiles, and live in the wildernesse without house or habitation . . . and all the land on the left hand of the said Volga . . . unto Astracan, and . . . to a land of the Tartars called Turkemen, is called the countrey of Mangat or Nagay. . . . All the countrey upon our right hand the river Volga . . . is the land of Crimme."

[44] Hakluyt, I, 326 (the same relation): "It is from the Mosco unto Astracan sixe hundreth leagues, or thereabout. . . . The towne of Astracan is situated in an Island upon a hill side, having a castle within the same, walled about with earth and timber, neither faire nor strong: The towne is also walled about with earth: the buildings and houses (except it be the captaines lodging, and certaine other gentlemens) most base and simple. The Island is most destitute and barren of wood and pasture, and the ground will beare no corne: the aire is there most infected, by reason (as I suppose) of much fish, and specially Sturgion, by which onely the inhabitants live, having great scarsitie of flesh and bread. They hang up their fish in their streets and houses to dry for their provision, which causeth such abundance of flies to increase there, as the like was never seene in any land, to their great plague. . . . This Astracan is the furthest hold that this Emperour of Russia hath conquered of the Tartars towards the Caspian sea, which he keepeth very strong, sending thither every yere provision of men, and victuals, and timber to build the castle. . . . This foresaid Island of Astracan is in length twelve leagues, and in bredth three. . . . We entred into the Caspian sea . . . being twentie leagues from Astracan aforesaid. . . . Volga hath seventie mouthes or fals into the sea."

[45] Hakluyt, I, 364 (Edwards, 1567): "So between S. Nicholas and the Caspian sea, are] 46. dayes iourney." Milton clearly distrusted this figure, which is much too small, and may have counted up for himself the time required on various English journeys to the Caspian. Hakluyt did not have Arthur Edwards's itinerary, printing only some letters and summaries. Jenkinson's first journey in 1558 took sixty-one days from Moscow, and seventy-three days to return. His later journey, 1562, took forty-six days from Moscow to the Caspian, and Milton may have substituted this figure for Edwards's.

West-ward from Saint *Nicholas*[46] 1200 miles, is the City *Novogrod*[47] 58 degrees, the greatest Mart-town of all this Dominion, and in bigness not inferior to *Mosco*.[48] The way thither[49] is through the western bottom of Saint *Nicholas* Bay, and so along the Shoar full of dangerous Rocks to the Monastery *Solofky,* wherein are at least 200 Monks; the People thereabout in a manner Savages, yet Tenants to those Monks. Thence to the [11] dangerous River *Owiga,* wherein are Waterfalls as steep as from a Mountain, and by the violence of their descent kept from freezing; so that the Boats are to be carried there a mile over land: which the Tenants of that Abby did by command, and were guides to the Merchants without taking any reward. Thence to the Town *Povensa* standing within a mile of the famous Lake *Onega* 320 miles long; and in some places 70, at narrowest 25 broad, and of great depth.[50] Thence

[46] (M) West. *Novogrod.* 365.] Hakluyt, I, 368 (Thomas Southam, 1566): "from Novogrod to S. Nicholas road [harbor], is by our accompt 1261. miles or versts."

[47] Hakluyt, I, 335 (Jenkinson, 1560): "Novogrod the great 58 deg. 26 min."

[48] Hakluyt, I, 251 (Chancellor, 1553): "Next unto Mosco, the Citie of Novogorode is reputed the chiefest of Russia: for although it be in Majestie inferior to it, yet in greatnesse it goeth beyond it. It is the cheifest and greatest Marte Towne of all Moscovie."

[49] Hakluyt, I, 365–68 ("The way discovered by water by us Thomas Southam & John Sparke, from the towne of Colmogro, by the Westerne bottome of the Baie of S. Nicholas, unto the citie of Novogrod . . . 1566"). Milton here touches only a few high spots of the voyage, which required many portages, and he does not add up the daily entries to discover that the voyage took forty days.

Ibid., I, 365: "[after seven days] we found many rocks: and if the great providence of God had not preserved us, wee had there perished, . . . our pilot none of the perfectest."

Ibid., I, 366: "[on the eighth day] we arrived at a monasterie named Solofky. . . . The people of all those parts are wild, and speake another kind of language, and are for the most part all tenants to the monasterie. . . . The number of monkes belonging to the monasterie are at the least 200."

"[in two days] we arrived . . . within the river of Owiga. . . . in the way . . . at a place where the water falleth from the rocks, as if it came steepe downe from a mountain, we were constrained to take out our goods and wares . . . to be caried a mile over land, and afterwards also had our boates in like sort caried or drawen over land by force of men which there dwelled, being tenants to the monasterie aforesaid. . . . the servant which we had at the Monasterie, . . . after that he had hired the boats, . . . hee departed from us without taking any reward for his paines."

Ibid., I, 367: "downe those dangerous rivers . . . in the Sommer it is impossible to cary downe any wares by reason of the great fals of water that doe descend from the rockes. Likewise in the Winter by reason of the great force and fall of waters which make so terrible raises, that in those places it never freezeth."

[50] Hakluyt, I, 367 (the same relation): "This towne of Povensa standeth within one mile of the famous lake or Ozera of Onega, which is 320. miles long, and in

by some Monasteries to the River *Swire;* then into the Lake *Ladiscay* much longer than *Onega:* after which into the River *Volhusky* which through the midst of *Novogrod* runs into this Lake, and this Lake into the *Baltick* sound by *Narv* and *Revel.*[51] Their other Cities toward the western bound are *Plesco, Smolensko* or *Vobsco.*[52] [12]

The Emperour exerciseth absolute power:[53] if any man die without male Issue, his Land returns to the Emperour. Any rich man who through age, or other impotence is unable to serve the Publick, being inform'd of, is turn'd out of his Estate, and forc'd with his Family to live on a small Pension, while some other more deserving, is by the Duke's authority put into possession.[54] The manner of

---

some places 70. miles over. . . . Hard aboord the shore . . . you shall have 40. and 45. fathoms of depth." (Only one of the four stops after Povensa was at a monastery): "and then entred into a river called Swire, at a Monastery." After two stops, not at monasteries, "We . . . entred upon the Lake of Ladiskaie, . . . which is farre longer then the lake of Onega, . . . and entred into the river of Volhuski, which river hath his beginning 20. miles above Novogrod, and runneth through the midst of the Citie, and so falleth into this lake. . . . This lake falleth into the sea that commeth from the Sound: where any vessel or boat, having a good pilot, may goe through the Sound into England." The Sound is the Gulf of Finland. Milton's condensed statement here gives a wrong impression. The party barely entered Lake Lagoda by the Svir river, leaving it to go upstream on the Volschov river 171 miles (I, 368) to Novgorod.

[51] Narve is mentioned at the end of Southam's relation (Hakluyt, I, 369) as 180 miles from Novgorod. Reval is mentioned with it in Henrie Lane's summary of the Russian voyages (I, 466, c.1584): "And at this time [1560] was the first traffike to the Narve in Livonia, which confines with Lituania, & all the dominions of Russia. . . . The trade to Rie, and Revel, of old time hath bene long since frequented by our English nation."

[52] Hakluyt, I, 475 (Fletcher, *Of the Russe Common Wealth,* as of 1588): Plesko and Smolensko are named as two of the "shires" of Russia. A little further on in Fletcher, Milton might have noted the conquest by Russia of Plesko and Smolensco in 1514 (Hakluyt, I, 485), and again (I, 486): "The foure castles of Smolensko, Vobsco, Cazan and Astracan, he hath made very strong [as frontier cities.]"

[53] (M) Governm. *Hac.* 240.] I do not find this exact phrase ("absolute power") in the English documents. Herberstein had not quite said it (*Notes upon Russia,* Hakluyt Society 10, [1851], p. 32, translated from the original of 1549): "He . . . holds unlimited control over the lives and property of all his subjects. . . . They openly confess that the will of the Prince is the will of God. . . . It is a matter of doubt whether the brutality of the people has made the prince a tyrant, or whether the people themselves have become thus brutal and cruel through the tyranny of their prince." Botero had written (1596; English translation, 1601, p. 135): "This government is more tyrannical than of any other Prince in the world for he is absolute Lord, and disposer of the bodies and goods of his subjects."

[54] Hakluyt, I, 240 (Chancellor, 1553): "Also, if any gentleman or man of living do die without issue male, immediately after his death the Duke entreth his land.

informing the Duke is thus. Your Grace, saith one, hath such a Subject, abounding with Riches, but for service of the State unmeet, and you have others poor and in want, but well able to doe their Country good service. Immediately the Duke sends forth to enquire, and calling the Rich man before him, Friend, saith he, you have too much Living, and are unserviceable to your Prince; less will serve you, and the rest maintain others [13] who deserve more. The man thus call'd to impart his Wealth, repines not, but humbly answers, that all he hath is God's, and the Duke's: as if he made restitution of what more justly was anothers, than parted with his own. Every Gentleman hath rule and justice over his own Tenants: if the Tenants of two Gentlemen agree not, they seek to compose it, if they cannot, each brings his Tenant before the high

---

. . . Also if there be a rich man, a fermour, or man of living, which is stricken in age or by chance is maimed, and be not able to doe the Duke [military] service, some other gentleman that is not able to live and more able to doe service, will come to the Duke and complayne, saying, your Grace hath such an one, which is unmeete to doe service to your Highnes, who hath great abundance of welth, and likewise your Grace hath many gentlemen which are poore and lacke living, and we that lacke are well able to doe good service, your Grace might doe well to looke upon him, and make him to helpe those that want. Immediately the Duke sendeth forth to inquire of his wealth: and if it be so proved, he shall be called before the Duke, and it shall bee sayd unto him, friend, you have too much living, and are unserviceable to your prince, lesse will serve you, and the rest will serve other men that are more able to serve. whereupon immediately his living shal be taken away from him, saving a little to find himselfe and his wife on, and he may not once repine thereat: but for answere he will say, that he hath nothing, but it is Gods and the Dukes Graces, and cannot say, as we the common people in England say, if wee have any thing; that it is Gods and our owne. . . . every gentleman hath rule and justice upon his owne tenants. And if it so fall out that two gentlemens servants or tenaunts doe disagree, the two gentlemen examine the matter, and have the parties before them, and soe give the sentence. And yet cannot they make the ende betwixt them of the controversie, but either of the gentlemen must bring his servant or tenant before the high judge or justice of that countrey, and there present them, and declare the matter and case. . . .

"Their order in one point is commendable. They have no man of Lawe to pleade their causes in any court: but every man pleadeth his owne cause, and giveth bill and answere in writing. . . . The complaint is in maner of a supplication, & made to the Dukes Grace, and delivered him into his owne hand."

Ibid., I, 241: "The duke giveth sentence himselfe upon all matters in the Law. . . . Yet notwithstanding it is wonderfully abused: and thereby the Duke is much deceived. . . . [many sentences upon trial by personal combat, or by champion; in special case of debt,] the Duke taketh the partie defendant home to his house, and useth him as his bond-man, and putteth him to labour, or letteth him for hier to any such as neede him, untill such time as his friends make provision for his redemption: or else hee remaineth in bondage all the dayes of his life."

Judge of that Country. They have no Lawyers, but every man pleads his own Cause, or else by Bill or Answer in writing delivers it with his own hands to the Duke: yet Justice by corruption of inferiour Officers is much perverted. Where other proof is wanting, they may try the matter by personal combat, or by champion. If a Debtor be poor, he becomes bondman to the Duke, who lets out his labour till it pay the dept; [14] till then he remains in bondage: [55] another tryal they have by lots.

The Revenues of the Emperour [56] are what he list, and what his Subjects are able; and he omits not the coursest means to raise them: for in every good Town there is a drunken Tavern, call'd a *Cursemay,* which the Emperour either lets out to farm, or [57] bestowes on some Duke, or Gentleman in reward of his Service; who for that time is Lord of the whole Town, robbing and spoiling at his pleasure; till being well enricht, he is sent at his own charge to the Wars, and there squeez'd of his ill-got wealth; by which means the waging of war is to the Emperour little or nothing chargeable.

The *Russian* armeth not less in [58] time of war than 300 thousand men; half of whom he takes with him into the Field, the rest bestows in Garrisons on the Bor- [15] ders. He presseth no Hus-

[55] (M) *Hac.* 309.] Hakluyt, I, 309: "The maner of Justice by lots in Russia, written by Master Henrie Lane, and executed in a controversie betweene him and one Sheray Costromitskey in Mosco. 1560." (a long account of a disputed debt, won in a court of law by an Englishman).

[56] (M) Revenues.] I do not find in Hakluyt an explicit statement that the czar's revenues are "what he list." In Avity we read (English version, 1615, pp. 692–93): "As for the king's riches, we may easily conjecture that he is lord and absolute maister of all things: he makes use of the labour of his subjects, and taketh what part of their goods he pleaseth . . . He hath infinit means to draw money."

[57] (M) *Hac.* 314.] Hakluyt, I, 314 (Jenkinson, 1558): "In every good towne there is a drunken Taverne called a Cursemay, which the Emperour sometime letteth out to farme, & sometimes bestoweth for a yeare or two on some duke or gentleman, in recompense of his service; and for that time he is Lord of all the towne, robbing and spoiling, and doing what pleaseth him: and then he being growen rich, is taken by the Emperor, and sent to the warres againe, where he shall spend all that which he hath gotten by ill meanes: so that the Emperour in his warres is little charged, but all the burden lieth upon the poore people." (For the word "Cursemay," see Harris Fletcher in *PQ,* XX [1941], 501–11.)

[58] (M) Forces. *Hac.* 239. 250.] Hakluyt, I, 239 (Chancellor, 1553): "he is able to bring into the field two or three hundred thousand men: he never goeth into the field himselfe with under two hundred thousand men. [and he stations 160,000 on the borders.] All his men are horsemen: he useth no footmen, but such as goe with the ordinance and labourers, which are thirtie thousand. The horsemen are all archers, with such bowes as the Turkes have, and they ride short as doe the Turkes. Their armour is a coate of plate, with a skull on their heads. Some of

bandman or Merchant, but the Youth of the Realm. He useth no Foot, but such as are Pioners, or Gunners, of both which sort 30 thousand. The rest being Horsemen, are all Archers, and ride with a short Stirrup after the *Turkish*. Their Armour is a Coat of Plate, and a Skull on their Heads. Some of their Coats are cover'd with Velvet, or cloth of Gold; for they desire to be gorgeous in Arms, but the Duke himself above measure: his Pavilion cover'd with cloth of Gold, or Silver, set with pretious Stones. They use little Drums at the Saddle bow instead of Spurs; for at sound thereof the Horses run more swiftly.

[59]They fight without order; nor [60]willingly give battail but by stealth or ambush; of cold and hard Diet marvelously patient; for

---

their coates are covered with velvet or cloth of gold: their desire is to be sumptuous in the field, and especially the nobles and gentlemen . . . but the Duke himselfe is richly attired above all measure: his pavilion is covered either with cloth of gold or silver, and so set with stones that it is wonderfull to see it."

Cf., ibid., I, 250 (Adams's report of Chancellor): "hee never armeth a lesse number against the enemie, then 300. thousand soldiers, 100. thousand whereof hee carieth out into the field with him, and leaveth the rest in garison in some fit places. . . . He presseth no husbandmen, nor Marchant: for . . . the youth of the Realme is sufficient for all his wars. . . . They fight not on foote, but altogether on horsebacke: their armour is a coate of maile, & a helmet: the coate of maile without is gilded, or els adorned with silke, although it pertaine to a commom soldier: they have a great pride in shewing their wealth. . . . They ride with a short stirrop, after the maner of the Turks. As for the furniture of the Emperour himselfe, it is then above all other times, most notable. The coverings of his tent for the most part, are all of gold, adorned with stones of great price, and with the curious workemanship of plumasiers."

But cf. ibid., I, 483 (Fletcher, *Of the Russe Common Wealth,* as of 1588), which points out that only generals and nobles are so luxurious, "while the comon horseman hath nothing els but his bow in his case under his right arme, & his quiver & sword hanging on the left side. The under captains wil have commonly some piece of armour besides, as a shirt of male, or such like."

[59] (M) *Hac.* 314.] Hakluyt, I, 314 (Jenkinson, 1558): "They use little drummes at their sadle bowes, by the sound whereof their horses use to runne more swiftly."

Cf. ibid., I, 484 (Giles Fletcher again): "The . . . chiefe horsemen, have every man a small drum of brasse at his saddle bowe, which he striketh when he giveth the charge, or onset." And cf. I, 388 (George Turberville, 1568): "the Russie hath his whippe / To rappe him on the ribbes, for though all booted bee, / Yet shall you not a paire of spurres in all the countrey see."

[60] (M) 250.] Hakluyt, I, 239 (Chancellor, 1553): "They are men without al order in the field. For they runne hurling on heapes, and for the most part they never give battell to their enemies: but that which they doe, they doe it all by stelth. But I beleeve they be such men for hard living as are not under the sun: for no cold wil hurt them. Yea and though they lie in the field two moneths, at such time as it shall freese more then a yard thicke, the common souldier hath neither tent nor any thing else over his head: the most defence they have against the

when the Ground is cover'd with Snow froz'n a yard thick, [16] the common Souldier will lie in the Field two months together without Tent, or covering over head; onely hangs up his Mantle against that part from whence the Weather drives, and kindling a little fire, lies him down before it, with his Back under the Wind: his Drink, the cold Stream mingl'd with Oat-meal, and the same all his Food: his Horse fed with Green Wood and Bark, stands all this while in the open Field, yet does his service. The Emperour gives no pay at all,[61] but to Strangers; yet repaies good deserts in war with certain Lands during life; and they who oftenest are sent to the wars, think themselves most favour'd, though[62] serving

---

weather is a felte, which is set against the winde and wether, and when Snowe commeth hee doth cast it off, and maketh him a fire, and laieth him down thereby. . . . hee himselfe shal live upon water & otemeale mingled together cold, and drinke water therto: his horse shal eat green wood, & such like baggage, & shal stand open in the cold field without covert, & yet wil he labour & serve him right wel."

Milton also drew upon the elaborated Adams report of Chancellor, ibid., I, 250: "they goe forth without any order at all: they make no wings, nor militarie divisions of their men, as we doe, but lying for the most part, in ambush, doe suddenly set upon the enemie. . . . this Russe hangs up his mantle, or souldiers coate, against that part from whence the winde and Snowe drives, and so making a little fire, lieth downe with his backe towards the weather."

[61] Hakluyt, I, 239–40 (Chancellor, 1553): "[The Emperour] giveth no wages, except to strangers. . . . But if any man [Russian] hath done very good service he giveth him a ferme or a piece of lande; for the which hee is bound at all times to bee readie with so many men as the Duke shall appoint."

Ibid., I, 250 (Clement Adams): "notwithstanding after his death, [the grant] returneth againe to the Emperour, if he die without a male issue."

[62] (M) *Hac.* 316.] Hakluyt, I, 316–17 (Jenkinson, 1557): "The 12 of December the Emperours Majestie and all his nobility came into the field on horsebacke, in most goodly order, having very fine Jennets and Turkie horses garnished with gold & silver abundantly. . . . there went 5000 harquebusiers. . . . the harquebusiers began to shoot off at the banke of ice [two foot thicke, and sixe foote high, and a quarter of a mile long] . . . who ceased not shooting, untill they had beaten all the ice flat on the ground.

"After the handguns, they shot off their wild fire up into the aire, which was goodly sight to behold. And after this, they began to discharge the smal pieces of brasse, beginning with the smallest and so orderly bigger and bigger, untill the last and biggest. . . . [and so three times around.] And note that before they had ended their shooting, the 2 houses that they shot unto were beaten in pieces, & yet they were very strongly made of Wood and filled with earth, being at the least 30 foote thicke. This triumph being ended, the Emperour departed and rode home in the same order. . . . The ordinance is discharged every yeare in the moneth of December."

Cf. also ibid., I, 316: "They have faire ordinance of brasse of all sortes, . . . they have six great pieces whose shot is a yard of height, which shot a man may easily discerne as they flee."

without Wages. On the 12*th* of *December* yearly the Emperour rides into the Field which is without the City, with all his Nobility on Jennets and Turky Horses in great state: before him [17] 5000 Harquebusiers, who shoot at a bank of Ice till they beat it down, the Ordnance, which they have very fair of all sorts, they plant against two wooden Houses fill'd with earth at least 30 foot thick, and beginning with the smallest, shoot them all off thrice over, having beat those two Houses flat. Above the rest 6 great Cannon they have, whose Bullet is a yard high, so that a man may see it flying; then out of Morter-pieces they shoot wild-fire into the Aire. Thus the Emperour having seen what his Gunners can doe, returns home in the same order.

[63]They follow the *Greek* Church, but with excess of Superstitions; their Service is in the *Russian* Tongue. They hold the Ten Commandments not to concern them, saying that God gave them under the Law, which *Christ* by his death on the Cross hath abro- [18] gated: the Eucharist they receive in both kinds; they observe 4 Lents, have Service in their Churches daily, from two hours before dawn to Evening;[64] yet for Whordom, Drunkenness and Extortion none worse than the Clergy.

They have many great and rich Monasteries, where they[65] keep great hospitality. That of *Trojetes* hath in it 700 Friers, and is

[63] (M) Religion. *Hac.* 253.] Hakluyt, I, 253, contains Adams's elaboration of Chancellor. Actually Milton follows Chancellor's own account, I, 241–42: "They doe observe the lawe of the Greekes with such excesse of superstition, as the like hath not bene heard of. They have no graven images in their Churches, but all painted, . . . but to their painted images they use such idolatrie, that the like was never heard of in England. . . . All their service in Churches is in their mother tongue. . . . Speake to them of the Commandements, and they wil say they were given to Moses in the law, which Christ hath nowe abrogated by his precious death and passion: therefore, (say they) we observe little or none thereof. . . . They have the Sacrament of the Lords Supper in both kindes. . . . They have foure Lents in the yeere. . . . They [the monks] have service daily in their Churches . . . [from] two houres before day . . . to supper."

[64] (M) 242, 321.] (Chancellor continues): "As for whoredome and drunkennesse there be none such living: and for extortion, they be the most abhominable under the sunne."

[65] (M) 320.] Hakluyt, I, 320 (Jenkinson, 1558): "They have both monks, friers and nunnes, with a great number of great & rich monasteries: they keepe great hospitalitie, and doe relieve much poore people day by day. I have bene in one of the monasteries called Troietes, which is walled about with bricke very strongly like a castle, and much ordinance of brasse upon the walles of the same. They told me themselves that there are seven hundred brethren. . . . The most part of the lands, towns, and villages which are within 40. miles of it, belong unto the same. . . . [321] The same monkes are as great merchants as any in the land of Russia."

wall'd about with Brick very strongly, having many Pieces of Brass Ordnance on the Walls; most of the Lands, Towns and Villages within 40 miles belong to those Monks, who are also as great Merchants as any in the Land. During Easter Holy-daies when two Friends meet they take each other by the hand; one of them saying, the Lord is risen; the other answering, it is so of a[66] truth; and then they kiss, whe- [19] ther Men or Women. The Emperour esteemeth the Metropolitan next to God, after our Lady, and Saint *Nicholas,* as being his spiritual Officer, himself but his temporal. But the [67]*Muscovites* that border on *Tartaria* are yet *Pagans.*

[68]When there is love between two, the Man among other trifling Gifts, sends to the Woman a Whip, to signify, if she offend, what she must expect; and it is a Rule among them, that if the Wife be not beaten once a week, she thinks her self not belov'd, and is the worse; yet are they very obedient, and stir not forth, but at some Seasons. Upon utter dislike, the Husband divorces; which Liberty

[66] (M) 318.] Hakluyt, I, 318: "For when two friends meete during the Easter holy dayes, they come & take one another by the hand: the one of them sayth, the Lord or Christ is risen, the other answereth, it is so of a truth, and then they kisse and exchange their [colored] egs both men and women, continuing in kissing 4 dayes together." [320] "The Metropolitane is next unto God, our Lady and S. Nicholas excepted: for the Emperors majesty judgeth & affirmeth him to be of higher dignitie then himselfe; for that, saith he, he is Gods spiritual officer, and I the Emperour am his temporall officer."

[67] (M) 320, 254.] Hakluyt, I, 254 (Adams's report of Chancellor, 1553): "There is a certaine part of Moscovie bordering upon the countreys of the Tartars, wherin those Moscovites that dwell are very great idolaters."

[68] (M) Marriages. *Hac.* 322.] Hakluyt, I, 322 (anonymous description of Russian manners, 1558): "Their matrimonie is nothing solemnized, but rather in most points abhominable, and as neere as I can learne, in this wise following. First, when there is love betweene the parties, the man sendeth unto the woman a small chest or boxe, wherein is a whip, needles, threed, silke, linnen cloth, sheares, and such necessaries as shee shall occupie when she is a wife, . . . giving her to understand, that if she doe offend, she must be beaten with the whip." [Then follows a lengthy account of wedding feasts.] ". . . but one common rule is amongst them, if the woman be not beaten with the whip once a weeke, she will not be good, and therefore they looke for it orderly, & the women say, that if their husbands did not beate them, they should not love them. . . . they use to keep their wives very closely, I meane those that be of any reputation, so that a man shall not see one of them but at a chance, when she goeth to church at Christmas or at Easter, or els going to visite some of her friends."

Cf. ibid., I, 314 (Jenkinson, first voyage to Russia, also 1558): "The women be there very obedient to their husbands, & are kept straightly from going abroad, but at some seasons."

no doubt [69]they receiv'd first with their Religion from the *Greek* Church, and the Imperial Laws.

[70]Their Dead they bury with new Shooes on their Feet, as to [20] a long Journey; and put Letters testimonial in their Hands to

[69] (M) 314.] Hakluyt, I, 314, says nothing of divorce, nor does the preceding passage above; nor does Lane or Fletcher later. Milton apparently drew upon other reading, though I do not find this specific sentence. In the *Commonplace Book* a note under divorce reads (fol. 112): "Joannes Basilii filius Moschorum dux, uxore repudiatâ, quod, quoties vult[x], illi moribus patriis licet, novam ducit. Thuan. hist. 1. 72, p. 417. [x]non regi solum sed cuivis. Baro ab Herber. de Mosch:"

De Thou was reporting (book 72, chap. xvii, date 1580) the sixth marriage of Ivan IV. The Herberstein citation reads simply: "They admit divorces, and grant a writ of repudiation, but they mostly conceal it, because they know it to be contrary to religion and the statutes" (Sigismund von Herberstein, *Rerum Moscoviticarum Commentarii,* Vienna, 1549, as translated by R. H. Major in Hakluyt Society 10 (1851), p. 93).

The most conclusive statement in the literature is that of Alessandro Guagnini, *De Moscoviticorum . . . religione, ritibus nuptiarum . . .* (Speyer, 1582; rep. in *Respublica Moscoviae,* Leiden, 1630, p. 111): "Divortia inter se frequenter celebrant, Episcopis permittentibus, literasque repudii datibus." The English understood that Ivan put away two wives by consigning them to nunneries (Jerome Horsey, *Travels,* ed. from MS more inclusive than the part printed by Hakluyt: Hakluyt Society 20 (1856), 163–64). Giles Fletcher wrote that a husband might go into a monastery and leave his wife to shift for herself (*Purchas His Pilgrimes,* III, 455).

Milton does not give a source for his statement that the tradition of the Greek Church permitted divorce. As for the Roman law, two references in his Commonplace Book to *Jus Graeco-Rom.* are conflicting: one to the excommunication of Leo the General for a remarriage (fol. 109), and one to a wife's right to remarriage after five years' absence of the husband (fol. 112).

[70] (M) Burial. 242, 254, 323.] Hakluyt, I, 242 (Chancellor, 1553): "And when any of them die, they have a testimoniall with them in the Coffin, that when the soule commeth to heaven gates it may deliver the same to Saint Peter, which declareth that the partie is a true and holy Russian."

Ibid., I, 254 (Adams's report of Chancellor, 1553): "when any man dyeth amongst them, they take the dead body and put it in a coffine or chest, and in the hand of the corps they put a litle scroule, and & in the same there are these wordes written, that the same man died a Russe of Russes, having received the faith, and died in the same. This writing or letter they say they send to S. Peter, who receiving it (as they affirme) reades it, and by and by admits him into heaven, and that his glory and place is higher and greater then the glory of the Christians of the Latine church, reputing themselves to be followers of a more sincere faith and religion then they."

Ibid., I, 323 (anonymous description of Russia, 1558): "When any man or woman dieth, they stretch him out, and put a new paire of shooes on his feete, because he hath a great journey to goe: then doe they winde him in a sheet, as we doe, but they forget not to put a testimonie in his right hand, which the priest giveth him, to testifie unto S. Nicholas that he died a Christian man or woman. And they put the coarse alwayes in a coffin of wood, although the partie be very

Saint *Nicholas,* or Saint *Peter,* that this was a *Russe* of *Russes* and dy'd in the true Faith; which, as they believe, Saint *Peter* having read, forthwith admits him into Heaven.

They have no Learning,[71] nor will suffer to be among them;[72] their greatest friendship is in drinking; they are great Talkers, Lyars, Flatterers and Dissemblers. They delight in gross Meats and noysom Fish; their Drink is better, being sundry sorts of Meath; the best made with Juice of a sweet and crimson Berry call'd *Maliena,* growing[73] also in *France;* other sorts with Black-cherry, or divers other Berries: another Drink they use in the Spring drawn from the Birch-tree Root, whose Sap after *June* dries up. But there is no People that live so miserably [21] as the Poor of *Russia;*[74] if

---

poore: and when they goe towards the Church, the friends and kinsemen of the partie departed carrie in their hands small waxe candles, and they weepe and howle, and make much lamentation. They that be hanged or beheaded, or such like, have no testimonie with them: how they are received into heaven, it is a wonder, without their pasport."

[71] Hakluyt, I, 253 (Adams's report of Chancellor, 1553): "all studies and letters of humanitie they utterly refuse: concerning the Latine, Greeke, and Hebrew tongues, they are altogether ignorant in them."

[72] (M) Manners. 241, 314.] Hakluyt, I, 253 (Adams): "for that sevennight [of fasting] they eate nothing but hearbes: but after that sevennights fast is once past, then they returne to their old intemperancie of drinking, for they are notable tospots."

Ibid., I, 314 (Jenkinson, 1557): "They have many sortes of meats and drinkes, when they banket and delight in eating of grosse meates, and stinking fishe. Before they drinke they use to blowe in the cup: their greatest friendship is in drinking: they are great talkers and lyers, without any faith or trust in their words, flatterers and dissemblers."

Cf. the following, ibid., I, 241 (Chancellor, 1553): "The poore is very innumerable, and live most miserably: for I have seen them eate the pickle of Hearring and other stinking fish: nor the fish cannot be so stinking nor rotten, but they will eate it and praise it to be more wholesome then other fish or fresh meate. In mine opinion there be no such people under the sunne for their hardnesse of living."

[73] (M) 323.] Hakluyt, I, 323 (anonymous description, 1558): [I do not find "their Drink is better, being sundry sorts of Meath."] "The first and principall meade is made of the juice or liccour taken from a berrie called in Russia, Malieno, which is of a marveilous sweete taste, and of a carmosant colour, which berry I have seene in Paris. The second meade. . . . The third meade. . . . The fourth meade. . . . is made of the wilde blacke cherry. . . . There is also a delicate drinke drawn from the root of the birch tree, . . . which drinke the noble men and others use in Aprill, May, and June . . . after those moneths, the sappe of the tree dryeth."

[74] Hakluyt, I, 323 (anonymous, 1558): "There are a great number of poore people among them which die daily for lacke of sustenance, which is a pitifull case to beholde: . . . for if they had had straw and water enough, they would make shift to live: for a great many are forced in the winter to drie straw and

they have Straw and Water they make shift to live; for Straw dry'd and stampt in Winter time is their Bread; in Summer Grass and Roots; at all times Bark of Trees is good Meat with them; yet many of them die in the Street for hunger, none relieving, or regarding them.

[75]When they are sent into Foreign Countries, or that Strangers come thither, they are very sumptuous in apparel, else the Duke himself goes but meanly.

[76]In Winter they travail onely upon Sleds, the Wayes being hard, and smooth with Snow, the Rivers all froz'n: one Horse with a Sled will draw a man 400 miles in 3 daies; in Summer the way is deep, and travailing ill. The *Russe* of better sort goes not out in Winter, but on his Sled; in Summer on his Horse: in his Sled he sits on a [22] Carpet, or a white Bears Skin; the Sled drawn with a Horse well deckt, with many Fox or Wolve Tayles about his Neck, guided by a Boy on his Back, other Servants riding on the tayle of the Sled.

The *Russian* Sea breeds a certain[77] Beast which they call a Morse; who seeks his Food on the Rocks, climing up with help of his Teeth; whereof they make as great account, as we of the Elephant's Tooth. [23]

---

stampe it, and to make bread thereof. . . . In the summer they make good shift with grasse, herbes and rootes: barks of trees are good meat with them at all times. There is no people in the world, as I suppose, that live so miserably . . . and the most part of them that have sufficient for themselves, and also to relieve others that need, are so unmerciful that they care not how many they see die of famine or hunger in the streets."

[75] (M) Habit. 239.] Hakluyt, I, 239 (Chancellor, 1553): "when they bee sent into farre or strange countreys, or that strangers come to them, they be very gorgious. Els the Duke himselfe goeth but meanly in apparell."

[76] (M) Travailing. 314.] Hakluyt, I, 314 (Jenkinson, 1558): "In the Winter time, the people travell with sleds, in towne and countrey, the way being hard, and smooth with snow: the waters and rivers are all frozen, and one horse with a sled, will draw a man upon it 400 miles, in three daies: but in the Summer time, the way is deepe with mire, and travelling is very ill. The Russe, if he be a man of any abilitie, never goeth out of his house in the winter, but upon his sled, and in Summer upon his horse: and in his sled he sits upon a carpet, or a white Beares skinne: the sled is drawen with a horse well decked, with many Foxes and Woolves tailes at his necke, & is conducted by a little boy upon his backe: his servants stand upon the taile of the sled."

[77] (M) Beasts. 252.] Hakluyt, I, 252 (Adams's report of Chancellor, 1553): "The sea adjoyning [the North partes of Russia], breedes a certaine beast, which they call the Mors, which seeketh his foode upon the rockes, climing up with the helpe of his teeth. The Russes use to take them, for the great vertue that is in their teeth, whereof they make as great accompt, as we doe of the Elephants tooth."

CHAP. II.

Of Samoedia, Siberia, *and other Countries*
north-east subject to the Muscovites.[1]

N ORTH-EAST of *Russia* lieth *Samoedia* by the River *Ob.*[2]
This Country was first discover'd by *Oneke* a *Russian;*
who first trading privately among them in rich Furrs got

[1] The source of this paragraph is Purchas, III, 522–25, sec. i of his chap. vii,
"A Description of the Countries of Siberia, Samoieda, and Tingoesia." Milton's
own heading may have put Samoedia first because it was discussed first in Purchas's chapter and in his own; but he may likewise have been struck by the large
capital letters of SAMOYEDA covering Russia's northeast frontier in the Jenkinson 1562 map of Russia, which had been printed in all the Ortelius atlases
from 1570 down to 1606, the English edition of which Milton certainly knew.
See George W. Whiting, *Milton's Literary Milieu* (Chapel Hill, 1939), chap. iii,
"The Use of Maps."

Purchas's chapter, sec. i, was a translation of the *Descriptio Siberiae, Samo-
jediae, &c,* by Isaac Massa, the first of three treatises published in Dutch (*Be-
schryvinge Vander Samoyeden Landt in Tartarien*) by Hessel Gerritz (Amsterdam,
1612), republished in Latin in the same year and again in 1613, republished as
well by Theodore de Bry as *Indiae Orientalis Pars X* (Frankfurt, 1613). Massa
was a long-time Dutch resident in Moscow. Though his name was not given in
the editions, it was listed, with the date 1612, on the detailed maps of Russia
printed by Blaeu and Janssen. It is not clear which edition of Massa Purchas
used, though the de Bry text alone has marginal headings; but Purchas's notes
are fuller than de Bry's and, much to Milton's purpose, often give the distance
or travel time (e.g., "five dayes journey").

Siberia here means the country as far as the Obi and Taz rivers, or west Siberia.

In the second sentence Milton writes Oneke for Purchas's Oneeko, which stands
for Massa's Anica: Purchas's marginal heading is "Arica or Oneeka." The founder
of the family was Anika Stroganoff (1498–1557); the first land grants were made
to the family by Ivan the Terrible in 1558 and 1564 in the region of Perm west
of the Urals (J. F. Baddeley, *Russia, Mongolia, China* (London, 1919), I, lvii).
This was of course well before the time of Boris Goudonov, and the famous
expedition of Yermak that captured the Tartar town of Sibir in 1582 took place
also in the time of Ivan IV.

[2] The first sentence is Milton's own. Milton has in this one paragraph reduced
to a brief abstract all of Purchas's chapter, "*Discoverie of* Siberia" (III, 522–25).
A more accurate abstract of the account of the new territory would have read:
This Country was first discovered by members of a merchant family, originally
peasants, the Oneekos, of Ustiug on the Dwina, who were attracted by the furs
brought by Samoeds to market there, and followed them home to the Obi River
region. Having gained wealth and made settlements there, they revealed the
discovery to Boris, brother of Pheodor and later emperor. Boris sent soldiers with

great Wealth, and the knowledge of their Country; then reveal'd
his discovery to *Boris* Protectour to *Pheodor,* shewing how ben-
eficial that Country gain'd, would be to the Empire. Who sending
Ambassadours among them gallantly attir'd, by fair means won
their subjection to the Empire; every Head paying yearly two Skins
of richest Sables. Those Messengers travailing also 200 leagues [24]
beyond *Ob* east-ward, made report of pleasant Countries, abounding with Woods and Fountains, and People riding on Elks and
Loshes, others drawn on Sleds by Rain-deer, others by Dogs as
swift as Deer.[3] The *Somoeds* that came along with those Messengers returning to *Mosco* admir'd the stateliness of that City, and
were as much admir'd for excellent Shooters, hitting every time the
breadth of a penny, as far distant as hardly could be discern'd.

The River *Ob* is reported by[4] the *Russes* to be in breadth the
sayling of a Summer's day: but full of Islands and Shoals, having
neither Woods, nor, till of late, Inhabitants. Out of *Ob* they turn
into the River *Tawze.* The *Russians* have here, since the *Samoeds*
yielded them subjection, two Governours with 3 or 400 Gunners;
have built Villages [25] and some small Castles; all which Place

---

the merchants to impress the Samoeds with the majesty of the empire and to gain
their goodwill; of their own accord the natives subjected themselves to the authority of the Moscovites and agreed to a tax of two sables yearly per person.

[3] Purchas, III, 523: "After this the Messengers passed over the river *Obi,* and
travelled beyond it almost two hundred leagues toward the East and North-east,
having seene by the way many wild beasts of strong [*sic*] shapes, most cleere
Fountaynes, extraordinary Plants and Trees, pleasant Woods, and *Samoieds* of
divers sorts, whereof some did ride on *Elkes* or *Loshes,* other were drawne in
Sleds by Raine Deere, and others also were drawne by Dogges, which are equall
to Harts for swiftnesse. . . . They [the Moscovites] marvelled at the
Samoieds . . . commanding them to make some shew of their cunning in shooting;
which they did so perfectly, that almost it seemed to any man incredible. For
taking a piece of Coyne lesse then our Pennie [marginal note: Stiver], and fastning
it to the stocke of a Tree, and then going as farre from the same, as they could
very hardly discerne it, they did every time that they did shoot so assuredly hit
the same, that they did not once misse it. . . . And on the other side, the *Samoieds*
as greatly wondred both at the *Moscovites* manner of living and fashions, as also
at the statelinesse of the Citie."

[4] (M) *Purch.* part 3. 543, 540. *Molgomsay.*] Purchas, III, 543 (Josias Logan,
voyage of 1612): "The River [Ob] is reported to be a Summer dayes sayling over
in bredth, and is full of Ilands: whereby they report it to be shoald."

Ibid., III, 540 (Richard Finch, the same voyage): "In the River of *Ob,* are
neither Woods nor Inhabitants, till they sayle so farre up the same, that they
come neere to *Siberia.* But there are Woods. When they are entred into this *Tawze*
River, [they have four days' sailing, or twelve days' rowing, to Mongosey,] with
the Villages, Townes, and all other places thereto belonging. . . . At this place

they call *Mongozey* or *Molgomzay.* Further up-land [5]they have also built other Cities of Wood, consisting chiefly of *Poles, Tartars* and *Russes,* fugitive or condemned men; as *Vergateria, Siber,* whence the whole [6]Country is nam'd, *Tinna,* thence *Tobolsca* on this side *Ob,* on the Rivers *Irtis,* and *Tobol,* chief Seat of the *Russian* Governour; above that, *Zergolta* in an Island of Ob, where they have a Custom-house, beyond that on the other side *Ob, Narim,* and *Tooina* [7]now a great City. Certain Churches also are erected in those Parts; but no man forc'd to Religion; beyond *Narim* eastward on the River *Telta* is built the Castle of *Comgoscoi,* and all this Plantation began since the year 1590. with many other Towns like these. And these are the Countries from whence [26] come all the Sables and rich Furrs.

---

are two Gentlemen or Governours, with three or foure hundred Gunners, and small Castles in severall places." (The Taz is an eastern parallel of the Obi; Mangazeia was founded on it in 1601.)

[5] (M) 524.] Purchas, III, 524 (returning to "A Description of the Countries of Siberia, etc."): ". . . there were builded certaine Castles enclosed with certaine strong beames, cut out of the Woods thereby, and fastned one in another in double rewes, filled betweene with earth, and fortified with Garrisons; And so great a multitude of men is duely sent thither, that in some places there are Cities assembled, consisting of *Poles, Tartars, Russes,* and other Nations mingled together. For, into these parts are sent all that are banished, Murtherers, Traitors, Theeves, and the scumme of such as deserve death."

[6] (M) 526.] Purchas, III, 525. Massa's second treatise, published with the first in 1612, was translated by Purchas, pp. 525–29, as "*A briefe Description of the wayes and Rivers, leading out of* Moscovia *toward the East and North-east,*" sec. ii of his chap. vii. The treatise has been retranslated by J. F. Baddeley, *Russia, Mongolia, China,* II, 3–12. "*Vergateria* is the first Towne of the Countrey of *Siberia,* and was begun to be builded with some other Townes within these one and twenty yeeres." (Purchas puts in the margin the date 1590, which gives Milton the initial date for the settlements in Siberia, noted toward the end of the paragraph. In fact, Verkhoturia was founded in 1598; Baddeley, *Russia, Mongolia, China,* II, 4, 13.)

[7] (M) 526, 527.] Purchas, III, 526–27 (the same): "And from thence they proceed farther to *Tinna.* . . . From *Tinna* they come to *Tobolsca,* the chiefe of all the Townes of *Siberia* . . . on the River *Yrtis.* . . . On the other side is the River *Tobol.* . . . they builded another [Towne] upon an Iland of the River *Oby,* called *Zergolta.* [We are now far up the Ob.] . . . Beyond *Obi* are *Narim, Tooma,* and divers other Cities." (Tooina is an obvious misprint for Tooma.)

Ibid., III, 526 (the same): "in divers places [in Siberia] there are Churches and Chappels erected. . . . But howsoever, no man is forced against his will to their Religion. [527] Also above *Narim* as men travaile toward the East, they meete with the River *Telta:* on the banke whereof they have builded a Castle, named Comgof-scoi" [Ketsk]. (The date 1590 is supplied from above; see n. 6. As for the country of furs, the whole discourse of Massa's *Description* concerns the expansion of the fur trade.)

The *Samoeds* have no Towns,[8] or certain place of abode, but
up and down where they find Moss for their Deer; they live in
companies peaceably, and are govern'd by some of the Ancientest

---

In dealing with Siberia, Milton has omitted the itineraries of the eastward
journeys to and over the Urals to reach it and does not even trouble, as he does
elsewhere, to add them up to reach a total of sixty days, mostly by water, from
Solvychegodsk on the Dvina river to Vergateria beyond the Urals. Siber or Isker
is well beyond, on the Ob River near Tobolsk.

Doubtless Milton glanced from one marginal heading to the next in Purchas,
picking up the names Tinna (Tiumen, or in Purchas's source, Tinnen, founded
1586); "*Tobolsca* the chiefe Towne of *Siberia*" (founded 1587); "*Zergolta* a town
builded in an Iland of the River Oby" (for Surgut, founded 1594); "*Narim* and
Tooma, beyond *Obi*" (Narym, founded 1598, and Tomsk, founded 1604); "*Telta*
River to the East beyond *Obi. Comgof-scoi* Castle" (old Ketsk, founded 1602).
A customhouse at Surgut is mentioned later by Pursglove in 1613: see n. 9 in
chap. 3, below.

It is difficult to see how Milton could follow these routes with any understanding
on the maps he had. Massa's 1612 map of Russia has few of these names on his
itinerary and indeed gives only Siberia, Oby, and Tobol of these place-names and
puts "Tobol metropolis Siberiae," in 65° north instead of 58°. Even the 1657 map
of Tartaria, as Siberia was then known, names only Sibier, Tumen, and Oby.
Without a modern map one can make nothing of Massa's itinerary or of Milton's
excerpt from it; it would be hard to tell even that the general direction of Purchas's
"wayes and Rivers" is eastward.

The Russian expansion may be followed in George V. Lantzeff, *Siberia in the
Seventeenth Century* (1943); Raymond H. Fisher, *The Russian Fur Trade,
1550–1700* (1943); and Robert J. Kerner, *The Urge to the Sea: The Course of
Russian History* (1946; all three books published by the University of California
Press, Berkeley).

[8] (M) Manners of the *Samoeds*. 522, 555.] Purchas, III, 522 (returning to the
description of Samoedia): "this [Samoed] people had not any Cities, but lived
together in Companies, and peaceably, and governed by some of the ancientest
among them; that they were lothsome in their feeding, and lived on the flesh of
such beasts as they tooke; that they had no knowledge of Corne or Bread, were
cunning and skilfull Archers, making their Bowes of a gentle and flexible kind
of Wood, and that their Arrowes were headed with sharpened stones or fish
bones: . . . that they sowed also with bones of fishes, serving them for Needles;
their thred being made of the sinewes of certaine small beasts, and so they sew
together the Furres, wherewith they cloath themselves: the Furrie side in Summer
turned outward, and in Winter inward."

Ibid., III, 555 (William Gourdon, sojourn in Pustozera, 1614–15): "Their Wives
they buy for Deere, and will have if hee have abilitie foure or five Wives, . . .
he is the richest man that hath most Deere or Daughters, selling them to any that
will give most for them. . . . It falleth out many times, that after they have had
their Wives halfe a yeere or a yeere, they will turn them backe to their Friends,
taking their Deeres againe, paying for the charge of the [wedding] Feast, which
is alwayes to bee made at her Fathers charge. . . . They have not knowledge of
the true God, but worship Blocks and Images of the Devill."

amongst them, but are Idolaters. They shoot wondrous cunningly; their Arrow heads are sharpned Stones, or Fish-bones, which latter serve them also for Needles, their Thread being the Sinews of certain small Beasts, wherewith they sowe the Furrs which cloath them; the furry side in Summer outward, in Winter inward. They have many Wives, and their Daughters they sell to him who bids most; which, if they be not lik't, are turn'd back to their Friends, the Husband allowing onely to the Father what the marriage Feast stood him in. [27] Wives are brought to bed there by their Husbands, and the next day go about as before. They till not the Ground; but live on the Flesh of those Wild Beasts which they hunt. They are the onely Guides to such as travaile ⁹*Jougoria, Siberia,* or any of those north-east parts in Winter; being drawn on Sleds with Bucks, riding post day and night, if it be Moonlight; and lodge on the Snow under Tents of Deer Skins in whatever place they find enough of white Moss to feed their Sled Staggs, turning them loose to dig it up themselves out of the deep Snow: another *Samoede* stepping to the next Wood, brings in store of Firing; round about which they lodge within their Tents, leaving the top open to vent Smoak; in which manner they are as warm as the Stoves in *Russia.* They carry Provision of Meat with them, [28] and partake besides of what Fowle or Venison the *Samoede* kills with shooting by the way; their Drink is melted Snow. Two Deer being yoak'd to a Sled riding post will draw 200 miles in 24 hours without resting, and laden with their Stuff will draw it 30 miles in 12.

Ibid., III, 556 (the same): "The Women be very hard of Nature; for at their Child-bearing, the Husband must play the Midwife, and being delivered, the Child is washed with cold water or Snow, and the next day the Woman able to conduct her Argish" [sleigh].

⁹ (M) 548.] Purchas, III, 548 (William Pursglove, by land from Pustozera west to Slobotca and Colmogro, 1612): "The *Samoieds* being the onely Guides in Winter either from *Pustozera* to *Slobotca,* or to any other places Eastward, as *Ougoria, Siberia,* or *Molgomsey.*"

Ibid., III, 547 (the same): "drawne the most part with two Deere in a Sled."

Ibid., III, 548 (the same): "and rid post all that day and night following, beeing Moone-light . . . [They know] where most store of white Mosse is growing: . . . there for that night they pitch their Tents, being for the most part made of Deere and Elkes skinnes. . . . This worke of pitching the tents belongeth unto the Women. In the meane time the men unyoake the Deere, and turne them loose to digge through the Snow, bee it never so deepe, for their food and sustenace [*sic*]. Then the *Samoieds* (of every Tent one) out of the next Wood, provide as much Fuell as shall serve their turnes. . . . Our lodgings were upon the Snow within our Tents, round about the Fire, having under us for our Beds the skinnes of Deere, covered with our day apparell."

Ibid., III, 555 (Gourdon, sojourn in Pustozera, 1614–15): "Two Deere being yoaked to a Sled, they will runne with such swiftnesse, and so long to continue, as is not to be beleeved, except to those that have seene the same. For riding post, they will ride without rest or sleepe, two hundred miles in four and twentie houres; but with their Argish or stuffe, thirtie miles in twelve houres; their Women usually doe guide their Argish, which is ten Sleds, and to every Sled a Bucke, all made fast one after another, the Men in the way doe provide Wood for firing, and doe hunt for all manner of Beasts & Fowle, which the women dresse. . . . Their Tent or Choome, is made in this manner [deerskins are cast about poles, weighted down with snow,] leaving the top open for to vent smoake, making a Fire in the middle, spreading Deere-skins, upon which they lye, in which manner, it is altogether as warme as the Stoves in *Russia*."

CHAP. III.

Of Tingoesia, *and the Countries adjoyning eastward, as far as* Cathay.

BEYOND *Narim and Comgoscoi*[1] the Souldiers of those Garrisons travailing by appointment of the *Russian* Governour in the year 1605. found many goodly Countries not inhabited; many vast Deserts, and Rivers, till at the end of ten weeks they spy'd [29] certain Cottages, and Herds, or companies of People, which came to them with reverent behaviour, and signify'd to the *Samoeds* and *Tartars,* which were Guides to the *Russian* Souldiers, that they were call'd *Tingoesi;* that their dwelling was on the [2]great River *Jenissey.* This River is said to be far bigger than [3]*Ob;* distant from the Mouth thereof 4 daies and nights [4]sayling; and likewise falls into the Sea of *Naramzie;* it hath high [5]Mountains on the East, some of which cast out Fire, to the West

---

[1] (M) *Pur.* par. 3. 527.] Purchas, III, 527 ("the wayes and Rivers," 1612): "the garrison Souldiers of which Castle [Comgof-scoi], together with the Inhabitants of *Narim,* about seven yeares past, were commanded by the Governour of Siberia to travell East, and diligently to search what unknowne Nations dwelt in those parts. Therefore travelling through certaine vast Deserts, for the space of tenne weekes or there abouts, passing in the way through many faire Countreys, many Woods, and Rivers, at length they espied certaine Cottages set up in the fields, and certaine Hords or Companies of people. . . . The people came unto them reverently, and with humble behaviour, and signified by the *Samoieds* and *Tartars* [the guides], that they were called *Tingoesi,* and that their dwelling was upon the banke of the great River *Jeniscè . . . Jeniscè* being a River farre bigger then *Obi.*"

From Narym and Tomsk on the upper (southern) Ob River to the Yenisei would be some three hundred miles; the latitude of Tomsk is some 56° north. The Tunguses are a Mongolian people, then nomad fur hunters, who roamed northern Asia from the Yenisei to the Pacific Ocean.

[2] (M) *Jennissey.*]

[3] (M) 527.] This refers to the last sentence cited in n. 1, above.

[4] (M) 551.] Purchas, III, 551 (William Pursglove, 1613): "From the mouth of *Ob* to the great River *Jenisce,* as a Russe told mee, is foure dayes and foure nights sayling."

[5] (M) 546.] This number has dropped down one line. Purchas, III, 546 (Josias Logan from Pechora, 1612): "the great River Yenisse . . . falleth into the Sea *Naromzie.*" Massa's map shows the Niaren More east of Nova Zembla; replacing Russian "more" with Dutch "zee" might give "Naromzie."

a plain and fertil Country, which [6]in the Spring time it overflowes
about 70 leagues; all that time the Inhabitants keep them in the
[7]Mountains, and then return with their Cattel to the Plain. The
Tingoesi are a very gentle Nation, they have great swoln Throats
[8]like those in *Italy* that live under the *Alpes;* at perswasion of the
[30] *Samoeds* they forthwith submitted to the *Russian* Government;
and at their request travailing the next year to discover still eastward, they came at length to a River, which the Savages of that
place call'd *Pisida,* somewhat less[9] than *Jenissey;* beyond which

---

[6] (M) 527.] This number should take the place now held by 546. Purchas, III,
527 (Siberia, 1612): "*Jeniscè* . . . hath high mountaines on the East, among which
are some that cast out fire and brimstone. The Countrey is plaine to the West,
and exceeding fertile, stored with plants, flowers, and trees of divers kinds. . . .
Jeniscè in the spring overfloweth the fields about seventie leagues, . . . as *Nilus*
doth *Egipt.* Wherewith the *Tingoesi* . . . doe keepe beyond the River, and in the
mountaines, untill it decrease, and then returne, and bring downe their heards
of Cattell into the plaines. The *Tingoesi* being a very gentle people, by the
perswasion of the *Somoieds* [*sic*], without delay submitted themselves to the same
Governours which they obeyed. . . . These people were deformed with swellings
under their throats, and in their speech they thratled like Turkie-cocks."

The high mountains would presumably be in fact on the south rather than on
the east; but since the ancient maps of Ptolemy showed an immense north-south
mountain range, Mons Imaus, dividing northern Asia, our narration assumed its
existence. The seventeenth-century maps continue to show it.

[7] (M) Manners.]

[8] (M) *Ibid.*] This must refer to 527 just above.

[9] (M) 528.] Purchas, III, 528 (the same): "The yeere following, the *Tingoesies*
sent divers of their owne people Eastward: who . . . at length found another
mightie River, somewhat lesser then *Jenisce,* but as swift as it . . . the *Tingoesies*
gathered, that that [Pisida, now the Piasina] should bee the name of the River. . . .
[The next year's expedition] durst not passe over the River *Pisida;* having now
plainly heard . . . the towling of Brazen Bells; and . . . they sometimes heard
the noyse of men and horses. Moreover they saw certayne sayles, though but a
few; . . . the sayles were square, like the Indian sayles, as wee suppose."

Purchas's marginal note: "The towling of brazen Bells: of which they have in
China, and perhaps in the North parts above it."

Ibid., III, 543 (Logan from Pustozera, 1612): "These *Tingusses* report . . . wherein
[the river Pisida] there are great ships, not unlike unto the *Russes* ships, that sayle
in it, having many Masts and Gunnes, which when they are shot off, make all
the earth shake with the noyse: which should seeme to be the *Chinians* that trade
thither in the Summer. . . . The like also affirmeth another, being a Russe."

The Piasina River rises in about 72° north latitude and falls into the Arctic
Ocean in about 74°. The armed sailing vessels reported there, if Chinese, would
have had to pass Bering Strait and sail over two-thirds of the Northeast Passage
from east to west. Nordenskiöld in the *Vega* in 1878–79 required a year to make
the voyage in the contrary direction, his ship frozen in during the winter. The
Tunguses must have referred to Russian vessels. The brazen bells and the horses
may have a simple explanation.

hearing ofttimes the towling of Brazen Bells, and sometimes the noise of Men and Horses, they durst not pass over; they saw there certain Sayles afar off, square, and therefore suppos'd to be like *Indian* or *China* Sayles, and the rather for that they report that great Guns have been heard shot off from those Vessels. In *April,* and *May* they were much delighted with the fair prospect of that Country, replenish't with many rare Trees, Plants and Flowers, Beasts and Fowle.[10] Some think here to be the Borders of *Tangut* in the north[11] of *Cathay.* Some of those *Sa-* [31] *moeds* about the Year 1610. [12]travail'd so far till they came in view of a White City, and heard a great din of Bells, and report there came to them Men all arm'd in Iron from head to foot. And in the Year 1611. divers out of *Cathay,* and others from *Alteen Czar* who stiles himself the golden King, came and traded at *Zergolta,* or *Surgoot* on the River

[10] Purchas, III, 528 ("the wayes and Rivers," 1612): "[returning from the Pisida (Piasina) River] . . . reporting, . . . That in the moneths of Aprill and May, they were very much delighted with the exceeding faire shew of that Countrey; And that they had seene therein many rare Plants, Flowers, Fruits, Trees, Fowles, and wild Beasts." This report can hardly refer to the tundra, described as "cold, desert, treeless plain" (*Encyclopaedia Britannica,* s.v.). The information clearly relates to regions much farther south, in the upper Yenisei valley rather than along the short Arctic course of the Piasina.

[11] (M) 543.] Purchas, III, 543 (Logan, report in Petzora of a Russian traveler, 1612): "I conjecture, that it is not farre from the Citie *Tangut* in *Cathay.*" Tangut was reported by Marco Polo (I, xl) as a province beyond the Gobi desert "between north and northeast"; he went on to describe the Tartar homeland north of the desert and seemed to continue north and northeast to Cathay; still farther beyond were Bargu on the northern ocean and Tenduc on the eastern ocean. These names are still retained on the Cluverius map of 1661. So Cathay was set in what would now be northeastern Siberia, with Cambaluc (Peking) in 60° north latitude, whereas China remained a separate country, the Serica Regio known to the Romans and reached by the Portuguese from the south, in the lower temperate latitudes.

Logan was therefore quite justified in believing that the due eastward exploring of the Russians was leading them straight to Cathay. Purchas admitted some doubts raised by a recent Jesuit mission to China by way of Tibet but continued to think Cathay separate (III, 801).

[12] (M) 546.] Purchas, III, 546 (Logan, 1612): "And the *Samoieds* report that they have travelled so farre, that they came within sight of a *White Citie* or Towne: which should seeme to be builded of stone, for they durst not goe to make triall: and they heard great ringing of Bels . . . there came people unto them all made of Iron, their heads, armes, hands, and legges . . . which, as I conjecture, were people in Armour. . . . By this you may gather, that they are not farre from *Cataia* and *China.*"

Again, the Samoeds must have gone far to the south, perhaps to Turkestan, which is however most unlikely.

Ob, bringing with them Plates of Silver.[13] Whereupon *Michael Pheodorowick* the *Russian* Emperour in the Year 1619. sent certain of his People from *Tooma* to *Alteen,* and *Cathay,* who return'd with Ambassadours from those Princes. [14]These relate, that from *Tooma* in ten daies and a half,[15] three daies whereof over a Lake, where Rubies and Saphirs grow, they came to the *Alteen* King, or King of *Alty;*[16] through his Land in five weeks they pass'd into the Country of *Sheromugaly* or *Mugalla,*[17] [32] where reigned a Queen

[13] Purchas, III, 552 (Pursglove, reporting from Pustozera, 1613): "From *Tobolsca* to *Surgout,* or *Sergalt,* is sixe Weekes journey up the River *Ob.* . . . *Abraham Michaelovich* was chiefe Customer at *Surgout,* 1611 . . . , he told me, that the people of *Cathay* doe trade to *Surgout,* and people from divers other Kingdomes, as from *Alteen Tzar,* or King *Alteen,* who among other things bring Plates of Silver and sell them."

"Customer" is customs collector. Milton's "*Alteen Czar* who stiles himself the golden King" comes from Purchas's heading of a part of the relation next quoted in note 14: "*The Copie of the* Altine Chars, *or golden Kings Letter to the Emperour of* Russia" (Purchas, III, 797).

[14] (M) 797.] Purchas, III, 797–802: "*A relation of two* Russe Cossacks *travailes, out of* Siberia *to* Catay," 1619. This is a version, presumably brought to England and translated by merchants of the Muscovy Company, of the Petlin-Mundoff mission to China in 1618–19. The reports are translated from the originals in the Russian archives by Baddeley, *Russia, Mongolia, China,* II, 73–80. Baddeley suggests that the English in Moscow may well have inspired the mission with an eye to trade possibilities.

The word "Catay" occurs only in Purchas, the Russian reports calling it China.

[15] Purchas, III, 799 (the same relation, 1618): "[passing by] the great Lake, (in which Lake Rubies or Saphires grow)." Baddeley translates, "the large lake where Ivan Petroff reported a self-colored (precious or semi-precious) stone" (II, 73). He identifies the lake as Ubsa-nor, at the northwest corner of Outer Mongolia.

[16] Purchas, III, 798 (the same relation): [The Governors of Tobolsko] "sent him from the Castle of *Tomo* [for Tomsk, founded 1604; Purchas's marginal note: "a new Castle beyond *Ob*"] to conduct the Kings *Altines* Ambassadours, as also to inquire or search the Kingdomes of Catay. . . . They . . . travelled from Tomo to Kirgis . . . tenne days, and . . . went halfe a day, and came . . . to the *Altine* King."

Baddeley (II, 62) notes this first stage of the journey as up a tributary of the Ob River to its source, then over a pass in the Sayan mountains and again in the Tannuola mountains to Ubsa-nor (lake), where the Altin Khan had his camp. This would mean a route slightly east of south from West Siberia into Outer Mongolia.

"Altin regn." does not appear on a map before the Witsen map of 1687, reproduced in *Remarkable Maps,* vol. 4 (Amsterdam, Frederik Muller, 1897), and again in *Imago Mundi,* vol. 11 (1954), opposite p. 98.

[17] Purchas, III, 798 (the same relation): "so they passed through his Land [the Altine King's] five weekes to the Country of *Sheremugaly;* where raigneth a Queene called *Manchika.* . . . they travelled foure dayes, and came into the Dominions of *Catay;* called *Crim,* where is a wall made of stone fifteene fathomes high, alongst the side of which wall they went ten dayes, where they saw pettie

call'd *Manchika;* whence in four daies they came to the Borders of *Cathay,* fenc't with a stone Wall, 15 fathom high; along the side of which, having on the other hand many pretty Towns belonging to Queen *Manchika,* they travail'd ten daies without seeing any on the Wall till they came to the Gate. Where they saw very great Ordnance lying, and 3000 men in watch. They traffick with other Nations at the Gate, and very few at once are suffered to enter. They were travailing from *Tooma* to this Gate 12 weeks; and from thence to the great City of *Cathay* ten daies. Where being conducted to the House of Ambassadours, within a few daies there came a Secretary from King *Tambur* with 200 Men well apparell'd, and riding on Asses, to feast them with divers sorts of Wine, and to de- [34] mand their Message; but having brought no Presents with them, they could not be admitted to his sight; onely with his Letter to the Emperour they return'd as is aforesaid, to *Tobolsca.* They report that the Land of *Mugalla* reaches from *Boghar* to the north [18]Sea, and hath many Castles built of Stone four-square, with

---

Townes and Villages belonging to the Queene *Manchika;* but in those ten dayes they saw no people upon the wall at all. At the end of these ten dayes, they came to the gate, wherein lye very great Peeces of Ordnance, [and] in watch three thousand men, and they come with their Merchandizes to traffique at the gate. The Altine men also come to the gate, with their Horses to sell to the *Catay* men; but are not permitted to come within the walls, except very few at once. Thus their whole travell from *Tomo* Castle to this gate, was twelve weekes, . . . and from the gate to the great Empire of *Catay* tenne dayes . . . and were lodged in the great Embassadors house: and . . . there used to come unto them a Secretary with two hundred men upon Asses very well apparelled, and did entertayne and feast them with Sacke and other Drinkes made of Grapes, and told them that the Emperour, or King *Tambur* had sent him to aske them wherefore they were come into the Dominions of *Catay.* Whereupon they answered that our great Lord and Emperour had sent them to discover the Dominions of *Catay,* and see the King thereof; but hee answered them againe, that without presents they could not see the King, and withall gave them a Letter, which Letter they brought with them to *Tolbosko.*"

"Sheremugaly" is shara or yellow Mongolia, Mugalia Flava on Witsen's map. "Crim" is glossed as Mongol kirim, Russian kreml (hence Kremlin), a wall. The gate is clearly the city of Kalgan (Mongolian halga, a gate), the traditional gateway from Mongolia to China. Ten days' travel brought the mission to "the Empire of Catay," that is, Peking; Baddeley translates, "great city of China."

Baddeley did not work out the itinerary, which seems most simply to have continued southeast across the Gobi Desert to what is now Inner Mongolia and so east to the Great Wall. The later Russian trade route to China continued east in Siberia to Lake Baikal, following the course now taken by the Trans-Siberian Railway, and then turned sharply south across the Gobi to Kalgan. See Raymond H. Fisher, *The Russian Fur-Trade, 1550–1700* (Berkeley, 1943).

[18] (M) 799.] Purchas, III, 799–800 (a second, more detailed relation): "The Land of *Mulgalla* is great and large from Bughar [Bokhara] to the sea; all the Castles

Towers at the Corners cover'd with glazed Tiles; and on the Gates
Alarum-Bells or Watch-Bells twenty pound weight of Metal; their
Houses built also of Stone, the Seelings cunningly painted with

---

are built with stone foure square; at the corners, Towers, the ground or foundation
is layd of rough, grey stone, and are covered with Tiles, the gates with count-
erwards as our *Russe* gates are, and upon the gates alarum Bels of Watch-bels
of twentie poode [p. 566: "A Pood is 37. pound, or the third part of a hundred
weight."] weight of metall, the Towers are covered with glazed Tiles; the houses
are built with stone foure cornerd high, within their Courts they have low Vaults,
also of stone, the seelings whereof, and of their houses are cunningly painted with
all sorts of colours, and very well set forth with flowres for shew." (Several
sentences follow on the Idols in the churches.)

   "As for bread in the Land of *Mugalla* there groweth all manner of Graine. . . .
for Fruit in *Mugalla* they have of all sorts. . . . toward *Bughar,* and towards the
Sea, the Towres are not to bee numbred, and every Towre standeth from another
about a flight shot distant. The said wall stretcheth downe towards the Sea foure
moneths travell. The people of *Catay* say, that this wall stretcheth alongst from
Bughar to the Sea, and the Towres upon it stand very thicke; it was made, as
they say, to be a border betweene *Mugalla* and *Catay.* The Towres upon it are
to the end, that when any enemy appeareth, to kindle fires upon them, to give
the people warning to come to their places where they are appointed upon the
wall. [Margin: Tower-becons]. . . . In the wall to *Catay* are five gates, both low,
and straight or narrow, a man cannot ride into them upright on horse-backe, and
except these five gates there is no more in all the wall; there all manner of people
passe into the Citie of *Shrokalga.*

   "Within the borders or wall is a Citie or Castle of *Catay,* called *Shirokalga,*
built of stone . . . the Castle is very high walled and artificially built; the Towres
are high after the manner of *Mosco* Castle, in the Loope-holes or Windowes are
Ordnance planted, as also upon the Gates or Towres; their Ordnance is but short,
they have also great store of small shot, and the Watchmen every-where upon
the Gates, Towres, and Wals, well appointed; and assoone as they perceive the
Sunne going downe, the Watch dischargeth their Peeces of Ordnance thrice, as
also at the breake of day in the morning. . . . Within the Castle are shops built
of stone, and painted cunningly with divers colours, wherein they have all manner
of Merchandizes, as Velvets, Damaskes, Dorogoes, Taffataes, Cloth of Gold, and
Tissue of divers colours, sundry sorts of Sugars, Cloves, &c.

   "And from *Shirokalga* to the Citie *Yara* is three dayes travell. . . . the Markets
in the Citie are well and richly accommodated, with Jewels, Merchandizes, Grocerie, or Spices. . . . their Markets have a very odiferous smell with Spices.

   "And from this Citie, to a Citie called *Tayth,* is three dayes journey." In its
market "are all manner of Merchandizes, Spices, or Grocerie, and precious things
more abundant then in the aforesaid Cities."

   Ibid., III, 801 (the same relation): *Shirooan* . . . from one Gate to the other
through the Citie is halfe a dayes going. . . . this Citie is adorned more with
precious things then the former mentioned, and much more populous." From
Tayth "to a Citie called *White Castle,* is two dayes travell: this Citie is built of
white stone."

   Shirokalga is identified as Kalgan. Shirooan remains unidentified. Yara is
thought to be Süan-hwa-fu; the White City is Sin-Pao-ngan. For Tayth, Bad-

Flowers of all Colours. The People are Idolaters; the Country exceeding fruitfull. They have Asses and Mules, but no Horses. The
People of *Cathay* say that this great Wall stretches from *Boghar*
to the north Sea four months journey with continual Towers a
flight-shot distant from each other, and Beacons on every [34]
Tower; and that this Wall is the bound between *Mugalla* and
Cathay. In which are but five Gates; those narrow, and so low,
that a Horse-man sitting upright cannot ride in. Next to the Wall
is the City *Shirokalga;* it hath a Castle well furnish't with short
Ordnance, and small Shot, which they who keep watch on the
Gates, Towers and Walls, duly at Sun-set and rising discharge
thrice over. The City abounds with rich Merchandize, Velvets,
Damasks, Cloth of Gold and Tissue, with many sorts of Sugars.
Like to this is the City *Yara,* their Markets smell odoriferously with
Spices, and *Tayth* more rich than that. *Shirooan* yet more magnificent, half a day's journey through, and exceeding populous.
From hence to *Cathaia* the imperial City is two daies journey,[19]
built of White-stone [35] four-square, in circuit four daies going,
corner'd with four White Towers, very high and great, and others
very fair along the Wall, white intermingl'd with blew, and Loop-
holes furnisht with Ordnance. In midst of this White City stands
a Castle built of Magnet, where the King dwels, in a sumptuous
Palace, the top whereof is overlaid with Gold. The City stands on
even ground encompass'd with the River *Youga,* 7 daies journey
from the Sea. The People are very fair, but not warlike, delighting

---

deley's original text reads Taimui (*Russia, Mongolia, China,* II, 81). Purchas had
transposed his account of Shirooan, putting it after Tayth; it is interesting that
Milton saw the mistake and put Shirooan in its proper place.

[19] Purchas, III, 801 (the same relation): "From this white Citie, or Castle, to
the greatest Citie of all *Cataya,* called *Catay,* is two dayes journey, where the
King himselfe dwelleth, it is a very great Citie, built of white stone foure square,
and in compasse it is foure dayes journey, upon every corner thereof are very
great Towres high built, and white, and alongst the wall are very faire and high
Towres, likewise white and intermingled with Blue or Azure. . . . the Loop-holes
or Windowes are well furnished with Ordnance, and a strong Watch. In the midst
of this white Citie standeth a Castle built of *Magnet,* or Load-stone, wherin the
King himselfe dwelleth, called *Tambun* [sic] . . . curiously set forth with all manner of artificiall and precious devices, in the middest whereof standeth the Kings
Palace, the top whereof is all gilt over with Gold. . . . The Citie . . . is built upon
an even plaine ground, and is incompassed round about with a River called
Youga, which falleth into the blacke Sea, which is from the Citie *Catay* seven
dayes travell. . . . the people are very faire but not warlike, timorous & most
their endevour is in great and rich traffick."

"The blacke Sea" is an error for "the red [that is, yellow] Sea," as given in
Baddeley's text.

most in rich Traffick. These Relations are referr'd hither, because we have them from *Russians;* who report also, that there [20]is a Sea beyond *Ob* so warm that all kind of Sea-Fowl live thereabout as well in Winter as in Summer. Thus much briefly of the Sea and Lands between *Russia,* and *Cathay.* [36]

[20] (M) 806.] Purchas, III, 806 (Russian reports to English merchants, 1584): "Furthermore, Master *Thomas Lynde* an honest and discreet *English* Merchant, which hath likewise lived many yeeres in those parts of *Moscovy,* saith, That this Sea beyond *Ob,* is by the report of the *Russes,* that are travailers, so warme, that all kinde of Sea fowles live there as well in the Winter as in the Summer, which report argueth, that this Sea pierseth farre into the South parts of *Asia.*"

At this early date, the rumor is either sheer speculation, if heard near the mouth of the Obi, and therefore relating to the northern ocean, or the transformation of news of a Siberian lake such as Lake Baikal.

CHAP. IV.

The Succession of Moscovia Dukes[1] and Emperours taken out of their Chronicles by a Polack with some later Additions.

THE great Dukes of *Muscovy* derive their Pedegree, though without ground, from *Augustus Cæsar:* whom they fable to have sent certain of his Kindred to be Governours over many remote Provinces; and among them, *Prussus* over *Prussia;* him to have had his Seat on the eastern *Baltick* Shoar by the River *Wixel;* of whom *Rurek, Sinaus,* and *Truuor* descended by the Fourth Generation, were by the *Russians* living then without Civil Government sent for in the Year 573. to bear rule over[2] them; at the perswasion of *Go-* [37] *stomislius* chief Citizen of *Novogrod.* They therefore taking with them *Olechus* their Kinsman divided those Countries among themselves, and each in his Province taught them Civil Government.

Ivorson[3] of *Rurek,* the rest dying without Issue, became Successour to them all; being left in nonage under the protection of *Olechus.* He took to wife *Olha* Daughter to a Citizen of *Plesco;* of whom he begat *Stoslaus;* but after that, being slain by his Enemies, *Olha* his Wife went to *Constantinople,* and was there baptiz'd *Helena.*

Stoslaus fought many Battails with his Enemies; but was at length by them slain, who made a Cup of his Scull engrav'n with

---

[1] (M) *Hac.* vol. I. 221.] Milton has adopted Hakluyt's title (I, 221–24), which read: "A briefe Treatise of the great Duke of Moscovia his genealogie, being taken out of the Moscovites manuscript Chronicles written by a Polacke." Milton condenses this treatise from some 3,000 to 1,500 words; it ends at his marginal date 1571.

The author of the chronicle is now identified as probably Daniel Printz von Buchau, his treatise (*Epitome*) published in *Edictum serenissimi Poloniae regis ad milites* (Cologne, 1580). See J. S. G. Simmons, in 2 Hakluyt Society 144 (1974), p. 163, n. 3.

[2] (M) 573.] The Hakluyt text has 572 (I, 221). The date now supposed is A.D. 862.

[3] Ivorson is an error for "Igor, son of" (Hakluyt, I, 221); doubtless a printer's error.

this Sentence in Gold; Seeking after other Mens he lost his own. His Sons were *Teropolchus, Olega* and *Volodimir.* [38]

Volodimir having slain the other two, made himself sole Lord of *Russia;* yet after that fact enclining to Christian Religion, had to wife *Anna* Sister of *Basilius* and *Constantine Greek* Emperours; and with all his People in the Year 988.[4] was baptiz'd, and called *Basilius.* Howbeit *Zonaras* reporteth that before that time *Basilius* the *Greek* Emperour sent a Bishop to them; at whose preaching they not being mov'd, but requiring a Miracle, he, after devout Prayers, taking the Book of Gospel into his hands, threw it before them all into the Fire: which remaining there unconsum'd, they were converted.

Volodimir had eleven Sons among whom he divided his Kingdom;[5] *Boristus* and *Glebus* for their holy Life register'd Saints; and their Feast kept every year in *November* [6] with great [39] solemnity. The rest through contention to have the sole Government, ruin'd each other; leaving onely *Jaroslaus* inheritour of all.

Volodimir Son of *Jaroslaus* kept his Residence in the ancient City *Kiow* upon the River *Boristenes.*[7] And after many conflicts with the Sons of his Uncles; and having subdu'd all was call'd *Monomachus.* He made war with *Constantine* the *Greek* Emperour, wasted *Thracia,* and returning home with great spoils to prepare new war, was appeas'd by *Constantine,* who sent *Neophytus* Bishop of *Ephesus,* and *Eustathius*[8] Abbot of *Jerusalem,* to present him with part of our Saviour's Cross, and other rich Gifts, and to salute him by the name of *Czar,* or *Cæsar:* with whom he thenceforth enter'd into league and amity. [40]

After him in order of descent *Vuszevolodus, George, Demetrius.*

Then *George,* his Son, who in the Year 1237. was slain in[9] battail by the *Tartar* Prince *Bathy,* who subdu'd *Muscovia* and made it tributary. From that time the *Tartarians* made such Dukes of *Russia,* as they thought would be most pliable to their ends; of whom they requir'd, as oft as Ambassadours came to him out of *Tartary,* to go out and meet them; and in his own Court to stand bareheaded, while they sate and deliver'd their Message. At which time the *Tartars* wasted also *Polonia, Silesia,* and *Hungaria,* till Pope

---

[4] (M) 988.]

[5] Hakluyt, I, 222: Borissus (not Boristus).

[6] Hakluyt, I, 222: the twelfth of November.

[7] Vladimir's dates of reign are 1113–25. Boristhenes is the classical name for the river now called Dnieper.

[8] Hakluyt, I, 222: Eustaphius (not Eustathius).

[9] (M) 1237.]

Innocent the Fourth obtain'd peace of them for 5 years. This *Bathy,* say the *Russians,* was the Father of *Tamerlan,* whom they call *Temirkutla.* [41]

Then succeeded *Jaroslaus* the Brother of *George,* then *Alexander* his Son.

Daniel the Son of *Alexander* was he who first made the City of *Mosco* his Royal Seat, builded the Castle, and took on him the Title of great Duke.[10]

John the Son of *Daniel* was sirnamed *Kaleta,* that word signifying a Scrip, out of which, continually carried about with him, he was wont to deal his Almes.

His Son *Simeon* dying without Issue left the Kingdom to *John* his next Brother; and he to his Son *Demetrius,* who left two Sons, *Basilius* and *George.*

Basilius reigning had a Son of his own name, but doubting lest not of his own Body, through the suspicion he had of his Wife's Chastity, him he disinherits, and gives the Dukedom to his Brother *George.* [42] *George* putting his Nephew *Basilius* in prison, reigns; yet at his death, either through remorse, or other cause surrenders him the Dukedom.

Basilius[11] unexpectedly thus attaining his supposed right, enjoy'd it not long in quiet; for *Andrew* and *Demetrius* the two Sons of *George* counting it injury not to succeed their Father, made war upon him, and surprizing him on a suddain, put out his Eyes. Notwithstanding which, the *Boiarens,* or Nobles kept their allegiance to the Duke though blind, whom therefore they call'd *Cziemnox.*

John Vasiliwich[12] his Son was the first who brought the *Russian* Name out of obscurity into renown. To secure his own Estate he put to death as many of his Kindred as were likely to pretend; and stil'd himself great Duke of *Wolodimiria, Muscovia,* [43] *Novogardia, Czar* of all *Russia.* He won *Plesco* the onely walled City in all *Muscovy,* and *Novogrod* the richest, from the *Lituanians,* to whom they had been subject 50 years before; and from the latter carried home 300 Waggons laden with Treasure. He had war with *Alexander* King of *Poland,* and with the *Livonians;* with him, on pretence of withdrawing his Daughter *Helena,* whom he had to wife, from the *Greek* Church to the *Romish;* with the *Livonians* for no other cause, but to enlarge his Bounds: though he were often

---

[10] Daniel died in A.D. 1263.
[11] Basilius the Blind reigned from 1425 to 1462.
[12] Ivan III reigned from 1462 to 1505.

foyl'd by *Plettebergius* great Master of the *Prussian* Knights. His
Wife was Daughter to the Duke of *Tyversky;* of her he begat *John;*
and to him resigned his Dukedom; giving him to wife the Daughter
of *Steven,* Palatine of *Moldavia;* by whom he had Issue *Demetrius,*
[44] and deceas'd soon after. *Vasiliwich* therefore reassuming the
Dukedom married a second Wife *Sophia* Daughter to *Thomas
Palæologus:* who is said to have receiv'd her Dowry out of the
Pope's Treasury, upon promise of the Duke to become *Romish.*

This Princess of a haughty mind, often complaining that she was
married to the *Tartars* Vassal, at length by continual perswasions,
and by a wile found means to ease her Husband, and his Country
of that Yoke. For whereas till then the *Tartar* had his Procurators,
who dwelt in the very Castle of *Mosco,* to oversee State-affairs,
she fain'd that from Heaven she had been warn'd, to build a Temple
to Saint *Nicholas* on the same place where the *Tartar* Agents had
their House. Being therefore delivered of a Son, she made it her
request to the Prince of *Tartary,* [45] whom she had invited to the
baptizing, that he would give her that House; which obtaining she
raz'd to the ground; and remov'd those Overseers out of the Castle:
and so by degrees dispossess'd them of all, which they held in
Russia. She prevail'd also with her Husband to transfer the Dukedom from *Demetrius* the Son of *John* deceas'd, to *Gabriel* his eldest
by her.

Gabriel no sooner Duke, but chang'd his name to *Basilius,* and
set his mind to doe nobly; he recover'd great part of *Muscovy* from
Vitoldus Duke of *Lituania;* and on the *Boristhenes* won *Smolensko*
and many other [13]Cities in the Year 1514. He divorc'd his first
Wife, and of *Helena* Daughter to Duke *Glinsky* begat *Juan
Vasiliwich.*[14]

Juan Vasiliwich being left a Child was committed to *George* [46]
his Unkle and Protector; at 25 years of age he vanquish'd the
Tartars of *Cazan* and *Astracan,* bringing home with him their
Princes captive; made cruel war in *Livonia* pretending right of
inheritance. He seem'd exceedingly devout, and whereas the *Russians* in their Churches use out of zeal and reverence to knock their

---

[13] (M) 1514.]

[14] Ivan IV, later to be known as Ivan the Terrible, reigned from 1533 to 1584.
Note that, according to sixteenth-century practice, what is now spelled Ivan
would then be printed Iuan; it is true that Hakluyt's later English reports came
to read Ivan. Purchas sometimes used the spelling Evanowich. We cannot be sure
what Milton, or Milton's printer, thought Juan meant, perhaps equating it with
the Spanish. At least the English form John Vasiliwich makes clear that Juan
was John or Johannes.

Heads against the ground, his Forehead was seldom free of swellings and bruzes, and very often seen to bleed. The cause of his
rigour in government, he alledg'd to be the malice and treachery
of his Subjects. But some of the Nobles incited by[15] his cruelty,
call'd in the Crim *Tartar* who in the Year 1571. broke into *Russia*,
burnt *Mosco* to the ground: he reigned 54 years; had three Sons,
of which the eldest being strook on a time by his Father, with grief
thereof dy'd;[16] his other Sons were *Pheo-* [47] *dor* and *Demetrius:*
in the time of *Juan Vasiliwich* the *English* came first by Sea into
the north parts of *Russia.*

   [17]*Pheodor Juanowick* being under age was left to the protection
of *Boris* Brother to the young Empress, and third Son by adoption
in the Emperour's Will. After 40 daies of mourning, the appointed
time of Coronation being come, the Emperour issuing out of his
Palace, the whole Clergy before him, enter'd with his Nobility the
Church of *Blaueshina* or blessedness; whence after Service to the
Church of *Michael,* then to our Lady Church being the Cathedral.
In midst whereof a Chair of Majesty was plac'd, and most un-
valuable Garments put upon him: there also was the imperial
Crown set on his Head by the Metropolitan, who out of a small
Book in his hand [48] read Exhortations to the Emperour, of justice
and peaceable government. After this rising from his Chair he was
invested with an upper Robe, so thick with Orient Pearls and
Stones as weigh'd 200 pounds, the Train born up by 6 Dukes; his
Staff imperial was of a Unicorn's Horn three foot and a half long,
beset with rich Stones: his Globe, and six Crowns carried before
him by Princes of the Bloud: his Horse at the Church door stood

   [15] (M) *Horsey's* Observations. 1571.]
   [16] Hakluyt, I, 466 (Jerome Horsey report, 1584): "the old Emperour Ivan Vasiliwich died, . . . having raigned 54. yeeres." (His heir Feodor is then mentioned,
and his son Demetrius by his second wife.)
   Purchas, III, 739 (summary of Ivan's cruelties, taken by Purchas from Ales-
sando Guagnini, *Rerum Polonicarum tomi tres* (Frankfurt, 1584): "[Ivan] dying
with griefe, as was thought, for the death of his eldest son *Iuan,* whom falsely
accused he struck with a staffe wrought with iron, whereof he dyed in a few days
after."
   [17] (M) 1584. *Hac.* vol. I. 466. *Horsey.*] Hakluyt, I, 466–69 (Horsey, report of
the coronation of Feodor, 1584; repeated by Purchas, III, 740–43): "the Prince
Boris Pheodorowich Godonova, [and five other nobles], . . . especially the Lord
Boris, whom he [Ivan] adopted as his third sonne, & was brother to the Em-
presse, . . . were appointed to dispose, & settle his sonne Pheodor Ivanowich . . . he
being of the age of 25. yeeres. . . . The time of mourning after their use being
expired, . . . or fortie orderlie dayes, the day of the . . . coronation . . . was
come." Milton then condenses the 1,500 words of Horsey's account of the ceremonies to the following nine sentences, about one-fourth.

ready with a Covering of imbroidered Pearl, Saddle and all suitable
to the value of 300 thousand Marks. There was a kind of Bridge
made three waies, 150 fathom long, three foot high, two fathom
broad, whereon the Emperour with his Train went from one
Church to another above the infinite throng of People making loud
Acclamations; At the Em- [49] perour's returning from those
Churches they were spread under-foot, with Cloth of Gold, the
Porches with Red Velvet, the Bridges with Scarlet and Stammel
cloth, all which, as the Emperour pass'd by, were cut and snatch't
by them that stood next; besides new minted Coines of Gold and
Silver cast among the People. The Empress in her Palace was plac't
before a great open Window in rich and shining Robes, among her
Ladies. After this the Emperour came into Parliament, where he
had a Banquet serv'd by his Nobles in princely order; two standing
on either side his Chair with Battel-axes of Gold; three of the next
Roomes great and large being set round with Plate of Gold and
Silver, from the ground up to the roof. This Triumph lasted a
week, wherein many royal Pastimes were seen: after [50] which,
election was made of the Nobles to new Offices and Dignities. The
conclusion of all was a Peal of 170 Brass Ordnance two miles
without the City, and 20000 Harquebuzes twice over: and so the
Emperour with at least 50 thousand Horse return'd through the
City to his Palace: where all the Nobility, Officers, and Merchants
brought him rich Presents. Shortly after, the Emperour by direction
of *Boris* conquer'd the large Country of *Siberia,* and took Prisoner
the King thereof:[18] he remov'd also corrupt Officers and former
Taxes. In sum, a great alteration in the Government follow'd, yet

[18] Hakluyt, I, 469 (the same): "shortly after the Emperor by the direction of
the prince Boris Pheodorowich, sent a power into the land of Siberia, where all
the rich Sables & Furres are gotten. This power conquered in one yeere and a
halfe, 1000. miles . . . there was taken prisoner the Emperor of the countrey
called Chare Sibersky. . . .
   "Hereupon the corrupt officers, Judges, Justices, captains and lieutenants
through the whole kingdom were remooved, and more honest men substituted. . . .
the great taskes, customes, and duties . . . were now abated, and some wholy
remitted, and no punishments commanded to be used, without sufficient and due
proofe. . . . In summe, a great alteration universally in the government folowed,
and yet all was done quietly, civilly, peaceably. . . .
   "These things being reported and caried to the eares of the kings and princes
that were borderers upon Russia, they grew so fearefull and terrible to them, that
the Monarch of all the Scythians called the Crimme Tartar or great Can himselfe . . . came . . . to the Emperor of Russia, accompanied with a great number
of his nobilitie well horsed, although to them that were Christians they seemed
rude, yet they were personable men, and valiant: . . . their entertainment was
honourable, the Tartar prince having brought with him his wives also.

all quietly, and without tumult. These things reported abroad strook such awe into the neighbour Kings, that the Crim *Tartar* with his Wives also and many Nobles valiant and personable men came to visit [51] the *Russian*. There came also 12 hundred *Polish* Gentlemen, many *Circassians,* and People of other Nations to offer service; Ambassadours from the *Turk,* the *Persian, Georgian,* and other *Tartar* Princes; from *Almany, Poland, Sweden, Denmark.* But this glory lasted not long through the treachery of *Boris,* who procur'd the death first of *Demetrius,* then of the Emperour himself, whereby the imperial Race after the succession of 300 years was quite extinguish't.

Boris, adopted, as before was said, third Son to *Juan Vasiliwich* without impeachment now ascended the Throne; but neither did he enjoy long, what he had so wickedly compass'd; [19]Divine revenge raising up against him a Counterfeit of that *Demetrius* whom he had caus'd to be murthered at *Ouglets.* This Up- [52] start strength'd with many *Poles* and *Cossacks* appears in arms to claim his right out of the hands of *Boris,* who sent against him an Army of 200 thousand Men; many of whom revolted to this *Demetrius: Peter Basman* the General returning to *Mosco* with the empty Triumph of a reported Victory. But the Enemy still advancing, *Boris* one day, after a plentifull Meal finding himself heavy and pain'd in his Stomach laid him down on his Bed; but 'ere his Doctours, who made great haste, came to him, was found speechless, and soon after dy'd, with grief, as is suppos'd, of his ill-success against *Demetrius.* Before his death, though it were speedy, he would be shorn, and new christn'd. He had but one Son, whom he lov'd so fondly, as not to suffer him out of sight; using to say he was Lord and Father of his Son, [53] and yet his Servant, yea

---

"Not long after, 1200. Polish gentlemen . . . came to Mosko offring their service to the Emperor, who were all entertained: and in like sort many Chirkasses, and people of other nations came and offred service. . . . thither came Ambassadors from the Turke, from the Persian, the Bogharian, the Crimme, the Georgian, and many other Tartar princes. There came also Ambassadors from the Emperor of Almaine, the Pole, the Swethen, the Dane, &c."

[19] (M) 1604. *Pur.* par. 3. 750.] Milton here condenses into one sentence Purchas's account of the rise of Boris to the throne, which Purchas had summarized (III, 744–46) from the *Historia sui temporis* of Thuanus (books 120, 135); but Purchas does not blame Boris for the death of Feodor. The account of the behavior and death of Boris, and of the triumph of Demetrius, is taken from the relation of the embassy to Russia in 1604–5 of Sir Thomas Smith, which Purchas reprinted, Smith having been in Russia at the time of Boris's death. Milton used part of the Smith narrative in Purchas (III, 749–50) for the rebellion of Demetrius, part (751–52) for the death of Boris, and part (752–53) for the triumph of Demetrius.

his Slave. To gain the Peoples love, which he had lost by his ill-getting the Empire, he us'd two Policies; first he caus'd *Mosco* to be fir'd in four places, that in the quenching thereof he might shew his great care and tenderness of the People; among whom he likewise distributed so much of his Bounty, as both new-built their Houses, and repair'd their Losses. At another time the People murmuring, that the great Pestilence which had then swept away a third part of the Nation, was the punishment of their electing him, a Murtherer, to reign over them, he built Galleries round about the utmost Wall of *Mosco;* and there appointed for one whole month 20 thousand pound to be given to the Poor; which well nigh stopt their Mouths. After the death of *Boris, Peter Basman* [54] their onely hope and refuge, though a Young man, was sent again to the Wars, with him many *English, Scots, French* and *Dutch;* who all with the other General *Goleeche* fell off to the new *Demetrius;* whose Messengers coming now to the Suburbs of *Mosco,* were brought by the Multitude to that spatious Field before the Castle Gate; within which the Council were then sitting; many of whom were by the Peoples threatning call'd out and constrain'd to hear the Letters of *Demetrius* openly read: which, long 'ere the end, wrought so with the Multitude, that furiously they broke into the Castle, laying violence on all they met; when strait appear'd coming towards them two Messengers of *Demetrius* formerly sent, pittifully whipt and roasted, which added to their rage. Then was the whole City in an [55] uproar, all the great Counselours Houses ransack't, especially of the *Godonova's* the Kindred and Family of *Boris.* Such of the Nobles that were best belov'd, by entreaty prevail'd at length to put an end to this Tumult. The Empress flying to a safer place had her Collar of Pearl pull'd from her Neck; and by the next Message command was given to secure her with her Son and Daughter. Whereupon *Demetrius* by general consent was proclaim'd Emperour. The Empress now seeing all lost, coun-sel'd the Prince her Son to follow his Father's example; who, it seems, had dispatch't himself by Poyson; and with a desperate courage beginning the deadly Health, was pledg'd effectually by her Son; but the Daughter onely sipping, escap'd. Others ascribe this deed to the secret Command of *Demetrius,* [56] and Self-murther imputed to them, to avoid the envy of such a Command.

Demetrius Evanowich, for so[20] he call'd himself, who succeeded,

---

[20] (M) *Pur.* par. 3. 764.] Passing over Purchas's lengthy account from Thuanus of the fall of Demetrius, Milton made use of one English report by an unidentified person (Purchas, III, 764), copied nearly verbatim.

was credibly reported the Son of *Gregory Peupoloy* a *Russe* Gentleman, and in his younger years to have been shorn a Fryar; but
escaping from the Monastery, to have travail'd *Germany* and other
Countries, but chiefly *Poland:* where he attain'd to good sufficiency
in Arms and other Experience; which rais'd in him such high
thoughts, as grounding on a common belief among the *Russians,*
that the young *Demetrius* was not dead, but convey'd away, and
their hatred against *Boris,* on this foundation with some other
circumstances, to build his hopes no lower than an Empire; which
on his first discovery found acceptation so generally, as planted
him at length on the Royal Seat; [57] but not so firmly as the fair
beginning promis'd; for in a short while the *Russians* finding themselves abus'd by an Impostor, on the sixth day after his marriage,
observing when his Guard of *Poles* were most secure, rushing into
the Palace before break of day, drag'd him out of his Bed, and
when he had confes'd the fraud, pull'd him to pieces; with him
Peter Basman was also slain, and both their dead Bodies laid open
in the Market-place. He was of no presence, but otherwise of a
princely disposition; too bountifull, which occasion'd some exactions; in other matters a great lover of justice, not unworthy the
Empire which he had gotten, and lost onely through greatness of
mind, neglecting the Conspiracy, which he knew the *Russians* were
plotting. Some say their hatred grew, for that they saw him [58]
alienated from the *Russian* Manners and Religion, having made
Buchinskoy a learned Protestant his Secretary.[21] Some report from
Gilbert's relation, who was a *Scot,* and Captain of his Guard, that
lying on his Bed awake, not long before the Conspiracy, he saw
the appearance of an aged man coming toward him; at which he
rose, and call'd to them that watch'd; but they denied to have seen
any such pass by them. He returning to his Bed, and within an
hour after troubl'd again with the same Apparition, sent for *Buchinskoy,* telling him he had now twice the same night seen an
aged man, who at his second coming told him, that though he were
a good Prince of himself, yet for the injustice and oppression of his
inferiour Ministers, his Empire should be taken from him.[22] The
Secretary counsell'd him to embrace [59] true Religion, affirming
that for lack thereof, his Officers were so corrupt. The Emperour
seem'd to be much mov'd, and to intend what was perswaded him.
But a few daies after, the other Secretary, a *Russian,* came to him
with a drawn Sword; of which the Emperour made slight at first;

[21] Purchas, III, 765 (an unidentified English witness).
[22] Purchas, III, 765 (an account taken by Purchas from Captain Gilbert).

but he after bold words assaulted him, strait seconded by other Conspiratours crying liberty. *Gilbert* with many of the Guard oversuddenly surpris'd retreated to *Coluga* a Town which they fortify'd; most of the other Strangers were massacr'd, except the *English,* whose mediation sav'd also *Buchinskoy. Shusky* who succeeded him reports in a Letter to King *James* otherwise of him; that his right name was *Gryshca* the Son of *Boughdan;* that to escape punishment for Villanies done, he turn'd Fryar, and fell at last to the Black art; [60] and fearing that the Metropolitan intended therefore to imprison him, fled into *Lettow;* where by counsel of *Sigismund* the *Poland* King, he began to call himself *Demetry* of *Ouglitts;*[23] and by many Libels and Spies privily sent into *Mosco,* gave out the same; that many Letters and Messengers thereupon were sent from *Boris* into *Poland,* and from the Patriarch, to acquaint them who the Runnagate was; but the *Polanders* giving them no credit, furnish't him the more with Arms and Money, notwithstanding the League; and sent the Palatine *Sandamersko* and other Lords to accompany him into *Russia,* gaining also a Prince of the Crim *Tartars* to his aide; that the Army of *Boris* hearing of his sudden death, yielded to this *Gryshca,* who taking to wife the Daughter of *Sandamersko,* attempted to root [61] out the *Russian* Clergy, and to bring in the *Romish* Religion, for which purpose many Jesuits came along with him. Whereupon *Shusky* with the Nobles and Metropolitans conspiring against him, in half a year gather'd all the Forces of *Moscovia,* and surprising him found in writing under his own hand all these his Intentions; Letters also from the Pope and Cardinals to the same effect, not onely to set up the Religion of *Rome,* but to force it upon all, with death to them that refus'd.

[24]*Vasily Evanowich Shusky* after the slaughter of *Demetry* or *Gryshca* was elected Emperour; having not long before been at the Block for reporting to have seen the true *Demetrius* dead and buried; but *Gryshca* not onely recall'd him, but advanc'd him, to be the instrument of his owne ruine. He was then about the age of [62] 50; nobly descended, never married, of great wisedom reputed, a favourer of the *English;* for he sav'd them from rifling in

---

[23] Purchas, III, 765–69 (still another history of Demetrius, written by the emperor Vasily Shuisky, who succeeded him, to King James: considerably condensed by Milton).

[24] (M) 1606.] Note that Milton here spells the emperor's patronymic Evanowich, which is Purchas's spelling of Ivanovich.

the former Tumults.[25] Some say he modestly refus'd the Crown, till[26] by lot four times together it fell to him; yet after that, growing jealous of his Title, remov'd by Poyson, and other means all the Nobles that were like to stand his Rivals; and is said to have consulted with Witches of the *Samoeds, Lappians* and *Tartarians,* about the same fears; and being warn'd of one *Michalowich,* to have put to death three of that name; yet a fourth was reserv'd by fate to succeed him; being then a Youth attendant in the Court, one of those that held the golden Axes, and least suspected. But before that time he also was supplanted by another reviving *Demetrius* brought in by the *Poles;* whose counterfeited [63] Hand, and strange relating of privatest Circumstances had almost deceiv'd *Gilbert* himself; had not their persons been utterly unlike; but *Gryshca's* Wife so far believ'd him for her Husband, as to receive him to her Bed.[27] *Shusky* besieg'd in his Castle of *Mosco,* was adventrously supply'd with some Powder and Ammunition by the *English;* and with 2000 *French, English* and *Scots,* with other Forces from *Charles* King of *Sweden.* [28]The *English* after many miseries of cold, and hunger and assaults by the way, deserted by the *French,* yielded most of them to the *Pole,* neer *Smolensko,* and serv'd him against the *Russ.* Mean [29]while this second *Demetrius*

[25] Purchas, III, 764 (Purchas's own information about Shuisky, presumably from English merchants).

[26] (M) *Purch.* part. 3. 769, &c.] Purchas, III, 769–70 (still apparently Thuanus): but the latter (book 135, chap. 10) deals only with the refusal of the crown and the later greedy acceptance ("cupide amplexatus est"). The crimes of Shuisky, now emperor, are not in Thuanus, whose history ends in 1607. Purchas's source for them (III, 769–70) is information from Captain Gilbert, a Scottish mercenary, as reported orally by an intermediary.

[27] From the same source (Purchas, III, 770).

[28] (M) 1609.] The history of the mercenaries and their surrender to the Poles is reported in Purchas (III, 772–79) in a relation by a participant.

[29] (M) 779.] The Polish siege and capture of Moscow, the end of Shuisky and of the second Demetrius, and the recapture of Moscow from the Poles are briefly summarized by Purchas (III, 779–80) from sources not indicated: "To make an end of this Storie of the Foxe and the Beare, the pretending *Demetrius* and contending *Suiskey;* it is reported, that Demetrius seeing these perplexities of *Suiskey,* raysed a great Armie of such Russes as voluntarily" (in margin: "Some say he had 100000. which is scarsly credible.") "fell to him (the *Pole* having now rejected him, except some Voluntaries) and againe laid siege to *Mosco; Zolkiewsky* for *Sigismund* [king of Poland], beleagred another part thereof with fortie thousand men, whereof one thousand and five hundred were *English, Scottish,* and *French. Suiskey* seeing no hope to withstand them, his Empire renouncing him, hee would seeme to renounce the Empire first, betaking himselfe to a Monasterie. But not the sanctitie of the place, nor sacred name of an Emperour might protect or secure him. The Muscovites yeelded up their Citie and his Person to the Pole,

being now rejected by the *Poles*, with those *Russians* that sided
with him laid siege to *Mosco: Zolkiewsky* for *Sigismund* King of
Poland Beleaguers on the other [64] side with forty thousand Men;
whereof 1500 *English, Scotch,* and *French*. *Shusky* despairing success betakes him to a Monastery; but with the City is yielded to
the *Pole;* who turns now his force against the Counterfeit *Deme-*
trius; he seeking to fly is by a *Tartar* slain in his Camp. *Smolensko*
held out a siege of two years, then surrender'd. *Shusky* the Emperour carried away into *Poland,* there ended miserably in prison.
But before his departure out of *Muscovy* the *Polanders* in his name
sending for the chief Nobility as to a last farewell, cause them to
be entertain'd in a secret place, and there dispatch'd: by this means
the easier to subdue the People. Yet the *Poles* were starv'd at length
out of those Places in *Mosco* which they had fortify'd. Wherein the
Russians who besieg'd them, found, as is reported, 60 Barrels of
Man's Flesh[30] [65] powder'd, being the Bodies of such as dy'd
among them, or were slain in fight.

---

and the Castle was manned for Sigismund. All joyne against *Demetrius*, who
betaketh him to his heeles, and by a Tartar (as before is sayd) was slaine in his
campe." An account of the capture of Smolensk by the Poles follows.

"*Suiskey* was carried into *Poland* and there imprisoned in *Waringborough*
Castle, and after the losse of libertie and his Empire, exposed to scorne and
manifold miseries, hee dyed in a forraine countrie. But before that Tragedie, the
Poles are said to have more then acted others. For when they held him prisoner
before his departure from *Moscovia,* they sent for many *Grandes* in *Suiskeys*
name, as if he had much desired to see them before his fatall farewell, to take
a friendly and honourable leave of them. They come, are entertayned, and in a
private place knocked on the head and throwne into the River: and thus was most
of the chiefe remayning Nobilitie destroyed. The *Poles* fortified two of the Forts
at *Mosco,* and burnt two others, as not able to man them. But the *Muscovite*
also there held them besieged till famine forced them to yeeld: the *Russians* finding
there sixtie barrels of pouldred mans flesh (it seemeth of such as had dyed, or
were slaine, that their death might give life to the Survivers) a just, but miserable
and tragicall spectacle."

[30] (M) *Jansonius*.] Purchas summarized this history from reports from various
sources. One was Jansonius: that is, an annual volume of news entitled *Mercurii*
Gallobelgici Sleidano Succenturiati sive Rerum in Gallia et Belgio . . . ab anno
1588 [to 1630] *gestarum,* 18 vols. (1590–1630, published at Cologne, later at
Frankfurt: the first volumes edited by A. P. Jansonius, and listed under his name
in the BN catalogue, but listed in the Library of Congress catalogue as by Isselt,
Michael van). Vol. IX, for 1611–12, reports the sieges of Moscow and Smolensk.
Purchas lists Jansonius in the margin, however, only for a detail of the siege of
Smolensk; the barrels of corpses are not in his history.

Another source, though not listed by Purchas, was presumably an English news
pamphlet, Henry Brereton's *News of the Present Miseries of Rushia* (1614; *STC*
3609). Possibly Muscovy Company reports, not to mention gossip, provided news

[31]After which the Empire of *Russia* broke to pieces, the prey of such as could catch, every one naming himself, and striving to be accounted that *Demetrius* of *Ouglitts*. Some chose *Vladislaus* King *Sigismund's* Son, but he not accepting, they fell to a popular Government; killing all the Nobles under pretence of favouring the *Poles*. Some overtures of receiving them were made, as some say, to King *James,* and Sir *John Meric,* and Sir *William Russel* imploy'd therein. Thus *Russia* remaining in this confusion, it happen'd that a mean Man, a Butcher dwelling in the North [32]about *Duina,* inveying against the baseness of their Nobility, and the corruption of Officers, uttered words, that if they would but choose a faithfull Treasurer [66] to pay well the Souldiers, and a good General (naming one *Pozarsky* a poor Gentleman, who after good service done liv'd not far off retir'd and neglected;) that then he doubted not to drive out the *Poles*.[33] The People assent, and choose that General; the Butcher they make their Treasurer who both so well discharg'd their Places, that with an Army soon gather'd they raise the siege of *Mosco,* which the *Polanders* had renew'd; and with *Boris Licin* another great Souldier of that Countrey fall into consultation about the choise of an Emperour, and chose at last *Michalowich,* or *Michael Pheodorowich,* the fatal Youth, whose name *Shusky* so fear'd.

Michael Pheodorowich thus elected[34] by the valour of *Pozarsky* and *Boris Licin,* made them both Generals of his Forces, joyning with them another great Com- [67] mander of the *Cossacks* whose aid had much befriended him; the Butcher also was made a Counselour of State. Finally a Peace was made up between the *Russians* and the *Poles;* and that partly by the mediation of King *James.* [68]

---

also. The final news item of the Polish corpses in barrels, for which no source is given, makes a more sensational climax in Purchas than in Milton, for Purchas supposes cannibalism by the starving Poles. Purchas's manipulative style is apparent here, as compared with Milton's swifter version.

A convenient collection of the contemporary English narratives of the Russian civil wars from 1604 to 1613 involving the Dmitri pretenders and Shuiskey was provided by Sonia E. Howe, *The False Dmitri* (London, 1916).

[31] (M) 1612.] Purchas, III, 782 (from Purchas's own elaborate moralizing, reduced to these two sentences of fact).

[32] (M) *Purch.* part 3. 790.] Purchas, III, 790 (apparently Purchas's own information, doubtless the result of much London talk).

[33] Purchas, III, 790–91 (apparently Purchas's paraphrase of material in Jansonius, vol. X).

[34] (M) 1613.]

CHAP. V.

The first discovery of Russia *by The*
North-east, 1553 *with the* English
Embassies, and Entertainments at that
Court, untill the Year 1604.

HE discovery of *Russia* by[1] the northern Ocean, made first,
of any Nation that we know, by *English* men, might have
seem'd an enterprise almost heroick; if any higher end than
the excessive love of Gain and Traffick, had animated the design.
Nevertheless that in regard that many things not unprofitable to
the knowledge of Nature, and other Observations are hereby come
to light, as good events ofttimes arise from evil occasions, it will
not be the worst labour to relate briefly the [69] beginning, and
prosecution of this adventurous Voiage; untill it became at last a
familiar Passage.[2]

When our Merchants perceiv'd the Commodities of *England* to
be in small request abroad, and foreign Merchandize to grow higher
in esteem and value than before, they began to think with themselves how this might be remedied.[3] And seeing how the *Spaniards*
and *Portugals* had encreas'd their Wealth by discovery of new
Trades and Countries, they resolv'd upon some new and strange
Navigation. At the same time *Sebastian Chabota,* a man for the
knowledge of Sea-affairs much renown'd in those daies, happen'd
to be in *London.* With him first they consult; and by his advice
conclude to furnish out three Ships for the search and discovery
of the northern parts. And having heard that a [70] certain Worm
is bred in that Ocean, which many times eateth through the stron-

---

[1] (M) *Hac.* vol. 1. 243. 234.] Hakluyt, I, 234–37, gives the record of the voyage
of Sir Hugh Willoughby, commander of the voyage of 1553, who wintered on the
Arctic coast just short of the White Sea but who did not survive the winter. I,
243–55, gives the formal account of the expedition, written by Clement Adams
in Latin from the reports of Richard Chancellor, who brought his ship into the
Gulf of Archangel, and journeyed overland to Moscow. Hakluyt translated the
Adams account and added Chancellor's own narrative at I, 237–42, with the
special details of his reception by the emperor.

[2] Passage in the sense of voyage.

[3] Here begins the abridgment of the Adams narrative.

gest Oak, they contrive to cover some part of the Keel of those Ships with thin sheets of Lead; and victual them for 18 months; allowing equally to their journey their stay, and their return. Arms also they provide and store of Munition, with sufficient Captains and Governours for so great an enterprise. To which among many, and some void of experience that offer'd themselves, Sir *Hugh Willowby* a valiant Gentleman earnestly requested to have the charge. Of whom before all others both for his goodly personage, and singular skill in the services of War, they made choise to be Admiral; and of *Richard Chancelor,* a man greatly esteem'd for his skill, to be chief Pilot. This man was brought up by Mr. *Henry Sid-* [71] *ney,* afterwards Deputy of *Ireland,* who coming where the Adventurers were gather'd together; though then a young man, with a grave and eloquent Speech commended *Chancelor* unto them.

After this, they omitted no enquiry after any person that might inform them concerning those north-easterly parts to which the Voiage tended; and two *Tartarians* then of the King's Stable were sent for; but they were able to answer nothing to purpose. So after much debate it was concluded that by the 20*th* of *May* the Ships should depart. Being come near *Greenwich* where the Court then lay, presently the Courtiers came running out, the Privy Council at the Windows, the rest on the Towers and Battlements. The Mariners all apparell'd in Watchet, or sky-coloured Cloth, dis- [72] charge their Ordnance; the noise whereof, and of the People shouting is answer'd from the Hills and Waters with as loud an Echo. Onely the good King *Edward* then sick beheld not this sight, but dy'd soon after. From hence putting into *Harwich,* they staid long and lost much time. At length passing by *Shetland,* they kenn'd a far off *Ægelands,* being an innumerable sort of Islands call'd *Rost Islands* in 66 degrees. Thence to *Lofoot* in 68. to *Seinam* in 70 degrees; these Islands belong all to the Crown of *Denmark.*[4] Whence departing Sir *Hugh Willowby* set out his Flag by which he call'd together the chief men of his other Ships to counsel; where they conclude, in case they happen'd to be scatter'd by Tempest, that *Wardhouse* a noted Haven in *Finmark* be the appointed place of their meeting.[5] [73] The very same day after noon so great a Tempest arose, that the Ships were some driv'n one way, some another in great peril. The General with his loudest voice call'd

---

[4] These two sentences put together material in the Willoughby report (Hakluyt, I, 235).

[5] The narrative returns to Adams (Hakluyt, I, 245).

to *Chancelor* not to be far from him; but in vain, for the admiral sayling much better than his Ship, and bearing all her Sayles was carried with great swiftness soon out of sight; but before that, the Ship-boat striking against her Ship was overwhelmed in view of the *Bonaventure* whereof *Chancelor* was [6]Captain. The third Ship also in the same Storm was lost. But Sir *Hugh Willowby* escaping that Storm, and wandring on those desolate Seas till the 18*th* of *September* put into a Haven where they had Weather as in the depth of Winter; and there determining to abide till Spring, sent out three men southwest to find Inhabitants; who journy'd three [74] daies but found none; then other three went westward four daies journey, and lastly three southeast three daies; but they all returning without news of People, or any sign of Habitation, Sir *Hugh* with the company of his two Ships abode there till *January,* as appears by a Will since found in one of the Ships; but then perish'd all with cold. This River or Haven was *Arzina* in *Lapland* neer to *Kegor,* where[7] they were found dead the year after by certain *Russian* Fishermen. Whereof the *English* Agent at *Mosco* having notice, sent and recover'd the Ships with the dead Bodies and most of the Goods, and sent them for *England;* but the Ships being unstanch, as is suppos'd, by their two years wintring in *Lapland,* sunk by the way with their Dead, and them also that brought them. But now *Chan-* [75] *celor* with his Ship and Company thus left, shap'd his course to *Wardhouse,* the place agreed on to expect the rest; where having staid 7 daies without tydings of them, he resolves at length to hold on his Voiage; [8] and sayl'd so far till he found no night, but continual day and Sun cleerly shining on that huge and vast Sea for certain daies. At length they enter into a great Bay, nam'd, as they knew after, from Saint *Nicholas;* and spying a Fisherboat, made after him to know what People they were. The Fishermen amaz'd with the greatness of his Ship, to them a strange and new sight, sought to fly; but overtak'n, in great fear they prostrate themselves, and offer to kiss his Feet; but he raysing them up with all signes and gestures of courtesie, sought to win their friendship. They no sooner dismist, but spread abroad [76] the arrival of a strange Nation, whose humanity they spake of with great affection; whereupon the People running to-

---

[6] (M) *Hac.* 235.] The narrative goes back to Willoughby (Hakluyt, I, 236–37).

[7] (M) *Hac.* 464.] The discovery and return of Willoughby's ships was reported in a survey of the Russian voyages made by Henry Lane, a Muscovy Company agent, in 1568 (Hakluyt, I, 464).

[8] The ensuing narrative is put together from the Adams relation (Hakluyt, I, 246–47).

gether, with like return of all courteous usage receive them; offering them Victuals freely; nor refusing to traffick, but for a loyal Custom which bound them from that, without first the consent had of their King. After mutual demands of each other's Nation they found themselves to be in *Russia* where *Juan Vasiliwich* at that time reign'd Emperour. To whom privily the Governour of that place sending notice of the strange Guests that were arriv'd, held in the mean while our Men in what suspence he could. The Emperour well pleas'd with so unexpected a Message, invites them to his Court, offring them Post-horses at his own charge, or if the journey seem'd overlong, [77] that they might freely traffick where they were. But 'ere this Messenger could return, having lost his way, the *Muscovites* themselves, loath that our men should depart which they made shew to doe, furnish't them with Guides and other Conveniences to bring them to their King's presence. *Chancelor* had now gon more than half his journey, when the Sled-man sent to Court meets him on the way; delivers him the Emperour's Letters; which when the *Russes* understood, so willing they were to obey the Contents thereof, that they quarrell'd and strove who should have the preferment to put his Horses to the Sled. So after a long and troublesome journey of 1500 miles he arriv'd at *Mosco*. After he had remain'd in the City about 12 daies, a Messenger was sent to bring them to the King's [78] House.[9] Being enter'd within the Court Gates, and brought into an outward Chamber, they beheld there a very honourable company to the number of a hunder'd sitting all apparell'd in Cloth of gold down to their Ancles: next conducted to the Chamber of presence, there sate the Emperour on a lofty and very royal Throne; on his Head a Diadem of gold, his Robe all of Goldsmiths work, in his Hand a chrystal Sceptre garnish'd and beset with precious Stones; no less was his Countenance full of majesty. Beside him stood his chief Secretary; on his other side the great Commander of silence, both in Cloth of gold; then sate his Council of 150 round about on high Seats, clad all as richly. *Chancelor* nothing abash'd made his obeysance to the Emperour after the *English* manner. The [79] Emperour having taken, and read his Letters, after some enquiry of King *Edward*'s Health, invited them to dinner, and till then dismiss'd them. But before dismission the Secretary presented their Present bareheaded; till which time they were all cover'd; and before admittance our men had charge not to speak, but when the Emperour

[9] Skipping Adams's account of the geography of Russia, Milton resumes the Adams narrative (Hakluyt, I, 249–50).

demanded ought. Having sat two hours in the Secretary's Chamber, they were at length call'd in to dinner; where the Emperour was set at Table, now in a Robe of silver, and another Crown on his Head. This place was call'd the golden Palace, but without cause, for the *English* men had seen many fairer; round about the room, but at distance, were other long Tables; in the midst a Cupboard of huge and massy goblets, and other Vessels of gold [80] and silver; among the rest four great Flagons nigh two yards high, wrought in the top with devices of Towers and Dragons heads. The Guests ascended to their Tables by three steps; all apparell'd in Linnen, and that lin'd with rich Furrs. The Messes came in without order, but all in Chargers of gold, both to the Emperour, and to the rest that din'd there, which were two hundred persons; on every Board also were set Cups of gold without number. The Servitors one hundred and forty were likewise array'd in gold, and waited with Caps on their heads. They that are in high favour sit on the same Bench with the Emperour, but far off. Before Meat came in, according to the custom of their Kings, he sent to every Guest a slice of Bread; whom the Officer naming saith thus, *John* [81] *Basiliwich* Emperour of *Russ,* &c. doth reward thee with Bread, at which words all men stand up. Then were Swans in several pieces serv'd in, each piece in a several Dish, which the great Duke sends about as the Bread, and so likewise the Drink. In dinner time he twice chang'd his Crown, his Waiters thrice their Apparel; to whom the Emperour in like manner gives both Bread and Drink with his own hands; which they say is done to the intent that he may perfectly know his own Houshold; and indeed when dinner was done, he call'd his Nobles every one before him by name; and by this time Candles were brought in, for it grew dark; and the *English* departed to their Lodgings from dinner, an hour within night.

[10]In the Year 1555. *Chancelor* made another voiage to this [82] Place with Letters from Queen *Mary;* had a House in *Mosco,* and Diet appointed him; and was soon admitted to the Emperour's presence in a large room spread with Carpets; at his entring and salutation all stood up, the Emperour onely sitting, except when the Queen's name was read, or spoken; for then he himself would

---

[10] (M) *Hac.* 258. 263. 465.] Hakluyt, I, 258, gives a translation of the letter of Philip and Mary to the emperor Ivan. The narrative of Chancellor's reception by the emperor, and of the trade negotiations, was written by George Killingworth (I, 263–65), but Milton drew for the reception upon the later history by Henry Lane (I, 464–65).

rise: at dinner he sate bareheaded; his Crown and rich Cap standing on a Pinacle by. *Chancelor* returning[11] for *England, Osep Napea* Governour of *Wologda* came in his Ship Ambassadour from the *Russe;* but suffering shipwrack in *Pettislego* a Bay in *Scotland, Chancelor* who took more care to save the Ambassadour than himself was drown'd, the Ship rifled, and most of her lading made booty by the People thereabout. [83]

In the Year 1557. *Osep* [12]*Napea* returned into his Countrey with *Antony Jenkinson* who had the command of four tall Ships. He reports of a Whirlpool between the *Rost Islands* and *Lofoot* call'd *Malestrand;* which from half ebb till half flood is heard to make so terrible a noise, as shakes the Door-rings of Houses in those Islands ten mile off; Whales that come within the Current thereof make a pittifull cry; Trees carried in and cast out again have the ends and boughs of them so beaten, as they seem like the stalks of bruized Hemp. About *Zeinam* they saw many Whales very monstrous hard by their Ships; whereof some by estimation sixty foot long; they roard hideously, it being then the time of their engendring. At *Wardhouse,* he saith, the Cattel are fed with Fish. Coming to *Mosco,* he [84] found the Emperour sitting aloft in a Chair of state, richly crown'd, a Staff of gold in his hand wrought with costly stone.[13] Distant from him sate his Brother, and a Youth the Emperour's son of *Casan* whom the *Russ* had conquer'd; there din'd with him diverse Ambassadours, Christian and Heathen, diversely apparell'd; his Brother with some of the chief Nobles sate with him at Table: the Guests were in all six hundred. In dinner time came in six Musicians; and standing in the midst, sung three several times, but with little or no delight to our men; there din'd at the same time in other Halls two thousand *Tartars* who came

[11] (M) 286.] Hakluyt, I, 285–86, gives the official account of the Russian envoy's voyage, here condensed to one sentence. Milton's statement that "*Chancelor* who took more care to save the Ambassadour than himself was drown'd" rather modifies the original: "The grand Pilot using all carefulnesse for the safetie of the bodie of the sayde Ambassadour and his trayne." Henry Lane's history says only that Chancellor was drowned (I, 465).

[12] (M) 310, &c.] Hakluyt, I, 310–14, gives Jenkinson's narrative. The account of the Maelstrom (I, 311), which Milton repeats in full, is in part at least hearsay, the "pittifull cry" of the whale especially seeming apocryphal. The account of the Muscostrom in Jakob Ziegler's *Schondia* (1532) is much less sensational: it was translated in Richard Eden, *The Decades of the newe worlde* (1555), fol. 274.

[13] This account of the court dinners mingles the two reports of the voyage of 1557: Hakluyt, I, 312, for the first half, Anthony Jenkinson's account; I, 316–17, for the second, an anonymous account. Milton's "the Messes were but mean" exaggerates the original, "As for costly meates I have many times seene better."

to serve the Duke in his Wars. The *English* were set at a small Table by themselves direct before the Emperour; who sent them diverse Bowles of Wine and Meath and many Dishes [85] from his own hand: the Messes were but mean, but the change of Wines and several Meaths were wonderfull. As oft as they din'd with the Emperour, he sent for them in the Morning, and invited them with his own mouth. On *Christmass* day [14]being invited, they had for other provision as before; but for store of gold and silver Plate excessive; among which were twelve Barrels of silver, hoop'd with fine gold containing twelve gallons apiece.

1560. Was the first *English* traffick to the *Narve* in *Livonia,* till then conceal'd by *Danskers* and *Lubeckers*.[15]

1561. The same *Antony Jenkinson* made another voiage to *Mosco;* and arriv'd while the Emperour was celebrating his marriage with a *Circassian* Lady; during which time the City Gates for three daies were kept [86] shut; and all men whatsoever straitly commanded to keep within their Houses; except some of his Houshold; the cause whereof is not known.[16]

1566. He made again the same voiage; which now men[17] usually made in a month from *London* to Saint *Nicholas* with good Windes, being seven hundred and fifty leagues.

1568. *Thomas Randolf,* Esq; went Embassadour to *Muscovy,*[18] from Queen *Elizabeth;* and in his passage by Sea met nothing remarkable save great store of Whales, whom they might see engendring together, and the Sperma-ceti swimming on the Water. At *Colmogro* he was met by a Gentleman from the Emperour, at whose charge he was conducted to *Mosco:* but met there by no man; not so much as the *English;* lodg'd in a fair House built for Ambassa- [87] dours; but there confin'd upon some suspicion which the Emperour had conceav'd; sent for at length after seventeen

---

[14] (M) 317.]

[15] Hakluyt, I, 465 (Lane's survey, Lane having, as it happened, reported to the company in that year).

[16] Hakluyt, I, 343–44 (Jenkinson's report, one sentence on the confinement).

[17] (M) 311.] Hakluyt, I, 311. This reference is to the second page of the report of Jenkinson's voyage of 1557, noting the distance to St. Nicholas (Archangel) from London as 750 leagues. Jenkinson's voyage of 1566 is noted at I, 372. For the length of the voyage, the earlier ones (1557, 1561, 1566) took two months, but in 1568, 1571, 1579, and 1583 the voyages took a little over a month, the first and the last counting, however, from Harwich. In 1582 William Borough, a chief pilot of the Muscovy Company, wrote, "If wee sende them [the ships] in the beginning of May, then may they be at Saint Nicholas by the fine of the same moneth" (I, 455).

[18] (M) 373.] Hakluyt, I, 376 (two sentences).

weeks delay, was fain to ride thither on a borrow'd Horse, his men on foot.[19] In a Chamber before the presence were sitting about three hundred Persons, all in rich Robes taken out of the Emperour's Wardrobe for that day; they sate on three ranks of Benches, rather for shew than that the Persons were of honour; being Merchants, and other mean Inhabitants. The Ambassadour saluted them, but by them unsaluted pass'd on with his Head cover'd. At the Presence door being receiv'd by two which had been his Guardians, and brought into the midst, he was there will'd to stand still, and speak his message from the Queen; at whose name the Emperour stood up, and demanded [88] her health: then giving the Ambassadour his Hand to kiss fell to many questions. The Present being deliver'd, which was a great silver Bowle curiously grav'n, the Emperour told him, he din'd not that day openly because of great Affairs; but, saith he, I will send thee my Dinner, and augment thy Allowance. And so dismissing him, sent a Duke richly apparell'd soon after to his Lodging with fifty Persons each of them carrying Meat in silver Dishes cover'd; which himself deliver'd into the Ambassadour's own hands tasting first of every Dish, and every sort of Drink; that done, set him down with his Company, took part, and went not thence unrewarded. The Emperour sent back with this Ambassadour another of his own call'd *Andrew Savin.* [89]

1571. *Jenkinson* made a third voiage; but was staid long at *Colmogro* by reason of the Plague in those Parts; at length had audience where the Court then was, near to *Pereslave;* to which place the Emperour was return'd from his *Swedish* War with ill success:[20] and *Mosco* the same year had been wholly burnt by the *Crim;* in it the *English* House, and diverse *English* were smother'd in the Sellars, multitudes of People in the City perish'd, all that were young led captive with exceeding spoil.[21]

---

[19] Hakluyt, I, 377–78 (condensed, but omitting the crucial passage on the embassy: after several audiences "I obtained at his hands my whole demands for large privileges in generall [for the English merchants], together with all the rest my particular requests").

[20] Hakluyt, I, 402–3 (condensed to three clauses).

[21] Hakluyt, I, 402 (report to the company agent Henry Lane, 1571): "The Mosco is burnt every sticke by the Crimme . . . and an innumerable number of people: and in the English house was smothered Thomas Southam, . . . to the number of 25. persons were stifeled in our Beere seller. . . . The Emperour fled out of the field, and many of his people were caried away by the Crimme Tartar: to wit, all the yong people, . . . and so with exceeding much spoile and infinite prisoners, they returned home againe."

[22] 1583. *Juan Basiliwich* having the year before sent his Ambassadour *Pheodor Andrewich* about matters of Commerce, the Queen made choice of Sir *Jerom Bowes,* one of her houshold, to go into *Russia;* who being attended with more than forty persons, and accompanied with the *Russe* re- [90] turning home, arriv'd at St. *Nicolas.* The *Dutch* by this time had intruded into the *Muscovy*-Trade; which by privilege long before had been granted solely to the *English;* and had corrupted to their side *Shalkan* the Chancellor, with others of the great ones; who so wrought, that a creature of their own was sent to meet Sir *Jerom* at *Colmogro,* and to offer him occasions of dislike: Until at *Vologda* he was receiv'd by another from the Emperour; and at *Yeraslave* by a Duke well accompanied, who presented him with a Coach and ten Geldings. Two miles from *Mosco* met him four Gentlemen with Two hundred Horse, who after short salutation, told him what they had to say from the Emperour, willing him to alight, which the Ambassadour soon refus'd, unless they also lighted; whereon they stood long deba- [91] ting; at length agreed, great dispute follow'd, whose foot should first touch the ground. Their Message deliver'd, and then embracing, they conducted the Ambassador to a house at *Mosco,* built for him purposely. At his going to Court he and his followers honourably mounted and apparell'd, the Emperour's Guard were set on either side all the way about 6000 shot. At the Court-gate met him four Noblemen in Cloth of Gold, and rich Furr-Caps, embroider'd with Pearl and Stone; then four others of greater degree, in which passage there stood along the Walls, and sate on Benches seven or eight hundred men in colour'd Sattins and Gold. At the Presence-dore met him the chief Herald, and with him all the great Officers of Court, who brought him where the Emperour sate: there were set by him three Crowns [92] of *Muscovy, Cazan* and *Astracan;* on each side stood two young Noblemen, costly apparell'd in White; each of them had a broad Axe on his shoulder; on the Benches round sate above a hundred Noblemen. Having giv'n the Ambassadour his hand to kiss, and enquir'd of the Queens Health, he will'd him to go sit in the place provided for him, nigh ten paces distant; from thence to send him the Queens Letters and Present. Which the Ambassadour thinking not reasonable, step'd forward; but the Chancellor meeting him, would have tak'n his Letters; to whom the Ambassadour said, that the Queen had directed no Letters to him; and so went on and deliver'd them to the

---

[22] (M) *Hac.* vol. I. 458.] Hakluyt, I, 458–63 (Sir Jerome Bowes's report, in later, bolder version of Hakluyt's second edition, here much condensed).

Emperour's own hands; and after a short withdrawing into the Council-Chamber, where he had Conference with some of the Council, he was call'd in to [93] dinner: about the midst whereof, the Emperour standing up, drank a deep Carouse to the Queens Health, and sent to the Ambassadour a great Bowl of Rhenish-Wine to pledge him. But at several times being call'd for to treat about Affairs, and not yielding ought beyond his Commission, the Emperour not wont to be gain-say'd, one day especially broke into passion, and with a stern countenance told him, he did not reckon the Queen to be his fellow; for there are, quoth he, her betters. The Ambassadour not holding it his part, whatever danger might ensue, to hear any derogate from the Majesty of his Prince, with like courage and countenance told him, that the Queen was equal to any in Christendom who thought himself greatest; and wanted not means to offend her Enemies whomsoever. Yea, quoth [94] he, what saist thou of the *French* and *Spanish* Kings? I hold her, quoth the Ambassadour, equal to either. Then what to the *German* Emperour? Her Father, quoth he, had the Emperour in his pay. This answer mislik'd the Duke so far, as that he told him, were he not an Ambassadour, he would throw him out of doors. You may, said the Ambassadour, doe your will, for I am now fast in your Countrey; but the Queen I doubt not will know how to be reveng'd of any injury offer'd to her Ambassadour. Whereat the Emperour in great sudden bid him get home; and he with no more reverence than such usage requir'd, saluted the Emperour, and went his way. Notwithstanding this, the *Muscovite,* soon as his mood left him, spake to them that stood by, many praises of the Am- [95] bassadour, wishing he had such a Servant, and presently after sent his chief Secretary to tell him that whatever had pass'd in words, yet for his great respect to the Queen, he would shortly after dispatch him with honour and full contentment, and in the mean while he much enlarg'd his entertainment. He also desir'd that the Points of our Religion might be set down, and caus'd them to be read to his Nobility with much approbation. And as the year before he had sought in marriage the Lady *Mary Hastings,* which took not effect, the Lady and her Friends excusing it, he now again renu'd the motion to take to wife some one of the Queen's Kinswomen either by sending an Embassage, or going himself with his Treasure into *England.* Now happy was that Nobleman whom Sir *Jerom Bowes* in pub- [96] lick favour'd; unhappy they who had oppos'd him: for the Emperour had beaten *Shalkan* the Chancelour very grievously for that cause, and threatn'd not to leave one of his race alive. But the Emperour dying soon after of a Surfeit,

Shalkan to whom then almost the whole Government was committed, caus'd the Ambassadour to remain close Prisoner in his House nine weeks. Being sent for at length to have his dispatch, and slightly enough conducted to the Council Chamber, he was told by *Shalkan* that this Emperour would condescend to no other agreements than were between his Father and the Queen before his coming: and so disarming both him and his Company, brought them to the Emperour with many affronts in their passage, for which there was no help but patience. The [97] Emperour saying but over what the Chancelour had said before, offer'd him a Letter for the Queen: which the Ambassadour, knowing it contain'd nothing to the purpose of his Embassy, refus'd, till he saw his danger grow too great; nor was he suffer'd to reply, or have his Interpreter. *Shalkan* sent him word that now the *English* Emperour was dead; and hasten'd his departure, but with so many disgraces put upon him, as made him fear some mischief in his journey to the Sea; having onely one mean Gentleman sent with him to be his Convoy; he commanded the *English* Merchants in the Queen's name to accompany him, but such was his danger, that they durst not. So arming himself and his Followers in the best wise he could, against any outrage, he at length recover'd the Shoar of [98] Saint *Nicholas*. Where he now resolv'd to send them back by his Conduct some of the affronts which he had receiv'd. Ready therefore to take Ship, he causes three or four of his valiantest and discreetest men to take the Emperour's Letter, and disgracefull Present, and to deliver it, or leave it at the Lodging of his Convoy, which they safely did; though follow'd with a great Tumult of such as would have forc'd them to take it back.

1584. At the Coronation of *Pheodor* the Emperour, *Jerom Horsey* being then Agent in *Russia,* and call'd for to court with one *John de Wale* a Merchant of the *Netherlands* and a Subject of *Spain,* some of the Nobles would have preferr'd the *Fleming* before the *English*.[23] But to that our Agent would in no case agree, saying he would rather have his Leggs cut off by [99] the Knees, then bring his present in course after a Subject of *Spain*. The Emperour and Prince *Boris* perceiving the controversy, gave order to admit *Horsey* first: who was dismiss'd with large Promises, and seventy Messes with three Carts of several Meath sent after him.

1588. Dr. *Giles Fletcher* went Ambassadour from the Queen to *Pheodor* then Emperour; whose Relations being judicious and ex-

---

[23] Hakluyt, I, 468–69 (following Horsey's account of the coronation). At the end of the passage, Milton has put "Meath" (mead) for Horsey's "drinks."

act, are best red entirely by [24]themselves. This Emperour upon report of the great learning of *John Dee* the Mathematician invited him to *Mosco* with offer of two thousand pound a year, and from Prince *Boris* one thousand Marks; to have his Provision from the Emperour's Table, to be honourably receiv'd, and accounted as one of the chief men in the Land. All which *Dee* accepted not.[25] [100]

1604. Sir *Thomas Smith* was sent Ambassadour from King *James* to *Boris* then Emperour;[26] and staid some daies at a place five miles from *Mosco* till he was honourably receiv'd into the City; met on horseback by many thousands of Gentlemen and Nobles on both sides the way; where the Ambassadour alighting from his Coach and mounted on his Horse, rode with his Trumpets sounding before him; till a Gentleman of the Emperour's Stable brought him a Gennet gorgeously trapt with gold, pearl and stone, especially with a great Chain of plated gold about his Neck, and Horses richly adorn'd for his Followers. Then came three great Noblemen with an Interpreter offring a Speech; but the Ambassadour deeming it to be ceremony, with a brief Complement found means to put it [101] by. Thus alighting all, they saluted, and gave hands mutually. Those three after a tedious preamble of the Emperour's Title thrice repeated brought a several Complement of three words apiece, as namely, the first, to know how the King did, the next, how the Ambassadour, the third, that there was a fair House provided him. Then on they went on either hand of the Ambassadour, and about six thousand Gallants behind them; still met within the City by more of greater quality to the very Gate of his lodging: where fifty Gunners were his daily Guard both at home and abroad. The Prestaves or Gentlemen assign'd to have the care of his entertainment, were earnest to have had the Ambassadour's Speech and Message given them in writing, that the Interpreter,

[24] (M) 508.] Giles Fletcher's relation begins at Hakluyt, I, 473. This gives first a summary of the privileges obtained by him from the emperor for the English, and Hakluyt adds most of Fletcher's book, *Of the Russe Common Wealth* (1591). This had been suppressed on the complaint of the English merchants that its critical view of Russia made their position there more difficult. Purchas reprinted most of the book, and a complete new edition was published separately in 1643.

[25] Hakluyt, I, 508 (a letter to John Dee, 1586, conveying the emperor's offer). Note that Milton has changed the "thousand rubbles" of the offer to "one thousand marks," which seems to have been the equivalent in Hakluyt's time at least; see T. S. Willan, *The Early History of the Russia Company, 1553–1603* (Manchester: Manchester University Press, 1956), p. 96, n.3.

[26] Purchas, III, 747–49 (mission of Sir Thomas Smith, 1604). The report is condensed to include the ceremony and the decorations.

as they pretended, might the [102] better translate it; but he admonish'd them of their foolish demand. On the day of his audience other Gennets were sent him and his Attendants to ride on, and two white Palfreys to draw a rich Chariot, which was parcel of the Present; the rest whereof was carried by his Followers through a lane of the Emperour's Guard; many Messengers posting up and down the while, till they came through the great Castle, to the uttermost Court gate. There met by a great Duke they were brought up stairs through a Stone-gallery, where stood on each hand many in fair Coats of *Persian* Stuff, Velvet and Damask. The Ambassadour by two other Counselors being led into the presence, after his obeysance done, was to stay and hear again the long Title repeated; then the particular Presents; and so deli- [103] ver'd as much of his Embassage as was then requisite. After which the Emperour arising from his Throne demanded of the King's health; so did the young Prince. The Ambassadour then deliver'd his Letters into the Emperour's own hand, though the Chancelour offer'd to have taken them. He bore the Majesty of a mighty Emperour; his Crown and Sceptre of pure gold, a Collar of Pearls about his Neck, his Garment of crimson Velvet embroider'd with precious stone and gold. On his right Side stood a fair Globe of beaten gold on a Pyramis with a Cross upon it; to which, before he spake, turning a little he crost himself. Not much less in splendour on another Throne sate the Prince. By the Emperour stood two Noblemen in Cloth of silver, high Caps of black Furr, and Chains [104] of gold hanging to their Feet; on their Shoulders two Poleaxes of gold; and two of silver by the Prince; the ground was all cover'd with Arras or Tapistry. Dismist, and brought in again to dinner they saw the Emperour and his Son seated in state, ready to dine; each with a Skull of Pearl on their bare Heads, their Vestments chang'd. In the midst of this Hall seem'd to stand a Pillar heap'd round to a great height with massy Plate curiously wrought with Beasts, Fishes and Fowl. The Emperour's Table was serv'd with two hundred Noblemen in Coats of gold; the Princes Table with young Dukes of *Casan, Astracan, Siberia, Tartaria* and *Circassia*. The Emperour sent from his Table to the Ambassadour, thirty Dishes of Meat, to each a Loaf of extraordinary fine Bread. Then follow'd a number more of strange [105] and rare Dishes pil'd up by half dozens, with boyl'd, roast and bak't, most part of them besawc't with Garlick and Onions. In midst of dinner calling the Ambassadour up to him he drank the King's health, who receiving it from his hand, return'd to his place, and in the same Cup being of fair Chrystal pledg'd it with all his Company. After dinner they were call'd up to drink of excellent and strong Meath from the Emperour's hand; of which when many did but sip, he urg'd it not; saying he was best pleas'd with what was most for their health. Yet after that, the same day he sent a great and glorious Duke, one of them that held the golden Poleax, with his Retinue, and sundry sorts of Meath to drink merrily with the Ambassadour, which some of the *English* did, untill the Duke and his Followers [106] light-headed, but well rewarded with thirty yards of Cloth of gold, and two standing Cups, departed. At second audience the Ambassadour had like reception as before: and being dismiss'd had dinner sent after him with three hundred several Dishes of Fish, it being Lent, of such strangeness, greatness and goodness as scarce would be credible to report.[27] The Ambassadour departing was brought a mile out of the City with like honour as he was first met; where lighting from the Emperour's Sled, he took him to his Coach, made fast upon a Sled; the rest to their Sleds an easy and pleasant passage.[28] [107]

Names of the Authours from whence these Relations have been taken; being all either Eye-witnesses, or immediate Relaters from such as were.

THE Journal of Sir Hugh Willowby.[29]
Discourse of Richard Chancelor.[30]
Another of Clement Adams *taken from the mouth of* Chancelor.[31]
Notes of Richard Johnson, *Servant to* Chancelor.[32]
The Protonotaries *Register.*[33]
Two Letters of Mr. Hen. Lane.[34]
The several Voiages of Jenkinson.[35]

[27] Purchas, III, 750–51 (the same, one sentence from the page).

[28] Purchas, III, 751 (one sentence out of a paragraph).

[29] The first eleven of these "Authours" are taken from Richard Hakluyt, ed., *The Principal Navigations,* vol. I, 1598. This Willoughby journal is I, 232–37, voyage of 1553.

[30] Hakluyt, I, 237–42 (voyage of 1553).

[31] Hakluyt, I, 243–55 (the same voyage; Hakluyt's first edition, 1589, gives the original Latin).

[32] Hakluyt, I, 283–85 (notes on the Samoeds, etc., from the voyage of 1556; Johnson's notes on Turkestan, etc., 1559, I, 335–37, were not used by Milton).

[33] Hakluyt, I, 285–90 (official account of the voyage and reception in England of the first Russian ambassador, Osep Napea, 1556).

[34] Hakluyt, I, 309 (on "the maner of Justice by lots in Russia," 1560), and I, 464–66 (c.1584, summarizing the Russia voyages from 1553).

[35] Jenkinson to Russia, 1557 (Hakluyt, I, 310–14, together with another anonymous account, I, 314–23); from Moscow to Bokhara, 1558 (I, 324–35); to Moscow and Persia, 1561–64 (I, 343–52, not used by Milton); to Russia, 1566–67 (I, 372–74); to Russia, 1571–72 (I, 402–11).

Southam *and* Sparks.[36]
The Journal of Randolf *the Embass.*[37] [108]
Another of Sir Jerom Bowes.[38]
The Coronation of Pheodor *written by* Jerom Horsey.[39]
Gourdon *of* Hull's *Voiage to* Pechora.[40]
The Voiage of William Pursglove, *to* Pechora.[41]
Of Josias Logan.
Hessel Gerardus, *out of* Purchas, *part 3, l. 3.*[42]
Russian *Relations in* Purch. 797. ibid. 806. ibid.[43]
The Embassage of Sir Thomas Smith.[44]
Papers of Mr. Hackluit.[45]
Jansonius.[46]

The End.   [109]

[36] Hakluyt, I, 365–69 (an inland voyage from Archangel to Novgorod, 1566).

[37] Hakluyt, I, 376–78 (1568).

[38] Hakluyt, I, 458–64 (1583).

[39] Hakluyt, I, 466–70 (1584).

[40] Purchas (1625), III, 530–34 (voyage of William Gourdon, 1611; followed by the report of Richard Finch, merchant on the same voyage to Pechora, III, 534–38, with accompanying information on northeastern Russia, III, 538–40).

[41] Purchas prints Josias Logan first, III, 541–47; then William Pursglove, III, 547–51, with further information, III, 551–52: both dealing with their winter trading in northeast Russia, 1611–15. Milton also drew upon a later narrative of William Gourdon in the same area, III, 553–56.

[42] Hessel Gerardus (for Hessel Gerritz) was the publisher of the two narratives of the Russian itineraries to and in Siberia that were translated from Russian by Isaac Massa of Haerlem (published Amsterdam, 1612). See chap. 2, n. 1, above.

[43] Russian *Relations* described journeys from Tobolsk to Peking, 1619 (Purchas, III, 797–802); besides a Russian report to an English merchant, Francis Cherry (1584), of a warm sea beyond the Obi River (III, 806).

[44] The mission to Moscow of 1604–5, the narrative published in London, 1605, reprinted in Purchas, III, 748–53.

[45] It has been estimated that some two-fifths of the material in *Purchas His Pilgrimes* were made up from Hakluyt's manuscripts collected for a new edition of *The Principal Navigations.* A specific reference to "Master Hackluyts Papers" is given for part of the story of Emperor Demetrius of Russia as published in Purchas (III, 764); but Purchas marked many of his items with "H" in his table of contents: for example, the Pechora narratives.

[46] Jansonius stands for *Mercurius Gallobelgicus,* 18 vols. (Cologne and Frankfurt, 1590–1630), an annual chronicle of European events, of which the first volume was edited by A. P. Jansonius (Janssen). Purchas quoted passages from vols. 9 and 10: report of the capture of Moscow by the King of Poland, 1611 (III, 789–90), and a note of the Russian embassy to the Holy Roman Empire, 1613 (III, 790–91). Milton does not seem to have looked behind Purchas to the original *Mercurius,* all his material coming from either Hakluyt or Purchas.

Milton might have added to his sources the *Historia sui temporis* of Thuanus (Jacques de Thou), from which Purchas quotes in his account of the civil wars to 1607 (III, 744–46, 769–70). It is true that Thuanus was not here an eyewitness, but neither was Jansonius.

MILTON'S OUTLINES FOR TRAGEDIES

(1639?–1642?)

Preface and Notes by John M. Steadman

I. THE JOTTINGS

Milton's dramatic notes occupy pages 35–41 in the Trinity College, Cambridge, manuscript.[1] These "seven pages of Jottings," as Masson termed them, are usually assigned to the early 1640s, primarily on the evidence of handwriting and secondarily on the more tenuous basis of theme and dramaturgy.[2]

On the first page of the notes (p. 35) Milton wrote three drafts of a drama on the fall—the first two subsequently cancelled—and entered three additional titles based on Genesis. In the upper left-hand column of the second page (p. 36) he listed the personæ for a tragedy on Dinah. In the right-hand column of this same page he added a catalogue of Old Testament subjects beginning with an episode from Exodus and following the order of Scripture. After filling this column, he continued the catalogue in the vacant portion of the left-hand column, under the earlier entry on "Thamar Πεπλοφόρος." After two pages of British subjects (pp. 37–38) he filled the next two pages (pp. 39–40) with detailed outlines for dramas on Abraham, Baptistes, Sodom, and "Adam unparadized." On the last page (p. 41), after five subjects on Scottish history, he inserted sketches for two other biblical dramas: "Moabitides" and "Christus patiens."

Covering over one hundred subjects drawn from sacred and national history, the notes fall into three distinct categories: biblical, British (including Anglo-Saxon and Danish as well as Romano-Celtic themes), and Scottish. Milton himself supplied the general headings for the "British" and "Scotch" sections as well as the serial numbers for the British entries. The majority of the subjects (approximately sixty-four) belong to biblical history, ranging from Adam's fall to Christ's resurrection. Most of these have been derived from the Old Testament—chiefly from Genesis, Numbers,

Judges, 1 and 2 Samuel, and 1 and 2 Kings. A few include arguments based on other books: Exodus, Joshua, Ruth, 2 Chronicles, Jeremiah, and Daniel. Only eight entries concern the New Testament: a drama on the execution of John the Baptist, another on the massacre of the innocents, and six episodes from the life of Christ. The national subjects constitute slightly over a third of the total: upward of thirty-three British and five Scottish entries. The earliest biblical entries usually follow the order observed in Hebrew and Protestant editions of the Old Testament, but the national subjects are not in a strictly chronological sequence.

The exact number of entries and their precise order and relative dates remain indefinite. Besides cancellations and repetitions, the manuscript contains insertions indicating additional subjects and/or alternative titles. The latter are not always distinguishable, and in several instances the inserted title may indicate a shift of emphasis to a different aspect of the same story or else a different, though related, episode. The entries on Samson, for example, may refer to merely two subjects, but they may conceivably denote three, four, or even five.[3]

Although the original order of the three groups—biblical, British, and Scottish—is not altogether clear, the chronological order within these groups is less ambiguous. Cancellations within a particular entry or cancellations of entire plans, such as the first two drafts for a drama on the fall of man, may sometimes serve as a guide to the order of entry of the notes themselves. Sometimes, as in the notes on the deluge,[4] Milton repeats an earlier entry with minor differences later in the list. In other cases (such as the entries on "Sodom," "Moabitides," and "Hezechias πολιορκούμενος"),[5] he merely jots down a title but later in the manuscript elaborates the subject in greater detail. Occasionally he adds cross-references to earlier and later notes on the same theme. After the initial entry on Hezekiah he inserts the word "infra" to connect it with the subsequent and fuller version of his plan.[6] Conversely, in the fourth sketch for a drama on the fall he calls for a comparison with the "former draught."[7] Milton's catalogue of British subjects likewise shows evidence of later revisions. An entry on the Roman conquest of Britain, inserted among events that occurred some four hundred years later, represents a later addition on an altogether different subject.[8] To initial entries on the later British kings Vortiger and Vortimer, the poet has inserted further notes on Vortiger's reign.[9]

As the manuscript indicates, Milton composed his notes for personal use, not for the edification of posterity. Additional subjects are not always distinguishable from variant titles. Numerous emendations and insertions sometimes disrupt the order and syntax of earlier entries, so that syntactical relationships between inserted passages and original entries are frequently ambiguous. Thus, in arranging these "jottings" for publication and in attempting to render them intelligible to modern readers, an editor may be seeking a degree of precision that Milton himself never anticipated and imposing upon them an artificial coherence alien to Milton's changing and incomplete designs.

II. SOURCES

Though Milton's primary source for the scriptural entries was the Bible itself, in two instances he refers to secondary works: for the tragedy of Dinah he cites Eusebius Pamphili, *Evangelicæ Præparationis Lib. XV;* [10] and for the tragedy of Ahab, Lavater's commentary on Chronicles.[11] The "Scotch stories" (as Masson correctly determined by the page numbers) [12] were based on "the English adaptation of Bellenden's translation of the *Scotorum Historiæ* of Hector Boethius, printed with Holinshed's *Chronicles.*"

The British subjects, on the other hand, present problems. For some of these Milton mentioned several authorities, and for others he offered a single reference. For the majority, however, he specified no sources at all. The proper names of the protagonists in his list, moreover, often differ widely in form from the names in his acknowledged sources. In several instances they show a closer resemblance to Stow (whom Milton cites only once) than to Speed or Holinshed, to whom he indicates greater specific indebtedness. Page numbers indicate that Milton read John Speed's *Historie of Great Britaine* in either the 1623 or the 1627 edition, and Raphael Holinshed's *Chronicles of England, Scotland, and Ireland* in the three-volume London edition of 1587. From the *Commonplace Book* and the *History of Britain,* we learn that Milton read John Stow's *Annales; or, a Generall Chronicle of England* in either the 1615 or the 1631 edition; for Bede and Geoffrey of Monmouth, he depended on Jerome Commelin's collection *Rerum Britannicarum* (Heidelberg, 1587); and for William of Malmesbury, he used another collection, Sir Henry Savile's *Rerum Anglicarum Scriptores post Bedam* (Frankfurt, 1601).[13]

III. IMPORTANCE

The majority of Milton's jottings are essentially notes rather than a program or plans. Most of the biblical entries are merely titles, generally accompanied with brief allusions to book and chapter. The poet's search for effective titles is apparent not only in his frequent insertion of variant and alternative titles under the same entry but also in his experiments with Greek and Latin epithets and with the noun-adjective formula conventional in the titles of classical and neoclassical tragedy. Such jaw-breaking combinations as "Salomon Gynæcocratumenus" (#[35]), "Elisæus Adoradocétos" (#[43]), "Achabæi Cunoboroomeni" (#[46]), and "Amaziah Doryalotus" (#[49]) may seem awkward and affected—a pedantic exaggeration of the conventions of humanist drama. Nevertheless, they embody many of the religious and æsthetic principles underlying Milton's later poetry. In their painstaking adaptation of Hebraic content to Hellenic form, they reflect a preoccupation of the Christian Renaissance that will be apparent elsewhere in Milton's work—evident not only in the classical structure of his more detailed dramatic sketches but also in the epics and drama of his major phase. In this immature list of titles—scriptural in matter and classical in style—Milton is foreshadowing the concerns of his maturity. He is testing his wings as a divine poet, though his plumage is still ungainly and unsightly.

In contrast to the biblical entries, the British and Scottish notes indicate subjects rather than titles. For the most part, they indicate the principal action and its protagonists. They range in complexity and detail from entries like "Sigher of the east saxons revolted from the faith and reclaim'd by Jarumang" (#4) or "Sebert slaine by Penda after he had left his kingdom" (#6) to the fuller notes on Godwin's revolt (#3) or the murder of Natholocus (#[1]). A few of them indicate thematic emphasis, such as Edward the Confessor's "slacknesse to redresse the corrupt clergie" and his "superstitious prætence of chastitie" (#33). Though these entries on secular history are fuller and more explicit than the majority of notes on scriptural subjects, none of them is as fully developed as the more detailed biblical plans.

Despite their brevity, his notes on the story of Thamar and Judah (#[10]), the sons of Eli (#[25]), Rehoboam (#[36]), Ahab's family (#[40]), Hezekiah (#[50]), Zedekiah (#[52]), Asa (#[54]), and Christ's agony in the garden of Gethsemane (#[67]) indicate the kind of dramatic or thematic emphasis he intended to give them. Other subjects he developed in greater detail. The entry on Dinah (#[9]) contained a list of dramatis personæ, including messenger and chorus. The entry on Abijah, the son of Jeroboam (#[37]), offered detailed suggestions for plot structure and the role of the chorus. The sketch for a drama on Phineas (#[122]) provided clear indications of plot structure and theme. The fullest dramatic sketches, however, were the drafts for tragedies on the sacrifice of Isaac (#[56]), the execution of John the Baptist (#[57]), the destruction of Sodom (#[58]), and the fall of man: "Paradise Lost" (#[3]) and "Adam unparadiz'd" (#[9]). In these the "economy" [14] or disposition of the plot has been developed in detail and the scene clearly indicated. Some of these sketches included suggestions for the prologue, and most of them contained notes on the chorus and on major and minor characters.

A decided preference for "divine" arguments as against national themes is apparent, then, not only in the numerical preponderance of biblical entries but (more significantly) in Milton's choice of subjects for further dramatic and thematic development. All of the more detailed plans concern biblical—and chiefly Old Testament— subjects. In this respect the differences between the sacred and secular lists are impressive. Except for minor insertions among the "British Tragedies," the secular list remains static while the sacred becomes increasingly selective. The first two drafts for a drama on the fall (#[1–2]) are canceled in favor of a third (#[3]); and a fourth (but not final) draft (#[65]) is added as an alternative. The scriptural list undergoes a continuous process of growth and development, selection and elaboration. [15]

With their predilection for sacred subjects, these dramatic notes pointed the direction that Milton's future literary enterprises would take. His concern with political and ecclesiastical issues, evident in both scriptural and national lists, would find its principal outlet in his prose treatises but would also characterize his historical and epic compositions. Some of the material for "British Tragedies" would be utilized in his *History of Britain.* His poetic development would continue along the lines foreshadowed by the biblical plans. Though none of the fuller dramatic plans would be followed in detail and most would lie idle, two subjects continued to interest him and would eventually bear fruit: The theme of the fall would find expression in narrative rather than dramatic form; and the seed of his only tragedy is to be found in one of the briefest entries in the scriptural list—"Dagonalia"—where the manuscript gives no indication that Milton appreciated its dramatic possibilities.

The dramatic notes suggest, however, a concept of tragedy considerably broader than the ordeal of heroic suffering central to *Samson Agonistes.* Though a drama on "Christ born" (#[59]) might possess elevation and gravity ("high seriousness") and tragic implications for the future, the tragic events themselves would appear to lie outside the scope of the fable. Though such stories as Tamar's pregnancy (#[10]), Abraham's sacrifice (#[56]), the ordeal of the Three Children (#[55]), and the resurrections of Lazarus (#[64]) and Christ (#[63]) portray suffering or death, all of them end happily; a tragedy on any of these themes would be a *tragedia di lieto fin.*[16] Tragedies on other subjects—the deluge (#[7]), Sodom (#[58]), "Gideon persuing" (#[19]), "Samson in Ramath Lechi" (#[21]), "Elisæus Hydrochóos" (#[42]), "Samaria Liberata" (#[45])—would have double endings for the just and the unjust, fortunate for the one but disastrous for the other.[17] In "Moabitides or Phineas" (#[66]), the tragic event lies outside the fable; it has occurred *before* the dramatic action. The object of the dramatist's imitation would appear to be not so much the tragic deed itself as its justification. Of the tragic stories that do conclude in death, several portray the downfall of the wicked—"Ahab" (#[40]), "Athaliah" (#[48]), "Achabæi Cunoboroomeni" (#[46]); while others—"Abias Thersæus" (#[37]), "Baptistes" (#[57]), the dramas of the passion of Christ (#[61, 62, 67])—center on the suffering of the just.

In making his initial entries—and especially in selecting a relatively small group for detailed elaboration—Milton must have been influenced by considerations of dramatic form as well as thematic content, by ideas of plot construction and tragic effect as well as by moral or political principles. Within a few years he would acknowledge the "laws" of drama and the importance of decorum in character and action. He would assert the "doctrinal and exemplary" value of "Dramatic constitutions . . . to a Nation." He would praise the poet's ability to portray "whatsoever hath passion or admiration in all the changes of that which is call'd fortune from without, or the wily suttleties and refluxes of mans thoughts from within." He would affirm the poet's mission to depict "what [God] works, and what he suffers to be wrought with high Providence in his Church," to describe "the victorious agonies of Martyrs and Saints" and "the deeds and triumphs of just and pious Nations doing valiantly through faith against the enemies of Christ," and to "deplore the general relapses of Kingdoms and States from justice and Gods true worship."[18] Most of these themes are implicit in Milton's biblical and British subjects, and in these dramatic notes several scholars have detected the same dedication to the moral and political functions of poetry that pervades *The Reason of Church-Government, Of Education,* and Milton's later prose.

Lack of a precise date for his dramatic entries leaves many of Milton's aesthetic beliefs also in doubt. We cannot assume that he had already formulated the views expressed in *The Reason of Church Government* or that he had already consulted the authorities on poetics mentioned in *Of Education*. On the other hand, we have no positive evidence to the contrary, and it is possible that some of the later plans may have been written *after* these prose treatises. On the whole, it seems not unlikely that in these jottings Milton was looking not only for dramatic subjects relevant to the political issues of the time (tyranny, civil war, reformation, prelatical and petticoat rule) or to more abiding moral values (chastity, patience, and faith) but—more specifically—for events capable of arousing the tragic emotions of "passion and admiration." The more detailed plans and many of the briefer entries do, in fact, contain *peripeteias* ("the changes of that which is call'd fortune from without") or instances of passionate inner debate ("the wily suttleties and refluxes of man's thoughts from within"). As Aristotle and Tasso had advised him, Milton seems to have selected his subjects with an eye to their affective potentialities (their ability to evoke pity, terror, or wonder) [19] and to the requirements of plot structure.

Milton's concern for plot structure is apparent in many of the detailed plans, and an examination of these may help to correct some of the critical misconceptions that have developed concerning his later poetry. In the first place, he exercises considerable liberty in reshaping his biblical materials to meet the requirements of dramatic form—inventing characters and episodes in the interests of structure, verisimilitude, and probability. Though he has been censured for observing a similar freedom in *Paradise Lost,* such license was inherent in Renaissance conceptions of poetic imitation; for many English and Italian critics, mimesis entailed the invention of fictions, probable circumstances, and other elements essential for a well-constructed plot.

In the second place, Milton reveals a marked concern for the "middle" of his plot. In two of the detailed plans—"Abias Thersæus" (#[37]) and "Moabitides or Phineas" (#[66])—he takes pains to describe the "Epitasis." [20] This was a term common in Terentian criticism, and Milton had probably encountered it during his schooldays at Saint Paul's. Traditionally applied to the structure of comedy but subsequently transferred to the analysis of tragedy, it denoted the middle portion of a drama, between the protasis and the catastrophe. It usually embraced the third and fourth acts but sometimes embraced the second act also and extended well into the fifth act. [21]

In both of these plans the epitasis is the poet's own invention;

it does not occur in his biblical source. In both instances, moreover, it presents an obstacle to the execution of the principal action and the final resolution of the plot. In the draft of "Adam unparadiz'd" (#[65]) it is apparent (though Milton does not employ the term here) in Adam's stubborn refusal to repent.

Neoclassical principles are not only evident in Milton's epitasis and his fidelity to the unities of time, place, and action. They are also apparent in his references to the functions of messengers, prologues, and chorus, in the Senecan roles of the ghosts of Philip ([#57]), Prince Alfred (#28), and King Duncan (#[5]), and in other reminiscences of dramatic situations in Greek or Latin tragedies. The queen's attempt to thwart Ahijah's (or Ahias's) (#[37]) prophecy concerning the death of her son parallels Jocasta's contempt for the oracle and Oedipus's scorn for the predictions of Tiresias. Milton's first Scottish entry similarly portrays the execution of a prophecy in spite of the disbelief and contumely with which it had first been received. The plot of *Samson Agonistes* likewise hinges on the fulfillment of a "divine prediction" that had hitherto seemed subject to doubt.[22]

Reversals contrary to expectation characterize the plots of "Baptistes" (#[57]) and "Abram from Morea" (#[56]). The king has intended to set the prophet at liberty but instead puts him to the sword; John's disciples, who have come to congratulate him on his release, remain to lament his death. In "Abram from Morea" the tragic event is averted by a *deus ex machina*—the intervention of an angel. In "Thamar Cúephorusa" (#[10]) another tragic event between members of the same family is prevented by a timely discovery (*anagnorisis*).[23] Sentenced to death by her father-in-law, Tamar produces the pledge that he had previously given her: "By the man, whose these are, I am with child. . . . And Judah acknowledged them, and said, She hath been more righteous than I." In this episode the *peripeteia* results directly from the discovery; a drama on this subject would therefore have a "complex" plot. In making this entry, Milton was probably impressed by the opportunities it might provide for a recognition scene in the classical manner.

The influence of postclassical dramatists is more difficult to trace. Though the entries reveal a general affinity with the divine and national dramas of the period,[24] there is little evidence of indebtedness to particular works. Milton had probably read humanistic dramas on biblical themes, some of them paralleling subjects on his own list. Buchanan had written a *Baptistes,* Beza had composed a drama on Abraham's sacrifice, a number of dramatists had

treated the theme of Adam's fall, and a *Christus Patiens* had been
attributed (dubiously, perhaps) to Saint Gregory Nazianzen.[25]
These did not deter him from considering the same subjects. One
wonders, nevertheless, whether the omission of other themes—the
career of Joseph, the passage through the Red Sea, Jephthah, Es-
ther, Judith, David and Goliath, the fate of Absalom—may not
have been conditioned by his awareness of their popularity with
earlier epic or dramatic poets.[26]

Several of the themes for "British Tragedies" significantly parallel entries that Milton made in his *Commonplace Book* [27] shortly
after his return from Italy. In both sets of notes, scholars have
been tempted to see Milton's personal response to the political
issues of the time.[28] In the Ceaulin entry (#15), Masson perceived
an oblique attack on the Bishops' Wars. The note for a drama on
Edward the Confessor (#33) stresses the danger of favoritism toward foreigners, shows sympathy to Godwin's rebellion, and
praises arbitration in civil conflicts as the better alternative to
violence. The entries on Vortiger (#2) and Ahab (#[46]) portray
the perils of royal marriages with women of alien nationality and
idolatrous religion. Both of these entries also depict rebellion
against tyranny and the tyrant's violent death. The entry on Hardicanute (#32) ascribes the king's sudden death to gourmandizing,
but in all probability a drama on this episode would also have
raised the issue of ship-money. In several entries stressing the power
exerted by Archbishop Dunstan and other prelates in the affairs
of state (#2, 12, 13, 16, 19, 33), Milton may have intended a
parallel with Archbishop Laud. The theme of government by
women ("gynæcocracy") is inherent in the note on Athaliah (#[48]).
The allied theme of royal subjection to a beautiful idolatress is
explicit in the very title "Salomon Gynæcocratumenus" (#[35]) and
implicit in several dramas on British history. Many of the same
themes would recur in the antiprelatical and antiroyalist tracts, in
the *Commonplace Book,* and in the *History of Britain.* They were
not, however, limited to a particular historical context. For the
most part, they represented abiding concerns in Milton's life and
thought. Along with other motifs inherent in the dramatic plans—
the opposition between chastity and lust, the conflict between true
religion and idolatry, the heroic pursuit of liberty, the trial of
patience and faith—they dominate his apprentice works as well as
his final masterpieces, in poetry as in prose.

The salient features of the dramatic notes are their historical
subject matter, their preference for "divine" over secular arguments, and their concern for specific political and ecclesiastical

themes. Equally impressive are the contrast between the titles of the biblical catalogue and the subjects of the British and Scottish lists, and the striking variations among the biblical entries in degree of elaboration and detail.[29]

Confused, ambiguous, tantalizing—these notes are no *lumen siccum,* no dry light. At best they are a sort of dark lantern. They suggest—rather than clearly illuminate—the full range of the poet's dramatic ambitions, the developing shape of his poetic theory, and his maturing designs for a drama on Adam's expulsion from the earthly paradise.

IV. TEXT AND FOOTNOTES

To present in a printed text exactly what Milton jotted down on pages 35–41 of the Trinity College manuscript is an elusive ideal rather than a realizable achievement. Like all sublunary things, Milton's notes have not escaped corruption. For more than three centuries the outer edges of the manuscript leaves have been crumbling away, obliterating significant letters, crucial words, and entire phrases. Comparison of the eighteenth-century editions of Birch and Peck, the nineteenth-century facsimiles of Sotheby and Wright, and the 1970 Scolar Press photographs provides as compelling an emblem of the ravages of time as the poetic allegories of Chaucer and Ariosto. Passages legible to early editors have become indecipherable; [30] Sotheby's tracings preserve readings no longer apparent in Wright's collotypes; and Wright preserves readings no longer present in the Scolar Press photographs. And within what has been preserved are further uncertainties in minor details. In capitalization, Milton's practice is inconsistent. The same letter, especially in the case of *l*'s and *c*'s and *s*'s, can be (and often has been) read by different editors either as capital or as lower case. In other instances, the identity of certain letters is subject to doubt.

My text I base primarily on Wright, the first reliable reproduction, since Sotheby's plates are tracings. Where Wright and Sotheby are not legible, the transcripts of earlier editors (Birch, Peck, Todd, and Masson) have been indispensable; and frequently useful in minutiae have been the twentieth-century editors (Hanford, Columbia, and Fletcher). Expanded abbreviations I have indicated by italics. For ease in determining the manuscript page, I have placed the numbers (in square brackets and black face type) at the head rather than at the foot of the page. Revisions, deletions, and other textual changes, as well as debatable readings, I describe and discuss in footnotes.

For most of the biblical subjects Milton himself specified his sources. Where he failed to do so, I have cited book and chapter in my footnotes to the text. In cases where Milton's titles echo biblical phraseology (such as "Gideon persuing" and "Thamar Cüephorusa"), I have quoted relevant titles in a 1612 edition of the Authorized Version: *The Holy Bible, Conteyning the Old Testament and the New* (London, 1612; HLH #32190), the edition that Milton owned. In glossing Greek and Latin terms, I have cited standard Renaissance lexicons as well as two modern reference works: Henricus Stephanus, *Thesaurus Græcæ Linguæ* (Geneva, 1572); Robertus Stephanus, *Thesaurus Linguæ Latinæ* (Basileæ, 1576–78); [31] Henry George Liddell and Robert Scott, *A Greek-English Lexicon*, rev. Henry Stuart Jones (Oxford, 1925); and *Harper's Latin Dictionary*, rev. C. T. Lewis and C. Short (New York, 1907).

In annotating the British and Scottish notes, I have quoted or summarized relevant passages in Milton's acknowledged sources and (since he may well have had more than one account in mind) in other histories cited in his list. For entries without a specific source-reference, I have quoted the closest accounts that I could find—usually from Speed or Holinshed and occasionally from Stow. Though I have noted some matters in Milton's *History of Britain,* I have kept quotations from this work to a minimum, trusting that the interested reader will consult the annotated edition edited by Professor French Fogle in *Complete Prose,* V. In my annotations I have used the following editions: Bede, *Historia Ecclesiastica,* and Geoffrey of Monmouth, *Historia Regum Britanniæ,* in *Rerum Britannicarum . . . Scriptores,* ed. Hieronymus Commelinus (Heidelberg, 1587); William of Malmesbury, *De Gestis Regum Anglorum,* in *Rerum Anglicarum Scriptores,* ed. Henricus Savile (Francofurti, 1601); Raphael Holinshed, *Chronicles of England, Scotland, and Ireland* (London, 1587); John Speed, *The Historie of Great Britaine,* 2nd ed. (London, 1623); and John Stow, *Annales; or, a Generall Chronicle of England* (London, 1631).

---

[1] For the provenance and structure of this manuscript, see the introductions to the Wright and Scolar Press facsimiles listed just below, and Maurice Kelley, "Milton's Later Sonnets and the Cambridge Manuscript," *MP,* LIV (1956–57), 20–25, and "Daniel Skinner and Milton's Trinity College Manuscript," *N&Q,* 222 (1977), 206–7.

For facsimiles, see Samuel Leigh Sotheby, *Ramblings in the Elucidation of the Autograph of Milton* (London, 1861), pp. 67–87, plates IV–IX from tracings by G. I. F. Tupper; William Aldis Wright, *Facsimile of the Manuscript of Milton's Minor Poems* (Cambridge, 1899), pp. 33–39, collotype facsimile and transcript; Harris F. Fletcher, *John Milton's Complete Poetical Works Reproduced in Pho-*

tographic Facsimile, 4 vols. (Urbana: University of Illinois Press, 1943–48), II, 12–29, facsimiles made from Wright with the transcript making use of Peck, Sotheby, and Wright; and *John Milton: Poems Reproduced in Facsimile from the Manuscript in Trinity College, Cambridge, with a Transcript* (Menston, Yorkshire: Scolar Press, 1970), pp. 33–39, facsimiles from photographs made in 1970. The deterioration of the manuscript is evidenced by page numbers 35, 36, 38, which are present in Sotheby but missing in Wright, and by "Abias Thersæus" and "Hesechia beseig'd" (p. 36), which are present in Wright but appear with several letters missing in Scolar. Scolar reprints the Wright transcript but adds several marginal emendations.

Publication of the plans began with Thomas Birch, "An Historical and Critical Account of the Life and Writings of Mr. John Milton," in *A Complete Collection of the Historical, Political, and Miscellaneous Works of John Milton,* 2 vols. (London, 1738), I, xxxix–xlv, and Francis Peck, *New Memoirs of the Life and Poetical Works of Mr. John Milton* (London, 1740), pp. 37–51, 88–97, 216–18, 278–79. The plans have since been reedited by Henry John Todd, *The Poetical Works of John Milton,* 6 vols. (London, 1801), I, 248–303, III, 489–94, IV, 501–11; by David Masson, *The Life of John Milton,* 7 vols. (London and New York, 1875–94), II, 104–21; and by Thomas Ollive Mabbott and J. Milton French, *The Uncollected Writings of John Milton,* in *The Works of John Milton,* 18 vols. (New York: Columbia University Press, 1931–38), XVIII, 228–45, 501–11.

[2] In Masson's opinion (*Life,* II, 120–21), Milton's consistent use of the Italian form of the letter *e* pointed to a date after the Italian journey; and though Helen Darbishire ("The Chronology of Milton's Handwriting," *Library,* XIV [1933], 229–35) has challenged this argument, maintaining that Milton's "use of the Italian *e . . .* was a practice begun before his journey," a majority of scholars still accept Masson's *terminus a quo.* James Holly Hanford (*A Milton Handbook* [1954], pp. 181–87), for instance, assigned the entries to 1640–42; and Parker (*Milton,* p. 190) believes that the notes were "probably made within a year or so after [Milton's] return from the Continent," basing his dating (p. 843) "largely on changes in Milton's handwriting (particularly his consistent use of the italic *e* after 1638) and on his spelling practices between 1634 and *c.* 1646." For Masson's further arguments, on theme and so on, see *Life,* II, 120–21.

[3] Below, p. 556, #[21]–[22].

[4] Below, p. 555, #[4]–[6], [7].

[5] Below, p. 555, 557, #[8], [15], [50].

[6] Below, p. 557, #[50].

[7] Below, p. 560, #[65].

[8] Below, p. 569, #[1a].

[9] Below, p. 569, #[2].

[10] Below, p. 555, #[9].

[11] Below, p. 556, #[40].

[12] Masson, *Life,* II, 115, n. 1.

[13] For these identifications, see *Complete Prose,* I, 381, 369, 370–71; V, xxxiii–xxxiv, 4, 10.

[14] Milton employs the term "oiconomie" in "Abram from Morea" (#[56]). For the significance of *oeconomia* in criticism of Terence's comedies, see Marvin T. Herrick, *Comic Theory in the Sixteenth Century* (Urbana: University of Illinois Press, 1964), pp. 101–6.

[15] Between *Paradise Lost* and the drafts in the Trinity MS there must have been a fifth dramatic plan, with a different beginning. Edward Phillips remem-

bered seeing its opening lines—verses that subsequently became the first six (or ten) lines of Satan's apostrophe to the sun in *Paradise Lost*. For different views on the number of plans between the Trinity MS and the epic, see Peck, *New Memoirs*, p. 14; Grant McColley, "Milton's Lost Tragedy," *PQ*, XVIII (1939), 70–79; and John S. Diekhoff, "The Trinity Manuscript and the Dictation of *Paradise Lost*," *PQ*, XXVIII (1949), p. 47. For discussion of the correction of "Six Verses" to "Ten Verses" in Phillips's *Life of Milton*, see Parker, *Milton*, p. 857.

[16] For the *tragedia di lieto fin* in Renaissance criticism, see Marvin T. Herrick, *Tragicomedy* (Urbana: University of Illinois Press, 1962), pp. 83–124.

[17] For Aristotle's criticism of the tragedy with "an opposite catastrophe for the good and for the bad," see S. H. Butcher, *Aristotle's Theory of Poetry and Fine Art*, 4th ed. (New York: Dover Publications, 1951), p. 47.

[18] For relevant passages in *The Reason of Church-Government*, see *Complete Prose*, I, 813–20; in *Of Education*, II, 403–6.

[19] In his entry on "Christus patiens" (#[67]) Milton comments that Christ's agony might receive some "noble expressions." According to Aristotle's classification, this drama would have been, apparently, a tragedy of suffering. Milton's note suggests, moreover, that like many Renaissance critics he regarded tragedy as an imitation not only of an action but also of character and passion as well. In the Scottish stories, witchcraft serves as a source for tragic wonder and fear. More frequently, however, Milton seeks the element of admiration in the Judaeo-Christian marvelous—in divine miracles, in the fulfillment of prophecies against normal probability and human expectation, in signal instances of divine justice, in the triumph of supernal providence, and in the victory of God's uncontrollable intent.

[20] For the significance of the term "Epitasis" in commentaries on Terence and in the critical works of Jonson and Dryden, see Herrick, *Comic Theory*, pp. 106–10, 119–22, and passim.

[21] It is significant that Milton employs the idiom of Terentian commentary rather than the Aristotelian term "complication" (δέσις).

[22] See J. C. Maxwell, "Milton's Samson and Sophocles' Heracles," *PQ*, XXXIII (1954), 90–91, on the oracle motif.

[23] Aristotle advises the poet (Butcher, *Aristotle's Theory*, pp. 49–53) to look for situations where "the tragic incident occurs between those who are near and dear to one another." The best type of tragic situation is to be found "when some one is about to do an irreparable deed through ignorance, and makes the discovery before it is done."

[24] In an appendix, "Zur literarhistorischen Stellung der Dramenpläne," Walther Schork (*Die Dramenpläne Miltons* [Freiburg im Breisgau, 1934], pp. 63–92) places Milton's subjects in the context of English and Continental dramatic traditions.

[25] See Thomas Kranidas, "Milton and the Author of *Christ Suffering*," *N&Q*, n.s., XV (1968), 99.

[26] The omissions in the British list are even more striking. The Trojan immigrants and early Celtic dynasties are notably absent. There are no entries on Brutus or on Brennus and Arviragus, on Lear or Gorboduc, on Boadicea or Cymbeline. The only entry concerning the Roman conquest is the note on Venutius and Cartismandua (#[1a])—a subject that would indirectly involve Caradoc. After a silence of four centuries, the list resumes with the period immediately before the Saxon invasion and continues through the "time of troubles" under Vortiger (#3) to his death in his mountain citadel. This episode would apparently

involve Merlin as well as Uther Pendragon and thus bring Milton's catalogue to the threshold of the Arthurian period. He skips this, however, and continues with entries from English and Saxon history. Such omissions may have resulted from his awareness of earlier dramatic versions of many of these stories, his intention to treat some of the Celtic material in narrative form, and his growing recognition that much of this material lacked historical foundation.

[27] For detailed studies, see J. H. Hanford, "The Chronology of Milton's Private Studies," *PMLA*, XXXVI (1921), 251–314, or *John Milton, Poet and Humanist*, ed. John S. Diekhoff (Cleveland: Press of Western Reserve University, 1966); Ruth Mohl, *Complete Prose*, I, 344–59, and *John Milton and His "Commonplace Book"* (New York: Frederick Ungar, 1969), p. 35; Parker, *Milton*, pp. 841–42; and French Fogle, *Complete Prose*, V, xxiv n., 9 n.–10 n., 138 n., 161 n.

[28] For Schork (*Die Dramenpläne Miltons*, p. 52) the character of these dramatic plans is polemical: In them Milton sought to give artistic expression to moral and political questions. See also Mohl, *Milton and His "Commonplace Book*," pp. 57, 107–11, 164–68, 207–8, 232–34, 243, 245, 269, 278–81; for Milton's defense of the dramatic arts, see pp. 312–14.

[29] Other recent studies of the plans and their relationship to Milton's later poetry include Edith Buchanan, "The Italian Neo-Senecan Background of *Samson Agonistes*" (Ph.D. diss., Duke University, 1952); Gretchen Ludke Finney, "Chorus in *Samson Agonistes*," *PMLA*, LVIII (1943), 649–64; "*Comus, Drama per Musica*," *SP*, XXXVII (1940), 482–500; Allan H. Gilbert, *On the Composition of "Paradise Lost"* (Chapel Hill: University of North Carolina Press, 1966); James Holly Hanford, *A Milton Handbook* (New York: Appleton-Century-Crofts, 1954), pp. 181–87, 269, 416–17, and "The Dramatic Element in *Paradise Lost*," in *Milton, Poet and Humanist*, pp. 224–43; Marguerite Little, "Some Italian Elements in the Choral Practice of *Samson Agonistes*" (Ph.D. diss., University of Illinois, 1946); Christopher C. Love, "The Scriptural Latin Plans of the Renaissance and Milton's Cambridge Manuscript" (Ph.D. diss., University of Toronto, 1950); Constance Nicholas, "Milton's Medieval British Readings" (Ph.D. diss., University of Illinois, 1951); William Riley Parker, "On Milton's Early Literary Program," *MP*, XXXIII (1935), 49–53; Maria Wickert, "Miltons Entwürfe zu einem Drama vom Sündenfall," *Anglia*, LXXIII (1955), 171–206; Balachandra Rajan, *The Lofty Rhyme* (London: Routledge and Kegan Paul, 1970), pp. 62, 83, 128, 180; Thomas B. Stroup, *Religious Rite & Ceremony in Milton's Poetry* (Lexington: University of Kentucky Press, 1968), p. 17. For other earlier studies, see Thomas Newton, "The Life of Milton," in *Paradise Lost*, 2 vols. (Philadelphia, 1777), II, 419, 427, 444; John Mitford, "The Life of Milton," in *The Works of John Milton*, 3 vols. (London and Boston, 1851), I, xlviii, lv, cii; Thomas Keightley, "Introduction to *Paradise Lost*," in *An Account of the Life, Opinions, and Writings of John Milton* (London, 1855), p. 400; Samuel Johnson, *Life of Milton*, in *A Johnson Reader*, ed. E. L. McAdam, Jr., and George Milne (New York: Pantheon Books, 1964), pp. 381–84; A. W. Verity, "Introduction to *Samson Agonistes*," in *John Milton's "Samson Agonistes": The Poem and Materials for Analysis*, ed. Ralph E. Hone (San Francisco: Chandler Publishing Co., 1966), pp. 122–26.

[30] For a notable instance of this sort concerning an important, partially obliterated sentence at the bottom of a page, see below, p. 556, #[40].

[31] Milton was familiar with both of these lexicons: The Greek he used in annotating his Aratus, and he amassed notes for a Latin thesaurus "to the emendation

of that done by Stephanus." On these matters, see Maurice Kelley and Samuel D. Atkins, "Milton's Annotations of Aratus," *PMLA,* LXX (1955), 1100, and Helen Darbishire, *The Early Lives of Milton* (London, 1932), p. 29.

[PLANS FOR BIBLICAL TRAGEDIES]

[1 Untitled. Cancelled]		[2 Untitled. Cancelled]	
the Persons		the Persons	
Michael.		Moses [1]	
Heavenly Love		Justice.[2] Mercie Wisdome [3]	
Chorus of Angels		Heavenly Love	
Lucifer		The Evening Starre Hesper-us [4]	
Adam	⎤	Chorus of Angels	
with the serpent	⎥	Lucifer	
Eve	⎦	Adam	
Conscience		Eve	
Death		Conscience [5]	
Labour	⎤	Labour	⎤
Sicknesse	⎥	Sicknesse	⎥
Discontent	⎥ mutes.	Discontent	⎥ mutes
Ignorance	⎥	Ignorance	⎥
with others	⎦	Feare	⎥
Faith		Death	⎦
Hope		Faith	
Charity.		Hope	
		Charity.	

---

[3] Paradise Lost   The Persons

Moses προλογίζει [6] recounting how he assum'd his true bodie,
that it corrupts not because of his with god in the mount
declares the like of Enoch and Eliah, besides the purity of yᵉ
pl[ace] that certaine pure winds, dues, and clouds præserve it
from corruption whence [ex]horts to the sight of god, tells they
cannot se Adam in the state of innocence by reason of thire
sin [7]

Justice [8]
Mercie | debating what should become of man if he fall
Wisdome
Chorus of Angels sing a hymne of yᵉ creation [9]
      Act 2.
Heavenly Love
Evening starre
chorus sing the mariage song and describe Paradice
      Act 3.

Lucifer contriving Adams ruine
  Chorus feares for Adam and relates Lucifers rebellion and fall
    Act 4.
Adam ⎤
        fallen ⎦
Eve
Conscience cites them to Gods Examination
  Chorus bewails and tells the good Adam hath lost
    Act 5
Adam and Eve, driven out of Paradice
  præsented by an angel with
  Labour greife hatred Envie warre famine Pestilence

sicknesse	mutes to whome he gives
discontent	thire names
[Ignor]ance	likewise winter, heat Tempest &c.
Feare	
Death [10]	enterd into ye world [11]
Faith ⎤	
Hope	comfort him and instruct him
Charity ⎦	

  chorus breifly concludes
[4–6] [12] other Tragedies
Adam in [13] Banishment [14]
The flood [15]
Abram in Ægypt. [16]

[MS p. **36**]

[7] The Deluge.   [8] Sodom. [17]
[9]   Dinah vide Euseb. præparat. Evang. 1. 9. c. 22. [18]
the Persons

Dina	Hamor
Debora rebeccas nurse	Sichem [19]
Jacob	counselors 2.
Simeon [20]	nuncius
Levi	Chorus

[10] Thamar [21] Cừephorusa [22] where Juda is found to have
bin [23] the author of that crime wch he condemn'd in Tamar,
Tamar excus'd in what she attempted
[11] [24] the golden calfe. or the massacre in Horeb. [25]
[12] the quails num. 11.
[13] the murmurers. Num. 14.
[14] Corah Dathan &c. Num. 16. 17. [26]
[15] Moabitides Num. 25. [27]
[16] Achan. Josue 7. et [28] 8.
[17] Josuah in Gibeon. Josu. 10.

[18] Gideon Idoloclastes [29] Jud. 6.[30] 7.

[19] Gideon *per*suing Jud.[31] 8

[20] Abimelech the usurper. Jud. 9.

[21][32] Samson pursophorus [33] or Hybristes,[34] or Samson marriing [35] or in Ramath Lechi Jud. 15 [36]

[22] Dagonalia.[37] Jud. 16.

[23] Comazontes [38] or the Benjaminits Jud. 19. 20. &c. or the Rioters.

[24] Theristria.[39] a Pastoral out of Ruth.

[25] Eliadæ [40] Hophni and Phinehas. Sam. 1. 2. 3. 4. beginning with the first overthrow of Israel by the Philistims, interlac't with Samuels vision concirning Eli's familie.

[26] Jonathan rescu'd [41] Sam. 1. 14.[42]

[27] Doeg slandering Sam. 1. 22.[43]

[28] the sheepshearers in Carmel a pastoral. 1 Sam. 25.

[29] Saul in Gilboa [44] 1 Sam. 28. 31.[45]

[30] David revolted [46] 1 Sam. from the 27 c. to the 31.

[31] David Adulterous 2 Sam. c. 11. 12.

[32] Tamar. 2 Sam. 13.

[33] Achitophel 2 Sam. 15. 16. 17. 18.

[34] Adoniah. 1 Reg. 2.

[35] Salomon Gynæcocratumenus [47] or Idolomargus [48] aut Thysiazusæ.[49] Reg. 1. 11.[50]

[36] Rehoboam 1 Reg. 12 wher is disputed of a politick religion [51]

[37] Abias [52] Thersæus 1 Reg. 14.

the queen after much dispute as the last refuge sent to the profit. Ahias of Shilo receavs the message the epitasis [53] in that shee hearing the child shall die as she comes home refuses to return thinking therby to elude the oracle. the former part is spent in bringing the sick Prince forth as it were desirous to shift his chamber and couch as dying men use his father telling him what sacrifize he had sent for his health to bethel and Dan, his fearlesnesse of Death and puting his father in mind to set [54] to Ah[i]ah [55] the chorus of the Elders of Isræel bemoning his vertues bereft them and at an other time wondr[ing why] [56] Jeroboam beeing bad himself sho[ul]d [57] so greive for his son that was good. [&c].[58]

[38] Imbres or the Showrs. 1 Reg. 18.[59]

[39] Naboth. συκοφαντούμενος [60] 1 Reg. 21.

[40] Ahab.[61] 1 Reg. 22. beginning at th[e] [62] synod of fals profets ending wi[th] [63] relation of Ahabs death his [bodie brought Zedechiah slain by Ahabs fr][64]einds for his seducing (See lavater 2 Chron. 18.) [65]

[41] [66] Elias in the mount. 2 Reg. 1. 'Ορειβάτης.[67] or better Elias Polemistes.[68]

[42] Elisæus Hydrochóos.[69] 2 Reg. 3. Hudrophantes [70] Aquator [71]

[43] Elisæus Adorodocétos.[72]

[44] Elisæus Menutes [73] sive in Dothaimis [74] 2 Reg. 6 [75]

[45] Samaria Liberata [76] 2 Reg. 7.

[46] Achabæi Cunoboroomeni.[77] 2 Reg. 9. the scene Jesrael. beginning from the watchmans discovery of Jehu till he go out in the mean while message of things passing brought to Jesebel &c. lastly the 70 heads of Ahabs [so]ns [78] brought in and message brought of Ahaziah brethren slain on the way c. 10

[47] Jehu Belicola.[79] 2 Reg. 10

[48] Athaliah 2 Reg. 11.

[49] Amaziah Doryalotus.[80] 2 Reg. 14. 2 chron. 25

[50] Hezechias [81] πολιορκούμενος [82] 2 Reg. 18. 19. infra [83] [H]esechia beseig'd. the wicked hypocrysy of Shebna spoken of in the 11 or therabout of Isaiah & the commendation of Eliakim will afford αφορμας λογου [84] together with a faction that sought help from Ægypt.

[51] Josiah Aiazomenos.[85] 2 Reg. 23.

[52] Zedechiah νεοτερίζων.[86] 2 Reg. but the story is larger in Jeremiah.

[53] [So]lymων Halosis [87] which may [be]gin [88] from a Message brought to [th]e [89] citty of the judgment upon Zedechiah [a]nd his children in Ribla, and so seconded with the burning and destruction of citty & [t]emple by Nabuzaradan. Lamented by [J]eremiah.[90]

[54] Asa or Æthiopes. 2 chron. 14 with the deposing his mother, and burning her Idol.

[55] Duræ [91] the three children Dan. 3.

[MS p. **39**]

[56] Abram from Morea, or Isack redeemd.[92] the oiconomie [93] may be thus the fift or sixt day after Abrahams departure, Eleazer Abrams steward [94] first alone and then with the chorus discours of Abrahams strange voiage thire mistresse sorrow and perplexity accompanied with frighfull [95] dreams, and tell the manner of his rising by night taking his servants and his son with him next may come forth Sarah her self, after the Chorus or Ismael or Agar next some shepheard or companie of merchants passing through the mount in the time that Abram was in the mid work relate to Sarah what they saw hence lamentations, fears, wonders, the matter in the mean while divulgd Aner or Eshcol, or mamre Abrams confederats come to the hous of Abram to be more certaine, or to bring

news, in the mean while discoursing as the world would of such an action divers ways, bewailing the fate of so noble a man faln from his reputation, either through divin justice, or superstition, or coveting to doe some notable act through zeal. at length a servant sent from Abram relates the truth, and last he himselfe comes in with a great Train of Melchizedec whose shepheards beeing secret eye witnesses of all passages had related to thir master, and he conducted his freind Abraham home with joy.

[57] Baptistes
    the Scene. the Court

Beginning from the morning of Herods birth day. Herod by some counseler or els the Queen may plot under prætense of begging for his liberty to seek to draw him into a snare by his freedom of speech [96] persuaded on his birth day to release John Baptist, purposes it causes him to be sent for to the court from prison, the Queens [97] hears of it, takes occasion to passe wher he is on purpose, that under prætence of reconsiling to him, or seeking to draw a kind retraction ffrom [98] him of his censure on the marriage, to which end she sends a courtier before to sound whether he might be persuaded to mitigate his sentence which not finding she her selfe craftily assays, and on his constancie founds an accusation to Herod of a contumacious affront on such a day before many peers, præpares the [99] K. to some passion, and at last by her daughters dancing effects it. there may prologize the spirit of Philip Herods brother. it may also be thought that Herod had well bedew'd himself with wine which made him grant the easier to his wives daughter. Some of his disciples also as to congratulate his liberty, may be brought in, with whom after certain [100] command of his death many compassioning words of his disciples bewailing his youth cut off in his glorious cours he telling them his work is don and wishing them to follow Christ his maister. [101]

[58] [102] Sodom.—the title Cupids funeral pile. Sodom Burning—[103] the Scene before Lots gate

the Chorus consists of Lots Shepherds com n [104] to the citty about some affairs await in the evening thire maisters return from his evenin[g] walk toward the citty gates, he brings with him 2 yong men or youth [105] of noble form after likely discourses præpares for thire entertainmen[t] by then Supper is ended, the Gallantry of the town passe by in Processi[on] with musick and song to the temple of Venus Urania or Peor [106] and understanding of tow noble strangers arriv'd they send 2 of thire choysest youth with the preist [107] to invite them to thire citty solemnities it beeing an honour that thire citty had decreed to fair personages, as being Sacred to

thir goddesse. the angels being askt by the preist whence they are
say they are of Salem the preist inveighs against ye strict raigne of
melchizedeck [108] Lot that knows thire drift answers thwartly at
last of which notice give[n] [109] to the whole assembly they hasten
thither taxe [110] him of præsumption, singularity, breach of citty
customs, in fine offer violence, the chorus of Shephe[rds] [111] [MS
p. **40**] præpare resistance in thire maisters defence calling the rest
of the serviture, but beeing forc't to give back, the Angels open
the dore rescue Lot, discover them selves, warne him to gather his
freinds and sons in Law out of ye citty, he goes and returns as
having met with some incredulous, some other freind or son in law
out of the way when Lot came to his house, overtakes him to know
his buisnes, heer is disputed of incredulity of divine judgements
& such like matter, at last is describ'd the parting from the citty
the Chorus depart with thir maister, the Angels doe the deed with
all dreadfull execution, the K. and nobles of the citty may come
forth and serve to set out the terror a Chorus of Angels concluding
and the Angels relating the event of Lots journy, & of his wife. the
first Chorus beginning may relate the course of the citty each eveing
every one with mistresse, or Ganymed, gitterning [112] along the
streets, or solacing on the banks of Jordan, or down the stream.[113]
at the preists [114] inviting ye Angels to ye Solemnity the Angels
pittying thir beauty may dispute of Love & how it differs from lust
seeking to win them in the last scene to ye king & nobles when the
firie [115] thunders begin aloft the Angel appeares all girt with flames
which he saith are the flames of true love & tells the K. who falls
down with terror his just suffering as also Athanes id est [116] Gener
lots son in law for dispising ye continuall admonitions of Lots then
calling to ye thunders lightnings [117] & fires he bids them heare the
call and command of god to come & destroy a godlesse nation [118]
he brings them down with some short warning to all other nations
to take heed
[59] Christ born
[60] Herod massacring.[119] or Rachel weeping Math. 2.
[61] Christ bound
[62] Christ Crucifi'd
[63] Christ risen.
[64] Lazarus Joan. 11.
[65] Adam unparadiz'd [120]
The angel Gabriel, either descending or entering, shewing since
this globe was created, his frequency as much on earth, as in heavn,
describes paradise. next next [121] the chorus shewing the reason of
his comming to keep his watch in Paradise after Lucifers rebellion

by command from god, & withall expressing his desire to see, & know more concerning this excellent new creature man. the angel Gabriel as by his name signifying a prince of power tracing paradise with a more free office [122] passes by the station of ye chorus & desired by them relates what he knew of man as the creation of Eve with thire love, & mariage. after this Lucifer appeares after his overthrow, bemoans himself, seeks revenge on man the chorus prepare resistance at his first approach at last after discourse of enmity on either side he departs wherat the chorus sings of the battell, & victorie in heavn against him & his accomplices, as before after the first act was sung a hymn of the creation. heer again may appear Lucifer relating, & insulting in what he had don to the destruction of man. [123] man next & Eve having by this time bin seduc't by the serpent appeares confusedly cover'd with leaves conscience in a shape accuses him, Justice cites him to the place whither Jehova call'd for him in the mean while the chorus enter-tains the stage, & his inform'd by some angel the manner of his fall heer the chorus bewailes Adams fall. [124] Adam then & Eve returne accuse one another but especially Adam layes the blame to his wife, is stubborn in his offence Justice appeares reason with him convinces him the chorus admonisheth Adam, & bids him beware by Lucifers example of impenitence [125] the Angel is sent to banish them out of paradice but before causes to passe before his eyes in shapes a mask of all the evills of this life & world he is humbl'd relents, dispaires. at last appeares Mercy comforts him [126] promises the Messiah, then calls in faith, hope, & charity, instructs him he repents gives god the glory, submitts to his penalty the chorus breifly concludes. compare this with the former draught.

[66] Moabitides or Phineas [127]   [MS p. **41**]

the Epitasis [128] wherof may lie in the contention first between ye father of Zimri & Eleazer whether [129] he to have slain his son without law. next ye Embassadors of ye Moabite[s] [130] expostulating about Cosby [131] a stranger & a noble woman slain by Phineas. it may be argud about reformation & punishment illegal & as it were by tumult after all arguments drivn home then the word of the lord may be brought acquitting & approving phineas.

[67] Christus patiens [132]

The Scene in ye garden beginning fro*m* ye comming thither till Judas betraies & ye officers lead him away ye rest by message & chorus. his agony may [133] receav noble expressions

---

¹ Written above canceled "Michael."
² Before "Justice.": "or" inserted with caret but subsequently canceled.

³ Inserted above "Mercie"; "Divine" inserted before "Wisdome" and above "Justice." but subsequently canceled.

⁴ The numerals 1 2 3 1 appear under these four words. Fletcher and Wright (tr.) omit the 1 under "The"; Birch reads "The Evening Starre Hesperus"; Masson and Hanford observe the same order but with modernized spelling. Peck and Columbia read "Hesperus the Evening Starre"; Columbia suggests that Milton first wrote "The Evening Starre," afterward attempted to alter "The" to "Hes," and then "added the name and indicated the proper order by adding subscript numerals 1 2 3 1."

⁵ "Death" written below "Conscience" but deleted when "Death" was later listed among the mutes.

⁶ Cf. the similar phrase Μωϋσῆς προλογίζει in Ezekiel's *Exagogue,* a Greek tragedy based on Exodus. See John M. Steadman, " 'Moses Prologizes': Milton and Ezekiel's *Exagogue," N&Q,* 209 (1964), 336–37.

⁷ "recounting . . . sin" added at upper right of προλογίζει. Within the passage are the following changes and differing transcriptions: "his" inserted with caret above canceled "a"; "because of his with god"—other transcriptions are Birch, "because 'tis with God," Peck, Masson, Columbia, "because of his [being] with God," Todd, "because of his [abode] with God," Hanford, "because of his [converse] with God"; "exhorts"—the "r" has been badly inscribed, and Columbia reads "he hasts"; the preceding letter, however, seems "o" rather than "a"; "the state"—Columbia, "this state"; "sin" deleted before "thire."

⁸ "mercie" deleted after "Justice."

⁹ "hymne . . . creation" written above "Angels . . . a."

¹⁰ "Labour . . . Death"; Birch and Columbia include all twelve of these characters in the list of mutes; Peck and Todd include the first eleven, omitting "Death"; Masson transcribes "Fear [as] Mutes, to whom" etc.

¹¹ "enterd . . . world": in MS this passage is directly below "likewise winter, heat Tempest &c." but directly opposite "Death." The passage, consequently, could be interpreted as referring only to "Death" or to "winter, heat Tempest &c." Peck, Masson, and Todd prefer the reading "Death entered into the world"; while Wright (tr.) and Hanford print the passage immediately under the reference to "winter" and on the same line with "Feare" rather than on the line with "Death." Fletcher, however, prints the passage on the same line with "Death," adding that the words "enterd into yᵉ world" have been "written in a different ink and at a later time, with the stroke to the top of the first running over the lower part of the brace to indicate that the words apply to *Death."* Though Wright and Hanford omit the dash after "Death," Columbia and Fletcher retain it and print "enterd . . . world" on the same line.

¹² These three subjects appear on p. 35 in the space between the double columns containing plans [1] and [2]. Unlike [1] and [2], [4–6] show no marks of cancelation. Fletcher, nevertheless, suggests that "all material above the rule was intended to be struck out, although the lines between the two are untouched."

¹³ "ex" deleted before "in."

¹⁴ Peck equates this subject with plan #[65], "Adam unparadiz'd."

¹⁵ Cf. plan #7. Columbia combines #[5] and #[7]: "The flood [*or*] The Deluge." Cf. Gen. 6–8.

¹⁶ Gen. 12.

¹⁷ Cf. plan #[8] with #[58]; Gen. 19.

¹⁸ For the Dinah story to which Milton refers, translated, see *Eusebii Pamphili Evangelicæ Præparationis,* ed. E. H. Gifford (Oxford, 1903), III, i, 458–59.

[19] "i" seems to have been written over original "e."

[20] Last three letters blurred in Sotheby and Wright; see Gen. 34, and particularly v. 25.

[21] After "Thamar": Πεπλοφόρος canceled and "Cûephorusa" written above. Columbia translates Πεπλοφόρος as "veiled." Gen. 38:14: "And she put her widowes garments off her, and covered her with a vaile."

[22] I.e., Cuophorusa. Masson and Columbia translate as "Pregnant"; cf. H. Stephanus, κυοφορέω, "idem significans quod Gravida sum, Uterum fero, &c."; Gen. 38:24—"behold, she is with child by whoredome: and Iudah said, Bring her forth, and let her be burnt." For Milton's "curious diaeresis" here and elsewhere in the MS, see W. W. Greg, *MLR*, XXXIX (1944), 417.

[23] "bin" inserted above line with caret.

[24] With #[11] Milton begins a new column at the top of the right half of the page.

[25] "in Horeb" added above line over "massacre"; see Exod. 32.

[26] The rebellion and destruction of Corah and Dathan occur in Num. 16; Num. 17 concerns the rods in the tabernacle, Aaron's rod serving as a token against the rebels.

[27] Cf. plan #[66] below.

[28] "et" inserted above line with caret.

[29] Masson and Columbia translate as "Gideon the Idolbreaker."

[30] "6" written over "7"; Judg. 6 describes Gideon's destruction of the altar and grove of Baal, whereas Judg. 7 narrates his victory over the Midianites.

[31] Possibly the abbreviation should be transliterated "pursuing"; cf. the same contraction for "parts" in Trinity MS (*Comus*, line 72). "Jos." deleted before "Jud."; for "*per*suing," see Judg. 8:4, "and Gideon came to Jordan, . . . yet pursuing them"; and Judg. 8:5, "I am pursuing after Zebah and Zalmunna, kings of Midian."

[32] The original entry appears to have been "Samson in Ramath Lechi Jud. 15"; subsequently the words "marriing or" were inserted with a caret before "in Ramath Lechi" and the entry amplified by the addition of further titles ("Samson pursophorus or Hybristes, or") to the left of the original title. This addition consists of two lines; as the top line ("Samson pursophorus") is on the same line as the "Samson in Ramath Lechi" title, the inserted lines seem to belong with this entry rather than with the following concerning the "Dagonalia." Editors, however, have varied widely in their versions of this insertion, with W. R. Parker ("The Trinity Manuscript and Milton's Plans for a Tragedy," *JEGP*, XXXIV [1935], 225–32) concluding that its "position on the page" cannot be "precisely ascertained."

[33] The first "p" in this word may have been superimposed on another letter. Masson translates as "Firebrand bringer." Cf. Judg. 15:4, "and tooke firebrands."

[34] Masson translates as "Violent"; Liddell and Scott, ὑβριστής, "violent, wanton, licentious, insolent." Parker, "Trinity Manuscript," observes that "the specific reference is vague, but the title shows a definite sympathy with Greek tragedy."

[35] Parker, "Trinity Manuscript," suggests that this title "refers to the woman of Timnath, and not Dalila." Samson's marriage to the former is described in Judg. 14, his affair with the latter in Judg. 16.

[36] See Judg. 15:14–19 for Samson's battle against the Philistines at this place.

[37] Parker, "Trinity Manuscript," observes that the "Dagonalia" refers "to the closing scene of Samson's life, at the feast in honor of Dagon. But what treatment

Milton had in mind is . . . beyond conjecture." In Parker's opinion, p. 228, "it is impossible to say with certainty just how many plays Milton had in mind. . . . Masson thinks there are only two; H. M. Percival suggests a trilogy; Verity admits there might be four; and J. H. Hanford believes there are five." For various views on this puzzling matter, see Allan H. Gilbert, "The Cambridge Manuscript and Milton's Plans for an Epic," *SP*, XVI (1919), 172–76; Hone, ed., *Milton's "Samson Agonistes,"* p. 123; J. H. Hanford, *John Milton, Englishman* (New York: Crown, 1949), pp. 124–27, 246, and passim; and Anthony Low, "Milton's *Samson* and the Stage, with Implications for Dating the Play," *HLQ*, XL (1977), 313–24.

[38] Liddell and Scott: κωμάζω, "revel, make merry." "Jud" deleted after "Comazontes."

[39] Columbia translates as "The Reaping Woman"; H. Stephanus, θερίστρια, fem. of θεριστής, "Messor."

[40] "the" deleted before "Eliadæ."

[41] Cf. 1 Sam. 14:45: the "people rescued Jonathan."

[42] 1 Sam. 14.

[43] 1 Sam. 22.

[44] "in Gilboa" written under canceled "Autodàictes"; H. Stephanus, αὐτοδάϊκτος, "A seipso interfectus."

[45] Columbia suggests that Milton may have originally written "34" and afterward emended it to "31."

[46] "from" deleted after "revolted."

[47] Masson translates as "Solomon Women-governed"; H. Stephanus, γυναικοκρατούμενοι, dicuntur etiam Uxorii . . . Qui in potestate mulierum."

[48] "or *Idolomargus" inserted in blank space left of original entry, its position indicated by asterisk before "Gynæcocratumenus"; Birch transcribes "Solomon, Idolomargus, or Gynæcocratumenos, aut Thysiazusæ." Masson and Columbia translate as "Idol-mad."

[49] Masson translates as "the Women-sacrificers"; Columbia as "the Women Sacrificing." Cf. H. Stephanus, θυσιάζω, "Sacrificio, Immolo."

[50] 1 Kings 11.

[51] "wher . . . religion" added later at right of original entry, the first five words on the same line, the last two on the line above.

[52] Columbia transcribes and translates as "Abijah(?) Sought for," commenting that Milton "almost surely meant to write 'Ahias' here." Though the title is probably correct as written (referring to the prince Abijah rather than the prophet Ahijah), the meaning and derivation of "Thersæus" are obscure. As Milton's draft stresses Abijah's "fearlesnesse of Death," the title probably means "Abijah of Good Confidence." Cf. H. Stephanus, θαρσέω, "Fiducia præditus sum, Fiduciam habeo, Confido. Non vereor, Sum bono animo." θαρσήεις, "Qui est fidenti animo, Qui est præsenti animo, Fidens." Like Milton's "Thersæus," some of the Aeolic forms read *Thers-* rather than *Thars-;* cf. also the Homeric form "Thersites."

[53] This is a technical term derived from criticism of Terence and denotes the middle portion of a drama, between the protasis (or proposition) and the catastrophe. Renaissance dramatic theory transferred these critical terms from comedy to tragedy.

[54] Peck and Todd, "to set (read, *send*)."

[55] In Sotheby the middle letter "i" is not clear; in Wright it has disappeared as the result of a long vertical tear in the lower right-hand corner of the page.

[56] In Wright the last three letters of "wondring" and the word "why" have disappeared as the result of a long vertical rent and a short horizontal tear at this point. In Sotheby they are clear.

[57] The "ul," missing because of the rent in Wright, is clear in the Sotheby tracing.

[58] "&c." only partly legible in Wright because of the vertical rent in the page but still clear in Sotheby.

[59] After "18." on the other side of the rent is a mark suggesting a 9 and an original reading of "18. 19." 1 Kings 18:41–46 relates how Elijah obtained rain through prayer.

[60] Inserted in blank space left of original entry, its position indicated by an X to the left of "Naboth." Masson translates as "falsely-accused"; Columbia as "calumniated." Liddell and Scott, συκοφαντέω, "prosecute vexatiously, black-mail; accuse falsely; oppress."

[61] This is the lowest entry in the right-hand column, with the final portion of the entry extended into the blank space at the bottom of the left-hand column and the Lavater reference entered in the left column above "[fr]einds." Several letters are missing in the left and right margins, and lower portions of other letters at the bottom of the page have disappeared. Apparently much of this passage was still legible for Birch and Peck but not for Sotheby and Wright.

[62] Birch, Peck, and Todd, "the"; the final "e" does not appear in Sotheby's tracing.

[63] Birch, Peck, and Todd, "with"; the "th" does not appear in Sotheby's tracing.

[64] In Sotheby, no words are legible after "Ahabs death his" until the final "einds for his seducing" and the Lavater reference; though the top parts of letters in the "Zedechiah" passage are still visible, the passage itself is illegible. Birch, Peck, and Todd, "his bodie brought; Zedechiah slain by Ahab's freinds for his seducing"; Masson and Columbia follow this version but substitute "Zedekiah" for "Zede-chiah." Wright and Fletcher read "his bodie brought alleluiah glory be &c." Where Wright reads "einds for his seducing," Fletcher reads "ends for his seducing." The reading "Zedechiah" seems preferable to "Zedekiah" in this passage—partly on the authority of Birch, Peck, and Todd but chiefly by analogy with Milton's use of "ch" in spelling "Hezechias" and "Zedechiah" in #[50], [52], [53].

[65] Ludovicus Lavater, *In Libros Paralipomenon sive Chronicorum commentarius* (Tiguri, 1573).

[66] With #[41], Milton returns to the left side of the page and starts a new column below #[10].

[67] Masson and Columbia translate as "the Mountain-Ranger"; cf. Liddell and Scott, ὀρειβάτης, "mountain ranging"; H. Stephanus, "Qui montes scandit seu pererrat."

[68] Masson and Columbia translate as "the Warrior"; cf. H. Stephanus, πολεμιστής, "Bellator, Habilis ad Bellum."

[69] Masson and Columbia translate as "the Water Pourer." The accent should be on the penult, but its position is not clearly indicated in Sotheby or Wright (facs.). Cf. H. Stephanus, ὑδροχόος, "Aquarius."

[70] Masson and Columbia translate as "Water-Prophet"; Liddell and Scott, ὑδροφάντης, "water-finder."

[71] Columbia translates as "Water Bringer"; Harper, "Aquator, a water-carrier."

[72] Final "o" in this word may have been written over another letter. In Sotheby the fifth letter is not clear and could be read as either "a" or "o"; in Wright it appears to be "o"; Birch, Peck, and Todd, "Adorodocétas"; Masson, Wright,

Fletcher, and Columbia, "Adorodocétos." Masson translates as "the Incorruptible"; Columbia as "Elisha refusing gifts." Cf. H. Stephanus, ἀδωροδόκητος, "Qui munera sordida non accipit, Qui munera sordida se corrumpi passus non est, Incorruptus. Unde ἀδωροδοκήτως, Sine munerum sordidorum acceptione, Incorruptè, Integrè." Milton's accenting apparently reflects a confusion between adjectival and adverbial forms.

[73] Masson and Columbia translate as "the Informer"; cf. Liddell and Scott, μηνυτής, "bringing to light; one who brings information, . . . informer."

[74] Masson and Columbia translate as "in Dothan."

[75] "6" written above "Dothaimis."

[76] Masson and Columbia translate as "Samaria Delivered."

[77] The letters following "r" seem to be "oo" rather than an omega, as Birch, Peck, Todd, and Masson read the word. Masson translates as "devoured by dogs"; Columbia as "The sons of Ahab eaten by dogs." See the prophecy in 1 Kings 21:19–24, "In the place where dogs licked the blood of Naboth, shall dogs lick thy blood. . . . Him that dieth of Ahab in the citie, the dogs shall eate."

[78] In Sotheby the entire word (at the beginning of the line) is still clearly legible. Scolar emends "Jesrael" (Wright tr.) to "Iesrael."

[79] Masson translates as "Jehu worshipping Baal"; Columbia as "Jehu Worshipper of Baal."

[80] Masson translates as "Captive of the Spear"; Columbia as "Amaziah Captive"; cf. H. Stephanus, δορυάλωτος, "Hasta captus, Bello captus, Captivus."

[81] "Assyrii" deleted before "Hezechias."

[82] Liddell and Scott, πολιορκέω, "to be besieged, in a state of siege"; H. Stephanus, "Obsidione cingo, Circumsedeo, Obsideo."

[83] Added later at right under the scriptural reference. The remainder of the entry ("[H]esechia . . . Ægypt.") appears below #[55] ("Duræ . . . 3.") in the left-hand column.

[84] Masson translates as "occasions for discourse"; Columbia as "occasion for discussion"; cf. Liddell and Scott, ἀφορμή, "starting point, origin, occasion, or praetext, ἀφορμαὶ λόγων"; H. Stephanus, "Iam verò ut Latinis Materia occasionem aliquando significat, sic & Græcis ἀφορμή."

[85] The letter ζ (zeta) is clearly legible in Sotheby and Wright (facs.); whether the letter "c" was written above it is uncertain. Columbia suggests that Milton "first changed ζ to c but returned" to "z"; Fletcher argues that Milton "first made the Greek letter zeta, which as he made it, looked like a xi, then perhaps later noting it looked like xi, wrote z over it. Masson translates as "Lamented"; Columbia as "Josiah Bewailed"; cf. Liddell and Scott, αἰάζω, "cry αἰαῖ, wail; . . . bewail"; H. Stephanus, αἰάζω, "Lugeo, Lamentor."

[86] Masson translates as "Revolutionising"; Columbia as "Zedekiah Revolting"; cf. Liddell and Scott, νεωτερίζω, "make innovations, take the law into one's own hands, attempt political changes, make revolutionary movements." 2 Kings 24:20: "Zedekiah rebelled against the King of Babylon."

[87] In Sotheby the letter "S" has partly disappeared, but the following letter is visible; it appears to be "o" but could conceivably be "a." In Wright (facs.) both letters have disappeared. Masson and Columbia translate as "the Taking of Jerusalem"; cf. Liddell and Scott, ἅλωσις, "capture"; H. Stephanus, "Captura, vel Captio . . . Item Expugnatio."

[88] In Sotheby this word is still entirely legible.

[89] In Sotheby the initial "t" is not clear; in Wright only the "e" remains.

[90] The "J" is gone in both Sotheby and Wright.

[91] In Wright the margin is badly torn; in Sotheby the word is still legible—the initial "D" is unmistakable, even though incomplete, and the remaining letters clearly read "uræ." Milton has preferred the locative form ("at Dura") to the nominative. Dan. 3:1: "in the plaine of Dura, in the province of Babylon."

[92] In Columbia this sketch is numbered fifth among the biblical subjects, immediately preceding "Sodom" (our #[8]) and following "Abram in Ægypt" (our #[6]). Cf. Gen. 22.

[93] Disposition or order; cf. R. Stephanus, "Oeconomia, Dispositio cuius rei."

[94] "with" deleted after "steward."

[95] The letter "t" inadvertently omitted in MS.

[96] "or els . . . speech" inserted above line at upper right, with caret after "counseler."

[97] In Sotheby and Wright the final letter appears to be "s" rather than "e."

[98] Sotheby and Wright show "ff"; Fletcher remarks that "the first *f* and perhaps both were written over."

[99] "for" deleted after "the."

[100] "me" deleted after "certain."

[101] In Sotheby this word is fully legible but slightly blurred in Wright. Part of this entry was added after Milton began the following entry; the last three lines show crowding and surround the title and scene for the "Sodom" sketch.

[102] Cf. #[8]. Title and scene have been entered on same line and at an earlier date than the final lines of the preceding entry. Columbia prints this draft as No. 6—between "Abram from Morea" (our #[56]) and "Dinah" (our #[9]).

[103] "the title . . . Burning" is an insertion, proposing alternative titles, and apparently represents an afterthought. It does not appear on p. 39 of the MS but is inserted (with indentation) at the top of the continuation of this draft on p. 40, immediately above the words "præpare resistance." Birch omits this addition; Peck prints it at the end of the entry; Todd inserts it between "Sodom" and the notation of the scene; Columbia places it immediately after the notation of scene. The dashes are supplied.

[104] "i" inadvertently omitted in what was intended as "in."

[105] In Sotheby and Wright "youth" (the last word on the right-hand margin) shows no final "s."

[106] "or Peor" inserted above line, with caret after "Urania."

[107] "with the preist" inserted above line, with two carets before "to."

[108] "the angels . . . melchizedeck" inserted at bottom right of preceding page (38); the location of the insertion is indicated by the symbol] after "goddesse." Though the "i" in "melchizedeck" is not visible in Sotheby, it does appear (at the end of the line) in Wright, the remainder of the name continuing on the next line.

[109] The final "n" in "given" (at the end of a line) is only partially present in Sotheby and Wright.

[110] Fletcher suggests that "the *x* was written over the start of another letter."

[111] Final "rds" (at end of line and page) is missing in Wright, and something like a small raised "r" is visible in Sotheby.

[112] I.e., playing on a cithern. Todd observes that "Milton uses the word *gitterning* because the *cittern* was a symbol of women that lived by prostitution." The *cithara* was associated with Venus and with the *meretrix* of Isa. 23:16. Scolar emends "them selves" (Wright tr.) to "themselves."

[113] Columbia reading "strëam" results from misinterpreting accidental marks in the MS as deliberate punctuation. In Sotheby and Wright four dots appear over this word, all of which seem to have been unintentional.

[114] "at the preists . . . heed" (the end of the entry) has been crowded into the space at bottom right, after "stream."

[115] Possibly "firce." In Wright the letter "i" appears to have been superimposed on "c" or vice versa; Sotheby's tracing reads "firce"; Birch and Peck, "firce"; Wright (tr.), "firie," suggesting that original "*firce* [was] changed to *firie*." Columbia maintains that Milton originally wrote "firie" and altered it later to "firce." Fletcher follows Wright in maintaining that "*firce* was written first and then *i* was written over *c* and *e* strengthened."

[116] "lots" deleted before "id"; "son" deleted before "est."

[117] Final "s" visible in Wright but not in Sotheby tracing.

[118] "he bids . . . godlesse nation" inserted (within enclosing line) on p. 41 in the left margin, under the list of Scottish stories. For biblical sources, see Gen. 19. Masson suggests that "Milton was thinking, analogically, of London and England."

[119] "m" deleted before "massacring."

[120] Written above canceled "Adams Banishment." Cf. #[1] through #[3]. Peck lists title as "Adam unparadiz'd, Adam's punishment: (or, Paradise Lost, the fourth plan)"; he also suggests that this subject is identical with the proposed "Adam in banishment" (#[4] above). Peck's division of this draft into five acts was taken over by Todd. The first act ends with Gabriel's account of the protoplasts' love and marriage, the second with the choral song concerning the battle in heaven, the third with the angelic account of Adam's fall, and the fourth with the choral admonition to Adam to beware of impenitence. On the basis of this arrangement Peck argued that Milton wrote much—perhaps all—of a drama on "Adam unparadiz'd" and that a large part of the epic could be put back into dramatic form. By excerpting dialogue from the epic and supplying stage directions, Peck attempted to reconstruct Act IV, scene 2, of the play that he believed Milton to have written. Hanford's act divisions, "suggested by those in the third draft," appear in his *Milton Handbook*. In his view, the second act begins with "The Angel Gabriel . . . tracing Paradise"; the third with Lucifer's first appearance "after his overthrow"; the fourth with Lucifer's reappearance "relating . . . what he had done to the destruction of Man"; and the fifth with Adam's and Eve's accusations.

[121] "on earth . . . next next" written at right in space above line ending "as much." The second "next" is written in left margin to the left of canceled "first"; Milton failed to cancel the additional "next." Or is the first "next" a catchword?

[122] "comes" deleted after "office."

[123] "heer again . . . destruction of man." added in left margin of following page (41) with symbol] indicating place of insertion.

[124] "heer the chorus . . . Adams fall." added at foot of page (40) with place of insertion indicated by caret.

[125] "the chorus admonisheth . . . impenitence" added at foot of page (40) with place of insertion indicated by a caret. Within the entry Wright finds *of* changed to *by;* Fletcher *by* "written over" *of*."

[126] "& brings in faith hope & charity" deleted after "him."

[127] Cf. #[15], above. Todd, Masson, and Columbia combine the two entries. Todd then numbers the combination 1v, which places it between "Sodom" and "Christus patiens" (our #[58] and #[67]); Masson and Columbia place it between "Corah" and "Achan" (our #[14] and #[16]). In the MS this entry (#[66]) appears in the blank space below "Scotch stories" on p. 41.

[128] On "Epitasis," see n. 53 to #[37] above.

[129] "cont" deleted before "whether."

[130] Final "s" not visible in Sotheby or Wright.

[131] Dot over "y" in Sotheby, Wright, and Scolar, which Wright, Scolar, and Fletcher print. Birch, Peck, Todd, and Masson read "Cosbi"; Columbia prints "Cosby" with comment that this form has been "changed from 'Cosbi.' " Num. 25 reads "Cozbi." Scolar emends "argud" (Wright tr.) to "argu'd."

[132] This draft follows "Moabitides or Phineas" (#[66]) in the space below the five "Scotch Stories" (MS p. 41); Todd places it between "Sodom" and "Christ born" (our #[58] and #[59]); Columbia between "Herod massacring." and "Christ bound" (our #[60] and #[61]).

[133] "make" deleted before "may."

[MS p. **37**]

British Trag.[1]

[1][2]

the cloister king Constans set up by Vortiger.[3]

[1a]

Venutius husband to Cartismandua.[4]

2 [5]

Vortimer. poison'd by Rôêna [6] Vortiger marrying Roena see Speed. reproov'd by Vodin archbishop of London Speed.[7]

3

Vortiger immur'd.[8] the massacre of the britains by Hengist in thire cups at Salisbyry plaine Malmsbyry.[9]

4

Sigher of the east saxons revolted from the faith and reclaim'd by Jarumang.[10]

5

Ethelbert of the east angles slaine by Offa the mercian k. see Holinsh: l. 6. c. 5.[11] Speed in the life of offa & ethelbert [12]

6

Sebert slaine by Penda after he had left his kingdom. see Holinshed. 116. p.[13]

7

Wulfer slaying his tow sons for beeing Christians.[14]

8

Osbert of Northumberland slain for ravishing the wife of Bernbocard and the Dans brought in. see stow. Holinsh. l. 6. c. 12. and especially Speed l. 8. c. 2 [15]

9

Edmond last k. of ye East angles martyr'd by Hinguar ye Dane. see speed. l. 8. c. 2.[16]

10

Sigebert tyrant of ye west Saxons. slain by a Swinheard.[17]

11

Edmund brother of Athelstan. slaine by a theefe at his owne table. Malmesb.[18]

12

Edwin son to Edward the yonger [19] for lust depriv'd of his kingdom. or rather by faction of monks whome he hated together the impostor Dunstan.[20]

13

Edward son of Edgar murderd by his stepmother [21] to which may be inserted the tragedie stirrd up betwixt the monks and preists about mariage. [22]

14

Etheldred son of Edgar a slothfull k. the ruin of his land by the Danes. [23]

15

Ceaulin k. of west saxons for tyrannie depos'd, and banish't & dying [24]

16

the slaughter of the monks of Bangor by Edelfride stirrd up as is said by Ethelbert, and he by Austine the monke because the Britain[s] would not receave the rites of the Roman Church. See Beda. Geffrey Monmouth. and Holinshed p. 104. wch must begin with the convocat[ion] of British clergie by Austin to determin *super*fluous points wch by them w[ere] refused. [25]

17

Edwin by vision promis'd the kingdom of Northumberland on promise of his conversion and therin establisht by Rodoald K. of East angles. [26]

18

Oswin k. of Deira slaine by Oswie his freind k. of Bernitia through instigation of flatterers. see Holinshed. p. 115. [27]

19

Sigibert of the East angles keeping companie with a *per*son excomunicated, slaine by the same man in his house according as the bishop Cedda had foretold. [28]

20

Egfride k. of the Northumbers slaine in battell against the Picts having before wasted Ireland and made warre for no reason on men that ever lov'd the English, forewarnd also by Cutbert not to fight with the Picts. [29]

21

Kinewulf k. of ye west Saxons slaine by Kineard in the house of one of his concubins. [30]

[MS p. **38**]

22

Gunthildis the danish ladie. with her husband Palingus and her son slaine by appointment of the traitor Edrick in k Ethelreds days. Holinshed. 7 l. c. 5. [31] together with the massacre of the danes at Oxford. Speed. [32]

23

Brightrick of west Saxons poyson'd by his wife Ethelburge Offa's daughter who dyes miserably also in beggery after adultery in an nunnery Speed in Bithric.[33]

24

Alfred in disguise of a ministrel discovers the danes negligence sets on with a mightie slaughter about the same tyme ye devonshire men rout Hubba & slay him.[34]

A Heroicall Poem may be founded somwhere in Alfreds reigne. especially at his issuing out of Edelingsey on the Danes. whose actions are wel like those of Ulysses [35]

25

Athelstan exposing his brother Edwin to the sea. and repenting.[36]

26

Edgar slaying Ethelwold for false play in woing wherin may be set out his pride, lust,[37] which he thought to close by favouring monks and building monasteries.[38] also the disposition of woman in Elfrida toward her husband.[39]

27

Swane beseidging London and Etheldred [40] repuls't by the Londoners [41]

28

Harold slaine in battel by William the norman [42] the first scene may begin with the ghost of Alfred the second son of Ethelred slaine in a cruel manner by Godwin Harolds father.[43] his mother and brother disuading him.[44]

29

Edmund Ironside defeating the danes at Brentford with his combat with Canute [45]

30

Edmund Ironside murder'd by Edrick the traitor and reveng'd by Canute.[46]

31

Gunilda daughter to k. Canute and Emma wife to Henry the third Emperour accus'd of inchastitie is defended by her English page in combat against a giantlike adversary. who by him at 2 blows is slaine &c. Speed in the life of Canute [47]

32

Hardiknute dying in his cups an example to riot.[48]

33

Edward Confessors divorsing and imprisoning his noble wife Editha Godwins daughter [49] wherin is shewed his over affection to strangers the cause of Godwin's insurrection,[50] his slacknesse to redresse the corrupt clergie and su*per*stitious prætence of chastitie.[51] wherin Godwins forbea[r]ance of battel [p]rais'd and the [En]glish moderatio*n* [on] both sides [m]agnifid [52]

[1] Sotheby reads "Traj."; Wright, "Troy."

[2] Unnumbered in MS, where the Vortiger entry is flush with the left margin and the Venutius entry has been inserted above the line at upper right, almost parallel with the "British Trag." heading. Though most editors print this as a single entry, Masson recognized the "large interval of time" between the two subjects (the Venutius entry involving events of A.D. 51, the Vortiger subject events of A.D. 408) and suggested that the Venutius entry was probably "an afterthought, intended as separate, but entered beside the other." That the Vortiger entry was first is virtually certain: It occurs at the normal position for the first entry (i.e., at the left margin on the line below the generic heading) and is closely linked with the events and persons mentioned in plans 2 and 3. Columbia (XVIII, 241) divides the two entries, numbering them 1 and 1a, but places the Venutius entry first. Birch and Todd omit the Venutius entry; Peck locates it after the Vortiger entry; Masson prints the Venutius entry first.

[3] Holinshed, "Constantius"; Geoffrey of Monmouth, "Constans." Holinshed prefers "Vortigern" but notes the variant "Vortigerus." Stow consistently uses "Vortiger." Though Milton prefers "Vortigern" in the *History of Britain,* he occasionally employs "Vortiger" in that work (*Complete Prose,* V, 148, 150–51). According to Holinshed, book V, chap. 1, pp. 76–77, Constantinus left three sons: Constantius, Aurelius Ambrosius, and Uter Pendragon. "Constantius was made a moonke in his fathers life time, because he was thought to be too soft and childish in wit, to have anie publike rule committed to his hands." After corrupting Constantius's foreign bodyguard "to murther the king," Vortigern himself was chosen "king of Britaine" instead of the rightful heirs. Holinshed depends largely on Geoffrey of Monmouth, *Historiæ Regum Britanniæ,* book VI, chaps. 6–9.

[4] Both names appear thus in Speed (book. V, chap. 6, p. 34): "*Venutius* . . . husband to *Cartismandua* . . . finding his bed abused by *Vellocatus* his servant and harnesse-bearer, raised his power against her, and her paramour. With him sided his *Brigants,* and the neighbour countries adioining, whose good will went generally with the lawful husband, fearing the ambitious authority of a lustfull woman. With her went the *Romans.*" The "warre continued to the *Romans,* the kingdome to *Venutius,* and the infamy with *Cartismandua.*"

[5] Entries 2–33 were numbered by Milton himself; all other plans in the MS were left unnumbered.

[6] Speed (book VII, chap. 12, p. 267): "*Rowena* the mother of the *Britaines* mischiefe, and the maintainer of the *Saxons* residence found the meanes to remove this worthy *Vortimer* away, and by poison caused the end of his life."

[7] "Vortiger . . . London Speed." inserted at right of original entry, apparently at the same time as additions to entry 3. Birch, Peck, Todd, and Masson insert this passage in entry 3 after "Vortiger immur'd." This entry represents a different subject from the Vortimer entry but is closely related in characters and themes. Speed (book VII, chap. 4, pp. 206–7) describes how Vortigern divorced his first wife in order to wed Rowena (daughter of the Saxon chieftain Hengist) and was reprimanded therefor by Vodine, archbishop of London, who "feared not to tell him that thereby he had *indangered both his soule & Crown:* which words by *Vortigern* were so digested, that shortly it cost the good Archbishop his life."

[8] After "Vortiger," "bele" deleted. Speed (book VII, chaps. 4, 12, pp. 208, 266) describes Vortigern's incestuous marriage to his daughter by Rowena, his flight to Wales, and his construction of "a strong Castle" in the mountains. His ultimate destruction is alternatively attributed to fire from heaven or to the action of Aurelius and Uter Pendragon as instruments of divine wrath.

[9] "the massacre . . . Malmsbyry." inserted to the right of "Vortiger immur'd." This passage constitutes an entirely different subject. Though closely associated with the events of entry 2, it is chronologically prior to Vortiger's immurement in his Welsh fortress. William of Malmesbury (book I, pp. 9–10) recounts: "Interea *Hengistus* vicio quodam humani ingenii ut quo plus habeas plus ambias fraude subornata generum ad convivium cum 300. suorum invitat: cumque frequentioribus poculis invitatos ad tumultum animasset, & unumquemque industria salsa dicacitate perstringeret, primo ad iurgia mox ad arma ventum est. Ita Brittones ad unum iugulati animas inter vina evomuere."

[10] "from the faith" inserted above the line. Wright reads the final letter of the final word as an abbreviation for "us" (Jarumanus). In the *History of Britain (Complete Prose,* V, 215) the form is Jarumannus. According to Speed (p. 235), "*Beda* reporteth, that upon a great mortality and plague, to appease the wrath of his *Gods, Sighere* became an *Apostata,* and forsooke the faith of Christ . . . yet by the diligent care of *Wulfere* king of the *Mercians, Sighere* and his people were reclaimed, throwing downe the *Temples* and *Altars* erected to Idolatrie, and opening againe the Christian Churches." According to Holinshed (book V, chap. 34, pp. 120–21), Sighere "falleth from . . . faith . . . Vulfhere king of Mercia sendeth bishop Iaroman to redresse that apostasie of the prince and people."

[11] Holinshed (book VI, chap. 5, p. 132): "Ethelbert king of the Eastangles commended for his vertues, Alfred the daughter of king Mercia [*sic*] is affianced to him, tokens of missehaps towards him, his destruction intended by queene Quendred. . . . Offa invadeth Ethelberts kingdome, Alfred his betrothed wife taketh his death grevouslie, and becommeth a nun."

[12] "Speed . . . ethelbert" apparently inserted later, crowded into the right margin after the Holinshed reference with the last six letters of "ethelbert" blotted. Speed (book VII, chap. 11, p. 263) relates how "This King being incited by *Offa* the *Mercian* . . . to marry *Elfryd* his daughter . . . came upon that purpose to *Offa* his court . . . and was by him there cruelly murthered at the instigation of *Quendrid* his unkind (intended) mother in Law."

[13] In Milton's *History of Britain (Complete Prose,* V, 234) this name appears as Sigebert; in Stow (p. 62) as Sebert. Holinshed (book V, chap. 30, pp. 115–16) recounts how Sigibert, king of the East Angles, growing old, became a monk; but when Penda, king of Mercia, made war upon them, the East Anglians "compelled Sigibert to come foorth of his monasterie, & to go with them into the field against Penda. Sigibert being thus constreined against his will, would not put on armour or beare anie other kind of weapon, than onelie a wand in his hand in steed of a scepter." He was killed in the ensuing battle.

[14] Speed (book VII, chap. 23, p. 307) relates how "King *Vulfere* of *Mercia* . . . understanding that *Vulfald* and *Rufin* his two sonnes, under pretence and colour of hunting, usually resorted to reverend *Chad,* to bee instructed in the fruitfull faith of Christ Iesus, and had at his hands received the Sacrament of Baptisme, at the perswasion of one *Werebod,* suddenly followed, and finding them in the Oratory of that holy man, in devout contemplations, slew them there with his owne hands. . . . But King *Vulfere* repenting this his most unhumane murther, became himself a Christian, and destroied al those Temples wherin his

heathen gods had beene worshipped." Speed's marginal gloss resembles Milton's wording, "*Vulfere* slaieth his two sonnes," and the index reads "*Wulfhere* Monarch of the Englishmen killeth his two sonnes, whiles they were in divine contemplation."

[15] According to Stow (p. 74), "This *Osbert* ravished a Lady of his Countrey, wife to *Bernebokard,* in revenge whereof, the same *Bernebokard* flying into Denmarke, returned againe with the Danes, *Hinguar* and *Hubba,* and arrived in Holy Island, and so came to Yorke, and there slew king *Osbright.*" As Milton "especially" notes Speed's account (book VIII, chap. 2, pp. "394–96"), he may have been impressed by the opportunities suggested for passion and admiration, as well as by the close analogy with the story of Lucretia: "*Osbright* a *Northumbrian* Vice-roy . . . came to the house of a Noble man, named *Beorn-Bocador,* whose Lady of passing feature (in his absence) gave him honourable entertainement." Speed's account is notable for the highly rhetorical tirade in which Beorn's wife laments her dishonor and exhorts him to seek revenge. The location of Holinshed's account is book VI, chap. 12, pp. 143–44. Faulty pagination in editions of Speed and Holinshed (nn. 15, 16, 43, 44, 47, 49, 51, 52) has been enclosed in quotation marks.

[16] Speed (book VIII, chap. 2, p. "397"): "Such was the murther of holy *Edmund,* King of the *East-Angles,* with *Danish* arrowes martyred to death as hee stood bound unto a stake, ever calling on the name of IESUS." The forms "Edmond" and "Hinguar" are those found in Stow (p. 64). "see . . . 2" perhaps added later.

[17] Speed (book VII, chap. 7, p. 229) recounts how Sigebert "wallowing in all sensuall pleasures, added exactions and cruelties upon his subiects, setting aside all lawes and rules of true pietie: of which vicious life, when hee was lovingly admonished by his most faithful Counsellor a worthy Earle called *Cumbra,* so farre was his minde from abandoning his impious courses, as that he caused this Noble Personage to be cruelly slaine; whereupon the rest of the Peeres . . . rebelliously rose up in Arms against him." Fleeing to the forest, Sigebert was "met with by a *Swine-heard* that was servant to *Cumbra*" and "slaine in revenge of his masters death." Other versions may be found in Holinshed (book VI, chap. 3, p. 131) and Stow (p. 77).

[18] "I" deleted before "11." According to William of Malmesbury (*De Gestis Regum Anglorum,* p. 54), King Edmund is slain by "latrunculus quidam *Leof,* quem propter latrocinia eliminaverat." Speed (book VII, chap. 39, p. 400) describes how Edmund "at his Manor of *Puclekerkes* . . . whiles hee interposed himselfe between his *Sewer* and one *Leove* to part a fray, was, with a thrust through the body, wounded to death." Holinshed, noting the discrepancies in various accounts of Edmund's death, offers another version (book VI, chap. 21, p. 157): "Other say, that keeping a great feast . . . as he was set at the table, he espied where a common robber was placed neere unto him, whome sometime he had banished the land, and now being returned without license, he presumed to come into the kings presence, wherewith the king was so moved with high disdaine, that he suddenlie arose from the table, and flew upon the theefe, and catching him by the heare of the head, threw him under his feet, wherewith the theefe, having fast hold on the king, brought him downe upon him also, and with his knife stroke him into the bellie, in such wise, that the kings bowels fell out of his chest, and there presentlie died."

[19] According to Holinshed, Stow, and Milton's *History of Britain* (*Complete Prose,* V, 319), Edwin (or Edwi) is not the son of Edward the younger but the son of Edmund and therefore grandson of Edward the elder.

[20] "or rather . . . Dunstan." added later in right margin. Holinshed (book VI, chap. 23, p. 158) reports Edwin's "beastlie and incestuous carnalitie with a kinswoman of his on the verie day of his coronation," how "he is reproved of Dunstane and giveth over the gentlewomans companie," how "Dunstane is banished for rebuking king Edwin for his unlawfull lust and lewd life, . . . what revenging mischiefs the king did for displeasure sake against the said Dunstane in exile," how "the middle part of England rebelleth gainst king Edwin, and erecteth his brother Edgar in roiall roome over them," and how (in contrast to Edwin) Edgar (p. 159) "was a great favourer of moonks, and speciallie had Dunstane in high estimation."

[21] Speed (book VII, chap. 43, p. 412) recounts how "King *Edward* for his disport was hunting in a forrest neere . . . a faire and strong Castle called *Corfe,* where his mother in law Queene *Elfrida* with his brother Prince *Ethelred,* were therein residing." Secretly leaving the hunt for a brief, solitary visit to his relatives, he refused the queen's invitation to remain overnight, craving "onely of his mother a cup of wine, that in his saddle hee might drinke to her and his brother, and so bee gone. The cuppe was no sooner at his mouth, then a knife in his backe, which a servant appointed by this trecherous Queene strooke into him; who feeling himselfe hurt set spurs to his horse, thinking to escape to his more faithfull company." But "fainting through losse of much blood," he soon "fell from his horse, and one foot intangled in the stirruppe, hee was thereby rufullie dragde up and downe through woods and lands; and lastly left dead at *Corfes*-gate."

[22] "to which . . . mariage." inserted apparently later below original entry. In the controversy between the monastic orders and the married canons and secular priests, King Edgar had backed the monastic orders. This quarrel became closely associated with the dispute over the succession to the crown; whereas the monastic party under Dunstan favored Edward over Ethelred, many of the latter's supporters aligned themselves on the side of the married clergy against the monks. For further details on this matter, see Speed, book VII, chap. 43, pp. 411–12, and Holinshed, book VI, chap. 25, pp. 162–63.

[23] Holinshed (book VII, chap. 1, pp. 164–65) stresses the same dual theme: "Egelred . . . his slouth and idlenes accompanied with other vices, the Danes arrive on the coasts of Kent and make spoile of many places. . . . through his negligent government, the state of the commonwealth fell into such decaie . . . that under him it may be said, how the kingdome was come to the uttermost point or period of old and feeble age, which is the next degree to the grave." Speed (book VII, chap. 44, p. 414) stresses the same vices as well as Dunstan's prophecy of the Danish invasion.

[24] According to Speed (book VII, chap. 17, pp. 290–91), "Cheuline the third king of the West-Saxons, and fifth monarch of the Englishmen" grew proud "through his many prosperous victories against his enemies, & tyrannizing over his own Subiects, the *West-Saxons,* fell into such contempt, that they ioyned with the *Britains* for his destruction." The two sides met in a battle at Wannesditch in Wiltshire, where defeated, he "is forced to flee before his conquered Captives, and to exile himself . . . and as a meane man, died in his banishment."

[25] Bede (book II, chap. 2, pp. 176–78) relates how Augustine was sent to Britain as papal legate and convoked a synod concerning the date of Easter and other discrepancies between British and Roman rites. A second synod included delegates from the monastery at Bangor, "septem Britonum episcopi, & plures viri doctissimi, maximè de nobilissimo eorum monasterio." To determine whether or not

Augustine was truly a man of God (*homo Dei*), the monks agreed in advance to judge him by the criterion of humility. When Augustine remained seated instead of rising to greet them, they concluded that he was *not* a man of God and accordingly opposed his arguments for submission and for joining him in evangelizing the English people. Augustine in turn threatened them with destruction at the hands of their enemies. Geoffrey of Monmouth (book XI, chaps. 12–13, p. 85) not only relates Abbot Dinoot's opposition to Augustine's demands but also adds that Ethelbert of Kent incited Edelfrid of Northumbria to avenge this affront to Augustine. Holinshed (book V, chap. 22, pp. 103–4) recounts that Edelferd "did more damage to the Britains than anie one other king of the English nation. . . . Of those moonks and priests which came to praie . . . there died at that battell about the number of 12 hundred, so that fiftie of them onelie escaped by flight. . . . Thus was the prophesie of Augustine fulfilled." Whereas Bede represents the massacre as divine justice, Geoffrey depicts it as martyrdom: "mille ducenti eorum in ipsa die martyrio decorati, regni cælestis adepti sunt sedem." In his *History of Britain* (*Complete Prose*, V, 192–94), Milton expresses uncertainty as to the causes of the massacre and as to whether Ethelfrid came to Westchester "of his own accord, or at the request of *Ethelbert* incens't by *Austin*." In Milton's entry, Fletcher suggests that in "with" the "w" is written over another letter.

²⁶ Fletcher believes that "Rodoald K." was written over some other letters. The second letter is probably "o" though one would have expected an "e." In Speed, Holinshed, and Milton's *History of Britain* (*Complete Prose*, V, 199, 201), this name appears as "Redwald." According to Speed (book VII, chaps. 9, 11, pp. 242–43, 260), Edwin aroused the suspicions of Ethelfrid, king of Northumbria, went into exile, and was "lastly received and succoured by *Redwald*, King of the *East-Angles*, who in his quarel forthwith assembled his forces, and meeting *Ethelfrid* in the field, slew him neere the River *Idle*." Edwin subsequently became King of Northumbria "and afterward Monarch of the *Englishmen*." His vision, as related by Bede, Speed summarizes: "whilest hee lay banished in king *Redwalds* Court," a mysterious stranger demanded the cause of his grief and offered to "shew him how to save his soule." Edwin promised to "bee ruled by him, that thus should free me from this present danger, set me upon the throne of a kingdome, and . . . also teach me the way to an eternall life." After enjoining Edwin to recall his vow when these things had been fulfilled, the stranger vanished; and, shortly thereafter, Redwald assembled his forces and slew Ethelfrid. Holinshed (book V, chap. 25, p. 107) also relates "The vision of Edwin . . . in the court of Redwald . . . whereby he was informed of his great exaltation and conversion to christian religion."

²⁷ Holinshed (book V, chap. 30, p. 115) reports that "King Oswie had one Oswin partener with him in government of the Northumbers . . . so that Oswie governed in Bernicia, and Oswin in Deira, continuing in perfect friendship . . . till at length, through the counsell of wicked persons . . . they fell at debate, and so began to make warres one against an other." Judging his forces insufficient to open battle, Oswin took refuge with "earle Hunwald, whome he tooke to have beene his trustie friend: but . . . Hunwald did betraie him unto Oswie, who by his captaine Edelwine slue the said Oswin and his servant."

²⁸ Relating how "Sigibert . . . is murthered of two brethren that were his kinsmen upon a conceived hatred against him for his good and christian life," Holinshed (book V, chap. 31, pp. 116–17) stresses two points, first, "how dangerous it is to keepe companie with an excommunicate person" and, secondly, how great

is "the authoritie of a bishop." In "this his innocent death" Sigibert was punished for an earlier offence "wherein he had suerlie transgressed the lawes of the church. For whereas one of them which slue him kept a wife, whome he had unlawfullie maried, and refused to put hir away at the bishops admonition, he was by the bishop excommunicated, and all other of the christian congregation commanded to absteine from his companie. This notwithstanding, the king being desired of him came to his house to a banket, and in his comming from thence met with the bishop. . . . Bicause (saith he) thou wouldst not absteine from entring the house of that wicked person being accurssed, thou shalt die in that same house: and so it came to passe." In his *History of Britain (Complete Prose,* V, 211), Milton correctly identifies Sigibert as king of the East-Saxons.

²⁹ According to Holinshed (book V, chap. 36, p. 125), "Egfride . . . sent an armie . . . into Ireland, the which wasted that countrie, sparing neither church nor monasterie, sore indamaging the people of that countrie, which had ever beene friends unto the English nation." The Irishmen, for their part, besought "God . . . that he would revenge their cause in punishing of such extreme iniuries . . . & so (peradventure) it fell out. For in the yeere following, the said Egfride had lead an armie into Pictland . . . and being trained into straits within hils and craggie mounteins, he was slaine with the most part of all his armie." Milton's *History of Britain (Complete Prose,* V, 223) cites Bede in his account of the warning of "Cudbert a famous Bishop of that Age." After "battell," "against" substituted for "with."

³⁰ Fletcher suggests that "the letters *wulf* were written over." Holinshed (book VI, chap. 6, p. 134) relates how Kinewulfe "confined one Kineard the brother of Sigibert, whose fame he perceived to increase more than he would have wished. . . . This Kineard dissembling the matter . . . watched his time, till he espied that king with a small number of his servants was come unto the house of a noble woman, whome he kept as paramour at Merton, whereupon the said Kineard upon the sudden beset the house round about." The king was slain, but one of his retainers survived to report the assassination to Osrike and other loyal nobles, who avenged the king's death by slaying Kineard and many of his fellow conspirators in a second skirmish at Merton.

³¹ "the danish ladie." inserted above line and indicated by a caret. According to Holinshed (book VII, chap. 5, pp. 170–71), "Gunthildis the sister of king Swaine was slaine, with hir husband & hir sonne, by the commandement of the false traitor Edrike. . . . she came hither into England with hir husband Palingus, a mightie earle, and received baptisme heere. . . . She was a verie beautifull ladie, and tooke hir death without all feare, not once changing countenance, though she saw hir husband and hir onelie sonne . . . first murthered before hir face." In the *History of Britain (Complete Prose,* V, 340), Milton adds the following comment: "Some say that this was done by the Traitor *Edric,* to whose custody she was committed, but the massacher was some years before *Edric's* advancement."

³² "together . . . Speed." added later at lower right of original entry. Speed (book VII, chap. 44, pp. 416–17) describes the "bloudy massacre" ordered by King Ethelred for November 13 and the slaughter at Oxford of the Danes who had taken refuge in the church of Saint Frideswide. According to Holinshed, however (book VII, chaps. 5, 8, pp. 170, 174), the massacre of the Danes at Oxford occurred in the year 1015, whereas the "generall slaughter of Danes" (and Gunthildis's murder) took place (in the opinion of Matthew of Westminster) on Saint Brice's day in the year 1012.

[33] "Brightrick" inserted with caret above and before canceled "Bithrick"; "of west Saxons" inserted above line, with place indicated by a caret; "who" inserted before "dyes." According to Speed (book VII, chap. 7, p. 230), "*Brithric . . .* maried *Ethelburga,* the daughter of great *Offa* the *Mercian* King. . . . It afterward chanced, that shee preparing poison to make an end of one of the Kings Minions, wrought therby (though unwittingly) the Kings death: for he by tasting the confection ended his life." After seeking refuge in France, she was "thrust into a Monastery" by the French king, "where not long after she abused her body by committing of adultery, and was shortly expelled, & in beggerly misery ended her life."

[34] "y^e" inserted above line. Speed (book VII, chap. 36, p. 386) relates how "this Prince . . . disguised himselfe in the habite of a common Minstrell, and in person repaired to the *Danes* Campe, who lay like *Senacheribs,* wallowing in wantonnesse, and secure in their owne conceit from impeach of danger . . .: whereby hee both saw their negligent security, and by diligent observance learned the designes that in their counsels they entended." After Alfred informed his own subjects of "how easie it was to recover againe their decaied estates," they "on the suddaine set upon the carelesse Campe of the *Danes* and made thereof a very great slaughter. . . . *Hubba,* that had harried the *English,* and now rowzed upon the newes of King *Elfreds* victory and life; with thirty three ships sailed from *Wales . . .* unto whom the *Devonshiere* men gave battle, and slew eight hundred and eighty persons of their retinue; where died the *Danish* King *Hubba.*"

[35] According to Holinshed (book VI, chap. 14, p. 146), "King Alured . . . builded a fortresse in the Ile of Edlingsey, afterward called Athelney, and breaking out oftentimes upon the enimies, distressed them at sundrie times with the aid of the Summersetshire men."

[36] According to Speed (book VII, chap. 37, p. 393), Edwine (fourth son of King Edward of the West-Saxons) "was very young when his father was buried, and his brother *Ethelstane* crowned. Notwithstanding a deep ielosie possessing the king, that his title was too neer the Crown, he caused him to bee put into a little Pinnesse, without either Tackle or Oares, one onely page accompanying him, that his death might bee imputed to the waves: whence the young Prince, overcome with griefe, and not able to master his own passions, cast himselfe headlong into the sea. . . . Which fact was much lamented by King *Ethelstan,* who greevously punished the suggestions of his own ielosie, and the procurers of his brothers death."

[37] After describing Edgar as "cruell to Citizens, and lecherous to maidens," Speed (book VII, chap. 42, pp. 406–8) recounts his "last lascivious Act, [which] was as *Davids* ioyned with bloud. . . . Fames lavish report of beauteous *Elfrida . . .* the only daughter of *Ordgarus* Duke of *Devonshire . . .* was heard into King *Edgars* court . . .: to trie the truth whereof, hee secretly sent his minion or favourite Earle *Ethelwold* of *East-Anglia . . .* with Commission, that if the Pearle proved so orient, it should bee seized for *Edgars* owne wearing, who meant to make her his Queene. . . . *Ethelwold . . .* himself began to wooe the Virgin, yea, and with her Fathers good liking. . . . *Ethelwold* returning, related that the maide indeed was faire; but yet her beauty much augmented by babling reports, and neither her feature or parts any wise befitting a King." On the strength of this report, Edgar abandoned his plan to wed Elfrida and subsequently granted Ethelwold permission to marry her. Nevertheless, reports of her beauty aroused the king's suspicions, and he resolved to visit Ethelwold and his bride on the pretext of a hunting trip. Angered by his courtier's deceit and smitten by the beauty of

his wife, Edgar concealed his passion and "passed on to his game, where having the false *Ethelwold* at advantage, he ranne him through with a Iaveline, and tooke faire *Elfrida* to his wife."

[38] According to Speed (book VII, chap. 42, p. 406), Edgar displayed "much devotion, but most especially toward the *Monks,* for whom, and for *Nunnes* he built and repaired forty seven *Monasteries.*"

[39] Speed (book VII, chap. 42, pp. 407–8) gives the following account of Elfrida's behavior toward her husband: "But *Ethelwold* mistrusting the cause of his [Edgar's] comming, thought by one policy to disappoint another: and therefore revealing the truth to his wife . . . requested her loving assistance to save his now endangered life," exhorting her to "conceale thy great beauty . . . and give him entertainement in thy meanest attires." Reflecting that her husband had not only slandered her beauty but also prevented her from becoming queen, Elfrida refused to "falsifie and bely Natures bounties, mine owne value, and all mens reports, onely to save his credite, who hath impaired mine. . . . And thus resolving to bee a right woman . . . made preparation to put it in practice. Her body shee endulced with the sweetest balmes, displaied her haire, and bespangled it with pearles, bestrewed her breasts & bosome with rubies and diamonds . . . And thus, rather Angell, then Lady-like, shee attended the approach and entrance of the King."

[40] Ethelred II ("the Unready"). In the MS the letter "r" has apparently been superimposed on "d." Columbia (XVIII, 513) suggests that the name was first written "Etheld"; and Fletcher that it was first "Ethelded" and the first "d" altered to "r." Wright reads "Etheldred' (the form occurring in #14 above and in Stow).

[41] According to Speed (book VII, chap. 44, p. 419), in the year 1013 King Swaine "came unto *London,* and presently begirt the walls with a strait siege. In the City lay unfortunate King *Ethelred.* . . . *Swaine* at his first comming fiercely assaulted the City, hoping his fortunes would have proved as before; but the presence of the King, and *London* the eye of the land, made the Citizens above measure couragious, who beat the *Danes* from their walles, and sallying forth of the Gates, slew them on heapes, so that *Swaine* himselfe was in great danger, had he not desperately runne through the midst of his enemies, and by flight escaped their swords."

[42] For Harold II's death at the Battle of Hastings, see Speed, book VII, chap. 44, p. 424.

[43] According to Speed (book VIII, chap. 4, p. "405" and index), "Prince *Alfred,* King *Canute* his Sonne, right heire to the Crowne of *England,*" was "entrapped by fraude, bereft of his eyes and cruelly tormented"; "Earle *Goodwin* met him, and binding his assurance with his corporall oath, became his liege-man, and guide to Queene *Emma;* but . . .trecherously led these strangers a contrary way, and at *Guilford* lodged them in severall companies, making known to the King what he had done: who forthwith apprehended them, even in their beds, and in the morning as chained prisoners, committing them to slaughter, . . . did spare and exempt onely every tenth man for service or sale: Prince *Alfred* himselfe was sent prisoner to the Isle of *Ely,* where having his eyes inhumanely put out, lived not long thereafter in torment and griefe." Vengeance for Alfred's death served as pretext for the Norman invasion. In Holinshed's account (book VIII, chap. 10, p. "174"), William's proclamation upon landing at Pevensey affirmed his duty "to revenge the death of his nephue Alured or Alfred . . . whome Goodwine earle of Kent and his adherents had most cruellie murthered."

[44] Speed (book VIII, chap. 7, p. "422") relates how King Harold II "with an

undaunted courage, led forth his Armie into *Sussex* (against the importunate suite
of his mother, who sought by all meanes to stay him)"; and according to Holinshed
(book VIII, chap. 10, pp. "174–75"), "Girth one of Harolds yoonger
brethren . . . advised his brother not to adventure himselfe at this present in the
battell."

⁴⁵ "murder'd" deleted before "defeating." Holinshed (book VII, chap. 9, pp.
176–77) relates how Edmund "fought with the Danes at Brentford, and gave
them a great overthrow"; and how (book VII, chap. 10, p. 177) "the title and
right of the realme of England is put to the triall of combat betweene Cnute and
Edmund, Cnute is overmatched, . . . both kings are pacified and the armies
accorded, [and] the realme divided betwixt Cnute and Edmund."

⁴⁶ While noting "the dissonant report of writers touching the maners of his
[Edmund's] death," Holinshed (book VII, chap. 10, pp. 177–80) asserts that the
"common report" is that "king Edmund was slaine at Oxford . . . that earle
Edrike was the procurer of this villainous act, and that (as some write) his sonne
did it. . . . In the yeare 1018, Edrike de Streona . . . was overthrowne in his
owne turne" after boasting to Canute that he had slain King Edmund. "At which
words Cnute . . . gave sentence against Edrike . . . And immediatlie he caused
his throat to be cut, and his bodie to be throwen out at the chamber window into
the river of Thames. But others say, that hands were laid upon him in the verie
same chamber or closet where he murdered the king" and his body "cast into a
common ditch called Houndsditch."

⁴⁷ "combat" inserted in left margin before "against". According to Speed (book
VIII, chap. 3, p. "403"), "*Gunhilda*, the daughter of King *Canute* and of *Emma*
his Queene, was the first wife of *Henry* the third *Romane* Emperour. . . . Shee
was a Lady of a surpassing beauty, which either mooved her husbands minde
to iealousie, or the overlavish report therof to breede surmize of incontinencie;
for accused she was of adulterie, and to defend her cause by combat, none could
be found, till lastly her Page, brought with her from *England,* seeing no other
would adventure for her innocencie, entred the list, himselfe but a Youth, in
regard of the other Combatant being a Giant-like man; yet in fight at one blow,
cutting the sinewes of his enemies legge, with another hee feld him to the
ground . . . and redeemed his Ladies life."

⁴⁸ On Hardicanute's character and death, Speed (book VIII, chap. 5, pp.
"407–8") reports "a great Epicure he was, and given much unto Cuppes, whereby
he trained the body to belly cheere, and sense to be subject to sloath and drunkennesse; foure times every day were his tables spred, and plenteously with all
Cates furnished." His "death was sodaine. . . . At the celebration of a great
marriage . . . and banquet, at *Lambeth* . . . revelling and carousing amidst his
cups, hee sodainely fell down without speech or breath: whose losse was the lesse
lamented for his excesse, riotousness, and unwonted exactions." In his *Commonplace Book* (*Complete Prose*, I, 367), Milton includes Hardiknute under the heading *Gula,* citing the histories of Holinshed and Jovius. Holinshed (book VII, chap.
15, p. 185) declares that "as he sat at the table in a great feast holden at Lambeth,
he fell downe suddenlie with the pot in his hand, so died not without some
suspicion of poison. . . . It hath been commonlie told, that Englishmen learned
of him their excessive gourmandizing & unmeasurable filling of their panches
with meates and drinkes, whereby they forgat the vertuous use of sobrietie."

⁴⁹ Speed reports (book VIII, chap. 6, p. "414") that "the King expulsed her his
Court and Bed and that with no little disgrace; for taking all her goods from her,
even to the uttermost farthing, committed her prisoner to the Monasterie of

Wilton, attended onely with one maid, where she, for a whole yeeres space almost, in teares and praiers expected the day of her release and comfort."

50 Holinshed (book VIII, chap. 2, pp. 187–88) relates how "a bloudie fraie" at Canterbury between the townsmen and Eustace earl of Boulogne led to a breach between King Edward and Godwin earl of Kent. Though the king commanded Godwin "foorthwith to go with an armie into Kent, and to punish them of Canturburie in most rigorous maner, yet he would not be too hastie, but refused to execute the kings commandement, both for that he bare a peece of grudge in his mind, that the king should favour strangers so highlie as he did; and againe, bicause heereby he should seeme to doo pleasure to his countriemen, in taking upon him to defend their cause."

51 Describing snow, earthquake, lightning, and dearth as "scourges sent from God upon the Land for sinne," Speed declares (book VIII, chap. 6, p. "413") that "both Princes, Pastors and people, had all severally their part thereof, as being ioyntly the causers of the same. For the King, in case of these Strangers, put the Land more than once in danger to be lost: and himselfe refraining the bed of his vertuous wife, committed thereby the offence forbidden by the Apostle, and caused her his Queene either to commit or to be accused to have committed adultery. The Clergie likewise altogether unlearned, wanton and vicious: for the Prelates, neglecting the offices of Episcopall function, . . . lived themselves idle, and covetous." According to Holinshed (book VIII, chap. 1, p. 187) "king Edward never had to doo with hir in fleshlie wise. But whether he absteined because he had happilie vowed chastitie . . . or for a private hate that he bare to her kin, men doubted."

52 "wherin Godwins . . . magnifid" added (apparently later) in lower left margin, without indication of the point at which it should be inserted in the text. Birch, Peck, Todd, and Masson interpolate this passage between the references to "Godwins insurrection" and "his slacknesse"; Columbia inserts it after "chastitie." As the square brackets indicate, several letters in the left margin have been lost. According to Speed (book VIII, chap. 6, p. "412"), "great preparation on both sides was made . . . the Battaile was prepared, and brought to the very point of hazard and ruine of all: For in that quarrell were assembled the greatest Peeres, and Lords of the Land, the Kings love swaying very much with many, but yet the hatred towards Strangers possessing the hearts of more. The beginning thus doubtfull, and the end like to prove dangerous; the matter both with great foresight and providence was referred unto Parliament, to be holden at *London* with all convenient hast."

Scotch stories or rather brittish of the north parts

[1]

Athirco slain by Natholochus whose daughters he had ravisht [1]
and this Natholocus usurping theron the kingdom seeks to slay the
kindred of Athirco who scape him & conspire against him [2] he
sends to a witch to know the event. the witch tells the messenger
that he is the man shall slay Natholochus he detests it but in his
journie home changes his mind, & *per*forms it &c. Scotch chron.
English. p. 68. 69.[3]

[2]

Duffe, & Donwald

a strange story of witchcraft, & murder discover'd, & reveng'd.
Scotch story. 149. &c.[4]

[3]

Haie the plow man

who with his tow sons that were at plow running to the battell that
was between the Scots & Danes in the next feild staid the flight of
his countrymen, renew'd the battell, & caus'd the victorie &c.
Scotch story. p. 155.[5]

[4]

Kenneth

who having privily poison'd Malcolm Duffe, that his own son
might succeed is slain by Fenela. Scotch hist. p. 157. 158. &c.[6]

[5]

Macbeth

beginning at the arrivall of Malcolm at Mackduffe. the matter of
Duncan may be express't by the appearing of his ghost.[7]

---

[1] Milton's reference is to the English adaptation of Bellenden's translation of
the *Scotorum Historiæ* of Hector Boethius, printed with Holinshed's *Chronicles*.
Milton's page numbers fit the 1587 edition of the *Chronicles*. According to Holinshed (p. 68), Athirco commenced his reign as a "verie sober, gentle, courteous"
monarch; but after "eight yeeres, he was quite altered," giving himself "wholie
to filthie pleasures and sensuall lusts of the bodie" and "not regarding at all the
nobilitie of his realme. . . . a noble man in Argile . . . named Natholocus, had
two faire yoong gentlewomen to his daughters: now the king . . . forced them
both . . . and not so content, delivered them afterwards to be abused in semblable
sort by his pages and servants. The father understanding this vilanie doone to
his daughters, . . . sent for his friends. . . . They being in a woonderfull furie to
heare of such an iniurie doone to their bloud, promised in revenge therof to spend

life, lands, & goods." At the news of their approach Athirco sought to escape to the western isles but "was by contrarie winds driven back againe to land, where doubting to come into his enimies hands, he chose rather to slea himselfe." He was not, as Milton's note reads, "slain by Natholochus."

² Holinshed (pp. 68–69) continues: having been elected monarch and having attainted Athirco's kindred of treason, Natholocus ruled his realm at will until "at length fortune began to shew a change of countenance after hir old accustomed guise. For Doorus the brother of Athirco . . . wrote certeine letters, signifieng his owne estate with the welfare of his nephues the children of Athirco unto certeine Scotish lords, whom he knew to favour his cause." Intercepting these communications, Natholocus caused the messenger to be "sacked and throwne into a river" and the addressees to be strangled. The friends and allies of the murdered nobles thereupon "procured the people to rebell: and so gathering them togither, they raised open and cruell warres against him." Here again Milton is not completely accurate, as Natholocus did not usurp the kingship.

³ Natholocus (Holinshed, p. 69) withdrew secretly to "Murrey land" to muster an army; desiring to "understand somwhat of the issue of this trouble," he "sent one of his trustie servants . . . unto a woman that dwelt in the Ile of Colmekill (otherwise called Iona) esteemed verie skilfull in forshewing of things to come, to learne of hir what fortune should hap of this warre." After consulting with her spirits, the witch declared "that the king should be murthered, not by his open enimies but by the hands of one of his most familiar friends. . . . The messenger demanding by whose hands that should be: Even by thine saith she. . . . The gentleman hearing these words, railed against hir verie bitterlie . . . but before he came where the king lay, his mind was altered, so that what for doubt on the one side, that if he should declare the trueth as it was told him, the king might happilie conceive some great suspicion, that it should follow by his means as she had declared, and thereupon put him to death first; and for feare on the other side, that if he keepe it secret, it might happen to be revealed by some other, and then he to run in as much danger of life as before; he determined with himselfe to worke the surest way, and so comming to the king, . . . he declared how he had sped; and then falling foorthwith upon Natholocus, with his dagger he slue him outright, and threw his bodie into a privie."

⁴ Before "witchcraft," "revenging" deleted. According to Holinshed (pp. 149–51) King Duffe had angered the nobility by ordering the thanes of the isles to purge their countries of "divers robbers and pillers of the common people." Shortly thereafter, when the king fell mysteriously ill, a rebellion broke out, in which the chief offenders "were those of Murrey land. . . . But about that present time there was a murmuring amongst the people, how the king was vexed with no naturall sicknesse, but by sorcerie and magicall art, practised by a sort of witches dwelling in a towne of Murrey land, called Fores." Through the exertions of Donwald ("capteine of the castell" at Forres in Morayshire) an attempt was made to detect and apprehend the witches. After a soldier's concubine had confirmed the plot against the king, Donwald's troops broke into a house at midnight and "found one of the witches rosting upon a woodden broch an image of wax at the fier, resembling . . . the kings person." When "examined for what purpose they went about such manner of inchantment, they answered, to the end to make away the king: for as the image did waste afore the fire, so did the bodie of the king breake forth in sweat. And as for the words of the inchantment, they served to keepe him still waking from sleepe, so that as the wax ever melted, so did the kings flesh: by which meanes it should have come to passe, that when the wax

was once cleane consumed, the death of the king should immediatlie follow. So were they taught by evill spirits, and hired to worke the feat by the nobles of Murrey land." The bystanders "streightwaies brake the image, and caused the witches . . . to bee burnt to death." After recovering health, King Duffe defeated the rebels in Morayshire and brought them back to Forres to be hanged. Among these were certain kinsmen of Donwald; and when the king refused his request for their pardon, "he conceived such an inward malice towards the king . . . that the same . . . ceased not, till through setting on of his wife . . . hee found meanes to murther the king within the foresaid castel of Fores." At his wife's instigation Donwald made the royal chamberlains drunk, bribing four servants to slay the king and hide his body under a river. In the morning "when the noise was raised in the kings chamber how the king was slaine," Donwald "ran thither" with the watch "as though he had knowne nothing of the matter, and . . . foorthwith slue the chamberleins, as guiltie of that heinous murther." Certain portents after the murder led Culene, prince of Cumberland, to vow vengeance on "the false inhabitants of Murrey land"; and by attempting to flee to Norway, Donwald revealed his guilt and thus stood "detected of manifest treason." After taking the castle of Forres, Culene "slue all that he found therein, and put the house to sacke and fire. Donwalds wife with his three daughters were taken" and put to the rack, where the woman "confessed the whole matter." Shortly thereafter "woord came that the traitor Donwald was by shipwracke cast upon the shore within foure miles of the castell." Immediately after he had been taken prisoner, "there came in divers lords of Rosse, bringing with them Donwalds foure servants, which . . . did execute the murther. Thus all the offendors being brought togither unto the place where the murther was both contrived and executed, they were arrained, condemned, and put to death."

⁵ After "tow," an illegible letter deleted; and after "feild," "recover'd the" deleted. According to Holinshed (p. 155) the Scottish and Danish forces fought near the river Tay, with King Kenneth himself governing the battle; Malcolm Duffe, prince of Cumberland, led the Scottish right wing, and Duncan lieutenant of Atholl the left: "there was in the next field at the same time an husbandman, with two of his sons busie about his worke, named Haie. . . . This Haie beholding the king with the most part of his nobles, fighting with great valiancie in the middle ward, now destitute of the wings, and in great danger to be oppressed by the great violence of his enimies, caught a plow-beame in his hand, and with the same exhorting his sonnes to doo the like, hasted towards the battell." Placing themselves athwart a lane near the battle where they "might best staie the flight," Haie and his sons "beat them backe whome they met fleeing, and spared neither friend nor fo: but downe they went all as came within their reach, wherewith diverse hardie personages cried unto their fellowes to returne backe unto the battell, for there was a new power of Scotishmen come to their succours. . . . The Danes being here staied in the lane by the great valiancie of the father and the sonnes, thought verely there had beene some great succors of Scots come to the aid of their king, and thereupon ceassing from further pursuite, fled backe in great disorder unto the other of their fellowes fighting with the middle ward of the Scots." In recompense, Haie and his two sons were awarded the "chiefest part" of the spoils, and the family was ennobled.

⁶ According to Holinshed (pp. 156–58), "the blind love he [Kenneth] bare to his owne issue, caused him to procure a detestable fact, in making away one of his neerest kinsmen. This was Malcolme the sonne of king Duffe, created in the beginning of Kenneths reigne prince of Cumberland, by reason wherof he ought

to have succeeded in rule of the kingdome after Kenneths death. Whereat the same Kenneth greeving not a little, for that thereby his sonnes should be kept from inioieng the crowne, found meanes to poison him." Kenneth was slain while lodging at the castle of Fethircarne, where he had been received by "Fenella ladie of the house, whose son . . . he caused to be put to death, for the commotion made betwixt them of Mernes and Angus. She was also of kin unto Malcolme Duffe, whome the king had made awaie, and in like manner unto Constantine and Grime, defrauded of their right to the crowne, by the craftie devise of the king. . . . This woman . . . long time before having conceived an immortall grudge towards the king . . . imagined night and day how to be revenged." Eventually she constructed a magnificent chamber, concealing "crossebowes set readie bent" behind "rich cloths of arras." In the midst of the chamber she placed a "goodlie brasen image" of Kenneth, "holding in the one hand a faire golden apple set full of pretious stones, devised with such art and cunning, that so soone as anie man should draw the same unto him, . . . the crossebowes would immediatlie discharge their quarrels upon him with great force and violence." Through this device she managed to ensnare and slay Kenneth, making her escape before the murder could be discovered.

⁷ Holinshed (pp. 174–75) relates Macduff's flight and interview with Malcolm Cammore. Earlier (p. 171) he relates the encounter of "Mackbeth" and "Banquho" with the three "weird sisters or feiries." Shortly thereafter, when King Duncan designated his elder son Malcolm as prince of Cumberland, "as it were thereby to appoint him his successor in the kingdome," Macbeth was "sore troubled herewith, for that he saw by this means his hope sore hindered (where, by the old lawes of the realme, the ordinance was, that if he that should succeed were not of able age to take the charge upon himselfe, he that was next of bloud unto him should be admitted)." Communicating "his purposed intent with his trustie friends, amongst whome Banquho was the chiefest," Macbeth "slue the king at Enverns, or (as some say) at Botgosuane, in the sixt yeare of his reigne."

NOTES ON MILTON'S *PARADISE LOST* AND OTHER

BIBLICAL SCENARIOS

By James Holly Hanford

EDITOR'S HEADNOTE

In preparing a new edition of Milton's dramatic plans, I am deeply grateful for the inspiration of Professor Hanford's scholarship and for Mrs. Hanford's generosity in making available to me his commentary on several scriptural subjects that Milton had significantly developed in detail. These are sketches for a drama on the fall of man ("Paradise Lost" and "Adam Unparadiz'd"); outlines for "Abram from Morea" and "Sodom"; plans for "Dinah" and "Thamar," "Baptistes" and "Christus Patiens." Professor Hanford's discussion throws additional light not only on the form and content of these projected tragedies but also on their relation to Milton's earlier and later poetry. In editing these comments (with minimal changes) for the benefit of other Miltonists, I should like to express my renewed admiration for a great scholar and dedicated humanist.

JOHN M. STEADMAN

I
"THE OUTLINES FOR A DRAMA ON THE FALL OF MAN."

There is some evidence that the three drafts on page 35 of the Trinity College manuscript were set down very soon after Milton's return from Italy in August, 1639. The handwriting is similar to that of the letter to Lukas Holste in the occasional use of a Greek "e." (There are apparently five such instances in these drafts.) Moreover, the play is reminiscent of the Italian *dramma per musica, sacra rappresentazione,* or oratorio. Resembling Andreini's *Adamo* in its use of allegorical figures, it differs significantly from the other dramas in the manuscript.

Milton's Italian experience is reflected in the operatic and allegorical character of the first three drafts for "Paradise Lost." In the fourth version certain simplifications have taken place, and the whole design has moved somewhat away from the Italianate conception. Heavenly Love and Evening Star do not appear as persons, and the matter of their songs is expressed by the angel Gabriel. There is no debate between Justice and Mercy; instead, they appear sequentially after Adam's fall. The specification of a scene of mutual recrimination between Adam and Eve, in the fourth draft, provides for a humanly dramatic element not suggested in the earlier versions. I take these changes to be the fruit of Milton's experience of working out some of the Biblical themes.

There is no escaping the conclusion that Milton, like Emerson's Brahma, could "keep, and pass, and turn again"; his dramatic plans show a kind of frustrated purposefulness. He weighs the possible choices of a poetic form and subject in *The Reason of Church-Government* (February 1642), and he is still speaking of postponed ideal achievement in *An Apology* (April 1642). After that, he is involved in the consequences of his ill-advised and hasty marriage, and we hear nothing further of poetic plans and promises. The personal passages in *Paradise Lost* are retrospective:

> Since first this Subject for Heroic Song
> Pleased me, long choosing and beginning late.

The hesitations and returns become more and more marked as the drafting of dramatic plans proceeds. The first three outlines on "Paradise Lost" had shown continuous progress toward a five-act play resembling Andreini's *Adamo*. In the following pages Milton's simple canvas of Biblical and historical subjects revealed a systematic exploration of possibilities, almost incidental to a rereading of Scripture. On the whole, however, his desire to model a Biblical episode along the lines of Greek tragedy resulted in a prolonged process of thinking and rethinking, which ended up by getting nowhere. There were too many choices of both subject and treatment. This is characteristically Miltonic, but nowhere else is there evidence that the poet was actually held up by it.

Yet the experimentation at least helped to define the problem. It shows a certain progression toward a solution, and a movement toward fuller realization of the human values of the materials.

"Paradise Lost"

The three first outlines for Milton's drama on the fall of man are lists of *dramatis personae* with changes and progressive amplification. Adam and Eve do not appear before their fall. In the third outline Moses prologuizes, explaining that in their state of innocence they are invisible to sinful mortals.

The First Plan contains few evidences (and these trifling) of hesitation or alteration. In the Second Plan the original sequence of persons seems to have been about the same as in the First Plan, with some amplification—notably "Justice, Mercy, Wisdom" after "Michael" and "the Evening Star Hesperus" following "Heavenly Love." Milton inserted "Moses or" above "Michael" cancelling the latter. Later in the plan he added "Fear" and "Death" to the list of mutes and (having done so) cancelled "Death" in its original position after "Conscience."

The Third Plan bears the title "Paradise Lost." The materials are now divided into five acts, and the contents partly indicated. In Act I Moses prologuizes, explaining his bodily presence in Paradise and declaring that Adam and Eve are invisible to the audience because of the latter's sin. Justice, Mercy and Wisdom are to debate "what is to become of man if he fall." At the end of Act I the chorus sings a hymn of creation.

Act II opens with "Heavenly Love" and "the Evening Star" and ends with the chorus singing the marriage song and describing creation. Act III presents Lucifer contriving Adam's ruin and the chorus who "fears for Adam and relates Lucifer's rebellion and fall." In Act IV Adam and Eve are fallen; Conscience "cites them to God's examination"; the chorus bewails and tells the good Adam has lost. In Act V Adam and Eve are driven out of Paradise by an angel who presents (and names) a much-elaborated collection of horrors. Faith, Hope, and Charity comfort and instruct him; the chorus "briefly concludes."

"Adam Unparadiz'd"

The fourth outline (on page 40) is later, but was written before "Sodom" (which, in turn, was set down before "Baptistes").[1] Milton returned to the subject of the Fall after an interval of canvassing other possible materials.

"Adam Unparadiz'd" reflects some experience with these explorations. It is not a list of persons, but a continuous scenario, like "Abram from Morea." Milton is discarding a considerable part of the allegorical machinery and moving toward the actual method of the epic, letting the chorus and dialogue of the divine and human actors carry the moral and religious ideas and lyric emotion. He is at the same time returning to the Biblical narrative. These are natural results of considering the other scriptural subjects as dramatic material, partly planning some of them and rather fully expounding others, such as "Abram from Morea."

In the Fourth Plan the scenario is written out consecutively under the title "Adam's Banishment" (which has been altered to "Adam Unparadiz'd"). Some interesting things have happened to Milton's earlier conception besides the change in title. He originally began with the chorus on guard in Paradise and expressing desire to know more concerning man. The angel Gabriel passes by their station and informs them. Later he inserted an expository prologue in the mouth of Gabriel. (It had been Michael in the first draft, Michael altered to Moses in the second, Moses in the third.)

Lucifer now enters, bemoaning his fall and plotting revenge on man. The chorus encounters him; there is discourse of enmity on each side and he departs. The chorus sings of the battle in Heaven, "as after the first act was sung a hymn of the creation." Milton is still evidently thinking of the act divisions in outline III, but is omitting the debate between Justice, Mercy, and Wisdom and the speaking parts of Heavenly Love and Evening Star, the material having been assigned to Gabriel. He seems to be tightening the action and arriving much earlier at the unparadising of Adam and Eve. This was perhaps due to the influence of Grotius' *Adamus Exul* as against the more fantastic and allegorical *Adamo* of Andreini. (His knowledge of the latter is less likely.)

The rest of the plot is hardly divisible into acts.[2] Adam and Eve appear covered with leaves, are accused by Conscience "in a shape," cited by Justice "to the place where Jehovah called for him." The judgment takes place off stage while the chorus, "informed by some angel the manner of his fall," laments. Satan appears again and boasts of his evil deed. Adam and Eve reenter and he impenitently accuses her. Justice appears again, reasons with, and convinces him. The chorus admonishes him to beware of Satan's example. An angel is sent to banish them and "causes to passe before his eyes in shapes a mask of all the evills of this life & world."

II

"DINAH"

According to the story as given in Genesis 34, Dinah—Jacob's daughter by Leah—was loved by Shechem, son of Hamor, who lay with her and defiled her. Shechem wished to marry Dinah and asked his father to obtain her for him. Learning that Dinah had been defiled, Jacob waited until his sons, Simeon and Levi, had returned from the fields. They gave a deceitful answer to Hamor:

"We cannot do this thing, to give our sister to one that is uncircumcised. . . ." The circumcision takes place. On the third day Simeon and Levi fall upon the males and destroy them. To Jacob's complaint that his sons have outraged the surrounding tribes who being many will destroy him and his house, the brothers reply: "Should he deal with our sister as with an harlot?" In Genesis 35:1–6 Jacob receives from his people the idols of the strange gods, buries them in Shechem, and at God's command flees to Bethel unpursued.

Why Milton selected this story and what he would have made of it had he carried it further is a matter of pure speculation. Except for three outlines for a "Paradise Lost" it is apparently his first attempt to deal with Old Testament episodes in dramatic form. Evidently his intention was to work closer to classical patterns than in the Italianate program for a drama on the Fall of Man, but we cannot even tell whether the chorus is composed of Shechemites or Hebrews. The messenger would doubtless have narrated the massacre and Rebecca's old nurse Deborah have prophesied the outcome—but where, when, and to whom? Milton is confronted with the difficulty of carving out a dramatic unit from the continuity of Hebrew history. In Eusebius he would have found a treatment in hexameter verses, which would have given him a certain authority for the literary use of the Dinah story. Nevertheless this too was narrative rather than dramatic—a portion of a verse hexaëmeron.

III
"THAMAR"

An early entry in the so-called "dramatic plans" which Milton set down in the Trinity College Manuscript shortly after his return from Italy shows him contemplating the shocking story of Tamar, wife of Judah's two eldest sons and mother of Judah's child in Genesis 38. The change in title—from "Thamar Peplophoros (Veiled)" to "Thamar Cùephorusa (Pregnant)" is characteristic. Milton visualized a scene which would have occurred early in the play: Tamar decoratively dressed and veiled as a harlot. His second title, on the other hand, refers to a later episode which might have served as the final scene of his drama: Judah confronted by Tamar with the pledges he had given her. The reasons underlying the alterations of title in the plans generally are complex and various.[3]

It is not possible to call "Thamar" an unwritten poem, though the two titles show that it had momentarily stirred his imagination.

The moral judgment made in the last sentence can be derived only by inference from scripture. Tamar is excused in what she attempted because her action is according to God's plan. One of Milton's persistent ideas is that human law and common ethics may be violated in the interests of a higher principle. The end justifies the means. This kind of casuistry recurs in other outlines and in many discussions in the later poetry and prose. *The Doctrine and Discipline of Divorce* begins with an indictment of custom and tradition as the great tyrants of man's thought. The notes in the Commonplace Book often propose questions or give examples which involve similar issues.[4]

IV
"ABRAM FROM MOREA" AND "SODOM"
TWO DRAMATIC SCENARIOS BY MILTON

Aside from the all-important plans for a drama on the Fall of Man, these two entries are the most interesting in the Trinity College Manuscript. Half-accomplished acts of the poetic imagination, they fill pages 39–40, along with "Baptistes" and "Adam Unparadiz'd." These four scenarios—written out at length in more or less complete sentences—differ from other entries and would seem to belong to a more advanced stage in Milton's exploration of the problem of reducing Biblical narrative to dramatic form. "Abram" is clearly written, without back-tracking; in "Sodom" Milton returns on himself, amplifying earlier scenes as if he were warming to the subject as he went along.

"Abram from Morea"

What strikes us first in Milton's outline is its remoteness from the essential spirit of the episode as given in Genesis 22. Milton has set the scene in Morea and constructed a dramatic plot which moves step by step to a purely external climax as Abram returns in triumph amid a host of friends and retainers. Of the religious meaning of Abram's obedience or of the conflicting emotions of his experience at the place of sacrifice Milton says nothing. He gives no hint of Isaac's moving inquiry or of the sudden release of tension at the moment of the miracle. The voice of God, which dominates everything, is unheard. The traditional interpretation of Abram as a type of Christ leaves no trace in Milton's plan.

On the other hand, Milton has created an interesting person in Sarah—a character unique in his poetry. Nowhere else does he portray a good but distracted woman torn by anxiety about her husband. Abram's friends are a little like Job's comforters, but it is difficult to make much out of their speculations. They talk "as the world would of such an action diverse ways." We may imagine a number of individual speakers commenting on one another's opinions and surmises, and groping for an explanation. Milton surely did not mean this to be mere space-filling talk. Instead, he must have intended to give the impression of puzzled minds groping for truth without the key till they are finally answered—not by a voice out of the whirlwind, but by the event itself. At the very least, this dialogue could increase the suspense, and the poet might have succeeded in making it interesting.

Compared with the original or with Milton's own *Samson Agonistes,* the proposed drama on Abram is a poor thing. Nevertheless, it is significant as one of a series of experiments, not fully worked out, toward the fusing of the Hebraic and the Hellenic. As such, it doubtless played a part in the poet's preparation for his chosen goal of creating for England a new literature, artistically disciplined and "doctrinal and exemplary to a nation."

"Sodom"

In considering this remarkable production we may note first the points which Milton has passed over in Genesis 19. He says nothing about Lot's offer to expose his daughters to the abuse of the men of Sodom; he omits the blinding of the Sodomites; and he overlooks Lot's lingering and his protest. Even though he might have mentioned these episodes in chorus or dialogue, he evidently did not regard them as necessary to the action. That Lot should have set the claims of hospitality above his ordinary morality would seem out of character to a seventeenth-century audience; such decorum would at least have demanded a dubious casuistical explanation. The comic blindness of the Sodomites "so that they wearied themselves to find the door" would apparently interrupt the sequence of events. Instead, in Milton's outline the angels pull Lot inside the house when he is sore pressed, then come forth and reveal themselves.

On the other hand, the poet has freely amplified some of the scenes and motives. There is little detail in Genesis about the corrupt life of the city, which Milton makes the most of, putting the description into the mouth of the chorus. The chorus itself is, of course, an innovation determined by the poet's general practice in the outlines. Genesis makes no mention of Lot's shepherds. In

Milton they play an important part in the action by providing for a pitched battle before the door.

The great theatrical climax at the end is made possible by the introduction of the king and nobles and an unbelieving son-in-law as individual victims of divine wrath. This and the battle constitute the two essential moments in the plot, and both are Miltonic inventions. Minor concrete additions to the Biblical story are found throughout. In Genesis there are no delegation of choice youths to invite Lot's guests to the festivities, no priest as spokesman for the mob, and no discourse of the angels to the men of Sodom.

More far-reaching is Milton's handling of the complex of ideas which led him to adopt the new title "Cupid's Funeral Pile" and to specify Venus Urania or Peor as the deities worshipped by the men of Sodom. The sources are both Biblical and Greek. Peor is mentioned once in Genesis, but the identification of the rites of the various Eastern cults depends on multiple references later in Scripture, on such accounts as that of Lucian in *De Dea Syria,* and on the long tradition of Scriptural interpretation down to Milton's time.

The poet had made use of these materials for many years. They furnish the demon lore of the *Nativity Ode* and the allegorical mysticism of the close of *Comus.* Later, in *Paradise Lost,* they are gathered and expanded in the enumeration of Satan's host. In each case they are adapted to the requirements of the subject, but there is also a progression of idea and feeling. "Sodom" presents the eternal conflict between good and evil more immediately than the youthful poems. In *Paradise Lost* the composite lore of the subject is integrated with the larger narrative and held at arm's length. Emphasis on the obscenity of the cults is lacking in the *Nativity Ode* and in *Comus,* but gives the main accent to "Sodom" and the passage in *Paradise Lost.* Nevertheless, in "Sodom" there is no space for the elaborate demonology of the epic. Instead, Milton concentrates on the moral corruption of the Sodomites and on the horror of God's vengeance; his dramatic use of demonology is conditioned by this predominantly ethical intent. To the obscene love associated with Astarte, Baal, Peor, and Chemosh he opposes the heavenly love embodied in the Platonic Aphrodite Urania.

For all its proclamation of divine love, "Sodom" is the most unmitigated representation of God's vengeance on the wicked to be found anywhere in Milton's works. In *Paradise Lost* Satan and the rebellious angels are routed with hideous ruin and combustion, but they continue to exist and plot in Hell. The lustful unbelievers in "Sodom," on the other hand, are completely annihilated.

V
"BAPTISTES" [5]

Act 1.   Herod, councillors, and Queen.
Act 2.   The Queen holds dialogue with John.
Act 3.   The Queen accuses John to Herod.
Act 4.   Salome dances before Herod.
Act 5.   John is condemned and bewailed by his disciples. John
         tells them his work is done.

VI
"CHRISTUS PATIENS"

This item (entered at the bottom of page 41 following "Moabitides") is virtually the only evidence of Milton's concern beyond mere titles ([59]–[64] [p. 559 above]) with the life of Christ in the entire body of material. It carries us back to the abortive ode on "The Passion" of about 1630, but represents something entirely different. One conjectures that if Milton had actually undertaken this drama as outlined, he would have found himself as much inhibited as he had been in the ode. Nowhere in his poetry does he respond emotionally and artistically to the suffering Christ. I believe this entry to have been made last, as if to recall that everything led to the fulfillment of God's purpose in the sacrifice and victory of Christ, the justification of his ways to men. On the other hand, sin, fierce retribution, and human conflict were the substance of the Old Testament plans.

When did Milton set down this plan? Though it is the last in the preserved list of dramatic subjects, there is nothing to show that it was later than the rest of the entries which are customarily dated 1640–42.

Though its subject and its emphasis on noble expressions for Christ's agony may link this play with *Paradise Regained,* there are nevertheless significant differences. To be sure, the agony in the Garden is one of the "temptations fierce, and former sufferings" mentioned in "The Passion"—themes that had been sounded by Vida's heroic trump but which the youthful Milton had rejected for mourning. Even though Christ's agony is analogous to his temptations in *Paradise Regained,* it is not identical in kind. In the dramatic sketch, Christ is not preparing for his mission; it has already been, in large part, fulfilled. In contrast to *Paradise Lost,* which still bears a notable resemblance to the projected dramas on this subject, *Paradise Regained* and "Christus Patiens" differ significantly not only in argument, but also in their central emphasis. In the dramatic "Paradise Lost" the promises to Adam occupy relatively the same place as in the epic. When Milton came to write *Paradise Regained,* it was not the *agony* of Christ which received "noble expressions."

¹ "The pages intervening between the first three outlines of 'Paradise Lost' and the fourth were presumably filled with the list of Biblical subjects on page 36 and those from British history on pages 37–38. Otherwise the fourth plan would naturally be found on the verso (page 36) or the recto (page 37)." [JHH]

² Professor Hanford's notes on "Adam Unparadiz'd" include a tentative division of this drama into five acts. As this differs from the act division suggested in *A Milton Handbook,* I quote it in full:

"Act I.
Prologue: Gabriel explains that since the creation he is present as often on earth as in Heaven. A chorus of angels say that they are stationed to guard Paradise and express a desire to know more of the new creature man. Gabriel passes by their station and relates the creation of Adam and Eve, their love and marriage. Angels sing a hymn of the Creation.

"Act II.
Satan bemoans his condition and plots revenge on man. The Chorus confront him, and he retires. The Chorus sing the battle in Heaven.

"Act III.
Satan reappears 'relating and insulting in what he had done to the destruction of Man.' Adam and Eve enter covered with leaves. Conscience accuses him, and Justice 'cites him to the place whither Jehovah called for him.' They go out. The Chorus are informed of the judgment by an angel and bewail man's fall.

"Act IV.
Adam and Eve return and accuse each other. Adam is impenitent, but Justice reasons with him and convinces him. The Chorus bid him 'beware Lucifer's example of impenitence.'

"Act V.
An angel is sent to banish them, but 'causes to pass before his eyes, in shapes, a masque of all the evils of this life and world.' Adam is humbled, 'relents, despairs.' At last Mercy comforts him, promises him the Messiah, calls in Faith, Hope, and Charity, and instructs him. Adam 'repents, gives God the glory, submits to his penalty. The Chorus briefly concludes.'

"The outline as thus given partly reveals Milton's progress toward a fully realized plot. He has omitted Justice, Mercy, and Wisdom in Act I. Adam and Eve are later to be cited by Justice (Act III), who appears again to reason with Adam (Act IV) after judgment has been pronounced by Jehovah off stage. Mercy comforts and instructs him (Act V). The substance of the raptures of Heavenly Love and Evening Star is expressed by Gabriel and the Chorus in Act I. This tightening makes possible the appearance of Lucifer at the beginning of Act II. Unless Milton again reduced the introductory material, this speech (which Edward Phillips believed to have constituted the very opening of the tragedy) was incorporated at the beginning of Book IV of the epic.

"There are other changes of importance. Originally Milton opened the scene with the angels guarding Paradise. He then inserted a sentence between the title and the first line, making Gabriel the prologue and thus returning to the idea of the first outline, where Michael introduces the drama. This was perhaps a step backward in simplifying the action. But the fifth act again shows evidence of compression, in that none of the shapes of evil are specified. Milton had, of course, already done so, increasing the list from the first to the third outline; the note at the end of the fourth outline—'compare this with the former draft'—suggests that Milton was divided between a kind of compulsion to get everything in and his awareness of the obvious difficulty of doing so without too much complicating the argument. Epic form was, of course, the ultimate solution. Moreover, if Milton had Grotius' *Adamus Exul* in mind (as seems probable), he would have been prewarned against the dangers of the plot." [JHH]

³ "The Tamar entry stands on page 36 (left-hand column) of the Trinity College Manuscript. Milton began this page with the mere titles 'The Deluge' and 'Sodom,' followed them with the *dramatis personae* of 'Dinah,' and then added the outline for a drama on Tamar. Originally this may have consisted of a title only, with spaces left for subsequent amplification. The title is centered in the column and written large, whereas the note itself is smaller and somewhat crowded. My conjecture is that before writing this note Milton had begun to survey scripture more swiftly, recording the subjects in the right-hand column, and had reached at least the Samson entries from Judges 15–16. The alternative titles for a Samson play are partly in the left column just after the note on Tamar. Proceeding then to the bottom of the right-hand column, Milton turned back to the left and continued until the page was almost filled. A small gap remained after the Tamar and added Samson titles. Had he wished to elaborate 'Thamar' further, he could have done so.

"We note first that the entries are in the approximate order of the Bible narrative from Genesis through Daniel, with large gaps. It looks as if Milton were first of all reviewing scripture for himself as part of the necessary preparation for the major work which he intended. In a large way this would be to pursue the theme of the Fall of Man, with its consequences in the punishment of sin and in the promise of redemption implied in it; in other words, he was studying God's plan for man. Having experimented with dramatic form on the Italian model, he is led to continue to do so with Greek tragedy in mind. From time to time he is intrigued by the literary possibilities of the different themes and pauses to work out a scenario. Confirmation of this theory is the fact that in later pages of the manuscript he develops certain given themes in fuller detail for their own sakes to the extent that we have in them what might have become the equivalents of *Samson Agonistes* and which can be studied in comparison with that tragedy, as the whole series may be studied for its bearing on the epic *Paradise Lost*. While Milton did not follow the program in the same way through the New Testament, he does include a 'Baptistes' and a 'Christus Patiens' among the later subjects." [JHH]

⁴ In his notes Professor Hanford cites entries under the headings "Of Lying" ("How far it is permitted") and "Of Marriage" ("To forbidd Polygamy to all hath more obstinat rigor in it then wisdom"). See *Complete Prose*, I, 384, 411.

⁵ Though this note was left incomplete, it is valuable for its tentative act division.

APPENDIX C

DIPLOMA ELECTIONIS S.R.M. POLONIÆ

Preface by Maurice Kelley

Reprinted below is the part of the Latin *Diploma Electionis S.R.M. Poloniæ* that Milton translated to form his *A Declaration, or Letters Patents,* 1674. In this reprint, ellipses indicate the omissions of names and titles that Milton did not include in his translation. Accents have been omitted and the occasional abbreviations expanded.

Those who wish to see the *Diploma* in its complete and original form can find it under the press mark Syng. XVIII–233–III in the Ossolineum, Wrocław, Poland. For identifying the document and locating this copy, I am indebted to the Slavonic Division of the New York Public Library. The Xerox copy from which my text is printed I owe to the courtesy of W. Brodzki, vice-director, and Dr. Janusz Albin, director of the Ossolineum. Copies of this Xerox are deposited in the New York Public and Princeton University libraries.

DIPLOMA
ELECTIONIS
S. R. M. POLONIÆ.[1]

In Nomine Sanctissimæ, & Individuæ Trinitatis, Patris, &
Filii, & Spiritus Sancti.

NOS ANDREAS TZREBICKI, Episcopus Cracoviensis, Dux Severiæ, Joannes Gembicki, Vladislaviens. & Pomeraniæ, . . . EPISCOPI. Stanislaus Warszycki, Castell. Cracoviensis, Alexander Michael Lubomirski, Cracoviensis, . . . PALATINI. Christophorus Grzymultovvski. Posnaniens. Alexander Gratus de Tarnovv, Sandomiriens. . . . CASTELLANI. Hilarius Polubinski, Supremus M. D. L. Mareschalcus, Christophorus Pac, Supremus M. D. L. Cancellarius, . . . SENATORES & OFFICIALES REGNI. . . .

Significamus præsentibus Literis Nostris quorum interest Universis
& singulis. Viduata iterum Respublica Nostra, per immaturum
Obitum Serenissimi olim Michaelis Poloniæ Regis, qui, vix unico
nec dum Integro Imperii Lustro exacto, die decima Mensis No-
vembris, Anno proxime elapso Leopoli, caducam istam immortali
Corona permutavit, in tam luctuosi funeris, & novæ Cladis acer-
rimo sensu, animo tamen erecto, suique inter præcipitia memor,
ire in remedia non destitit, ut crescere per ipsa Lechiam damna
compertum haberet Orbis. Auspicari imprimis placuit servandæ
& ultimis Interregni Casibus eripiendæ Patriæ, Consilia, ab ex-
orato Divino Numine, cujus unico velut digiti motu, Regna de
Gente in gentem transferri, Reges e Solo ad Solium provehi, solenne
& in proclivi est. Cœptum de hinc ingens Negotium Patriis Legibus,
& Majorum Institutis, post per actam Omnium Regni Ordinum
Varsaviæ Mense Februario Convocationem, Communi eorundem
Ordinum consensu die Electioni XX. Aprilis, A. præsen. 1674.
decreta ad famam celeberrimi Actus quasi dato Classico & erecto
virtutis trophæo Externorum Principum Vota & Cupidines in
Campo Libertatis Polonæ insigni Meritorum & Officiorum erga

---

[1] These three lines constitute the title page of the *Diploma*. The text begins on a new page, headed by a row of ornaments.

Rempubl. certamine, Sua quisque decora, in publicum commoda, & dona ferentes, ultro prodiere. Verum proximi Interregni effuso ambitu, & Partium studiis, Animorumque discidiis Respub. so- lertior, nec futuri socors, firma an dubia promitterentur, secum meditari, an vetera & recens parta Sarmatiœ decora in exterorum possessionem trudere, an Gloriam Militarem, & Orbi vix auditum ex Turcis Triumphum, fusumque bellis Sanguinem in Purpuram otiosi alicujus Principis transfundere, e prœsenti Statu videretur. Scilicet aliquis Caritatem Patriœ statim accipiat, non suœ & in- imica adeo Genti, famœque suœ sola Polonia sit, ut Exteris magis, quam suis faveat, utque reperta in Regno hoc Virtute, novœ potentiœ Hospitem superbire patiatur. Vertit exinde cogitationem in cives, & impositam arcani specie contumeliam, non posse Reges Poloniœ nisi extra Poloniam natos creari, quod priori Electione cœptavit tandem iterum abolevit. Neque inter Cives diu quœsivit, quem Civibus prœponeret; non enim incerta & suspensa hœc Elec- tio, non cunctationi locus, cum in hac licet œqualitate Nobilitatis Nostrœ, supra œquales Herois virtus prœmineret; ergo ora omnium & studia libenter ac Divinitus plane versa in Supremum Regni Mareschalcum Generalissimum Exercitus Ducem JOANNEM SO- BIESKI, admiranda Viri virtus, Mareschalci suprema in Aula potestas, cum armorum Dictatura, Senatoria amplitudo, cum Civili modestia, Natalium & Fortunarum exuberans splendor, cum obvia comitate, in comparabilis prudentia, invicta Fortitudo, in Deum pietas, in Concives amor, in dictis factisque constantia, in ipsos etiam hostes fides & clementia, ac quicquid de Heroe summum dici potest, aureas veluti compedes omnium animis & linguis adeo imposuere, ut eundem nullo ambitu, non prœcipitato consilio, sed matura & tertium in diem protracta, expensaque deliberatione Senatus Populusque Polonus & Magni D. Lit. concordibus votis & Suffragiis, Regem suum dicerent, eligerentque. Sane militavit in SERENISSIMI ELECTI *decus, in liberrimœ Electionis fidem, ac œviternam Electoris populi laudem, non una die, neque seriore vespera, aut in umbra noctis, nec uno fortuito impetu, transactum ingens sœculorum negotium: fas enim minime erat, Heroem sœculi momento temporis, & velut aleœ jactu in Regem evadere, cum nec una nocte generari Herculem, vetere scito antiquitas prodiderit, atque Electionem in aperto sub Jove libero, media luce sincerius enitescere docuerit. Quin & ipse Serenissimus Electus Nomina- tionem in tertium diem protelari modeste tulisse, imo ambivisse visus, ne subita facilitas suspecta judicio detraheret, & certiore argumento Orbis in fidem impelleretur, procul ambitu & corruptœ libertatis invidia Electum qui taliter eligeretur. An & destinato*

Superum consilio triduum integrum a Sabatho ad diem Lunæ hæc trutina duravit, quasi cæpta Sabatho Chotimensis Victoria, tertia demum die post captam Arcem Chotimensem Victoriam claudens, Regalis hujusce adoreæ augurium fecisset & auspicato Omine tri- nus Electionis dies JOANNIS TERTII *Regio Nomini allusisset. Munivit ad Coronam aditum, firmavitque huic Serenissimo Electo Suffragiorum favorem inclyta bellorum gloria, dum primus Polo- norum monstravit, posse stataria pugna pernicitatem Scythicam omnibus retroacti mundi Monarchiis gravem cohiberi, posse for- mitandas Turcarum phalanges uno ictu frangi & deleri. Ut vetera Militiæ Rudimenta quæ ductu & auspiciis alienis in Suecos, Mos- chos, Borussos, Transylvanos, Cosacos fortiter & gloriose gessit, sileantur, ut receptæ ex Cosacis Sexaginta circiter Civitates minus in ore famæ versentur: tamen hæc crebra & prospera prælia maximis post hominum memoriam victoriis præludium fuere. Inundaverant ante Sexennium prædatoriis turmis Podoliæ oras Scythicæ Myri- ades, omnia ferro & flamma late sternebantur, cum parva tunc manus & laceræ Legiones impetui hostili non sufficerent, noster tamen cedere nescius novo bellandi consilio se Podhaieci, angusta Arce, & tumultuaria munitione iuclusit [sic], quo sævitiam in vis- cera Regni festinantem excluderet. Ita clusus & fractus Barbarus Pacis Leges accepit, quasi ad id tantum irruisset, ut Serenissimo Electo Victoriæ materiam, gloriæque fegetem afferret. Posteriore Quadriennio, singulos Imperii bellici Annos inclytæ ex Cosacis & Tartaris simul junctis Sobiescianæ Victoriæ insignivere, recepta ex hoste Cosaco, quam late inter Hypanim & Tyram protenditur Urbibus & bellatore Populo Validissima Braclaviensis Provincia, ac supra fidem plane sunt, quæ annis abhinc duobus Serenissimus Electus post occupatam Kameneciam. Leopoli obsidione cincta in- territus, vix trium Millium Exercitus Polonici audacia & forti- tudine ad miraculum plane peregit, cum quinque dierum & noctium continuo cursu, absque ullo cibo, herbis duntaxat silvestribus, vi- tam trahendo Tartaros adortus, Narulum, Niemicroviam, Ko- marnum, Kalussiam, obscura quondam Oppidorum vocabula ingentibus Barbarorum cladibus illustravit, tres Crimenses Sol- tanos e Regnatrice Giercia Domo occidit, & robur illud Scytharum adeo protrivit, ut posterioribus hisce Annis recipere Animos & vires recolligere nequiverint. Sed Victorias omnes præteriti Au- tumni vicit felicitas: cum famosæ olim ad Chocimum munitiones Quadraginta Turcarum Millibus occupatæ, & firmatæ, in quibus ante tres & quinquaginta Annos totius Imperii Ottomanici ex Asia, Africa, & Europa coactas vires Poloni sustinuerant, & retuderant, nunc unicæ post Deum Imperatoriæ virtuti, & prudentiæ*

Sobiescianæ, paucas intra horas succubuere. Quippe ille vigilias obire, Stationes ordinare, tormentorum bellicorum apparatum præsens inspicere, Militem fame cælique injuriis & pertinaci in tertium diem statione fatigatum manu, voce, vultu accendere, ille quod maxime stupendum, pedes ante pedestres Legiones ad vallum penetrare, & eniti, & devotum pro Deo & Patria Caput in alcam fati mittere, palmarium duxit, moxque atrocissimam, intra munimenta Castrorum, stragem edidit, cum desperatio Turcarum acueret virtutem, & ipse fortissimi & providi Ducis omnia munia impleret, quo tempore tres Bassæ occisi, quartus vix effugio, Tyræ vortices superavit, cæsa internecione Janizarorum octo, Spachiorum selectissimorum, præter Militare vulgus. Viginti Millia, Castra cum omni apparatu & tormentis bellicis, & Assiriis, ac Phrigiis luxuriantis Asiæ operibus capta ac direpta, Famosa Chotimensis Arx, Pons per Tyram, ac utrinque firmissima instar Artium propugnacula additamentum Victoriæ fuere. Quid ni ergo tam inclyta & heroica virtus dignissimo Diadematis præmio Coronetur? Præivit Nobis exemplo tota olim Christianitas, quæ ad recuperationem Ierozolimorum Duce Godefredo Bullioneo, excita, Regnum illud eidem sponte detulit, eo quod primus Mœnia Urbis conscenderit. Non inferior gloria Serenissimus Electus Noster primus quoque binum hostile Vallum superavit. Ornat inauditam a multis retro sæculis Victoriam ipsius temporis momentum, quo Serenissimus REX MICHAEL *pridie vita excesserat, veluti commonstrans, Se tantæ virtuti ultro cedere, ut suis jam auspiciis ille Victor, a Galea ad Coronam, a Capulo ad Sceptrum, a Cespite Castrensi ad Regale Solium, tanto gloriosius transiret. Revocavit Respub. gratam sibi, ac nullo temporis ritio obliterandam memoriam inclyti Parentis Illustrissimi & Excellentissimi olim Jacobi Sobieski Castellani Cracoviensis, Vir cum cura scribendi, qui aurea suada in togatis Reipubl. Consiliis, in arena Martis invicta dextera, fortunam Remquepubl. toties auxerat, & gentilitio plane Scuto suo protexerat. Neque sine Numine evenisse credamus, ut quo loco tribus ab hinc & quinquaginta Annis Magnus Parens, Reipubl. Polonæ Legatus, Pacem & Pacta cum Osmano Turcarum Imperatore sanxerat, Maximus Filius, cælo ipso perfidiam hostibus exprobante, abruptæ pacis scelus, vindice ferro ulcisceretur. Cæteri Avi & Proavi ac innumera Clarissimorum Senatorum & Officialium Nomina, lucem velut Sereniss. Electo protulere, æmula Maternæ Stirpis magnitudine & gloria, præsertim Stanislai Zolhievii Supremi Cancellarii Regni, & Exercituum Imperatoris, cujus Sarcophago proximis campis, in quibus ille rabie Turcicæ Anno 1920. occubuerat, tam insigni hostium strage Victor Nepos parentavit. Congeminavit avi-*

tam gloriam ornatissimi Avunculi Stanislai Danilovicii, Palatinidæ Russiæ immortalis virtus & fatalis pro Patria An. 1635. occasus, quem egregius & juvenilis ardor bellicæ Laureæ avidum & Pacis, cui tunc secura Polonia altum indormiebat, haud tolerantem, Tauricanos in campos privatis opibus viribusque ultro propulerat, ut vetere illa Martis Poloni Eruditrice arena per vestigia sua Sobiescianis Meritis iter signaret, atque Nobilissimo Sanguine, ipsius Cantimiri Tartarorum Hani dextera in ultionem occisi filii mactatus, purpuræ jam præsenti fulgorem commodaret. Neque excidit Populo Polono Illustrissimus olim Marcus Sobieski, Serenissimi Electi Nostri Germanus natu major, qui profligato a Barbaris ad Batoum Exercitu Polono, etsi evadendi non deesset occasio, maluit tamen magnæ Cladi fortissimorum Virorum immori, & victima pro Patria occumbere, quam indecoro receptu vitam mercari; an forte ita disponentibus Divinis Judiciis, quibus res & Personas interire, Causas & eventus eosdem recurrere Ordo est, ut repetito Huniadum fato Major Summæ indolis Frater, miseranda cæde submotus, minori superstiti ad Thronum Regium expeditiorem viam relinqueret. Quod igitur Orthodoxæ Reipublicæ Nostræ ac Universæ Christianitati felix, faustum, fortunatumque sit, tam eximiis dotibus, meritis, & splendoribus cumulatissimum JOANNEM in Zolkievv & Zloczovv SOBIESKI, Supremum Regni Mareschalcum, Generalissimum Exercituum Ducem, Mævensem, Barensem, Stryensem, Javorouien, Kalusien Gubernatorem, liberis, concordibusque votis vocibus, & suffragiis, nemine contraveniente, omnibus consentientibus & applaudentibus, pro Jure liberæ Electionis, Vocatorum non Comparentium, absentia non obstante, nullo privato respectu ducti, sed Dei duntaxat gloriam, priscæ Religionis Catholicæ Incrementum, Reipublicæ salutem, ac Gentis Nominisque Poloni dignitatem præ oculis habentes, in Regem Poloniæ, Magnum Ducem Lithuaniæ, Russiæ, Prussiæ, Mazoviæ, Samogitiæ, Kijoviæ, Volhiniæ, Podlachiæ, Podoliæ, Livoniæ, Smolensciæ, Severiæ, Czerniechoviæque eligendum, creandum, nominandum duximus, prout elegimus, creavimus, renunciavimus, nominavimus, me prædicto Episcopo Cracovien. vacante pro tunc Archiepiscopali Sede. Munus & Prærogativam Primatialem exercente, & de Consensu omnium Ordinum, per trinam interrogationem, a nemine impugnatam, ab omnibus & singulis approbatam, Electionem concludente. Bona fide promittentes quod eidem Serenissimo & Potentissimo Principi, Dn. JOANNI III. Regi nostro, eandem fidem, subjectionem, obedientiam & obsequia debita, secundum Jura & Libertates Nostras, semper exhibebimus, quam Divis Suæ Majes-

tatis Prædecessoribus exhibuimus. Tum etiam quod eundem Serenissimum in Comitiis proximis Cracoviæ eo fine celebrandis tanquam verum Regem & Dominum Nostrum, Regio diademate, quo Reges Poloniæ Coronari solent, insigniemus, & de more, quem Catholica Romana Ecclesia in unguendis, & inaugurandis Regibus, ante hac servavit, ungemus, & inaugurabimur: Ita tamen si primum Omnium Jura, Immunitates Ecclesiasticas & Seculares, per Divos Antecessores Nobis Concessas & donatas, & quæ Nos ipsi præteritorum & præsentis Interregni tempore pro Jure Libertatis nostræ, Statuque Reipublicæ melius conservando sancivimus, manu tenebit, & observabit. Si præterea idem Serenissimus Electus, conditionibus a Nobis cum Legatis Suæ Majestatis conclusi ante exhibitionem præsentis Decreti Electionis, se satisfacturum Juramento obstringet, & literis suis authenticis omni meliori modo cavebit. Quod quidem Decretum Electionis Nostræ auxilio Divino exequi cupientes, de communi concordia Nostra ad tradendum illud in manus Serenissimi Regis Electi mittimus cum Illustrissimo, & Reverendissimo Dn. Episcopo Cracoviensi nonnullos Senatores & Officiales, & Illustrem ac Magnificum Benedictum Sapicha, M.D.L. Curiæ Thesaurarium, Equestris Ordinis Mareschalcum Committentes illis id ipsum Decretum intimandi, Juramentum super præmissis ab ipso, & subscriptionem recipiendi; tum demum in manus ejusdem Electi ipsum, Decretum dandi, & tradendi, ac cætera quæ hoc ipsum Negotium requirit, agendi & perficiendi. In cujus rei fidem præsentium Dominorum Senatorum, & ex Equestri Ordine ad sigillandum Deputator, Sigilla sunt appensa. Datum per manus Illust. & Reverend. in Christo Patris Dn. Andreæ Olszcovvski. Episcopi Culmensis & Pomesanien. Pro-Cancellarii Regni in Conventu Electionis Novi Regis Generali Ordinario Regni, & M.D.L. ad Varsaviam Die XXII. Mensis Maij, Anno Domini 1674. Præsentibus, Francisco Prazmovvski, Præposito Genesnensi, Abbate Sleciechovien, Secretario Regni Majore, Joanne Malachovvski, Abbate Mogilnens. Regni Cypriano Paulo Brzovvski M.D.L. Referendariis. . . . Ceterisque plurimis Officialibus, Capitaneis, Secretariis, & Aulicis Regiis. Incolisque Regni & M.D.L. ad præsentem Conventum Electoris Regni, & M.D.L. Varsaviæ congregatis.

ADSTITERUNT solenni juramento die V. Mensis Junii, in Basilica Varsaviensi super Pacta Conventa seu Capitulationem post traditum hocce Diploma a Regia Majestate præstito, Reverendissimi, Excellentissimi, Domini. Franciscus Bonuisi, Archiepiscopus Tessalonicen, Nuntius Apostolicus. Christophorus Comes a Schaffgotsch. Cæsareus. Tussanus de Forbin, de Janson, Episcopus Masiliensis, Gallicus. Joannes Liber Baro ab Houerbeck, Brandeburgicus. Legati:

aliique Principum Externorum Ablegati Ministri.

F I N I S.

Appendix D

RUSSIAN-LANGUAGE CRITICISM OF MILTON'S

MOSCOVIA

By John B. Gleason

Milton's *Brief History of Moscovia* was first brought to the notice
of the Russian reading public by Mikhail Petrovich Poludenskiĭ,
a well-connected young book collector who owned a copy of the
1682 edition and had an amateur interest in his country's history.[1]
Poludenskiĭ described Milton's book in an article, "Russkaia istoriia
Mil'tona" [Milton's Russian history], which appeared in the widely
read periodical *Russkiĭ vestnik*, XXVI (April 1860), 533–45. This
more popular account had in fact been preceded by a brief factual
description in Friedrich von Adelung, *Kritisch-historische Übersicht
der Reisenden in Russland bis 1700*, 2 vols. (St. Petersburg and
Leipzig, 1846), but Poludenskiĭ made high claims for Milton's history as an original source for Russian historians because Milton
"had access to many accounts of Russia which have remained
unpublished down to our own day" (p. 533). The body of the article
consists almost wholly of extracts, taken mainly from Milton's first
and fifth chapters. Of the information on Russian government and
daily life given by Milton, Poludenskiĭ observes in passing (p. 535)
that "the greater part of the information is incorrect and some of
it is absurd"; he nevertheless devotes several pages to it, apparently
as a curiosity to the Russian reader. He devotes another six pages
to a summary, with quotations, of Milton's fifth chapter, which
he feels is "the most curious one for us [Russians]" (p. 537). On the
last page he reprints Milton's list of sources, in English and without
translation. He makes no effort anywhere to justify the claim he
had made at the outset for the book's value as a historical source.

Poludenskiĭ's article, though of little value in itself, awakened
considerable interest of both a semipopular and a scholarly kind.
A prolific journalist, E. P. Karnovich, rushed into print with a
translation a few months later in another important national mag-
azine, the *Otechestvennye Zapiski*.[2] Karnovich accepted Poludenskiĭ's high estimate of the *Moscovia* and was quite ignorant of all
that that work omitted. He goes so far as to say (p. 102) that the

Moscovia had a "special significance" for the Englishmen of the seventeenth century because it was a "complete collection of all the remarkable information concerning Russia that was available at that time in English writers." [3] As Milton "definitely" used "whatever had been written up to that time by his countrymen," his book "was, so to speak, a scholarly summary of the almost century-long continuous relations between Russia and England, both diplomatic and commercial." Karnovich's translation has no commentary and a solitary footnote, which corrects Milton's mistaking a Russian patronymic for a surname. As an educated Russian, Karnovich must have been aware how far the book was from living up to its ambitious preface, and he cast about for another explanation of its significance. Karnovich was thus the first to speculate on the purpose of the *Moscovia*. He noted that although the book has no independent historical value, it depicts the way of life in Muscovy and adjacent lands and especially their trade relations. Thus, the book would have been useful for the English and for the Dutch, both commercial powers, since the English were at that time the only people who were gathering, through the Russians, information about the Far East. Karnovich made no attempt to determine the relation of Milton's account to its sources (pp. 102–3).

Meanwhile, a really serious student of Anglo-Russian relations, IUriĭ Tolstoĭ, had also read Poludenskiĭ's enthusiastic article and was preparing a reply very different in tone and substance from Karnovich's. This essay, called "Zametka po povodu stat'i g. Poludenskago 'Russkaia istoriia Mil'tona' " [Note apropos of Mr. Poludenskiĭ's article, "Milton's Russian History"], was ready for publication in 1861 and was intended for the *Chteniia* [Papers] of the Moscow University Society for Russian History and Antiquities. Unfortunately, political events prevented publication at that time. The *Chteniia* had already been suspended once, in 1848, for publishing a translation of Giles Fletcher's *The Russe Common Wealth,* obviously because of Fletcher's sharp criticism of Russia's backward institutions, published in the revolutionary atmosphere of that year.[4] Eighteen sixty-one was likewise a tense year, the year in which the serfs were to be liberated. Under those circumstances the Society must have felt it more prudent to defer publication of Tolstoĭ's translation of the similarly critical *Brief History of Moscovia* with which Tolstoĭ accompanied his critique of Poludenskiĭ. In the event, neither the critique nor the translation saw print until the *Chteniia* for 1874.[5] The translation may have benefited from the delay, however, because it was fortified with copious annotation, and Tolstoĭ's contribution seems to have settled for Russian readers any question as to the historical value of Milton's work.

Tolstoĭ states that during two years previously spent in London doing research on Anglo-Russian relations he had of course come upon Milton's book but had dismissed it almost at once as valueless for serious purposes. It was a work that "not only offers no new information, but often even transmits existing information inaccurately and distortedly" (p. 2). The valuelessness of the *Moscovia* is thoroughly demonstrated, mainly by showing how much better sources are available to the Russian historian for the topics touched on by Milton than anything appearing in the latter writer. Thus, exposure of Milton's errors and conceptual inadequacies is only incidental to the refutation of Poludenskiĭ's absurd claims for the *Moscovia*. Nevertheless, Tolstoĭ's detailed notes to his translation, together with the critical essay, show how singularly imperfect Milton's work is. Tolstoĭ, not so inhibited by respect for the great poet as the English critic is likely to be, wonders whether the *Moscovia* is not merely a seventeenth-century potboiler—"speculation" is his word—aimed at a curious but ignorant public and compiled "with an extraordinary lack of conscientiousness" (p. 2).

Only one later essay has raised again the question of the value of the *Moscovia* for history, and then in a perfunctory way. M. P. Alekseev has published a survey of all the European writers and travelers from the thirteenth to the seventeenth centuries who dealt in any way with Siberia, where his study was published in Irkutsk.[6] The enumeration of these writers leads in due course to the short thirtieth chapter devoted to Milton. Alekseev dates the *Moscovia* to 1649–52. However, he also records his interest in the suggestion, made earlier by Alfred Stern,[7] that Milton may have had an additional oral source in his friend Andrew Marvell, who was secretary of an embassy to Russia in 1663 (p. 305). Alekseev does not try to reconcile this possibility with his own dating to 1649–52. Again following a hint by Stern,[8] the Soviet scholar sees the *Moscovia* as deliberately adapted to a wider reading public. Thus, the *Moscovia* may be seen as an early example of the popularization of a serious subject expressive of the democratic tendencies of the Puritan revolutionary period (p. 302). Alekseev explains the book's publication so many years after it was presumably written as showing that Milton, realizing the importance of reaching a wider public with serious popularizations, wanted to be sure that the book was actually published. Not only did the *Moscovia* have a certain impact on Milton's imagination, but it also diffused widely its picture of Russia to the many English readers who were, Alekseev affirms, attracted to it by their admiration for Milton's poetry.

With the exception of Alekseev, who was committed to covering the ground by mentioning every early English writer who had anything to say about Siberia, there has been no further show of interest in the *Moscovia* by Russian scholars since 1874, when Tolstoĭ's extended critique apparently settled the matter once for all. One would have supposed that the great poet's parergon would have retained at least some curiosity value for Russians, but such is not the case. The standard multivolume *Istoriia angliĭskoĭ literatury* [History of English literature] published by the Academy of Sciences of the USSR (3 vols. in 5; Moscow and Leningrad, 1943–58), has only a half-sentence for the *Moscovia:* Milton "worked on" a history of England "and, what is especially interesting, on a *Brief History of Moscovia* printed in 1682" (vol. I, pt. 2, p. 179). The expression, "worked on" (*rabotal nad*), permits, if it does not require, the inference that both histories are incomplete. Equally succinct is the notice in the current (3rd) edition of the *Bol'shaia sovetskaia entsiklopediia* [Large Soviet encyclopedia], XVI (1974), 265: "Milton aroused interest in Russia through devoting to the country a *Brief History of Moscovia.*" The only periodical article cited in the bibliography to this entry, I. S. Kon, "Dzhon Mil'ton kak sotsial'no-politicheskiĭ myslitel' " [John Milton as a sociopolitical thinker], *Voprosy istorii* [Questions of history], XIII (1959), 110–20, does not mention the *Moscovia.*[9] Finally, the only recent book-length study of Milton in Russian, R. M. Samarin's *Tvorchestvo Dzhona Mil'tona* [John Milton's literary work] (Moscow, 1964), contains in its 485 pages only these two references to the *Moscovia:* on p. 127 Samarin mentions it as a "compilation" along with *Accedence Commenc't Grammar* and the *Art of Logic;* and on p. 195 he remarks, in the course of discussing a different topic, that "the composition of the *History of Moscovia* is diversified by information of a geographical and economic character."

The only other Russian-language study of the *Moscovia* known to me is in fact by a Hungarian scholar, but as it seems to be available only in the Russian language it may serve as an appendix to the present survey. This essay, by M. Szenczi, was published in a *Festschrift* dedicated to Professor Alekseev in 1966.[10] Szenczi's study is of interest as being the only Russian-language study of the *Moscovia* that tries to discover the literary reasons for what he considers the "attractiveness" of Milton's history. What Cawley and Thompson admire as skillfulness in compression and resolute elimination of nonessentials, Szenczi sees as essentially negative qualities. It is worth observing that this latest Russian-language essay does not take up the question of the *Moscovia*'s historical value, the question that was almost the sole interest of the Russian writers whose work has been surveyed in this note.

[1] Accounts of Poludenskiĭ, and also of Karnovich, mentioned below, may be found in the *Russkiĭ biograficheskiĭ slovar'* [Russian biographical dictionary], 25 vols. (St. Petersburg, 1896–1913).

[2] "Sochinenie Mil'tona o Rossii" [Milton's work concerning Russia], *Otechestvennye Zapiski*, 3rd ser., CXXXI (July 1860), 101–42. I owe my knowledge of this translation to a reference by Alekseev in his essay discussed below. Alekseev's reference is seriously astray, however; the interested student should be warned that the translation appears, as here noted, in vol. CXXXI, *not* XXI, and that the pagination is 101–42, *not* 1–142.

[3] Karnovich, unlike Poludenskiĭ, assumes that the work was composed before Milton became blind.

[4] See article, "Fletcher, Dzhilz" [i.e., Giles Fletcher], *Bol'shaia Sovetskaia Entsiklopediia*, 2nd ed., XLV (1957), 242.

[5] Both essay and translation appear in part 3 of the *Chteniia* of the Moscow University Society for Russian History and Antiquities, each with separate pagination.

[6] M. P. Alekseev, *Sibir' v izvestiiakh zapadno-evropeĭskikh puteshestvennikov i pisateleĭ: Vvedenie, teksty i kommentarii XIII–XVII v.v.* [*Siberia in the accounts of Western-European travelers and writers: Introduction, texts and commentaries XIII–XVII centuries*], 2nd ed. (Irkutsk, 1941).

[7] *Milton und seine Zeit*, 2 vols. (Leipzig, 1877–79), II, 178.

[8] Ibid.

[9] I have not seen the same writer's "Politicheskie vozzreniia Dzhona Mil'tona" [The political views of John Milton], *Uchënnye zapiski Vologodskogo Gosudarstvennogo Pedagogicheskogo Instituta* [*Scholarly annals of the Vologda State Pedagogical Institute*], no. 9 (1951).

[10] M. Sentsi [i.e., Szenczi], "Mil'ton o Rossii" [Milton on Russia], in *Russko-evropeĭskie literaturnye sviazy: Sbornik stat'eĭ k 70-letiiu so dnia rozhdeniia Akademika M. P. Alekseeva* [*Russo-European literary relations: A collection of essays for the seventieth birthday of Academician M. P. Alekseev*] (Moscow and Leningrad, 1966), pp. 284–92.

INDEX TO AUTHORS AND WORKS

Most works are indexed under the authors' names. Editors and translators are cross referenced to authors. For many works short titles have been used. Starred page references indicate that the longer titles or additional bibliographical information will be found on the cited pages. Known dates of publication are included in the index for works published during or close to Milton's lifetime.